A TO Z
ALL
the
NAMES
in the
BIBLE

THOMAS NELSON
Since 1798

NASHVILLE   DALLAS   MEXICO CITY   RIO DE JANEIRO

Published in Nashville, Tennessee, by Thomas Nelson. Thomas Nelson is a registered trademark of HarperCollins Christian Publishing, Inc.

Typesetting by Rainbow Graphics, Kingsport, Tennessee

Thomas Nelson titles may be purchased in bulk for educational, business, fund-raising, or sales promotional use. For information, please e-mail SpecialMarkets@ThomasNelson.com.

ISBN: 978-0-5291-0650-6

Printed in the United States of America

14 15 16 17 18 RRD 5 4 3 2 1

Contents

Aaron...... 1	Abimelech...... 11
Aaronites...... 2	Abinadab...... 12
Ab 3	Abiner 13
Abaddon 3	Abinoam 13
Abagtha...... 3	Abiram 13
Abana 3	Abishag 13
Abanah...... 3	Abishai/Abshai...... 13
Abarim 3	Abishalom...... 14
Abba 3	Abishua 14
Abda 4	Abishur 14
Abdeel 4	Abital 14
Abdi...... 4	Abitub...... 14
Abdiel...... 5	Abiud 14
Abdon 5	Abner...... 14
Abed-nego 5	Abomination of Desolation...... 14
Abel 5	Abraham 15
Abel Acacia Grove 6	Abram 19
Abel-beth-maachah...... 7	Abronah/Ebronah...... 19
Abel-cheramim 7	Absalom 19
Abel-keramim 7	Absalom's Pillar...... 21
Abel-maim...... 7	Abyss 21
Abel-meholah 7	Acacia Grove 21
Abel-mizraim 7	Acacias, Valley of 21
Abel-shittim 7	Accad/Akkad...... 21
Abez/Ebez...... 7	Accaron 22
Abi, Abia, Abiah...... 7	Accho 22
Abi-albon 8	Acco...... 22
Abiasaph 8	Accuser 22
Abiathar 8	Aceldama 22
Abib 8	Achaia 22
Abida/Abidah...... 8	Achaicus...... 22
Abidan...... 8	Achan 23
Abiel 9	Achar 23
Abiezer 9	Achaz 23
Abiezrite 9	Achbor 23
Abigail 9	Achim 23
Abigal 10	Achish 23
Abihail 10	Achmetha 24
Abihu...... 10	Achor...... 24
Abihud 10	Achsah, Achsa...... 24
Abijah/Abi/Abia/Abiah...... 10	Achshaph 24
Abijam...... 11	Achzib...... 24
Abilene/Abila 11	Acrabbim 24
Abimael...... 11	Acre 25

Acsah.................................. 25
Adadah................................ 25
Adah.................................. 25
Adaiah................................ 25
Adalia................................ 25
Adam.................................. 25
Adamah................................ 27
Adami-nekeb........................... 27
Adar.................................. 27
Adar, Addar........................... 27
Adbeel................................ 27
Addan, Addon.......................... 27
Addar................................. 27
Addi.................................. 27
Addon................................. 27
Ader.................................. 27
Adida................................. 27
Adiel................................. 27
Adin.................................. 27
Adina................................. 28
Adino................................. 28
Adithaim.............................. 28
Adlai................................. 28
Admah................................. 28
Admatha............................... 28
Adna.................................. 28
Adnah................................. 28
Adonai................................ 28
Adoni-bezek........................... 28
Adonijah.............................. 29
Adonikam.............................. 29
Adoniram.............................. 29
Adoni-zedek, Adoni-zedec.............. 30
Ador, Adora........................... 30
Adoraim............................... 30
Adoram................................ 30
Adrammelech........................... 30
Adramyttium........................... 30
Adria................................. 30
Adriatic.............................. 30
Adriel................................ 30
Adullam............................... 30
Adullamite............................ 30
Adummim............................... 31
Aeneas................................ 31
Aenon................................. 31
Agabus................................ 31
Agag.................................. 31
Agagite............................... 31
Agar.................................. 31
Agee.................................. 31

Agrippa............................... 31
Agur.................................. 31
Ahab.................................. 31
Aharah................................ 33
Aharhel............................... 33
Ahasai, Ahzai......................... 33
Ahasbai............................... 33
Ahashverosh........................... 33
Ahasuerus............................. 33
Ahava................................. 34
Ahaz, Achaz........................... 34
Ahaz, Dial of......................... 35
Ahaziah............................... 35
Ahban................................. 36
Aher.................................. 36
Ahi................................... 36
Ahiah................................. 36
Ahiam................................. 36
Ahian................................. 36
Ahiezer............................... 36
Ahihud................................ 37
Ahijah, Ahiah......................... 37
Ahikam................................ 38
Ahilud................................ 38
Ahimaaz............................... 38
Ahiman................................ 38
Ahimelech............................. 38
Ahimoth............................... 39
Ahinadab.............................. 39
Ahinoam............................... 39
Ahio.................................. 39
Ahira................................. 39
Ahiram................................ 39
Ahiramites............................ 39
Ahisamach............................. 39
Ahishahar............................. 39
Ahishar............................... 39
Ahithophel............................ 39
Ahitub................................ 40
Ahlab................................. 40
Ahlai................................. 40
Ahoah................................. 40
Ahohi................................. 40
Ahohite............................... 40
Aholah................................ 40
Aholiab............................... 40
Aholibah.............................. 40
Aholibamah............................ 40
Ahumai................................ 40
Ahuzam, Ahuzzam....................... 41
Ahuzzath.............................. 41

Ahzai, Ahasai 41
Ai, Hai 41
Aiah, Ajah 41
Aiath 41
Aija 41
Aijalon, Ajalon 42
Ain 42
Ajah 42
Ajalon 42
Akan 42
Akeldama, Aceldama 42
Akkad 42
Akkub 42
Akrabbim 43
Alabaster 43
Alameth 43
Alammelech 43
Alemeth, Alameth 43
Alexander 43
Alexandria 44
Alexandrians 44
Aliah 44
Alian 44
Allammelech, Alammelech 44
Allon 44
Allon-bachuth, Allon-bacuth 44
Almighty 45
Almodad 45
Almon 45
Almon-diblathaim 45
Aloth, Bealoth 45
Alphaeus 45
Alush 45
Alvah, Aliah 45
Alvan, Alian 45
Amad 45
Amal 45
Amalek 46
Amalekites 46
Amam 46
Amana 46
Amariah 46
Amasa 46
Amasai 47
Amashai 47
Amashsai 47
Amasiah 47
Amaziah 47
Ami 47
Aminadab 47
Amittai 47

Ammah 48
Ammi 48
Ammiel 48
Ammihud 48
Amminadab, Aminadab 48
Ammishaddai 48
Ammizabad 48
Ammon 48
Ammonites 49
Ammonitess 49
Amnon 49
Amok 49
Amon 49
Amorites 50
Amos 50
Amoz 51
Amphipolis 51
Amplias 51
Amram 52
Amramites 52
Amraphel 52
Amzi 52
Anab 52
Anah 52
Anaharath 53
Anaiah 53
Anak 53
Anakim 53
Anamim 53
Anammelech 53
Anan 53
Anani 53
Ananiah 53
Ananias 54
Anath 54
Anathoth 55
Anathothite 55
Ancient of Days 55
Andrew 55
Andronicus 56
Anem 56
Aner 56
Anethothite, Anetothite 56
Angel of the Lord, Angel of God 56
Aniam 57
Anim 57
Anna 57
Annas 58
Antediluvians 58
Anthothijah, Antothijah 59
Antichrist 59

Antioch of Pisidia 59
Antioch of Syria 60
Antiochus 61
Antipas 61
Antipatris 62
Antonia, Tower of 62
Antothijah 62
Antothite 62
Anub 62
Apelles 62
Apharsachites, Apharsathchites 62
Aphek 62
Aphekah 62
Aphiah 63
Aphik 63
Aphrah, Beth-le-aphrah 63
Aphses 63
Apis 63
Apollonia 63
Apollos 63
Apollyon 63
Apostle 64
Apostolical Council 64
Appaim 64
Apphia 64
Appian Way 64
Appiiforum 64
Aqaba, Gulf of 64
Aquila 64
Ar 65
Ara 65
Arab 65
Arabah 65
Arabia 65
Arad 65
Aradus 66
Arah 66
Aram 66
Aram Dammesek 66
Arameans 66
Aramitess 66
Aram-maacah 66
Aram-naharaim 67
Aram-zobah 67
Aran 67
Ararat 67
Araunah, Ornan 67
Arba 67
Arbah 67
Arbathite 68
Arbite 68

Archelaus 68
Archevites 68
Archi 68
Archippus 68
Archite 68
Arcturus 68
Ard 68
Ardites 68
Ardon 68
Areli 68
Arelites 68
Areopagite 68
Areopagus 69
Aretas 69
Argob 69
Aridai 69
Aridatha 69
Arieh 69
Ariel 69
Arimathaea 69
Arioch 70
Arisai 70
Aristarchus 70
Aristobulus 70
Arkite 70
Armenia 70
Armoni 70
Arnan 70
Arni 70
Arnon 70
Arod, Arodi 70
Arodites 71
Aroer 71
Aroerite 71
Arpachshad 71
Arpad, Arphad 71
Arphaxad, Arpachshad 71
Artaxerxes 71
Artemas 72
Artemis 72
Aruboth 72
Arumah 72
Arvad 72
Arvadite 72
Arza 72
Asa 72
Asahel 72
Asahiah 73
Asaiah 73
Asaph 73
Asaph, Sons of 73

Asaphite 73
Asareel.................................... 73
Asarelah, Asharelah.................. 73
Ascalon 74
Ascent of Akrabbim 74
Asenath 74
Aser 74
Ashan 74
Asharelah 74
Ashbea.................................... 74
Ashbel 74
Ashbelites................................ 74
Ashchenaz 74
Ashdod.................................... 74
Ashdodites, Ashdothites............ 75
Ashdoth-pisgah........................ 75
Asher 75
Asherah 75
Asherite 75
Ashhur 75
Ashima 75
Ashkelon, Askelon.................... 75
Ashkenaz 76
Ashnah 76
Ashpenaz 76
Ashriel.................................... 76
Ashtaroth 76
Ashterathite 76
Ashteroth-karnaim.................... 76
Ashtoreth 76
Ashur, Ashhur.......................... 77
Ashurbanipal........................... 77
Ashurites................................. 77
Ashurnasirpal........................... 77
Ashvath 77
Asia.. 77
Asia Minor............................... 77
Asiarchs.................................. 78
Asiel....................................... 78
Askelon 78
Asnah 78
Asnapper, Osnapper................. 78
Aspatha 78
Asriel, Ashriel.......................... 78
Asrielites 78
Asshur 78
Asshurim 78
Assir....................................... 78
Assos...................................... 78
Assur 78
Assyria, Asshur, Assur 79
Astaroth 80
Astarte.................................... 80
Asuppim 80
Asyncritus................................ 80
Atad 80
Atarah..................................... 80
Ataroth 80
Ataroth-addar 81
Ater.. 81
Athach 81
Athaiah.................................... 81
Athaliah 81
Athenians................................ 82
Athens 82
Athlai...................................... 83
Atroth 83
Atroth-beth-joab 83
Atroth-shophan 83
Attai....................................... 83
Attalaia 83
Augustus 84
Ava 84
Aven....................................... 84
Avim 84
Avites 84
Avith 84
Avva, Ava 84
Avvim, Avim 84
Ayyah 85
Azal.. 85
Azaliah 85
Azaniah 85
Azarael 85
Azareel, Azarel......................... 85
Azarel 85
Azariah.................................... 85
Azaz 87
Azaziah 87
Azbuk 87
Azekah 87
Azel, Azal 87
Azem 87
Azgad 87
Aziel....................................... 87
Aziza 87
Azmaveth................................. 87
Azmon..................................... 88
Aznoth-tabor 88
Azor 88
Azotus 88
Azriel...................................... 88

Azrikam 88
Azubah 88
Azur 88
Azzah 88
Azzan 88
Azzur, Azur 88

Baal 89
Baalah 89
Baalath 89
Baalath-beer 90
Baal-berith 90
Baale 90
Baal-gad 90
Baal-hamon 90
Baal-hanan 90
Baal-hazor 90
Baal-hermon 90
Baalim 90
Baalis 90
Baal-meon 90
Baal-peor 90
Baal-perazim 91
Baal-shalishah 91
Baal-tamar 91
Baal-zebub 91
Baal-zephon 91
Baana 91
Baanah 91
Baara 91
Baaseiah 91
Baasha 92
Babel, Tower of 92
Babylon, City of 93
Babylonia 96
Baca 97
Bachrites 97
Baharumite 97
Bahurim 97
Bajith 97
Bakbakkar 98
Bakbuk 98
Bakbukiah 98
Balaam 98
Balac 99
Baladan 99
Balah 99
Balak 99
Bamoth 99
Bamoth-baal 100
Bani 100

Barabbas 100
Barachel 100
Barachiah, Barachias 100
Barak 100
Barhumite 101
Bariah 101
Bar-Jesus 101
Bar-Jona 101
Barkos 101
Barnabas 101
Barsabas 102
Barsabbas 102
Bartholomew 102
Bartimaeus 102
Bartimeus 102
Baruch 102
Barzillai 103
Basemath 103
Bashan 103
Bashan-havoth-jair 104
Bashan, Mountain of 104
Bashemath 104
Basmath 104
Bath-rabbim 104
Bathsheba 104
Bath-shua 105
Bavai, Bavvai 105
Bazlith 105
Bealiah 105
Bealoth 105
Beautiful Gate 105
Bebai 105
Becher 106
Becherites 106
Becorath, Bechorath 106
Bedad 106
Bedan 106
Bedeiah 106
Beeliada 106
Beelzebub 106
Beelzebul 106
Beer 106
Beera 106
Beerah 106
Beer-elim 107
Beeri 107
Beer-lahai-roi, Lahai-roi 107
Beeroth 107
Beeroth-bene-jaakan 107
Beerothite 107
Beersheba 107

Beesh-terah 108
Beker 108
Bel 108
Bela 108
Belah 108
Belaites 108
Belshazzar 108
Belteshazzar 108
Ben 109
Ben-abinadab 109
Benaiah 109
Ben-ammi 109
Ben-deker 109
Bene-berak 109
Bene-jaakan 109
Bene-kedem 109
Ben-geber 109
Ben-hadad 110
Ben-hail 110
Ben-hanan 110
Ben-hayil 110
Ben-hesed 110
Ben-hur 110
Beninu 110
Benjamin 110
Benjamin, Gate of 111
Benjamin, Tribe of 111
Benjamite 112
Beno 112
Ben-oni 112
Ben-zoheth 112
Beon 112
Beor 112
Bera 112
Beracah 112
Berachah 112
Berachiah 112
Beraiah 112
Berea 112
Berechiah 112
Bered 113
Berenice 113
Beri 113
Beriah 113
Beriites 113
Berites 113
Berith 113
Bernice, Berenice 113
Berodach-baladan 114
Beroea 114
Berothah 114

Berothai 114
Berothite 114
Berutha 114
Besai 114
Besodeiah 114
Besor 114
Betah 114
Beten 114
Bethabara 114
Beth-acacia 114
Beth-anath 115
Beth-anoth 115
Bethany 115
Beth-aphrah 115
Beth-arabah 115
Beth-aram 115
Beth-arbel 115
Beth-aven 115
Beth-azmaveth 115
Beth-azmoth 115
Beth-baal-meon 116
Beth-barah 116
Beth-birei 116
Beth-car 116
Beth-dagon 116
Beth-diblathaim 116
Beth-eden 116
Beth-el 116
Beth-elite 118
Beth-emek 118
Bethesda 118
Beth-ezel 118
Beth-gader 118
Beth-gamul 118
Beth-gilgal 118
Beth-haccherem, Beth-haccerem ... 118
Beth-haggun 118
Beth-hakkerem 118
Beth-haram 118
Beth-haran 118
Beth-hoglah 119
Beth-horon 119
Beth-jeshimoth 119
Beth-jesimoth 119
Beth-le-aphrah 119
Beth-lebaoth 119
Bethlehem 119
Bethlehemite 120
Bethlehem-judah 120
Beth-maachah 120
Beth-marcaboth 121

x CONTENTS

Beth-meon.................................121
Beth-nimrah..............................121
Beth-ophrah.............................121
Beth-palet................................121
Beth-pazzez..............................121
Beth-pelet................................121
Beth-peor................................121
Bethphage...............................121
Beth-phelet..............................121
Beth-rapha...............................121
Beth-rehob..............................121
Bethsaida...............................121
Beth-shean, Beth-shan...............122
Beth-shemesh, Ir-shemesh...........122
Beth-shemite............................123
Beth-shittah.............................123
Beth-tappuah...........................123
Bethuel...................................123
Bethul.....................................123
Beth-zur..................................123
Betonim...................................123
Beulah.....................................123
Bezaanannim............................123
Bezai.......................................123
Bezaleel, Bezalel.......................123
Bezek......................................124
Bezer......................................124
Bichri......................................124
Bidkar.....................................124
Bigtha.....................................124
Bigthan, Bigthana.....................124
Bigvai......................................124
Bildad.....................................124
Bileam.....................................125
Bilgah.....................................125
Bilgai......................................125
Bilhah.....................................125
Bilhan.....................................125
Bilshan....................................125
Bimhal.....................................125
Binea.......................................125
Binnui.....................................125
Birsha.....................................126
Bir-zaith, Bir-zavith...................126
Bishlam...................................126
Bithiah....................................126
Bithron....................................126
Bithynia...................................126
Biziothiah.................................126
Bizjothjah.................................126
Biztha......................................126

Blastus.....................................126
Boanerges................................126
Boaz.......................................126
Bocheru...................................127
Bochim....................................127
Bohan......................................127
Bokeru....................................127
Bokim......................................127
Booz..127
Bor-ashan................................127
Boscath....................................127
Bosor.......................................127
Bozez......................................127
Bozkath, Boscath.......................127
Bozrah.....................................127
Brazen Sea...............................128
Bronze Sea...............................128
Bukki.......................................128
Bukkiah....................................128
Bul..128
Bunah......................................128
Bunni......................................128
Buz...128
Buzi...129
Buzite......................................129

Cabbon....................................130
Cabul.......................................130
Caesar.....................................130
Caesarea...................................130
Caesarea Philippi.......................131
Caiaphas...................................132
Cain..132
Cainan.....................................133
Calah.......................................133
Calcol......................................133
Caleb.......................................133
Caleb-ephratah..........................134
Caleb-ephrathah.........................134
Calebite....................................134
Calneh......................................134
Calno.......................................134
Calvary.....................................134
Camon......................................136
Cana..136
Canaan.....................................136
Canaanite..................................137
Canaanitess...............................138
Cananaean, Canaanite..................138
Candace....................................138
Canneh.....................................138

Capernaum 138
Caphtor 139
Caphtorim, Caphthorim 139
Cappadocia 139
Carcas 139
Carchemish 139
Careah 140
Carites 140
Carkas 140
Carmel 140
Carmelite 141
Carmelitess 141
Carmi 141
Carmites 141
Carnaim 141
Carpus 141
Carshena 141
Casiphia 141
Casluhim 141
Castor and Pollux 141
Cauda 141
Cedron 141
Cenchrea 141
Cenchreaa 142
Cephas 142
Chalcol 142
Chaldea 142
Chaldean 142
Chaldees 142
Champaign 142
Chanaan 142
Charashim 143
Charchemish 143
Charran 143
Chebar 143
Chedorlaomer 143
Chelal 143
Chelluh 143
Chelub 143
Chelubai 144
Cheluh 144
Cheluhi 144
Chemarim 144
Chemosh 144
Chenaanah 144
Chenani 144
Chenaniah 144
Chephar-ammoni 144
Chephar-haamonnai 144
Chephirah 144
Cheran 145

Cherethites 145
Cherith 145
Chesalon 145
Chesed 145
Chesil 145
Chesulloth 145
Cheth 145
Chezib 145
Chidon 145
Chileab 145
Chilion 145
Chilmad 146
Chimham 146
Chinnereth, Chinneroth,
    Cinneroth 146
Chios 146
Chisleu 146
Chislev 146
Chislon 146
Chisloth-tabor 146
Chithlish 146
Chittim 146
Chiun 147
Chloe 147
Chorashan 147
Chorazin 147
Chozeba 147
Christ 147
Christian 147
Chub 148
Chun 148
Chushan-rishathaim 148
Chuza 148
Cilicia 148
Cinneroth 148
Cis 148
Cities of the Plain 148
City of Moab 149
City of Salt 149
Clauda 149
Claudia 149
Claudius 149
Claudius Lysias 149
Clement 149
Cleopas 149
Cleophas 149
Clopas 149
Cnidus 150
Colhozeh 150
Colosse 150
Conaniah 150

Coniah..................................... 151
Cononiah................................. 151
Consolation............................. 151
Coos 151
Corashan................................. 151
Core....................................... 151
Corinth................................... 151
Cornelius 153
Cos.. 154
Cosam 154
Court of the Gentiles................. 154
Coz.. 154
Cozbi 154
Cozeba, Chozeba 154
Crescens 154
Cretans 155
Crete 155
Cretes 155
Crispus 155
Cub 155
Cun 155
Cush 155
Cushan-rishathaim,
    Chushan-rishathaim 156
Cushi 156
Cushite 156
Cuth, Cuthah........................... 156
Cuza....................................... 156
Cyprus.................................... 156
Cyrene.................................... 156
Cyrenian 156
Cyrenius.................................. 156
Cyrus 157

Dabareh.................................. 158
Dabbasheth.............................. 158
Dabbesheth.............................. 158
Daberath 158
Dagon..................................... 158
Dalaiah 158
Dale, The King's 158
Dalmanutha............................. 158
Dalmatia 158
Dalphon 158
Damaris................................... 158
Damascene 159
Damascus 159
Dan.. 161
Daniel..................................... 161
Danite..................................... 163
Dan-jaan 163

Dannah 163
Dara....................................... 163
Darda...................................... 163
Darius..................................... 163
Darkon 163
Dathan 163
David 163
David, City of........................... 167
David, Tower of......................... 167
Daystar 167
Dead Sea 167
Debir 168
Deborah 168
Decapolis 169
Decision, Valley of..................... 169
Dedan..................................... 169
Dedanim 170
Dedanites 170
Dedication, Feast of.................... 170
Dehaites, Dehavites 170
Deker, Dekar 170
Delaiah, Dalaiah 170
Delilah.................................... 170
Demas 171
Demetrius 171
Derbe...................................... 171
Desire of all Nations................... 171
Destroyer 171
Destruction 171
Deuel 171
Devil 171
Dial of Ahaz 172
Diana 172
Dianites 172
Diblah, Diblath 172
Diblaim 172
Diblath 172
Dibon 172
Dibon-gad 172
Dibri 173
Didymus 173
Diklah 173
Dilean 173
Dimnah 173
Dimon 173
Dimonah.................................. 173
Dinah 173
Dinhabah 173
Dionysius 173
Diotrephes 173
Diphath................................... 173

Dishan 173
Dishon 173
Diviner's Terebinth Tree 174
Dizahab 174
Dodai 174
Dodanim, Rodanim 174
Dodavah 174
Dodo 174
Doeg 174
Dophkah 174
Dor 174
Dorcas 174
Dothaim 175
Dothan 175
Dragon's Well 175
Drusilla 175
Dumah 175
Dura 175

Earth 176
East, Children of the 176
East Country 176
Easter 176
Eastern Sea 176
East Gate 176
Ebal 176
Ebed 177
Ebed-melech 177
Ebenezer 177
Eber, Heber 177
Ebez 177
Ebiasaph 177
Ebron 177
Ebronah 177
Ecbatana 177
Ed 177
Edar 177
Edar, Tower of 177
Eden 178
Eder, Edar, Ader 179
Edom 179
Edomites 181
Edrei 181
Eglah 181
Eglaim 181
Eglath-shelishiyah 181
Eglon 181
Egypt 182
Egypt, Brook of 182
Egyptian 183
Ehi 183

Ehud 183
Eker 183
Ekron 183
Ekronite 183
El 183
Eladah, Eleadah 183
Elah 183
Elah, The Valley of 184
Elam 184
Elamites 185
Elasah 185
Elath, Eloth 185
El-berith 185
El-bethel 185
Eldaah 185
Eldad 185
Elead 186
Eleadah 186
Elealeh 186
Eleasah 186
Eleazar 186
Elect Lady 187
El-elohe-israel 187
Eleph 187
Elhanan, Elthanan 187
Eli 187
Eliab 188
Eliada 188
Eliadah 188
Eliah 188
Eliahba 188
Eliakim 188
Eliam 189
Elias 189
Eliasaph 189
Eliashib 189
Eliathah 189
Elidad 189
Eliehoenai 189
Eliel 189
Elienai 190
Eliezer 190
Elihoenai 190
Elihoreph 190
Elihu 191
Elijah 191
Elika 194
Elim 194
Elimelech 194
Elioenai 194
Eliphal 194

Eliphalet 194
Eliphaz 195
Elipheleh 195
Eliphelehu 195
Eliphelet 195
Elisabeth 195
Elisha 195
Elishah 197
Elishama 197
Elishaphat 198
Elisheba 198
Elishua 198
Eliud 198
Elizabeth 198
Elizaphan 198
Elizur 198
Elkanah 198
Elkosh 199
Ellasar 199
Elmodam 199
Elnaam 199
Elnathan 199
Elohim 199
Elon 200
Elon-beth-hanan 200
Elonites 200
Eloth 200
Elpaal 200
Elpalet 200
Elparan 200
Elpelet 200
Eltekeh 200
Eltekon 200
Eltolad 200
Elul 200
Eluzai 200
Elymas 201
Elzabad 201
Elzaphan 201
Emek-keziz 201
Emim 201
Emmanuel 201
Emmaus 201
Emmor 201
Enaim 201
Enam 201
Enan 202
Endor 202
En-eglaim 202
En-gannim 202
En-gedi 202

En-haddah 202
En-hakkore 202
En-hazor 202
En-mishpat 202
Enoch 202
Enos 202
Enosh 203
En-rimmon 203
En-rogel 203
En-shemesh 203
Entappuah 203
Ep-aenetus, Ep-enetus 203
Epaphras 203
Epaphroditus 203
Ep-enetus 203
Ephah 203
Ephai 204
Epher 204
Ephes-dammim 204
Ephesian 204
Ephesus 204
Ephlal 206
Ephod 206
Ephraim 206
Ephraim, City of 206
Ephraim, Forest of 206
Ephraim, Gate of 207
Ephraimite 207
Ephraim, Mountains of 207
Ephraim, Tribe of 207
Ephrain 207
Ephratah 207
Ephrath 207
Ephrathah 207
Ephrathite 207
Ephron 207
Epicureans 208
Er 208
Eran 208
Eranites 208
Erastus 208
Erech 208
Eri 208
Esarhaddon 208
Esau 209
Esau's Wives 209
Esdraelon, Plain of 210
Esek 210
Eshan, Eshean 210
Eshbaal 210
Eshban 210

Eshcol 210
Eshean 210
Eshek 210
Eshkalonite 210
Eshtaol 210
Eshtaulite 210
Eshtemoa 210
Eshtemoah 211
Eshton 211
Esli 211
Esrom 211
Essenes 211
Esther 211
Etam 212
Etham 212
Ethan 212
Ethanim 212
Ethbaal 213
Ether 213
Ethiopia 213
Ethiopian 213
Ethiopian Eunuch 213
Eth-kazin 213
Ethnan 213
Ethnarch 213
Ethni 213
Eubulus 213
Eunice 213
Euodias 214
Euphrates 214
Euraquilo 214
Euroclydon 214
Eutychus 214
Eve 215
Evi 215
Evil-merodach 215
Evil One 215
Ezar 215
Ezbai 215
Ezbon 215
Ezekias 215
Ezekiel 215
Ezel 216
Ezem, Azem 216
Ezer, Ezar 216
Ezion-gaber 216
Ezion-geber 216
Eznite 217
Ezra 217
Ezrah 218

Ezrahite, Ezrarite 218
Ezri 218

Fair Havens 219
False Prophet, The 219
Father, God the 219
Felix 219
Festus, Porcius 219
Field of Sharp Swords 219
Fire, Lake of 220
First Gate 220
Fish Gate 220
Former Gate 220
Fortunatus 220
Foundation Gate 220
Fuller's Field 220
Furnaces, Tower of the 220

Gaal 221
Gaash 221
Gaba 221
Gabbai 221
Gabriel 221
Gad 221
Gad, Ravine of 222
Gadara 222
Gadarenes 222
Gaddi 222
Gaddiel 222
Gadi 222
Gadites 222
Gaham 223
Gahar 223
Gai 223
Gaius 223
Galaad 223
Galal 223
Galatia 223
Galeed 224
Galilaean, Galilean 224
Galilee 224
Galilee, Sea of 226
Gallim 227
Gallio 227
Gamaliel 227
Gammad 227
Gammadim 227
Gamul 227
Garden of Eden 228
Gareb 228
Garmite 228

Gashmu................................228
Gatam..................................228
Gates of Jerusalem..............228
Gath....................................229
Gath-hepher........................229
Gath-rimmon......................229
Gaulanitus..........................229
Gaza....................................229
Gazathite............................230
Gazer..................................230
Gazez..................................230
Gazite..................................230
Gazzam..............................230
Geba, Gaba........................230
Gebal..................................231
Gebalites............................231
Geber..................................231
Gebim................................231
Gedaliah............................231
Gedeon..............................232
Geder..................................232
Gederah..............................232
Gederathite........................232
Gederite..............................232
Gederoth............................232
Gederothaim......................232
Gedor..................................232
Geharashim........................232
Gehazi................................232
Gehenna..............................232
Geliloth..............................233
Gemalli..............................233
Gemariah............................233
Gennesaret..........................233
Gentiles..............................233
Gentiles, Court of..............234
Genubath............................234
Gera....................................234
Gerar..................................234
Gerasa................................234
Gerasenes............................234
Gergesenes..........................234
Gerizim..............................234
Gerizites..............................235
Gershom............................235
Gershomites........................235
Gershon..............................235
Gershonites..........................236
Geruth Kimham..................236
Gerzites..............................236
Gesham..............................236

Geshan................................236
Geshem..............................236
Geshur................................236
Geshurites............................236
Gether................................236
Gethsemane........................236
Geuel..................................237
Gezer..................................237
Gezrite................................237
Ghost, Holy........................237
Giah....................................237
Giants, Valley of................237
Gibbar................................237
Gibbethon..........................237
Gibea..................................237
Gibeah, Gibeath................238
Gibeath..............................238
Gibeath Elohim..................238
Gibeathite..........................238
Gibeon................................238
Gibeon, Pool of..................239
Gibeonites..........................240
Giblite................................240
Giddalti..............................240
Giddel................................240
Gideon................................240
Gideoni..............................242
Gidom................................242
Gihon................................242
Gilalal................................243
Gilboa................................243
Gilead................................243
Gileadites............................244
Gilgal..................................244
Giloh..................................245
Gilonite..............................245
Gimzo................................245
Ginath................................245
Ginnetho............................245
Ginnethoi............................245
Ginnethon..........................245
Girgashites..........................245
Girzite................................246
Gishpa................................246
Gispa..................................246
Gittah-hepher....................246
Gittaim..............................246
Gittite................................246
Gizonite..............................246
Gizrites..............................246
Glass, Sea of......................246

Goah.. 246
Goath...................................... 246
Gob... 246
God... 246
God, Children of....................... 250
Godhead 250
God, Names of 250
God, Sons of 251
Gods, Pagan............................ 251
Gog... 252
Goiim 253
Golan...................................... 253
Golgotha 253
Goliath 253
Gomer 253
Gomorrah................................ 254
Goshen 254
Gozan 254
Grecians 255
Greece 255
Greek...................................... 256
Greeks 256
Guard, Gate of the 256
Guni.. 256
Gur, Ascent to 256
Gur-baal................................. 256

Haahashtari 257
Habaiah................................... 257
Habakkuk 257
Habaziniah 257
Habazziniah 257
Habor 257
Hacaliah.................................. 257
Hachaliah................................ 257
Hachilah.................................. 257
Hachmoni................................ 257
Hacmoni.................................. 258
Hadad..................................... 258
Hadadezer............................... 258
Hadadrimmon 258
Hadar...................................... 258
Hadarezer 258
Hadashah................................ 258
Hadassah................................. 258
Hades...................................... 258
Hadid...................................... 258
Hadlai..................................... 258
Hadoram.................................. 258
Hadrach 259
Hagab 259

Hagaba 259
Hagabah 259
Hagar...................................... 259
Hagarene................................. 260
Hagarite 260
Hagerite................................... 260
Haggai 260
Haggedolim 260
Haggeri.................................... 260
Haggi 260
Haggiah................................... 260
Haggites 260
Haggith 260
Hagri 260
Hagrite 260
Hahiroth 260
Hai 260
Haines 261
Hakilah.................................... 261
Hakkatan 261
Hakkoz.................................... 261
Hakupha 261
Halah...................................... 261
Halak...................................... 261
Half-Tribe 261
Halhul 261
Hali 261
Hallohesh, Halohesh 261
Halohesh 261
Ham.. 261
Haman..................................... 262
Hamath, Hemath 262
Hamathites 263
Hamath-zobah 263
Hamites................................... 263
Hammath.................................. 263
Hammedatha............................ 263
Hammelech 263
Hammolecheth 263
Hammoleketh 263
Hammon................................... 263
Hammoth-dor........................... 263
Hammuel.................................. 263
Hammurabi 263
Hamonah 264
Hamon-gog 264
Hamor 264
Hamran 264
Hamuel.................................... 264
Hamul 264
Hamulites................................. 264

Hamurapi 264
Hamutal 264
Hanameel 264
Hanamel 264
Hanan 264
Hananeel 265
Hananel 265
Hanani 265
Hananiah 265
Haniel 266
Hannah 266
Hannathon 266
Hanniel 266
Hanoch 266
Hanochites 266
Hanun 266
Hapharaim 267
Haphraim 267
Happizzez 267
Hara 267
Haradah 267
Haran 267
Hararite 268
Harbona 268
Harbonah 268
Hareph 268
Hareth, The Forest of 268
Harhaiah 268
Harhas 268
Harhur 268
Harim 268
Hariph 268
Harmon 269
Harnepher 269
Harod 269
Harodite 269
Haroeh 269
Harorite 269
Harosheth Hagoyim 269
Harsha 269
Harum 269
Harumaph 269
Haruphite 269
Haruz 269
Hasadiah 269
Hasenuah 269
Hashabiah 270
Hashabnah 270
Hashabneiah 270
Hashabniah 270
Hashbadana 270

Hashbaddana 270
Hashem 270
Hashmonah 270
Hashub 270
Hashubah 271
Hashum 271
Hashupha 271
Hasmonean 271
Hasrah 271
Hassenaah 271
Hassenuah, Hasenuah 271
Hasshub, Hashub 271
Hassophereth 271
Hasupha, Hashupha 271
Hatach 272
Hathach 272
Hathath 272
Hatipha 272
Hatita 272
Hattil 272
Hattush 272
Hauran 272
Havilah 272
Havoth-jair 272
Havvoth-jair 273
Hazael 273
Hazaiah 273
Hazar-addar 273
Hazar-enan 273
Hazar-enon 273
Hazar-gaddah 273
Hazar-hatticon 273
Hazarmaveth 273
Hazar-shual 273
Hazar-susah 273
Hazar-susim 273
Hazazon-tamar 274
Hazelel-poni 274
Hazer-hatticon 274
Hazerim 274
Hazeroth 274
Hazezon-tamar 274
Haziel 274
Hazo 274
Hazor 274
Hazor-hadattah 275
Hazzelel-poni 275
Heaven, The Heavens 275
Heavenly City 275
Heber 275
Heberites 276

Hebrew 276
Hebron 276
Hebronites 277
Hegai 277
Hege 277
Helah 277
Helam 277
Helbah 277
Helbon 277
Heldai 278
Heleb 278
Helech 278
Heled 278
Helek 278
Helekites 278
Helem 278
Heleph 278
Helez 278
Heli 278
Heliopolis 278
Helkai 278
Helkath 279
Helkath-hazzurim 279
Hell 279
Helon 279
Hemam 279
Heman 279
Hemath 279
Hemdan 279
Hena 280
Henadad 280
Henoch 280
Hepher 280
Hepherites 280
Hephzibah 280
Heres 280
Heresh 280
Hereth 280
Hermas 280
Hermes 280
Hermogenes 281
Hermon 281
Hermonites 281
Herod 281
Herodians 285
Herodias 286
Herodion 286
Hesed 286
Heshbon 286
Heshmon 286
Hesron 286

Heth 286
Hethlon 286
Hezeki 286
Hezekiah 286
Hezekiah's Water Tunnel 288
Hezion 289
Hezir 289
Hezrai 289
Hezro 289
Hezron 290
Hiddai 290
Hiddekel 290
Hiel 290
Hierapolis 290
High Gate 290
Hilen 290
Hilkiah 290
Hillel 291
Hill of Foreskins 291
Hill of God 291
Hinnom, Valley of 291
Hirah 291
Hiram, Huram 292
Hittites 292
Hittite, Uriah the 293
Hivites 293
Hizki 293
Hizkiah 293
Hizkijah 293
Hobab 293
Hobah 293
Hobaiah 293
Hod 293
Hodaiah 293
Hodaviah 293
Hodesh 294
Hodevah 294
Hodiah 294
Hodijah 294
Hoglah 294
Hoham 294
Holon 294
Holy of Holies 294
Holy Place 294
Holy Spirit 294
Homam 296
Hophni 296
Hophra 296
Hor, Mount 296
Horam 297
Horeb 297

Horem 297
Horesh 297
Hor-haggidgad 297
Hor-hagidgad 297
Hori 297
Horims 297
Horites 297
Hormah 297
Horonaim 297
Horonite 297
Horse Gate 297
Hosah 298
Hosea 298
Hoshaiah 298
Hoshama 298
Hoshea 298
Hosts, Lord of 299
Hotham 299
Hothan 299
Hothir 299
Hozai 299
Hukkok 299
Hukok 299
Hul 299
Huldah 299
Humtah 299
Hundred, Tower of the 299
Hupham 299
Huphamites 299
Huppah 300
Huppim 300
Hur 300
Hurai 300
Huram 300
Huri 300
Hurrians 300
Hushah 300
Hushai 300
Husham 300
Hushathite 300
Hushim 301
Huz 301
Hymenaeus 301

I Am, I am that I Am 302
Ibhar 302
Ibleam 302
Ibneiah 302
Ibnijah 302
Ibri 302
Ibsam, Jibsam 302

Ibzan 302
Ichabod 302
Iconium 303
Idalah 303
Idbash 303
Iddo 303
Idumaea 303
Idumea 303
Iezer 303
Igal 304
Igdaliah 304
Igeal 304
Iim 304
Ije-abarim 304
Ijim 304
Ijon 304
Ikkesh 304
Ilai 304
Illyricum 304
Imla 305
Imlah 305
Immanuel, Emmanuel 305
Immer 305
Imna 305
Imnah 305
Imrah 306
Imri 306
India 306
Inspection Gate 306
Iob 306
Iphdeiah 306
Iphedeiah 306
Iphtah 306
Iphtahel 306
Ir 306
Ira 306
Irad 307
Iram 307
Ir Ha-heres 307
Iri 307
Irijah 307
Ir-nahash 307
Irpeel 307
Ir-shemesh 307
Iru 307
Isaac 307
Isaiah 309
Iscah 311
Iscariot 311
Ishbah 311
Ishbak 311

Ishbi-benob 311
Ish-bosheth...................................... 311
Ishhod, Ishod 312
Ishi.. 312
Ishiah.. 312
Ishijah... 312
Ishma... 312
Ishmael.. 312
Ishmaelite 314
Ishmaiah.. 314
Ishmeelite 314
Ishmerai 314
Ishod... 314
Ishpah... 314
Ishpan... 314
Ishtar 314
Ishtob... 314
Ishuah... 314
Ishuai... 314
Ishui... 314
Ishvah 314
Ishvi 315
Ishyo 315
Ismachiah 315
Ismaiah... 315
Ispah 315
Israel.. 315
Israel, God's Covenant People........ 316
Israelite... 319
Issachar 319
Issachar, Tribe of............................ 319
Isshiah 319
Isshijah.. 319
Isuah.. 319
Isui... 320
Italy.. 320
Ithai 320
Ithamar.. 320
Ithiel 320
Ithlah... 320
Ithmah... 320
Ithnan.. 320
Ithra 320
Ithran... 320
Ithream.. 320
Ithrite... 320
Ittah-kazin 321
Ittai 321
Ituraea 321
Ivah.. 321
Ivvah.. 321

Iye-abarim, Ije-abarim 321
Iyim 321
Izhari, Izehar 321
Izliah, Jezliah.................................. 321
Izrahiah... 321
Izrahite.. 322
Izri 322
Izziah, Jeziah 322

Jaakan 323
Jaakobah 323
Jaala 323
Jaalah 323
Jaalam 323
Jaanai 323
Jaar 323
Jaare-oregim 323
Jaareshiah.. 323
Jaasai 323
Jaasau 323
Jaasiel 323
Jaasu 323
Jaazaniah, Jezaniah......................... 323
Jaazer... 324
Jaaziah... 324
Jaaziel, Aziel 324
Jabal... 324
Jabbok 324
Jabesh 324
Jabesh-gilead................................... 324
Jabez 325
Jabin... 325
Jabneel... 325
Jabneh.. 325
Jacan 325
Jachan 325
Jachin... 325
Jachin and Boaz 325
Jachinites.. 326
Jackal's Well 326
Jacob.. 326
Jacob's Well 328
Jada 328
Jadai 328
Jaddua 328
Jadon 328
Jael 328
Jagur 328
Jah 328
Jahaleleel... 328
Jahath 328

Jahaz 329
Jahaza 329
Jahazah 329
Jahaziah 329
Jahaziel 329
Jahdai 329
Jahdiel 329
Jahdo 329
Jahleel 329
Jahleelites 329
Jahmai 329
Jahzah 329
Jahzeel 330
Jahzeelites 330
Jahzeiah 330
Jahzerah 330
Jahziel 330
Jair 330
Jairite 330
Jairus 330
Jakan 330
Jakeh 330
Jakim 330
Jalam 330
Jalon 330
Jambres 330
James 331
James the Less 333
Jamin 333
Jaminites 333
Jamlech 333
Jamnia 333
Janai 333
Janim 333
Janna 333
Jannai 333
Jannes and Jambres 333
Janoah, Janohah 334
Janum 334
Japheth 334
Japhia 334
Japhlet 334
Japhleti 334
Japhletite 334
Japho 334
Jarah 334
Jareb 334
Jared 334
Jaresiah 334
Jarha 334
Jarib 335

Jarmuth 335
Jaroah 335
Jashar 335
Jashen 335
Jasher 335
Jashobeam 335
Jashub 335
Jashubi-lehem 336
Jashubites 336
Jasiel 336
Jason 336
Jathniel 336
Jattir 336
Javan 336
Jazer, Jaazer 336
Jaziz 336
Jearim 336
Jeaterai 336
Jeatherai 336
Jeberechiah 336
Jebus 336
Jebusi 337
Jebusite 337
Jecamiah 337
Jechiliah 337
Jecholiah 337
Jechoniah 337
Jechonias 337
Jecoliah 337
Jeconiah 337
Jedaiah 337
Jediael 337
Jedidah 338
Jedidiah 338
Jeduthun 338
Jeezer 338
Jeezerite 338
Jegar-sahadutha 338
Jehaleleel 338
Jehalelel 338
Jehallelel 338
Jehdeiah 338
Jehezekel 338
Jehezkel 339
Jehiah 339
Jehiel 339
Jehieli 339
Jehizkiah 339
Jehoadah 339
Jehoaddah 339
Jehoaddan, Jehoaddin 339

Jehoahaz...340
Jehoash..340
Jehohanan..340
Jehoiachin.......................................340
Jehoiada 341
Jehoiakim 341
Jehoiarib...342
Jehonadab..342
Jehonathan.......................................342
Jehoram..342
Jehoshabeath 342
Jehoshaphat 342
Jehoshaphat, Valley of.....................344
Jehosheba...344
Jehoshua...344
Jehoshuah 344
Jehovah...344
Jehovah-jireh...................................344
Jehovah-nissi 344
Jehovah-shalom 344
Jehozabad...344
Jehozadak...345
Jehu..345
Jehubbah..346
Jehucal..346
Jehud 346
Jehudi 346
Jehudijah..346
Jehush...346
Jeiel 346
Jekameam 347
Jekamiah, Jecamiah 347
Jekuthiel...347
Jemima..347
Jemimah..347
Jemuel...347
Jephthae 347
Jephthah..347
Jephunneh..348
Jerah 348
Jerahmeel...348
Jerahmeelites 348
Jered...348
Jeremai 348
Jeremiah..348
Jeremias..350
Jeremoth 350
Jeremy 351
Jeriah 351
Jeribai 351
Jericho 351

Jeriel...353
Jerijah 353
Jerimoth 353
Jerioth...353
Jeroboam...353
Jeroham..355
Jerubbaal 356
Jerubbesheth....................................356
Jeruel 356
Jerusalem 356
Jerusalem Council, The....................361
Jerusalem, New 362
Jerusha 362
Jerushah 362
Jesaiah 362
Jeshaiah 362
Jeshanah 362
Jeshanah Gate 362
Jesharelah 363
Jeshebeab 363
Jesher 363
Jeshiah 363
Jeshimon 363
Jeshishai 363
Jeshohaiah..363
Jeshua 363
Jeshurun, Jesurun 364
Jesiah 364
Jesimiel...364
Jesse 364
Jesshiah 364
Jesui 364
Jesuites...364
Jesurun 364
Jesus...365
Jesus Christ......................................365
Jesus Justus 384
Jether 384
Jetheth 384
Jethlah 384
Jethro 384
Jetur 385
Jeuel 385
Jeush, Jehush 385
Jeuz 385
Jew 385
Jewess 385
Jewish 385
Jewry..385
Jezaniah..386
Jezebel 386

Jezer 386
Jezerites 386
Jeziah 387
Jeziel 387
Jezliah 387
Jezrahiah 387
Jezreel 387
Jezreelite 388
Jezreelitess 388
Jibsam 388
Jidlaph 388
Jimna 388
Jimnah 388
Jiphtah 388
Jiphthah-el 388
Jishui 388
Jisshiah 388
Jithlah 388
Jithra 388
Jithran 388
Jizliah 388
Jizri 388
Joab 388
Joah 390
Joahaz 390
Joanan 390
Joanna 390
Joannas 390
Joash, Jehoash 390
Joatham 391
Job 391
Jobab 392
Jochebed 393
Joda 393
Joed 393
Joel 393
Joelah 394
Joezer 394
Jogbehah 394
Jogli 394
Joha 394
Johanan 394
John 394
John Mark 395
John the Apostle 395
John the Baptist 397
Joiada 399
Joiakim 399
Joiarib, Jehoiarib 399
Jokdeam 400
Jokim 400

Jokmeam 400
Jokneam 400
Jokshan 400
Joktan 400
Joktheel 400
Jona 400
Jonadab, Jehonadab 400
Jonah 400
Jonam, Jonan 401
Jonas 401
Jonathan 401
Joppa 403
Jorah 404
Jorai 404
Joram, Jehoram 404
Jordan 404
Jorim 405
Jorkeam 405
Jorkoam 405
Josabad 405
Josaphat 405
Jose 405
Josech 406
Josedech 406
Joseph 406
Joses 408
Joshah 409
Joshaphat 409
Joshaviah 409
Joshbekashah 409
Josheb-basshebeth 409
Joshibiah, Josibiah 409
Joshua 409
Joshua, Gate of 410
Josiah 410
Josias 411
Josibiah 411
Josiphiah 411
Jotbah 412
Jotbath 412
Jotbathah 412
Jotham 412
Jozabad 412
Jozacar 412
Jozachar 412
Jozadak 412
Jubal 413
Jubilee 413
Jucal 413
Juda 413
Judaea 413

Judah 413	Kenezite 423
Judah, Kingdom of 415	Kenite 423
Judaizers 415	Kenizzite 423
Judas 415	Keren-happuch 424
Judas Iscariot 416	Kerioth 424
Judas Maccabaeus 417	Kerioth-hezron 424
Jude 417	Keros 424
Judea 417	Keturah 424
Judge 418	Kezia 424
Judith 418	Keziah 424
Julia 418	Keziz 424
Julius 418	Kibroth-hattaavah 424
Junias, Junia 418	Kibzaim 425
Jupiter 418	Kidron 425
Jushab-hesed 418	Kinah 425
Justus 418	Kir 426
Jutah 419	Kir-haraseth 426
Juttah 419	Kir-haresh 426
	Kir-heres 426
Kabzeel 420	Kiriath 426
Kadesh 420	Kiriathaim 426
Kadesh, Kadesh-barnea 420	Kiriath-arba 426
Kadmiel 421	Kiriath-baal 426
Kadmonites 421	Kiriath-huzoth 426
Kain 421	Kiriath-jearim 426
Kalai 421	Kiriath-sannah 426
Kallai 421	Kiriath-sepher 426
Kamon 421	Kirjath 427
Kanah 422	Kirjath-arba 427
Kareah 422	Kirjath-huzoth 427
Karka 422	Kirjath-jearim 427
Karkaa 422	Kirjath-sannah 427
Karkor 422	Kirjath-sepher 427
Kartah 422	Kir of Moab 427
Kartan 422	Kiroth 427
Kattath 422	Kish 427
Kedar 422	Kishi 428
Kedemah 422	Kishion 428
Kedemoth 422	Kishon 428
Kedesh 422	Kison 428
Kedron 423	Kithlish 428
Kefr Kenna 423	Kitron 428
Kehelathah 423	Kittim 428
Keilah 423	Koa 428
Keilah the Garmite 423	Kohath 429
Kelaiah 423	Kohathites 429
Kelita 423	Kolaiah 429
Kemuel 423	Korah 429
Kenan 423	Korahite 429
Kenath 423	Korathite 429
Kenaz 423	Kore 429

Korhite 429
Koz... 429
Kushaiah 429

Laadah..................................... 430
Laadan..................................... 430
Laban....................................... 430
Lachish.................................... 431
Ladan....................................... 431
Lael 431
Lahad....................................... 431
Lahai-roi 431
Lahmas.................................... 431
Lahmi...................................... 431
Laish 431
Laishah.................................... 431
Lake of Gennesaret................. 431
Lakkum 431
Lakum 431
Lamech.................................... 431
Laodicea.................................. 432
Lapidoth.................................. 433
Lappidoth 433
Lasea....................................... 433
Lasha 433
Lasharon 433
Lazarus.................................... 433
Leah 434
Lebana..................................... 434
Lebanah................................... 434
Lebanon 434
Lebaoth 435
Lebbaeus 435
Leb Kamai............................... 435
Lebonah 435
Lecah 435
Lehabim 435
Lehi... 435
Lemuel 435
Leshem 435
Letushim 435
Leummim 435
Levi 436
Leviathan 436
Levites 437
Levitical Cities........................ 437
Libanus.................................... 437
Libertines................................ 437
Libnah 437
Libni 438
Libnites.................................... 438

Libya....................................... 438
Likhi 438
Linus....................................... 438
Lo-ammi.................................. 438
Lod.. 438
Lodebar 438
Lois 438
Lord 438
Lord, Jesus is........................... 440
Lord of Hosts.......................... 441
Lo-ruhamah 441
Lot... 441
Lotan 442
Lowland 442
Lubim 442
Lucas....................................... 442
Lucifer 442
Lucius...................................... 443
Lud.. 443
Ludim 443
Luhith 443
Luke 443
Luz.. 444
Lycaonia 445
Lycia 445
Lydda...................................... 445
Lydia 445
Lydians 445
Lysanias................................... 445
Lysias Claudius 445
Lystra...................................... 445

Maacah, Maachah.................... 447
Maachathite, Maacathite 447
Maadai 447
Maadiah 448
Maai.. 448
Maaleh-acrabbim..................... 448
Maarath................................... 448
Maasai 448
Maaseiah 448
Maasiai 449
Maath 449
Maaz 449
Maaziah................................... 449
Macbannai............................... 449
Maccabees, The........................ 449
Macedonia............................... 449
Macedonians 450
Machaerus 450
Machbanai............................... 450

Machbena 450
Machbenah 450
Machi 450
Machir 450
Machirites 450
Machnadebai 450
Machpelah 450
Madaba 451
Madai 451
Madian 451
Madmannah 451
Madmen 451
Madmenah 451
Madon 451
Magadan 451
Magbish 451
Magdala 451
Magdalene 451
Magdiel 452
Magog 452
Magor-missabib 452
Magpiash 452
Mahalab 453
Mahalah 453
Mahalaleel 453
Mahalath 453
Mahali 453
Mahanaim 453
Mahaneh-dan 453
Maharai 453
Mahath 454
Mahavite 454
Mahazioth 454
Maher-shalal-hash-baz 454
Mahlah 454
Mahli 454
Mahlites 454
Mahlon 454
Mahol 454
Mahseiah 454
Makaz 454
Makheloth 455
Makkedah 455
Maktesh 455
Malachi 455
Malcam 455
Malcham 455
Malchiah 455
Malchiel 455
Malchijah, Malchiah 455
Malchiram 456

Malchishua 456
Malchus 456
Maleleel 456
Malkijah 456
Mallothi 456
Malluch 456
Malluchi 456
Malta 457
Mammaias 457
Mamre 457
Manaen 457
Manahath 457
Manahathites 457
Manahethites 457
Manasseh 457
Manasses 459
Manassites, The 459
Manoah 459
Manuhoth 459
Maoch 459
Maon 459
Maonites 459
Mara 459
Marah 459
Maralah 459
Mareal 459
Mareshah 459
Marheshvan 460
Mark, John 460
Market of Appius 461
Maroth 461
Marsena 461
Mars' Hill 461
Martha 461
Mary 462
Mash 466
Mashal 466
Maskil 466
Masrekah 466
Massa 466
Massah 466
Mathusala 466
Matred 466
Matri 466
Mattan 466
Mattanah 466
Mattaniah 467
Mattathah 467
Mattathiah 467
Mattathias 467
Mattattah 467

Mattenai 467
Matthan 467
Matthat 468
Matthew 468
Matthias 468
Mattithiah 469
Mazzaroth 469
Meah 469
Mearah 469
Mebunnai 469
Mecherathite 469
Meconah 469
Medad 469
Medan 469
Mede, Median 469
Medeba 470
Media 470
Mediterranean Sea 470
Megiddo 471
Megiddon 472
Mehetabeel 472
Mehetabel 472
Mehida 472
Mehir 472
Meholathite 472
Mehujael 472
Mehuman 472
Mehunim 473
Me-jarkon 473
Mekonah 473
Melatiah 473
Melchi 473
Melchiah 473
Melchisedec 473
Melchishua 473
Melchizedek 473
Melea 474
Melech 474
Melichu, Melicu 474
Melita 474
Melzar 474
Memphis 474
Memucan 474
Menahem 474
Menan 475
Meni 475
Menna 475
Menuhoth 475
Meonenim 475
Meonothai 475
Mephaath 475

Mephibosheth 475
Merab 476
Meraiah 476
Meraioth 476
Merari 476
Merarites 477
Merathaim 477
Mercurius 477
Mercury 477
Mered 477
Meremoth 477
Meres 477
Meribah 477
Meribah-kadesh 477
Merib-baal 478
Merodach 478
Merodach-baladan 478
Merom, Waters of 478
Meronothite 478
Meroz 478
Mesech 478
Mesha 478
Meshach 478
Meshech 479
Meshelemiah 479
Meshezabeel 479
Meshezabel 479
Meshillemith 479
Meshillemoth 479
Meshobab 479
Meshullam 479
Meshullemeth 480
Mesobaite 480
Mesopotamia 480
Messiah 480
Messias 481
Metheg-ammah 481
Methusael 481
Methuselah 481
Methushael 482
Meunim 482
Meunites 482
Mezahab 482
Mezobaite 482
Miamin 482
Mibhar 482
Mibsam 482
Mibzar 482
Micah 482
Micaiah 483
Michael 484

Michah 485
Michaiah 485
Michal 485
Michmash 486
Michmethath 486
Michri 486
Middin 486
Middle Gate 486
Midian 486
Midianites 486
Migdal-el 486
Migdal-gad 486
Migdol 486
Migron 487
Mijamin 487
Mikloth 487
Mikneiah 487
Milalai 487
Milcah 487
Milcom 487
Miletus, Miletum 487
Millo 488
Miniamin 488
Minjamin 488
Minni 488
Minnith 488
Miphkadgate 488
Miriam 488
Mirma 489
Mirmah 489
Misgab 489
Mishael 489
Mishal 489
Misham 489
Misheal 489
Mishma 489
Mishmannah 489
Mishraites 489
Mispar 490
Misperreth 490
Misrephoth-maim 490
Mithcah 490
Mithkah 490
Mithnite 490
Mithredath 490
Mitylene 490
Mizar 490
Mizpah 490
Mizpar 491
Mizpeh 491
Mizraim 491

Mizzah 491
Mnason 491
Moab 491
Moabites 492
Moadiah 492
Modin 492
Moladah 492
Molech 492
Molid 492
Moloch 493
Molten Sea 493
Morashtite 493
Morasthite 493
Mordecai 493
Moreh 494
Moresheth-gath 494
Moriah 494
Morning Star 494
Moserah 495
Moseroth 495
Moses 495
Most High 501
Mountain of the Valley 501
Mountains of the Amalekites 501
Mountains of the Amorites 501
Mount Baal Hermon 501
Mount Ephraim 501
Mount Heres 501
Mount of Beatitudes 501
Mount of Congregation 501
Mount of Corruption 501
Mount of Olives 502
Moza 503
Mozah 504
Muppim 504
Mushi 504
Mushites 504
Muster Gate, Mustering Gate 504
Myra 504
Mysia 504

Naam 505
Naamah 505
Naaman 505
Naamathite 506
Naamite 506
Naarah 506
Naarai 506
Naaran 506
Naarath 506
Naashon 506

Naasson 506
Nabajoth 506
Nabal 506
Nabatea 506
Nabopolassar 507
Naboth 507
Nabuchodonosor 507
Nachon 507
Nachor 507
Nacon 507
Nadab 507
Naggai 508
Nagge 508
Nahalal 508
Nahaliel 508
Nahallal 508
Nahalol 508
Naham 508
Nahamani 508
Naharai 508
Nahari 508
Nahash 508
Nahath 508
Nahbi 509
Nahor 509
Nahshon 509
Nahum 509
Nain 510
Naioth 510
Naomi 510
Naphathdor 510
Naphish 510
Naphtali 510
Naphtuhim 511
Narcissus 511
Nathan 511
Nathanael 512
Nathan-melech 512
Naum 512
Nazarene 512
Nazareth 512
Nazarite 514
Nazirite 514
Neah 514
Neapolis 514
Neariah 514
Nebai 514
Nebaioth 514
Nebajoth 515
Neballat 515
Nebat 515

Nebo 515
Nebuchadnezzar 515
Nebuchad-rezzar 516
Nebushasban 516
Nebushazban 516
Nebuzaradan 516
Necho 516
Nechoh, Neco, Necoh 516
Nedabiah 516
Negev, The 516
Nehelamite 517
Nehemiah 517
Nehum 518
Nehushta 518
Neiel 518
Nekeb 518
Nekoda 518
Nemuel 518
Nemuelites 519
Nepheg 519
Nephilim 519
Nephish 519
Nephishesim 519
Nephisim, Nephusim,
    Nephushesim 519
Nephthalim 519
Neph-toah 519
Ner 519
Nereus 519
Nergal 519
Nergal-sharezer 519
Neri 519
Neriah 520
Nero 520
Netaim 520
Nethaneal 520
Nethaneel 520
Nethanel 521
Nethaniah 521
Nethinim 521
Netophah 521
Netophathite 521
New Gate 521
New Jerusalem 521
Neziah 522
Nezib 522
Nibhaz 522
Nibshan 522
Nicanor 522
Nicodemus 522
Nicolaitans 523

Nicolas 523
Nicolaus 523
Nicopolis............................. 523
Niger................................... 523
Nile 523
Nimrah................................ 524
Nimrim 524
Nimrod 524
Nimshi................................ 524
Nineveh............................... 524
Ninevites............................. 525
Nisan 525
Nisroch............................... 525
No 526
Noadiah 526
Noah.................................... 526
No-amon.............................. 527
Nob...................................... 527
Nobah.................................. 528
Nobai................................... 528
Nod...................................... 528
Nodab.................................. 528
Noe 528
Nogah.................................. 528
Nohah.................................. 528
Non...................................... 528
Noph.................................... 528
Nophah................................ 528
Nun...................................... 528
Nymphas.............................. 528

Obadiah 529
Obal..................................... 530
Obed.................................... 530
Obed-edom 530
Obil..................................... 530
Oboth 530
Ochran 530
Ocran 530
Oded.................................... 530
Odollam............................... 531
Og 531
Ohad.................................... 531
Ohel..................................... 531
Oholah 531
Oholiab 531
Oholibah.............................. 531
Oholibamah 531
Old Gate.............................. 531
Olivet................................... 531
Olympas............................... 531

Omar.................................... 531
Omri.................................... 532
On.. 532
Onam 532
Onan.................................... 533
Onesimus............................. 533
Onesiphorus 533
Onias................................... 533
Ono...................................... 533
Ophel................................... 533
Ophir................................... 534
Ophni................................... 534
Ophrah................................. 534
Oreb..................................... 534
Oren 534
Orion 534
Ornan................................... 535
Orontes 535
Orpah................................... 535
Osee..................................... 535
Oshea................................... 535
Osnapper 535
Ostia.................................... 535
Othni.................................... 535
Othniel................................. 535
Ovens, Tower of the 536
Ozem 536
Ozias.................................... 536
Ozni..................................... 536
Oznites................................. 536

Paarai................................... 537
Padan, Paddan 537
Padan-aram 537
Padon 537
Pagiel................................... 537
Pahath-moab......................... 537
Pai 537
Palal 537
Palestina 538
Palestine............................... 538
Pallu.................................... 538
Palluites............................... 538
Palti..................................... 538
Paltiel................................... 538
Paltite.................................. 538
Pamphylia 539
Paphos................................. 539
Parah 539
Paran 539
Parbar.................................. 540

Parmashta 540
Parmenas 540
Parnach 540
Parosh 540
Parshandatha 540
Parthians 540
Paruah 540
Parvaim 540
Parzites 540
Pasach 540
Pasdammim 540
Paseah 541
Pashhur 541
Pashur 541
Passover 541
Patara 542
Pathros 542
Pathrusim 542
Patmos 542
Patrobas 542
Pau 542
Paul, The Apostle 542
Paulos 557
Paulus, Sergius 557
Pedahel 557
Pedahzur 557
Pedaiah 557
Pekah 558
Pekahiah 559
Pekod 559
Pelaiah 559
Pelaliah 559
Pelatiah 559
Peleg 559
Pelet 560
Peleth 560
Pelethites 560
Pella 560
Pelonite 560
Peniel 560
Peninnah 560
Pentecost 560
Penuel 561
Peor 561
Peraea 561
Perazim 561
Perea 561
Peresh 561
Perez 561
Perezites 561
Perez-uzza, Perez-uzzah 561

Perga 561
Pergamos 562
Pergamum 563
Perida 563
Perizzites 563
Persia 563
Persis 565
Peruda 565
Peter, Simon 565
Pethahiah 568
Pethor 569
Pethuel 569
Petra 569
Peullethai 569
Peulthai 569
Phalec 569
Phallu 569
Phalti 569
Phaltiel 569
Phanuel 569
Pharaoh 569
Pharaoh's Daughter 572
Pharaoh, Wife of 572
Phares 572
Pharisees 572
Pharosh 573
Pharpar 573
Pharzites 573
Phaseah 573
Phebe 573
Phenice 573
Phenicia 573
Phichol 573
Phicol 573
Philadelphia 573
Philemon 574
Philetus 574
Philip 574
Philippi 575
Philippians 576
Philistia 577
Philistines 577
Philologus 580
Phinehas 580
Phlegon 580
Phoebe 580
Phoenicia 580
Phoenicians 581
Phoenix 581
Phrygia 581
Phurah 582

Phurim 582
Phut 582
Phuvah 582
Phygellus, Phygelus 582
Pi-beseth 582
Pi-hahiroth 582
Pilate, Pontius.................................. 582
Pildash.. 584
Pileha.. 584
Pilha.. 584
Pillar of Fire and Cloud 584
Piltai 584
Pinon... 584
Piram 584
Pirathon 584
Pirathonite 584
Pisgah 584
Pishon 584
Pisidia... 584
Pison 584
Pispah... 585
Pithom.. 585
Pithon... 585
Pleiades 585
Pochereth-hazzebaim....................... 585
Pollux 585
Pontius Pilate.................................... 585
Pontus 585
Pool of Gibeon 586
Poratha 586
Porcius Festus................................... 586
Potiphar 586
Potiphera... 586
Potipherah 586
Potsherd Gate................................... 586
Potter's Field 586
Preparation Day................................ 586
Prisca.. 586
Priscilla 586
Prison, Gate of the............................ 586
Prochorus 587
Promised Land................................... 587
Prophet, False.................................... 587
Ptolemais 587
Ptolemy... 587
Pua.. 587
Puah 587
Publius 587
Pudens... 587
Puhites 587
Pul... 587

Punites 587
Punon.. 587
Purah... 588
Purim 588
Put 588
Puteoli 588
Puthites 588
Putiel 588
Puvah 588
Pyrrhus.. 588

Quartus 589
Queen of Heaven.............................. 589
Queen of Sheba................................. 589
Quicksands.. 589
Quirinius, Cyrenius........................... 589
Qumran, Khirbet............................... 589

Raamah, Raama................................. 590
Raamiah... 590
Raamses... 590
Rabbah 590
Rabbi, Rabboni 590
Rabbith.. 590
Rabboni... 590
Rabdai 590
Rabmag 590
Rabsaris... 591
Rabshakeh 591
Racal.. 591
Rachab... 591
Rachal.. 591
Rachel.. 591
Ragau... 592
Raguel.. 592
Rahab 592
Rahab-hem-shebeth........................... 593
Rahab the Dragon 593
Raham.. 593
Rahel.. 593
Rakem.. 593
Rakkath.. 593
Rakkon... 593
Ram 593
Rama 594
Ramah 594
Ramath... 595
Ramathaim-zophim 595
Ramathite 595
Ramath-lehi....................................... 595
Ramath-mizpah.................................. 595

Ramath-mizpeh 596
Ramath-negeb 596
Ramath of the South 596
Rameses 596
Ramiah 596
Ramoth 596
Ramoth Gilead 596
Ramoth-mizpah 597
Ramoth-negeb 597
Ramses 597
Rapha 597
Raphael 597
Raphah 597
Raphu 597
Reaia 597
Reaiah 597
Reba 597
Rebecca 597
Rebekah 597
Recab 598
Recah 598
Rechab 598
Rechabites 599
Rechah 599
Red Sea 599
Reelaiah 600
Regem 600
Regem-melech 600
Rehabiah 600
Rehob 600
Rehoboam 600
Rehoboth 602
Rehoboth by the River 602
Rehoboth-ir 602
Rehum 602
Rei 602
Rekem 602
Release, Year of 603
Remaliah 603
Remeth 603
Remmon, Remmon-methoar 603
Remnant 603
Remphan 604
Rephael 604
Rephah 604
Rephaiah 604
Rephaim 604
Rephan, Remphan 604
Rephidim 604
Resen 605
Resheph 605

Reu 605
Reuben 605
Reubenites 606
Reuel 606
Rezeph 606
Rezia 606
Rezin 606
Rezon 606
Rhegium 606
Rhesa 607
Rhoda 607
Rhodes 607
Ribai 607
Riblah 607
Rimmon 607
Rimmon-methoar 608
Rimmon-parez 608
Rimmon-perez 608
Rimmon, Rock of 608
Rinnah 608
Riphath 608
Rissah 608
Rithmah 608
River of Egypt 608
Rizia 608
Rizpah 608
Roboam 608
Rodanim 608
Rogelim 608
Rohgah 609
Romamti-ezer 609
Roman 609
Roman Empire 609
Rome, City of 610
Rosh 612
Rufus 612
Ruhamah 612
Rumah 612
Ruth 612

Sabaoth 614
Sabbath 614
Sabeans 615
Sabtah, Sabta 615
Sabteca 615
Sabtecha 615
Sacar 615
Sachar 615
Sachia 615
Sachiah 615
Sadducees 615

Sadoc 615
Sakia 616
Sala 616
Salah 616
Salamis 616
Salathiel 616
Salcah 616
Salchah, Salecah 616
Salem 616
Salim 616
Sallai 616
Sallu 616
Salma 616
Salmai 617
Salmon 617
Salmone 617
Salome 617
Salt, City of 617
Salt Sea 618
Salt, Valley of 618
Salu 618
Samaria, City of 618
Samaria, Region of 620
Samaritan 620
Samgar-nebo 621
Samlah 621
Samos 621
Samothrace 621
Samson 621
Samuel 622
Sanballat 625
Sanctuary 625
Sanhedrin 625
Sansannah 626
Saph 626
Saphir 626
Sapphira 626
Sarah, Sarai 626
Saraph 627
Sardis 627
Sardites 627
Sarepta 627
Sargon 627
Sarid 628
Saron 628
Sarsechim 628
Saruch 628
Satan 628
Saul 629
Sceva 631
Scythian 632

Sea, Brazen 632
Sea, Chinnereth 632
Sea, Dead 632
Sea, Molten 632
Sea of Galilee 632
Sea of Glass 632
Sea of Jazer 632
Sea, Salt 632
Sea, The Great 632
Sea, Tiberius 632
Seba 632
Sebam 632
Sebat 632
Secacah 632
Sechu 632
Second Death 632
Second Quarter, The 633
Secu 633
Secundus 633
Segub 633
Seir 633
Seirah 634
Seirath 634
Sela 634
Sela-hammahlekoth 634
Seled 634
Seleucia 634
Sem 635
Semachiah 635
Semei 635
Semein 635
Senaah 635
Seneh 635
Senir 635
Sennacherib 635
Senuah 636
Seorim 636
Sephar 636
Sepharad 636
Sepharvaim 636
Sepharvites 636
Serah 636
Seraiah 636
Seraphim 637
Sered 637
Seredites 637
Sergius Paulus 637
Serpent Well 637
Serug 638
Seth 638
Sethur 638

Seven Churches of Revelation 638
Seveneh 638
Shaalabbin 638
Shaalbim 639
Shaalbonite 639
Shaalim, Shalim 639
Shaaph 639
Shaaraim 639
Shaashgaz 639
Shabbethai 639
Shachia 639
Shad'dai 639
Shadrach 639
Shagee, Shage 640
Shageh 640
Shaharaim 640
Shahazimah 640
Shahazumah 640
Shalem 640
Shalim 640
Shalisha 640
Shalishah 640
Shallecheth 640
Shallum 640
Shallun 641
Shalmai 641
Shalman 641
Shalmaneser 641
Shama 641
Shamariah 641
Shamed 642
Shamer 642
Shamgar 642
Shamhuth 642
Shamir 642
Shamlai 642
Shamma 642
Shammah 642
Shammai 642
Shammoth 642
Shammua, Shammuah 643
Shamsherai 643
Shapham 643
Shaphan 643
Shaphat 643
Shapher 644
Shaphir, Saphir 644
Sharai 644
Sharaim 644
Sharar 644
Sharezer 644
Sharon 644
Sharonite 644
Sharuhen 644
Shashai 645
Shashak 645
Shaul 645
Shaulites 645
Shaveh 645
Shaveh Kiriathaim 645
Shavsha 645
Sheal 645
Shealtiel 645
Sheariah 645
Shear-jashub 645
Sheba 646
Sheba, Queen of 646
Shebah 646
Shebam 646
Shebaniah 647
Shebarim 647
Shebat 647
Sheber 647
Shebna 647
Shebuel 647
Shecaniah, Shechaniah 647
Shechem 648
Shechemites 649
Shedeur 650
Sheep Gate 650
Sheerah, Sherah 650
Shehariah 650
Shelah 650
Shelanites 650
Shelemiah 650
Sheleph 651
Shelesh 651
Shelomi 651
Shelomith, Shelomoth 651
Shelumiel 651
Shem 651
Shema 652
Shemaah 652
Shemaiah 652
Shemariah 654
Shemeber 654
Shemed 654
Shemer 654
Shemida 654
Shemidah 654
Shemidaites 654
Shemiramoth 654

Shemuel.............................. 655
Shen.................................. 655
Shenazar............................ 655
Shenazzar........................... 655
Shenir............................... 655
Sheol................................ 655
Shepham 656
Shephatiah 656
Shepher 657
Shephi, Shepho 657
Shephupham 657
Shephuphan......................... 657
Sherah 657
Sherebiah 657
Sheresh 657
Sherezer............................. 657
Sheshach 657
Sheshai 658
Sheshan 658
Sheshbazzar 658
Sheth................................ 658
Shethar 658
Shethar-bozenai 658
Shethar-boznai 658
Sheva 658
Shibmah............................. 658
Shicron 658
Shihor............................... 658
Shihor-libnath 659
Shikkeron........................... 659
Shilhi 659
Shilhim.............................. 659
Shillem 659
Shillemites 659
Shiloah 659
Shiloh 659
Shiloni 660
Shilonite 660
Shilshah............................. 660
Shimea, Shimeah 660
Shimeam 661
Shimeath 661
Shimeathites 661
Shimei 661
Shimeites 662
Shimeon 662
Shimhi............................... 662
Shimi 662
Shimites 662
Shimma.............................. 662
Shimon.............................. 662

Shimrath 662
Shimri................................ 662
Shimrith 662
Shimrom............................. 662
Shimron 663
Shimronites 663
Shimron-meron 663
Shimshai 663
Shinab 663
Shinar 663
Shion 663
Shiphi 663
Shiphmite............................ 663
Shiphrah 663
Shiphtan............................. 663
Shisha 663
Shishak.............................. 663
Shitrai 663
Shittim 664
Shiza 664
Shoa................................. 664
Shobab............................... 664
Shobach............................. 664
Shobai............................... 664
Shobal............................... 664
Shobek............................... 664
Shobi................................ 664
Shocho, Shochoh, Socoh 664
Shoham 665
Shomer 665
Shophach 665
Shophan 665
Shua................................. 665
Shuah................................ 665
Shual................................ 665
Shubael.............................. 665
Shuhah............................... 665
Shuham 665
Shuhamites 665
Shuhite 665
Shulamite 665
Shulammite.......................... 666
Shumathites......................... 666
Shunammite 666
Shunem.............................. 666
Shuni 666
Shunites.............................. 666
Shupham 666
Shuphamite.......................... 666
Shuppim.............................. 666
Shur 666

Shushan.................................... 666
Shushanchites........................... 666
Shuthalhites.............................. 666
Shuthelah 667
Sia, Siaha.................................. 667
Sibbecai.................................... 667
Sibbechai.................................. 667
Sibmah 667
Sibraim..................................... 667
Sichem...................................... 667
Siddim...................................... 667
Sidon 667
Sidonians 667
Sihon 668
Sihor 668
Silas... 668
Silla 668
Siloam 668
Siloam, Tower of 668
Silvanus.................................... 668
Simeon 668
Simon 669
Simon Peter 670
Simri 670
Sin.. 670
Sin, Wilderness of...................... 671
Sina.. 671
Sinai... 671
Sinim 672
Sinite.. 672
Sion.. 672
Siphmoth 672
Sippai....................................... 672
Sirah 672
Sirion 672
Sisamai 672
Sisera 673
Sismai 673
Sithri.. 673
Sitnah 673
Sivan 673
Siyon.. 673
Skull, Place of the...................... 673
Slaughter, Valley of 673
Smyrna..................................... 673
So 673
Sochoh, Socoh, Soco 673
Sodi.. 674
Sodom...................................... 674
Sodomite................................... 675
Solomon.................................... 675

Solomon's Porch........................ 679
Son of God................................ 679
Son of Man 679
Sons of God 679
Sopater 679
Sophereth................................. 679
Sorek.. 679
Sosipater 680
Sosthenes 680
Sotai... 680
South, The................................. 680
South Gate 680
South Ramoth 680
Spain.. 680
Spirit.. 680
Spirit, Holy 682
Stachys..................................... 682
Star of Bethlehem 682
Stephanas 682
Stephen 682
Straight Street........................... 684
Suah... 684
Sucathite 684
Succoth..................................... 684
Succoth-benoth.......................... 684
Suchathite................................. 684
Sukkiim 684
Sukkites 685
Sundial of Ahaz......................... 685
Suph... 685
Suphah 685
Supper, Lord's 685
Sur... 685
Susa... 685
Susanchites 685
Susanna 685
Susi.. 685
Sychar...................................... 685
Sychem 685
Syene 685
Symeon 685
Syntyche................................... 685
Syracuse 685
Syria... 685
Syrian 686
Syrophoenician 686
Syrtis Sands, The........................ 686

Taanach 687
Taanath-shiloh 687
Tabbaoth 687

Tabbath 687
Tabeel 687
Taberah 687
Tabernacle of Meeting 687
Tabernacle of the Congregation 688
Tabernacles, Feast of 688
Tabitha 688
Tabor 688
Tabrimmon 688
Tachmonite 688
Tadmor 689
Tahan 689
Tahanites 689
Tahapanes 689
Tahash 689
Tahath 689
Tahchemonite 689
Tahkemonite 689
Tahpanhes 689
Tahpenes 689
Tahrea 690
Tahtim-hodshi 690
Talmai 690
Talmon 690
Tamah 690
Tamar 690
Tammuz 690
Tanach 691
Tanhumeth 691
Taphath 691
Tappuah 691
Tarah 691
Taralah 691
Tarea 691
Tarpelites 691
Tarshish 691
Tarshisha 692
Tarsus 692
Tartak 693
Tartan 693
Tattenai 693
Taverns, Three 693
Tebah 693
Tebaliah 693
Tebeth 693
Tehaphnehes 693
Tehinnah 693
Tekoa 693
Tekoah 694
Tekoite 694
Tel-abib 694

Telah 694
Telaim 694
Telassar 694
Telem 694
Tel-haresha 694
Tel-harsa 694
Tel-harsha 694
Tel-melah 694
Tema 694
Temah 695
Teman 695
Temani 695
Temanite 695
Temeni 695
Tent of Meeting 695
Terah 695
Teresh 695
Tertius 695
Tertullus 696
Tetrarch 696
Thaddaeus 696
Thahash 696
Thamah 696
Thamar 696
Thara 696
Tharshish 696
Thebes 696
Thebez 696
Thelasar 696
Theophilus 696
Thessalonica 696
Theudas 698
Thimnathah 698
Thomas 698
Three Inns 699
Three Taverns 699
Thunder, Sons of 699
Thyatira 699
Tiberias 699
Tiberias, Sea of 699
Tiberius Caesar 699
Tibhath 699
Tibni 699
Tidal 699
Tiglath-pileser 699
Tigris 700
Tikvah 700
Tikvath 700
Tilgath-pilneser 700
Tilon 700
Timaeus 700

Timeus 701
Timna 701
Timnah 701
Timnath-heres 701
Timnath-serah 701
Timnite 701
Timon 701
Timotheus 701
Timothy 701
Tiphsah 703
Tiras 703
Tirathites 703
Tirhakah 703
Tirhanah 703
Tiria 703
Tirshatha 703
Tirzah 703
Tishbite 703
Tishri 703
Titius Justus 704
Titus 704
Titus Justus 705
Tizite 705
Toah 705
Tob 705
Tob-adonijah 705
Tobiah 705
Tobijah 705
Tochen 705
Togarmah 705
Tohu 706
Toi 706
Tokhath 706
Tola 706
Tolad 706
Tolaites 706
Tophel 706
Tophet 706
Topheth 707
Tou 707
Tower of Babel 707
Tower of the Furnaces 707
Trachonitis 707
Transjordan 707
Tree of Knowledge 707
Tree of Life 707
Tribulation, The Great 708
Trinity 708
Tripolis, Men of the 708
Troas 708
Trogyllium 709

Trophimus 709
Trumpets, Feast of 709
Tryphaena 709
Tryphena 709
Tryphosa 709
Tubal 709
Tubal-cain 709
Tychicus 709
Tyrannus 710
Tyre 710

Ucal 712
Uel 712
Ulai 712
Ulam 712
Ulla 712
Ummah 712
Unni 712
Unno 712
Uphaz 712
Upper Gate 712
Ur 713
Urbane 713
Urbanus 713
Uri 713
Uriah 713
Uriel 714
Urijah 714
Uthai 714
Uz 714
Uzai 714
Uzal 714
Uzza, Uzzah 715
Uzza, Garden of 715
Uzzen-sheerah 715
Uzzi 715
Uzzia 715
Uzziah 716
Uzziel 717
Uzzielites 717

Vaheb 718
Vajezatha 718
Valley Gate 718
Valley of Slaughter 718
Vaniah 718
Vashni 718
Vashti 718
Vedan 718
Via Dolorosa 718
Vineyards, Plain of 719
Vophsi 719

Weeks, Feast of.................................. 720
Wilderness of the Wandering 720
Willows, Brook of the 720
Wise Men.. 720

Xerxes.. 721

Yah... 722
Yahweh... 722
Year of Jubilee.................................. 722
Yhwh.. 722

Zaanaim... 723
Zaanan... 723
Zaanannim.. 723
Zaavan... 723
Zabad 723
Zabbai 723
Zabbud... 723
Zabdi.. 724
Zabdiel... 724
Zabidah... 724
Zabud... 724
Zabulon... 724
Zaccai 724
Zacchaeus... 724
Zacchur 724
Zaccur 724
Zachariah.. 725
Zacharias 725
Zacher 725
Zadok 725
Zaham 726
Zair 726
Zalaph 726
Zalmon.. 726
Zalmon, Mount................................ 727
Zalmonah 727
Zalmunna 727
Zamzummim 727
Zanoah 727
Zaphenath-paneah 727
Zaphnath-paaneah 727
Zaphon... 727
Zara, Zarah....................................... 727
Zareathite.. 727
Zared 727
Zarephath 727
Zaretan... 728
Zarethan.. 728
Zareth-shahar................................... 728

Zarhite.. 728
Zartanah 728
Zarthan 728
Zattu 728
Zavan.. 728
Zaza 728
Zealot 728
Zebadiah.. 729
Zebah and Zalmunna....................... 729
Zebaim 729
Zebedee... 730
Zebina 730
Zeboiim 730
Zebudah... 730
Zebul 730
Zebulun.. 730
Zebulunite 731
Zechariah... 731
Zecher 733
Zedad 733
Zedekiah 733
Zeeb... 735
Zelah.. 735
Zelek.. 735
Zelophehad.. 735
Zelotes 735
Zelzah.. 735
Zemaraim 735
Zemarite.. 735
Zemirah 735
Zenan 735
Zenas 735
Zephaniah.. 736
Zephath 736
Zephathah 736
Zephi, Zepho..................................... 736
Zephon... 736
Zer 736
Zerah 736
Zerahiah... 737
Zered 737
Zereda 737
Zeredah 737
Zeredathan 737
Zererah.. 737
Zererath 737
Zeresh... 737
Zereth.. 737
Zereth-shahar................................... 737
Zeri... 738
Zeror.. 738

Zeruah...738
Zerubbabel 738
Zeruiah 739
Zetham..739
Zethan...740
Zethar..740
Zeus..740
Zia...740
Ziba...740
Zibeon...740
Zibia 740
Zibiah 740
Zichri...740
Ziddim 741
Zidkijah...741
Zidon...741
Zidonians...741
Zif 741
Ziha 741
Ziklag 741
Zillah 742
Zillethal, Zilthai 742
Zilpah 742
Zilthai..742
Zimmah 742
Zimran 742
Zimri 742
Zin 743
Zina 743
Zion 743
Zior..744
Ziph 744
Ziphah...744

Ziphims...744
Ziphion 744
Ziphites 744
Ziphron 744
Zippor 744
Zipporah 744
Zithri 745
Ziv...745
Ziz, Ascent of 745
Ziza...745
Zizah..745
Zoan 745
Zoar...746
Zoba, Zobah 746
Zobebah 746
Zohar...746
Zoheleth 746
Zoheth 746
Zophah...746
Zophai...746
Zophar...746
Zophim 747
Zorah...747
Zorathite 747
Zoreah 747
Zorites 747
Zorobabel 747
Zuar...747
Zuph 747
Zur...747
Zuriel...747
Zurishaddai 748
Zuzim, The 748

A

Aaron [Aa'ron], *enlightened or bright*—First high priest of the Hebrew nation. Aaron was the oldest son of Amram and Jochebed, of the tribe of Levi (Ex. 6:16–27). He was three years older than his brother, Moses (Ex. 7:7), and younger than his sister, Miriam. He married Elisheba, a woman of the tribe of Judah, by whom he had four sons—Nadab, Abihu, Eleazar, and Ithamar (Ex. 6:23).

When God called Moses to lead the Hebrew people out of slavery in Egypt, Moses protested that he would not be able to speak convincingly to the pharaoh. So Aaron was designated by God as Moses' official spokesman (Ex. 4:14–16). At Moses' instruction, Aaron also performed miracles as signs for the release of the Hebrews. Aaron's rod turned into a serpent that swallowed the rods of the Egyptian magicians (Ex. 7:8–20). Aaron also caused frogs to cover the land by stretching his rod over the lakes and streams of Egypt (Ex. 8:6).

Aaron held an important place of leadership because of his work with his brother, Moses. A central figure in the exodus from Egypt, he also received instructions from God for observing the first Passover (Ex. 12:1). In the wilderness he assisted Moses in keeping order and rendering judgments over the people (Num. 15:33).

In Israel's first recorded battle with the Amalekites, Aaron and Hur supported the hands of Moses to keep them raised in the air, which ensured Israel's victory (Ex. 17:12).

Both he and Moses were singled out when the people complained about the harsh conditions of these wilderness years (Num. 14:2).

When the priesthood was instituted in the wilderness, Moses consecrated Aaron as the first high priest of Israel (Ex. 28–29; Lev. 8–9). The priesthood was set within the tribe of Levi, from which Aaron was descended. Aaron's sons (Nadab, Abihu, Eleazar, and Ithamar) inherited the position of high priest from their father (Num. 3:2–3).

Aaron was given special robes to wear, signifying his status within the priesthood (Lev. 8:7–9). At his death the robes were transferred to his oldest living son, Eleazar (Num. 20:25–28). The tabernacle, the main sanctuary of worship, was placed under Aaron's supervision (Num. 4). He received instructions from God on the functions of the priesthood and the tabernacle (Num. 18). He alone, serving in the capacity of high priest, went into the Holy of Holies once a year to represent the people on the Day of Atonement.

In spite of his responsibility for the spiritual leadership of the nation, Aaron committed a serious sin in the wilderness surrounding Mount Sinai. While Moses was on the mountain praying to God and receiving His commandments, the people demanded that Aaron make one or more gods for them to worship. Aaron made no attempt to stop the people and made a golden calf for them (Ex. 32:1–10). Aaron was saved from God's wrath only because Moses interceded on his behalf (Deut. 9:20).

After all their years of leading the people, neither Moses nor Aaron was permitted to enter the promised land. Apparently this was because they did not make it clear that God would provide for the Hebrews' needs when they believed they would die for lack of water in the wilderness (Num. 20:12).

Upon arriving at Mount Hor from the wilderness of Kadesh, Aaron was accompanied by Moses and his son Eleazar to the top of the mountain. There he was stripped of his high priestly garments, which were transferred to Eleazar. He died there on Mount Hor at age 123. After Aaron's death, the community mourned for 30 days (Num. 20:22–29).

The book of Hebrews explains how the perfect priesthood of Jesus Christ replaces the faulty and human priesthood of Aaron and his descendants (Heb. 5:2–5; 7:11–12). In contrast with the priesthood of Aaron, the priesthood of Christ is compared with the mysterious figure of Melchizedek, King of Salem and priest of God (Gen. 15:18–20; Ps. 110:4). Melchizedek's priesthood had no beginning and no end; in the same way, the priesthood of Christ is eternal and continuous (Heb. 7:1–3).

Aaronites [Aa′ron·ites]—The priestly descendants of Aaron, part of the tribe of Levi. A large company of Aaronites, under the leadership of

Jehoida, came to David's support when he was anointed king at Hebron (1 Chron. 12:27).

Ab [Ab], *to be fruitful*—The name of the fifth sacred and eleventh civil month of the Jewish calendar. It is a Chaldean name and was not used until after the Babylonian exile.

Abaddon [A·bad'don], *destruction*—Angel of the abyss or bottomless pit, called *Apollyon* in Greek (Rev. 9:11). Several times this word is accompanied by the word *Sheol*, which is often translated *hell* or *the grave* (Prov. 15:11; 27:20).

Abagtha [A·bag'tha], *father of the wine-press*—One of the seven eunuchs of King Ahasuerus (Xerxes), the guardians of the royal harem (Est. 1:10–11).

Abana [Ab'a·na], *stony*—A river of Damascus, probably the present Barada. It rises on a high plain on Anti-Lebanon, 23 miles from Damascus, flows through the city, and gives fertility to the surrounding plain. The Abana is one of the rivers mentioned by the Syrian official, Naaman the leper, when he was complaining about being told to bathe in the Jordan River in order to be cleansed from leprosy (2 Kings 5:12). See also **Pharpar.**

Abanah [Ab' a·nah]—A variation of Abana.

Abarim [Ab'a·rim], *regions beyond*—A mountainous area east of the Jordan and the Dead Sea. One of the encampments of the Israelites was in this region (Num. 21:11). The tribe of Reuben was given settlements within it (Num. 32:2–37). Moses viewed the promised land from the heights of Mount Nebo, a part of this mountain range (Deut. 32:49).

Abba [Ab'ba], *father*—As the everyday language of first-century Jews—the language of Christ and the disciples—Aramaic is the first "Christian" language. This Semitic tongue, closely related to Hebrew, was soon to be superseded by the common (*Koine*) Greek of the Roman Empire, especially in the east. As the faith attracted more and more Gentiles, the Jewish and Aramaic flavor became more and more diluted.

One of the few early Aramaic expressions to survive in the New Testament was the word *abba,* "father." In the Old Testament, God was sometimes seen as the Father of the nation Israel, but it was Christ who revealed that all believers are individually children of God by redemption. In a lesser sense, all people are children of God by creation, but in the sense of the model prayer, the "Our Father," only believers can claim that revealed relationship. Abba, *Father*, is used three times in the New Testament, once in the Gospels and twice by Paul; the Aramaic term being used with a translation. Abba is the most intimate term for Father, one of the first words a child would learn. It is akin to our word "Daddy." This word indicates how close the Father wants His children to feel toward Him.

Mark 14:36. In the Garden of Gethsemane, His "soul . . . exceedingly sorrowful, even to death," Jesus prayed, "Abba, Father, all things are possible for You. Take this cup away from Me; nevertheless, not what I will, but what You will." At this crisis in His ministry, facing betrayal by Judas and shameful death on the cross, the Lord reverted to the tender word He had first used at Mary's and Joseph's knees: *Abba*.

Romans 8:14–16. In one of the most beloved chapters in the Bible, Paul relates a word he no doubt learned as a tiny child to the believer's acceptance as a mature son by adoption, as well as a child by new birth. These blessings come through the third Person of the Trinity: "For as many as are led by the Spirit of God, these are sons of God. For you did not receive the spirit of bondage again to fear, but you received the Spirit of adoption by whom we cry out, 'Abba, Father.' The Spirit Himself bears witness with our spirit that we are children of God."

Galatians 4:6. Paul's other use is similar, only here sonship is contrasted with slavery. We are not merely slaves of God, although we should serve on that level of submission; we are sons. As God's sons and daughters we can boldly say, "Abba, Father!"

Abda [Ab'da], *servant*—Two Old Testament men:

1. The father of Adoniram (1 Kings 4:6).

2. A Leviate, the son of Shammua (Neh. 11:17). He is called Obadiah, the son of Shemaiah in 1 Chronicles 9:16.

Abdeel [Ab'deel], *servant of God*—The father of Shelemiah, who was one of the three appointed to arrest Baruch and Jeremiah (Jer. 36:26).

Abdi [Ab'di], *servant of Jehovah*—Two or three Old Testament men bear this name:

1. A Levite of the family of Merari and grandfather of Ethan, the singer (1 Chron. 6:44).

2. A Levite and father of Kish, contemporary of Hezekiah, king of Judah. He may be the same person as No. 1 (2 Chron. 29:12).

3. A son of Elam who divorced his foreign wife (Ezra 10:26).

Abdiel [Ab'di·el], *servant of God*—The son of Guni, a Gadite who lived in Gilead (1 Chron. 5:15).

Abdon [Ab'don], *servile*—The name of four Old Testament men and one city.

1. Son of Hillel of the tribe of Ephraim, a native of Pirathon, and judge of Israel for eight years. He had forty sons and thirty nephews who rode on asses, an indication of affluence (Judg. 12:13–15).

2. The son of Shashak, a Benjamite chief (1 Chron. 8:23).

3. The firstborn son of Jehiel of Gibeon, a Benjamite and ancestor of Saul (1 Chron. 8:30; 9:35–36).

4. The son of Micah who was sent by Josiah to enquire of Huldah concerning the Book of the Law found in the temple (2 Chron. 34:20). He is also referred to as Achbor (2 Kings 22:12).

5. A town of Asher awarded to the Gershonite Levites, also called Ebron (Josh. 21:30).

Abed-nego [A·bed'-ne·go], *a servant of Nebo*—The Chaldean name given to Azariah in King Nebuchadnezzar's court when he was chosen as one of the king's servants (Dan. 1:7; 2:49). With Shadrach and Meshach, Abed-nego was thrown into the fiery furnace for refusing to bow down and worship a golden image. The three men were miraculously protected from the fire (Dan. 3:12–30) and restored to their former positions. Like the three Hebrew men in the fiery furnace, the nation of Israel endured the captivity and were miraculously protected by God.

Abel [A'bel], *breath or vapor*—The name of a person and two places in the Old Testament:

1. The second son of Adam and Eve, and a shepherd. His brother Cain, who was a farmer, brought an offering of his produce to the Lord. Abel, brought to the Lord an offering "of the firstlings [the best quality] of his flock." The Lord respected Abel and his offering, but he did not respect Cain and his offering (Gen. 4:4–5). Envious of Abel, Cain killed his brother and was cursed by God for the murder.

Abel is described by Jesus as a righteous man, and the first martyr (Matt. 23:35; Luke 11:51; 1 John 3:12). He is listed in the "Hall of Faith," as one who "offered a more excellent sacrifice than Cain" (Heb. 11:4). Cain murdered his brother Abel, wrote John, "because his [Cain's] works were evil and his brother's [Abel's] righteous" (1 John 3:12). It is intimated that righteous Abel's death as a martyr was a foreshadowing of the death of Christ. The blood of Christ, however speaks of better things than the blood of Abel; it speaks of salvation rather than vengeance (Heb. 12:24).

2. A great stone near Beth-shemesh, in the field of a man named Joshua. When the Philistines returned the ark of the covenant to Israel, the Israelites placed the ark upon this stone, and offered sacrifices to the Lord (1 Sam. 6:18).

3. A fortified city in northern Israel, which Joab besieged after the rebellion of Sheba (2 Sam. 20:14–15, 18). This city, called Abel of Beth Maachah, is probably the same place as Abel-beth-maachah.

Abel Acacia Grove [A'bel A·ca'ci·a Grove], *meadow of the acacia*—Also called Abel Shittim (Num. 33:49; Mic. 6:5). Abel Acacia Grove was a site located on the plains of Moab, to the north and east of the Dead Sea, across the Jordan River from the city of Jericho. At the end of the forty years of wandering in the desert, the Israelites made their last camp at Shittim, on the banks of the Jordan. This is where they were staying when the Israelites began to indulge in sexual immorality with the Moabite women, and were enticed into worshipping the Baal of Peor with them.

As a result, 24,000 Israelites were killed by a plague (Num. 25:9). Here also, Moses numbered the fighting men of Israel, counting all those who were twenty years of age or older (Num. 26:2). While Israel was camped at Abel Acacia, God told Moses that he would not be allowed to enter the promised land, but that he would die, leaving Joshua as his successor and the leader of the people (Num. 27:12–23).

After Moses's death, Joshua sent out two spies from Abel Acacia, to discover the state of the people, and the strength of the armies and fortifications they would have to face in the new land they were setting out to conquer (Josh. 2:1). These two spies were sheltered by the woman

Rahab, in the city of Jericho. After their return, Israel broke camp, and following the ark of the covenant, they at last crossed the Jordan River into the promised land (Josh. 3:1).

Abel-beth-maachah [A'bel-beth-ma'a·chah], *meadow of the house of Maachah*—A town in the north of Israel, in the territory of Naphtali (2 Sam. 20:15; 1 Kings 15:20; 2 Kings 15:29). When his revolt against David failed, Sheba fled to this place. Joab, David's captain, threatened to assault the town to secure Sheba but spared it when assured that the rebel would be put to death. After the division of the nation, in the days when the godly king Asa ruled Judah, Ben-hadad, king of Amram, seized this town from evil king Baasha of Israel (1 Kings 15:20). Later, Tiglath-pileser, king of Assyria, captured Abel-beth-maachah and several other towns, and mentioned the fact in his annals (2 Kings 15:29).

Abel-cheramim [A·bel-cher'a·mim]—A form of Abel-keramim.

Abel-keramim [A·bel-ker'a·mim], *meadow of the vineyards*—A town near Minnith east of the Jordan to which Jephthah pursued the Ammonites, called *plain of the vineyards* in the King James Version (Judg. 11:33).

Abel-maim [A·bel-ma'im]—A town in northern Israel (2 Chron. 16:4), usually referred to as Abel-beth-maacah.

Abel-meholah [A'bel-me·ho'lah], *meadow of dancing*—The home of Elisha (Judg. 7:22; 1 Kings 19:16). It was probably about ten miles south of Bethshan on the west side of the Jordan.

Abel-mizraim [A'bel-miz'ra·im]—See Atad.

Abel-shittim [A'bel-shit'tim], *meadow of acacias*—It is also called Shittim (Num. 25:1; Josh. 2:1; Mic. 6:5). It was the final stopping place of the Israelites (Num. 33:49) and where Israel's idolatry was punished by a plague in which 24,000 died. See Abel Acacia Grove.

Abez/Ebez [A'bez/E'bez], *white*—A town of Issachar (Josh. 19:20), also called Ebez.

Abi, Abia, Abiah [A'bi, A·bi'a, A·bi'ah]—See Abijah.

Abi-albon [A′bi-al′bon], *father of strength*—One of David's mighty men (2 Sam. 23:31), called Abiel in 1 Chronicles 11:32.

Abiasaph [A·bi′a·saph], *father of gathering*—A son of Korah, the Levite (Ex. 6:16, 18, 21, 24). He may be the same person as Ebiasaph (1 Chron. 6:23; 9:19).

Abiathar [A·bi′a·thar], *father of abundance*—One of two chief priests in the court of David. Abiathar was the son of Ahimelech of the priestly clan of Eli from Shiloh (1 Sam. 22:20). When the residents of the priestly village of Nob were massacred by Saul for helping David, Abiathar was the only one to escape (1 Sam. 22:6–23). When David eventually became king, he appointed Abiathar, along with Zadok, as priests in the royal court (2 Sam. 8:17; 1 Chron. 18:16).

When David's son Absalom tried to take his throne by force, David was forced to leave Jerusalem. Zadok and Abiathar carried the ark of the covenant out of the capital city but later returned it at the command of David (2 Sam. 15:29). Both priests remained in Jerusalem to inform David of Absalom's plans (2 Sam. 15:34). After Absalom's death, Abiathar and Zadok carried the message of reconciliation to Amasa and the elders of Judah (2 Sam. 19:11–14).

During the struggle over who would succeed as king, Abiathar supported Adonijah. When Solomon emerged as the new ruler, Zadok was appointed priest of the royal court, while Abiathar escaped execution only because of his earlier loyalty to David. He and his family were banished to Anathoth, and his rights and privileges as a Jerusalem priest were taken away (1 Kings 1:7–25; 2:22–35).

Some scholars believe Abiathar may have written portions of 1 and 2 Samuel, especially the sections describing the royal court life under David.

Abib [A′bib], *an ear of corn*—The first month of the Jewish sacred year (Ex. 13:4), after the Exile called Nisan (Neh. 2:1; Est. 3:7).

Abida/Abidah [A·bi′da/A·bi′dah], *father of knowledge*—One of the sons of Midian, who was the son of Abraham and Keturah (Gen. 25:4; 1 Chron. 1:33).

Abidan [A·bi′dan], *the father judges*—Son of Gideoni, a prince of the tribe of Benjamin. He was the representative chosen by God to recount the history of his family and tribe when the census of Israel was taken in the wilderness (Num. 1:11; 2:22; 10:24).

Abiel [A·bi'el], *father of strength*—Two Old Testament men.

1. The father of Kish and Ner and grandfather of Saul and Abner according to 1 Samuel 9:1; 14:51, but he may have been the grandfather of Kish since Ner is listed as the father of Kish in 1 Chronicles 8:33; 9:39.

2. One of David's mighty men (1 Chron. 11:32), called Abialbon, the Arbathite, in 2 Samuel 23:31.

Abiezer [A·bi·e'zer], *father of help*—Two men of the Old Testament.

1. Son of Hammoleketh, a descendant of Manasseh. One of his descendants was the famous Gideon who was led by God to defeat the Midianite army with only three hundred men (Josh. 17:2; 1 Chron. 7:18). The name is sometimes abbreviated to Jeezer or Iezer (Num. 26:30).

2. One of David's mighty men. He is described as an Anathothite, from the tribe of Benjamin (2 Sam. 23:27; 1 Chron. 27:12). Much later, the prophet Jeremiah lived in the town of Anathoth (Jer. 1:1).

Abiezrite [A·bi·ez'rite]—A member of the family of Abiezer (Judg. 6:11, 24; 8:32), also called Jeezerite but more properly Iezrite.

Abigail [Ab'i·gail], *father of joy*—Two Old Testament women had this delightful name.

1. Wife of Nabal the Carmelite and, after his death, of David (1 Sam. 25:3, 14–42; 2 Sam. 2:2; 1 Chron. 3:1). Abigail's husband, Nabal, was an ill-tempered, drunken man. When David was hiding from the jealous King Saul, he asked Nabal for food for himself and his men. Nabal blatantly refused. Angered, David threatened to plunder Nabal's possessions and kill Nabal himself. Abigail, in her wisdom, gathered enough food for David's men, rode out to meet David, and bowed before him to show her respect.

By agreeing with David that Nabal had acted with great disrespect, she stemmed David's anger. To Abigail's credit, she did not leave her godless husband. When Nabal died, apparently from shock at discovering his near brush with death, David married Abigail and she later bore him a son, Chileab, called Daniel in 1 Chronicles 3:1. At one point after this she was taken captive by the Amalekites when they seized Ziklag but was rescued by David (1 Sam. 30:5, 18).

2. A sister or half sister of David and mother of Amasa, whom Absalom made captain of the army instead of Joab (2 Sam. 17:25; Abigal, NRSV, REB; 1 Chron. 2:16–17). She may be the same person as No. 1.

Abigal [Ab′i·gal]—See Abigail.

Abihail [Ab′i·ha·il], *father of strength*—Two women and three men of the Old Testament.

1. The father of Zuriel, a Levite of the family of Merari (Num. 3:35).

2. Wife of Abishur and mother of Ahban and Molid; of the tribe of Judah, descended through Hezron (1 Chron. 2:29).

3. A chief of the family of Gad in Bashan, the son of Huri (1 Chron. 5:14).

4. The daughter of David's brother Eliab (2 Chron. 11:18). It is a little unclear whether she was wife of Rehoboam, or the wife of David's son Jerimoth, and the mother of Rehoboam's wife, Mahalath.

5. Father of Esther and uncle of Mordecai (Est. 2:15; 9:29).

Abihu [A·bi′hu], *God is father*—One of the four sons of Aaron who were consecrated as the priestly family (Ex. 6:23; 24:1; 28:1). He and his brother Nadab used "strange" fire at the altar and were struck dead (Lev. 10:1–7). Since immediately afterward a law was pronounced prohibiting priests from using strong drink in the tabernacle (Lev. 10:9), it is possible that the sin of the two brothers was committed while they were intoxicated.

Abihud [A·bi′hud], *father of renown*—A descendant of Benjamin's son Bela (1 Chron. 8:3).

Abijah/Abi/Abia/Abiah [A·bi′jah/A′bi/A·bi′a/A·bi′ah], *The Lord is my father*—Nine people in the Old Testament bore this name:

1. A descendant of Eleazar whose family was eighth of the twenty-four courses into which the priests were divided. He served in David's time (1 Chron. 24:1, 10).

2. The wife of Hezron of Judah, and mother of Ashur (1 Chron. 2:24).

3. The second son of Samuel, and an unworthy judge in Beersheba (1 Sam. 8:2; 1 Chron. 6:28).

4. A descendant of Benjamin through Becher (1 Chron. 7:8).

5. A son of King Jeroboam. When the child became ill, Jeroboam sent his wife to Ahijah, the prophet, to inquire as to the outcome. Ahijah spoke the judgment of God upon Jeroboam for his idolatry, declaring the child would die (1 Kings 14:1–18).

6. The son and successor of King Rehoboam and grandson of Solomon (1 Chron. 3:10; 2 Chron. 12:16; 13:1–14:1), also called Abijam. His mother was Absalom's granddaughter Maacah (2 Chron. 11:20–22). During his three-year reign he followed the evil ways of his father and fought against King Jeroboam of Israel (1 Kings 15:6–7), a war in which Israel lost half a million men (2 Chron. 13:16–20). He had fourteen wives, twenty-two sons, and sixteen daughters (2 Chron. 13:21). Also called Abia (Matt. 1:7).

7. The mother of Hezekiah, king of Judah. Also called Abi (2 Kings 18:2; 2 Chron. 29:1).

8. One of the priests who set his seal upon Nehemiah's covenant (Neh. 10:7).

9. A priest who returned to Jerusalem from Babylon with Zerubbabel (Neh. 12:4, 7). Later, a priestly family bore this name (Neh. 12:17) and to this family belonged Zacharias, the father of John the Baptist (Luke 1:5).

Abijam [A·bi'jam]—See Abijah, No. 6.

Abilene/Abila [Ab·i·le'ne/A·bi·la], *meadow*—A district of Coele-Syria on the eastern side of Anti-Lebanon. Its capital, Abila, was on the Abana (modern Barada) River, about twenty miles northwest of Damascus. Lysanius was the governor at the time John the Baptist began to minister (Luke 3:1).

Abimael [A·bim'a·el], *father of Mael*—A descendant of Shem. One of Joktan's thirteen sons, and founder of an Arabian tribe (Gen. 10:28; 1 Chron. 1:22).

Abimelech [A·bim'e·lech], *royal father*—The name of five men in the Old Testament:

1. The king of Gerar in the time of Abraham (Gen. 20:1–18; 21:22–34). When Abraham was traveling through the area ruled by Abimelech, he was afraid that someone might kill him because of Sarah's beauty, so he declared Sarah to be his sister. Abimelech claimed Sarah for his harem, only to be warned in a dream that he had taken the wife of another man. Then Abimelech returned Sarah to Abraham. The two men made a covenant with each other, and Abraham asked God to reward the king by giving him many children, for God had closed all the wombs in his household because of Sarah. Many scholars believe that the word Abimelech is not a proper name but a royal title of the Philistine kings, just as pharaoh was a title for Egyptian kings.

2. Another Philistine king of Gerar, perhaps son of the preceding, with whom Isaac had a very similar experience to Abraham (Gen. 26:1–33).

3. The ruler of the city of Shechem during the period of the judges (Judg. 8:30–10:1; 2 Sam. 11:21). Abimelech was a son of Gideon by a concubine from Shechem. Abimelech tried to become king, and he did reign over Israel for three years (Judg. 9:22). In order to eliminate all who might challenge his authority, assisted by relatives of his mother he killed all the other sons of Gideon—his brothers and half brothers—who were potential successors of his father (Judg. 9:5). Abimelech was killed in a battle at Thebez, a city northeast of Shechem, which he surrounded with his army. When Abimelech ventured too close to the city tower, a woman dropped a millstone on his head, crushing his skull, fatally wounding but not killing him immediately. Abimelech commanded his armorbearer to kill him so it could not be said that he died at the hands of a woman (Judg. 9:50–54; 2 Sam. 11:21).

4. A priest, the son of Abiathar, whose name should probably read Ahimelech (1 Chron. 18:16; 24:6). He served during David's time.

5. In the title of Psalm 34, the name Abimelech is used, apparently as a title for Achish, king of Gash (1 Sam. 21:10–15).

Abinadab [A·bin′a·dab], *father of generosity*—Four men of the Old Testament.

1. A man of Kirjath-jearim in whose house the ark was kept after the Philistines returned it (1 Sam. 7:1–2; 2 Sam. 6:3; 1 Chron. 13:7).

2. A son of Jesse and older brother of David who served in Saul's army when David slew Goliath (1 Sam. 16:8; 17:13).

3. A son of Saul who was slain with his father at Gilboa (1 Sam. 31:2).

4. The father of Ben-abinadab who married a daughter of Solomon. Ben-abinadab was in charge of the district of Dor (1 Kings 4:11). See Ben-abinadab.

Abiner [Ab'i·ner]—See Abner.

Abinoam [A·bin'o·am], *father of grace*—The father of Barak, the judge (Judg. 4:6; 5:12). He was of the tribe of Naphtali.

Abiram [A·bi'ram], *father of elevation*—Two Old Testament men.

1. A Reubenite, son of Eliab. He and his brother Dathan joined Korah in his rebellion. He and his family were destroyed in an earthquake as punishment for their sin (Num. 16; 26:9–10).

2. The oldest son of Hiel, the Beth-elite. A curse had been pronounced upon the posterity of anyone who should attempt to rebuild Jericho. Hiel undertook to do this, and the curse was fulfilled. When the foundations were laid, his oldest son Abiram died; when the gates were set up, his youngest son Segub died (Josh. 6:26; 1 Kings 16:34).

Abishag [Ab'i·shag], *father of error*—A beautiful young woman brought from her home in Shunem to serve David in his old age (1 Kings 1:1–4). Following David's death, his son, Adonijah, desired to marry her and sought the permission of Solomon. Since she had been the wife of David, this request was regarded as leading to a claim for the throne and Adonijah was put to death (1 Kings 2:13–25).

Abishai/Abshai [Ab'i·shai/Ab'shai], *father of a gift*—The son of David's sister or half sister, Zeruiah, and brother of Joab and Asahel (2 Sam. 2:18; 1 Chron. 2:16). He led David to where Saul was sleeping and asked permission to slay him but David refused (1 Sam. 26:5–9). When David came to the throne, Abishai entered the army under Joab. He is listed as one of David's mighty men (2 Sam. 23:18; 1 Chron. 11:20). Among other exploits, he slew eighteen thousand Edomites in the Valley of Salt and fortified that country (1 Chron. 18:12–13). Abishai remained true to David when Absalom rebelled, and wanted to kill Shimei for cursing David (2 Sam. 16:9–10; 19:21–22). When Sheba son of Bichri tried to take over the kingdom, Abishai led forces to subdue the rebel (2 Sam. 20:2, 6). All three of the sons of Zeruiah seem to have had a reputation for being impulsive and hot-headed, but they served David with remarkable loyalty.

Abishalom [A·bi'sha·lom]—A form of the name Absalom (1 Kings 15:2, 10). See Absalom.

Abishua [A·bi'shu·a], *father of salvation*—Two Old Testament men:

1. A Benjamite of the family of Bela (1 Chron. 8:4). He was the ancestral head of a Benjamite clan.

2. A son of Phinehas, he became the fourth high priest (1 Chron. 6:4–5, 50; Ezra 7:5).

Abishur [A·bi'shur], *father is a wall*—A son of Shammai of Judah (1 Chron. 2:28–29).

Abital [A·bi'tal], *father of the dew*—A wife of David, the mother of Shephatiah who was the fifth of the six sons born to David at Hebron (2 Sam. 3:4; 1 Chron. 3:3).

Abitub [A·bi'tub], *father of goodness*—The son of Shaharaim and Hushim, part of the geneology of Saul (1 Chron. 8:8–11).

Abiud [A·bi'ud], *father of praise*—Son of Zerubbabel, in the geneology of Christ (Matt. 1:13).

Abner [Ab'ner], *father of light*—The son of Ner and cousin of King Saul. He was commander-in-chief of Saul's army (1 Sam. 14:51) and was present when David slew Goliath (1 Sam. 17:55–58). After Saul's death, Abner placed Ish-bosheth on the throne (2 Sam. 2:8). David's captain, Joab, defeated Abner (2 Sam. 2:12–32) and when the latter was retreating from the battle, he killed Asahel, a brother of Joab, in self-defense. Later Abner had a disagreement with his king and switched his allegiance to David. David was willing to accept him, but before Abner could fulfill his promise to rally Israel around David, Joab slew Abner in revenge for his brother's death. David was horrified by Joab's treachery, and mourned for Abner, but left Solomon to deal with the crime (2 Sam. 3:6–39; 1 Kings 2:5, 28–34).

Abomination of Desolation [A'bom·i·na'tion of Des·o·la'tion]—Daniel the prophet foretold an "abomination of desolation" which would be placed in the sanctuary of the Lord, defiling it (Dan. 11:31; 12:11). This would occur during a time of great trouble in Israel, when one who opposed the covenant of God would make an end of the sacrifices, and blaspheme God (Dan. 11:28–35). The same term "abomination of desolation" was used by Jesus when He instructed His disciples concerning the last days, quoting Daniel's prophecy as something yet to come (Matt. 24:15–16; Mark 13:14). This misuse of the temple was to be a sign of the terrors to come, and those who were in Jerusalem should flee.

The Jews saw the defilement of the temple by Antiochus Epiphanes (168 B.C.) as the fulfillment of Daniel 11:31. Antiochus Epiphanes sacrificed a pig on the altar of the temple, and erected an idolatrous altar to Jupiter Olympius. These certainly were times of great unrest and persecution of God's people. However, since Jesus still referred to Daniel's prophecy as future, nearly two hundred years after Antiochus Epiphanes' deplorable action, many believe that the fulfillment occurred in A.D. 70 when the Romans destroyed the temple (Luke 21:5–7, 20–22).

Certainly, the sacrifices ceased at that time, and have never been resumed; the temple is desolate. Still others believe that the abomination of desolation is yet to come, when the "man of sin" will sit in the temple, claiming to be God and requiring worship (2 Thess. 2:3–4). This final act of rebellion and defilement would be the mark of the beginning of the end of the age.

Abraham, originally Abram **[A′bra·ham/A′bram]**, *father of a multitude,* originally *exalted father*—The first great patriarch of ancient Israel and a primary model of faithfulness for Christianity. A descendant of Shem's son Arphaxad (Gen. 11:10–32). Seven generations after Arphaxad, Terah became the father of Abram, Nahor, and Haran. The family lived in Ur of the Chaldees in southern Babylonia. Later, Terah moved his family to Haran on their way to the land of Canaan. The accounts about Abraham are found in Genesis 11:26–25:11, with the biblical writer focusing on four important aspects of his life.

1. The Migration: Abraham's story begins with his migration with the rest of his family from Ur of the Chaldeans in ancient southern Babylonia (Gen. 11:31). He and his family moved north along the trade routes of the ancient world and settled in the flourishing trade center of Haran, several hundred miles to the northwest.

While living in Haran, at the age of 75 Abraham received a call from God to go to a strange, unknown land that God would show him. The Lord promised Abraham that He would make him and his descendants a great nation. The Messiah, the Savior of the world, would be brought forth from the nation of which Abraham was the founder (Gen. 12:1-3).

The promise must have seemed unbelievable to Abraham because his wife Sarah (called Sarai in the early part of the story) was childless (Gen. 11:30-31; 17:15). But Abraham obeyed God with no hint of doubt or disbelief. He took his wife and his nephew, Lot, and went to the land that God would show him.

Abraham moved south along the trade routes from Haran, through Shechem and Beth-el in the land of Canaan. Canaan was a populated area at the time, inhabited by the warlike Canaanites; so Abraham's belief that God would ultimately give this land to him and his descendants was an act of faith. The circumstances seemed quite difficult, but Abraham's faith in God's promises allowed him to trust in the Lord (Heb. 11:8).

2. The Famine and the Separation from Lot: Because of a severe famine in the land of Canaan, Abraham moved to Egypt for a short time (Gen. 12:10-20). During this trip, Abraham introduced Sarah to the Egyptians as his sister rather than as his wife in order to avoid trouble. Pharaoh, the Egyptian ruler, then took Sarah as his wife. It was only because "the Lord plagued Pharaoh and his house with great plagues because of Sarai, Abram's wife" (Gen. 12:17), that Sarah was returned to Abraham.

Upon his return from Egypt, Abraham and his nephew, Lot, quarreled over pasturelands and went separate ways (Gen. 13:8-9). Lot settled in the Jordan River valley, while Abraham moved into Canaan. After this split, God reaffirmed His promise to Abraham: "And I will make your descendants as the dust of the earth; so that if a man could number the dust of the earth, then your descendants also could be numbered" (Gen. 13:16).

Apparently Abraham headed a strong military force by this time as he is called "Abram the Hebrew" (Gen. 14:13). He succeeded in rescuing his nephew Lot from the kings who had captured him while raiding the cities of Sodom and Gomorrah (Gen. 14:14-17).

3. The Promise Reaffirmed: In Genesis 15 the Lord reaffirmed His promise to Abraham. The relationship between God and Abraham should be understood as a covenant relationship—the most solemn form of arrangement between individuals in the ancient world. According to such an arrangement, individuals or groups agreed to abide by certain conditions that governed their relationship to each other. In this case Abraham agreed to go to the land that God would show him (an act of faith on his part), and God agreed to make Abraham a great nation (Gen. 12:1–3). However, in Genesis 15 Abraham became anxious about the promise of a nation being found in his descendants because of his advanced age. The Lord thus reaffirmed the earlier covenant.

As we know from recent archaeological discoveries, a common practice of that time among heirless families was to adopt a slave who would inherit the master's goods. Therefore, because Abraham was childless, he proposed to make a slave, Eliezer of Damascus, his heir (Gen. 15:2). But God rejected this action and challenged Abraham's faith: "Then he [God] brought him [Abraham] outside and said, 'Look now toward heaven, and count the stars if you are able to number them.' And He said to him, 'So shall your descendants be'" (Gen. 15:5). Abraham's response is the model of believing faith. "And he [Abraham] believed in the Lord, and He [God] accounted it to him for righteousness" (Gen. 15:6).

The rest of chapter 15 consists of a ceremony between Abraham and God that was commonly used in the ancient world to formalize a covenant (Gen. 15:7–21).

According to Genesis 16, Sarah, because she had not borne a child, provided Abraham with a handmaiden. This also appears to be a familiar custom of the ancient world. According to this custom, if the wife had not had a child (preferably a male) by a certain time in the marriage, she was obligated to provide a substitute (usually a slavewoman) to bear a child to her husband and thereby ensure the leadership of the clan. Thus, Hagar, the Egyptian maidservant, had a son by Abraham. The boy was named Ishmael. Although Ishmael was not understood to be the child that would carry on the line promised to Abraham, he was given a favorable blessing (Gen. 16:10–13; 17:20).

Abram would have to wait fourteen more years for this child. When he was ninety-nine years old, God spoke to him again about the covenant, changing his name to Abraham (and Sarai's name to Sarah), and instituting the sign of circumcision.

The most substantial account of the covenant between Abraham and God is given in Genesis 17—a covenant that extended the promise of the land and descendants to further generations. This covenant required Abraham and the male members of his household to be circumcised as the sign of the agreement (Gen. 17:10–14). The name of the son whom God promises that Sarah will bear is designated as Isaac (Gen. 17:19–21). The practice of circumcision instituted at this time is not unique to the ancient Hebrews, but its emphasis as a religious requirement is a unique feature of God's covenant people. It became a visible symbol of the covenant between Abraham and his descendants and their redeemer God.

When Abraham was one hundred years old and Sarah ninety, their son Isaac was born (Gen. 21:1–7). Isaac was the promised son, through whom God's covenant with Abraham would be fulfilled). Sarah was unhappy with the presence of Hagar and Ishmael. She asked Abraham to cast them out of the family, which he did after the Lord told him they would have His protection. Ishmael does not play an important role in the rest of Abraham's story, though he does reenter the picture in Genesis 25:9, accompanying Isaac at Abraham's death.

4. The Supreme Test: When Isaac was a young boy God commanded Abraham to sacrifice his beloved son Isaac as a crucial test of his faith. Abraham was willing to give up his son in obedience to God, although at the last moment the Lord intervened to save Isaac (Gen. 22:1–13). The Lord's promise of descendants as numerous as the stars of the heavens was once again reaffirmed as a result of Abraham's unquestioning obedience (Gen. 22:16–18).

Abraham did not want Isaac to marry a woman from one of the local tribes. Possibly he feared this would introduce Canaanite religious practices into the Hebrew clan. Thus, Abraham sent a senior servant to Haran, the city from which he had migrated, to find a wife for Isaac. This mission was successful, and Isaac eventually married Rebekah, the sister of Laban (Gen. 24:1–67).

Sarah had died some time earlier, when Abraham was 137 years old (Gen. 23:1–20). Abraham eventually remarried and fathered several children by Keturah, named Zimran, Jokshan, Medan, Midian, Ishbak, and Shua (Gen. 25:1–6). Abraham died at the age of 175 and was buried alongside Sarah in the cave of Machpelah, near Hebron (Gen. 25:7–11).

In summary, Abraham was the father of the Hebrews and the prime example of a righteous man. In spite of impossible odds, Abraham had faith in the promises of God. Therefore, he is presented as a model for human behavior. Hospitable to strangers (Gen. 18:1–8), he was a God-fearing man (Gen. 22:1–18) who was obedient to God's laws (Gen. 26:5).

The promises originally given to Abraham were passed on to his son Isaac (Gen. 26:3), and to his grandson Jacob (Gen. 28:13; 35:11–12).

Abraham's descendants remained the chosen people of God; the subsequent chapters of Genesis and the rest of the Old Testament describe God's working with this people, forging them into a nation, teaching them to obey His commandments, and preparing the way for the coming Messiah. In later biblical references, the God of Israel is frequently identified as the God of Abraham (Gen. 26:24), and Israel is often called the people "of the God of Abraham" (Ps. 47:9; 105:6). Abraham was such an important figure in the history of God's people that when they were in trouble, Israel appealed to God to remember the covenant made with Abraham (Ex. 32:13; Deut. 9:27; Ps. 105:9).

In the New Testament, Abraham is presented as the supreme model of vital faith and as the prime example of the faith required for the Christian believer (Rom. 4:11; Gal. 3:6–9; 4:28). He is viewed as the spiritual father for all who share a similar faith in Christ (Matt. 3:9; Luke 13:16; Rom. 11:1). If anyone deserves to be called God's "friend," it is Abraham (Isa. 41:8).

Abram [A'bram], *exalted father*—Abraham's name before the covenant of circumcision (Gen. 17:5). See Abraham.

Abronah/Ebronah [Ab·ro'nah/Eb·ro'nah], *passage*—An encampment of the Israelites in the wilderness (Num. 33:34–35).

Absalom [Ab'sa·lom], *father of peace*—David's third son by Maacah, the daughter of the king of Geshur (2 Sam. 3:3; 1 Chron. 3:2). Of royal descent on both sides, Absalom was a potential heir to the throne. Attractive in appearance and charming in manners, Absalom was also a popular prince with the people and a favorite of his father. He was especially noted for his beautiful long hair, in which he took great pride (2 Sam. 14:25–26).

During the height of Israel's prosperity under David's rule, another of David's sons, Amnon, raped his half sister Tamar—Absalom's sister (2 Sam. 13:1–22). Absalom took it upon himself to avenge this dishonor, eventually succeeding after two years in having Amnon murdered by his servants (2 Sam. 13:23–29). Fearing his father's wrath, Absalom fled into exile. He stayed with his grandfather Talmai in Geshur for three years (2 Sam. 13:37–38).

Since Absalom was one of David's favorite sons, the king longed for his return (2 Sam. 13:39) in spite of his crime. Joab, one of David's advisors, urged that Absalom be allowed to return to Jerusalem on probation but that he not be allowed to appear before David.

Absalom did return to Jerusalem, but this turned out to be an ill-advised move on David's part. Absalom secretly plotted a revolt against the throne. Taking advantage of his natural appeal and his handsome appearance to win the favor of the people, he also aroused discontent by implying that he could rule more justly than his father. When the plot was ready, Absalom obtained permission to go to Hebron to worship. Meanwhile, he had sent spies throughout the tribes, inviting those favorable to him to meet at Hebron (2 Sam. 15:7–11). After gathering these warriors, he then enlisted Ahithophel, a disloyal official of David, as his aide and advisor (2 Sam. 15:12).

When David learned of these rebellious acts, he fled to Mahanaim, beyond the Jordan River (2 Sam. 17:24). Under Ahithophel's advice, Absalom entered Jerusalem and publicly took possession of the wives in his father's harem who had been left in the city. By this act Absalom demonstrated that he would never be reconciled with his father, and even more of the people rallied to his cause.

Absalom then called a council to determine what action to take against David. Present at this meeting was Hushai, a loyal advisor to David who pretended to follow Absalom in order to spy on the proceedings. Ahithophel advised that Absalom move against the retreating king as quickly as possible, but Hushai countered by pointing out that if the attack failed, his revolt would fail. He advised instead that Absalom gather all his forces for one full-scale attack. Absalom heeded Hushai's counsel, giving David time to assemble an army. Absalom was formally anointed king after taking Jerusalem (2 Sam. 19:10). He appointed Amasa as captain of his army, then crossed the Jordan to meet his father's forces.

The battle took place in the woods of Ephraim, where Absalom's recruits were no match for David's veterans. Absalom's army was defeated, and 20,000 of his men were killed (2 Sam. 18:6–7).

Absalom tried to flee from the forest on a mule, but his head caught in the thick boughs of a terebinth tree. Joab, the captain of David's army, found then killed Absalom as he hung there in spite of David's request that he not be harmed. Upon hearing the news of his death,

David moaned, "O my son Absalom—my son, my son Absalom—if only I had died in your place! O Absalom my son, my son!" (2 Sam. 18:33). These are some of the saddest words in the Bible.

Absalom had many talents and abilities. But he was also spoiled, impatient, and overly ambitious. These, along with his vanity and pride, led to his tragic death. His body was cast into a pit, over which a great heap of stones was piled as a sign of contempt (2 Sam. 18:17). A large mausoleum erroneously called Absalom's Monument, located in the Kidron Valley east of Jerusalem, was built centuries after Absalom's death. It can still be seen today.

Absalom's Pillar [Ab'sa·lom's Pillar]—Also called Absalom's monument. Absalom had this edifice set up as a memorial to himself, since at the time he had no sons (2 Sam. 18:18). It was located in the King's Valley, and bears a tragic contrast to his dishonored grave.

Abyss [A·byss'], *bottomless*—The place of the dead—Hades—also called the bottomless pit; especially the place of evil spirits under Apollyon—Satan (Rev. 9:11; 17:8; 20:1–3). Apparently it is a place that the demons fear, for the demons that Jesus drove out of the Gadarene man begged Him not to send them to the abyss (Luke 8:31). The Septuagint (the Greek version of the Old Testament) uses the word *abyss* to translate the word that English Bibles usually translate *the deep* (Gen. 1:2).

Acacia Grove [A·ca'cia Grove]—See Abel Acacia Grove.

Acacias, Valley of [A·ca'ci·as, Valley of]—Through the prophet Joel, God described the peace and plenty that would follow the restoration of Israel. The land would flow with wine and milk, all the brooks would be full, and a fountain would come from the temple and water the Valley of Acacias. Apparently this valley was very dry. It may have acquired its name because nothing but acacias, a specific type of tree, would grow there (Joel 3:18).

Accad/Akkad [Ac'cad/Ak'kad], *subtle*—One of the four towns in Shinar which formed the kingdom of Nimrod (Gen. 10:10). The name was also applied to the district called the land of Accad. It embraced at one time northern Babylonia and the cities of Babylon and Cutha; the area between the Tigris and Euphrates Rivers. The Accadian language is considered to be one of the earliest written Semitic languages—Babylonian and Assyrian are two of its dialects, as is the Aramaic that was spoken by Jesus and His disciples in New Testament days. The location of ancient Accad is thought to be only a few miles from modern Baghdad.

Accaron [Ac'caron]—See Ekron.

Accho [Ac'cho]—See Acco.

Acco [Ac'co], *hot sand*—A city allotted to the tribe of Asher, located south of Tyre, and about eight or nine miles north of Mount Carmel. Even though this city was supposed to be a part of Asher's territory, they never managed to drive out the Canaanite inhabitants. It was taken by Shalmaneser when the Assyrians invaded Israel in the reign of Hoshea. Its name was changed to Ptolemais during the time of the Greek Empire. It came under Roman rule in 65 B.C. It held an important geographical position as a seaport at the entrance to the valley of Jezreel. A Christian community was established in Acco, and on his third missionary journey Paul spent a day there (Acts 21:7). The city is now called Acre.

Accuser—See Satan.

Aceldama [A·cel'da·ma]—See Akeldama.

Achaia [A·chai'a], *trouble*—Originally the northern part of the Peloponnesus, but the name was applied by the Romans (146 B.C.) to all of Greece and Macedonia. Augustus divided the whole into two provinces. The northern province was Macedonia; it extended westward to the Adriatic. In the south was Achaia, with Corinth as its capital. The latter division is the province referred to in the New Testament (Acts 18:12–17; 19:21; Rom. 15:26; 2 Cor. 1:1; 1 Thess. 1:7).

While Paul was living in Corinth, the Jews brought him before Gallio, the proconsul of Achaia, accusing him of teaching false religion. Gallio refused to pay attention to their charge, and Paul was set free. The region of Achaia was apparently well evangelized, for when Apollos wanted to go there, the Christians in Ephesus were able to send him to other believers in Achaia for hospitality and help (Acts 18:27).

Achaicus [A·cha'i·cus], *belonging to Achaia*—A Christian of Corinth. He rendered Paul a service, along with Stephanas and

Fortunatus, and is kindly spoken of in the first letter to the Corinthians (1 Cor. 16:17).

Achan [A'chan], *trouble*—A son of Carmi of the tribe of Judah who, after the fall of Jericho, stole a wedge of gold and a Babylonian mantle. God had specifically commanded the Israelites not to take any plunder of any kind from the city, but rather to consider everything as belonging to God. Achan's disobedience caused the defeat of Joshua at Ai. After God had showed Joshua through the casting of lots who the culprit was, Achan confessed his sin and was stoned to death (Josh. 7:1–26).

Achar [A'char]—See Achan.

Achaz [A'chaz]—See Ahaz.

Achbor [Ach'bor], *mouse*—Two or possibly three Old Testament men:

1. The father of Baal-hanan, king of Edom (Gen. 36:38; 1 Chron. 1:49).

2. Son of Micaiah and father of Elnathan. In 2 Chronicles 34:20 he is called Abdon. He was an officer of Josiah, and one of the five men sent to inquire of the prophetess Huldah about the Book of the Law which had been found in the temple (2 Kings 22:12, 14; Jer. 26:20–23; 36:12).

3. The father of Elnathan, who was one of the men sent by Jehoiakim king of Judah to bring the prophet Urijah back from Egypt in order that he might be put to death (Jer. 26:20–23; 36:12). Since Jehoiakim was the son of Josiah, it is possible that Elnathan's father was the same person as No. 2.

Achim [A'chim], *whom God makes firm*—Born after Israel was taken into captivity in Babylon, son of Zadok and father of Eliud; part of the genealogy of Jesus (Matt. 1:14).

Achish [A'chish], *serpent charmer*—The king of Gath, a Philistine city, to whom David fled when he was pursued by Saul. David feared for his life when he saw that Achish remembered his reputation as Goliath's killer, and pretended to be insane.

Achish was apparently deceived and took no interest in a mad former hero, other than to order that David be taken out of his sight (1 Sam. 21:10–15; 27:1–12; 29:1–11). He is called Abimelech in the title of Psalm 34, but it seems likely that this was a title rather than a name, as Pharaoh was for the kings of Egypt.

Achmetha [Ach·me'tha], meaning *Ecbatana*—The capital of northern Media. It is the same as Ecbatana, a treasure city and the summer residence of the Persian kings. When the Samaritans were hindering the building of the second temple, the Jews declared that Cyrus had issued a decree that the temple should be built. Darius ordered that the claim be investigated, and when nothing could be found in Babylon to establish the veracity of this report, the search was continued in Achmetha. There, in the palace, the decree was found (Ezra 5:6–6:2). The city was conquered in 330 B.C. by Alexander the Great, and destroyed. Today, the site is occupied by the Iranian city of Hamadan.

Achor [A'chor], *trouble*—A valley south of Jericho on the northern boundary of Judah. It was here that Achan was stoned to death (Josh. 7:24–26; 15:7). The prophets spoke of the valley of Achor as a place which would be a "door of hope" (Hos. 2:15), and a peaceful place for herds to lie down (Isa. 65:10) when the restoration of Israel came about. See Achan.

Achsah, Achsa [Ach'sah, Ach'sa], *anklet*—Caleb's daughter, who was offered in marriage to the one who should capture Kirjath-sepher (also called Debir). Caleb's near relative, Othniel, the first of the judges, succeeded and won the daughter. She received from her father as her dowry a portion of the Negev, and upon her request he also gave her the valley of springs (Josh. 15:16–19; Judg. 1:12–15; 1 Chron. 2:49).

Achshaph [Ach'shaph], *enchantment*—A city of Canaan (Josh. 11:1; 12:7, 20; 19:24–25). It was part of the land given to the tribe of Asher, in the north.

Achzib [Ach'zib], *deceit*—Two Israelite towns:

1. A town in the southern section of Palestine included in the territory of Judah, also called Chezib (Gen. 38:5; Josh. 15:44; Mic. 1:14), probably the same as Chozeba (1 Chron. 4:22).

2. A seacoast town in Asher, which would be western Galilee (Josh. 19:29) from which the Canaanites were not driven (Judg. 1:31).

Acrabbim [Ac·rab'bim]—Joshua 15:3. See Maaleh-acrabbim.

Acre [A·cre′]—See Acco.

Acsah [Ac′sah]—See Achsah.

Adadah [A·da′dah], *festival*—A town in the southern part of the territory of Judah (Josh. 15:22).

Adah [A′dah], *beauty*—Two Old Testament women:
1. A wife of Lamech and mother of Jabal and Jubal (Gen. 4:19–23).
2. Daughter of Elon, the Hittite, a wife of Esau. Her oldest son was Eliphaz, from whom the Edomites descended (Gen. 36:2–4).

Adaiah [A·dai′ah], *Jehovah hath adorned*—Eight Old Testament men:
1. A man of Bozcath, father of Jedidah who was the mother of Josiah, king of Israel (2 Kings 22:1).
2. A Levite descended from Gershom, and an ancestor of Asaph (1 Chron. 6:41–42).
3. A Benjamite, son of Shimhi (1 Chron. 8:21).
4. Two members of the families of Bani and Binnui who divorced their foreign wives (Ezra 10:29, 39).
5. The father of Maaseiah who helped to put Joash on the throne of Judah (2 Chron. 23:1).
6. Son of Joiarib (Neh. 11:5).
7. A Levite of the family of Aaron (1 Chron. 9:12).

Adalia [A·da′li·a], *I shall be drawn up of Jah*—One of Haman's ten sons; he and his brothers were hanged along with their father (Est. 9:8).

Adam [Ad′am], *red or ground*—The name of a man and a city in the Old Testament:
1. The first man, created by God on the sixth day of creation, and placed in the garden of Eden (Gen. 2:19–23; 3:8–9, 17, 20–21; 4:1, 25; 5:1–5). He and his wife Eve, created by God from one of Adam's ribs (Gen. 2:21–22), became the ancestors of all people now living on the earth. Adam was unique and distinct from the animals in several ways. His creation is described separately from that of the animals and the rest of God's creative acts (Gen. 1:3–27; 2:7).

God breathed into Adam's body of "dust" the divine "breath of life; and man became a living being" (Gen. 2:7). God also made man in his own image and likeness. The exact words are "Let Us make man in Our image, according to Our likeness" (Gen. 1:26). The apostle Paul interprets this to mean that God created man with spiritual, rational, emotional, and moral qualities (Eph. 4:24–32; Col. 3:8–10).

God placed Adam in the garden of Eden where he was to work the ground (Gen. 2:5, 15) and take care of the animals (Gen. 1:26–28; 2:19–20). God made Eve as a "helper comparable to" Adam (Gen. 2:20), creating her out of one of Adam's ribs so they were "one flesh" (Gen. 2:24).

God told the human pair, "Be fruitful and multiply; fill the earth" (Gen. 1:28). As a consequence, they had a number of children: Cain, Abel, Seth, and a number of other sons and daughters (Gen. 4:1–2; 5:3–4). Created in innocence, they did not know sin (Gen. 2:25).

Genesis 3 tells how Adam failed to keep God's command not to eat of the Tree of Knowledge of Good and Evil. The consequence of this disobedience was death (Gen. 2:17), both physical (Gen. 5:5) and spiritual (Eph. 2:1). Eve disobeyed first, lured by pride and the desire for pleasure (Gen. 3:5–6; 1 Tim. 2:14). Then Adam, with full knowledge of the consequences, joined Eve in rebellion against God (Gen. 3:6).

The consequences of disobedience were: (1) loss of innocence (Gen. 3:7); (2) continued enmity between the seed of the woman [Christ] (Gen. 3:15; Gal. 3:16) and the seed of the serpent [Satan and his followers] (John 8:44); (3) the cursing of the ground and the resultant hard labor for man (Gen. 3:17–19); (4) the hard labor of childbirth (Gen. 3:16); (5) the submission of woman to her husband (Gen. 3:16; Eph. 5:22–23); and (6) separation from God (Gen. 3:23–24; 2 Thess. 1:9). Adam lived 930 years (Gen. 5:5).

The New Testament emphasizes the oneness of Adam and Eve (Matt. 19:3–9), showing that Adam represented man in bringing the human race into sin and death (Rom. 5:12–19; 1 Cor. 15:22). In contrast, Christ, the "last Adam," represented His redeemed people in bringing justification and eternal life to them (Rom. 5:15–21).

2. A city located "beside Zaretan" (Josh. 3:16), near the junction of the Jabbok River and the Jordan River, about 30 kilometers (18 miles) north of Jericho.

Also, considered a gender neutral term simply meaning "human" (Gen. 5:2).

Adamah [Ad′a·mah], *soil*—A fortified city of Naphtali, northwest of the Sea of Galilee (Josh. 19:36).

Adami-nekeb [Ad′a·mi-nekeb], *man of the pass*—A town of Naphtali, near the lower border (Josh. 19:33).

Adar [A′dar], *glorious*—Twelfth month of the Hebrew sacred year (Ezra 6:15; Est. 3:7, 13; 9:15). It extended from the new moon in February to the new moon in March.

Adar, Addar [A′dar, Ad′dar], *height or top*—A place on the southern boundary of Judah (Josh. 15:3), also called Hazar–addar in Numbers 34:4.

Adbeel [Ad′beel], *a miracle of God*—One of the twelve sons of Ishmael and head of a tribe (Gen. 25:13; 1 Chron. 1:29).

Addan, Addon [Ad′dan, Ad′don], *strong* or *firm*—A place in Babylonia (Ezra 2:59; Neh. 7:61). It was the home of certain persons who returned to Israel from exile but were unable to produce genealogies proving that they were truly Israelites.

Addar [Ad′dar], *a wide place*—A town on the southern boundary of Judah (Num. 34:4; Josh. 15:3), also called Adar and Hazar–addar. Also a Benjamite in Numbers 26:49 and 1 Chronicles 8:3—see Ard.

Addi [Ad′di]—An ancestor of Jesus, the Greek form of IDDO (Luke 3:28).

Addon [Ad′don]—See Addan.

Ader [A′der]—See Eder.

Adida [Ad′i·da]—See Adithaim.

Adiel [Ad′i·el], *ornament of God*—Three Old Testament men:
1. Head of a family of Simeon (1 Chron. 4:36).
2. A priest, son of Jahzerah and father of Maasai (1 Chron. 9:12).
3. The father of Azmaveth (1 Chron. 27:25).

Adin [A′din], *effeminate*—The head of a family, many of which returned from Babylon with Zerubbabel and Ezra (Ezra 2:15; 8:6; Neh. 7:20). A chief of the family signed the covenant with Nehemiah (Neh. 10:16).

Adina [Ad′i·na], *delicate*—One of David's mighty men, the son of Shiza the Reubenite (1 Chron. 11:42).

Adino [Ad′i·no], *his ornament*—Chief of David's mighty men. The name of Adino the Eznite was given to Josheb-Basshebeth, the Tachmonite, when he killed eight hundred men at one time (2 Sam. 23:8).

Adithaim [Ad·i·tha′im], *double prey*—A town of Judah, sometimes identified with Adida (Josh. 15:36).

Adlai [Ad·la′i], *God's justice*—The father of Shaphat. Shaphat was David's servant, one of two men who were in charge of all David's herds (1 Chron. 27:29).

Admah [Ad′mah], *red earth*—A city in the vale of Siddim—one of the cities of the plain (Gen. 10:19; 14:2, 8). It was destroyed with Sodom (Gen. 19:25, 28–29; Deut. 29:23; Hos. 11:8).

Admatha [Ad·ma′tha], *unconquered* or *God-given*—A prince of Persia under Ahasuerus at Shushan; one of the seven with privileged access to the king (Est. 1:14).

Adna [Ad′na], *pleasure*—Two Old Testament men:

1. A priest, the son of Harim, who returned from captivity during the time Joiakim was high priest (Neh. 12:15).

2. A son of Pahath-moab who divorced his foreign wife (Ezra 10:30).

Adnah [Ad′nah], *pleasure*—Two Old Testament men:

1. A man of Judah and high officer in the army of Jehoshaphat (2 Chron. 17:14).

2. A man of Manasseh who joined David at Ziklag (1 Chron. 12:20).

Adonai [A·do·nai], *lord*—See God, Names of.

Adoni-bezek [Ad′o·ni-be′zek], *lord of Bezek*—A king of Bezek. He was captured by soldiers of the tribes of Judah and Simeon, who cut off his thumbs and big toes. Adoni-bezek saw this as a just punishment from God, because he himself had served seventy kings with the same treatment (Judg. 1:4–7).

Adonijah [Ad·o·ni′jah], *the Lord is my Lord*—The name of three men in the Old Testament:

1. The fourth of the six sons born to David while he was at Hebron (2 Sam. 3:4). Adonijah's mother was Haggith. With the exception of Absalom, David apparently favored Adonijah over his other five sons. When David was old, Adonijah attempted to seize the throne, although he probably knew that his father intended Solomon to succeed him (1 Kings 1:13).

Adonijah won two important people to his cause—Joab, the captain of the army, and Abiathar, the priest. At an open-air feast at the stone of Zoheleth beside En Rogel, he had himself proclaimed king. But Adonijah had not won over Zadok the priest, Benaiah the commander of the royal bodyguard, or Nathan the prophet. Bathsheba, Solomon's mother, and Nathan told David of Adonijah's activities; David immediately ordered Solomon, who had been divinely chosen as David's successor, to be proclaimed king. When Adonijah sought sanctuary at the altar (1 Kings 1:5–50), Solomon forgave him.

Adonijah, however, foolishly made another attempt to become king—this time after David's death. He asked that the beautiful Abishag, who had taken care of David during his final days, be given to him in marriage. According to the custom of the day, claiming a king's wife or concubine amounted to the same thing as claiming his throne. This time Solomon ordered that Adonijah be killed (1 Kings 2:13, 25).

2. One of the Levites sent by Jehoshaphat to instruct the people of Judah in the law (2 Chron. 17:8).

3. A chieftain who, with Nehemiah, sealed the covenant (Neh. 10:14–16); he is also called Adonikam (Ezra 2:13).

Adonikam [Ad·o·ni′kam], *the Lord arises*—The founder of a family, members of which returned from exile with Nehemiah and Ezra (Ezra 2:13; 8:13; Neh. 7:18), probably the same person as the Adonijah of Nehemiah 10:16.

Adoniram [Ad·o·ni′ram], *the Lord is exalted*—One who had charge of tribute under David and Solomon, also known as Adoram (2 Sam. 20:24) and Hadoram (2 Chron. 10:18). He was stoned to death when he attempted to deal with the ten tribes at the time of revolt (1 Kings 4:6; 12:18).

Adoni-zedek, Adoni-zedec [Ad'o·ni-ze'dek, Ad'o·ni-ze'dec], *lord of righteousness*—King of Jerusalem who joined a confederacy of Amorite kings against Joshua. They were defeated (Josh. 10:1–27).

Ador, Adora—See Adoraim.

Adoraim [Ad·o·ra'im], *double honor*—A lowland city of Judah, fortified and rebuilt by Rehoboam, son of Solomon. It is about five miles southwest of Hebron and is now named Dura (2 Chron. 11:9).

Adoram [Ad'o·ram]—See Adoraim.

Adrammelech [A·dram'me·lech], *honor of the king*—
    1. An idol of the Sepharvites (2 Kings 17:31).
    2. Son of Sennacherib, king of Assyria. Adrammelech and his brother Sharezar killed their father the king (2 Kings 19:37; Isa. 37:38).

Adramyttium [Ad·ra·myt'ti·um], *I shall abide in death*—A city of Mysia in Asia Minor. Paul sailed in a ship of this city as a prisoner on his way to Rome (Acts 27:2).

Adria [A'dri·a]—See Adriatic.

Adriatic [A'dri·a'tic], *without wood*—The Adriatic Sea is the portion of the Mediterranean Sea east of Italy—so named from the old Etruscan town of Atria (Adria). By New Testament times it included also that portion of the Mediterranean north of a line joining Malta and Crete (Acts 27:27).

Adriel [A'dri·el], *flock of God*—A man of the tribe of Issachar. Saul's daughter Merab was given him in marriage (1 Sam. 18:19).

Adullam [A·dul'lam], *resting place*—A town of Judah which was inhabited by Canaanites in the time of Jacob (Gen. 38:1–2). It was conquered by Joshua (Josh. 12:15) and was fortified by Rehoboam (2 Chron. 11:7). After the Exile, it was occupied by Jews (Neh. 11:30). Near the city was a cave in which David hid for a long time and where he was joined by many of his adherents (1 Sam. 22; 2 Sam. 23:13; 1 Chron. 11:15).

Adullamite [A·dul'lam·ite]—A native or inhabitant of Adullam. Judah's friend Hirah is the only Adullamite mentioned in the Bible (Gen. 38:1, 12, 20).

Adummim [A·dum′mim], *red things*—A pass on the boundary between the territories of Benjamin and Judah. In this region was laid the scene of the parable of the good Samaritan (Josh. 5:7; 18:17; Luke 10:30).

Aeneas [Ae·ne′as], *laudable*—A man at Lydda afflicted with palsy for eight years. His restoration through Christ resulted in growth of the church (Acts 9:32–35).

Aenon [Ae′non], *fountains*—A locality near Salim which abounded with springs and where many came to be baptized by John the Baptist and to hear him preach (John 3:23).

Agabus [Ag′a·bus], *locust*—A prophet of Jerusalem in the time of Paul. He predicted the famine which occurred during the reign of Claudius (Acts 11:28); and warned Paul about what would happen to him in Jerusalem (Acts 21:10–11).

Agag [A′gag], perhaps *flaming*—

1. A king of Amalek mentioned by Balaam (Num. 24:7).

2. The Amalekite king who was spared by Saul and slain by Samuel (1 Sam. 15:9–33). The word may be the title of these kings as Pharaoh was the title for the kings of Egypt.

Agagite [Ag′a·gite]—Epithet applied to Haman (Est. 3:1, 10; 8:3–5).

Agar [Ag′ar]—See Hagar.

Agee [A′gee], *fugitive*—A Hararite and father of Shammah, one of David's warriors (2 Sam. 23:11).

Agrippa [A·grip′pa]—See Herod.

Agur [A′gur], *hired* or *gatherer*—Son of Jakeh who uttered the wisdom in Proverbs 30.

Ahab [A′hab], *father is brother*—The name of two men in the Old Testament:

1. The son of Omri and the seventh king of Israel, his reign began during the closing years of King Asa of Judah (1 Kings 16:29–30). Under the influence of Jezebel, his wife, Ahab gave Baal equal place with God. Ahab also built a temple to Baal in which he erected a "wooden image" of the Canaanite goddess Asherah (1 Kings 16:33). At Jezebel's urging,

Ahab opposed the worship of the Lord, destroyed His altars, and killed His prophets. He reigned over Israel in Samaria for twenty-two years (873–852 B.C.) (1 Kings 16:29).

Ahab strengthened the friendly relations with Phoenicia that David had begun when he was king of the united kingdom. He sealed the friendship between the two nations with a political marriage to Jezebel, the notoriously wicked daughter of Ethbaal, king of the Sidonians (1 Kings 16:31). Ahab may have been the first king of Israel to establish peaceful relations with Judah.

False religion soon led to immoral civil acts. Because Jezebel had neither religious scruples nor regard for Hebrew civil laws (Lev. 25:23–34), she had Naboth tried unjustly and killed so that Ahab could take over his property (1 Kings 21:1–16).

Throughout Ahab's reign, the prophet Elijah stood in open opposition to Ahab and the worship of Baal. During this time, at Mt. Carmel Elijah called on the Lord to bring down miraculous fire on his sacrifice, whereas the priests of Ahab and Baal could not (1 Kings 18:36). Ahab also had frequent conflicts with Ben-hadad, king of Syria, who once besieged Ahab's capital city, Samaria, but was driven off (1 Kings 20:1–21).

Later, Ahab defeated Ben-hadad in a battle at Aphek (1 Kings 20:22–34); but Ahab was lenient with him, perhaps in view of a greater threat, Shalmaneser III of Assyria. In 853 B.C., Ahab and Ben-hadad joined in a coalition to stop Shalmaneser's army at Qarqar on the Orontes River in Syria. Ahab contributed 2,000 chariots and 10,000 soldiers to this coalition. Still later, Ahab fought Ben-hadad again. In spite of his precautions, Ahab was killed at Ramoth Gilead (1 Kings 22:1–38).

Ahab was a capable leader and an avid builder. He completed and adorned the capital city of Samaria, which his father Omri had begun. Archaeological discoveries show that Ahab's "ivory house" (1 Kings 22:39; Amos 3:15) was faced with white stone, which gave it the appearance of ivory. It also was decorated with ivory inlays. The ivory fragments that have been found show similarities with Phoenician ivories of the period. These findings illustrate the close political and social ties that existed between Israel and Phoenicia. Archaeology has also shown that Ahab refortified the cities of Megiddo and Hazor, probably in defense against growing threats from Syria and Assyria.

Ahab's story is particularly sad because of his great potential. His tragedy was forming an alliance with Jezebel and turning from God to serve idols.

2. The son of Kolaiah and one of two false prophets denounced by Jeremiah (Jer. 29:21–23). Because Ahab prophesied falsely in God's name, Jeremiah declared that he would die at the hand of Nebuchadnezzar, king of Babylon, and would be cursed by all Babylonian captives from Judah.

Aharah [A·har′ah], a *following brother*—Third son of Benjamin (1 Chron. 8:1), called Ehi in Genesis 46:21 and Ahiram in Numbers 26:38.

Aharhel [A·har′hel], a *following host*—Son of Harum (1 Chron. 4:8).

Ahasai, Ahzai [A·ha′sai, Ah′zai], *my holder* or *protector*—A priest of the family of Immer whose descendants dwelt at Jerusalem after the captivity (Neh. 11:13), possibly the same as Jahzerah (1 Chron. 9:12).

Ahasbai [A·has′bai], *brother of my encompassers*—A Maachathite, father of Eliphelet, one of David's warriors (2 Sam. 23:34).

Ahashverosh [A·hash·ve′rosh]—A form of Ahasuerus (Ezra 4:6).

Ahasuerus [A·has·u·e′rus], *mighty man*—The name of two kings in the Old Testament:

1. A king of Persia and the husband of the Jew Esther. Scholars generally agree that Ahasuerus is the same person as Xerxes I (485–464 B.C.).

The picture of Ahasuerus presented in the book of Esther—the vastness of his empire (1:1), his riches (1:4), his sensuality and feasting (1:5–12), and his cruelty and lack of foresight (1:13–22)—is consistent with the description of Xerxes provided by the Greek historian Herodotus. Ahasuerus succeeded his father, Darius Hystaspis, in 485 B.C. The book of Esther tells the story of how Ahasuerus banished his queen, Vashti, because of her refusal to parade herself before the drunken merrymakers at one of his feasts. Following a two-year search for Vashti's replacement, Ahasuerus chose Esther as his queen. Esther and her people, the Jews, were in Persia as a consequence of the fall of Jerusalem (in 586 B.C.) and the scattering of the Jews into captivity in foreign lands.

Ahasuerus's advisor, Haman, hated the Jews; he prevailed upon Ahasuerus to order them to be wiped out—an order that the king gave with little concern for its consequences. During a sleepless night, Ahasuerus sent for his royal records and read of how the Jew Mordecai, Esther's guardian, had uncovered a plot to kill the king and thus had saved his life. Ahasuerus's discovery led to Mordecai's being raised to a position of honor in the kingdom. Haman's treachery soon led to his own fall, and he and his ten sons were hanged on the gallows he had previously prepared for Mordecai. In 464 B.C. a courtier murdered Ahasuerus, and his son, Artaxerxes Longimanus, succeeded him. In Ezra 4:6, the reign of Ahasuerus is mentioned chronologically between Cyrus (v. 5) and Artaxerxes (v. 7).

2. A king of the Medes and the father of Darius (Dan. 9:1).

Ahava [A·ha'va], *I shall subsist*—A river beside which Ezra gathered the company that returned with him to Jerusalem on the second expedition (Ezra 8:15, 31). It was probably north of Babylon.

Ahaz, Achaz [A'haz, A'chaz], *possessor*—The name of two men in the Old Testament:

1. A son of Jotham and the 11th king of Judah (2 Kings 15:38; 16:1–20; Achaz, KJV). He was an ungodly king who promoted the worship of Molech, with its pagan rites of human sacrifice (2 Chron. 28:1–4).

The reign of Ahaz probably overlapped the reign of his father Jotham and possibly the reign of his own son Hezekiah. His age when he became king was 20 and he reigned for 16 years, beginning about 735 B.C. Early in his reign Ahaz adopted policies that favored Assyria. When he refused to join the anti-Assyrian alliance of Pekah of Israel and Rezin of Syria, they invaded Judah and besieged Jerusalem, threatening to dethrone Ahaz and replace him with a puppet king (Isa. 7:1–6). Pekah and Rezin killed 120,000 people and took 200,000 captives. However, through the intervention of Oded the prophet, the captives were released immediately (2 Chron. 28:5–15).

In view of his precarious circumstances, Ahaz requested help from Tiglath-pileser III, king of Assyria, offering him silver and gold. At first the plan worked, and Assyria invaded Israel and Syria (2 Kings 15:29). Ultimately, however, Assyria "distressed" Ahaz, demanding excessive tribute (2 Chron. 28:20–21).

Spiritually, Ahaz stopped following in the ways of the four relatively good kings who had preceded him (Joash, Amaziah, Azariah, and Jotham). He made images of Baal, offered infant sacrifices in the Valley of Hinnom, and sacrificed on the high places, including his own son (2 Chron. 28:1–4, 1 Kings 16:3–4). He came under further pagan influence at Damascus where he had gone to meet Tiglath-pileser III. Seeing a pagan altar there, he commanded Uriah the priest at Jerusalem to build a copy of it. He then installed it next to the bronze altar in the Jerusalem temple.

It was to King Ahaz that Isaiah's announcement of the promised Immanuel was made (Isa. 7:10–17). The prophet Isaiah sent a message to the terrified Ahaz, but Ahaz would not turn to God and trust Him for deliverance. Instead, he plunged deeper into idolatry and self-destruction. Ahaz's conduct brought divine judgment to Judah in the form of military defeats. Edom revolted and took captives from Judah. The Philistines invaded Judah, capturing several cities. Rezin of Damascus seized control of Elath, Judah's port on the Gulf of Aqaba (2 Kings 16:5–6).

At his death, Ahaz was buried without honor in Jerusalem. He was not deemed worthy of a burial in the royal tombs (2 Chron. 28:27).

2. A Benjamite and descendant of King Saul. Ahaz was a son of Micah and the father of Jehoaddah (1 Chron. 8:35–36; 9:42).

Ahaz, Dial of [A'haz, Dial of]—See Dial of Ahaz.

Ahaziah [A·ha·zi'ah], *the Lord sustains*—The name of two kings in the Old Testament:

1. The son and successor of Ahab and the ninth king of Israel (1 Kings 22:40, 49, 51). Ahaziah reigned from 853 to 852 B.C. The son of Jezebel, Ahaziah followed policies that showed evidence of his mother's pagan influence. After reigning only two years, he "fell through the lattice of his upper room in Samaria" (2 Kings 1:2) and was seriously injured. Sending his messengers to ask Baal-zebub, the god of Ekron, about his recovery, Ahaziah was frustrated when the prophet Elijah interrupted their mission and prophesied Ahaziah's death.

Enraged by Elijah's predictions, Ahaziah tried to seize him, but the men sent to capture the prophet were destroyed by fire from heaven and Elijah's prophecy was quickly fulfilled (2 Kings 1:9–17).

At the time of Ahaziah's ascent to the throne, Mesha, the king of Moab, rebelled because of the tribute imposed on him by Omri, Ahaziah's grandfather (2 Kings 1:1; 3:4–5). Ahaziah formed an alliance with Jehoshaphat, king of Judah, to build ships and trade with other nations. God judged this effort and it failed (1 Kings 22:49).

2. The son and successor of Joram and the nephew of Ahaziah No. 1 (2 Kings 8:24–26). Ahaziah is also called Jehoahaz (2 Chron. 21:17; 25:23) and Azariah (2 Chron. 22:6). The sixth king of Judah, Ahaziah reigned for only one year (841 B.C.).

Ahaziah became king at age twenty-two (2 Kings 8:26; 2 Chron. 22:1). His wicked reign was heavily influenced by his mother, Athaliah, who was the evil power behind his throne: "He walked in the way of the house of Ahab" (2 Kings 8:27).

Ahaziah cultivated relations with Israel and joined with his uncle, King Jehoram (2 Kings 1:17; 9:24; 2 Chron. 22:5–7), in a military expedition at Ramoth Gilead against Hazael, king of Syria. Jehoram was wounded and returned to Jezreel, near Mount Gilboa, to convalesce. While visiting his uncle Jehoram, Ahaziah was killed by Jehu, Israel's captain, who had been ordered by God to exterminate the house of Ahab (2 Kings 9:4–10).

Ahban [Ah′ban], *brother of an understanding (intelligent) one*—A man of Judah of the family of Hezron (1 Chron. 2:29).

Aher [A′her], *another*—A Benjamite (1 Chron. 7:12), probably to be identified with Ahiram.

Ahi [A′hi], *brother of Jehovah*—Two Old Testament men:
   1. A Gadite chief in Gilead, the son of Abdiel (1 Chron. 5:15).
   2. A chief of the tribe of Asher, the son of Shamer (1 Chron. 7:34).

Ahiah [A·hi′ah]—See Ahijah.

Ahiam [A·hi′am], *mother's brother*—A son of Sharar, the Hararite, one of David's warriors (2 Sam. 23:33; 1 Chron. 11:35).

Ahian [A·hi′an], *brotherly*—One of the four sons of Shemidah who was a member of the sons of Manasseh (1 Chron. 7:19).

Ahiezer [A·hi·e′zer], *brother of help*—Two Old Testament men:

1. A chief of the tribe of Dan, the son of Ammishaddai (Num. 1:12; 2:25; 7:66).

2. A Benjamite chief who allied himself with David at Ziklag (1 Chron. 12:3).

Ahihud [A·hi′hud], *brother of renown*—Two Old Testament men:

1. The prince who represented the tribe of Asher when the land was divided (Num. 34:27).

2. A descendant of Bela of Benjamin (1 Chron. 8:7).

Ahijah, Ahiah [A·hi′jah, A·hi′ah], *my brother is the Lord*—The name of nine men in the Old Testament:

1. The performer of High Priestly functions at Gibeah during part of Saul's reign (1 Sam. 14:3, 18). Many scholars identify him with Ahimelech, the priest at Nob who is also identified as a son of Ahitub (1 Sam. 22:9). Ahijah's name is usually spelled Ahiah, a variant of Ahijah.

2. A secretary or scribe in Solomon's reign and a son of Shisha (1 Kings 4:3); also spelled Ahiah.

3. The prophet from Shiloh who prophesied Israel's division into two kingdoms because of its idolatries (1 Kings 11:29–39). While Solomon was king, Jeroboam rebelled against him. Ahijah tore his own garment into twelve pieces and instructed Jeroboam to take ten of them. This symbolic action indicated that Jeroboam would be king over the ten tribes that would be known as the northern kingdom of Israel. Ahijah stood up for the people in the face of their oppression under Solomon and Rehoboam.

Later, King Jeroboam disguised his queen and sent her to the aging and nearly blind prophet to ask whether their sick child would recover. Ahijah prophesied that because of Jeroboam's wickedness the child would die (1 Kings 14:1–18). His prophecies were also put into writing (2 Chron. 9:29).

4. The father of Baasha, who killed Jeroboam's son Nadab. He then reigned over Israel in his stead (1 Kings 15:27).

5. A man of the tribe of Judah and a son of Jerahmeel (1 Chron. 2:25).

6. A Benjamite who helped carry off the inhabitants of Geba (1 Chron. 8:7).

7. One of David's mighty men (1 Chron. 11:36).

8. A Levite during David's reign (1 Chron. 26:20) who kept the temple treasury.

9. One of the priests who, with Nehemiah, sealed the covenant (Neh. 10:26).

Ahikam [A·hi′kam], *a brother has appeared*—An official of Judah (2 Kings 22:12). When Jeremiah's life was threatened by false prophets and priests, he was protected by Ahikam (Jer. 26:24).

Ahilud [A·hi′lud], *brother of one born*—Father of Jehoshaphat. The latter was David's and Solomon's recorder (2 Sam. 8:16; 20:24; 1 Kings 4:3). It is quite likely that this Alihud was also the father of Baana, a purveyor of Solomon (1 Kings 4:12).

Ahimaaz [A·hi′ma·az], *brother of anger*—Three Old Testament men:

1. Father of Ahinoam, Saul's wife (1 Sam. 14:50).

2. Son of Zadok and supporter of David during Absalom's rebellion, who carried to David the news of Joab's victory (2 Sam. 15:27, 36; 17:20; 18:19–30).

3. Solomon's purveyor in Naphtali who married Basmath, Solomon's daughter (1 Kings 4:15).

Ahiman [A·hi′man], *brother is a gift*—Two Old Testament men:

1. Son of Anak (Num. 13:22).

2. A Levite porter of the sanctuary (1 Chron. 9:17).

Ahimelech [A·him′e·lech], *brother of a king*—Two Old Testament men:

1. Son of Ahitub, the chief priest at Nob. He was slain by Saul for befriending David when the latter fled from Saul. David gave him to understand that he was performing a duty for the king, and being in need of food, was given the showbread (1 Sam. 21:1–9; Matt. 12:4). Doeg, the Edomite, reported the matter, and Saul, assuming that the priests were disloyal, ordered them slain. Abiathar, son of Ahimelech, escaped (1 Sam. 21:7; 22:7–23). Many believe that the names Abiathar and Ahimelech have been interchanged in 2 Samuel 8:17 and that Ahimelech is intended in Mark 2:26.

2. A follower of David, a Hittite (1 Sam. 26:6).

Ahimoth [A·hi'moth], *brother of death*—Son of Elkanah, a Levite, and descendant of Kohath (1 Chron. 6:25).

Ahinadab [A·hin'a·dab], *liberal brother*—A purveyor of Solomon in Mahanaim (1 Kings 4:14).

Ahinoam [A·hin'o·am], *pleasant brother*—Two Old Testament women:
1. Daughter of Ahimaaz (1 Sam. 14:50).
2. A wife of David (1 Sam. 25:43), captured by the Amalekites at Ziklag (1 Sam. 30:5).

Ahio [A·hi'o], *brotherly*—Three Old Testament men:
1. A son of Abinadab who, with his brother, Uzzah, drove the cart that brought the ark to Jerusalem (2 Sam. 6:3–4).
2. A Benjamite, son of Jehiel (1 Chron. 8:29, 31; 9:35, 37).
3. A Benjamite, son of Elpaal (1 Chron. 8:14).

Ahira [A·hi'ra], *brother of evil*—The head of the tribe of Naphtali in the wilderness (Num. 1:15; 7:78; 10:27).

Ahiram [A·hi'ram], *exalted brother*—A founder of a family of the tribe of Benjamin (Num. 26:38), probably the same as Ehi (Gen. 46:21) and Aharah (1 Chron. 8:1).

Ahiramites [A·hi'ram·ites]—Descendants of Ahiram (Num. 26:38).

Ahisamach [A·his'a·mach], *brother of support*—The father of Aholiab (Ex. 31:6).

Ahishahar [A·hi'sha·har], *brother of the dawn* or *early*—A son of Bilhan, a Benjamite (1 Chron. 7:10).

Ahishar [A·hi'shar], *brother of a singer*—In a list of "princes" he is named as controller of Solomon's household (1 Kings 4:6), a position of importance.

Ahithophel [A·hith'o·phel], *foolish brother*—A counselor of David who lived in Giloh (2 Sam. 15:12). At the time of Absalom's rebellion he deserted David, but when he saw that the rebellion would be crushed, he committed suicide, thus winning the title *Judas of the Old Testament* (2 Sam. 15:12, 31–34; 16:15; 17:23). He may have been the grandfather of Bathsheba (2 Sam. 11:3; 23:34).

Ahitub [A·hi'tub], *brother of goodness*—Three Old Testament men:

1. Son of Phinehas, grandson of Eli, and father of Ahimelech, the priest (1 Sam. 14:3; 22:9).

2. Son of Amariah and father of Zadok, the priest (2 Sam. 8:17).

3. Grandfather of another Zadok (1 Chron. 6:11–12; Neh. 11:11).

Ahlab [Ah'lab], *fertile place*—A town of the tribe of Asher from which the Canaanites were not expelled (Judg. 1:31).

Ahlai [Ah'la·i], *O! would that!*—A man and a woman of the Old Testament:

1. Apparently the daughter of Sheahan the Judahite who became the wife of her father's Egyptian slave (1 Chron. 2:31, 34–35).

2. The father of one of David's warriors (1 Chron. 11:41).

Ahoah [A·ho'ah], *brother of rest*—The son of Bela, the son of Benjamin (1 Chron. 8:4), called Ahiah (1 Chron. 8:7).

Ahohi [A·ho'hi]—See Ahohite.

Ahohite [A·ho'hite]—A descendant of Ahoah (2 Sam. 23:9, 28).

Aholah [A·ho'lah], *her tent*—The harlot who was made a symbol of Samaria (Ezek. 23:4–5, 36, 44).

Aholiab [A·ho'li·ab], *tent of his father*—A Danite, son of Ahisamach. He and Bezaleel had the supervision of the construction of the tabernacle (Ex. 31:6; 35:34; 38:23).

Aholibah [A·hol'i·bah], *my tent is in her*—The harlot who was made a symbol of Judah (Ezek. 23:1–49).

Aholibamah [A·hol·i·ba'mah], *tent of the height*—A man and a woman of the Old Testament:

1. The granddaughter of Zibeon the Hittite and one of the wives of Esau (Gen. 36:2). In Genesis 26:34 she is called Judith, the daughter of Beeri the Hittite. Possibly Judith was her original name and Aholibamah one she assumed after marriage to Esau.

2. A duke who descended from Esau (Gen. 36:41).

Ahumai [A·hu'mai], *brother of water*—A man of Judah and son of Jahath (1 Chron. 4:2).

Ahuzam, Ahuzzam [A·hu′zam, A·huz′zam], *possessor*—Son of Ashur of Judah. His mother was Naarah (1 Chron. 4:5–6).

Ahuzzath [A·huz′zath], *possession*—A friend of Abimelech of Gerar (Gen. 26:26).

Ahzai, Ahasai [Ah′zai, A·ha′sai], *my holder* or *protector*—A priest (Neh. 11:13).

Ai, Hai [A′i, Ha′i], *the ruin*—The name of two cities in the Old Testament:

1. A Canaanite city (Josh. 10:1) located east of Beth-el (Gen. 12:8), "beside Beth Aven" (Josh. 7:2), and north of Michmash (Isa. 10:28). Many years before Joshua's time, Abraham pitched his tent at Ai before journeying to Egypt (Gen. 12:8).

Ai figures prominently in the story of Israel's conquest of Canaan. After Joshua conquered Jericho, he sent men to spy out Ai and the surrounding countryside. Because Ai was small, the spies assured Joshua that he could take Ai with only a handful of soldiers. Joshua dispatched about 3,000 soldiers to attack Ai. This army was soundly defeated, due to Achan's sin of taking spoils from Jericho contrary to God's commandment. When God singled out Achan and his family, the people stoned them to death. Joshua then sent 30,000 soldiers against Ai and captured the city by a clever military tactic—an ambush (Josh. 7–8).

Although Ai has been identified with modern et-Tell, situated southeast of Beth-el, recent archaeological discoveries conflict with this placement and make this identification uncertain. Nearby Khirbet Nisya is another possible location for Ai. Ai is also called Aiath (Isa. 10:28, KJV), Aija (Neh. 11:31, KJV), and Hai (Gen. 12:8; 13:3, KJV).

2. An Ammonite city in Moab (Jer. 49:3).

Aiah, Ajah [Ai′ah, A′jah], *vulture*—Two Old Testament men:

1. Son of Zibeon, a Horite (Gen. 36:24; 1 Chron. 1:40).
2. The father of Saul's concubine, Rizpah (2 Sam. 3:7; 21:8–11).

Aiath [Ai′ath]—The feminine form of Ai. It is probably the same as Ai, a town near Beth-el (Isa. 10:28).

Aija [Ai′ja]—A town mentioned as near Beth-el, most likely the same place as Ai (Neh. 11:31).

Aijalon, Ajalon [Ai′ja·lon, Aj′a·lon], *place of harts*—Three geographical locations in the Old Testament land of Israel:

1. A valley in Dan over which the moon stood still at the command of Joshua in battle with the five kings of the Amorites (Josh. 10:12).

2. A Levitical city of the Kohathites near the valley of Aijalon (Josh. 21:20, 24; 1 Chron. 6:69). When the kingdom was divided, it became part of Benjamin (1 Chron. 8:13; 2 Chron. 11:10) and was taken by the Philistines in the reign of King Ahaz (2 Chron. 28:18).

3. A place in Zebulun where Elon, the judge, was buried (Judg. 12:12).

Ain [A′in], *eye* or *spring*—Two geographical locations in the Old Testament land of Israel:

1. A place west of Riblah, perhaps near the source of the Orontes (Num. 34:11).

2. A town near Rimmon in Judah (Josh. 15:32), transferred to Simeon and made a priestly city (Josh. 19:7; 21:16).

Ajah [A′jah]—See Aiah.

Ajalon [Aj′a·lon]—See Aijalon.

Akan [A′kan]—See Jaakan.

Akeldama, Aceldama [A·kel′da·ma, A·cel′da·ma], *field of blood*—A small field near Jerusalem purchased by the priests with the thirty pieces of silver thrown away by Judas. It is called the potter's field and the field of blood because it was here that Judas hanged himself. Traditionally, it is located on the southern side of the Valley of Hinnom (Matt. 27:7–8; Acts 1:18–19).

Akkad [Ak′kad]—See Accad.

Akkub [Ak′kub], *cunning*—Four Old Testament men:

1. Son of Elioenai of the family of David (1 Chron. 3:23–24).

2. A Levite who founded a family of temple porters (Ezra 2:42; Neh. 12:25).

3. The head of a family of Nethinim (Ezra 2:45).

4. A Levite, appointed by Ezra to instruct the people (Neh. 8:7).

Akrabbim [Ak·rab'bim]—An ascent near the southern point of the Dead Sea, east of Beersheba, north of the desert of Zin; also called Maaleh–Acrabbim (Num. 34:4; Josh. 15:3).

Alabaster [Al'a·bas'ter]—A name possibly derived from a place in Egypt called Alabastrum or Alabastron where small vessels for perfumes were made. Modern alabaster is a form of gypsum or sulphate of lime, but Oriental alabaster was carbonate of lime. This white stone was much used in antiquity in the ornamentation of buildings, and was the expensive material out of which vases and bottles for the holding of precious ointments were made. The box that contained the perfume used in the anointing of Jesus at Bethany was of alabaster (Matt 26:7; Mark 14:3).

Alameth [Al'a·meth]—See Alemeth.

Alammelech [A·lam'me·lech]—See Allammelech.

Alemeth, Alameth [Al'e·meth, Al'a·meth], *covering*—Two men and a town of Old Testament Israel:

    1. A Benjamite, descendant of Becher (1 Chron. 7:8).

    2. The grandson of Ahaz, a descendant of Saul (1 Chron. 8:36; 9:42).

    3. A town (1 Chron. 6:60). See Almon.

Alexander [Al·ex·an'der], *defending men*—

    1. Alexander the Great, who followed his father, Philip, as king of Macedonia in 336 B.C. In his youth he was a pupil of Aristotle. He conquered all of the eastern world in thirteen years. According to Josephus, though questioned by many scholars, Alexander entered Jerusalem but was generous toward the Jews and extended many privileges to them in his newly founded city of Alexandria in Egypt.

    At the age of thirty-three Alexander died in Babylon (323 B.C.) and his vast empire was divided between his four generals, each taking the title of king—Ptolemy in Egypt, Seleucus in Syria, Antipater in Macedonia, and Philetaerus in Asia Minor. Palestine was annexed to Egypt and thus came under the rule of the Ptolemies and afterward under the Syrian kings. Daniel 8 prophesies the story of Alexander in a vision.

    2. A son of Simon of Cyrene. His father was compelled to carry the cross of Jesus (Mark 15:21).

3. A prominent person in Jerusalem at the time that John and Peter were brought before the authorities (Acts 4:6).

4. A man who was with Paul during the disturbance at Ephesus (Acts 19:33).

5. A convert to Christianity who renounced his faith and became a blasphemer. He was excommunicated by Paul (1 Tim. 1:19–20).

Alexandria [Al·ex·an′dri·a]—A city named after Alexander the Great who founded it in 332 B.C. Situated on the northern coast of Egypt west of the Nile, an advantageous site for commercial purposes, it was considered the second city of the Roman Empire and had a population of over half a million—Egyptians, Greeks, Jews and Romans.

With its famous library of several hundred thousand volumes, founded by the Ptolemies, it was regarded as one of the greatest intellectual centers of the world. It was here that the Hebrew Scriptures were translated into Greek. Called the Septuagint (Version of the Seventy), it was begun in the reign of Ptolemy Lagos and finished in the reign of Ptolemy Philadelphus, about 285 B.C.

Through close contact with the Greeks in this Hellenistic center, Judaism became affected by Greek philosophy. The Alexandrian Jews had a synagogue in Jerusalem which participated in the persecution of Stephen (Acts 2:10; 6:9), and Apollos, who labored at Corinth, was an Alexandrian Jew (Acts 18:24–25).

Alexandrians [Al·ex·an′dri·ans]—Residents of the city of Alexandria (Acts 6:9).

Aliah [A·li′ah]—See Alvah.

Alian [Al′i·an]—See Alvan.

Allammelech, Alammelech [Al·lam′me·lech, A·lam′me·lech], perhaps *king's oak*—A town of Asher (Josh. 19:26).

Allon [Al′lon], *an oak*—A man and a place of the Old Testament:

1. A Simeonite, the son of Jedaiah (1 Chron. 4:37).

2. A place listed among the cities of Naphtali (Josh. 19:33).

Allon-bachuth, Allon-bacuth [Al′lon-ba·chuth, Al′lon-ba·cuth], *oak of weeping*—The oak under which Deborah, the nurse of Rebekah, was buried (Gen. 35:8).

Almighty [Al·migh′ty]—See God, Names of.

Almodad [Al·mo′dad], *not measured*—The son of Joktan of the line of Shem and progenitor of an Arabian tribe (Gen. 10:26; 1 Chron. 1:20).

Almon [Al′mon], *hidden*—A town of Benjamin (Josh. 21:18), called Alemeth in 1 Chronicles 6:60. It is between Geba and Anathoth.

Almon-diblathaim [Al′mon-dib·la·tha′im], *concealing the two cakes*—One of the stations or encampments of the Israelites between Shittim and the Arnon (Num. 33:46).

Aloth, Bealoth [A′loth, Be·a′loth], *ascents*—Part of a district in northern Israel from which Solomon received supplies (1 Kings 4:16).

Alphaeus [Al·phae′us], *successor*—Two New Testament men:
   1. Husband of the Mary that stood by the cross of Jesus and father of James the Less and Joses (Matt. 10:3; Mark 15:40). Through the comparison of the Gospels (Matt. 27:56, Mark 3:18, and Luke 6:15), it has been ascertained that Mary, the wife of Cleophas and Mary, the mother of James the Less, were the same. Some have said that Mary, the wife of Cleophas, and the sister of Mary, the mother of Jesus, were the same person, but it is improbable that two sisters should have the same name. Hence it is assumed that Alphaeus was also called Cleophas.
   2. Father of Levi who was later called Matthew, one of the apostles (Matt. 9:9; Mark 2:14).

Alush [A′lush], *I will knead (bread)*—A place between Egypt and Sinai where Israel encamped during the wanderings in the wilderness (Num. 33:13–14).

Alvah, Aliah [Al′vah, Al′i·ah], *evil*—A chieftain of Edom, a descendant of Esau (Gen. 36:40; 1 Chron. 1:51).

Alvan, Alian [Al′van, Al′i·an], *high* or *tall*—A son of Shobal (Gen. 36:23; 1 Chron. 1:40).

Amad [A′mad], *station*—A town near the border of Asher (Josh. 19:26).

Amal [A′mal], *sorrow*—One of the four sons of Helem of the tribe of Asher (1 Chron. 7:35).

Amalek [Am′a·lek], *dweller in a valley*—Son of Eliphaz by his concubine Timna and the grandson of Esau (Gen. 36:12; Ex. 17:8; 1 Chron. 1:36).

Amalekites [A·mal′ek·ites]—Descendants of Esau, a nomadic people, inhabiting the peninsula of Sinai and the wilderness between the southern portion of Palestine and Egypt (Gen. 36:12; Num. 13:29; 1 Sam. 15:7). About the time of the exodus they occupied the region near Kadesh-barnea. Israel's first battle was fought with these people at Rephidim on their way to Sinai. The Amalekites were defeated but in the next encounter, when the Israelites were at Kadesh, the Amalekites were victorious (Ex. 17:8; Num. 14:45).

In the time of the judges they were the ally of the Midianites when the latter invaded and oppressed Israel (Judg. 3:13; 6:3, 33). They suffered a crushing defeat by Saul (1 Sam. 15), and were completely suppressed by David (1 Sam. 27:8; 30:1–20).

Amam [A′mam], *gathering spot*—A town in the southern section of Judah (Josh. 15:26).

Amana [A·ma′na], *fixed* or *established*—A mountain where the Abana River has its source (2 Kings 5:12; Song 4:8). See also Abana.

Amariah [Am·a·ri′ah], *Jehovah hath said*—Nine Old Testament men:

1. Son of Meraioth in the line of the high priests (1 Chron. 6:7, 52).
2. A priest, son of Azariah (1 Chron. 6:11; Ezra 7:3).
3. A Levite, a descendant of Kohath (1 Chron. 23:19; 24:23).
4. A Levite appointed to distribute the freewill offerings (2 Chron. 31:14–15).
5. A priest who accompanied Zerubbabel to Jerusalem (Neh. 12:2, 7).
6. A priest who sealed the covenant with Nehemiah (Neh. 10:3).
7. A man who divorced his foreign wife (Ezra 10:42).
8. A descendant of Judah through Pharez (Neh. 11:4).
9. An ancestor of the prophet, Zephaniah (Zeph. 1:1).

Amasa [A·ma′sa], *burden bearer*—Two Old Testament men:

1. A cousin of Joab and the son of Abigail, the half sister of David. He joined Absalom in his rebellion and was captain of his army (2 Sam.

17:25). Later he served David as a captain (2 Sam. 19:13). He was slain by Joab (2 Sam. 20:1–13).

2. A prince of Ephraim and son of Hadlai. He opposed bringing into Samaria the prisoners whom Pekah of Israel had taken in his campaign against Ahaz (2 Chron. 28:12).

Amasai [A·ma′sai], *burdensome*—Four Old Testament men:

1. A Kohathite ancestor of Heman, the singer (1 Chron. 6:35).

2. A captain who joined David at Ziklag (1 Chron. 12:18).

3. A priest who blew the trumpet when David brought the ark from the home of Obededom (1 Chron. 15:24).

4. A Kohathite (2 Chron. 29:12).

Amashai [A·ma′shai]—The son of Azareel and a priest who lived in Jerusalem (Neh. 11:13).

Amashsai [A·ma′shsai]—See Amashai.

Amasiah [Am·a·si′ah], *Jehovah hath borne*—Son of Zichri, a military officer of high rank under Jehoshaphat of Judah (2 Chron. 17:16).

Amaziah [Am·a·zi′ah], *Jehovah is strong*—Four Old Testament men:

1. King of Judah, son of Joash, who took the reins of government when his father, on account of sickness, was unable to rule (2 Kings 14:1). After defeating the Edomites in the Valley of Salt, he brought back the idols of Edom and worshipped them. He was defeated by King Jehoash of Israel. A conspiracy was formed against him which caused him to flee but his life was ended by assassins (2 Kings 14:1–20; 2 Chron. 25:1–27).

2. A Levite of the family of Merari (1 Chron. 6:45).

3. A priest of Beth-el who brought charges against Amos (Amos 7:10–17).

4. A Simeonite (1 Chron. 4:34).

Ami [A′mi]—See Amon.

Aminadab [A·min′a·dab]—See Amminadab.

Amittai [A·mit′tai], *true*—The father of Jonah, the prophet (2 Kings 14:25; Jonah 1:1).

Ammah [Am'mah], *beginning*—A hill to which Joab and Abishai came (2 Sam. 2:24).

Ammi [Am'mi], *my people*—The name to be applied to Israel at the time of the restoration (Hos. 2:1).

Ammiel [Am'mi·el], *people of God*—Four Old Testament men:
1. The one who represented the tribe of Dan when the twelve spies were sent to Canaan from Kadesh-barnea (Num. 13:12).
2. The father of Machir (2 Sam. 9:4–5; 17:27).
3. A son of Obed–edom (1 Chron. 26:5).
4. The father of Bathsheba, a wife of David and mother of Solomon (1 Chron. 3:5).

Ammihud [Am'mi·hud], *kinsman of praiseworthiness*—Five Old Testament men:
1. An Ephraimite, father of Elishama (Num. 1:10).
2. A Simeonite, father of Shemuel (Num. 34:20).
3. A man of Naphtali, father of Pedahel (Num. 34:28).
4. Father of Talmai, king of Geshur. To him Absalom fled after slaying his brother (2 Sam. 13:37).
5. A man of Judah, a descendant of Pharez (1 Chron. 9:4).

Amminadab, Aminadab [Am·min'a·dab, A·min'a·dab]—Three Old Testament men:
1. Father of Nahshon (Num. 1:7; 2:3; Matt. 1:4), an ancestor of David (Ruth 4:19–20; 1 Chron. 2:10). He was probably the Amminadab whose daughter was the wife of Aaron (Ex. 6:23).
2. A Levite, the son of Kohath (1 Chron. 6:22).
3. A Levite who was one of those appointed by David to bring the ark to Jerusalem (1 Chron. 15:10–11).

Ammishaddai [Am·mi·shad'dai], *the Alimight, an ally*—The father of Ahiezer, a Danite (Num. 1:12; 2:25).

Ammizabad [Am·mi'za·bad], *people of endowment*—A son of Benaiah and one of David's warriors (1 Chron. 27:6).

Ammon [Am'mon], *kinsman or people*—The land of Ammon, settled by those who were descended from Ben-ammi, Lot's son. Ben-ammi was born in a cave near Zoar (Gen. 19:30–38), a city near the southern end of the Dead Sea. The land of the Ammonites generally was located in the area north and east of Moab, a region between the river Arnon and the river Jabbok. Its capital city was Rabbah (Deut. 3:11; 2 Sam. 11:1). Amman, the name of the capital of the modern Hashemite kingdom of Jordan, is a continuing use of this ancient name.

Ammonites [Am'mon·ites]—A Semitic people located east of the Jordan between the land of Moab and the river Jabbok, represented as descendants of Ben-ammi, a son of Lot (Gen. 19:38). It appears that they had not been long in this land when Israel captured Jericho. Through the following centuries they had many clashes with the Hebrews, notably in the time of Jephthah (Judg. 11:4–33) and David (2 Sam. 10:6–14; 12:26–31). After the Exile they became an object of hatred for their alleged participation in the destruction of the kingdom (Ezek. 25:1–7). They obstructed the rebuilding of the walls of Jerusalem (Neh. 4:3, 7).

Ammonitess [Am'mon·it·ess]—An Ammonite woman. Solomon's wife Naamah, the mother of Rehoboam, was an Ammonitess (1 Kings 14:21), as was Shimeath, the mother of Zabad (2 Chron. 24:26).

Amnon [Am'non], *faithful*—Two Old Testament men:

  1. Son of David and Ahinoam, born while David was ruling over Judah at the beginning of his reign. He was murdered by Absalom because of his disgraceful treatment of Tamar, Absalom's half sister (2 Sam. 13).

  2. Son of Shimon of the family of Caleb (1 Chron. 4:20).

Amok [A'mok], *deep*—One of the priests who came with Zerubbabel from Babylon (Neh. 12:7).

Amon [A'mon], *workman*—The name of three men in the Old Testament:

  1. A governor of Samaria (1 Kings 22:26; 2 Chron. 18:25). When the prophet Micaiah prophesied that Ahab, king of Israel, would be killed in battle, he was sent to Amon as a prisoner.

  2. A son of Manasseh and a king of Judah (2 Kings 21:18–26; 2 Chron. 33:20–25). Amon became king at the age of twenty-two and reigned for only two years. His reign was characterized by idolatry. His wicked father may have deliberately named him after the Egyptian god Amun.

Amon's own servants conspired together and killed him, possibly because his corruption and idolatry had made him a weak king and they hoped to claim the throne for themselves. However, after Amon was assassinated, the people of Judah killed the conspirators and set Amon's eight-year-old son, Josiah, on the throne. Amon is mentioned in the New Testament as an ancestor of Jesus (Matt. 1:10).

3. The head of a captive family that returned to Israel from Babylon (Neh. 7:59). He was a descendant of one of Solomon's servants. He is also called Ami (Ezra 2:57).

Amorites [Am'o·rites], *mountaineers*—A powerful Semitic people who inhabited Canaan prior to the conquest of Joshua (Gen. 15:21; Ex. 3:8). In the time of Abraham they held a strong position in the hill country and the name was applied to the inhabitants of that region (Gen. 15:16) but, later, to the inhabitants of all Canaan in general (Josh. 7:7; Judg. 6:10).

Prior to the exodus they conquered districts east of the Jordan (Num. 21:26–30). They seized the land from the Arnon to Hermon (Josh. 2:10; 9:10; Judg. 11:22) and were settled between Jerusalem and Hebron and westward to the Shephelah and to the territory of Ephraim in the north (Josh. 10:5–6; 11:3; Judg. 1:35). They were not completely expelled by Joshua (Judg. 1:35; 3:5) and became a test of the loyalty of Israel to the Lord.

Amos [A'mos], *burden bearer*—One of two men in the Old Testament.

1. One of the twelve minor prophets of the Old Testament, he denounced the people of the northern kingdom of Israel for their idol worship, graft and corruption, and oppression of the poor. He was probably the earliest of the writing prophets. His prophecies and the few facts known about his life are found in the book of Amos.

Although he prophesied to the Northern Kingdom, Amos was a native of Judah, Israel's sister nation to the south. He came from the village of Tekoa (Amos 1:1), situated about 16 kilometers (10 miles) south of Jerusalem.

On one occasion, Amos's authority in Israel was questioned by a priest who served in the court of King Jeroboam II, and Amos admitted he was not descended from a line of prophets or other religious officials. By vocation, he claimed to be nothing but "a herdsman and a tender of sycamore fruit" (Amos 7:14), but he pointed out that his right to speak came from the highest authority of all: "The Lord took me as I followed the flock, and the Lord said to me, 'Go, prophesy to My people Israel' " (Amos 7:15).

Amos spoke because the Lord had called him to deliver His message of judgment. This is one of the clearest statements of the compulsion of the divine call to be found in the Bible. The theme of Amos's message was that Israel had rejected the one true God in order to worship false gods. He also condemned the wealthy class of the nation for cheating the poor through oppressive taxes (Amos 5:11) and the use of false weights and measures (Amos 8:5). He urged the people to turn from their sinful ways, to acknowledge God as their Maker and Redeemer, and to restore justice and righteousness in their dealings with others.

Amaziah the priest, who served in the court of King Jeroboam, made a report to the king about Amos and his message, saying he was guilty of conspiracy and a menace to the kingdom (Amos 7:10–13). This probably indicates that the prophet's stern warning created quite a stir throughout the land. But there is no record that the nation changed its ways as a result of Amos's message. About forty years after his prophecies, Israel collapsed when the Assyrians overran their capital city, Samaria, and carried away the leading citizens as captives.

After preaching in Israel, Amos probably returned to his home in Tekoa. No facts are known about his later life or death.

Amoz [A′moz], *strong*—Father of Isaiah (Isa. 1:1; 13:1; 38:1). Jewish tradition says that Amoz was also a prophet, and the brother of Amaziah, king of Judah.

Amphipolis [Am·phip′o·lis], *about the city*—An important city of Macedonia. Deriving its name from the fact that it was almost surrounded by the Strymon River, it was founded in the fifth century B.C. Paul and Silas passed through it as they were traveling from Philippi to Thessalonica. It was about thirty miles southwest of Philippi (Acts 17:1).

Amplias [Am′pli·as], *enlarged*—A Christian of the church at Rome (Rom. 16:8).

Amram [Am′ram], *exalted people*—Three Old Testament men:

1. Son of Kohath of the tribe of Levi, the husband of Jochebed and father of Moses, Aaron, and Miriam. He died at the age of 137 years (Ex. 6:20). The Amramites were strong in number in the time of Moses (Num. 3:17, 19, 27).

2. A son of Bani, who put away his foreign wife (Ezra 10:34).

3. Another spelling for the name Hamran, one of the descendants of Esau (1 Chron. 1:41). In Genesis 36:26, he appears as Hemdan.

Amramites [Am′ram·ites]—Descendants of Amram (Num. 3:27; 1 Chron. 26:23), a branch of the Kohathite family of priests.

Amraphel [Am·ra′phel], *sayer of darkness* or *fall of the sayer*—King of Shinar and ally of Chedorlaomer in the invasion of Palestine when Lot was taken prisoner (Gen. 14:1, 5, 9). The name has often been identified with that of Ammurabi or Hammurabi, lawgiver, king, and founder of the old Babylonian Empire. Hammurabi conquered the Elamites, seized Larsa, and brought all Babylon under his rule. He greatly improved and strengthened his country, built temples, and so contributed to the welfare of his people that he was called father to his people.

His code of laws, known as the "Hammurabi Code," discovered in 1902, is the oldest code of laws that has come to light. It has attracted special attention because of its close resemblance to the Mosaic Code (Ex. 20:23–23:33). Since Hammurabi was king of Babel about 1955 B.C., he must have antedated Moses by several centuries. The remarkable thing in this resemblance of the two codes is that the less fortunate members of society were regarded by both Babylonians and Israelites as possessing rights that could be recognized by the state. See Hammurabi.

Amzi [Am′zi], *strong*—Two Old Testament men:

1. A descendant of Merari of the tribe of Levi (1 Chron. 6:46).

2. A priest of the course of Malchijah (Neh. 11:12).

Anab [A′nab], *place of grapes*—A mountain town of Judah from which the Anakim were driven by Joshua (Josh. 11:21; 15:50).

Anah [A′nah], *answering*—Two men and one woman in the Old Testament:

1. Daughter of Zibeon and mother of Esau's wife, Aholibamah (Gen. 36:2, 14).

2. Son of Zibeon who discovered the hot springs ("mules" in King James Version) in the wilderness (Gen. 36:24; 1 Chron. 1:40).

3. A Horite chief, the son of Seir (Gen. 36:20; 1 Chron. 1:38).

Anaharath [A·na′ha·rath], *pass*—A town of Issachar (Josh. 19:19).

Anaiah [A·nai′ah], *Jehovah hath answered*—Two Old Testament men:

1. One, perhaps a priest, who stood beside Ezra as he read the law to the people (Neh. 8:4).

2. A Jew who signed the covenant (Neh. 10:22).

Anak [A′nak], *long-necked*—In Numbers 13:22, 28 he appears to have been the founder of Kirjath-arba (Hebron) and ancestor of the race of giants called Anakim. The name usually denotes the Anakim collectively.

Anakim [An′a·kim]—A race of giants, the descendants of Arba (Josh. 15:13; 21:11). They are called the sons of Anak (Num. 13:22). The Israelites were terrified by them (Num. 13:28; Deut. 9:2) but, under the leadership of Joshua, drove them out (Josh. 10:36, 39) and they settled in the country of the Philistines (Josh. 11:21–22). Caleb expelled three families of them from Hebron (Josh. 15:14).

Anamim [An′a·mim]—Descendants of Mizraim (Gen. 10:13; 1 Chron. 1:11).

Anammelech [A·nam′me·lech], *Anu is king*—One of the gods worshipped by the people who were brought into Samaria after the fall of Israel (2 Kings 17:31).

Anan [A′nan], *a cloud*—One who sealed the covenant with Nehemiah (Neh. 10:26).

Anani [A·na′ni]—The seventh son of Elioenai, a descendant of Zerubbabel (1 Chron. 3:24).

Ananiah [An·a·ni′ah], *Jehovah hath covered*—Two Old Testament men:

1. An ancestor of Azariah who assisted Nehemiah in rebuilding the walls of Jerusalem (Neh. 3:23).

2. A town of Benjamin between Nob and Hazer, believed to be the Old Testament name for Bethany (Neh. 11:32).

Ananias [An·a·ni′as], *Jehovah is gracious*—The name of three New Testament men:

1. A Christian in the early church at Jerusalem (Acts 5:1–11). With the knowledge of his wife, Sapphira, Ananias sold a piece of property and brought only a portion of the proceeds from its sale to Peter, claiming this represented the total amount realized from the sale. When Peter rebuked him for lying about the amount, Ananias immediately fell down and died. Sapphira later repeated the same falsehood, and she also fell down and died. Apparently, their pretense to be something they were not caused God to strike Ananias and Sapphira dead.

2. A Christian disciple living in Damascus at the time of Paul's conversion (Acts 9:10–18; 22:12–16). In a vision the Lord told Ananias of Paul's conversion and directed him to go to Paul and welcome him into the church. Aware of Paul's reputation as a persecutor of Christians, Ananias reacted with alarm. When the Lord informed him that Paul was "a chosen vessel of Mine" (Acts 9:15), Ananias went to Paul and laid his hands upon him. Paul's sight was restored immediately, and he was baptized (Acts 9:18).

3. The Jewish high priest before whom Paul appeared after his arrest in Jerusalem following his third missionary journey, about A.D. 58 (Acts 23:2). Ananias was also one of those who spoke against Paul before the Roman governor Felix (Acts 24:1). Ananias was appointed high priest about A.D. 48 by Herod. In A.D. 52 the governor of Syria sent Ananias to Rome to be tried for the Jews' violent treatment of the Samaritans. Ananias was acquitted of the charges through Agrippa's influence, and he was returned to his office in Jerusalem. About A.D. 59 Ananias was deposed by Agrippa. Known to the Jews as a Roman collaborator, Ananias was murdered by a Jewish mob at the beginning of the Jewish–Roman War of A.D. 66–73.

Anath [A′nath], *answer*—Father of Shamgar, third judge of Israel; or possibly the town from which Shamgar came (Judg. 3:31; 5:6).

Anathoth [An'a·thoth], *answers*—The name of two men and one city in the Old Testament:

1. A city in the tribe of Benjamin given to the Levites (1 Kings 2:26). Abiathar lived here (1 Kings 2:26), and it was also the birthplace of the prophet Jeremiah (Jer. 1:1; 29:27). During a time of siege, the Lord instructed Jeremiah to purchase a field in Anathoth. This was to serve as a sign of God's promised redemption of Israel (Jer. 32:7–9). Anathoth was located about 5 kilometers (3 miles) northeast of Jerusalem and is now called Anata.

2. A son of Becher (1 Chron. 7:8).

3. A leader of the people who placed his seal on the covenant, along with Nehemiah (Neh. 10:19).

Anathothite [An'a·thoth·ite]—One who lives in or comes from Anathoth (2 Sam. 23:27; 1 Chron. 27:12).

Ancient of Days—One of the names of God, used by Daniel to describe God sitting on His throne to judge the world (Dan. 7:9, 13, 22). The name emphasizes the fact that God has been here since before time began; He has seen all that has ever happened on this earth. See God, Names of.

Andrew [An'drew], *manly*—Brother of Simon Peter and one of Jesus' first disciples. Both Andrew and Simon Peter were fishermen (Matt. 4:18; Mark 1:16–18) from Bethsaida (John 1:44), on the northwest coast of the Sea of Galilee. They also had a house at Capernaum in this vicinity (Mark 1:29).

According to the gospel of John, Andrew and an unnamed friend were among the followers of John the Baptist (John 1:35–40). When John the Baptist identified Jesus as the Lamb of God, both he and Andrew followed Jesus (John 1:41). Andrew then brought his brother Simon Peter to meet the Messiah (John 1:43–51).

At the feeding of the five thousand, Andrew called Jesus' attention to the boy with five barley loaves and two fish (John 6:5–9). Later Philip and Andrew decided to bring to Jesus the request of certain Greeks for an audience with Him (John 12:20–22). Andrew is mentioned a final time in the Gospels, when he asked Jesus a question concerning last things in the company of Peter, James, and John (Mark 13:3–4).

All lists of the disciples name Andrew among the first four (Matt. 10:2–4; Mark 3:16–19; Luke 6:14–16; Acts 1:13). According to tradition, Andrew was martyred at Patrae in Achaia, in Greece, by crucifixion on an X-shaped cross. According to Eusebius, Andrew's field of labor was Scythia, the region north of the Black Sea. For this reason he became the patron saint of Russia. He is also considered the patron saint of Scotland.

Andronicus [An·dro·ni′cus]. *man conquering*—A Christian at Rome (Rom. 16:7).

Anem [A′nem], *two fountains*—A town of Issachar assigned to the sons of Gershom (1 Chron. 6:73).

Aner [A′ner], *boy*—Two Old Testament men:
  1. A town of Manasseh west of the Jordan (1 Chron. 6:70).
  2. An Amorite ally of Abraham in his conflict with Chedorlaomer (Gen. 14:13–14).

Anethothite, Anetothite [An·e·tho′thite, An·e·to′thite]—An inhabitant of Anathoth (2 Sam. 23:27; 1 Chron. 27:12).

Angel of the Lord, Angel of God—The Angel of the Lord in the Old Testament is a mysterious being, whose precise nature is unknown. He appears to be an audible and sometimes visible manifestation of God to man. In some way, the God whom no man can see in all His glory and still live (Ex. 33:20), arranged a way to show Himself to humans.

The Angel of the Lord is frequently referred to as one who appeared to be a man (Gen. 18:1–2; Josh. 5:13–15). Unlike the angel that showed John the revelation of the end times (Rev. 19:10; 22:8), the Angel of the Lord accepted worship (Josh. 5:14). When the Angel of the Lord is speaking to humans, the text uses the term "LORD" and "Angel of the LORD" interchangeably (Ex. 3:1–8). At the same time, there are times when the Angel of the Lord seems to be distinct from God, as when He interceded with God for men (Zech. 1:12; 3:1–5).

Many believe that the Angel of the Lord was a pre-incarnate appearance of Christ, although Scripture does not specifically say so. The description of the "one like the Son of God" who was with Daniel's three friends in the fiery furnace is assumed to be the Angel of the Lord, and the title "Son of God," of course, belongs to Christ. The following is a list of encounters with the Angel of the Lord as recorded in Scripture.

1. Genesis 16:7-10—Instructed Hagar to return to Sarah and told her she would bear many descendants

2. Genesis 18:1-19:2; 22:11-13—Promised Isaac's birth, and warned of the destruction of Sodom and Gomorrah; prevented Abraham from sacrificing his son Isaac

3. Genesis 32:24-30—Wrestled with Jacob through the night and blessed him at daybreak

4. Exodus 3:1-8—Spoke to Moses from the burning bush, promising to deliver Israelites from enslavement

5. Exodus 14:19-20—Protected the children of Israel from the pursuing Egyptians

6. Exodus 23:20-23—Prepared the children of Israel to enter the promised land

7. Numbers 22:22-35—Blocked Balaam's path, then sent him to deliver a message to the prince Balak

8. Joshua 5:13-15—Reassured Joshua in his role as commander of the army of the Lord

9. Judges 2:1-3—Announced judgment against Israelites for their sinful alliance with the Canaanites.

10. Judges 6:11-24—Commissioned Gideon to fight against the Midianites

11. 1 Kings 19:4-8—Provided food for Elijah in the wilderness

12. 1 Chronicles 21:16-22—Appeared to David on the threshing floor of Ornan, where David built an altar

13. Isaiah 37:36—Delivered the citizens of this city from the Assyrian army

Aniam [A·ni'am], *sighing of the people*—A son of Shemida of the tribe of Manasseh (1 Chron. 7:19).

Anim [A'nim], *fountains*—A town in the hill country of Judah probably about eleven miles west of Hebron (Josh. 15:50).

Anna [An'na], *grace*—A prophetess in Jerusalem. She was of the tribe of Asher, a widow, and daughter of Phanuel. When the child Jesus was brought to the temple to be presented before the Lord, she immediately recognized Him as the Messiah, and praised God (Luke 2:36-38).

Annas [An'nas], *grace of the Lord*—One of the high priests at Jerusalem, along with Caiaphas, when John the Baptist began his ministry, about A.D. 26 (Luke 3:2). Quirinius, governor of Syria, appointed Annas as high priest about A.D. 6 or 7. Although Annas was deposed by Valerius Gratus, the Procurator of Judea, about A.D. 15, he was still the most influential of the priests and continued to carry the title of high priest (Luke 3:2; Acts 4:6).

After his removal, Annas was officially succeeded by each of his five sons, one grandson, and his son-in-law Caiaphas, the high priest who presided at the trial of Jesus (Matt. 26:3, 57; John 18:13–14). During His trial, Jesus was first taken to Annas, who then sent Jesus to Caiaphas (John 18:13, 24). Both Annas and Caiaphas were among the principal examiners when Peter and John were arrested (Acts 4:6). Some believe that Caiaphas was the actual high priest and that Annas was president of the Sanhedrin.

Antediluvians [An'te·di·lu'vi·ans], *before the deluge*—The people who lived before the Flood. The first people, Adam and Eve, and their descendants had obeyed the command to multiply and fill the earth, but the offspring of the first couple were tainted with the sin they had brought into the world. Beginning with Cain murdering Abel, their descendants grew more and more wicked. In spite of their wickedness, the antediluvians were clever and made advances in technology.

We cannot know how advanced they were, but we know that they built cities, raised flocks and herds, played musical instruments, and worked with bronze and iron (Gen. 4:16–22). Therefore, they must have had mines and smelters, and sharp tools for carving the harps and flutes. They must have had some engineering skills in order to build cities, or for Noah to have constructed something so large as the ark. The antediluvian people also lived for a very long time, most of them for hundreds of years. The oldest man of all was Methuselah, who lived to be 969 years old. Not all the people were entirely wicked.

Both Noah and Enoch were righteous men (Gen. 5:24; 6:9), who preached of God to the corrupt and disobedient people around them (2 Peter 2:5; Jude 14–15). However, their preaching was not well received, and Noah made ready to escape God's wrath on the ark, as he had been commanded; only his wife and his sons and their wives accompanied him. Noah was the only righteous man that God could find on the entire earth at that time.

The antediluvians did not believe Noah's warning, and they were eating and drinking and making merry right up until the last moment. People today react in the same way to the message of the gospel. Jesus warned His followers that when the last day comes, people will be like the antediluvians, wrapped up in their everyday affairs and ignoring the coming wrath of God which will punish their corruption (Matt. 24:37–41; Luke 17:26). Believers need to have a different attitude, to be watchful and ready (1 Thess. 5:5–11).

Anthothijah, Antothijah [An·tho·thi'jah, An·to·thi'jah], *answers of Jehovah*—A Benjamite descended through Shashak (1 Chron. 8:24).

Antichrist [An'ti·christ]—The word signifies *against Christ*, an *enemy of Christ, in the place of Christ* (1 John 2:18, 22; 4:3; 2 John 7). The coming of Antichrist, according to John's statement, will mark "the last days" before the second coming of Christ. The Antichrist is apparently a specific person and John emphasizes the spirit of Antichrist as it manifests itself in the denial of Jesus's incarnation and messiahship.

While the term is used by John alone, he is not the only one who teaches this doctrine. Christ uttered a warning regarding "false Christs" (Matt. 24:23–24; Mark 13:21–22). Paul clearly describes the Antichrist and his satanic claims and operations (2 Thess. 2:3–12), stating that the lawless one, the masterpiece of Satan, will appear before the second coming of Christ.

John describes the same person as the "beast" (Rev. 13) and both Paul and John declare he will be destroyed by Christ at His second coming. According to these teachings Christ will return to the world when apostasy and iniquity come to full expression in the Antichrist.

Antioch of Pisidia [An'ti·och of Pi·sid'ia]—A city of southern Asia Minor in Phrygia, situated just north of the territory of Pisidia. Antioch was an important first-century commercial center and an important center for the spread of the gospel. Founded by Seleucus I Nicator (about 300 B.C.) and named for his father Antiochus, it became a great center for commerce and was inhabited by many Jews. It was called the Pisidian Antioch to distinguish it from the Syrian Antioch (see below) and it was called Caesarea by the Romans, due to its military importance.

The apostle Paul preached in this city's synagogue and founded a church there during his first missionary journey (Acts 13:14–49). Just as Antioch exerted great cultural and political influence over the surrounding area, so also it became a strong base from which to launch the church's evangelistic outreach (Acts 13:42–49). In reaction to Paul's success, the Jews at Antioch caused some influential women to turn against the gospel and had Paul driven out of the city (Acts 13:50).

Antioch of Syria [An'ti'och of Syr·i·a]—The capital of the Roman province of Syria that played an important part in the first-century expansion of the church. Antioch was situated on the east bank of the Orontes River, considered part of an important trade route, and was about 27 kilometers (16.5 miles) from the Mediterranean Sea and 485 kilometers (300 miles) north of Jerusalem. The city was founded about 300 B.C. by Seleucus I Nicator, one of the three successors to Alexander the Great, and named for his father Antiochus.

With a population of more than half a million, it was the third largest city of the Roman Empire, ranking behind only Rome and Alexandria. Under the Roman rulers, Antioch became one of the most beautiful cities of the Roman Empire. Its main street, about two miles long, was paved with marble and flanked on both sides by hundreds of columns, which supported ornamented porches and balconies. Its cultural splendor and beautiful buildings, including the temple of Artemis, the amphitheater, and royal palaces, contributed to its reputation as the "Paris of the Ancient World" among scholars and researchers.

The early history of the church is closely connected with Antioch of Syria. One of the first seven "deacons," Nicolas, was a "proselyte from Antioch" (Acts 6:5). After the stoning of Stephen (Acts 7:54–60), great persecution caused certain disciples to flee from Jerusalem to Antioch, known for its tolerance, where they preached the gospel to the Jews (Acts 8:1; 11:19). Others arrived later and had success preaching to the Gentiles (Acts 11:20–21). When the church leaders at Jerusalem heard of this success in Antioch, they sent Barnabas to visit the church there (Acts 11:25–26).

Because this church was made up of both Gentiles and Jews, city officials sought a name that would distinguish them from other religious groups. They nicknamed them "Christians," meaning "Christ Followers" or "People of Christ," and the name stuck. According to the book of Acts, "the disciples were first called Christians in Antioch" (Acts 11:26).

Apparently, Paul and Barnabas used Antioch as the base for their missionary journeys into Asia Minor (Acts 13:1–3; 15:36–41; 18:22–23). Following the first missionary journey, Antioch became the scene of an important dispute. Certain men from Judea taught that Gentile converts must be circumcised and follow other rules for converts to Judaism before becoming Christians (Acts 15:1–2). This theological disagreement led to a church council at Jerusalem. Paul and Barnabas were sent here to report how God had given them success in bringing the gospel to the Gentiles. The council decided that Gentile converts did not have to be circumcised.

Antioch flourished under the Seleucid kings and contained magnificent buildings. It was made a free city by Pompey. Antioch is now known as Antakya, in modern-day Turkey.

Antiochus [An·ti′o·chus], *endurer*—Thirteen Syrian rulers of the Seleucid dynasty were named Antiochus. Two of them were particularly associated with Israel:

1. *Antiochus the Great.* He came to the throne of Syria in 223 B.C. and was the sixth ruler of the Seleucidan dynasty. After the death of Ptolemy IV he seized Palestine in 198 B.C. He invaded Europe but was defeated in the battle of Magnesia (190 B.C.) and forced to pay Rome an excessive tribute. While plundering a temple in 187 B.C., he was murdered by a mob.

2. *Antiochus Epiphanes.* The youngest son of Antiochus the Great. A hostage at Rome for fifteen years, he was released shortly after his father's death and came to the throne in 175 B.C., obtaining his kingdom by flatteries (Dan. 11:21). He enraged the Jews by looting the temple, setting up in it a statue of Jupiter, sacrificing swine on the altar, and destroying the walls of Jerusalem. These insults he followed with a frightful massacre of the Jews and this action precipitated the revolt of the Maccabees.

Antipas [An′ti·pas], *like a father*—Two men of the New Testament era:

1. A Christian martyr of Pergamos (Rev. 2:12–13). According to tradition he was the bishop of that place.

2. Son of Herod the Great. See Herod.

Antipatris [An·tip′a·tris], *city of Antipater*—The town to which Paul was taken by night (Acts 23:31). Its Old Testament name was Aphek (Josh. 12:18; 1 Sam. 4:1; 29:1).

Antonia, Tower of [An·to′ni·a]—A castle at the northwestern corner of the temple area. It rose forty cubits above the rock. Here Paul was brought after his rescue from the mob (Acts 21:30).

Antothijah [An·to·thi′jah]—See Anthothijah.

Antothite [An′to·thite]—An inhabitant of Anathoth (1 Chron. 11:28).

Anub [A′nub], *confederate*—Son of Coz (Hakkoz) (1 Chron. 4:8).

Apelles [A·pel′les], *called*—A Christian in Rome to whom Paul sent a salutation (Rom. 16:10). According to tradition he was bishop of Smyrna.

Apharsachites, Apharsathchites [A·phar·sa′chites, A·phar·-sath′chites], *as causers of division* or *I will divide the deceivers*—Probably Assyrian tribes from which came certain of those who settled in Samaria after the fall of the northern kingdom of Israel (Ezra 4:9; 5:6).

Aphek [A′phek], *fortress*—Four Old Testament cities:

1. A city of the Canaanites (Josh. 12:18), probably the same as Aphekah in Joshua 15:53.

2. A city of Asher near Sidon (Josh. 19:30; Judg. 1:31), also called Aphik.

3. A place near Shiloh where the Philistines gathered before the battle in which the ark was captured (1 Sam. 4:1).

4. A town near Jezreel (1 Sam. 29:1).

5. A city six miles east of the Sea of Galilee (1 Kings 20:26).

Aphekah [A·phe′kah], *fortress*—A city in the hill country of Judah (Josh. 15:53).

Aphiah [A·phi'ah], *I will make to breathe*—An ancestor of Saul, a Benjamite (1 Sam. 9:1).

Aphik [A'phik]—See Aphek.

Aphrah, Beth-le-aphrah [Aph'rah, Beth-le-aph'rah]—A town mentioned in Micah 1:10.

Aphses [Aph'ses], *to break*—The priests were divided into twenty-four families. Aphses was the head of the eighteenth (1 Chron. 24:15). A form of Happizzez.

Apis [A'pis]—One of the gods worshipped by the ancient Egyptians, the sacred bull-god of Noph (Memphis). It has been supposed that the golden calf that the Israelites made in the wilderness (Ex. 32) was modeled after the Apis-bull.

Apollonia [Ap·ol·lo'ni·a], *pertaining to Apollo*—A city of Macedonia about forty miles from Thessalonica (Acts 17:1).

Apollos [A·pol'los], *destroyer*—A learned and eloquent Jew from Alexandria in Egypt and an influential leader in the early church. Well-versed in the Old Testament, Apollos was a disciple of John the Baptist and "taught accurately the things of the Lord" (Acts 18:25). His preaching that Jesus was the Christ was attended with great success in Corinth and throughout Achaia. However, while Apollos knew some of Jesus' teaching, "he knew only the baptism of John" (Acts 18:25).

When Priscilla and Aquila, two other leaders in the early church, arrived in Ephesus, they instructed Apollos more accurately in the way of God (Acts 18:26). In Corinth, Apollos publicly contended with the Jewish leaders and refuted their objections to Christian teaching. He was apparently quite popular in Corinth, for in 1 Corinthians 1:12 Paul wrote of four parties into which the church at Corinth had become divided: one "following" Apollos, one Paul, one Cephas (Peter), and one Christ. In dealing with this division, Paul compared himself to the one who planted and Apollos to the one who watered what was already planted (1 Cor. 3:6). Some believe that he was the author of the epistle to the Hebrews.

Apollyon [A·pol'ly·on], *destroyer*—The Greek form of the Hebrew word *Abaddon*, the angel of the bottomless pit (Rev. 9:11).

Apostle [A·pos'tle], *one who is sent* or *a messenger*—The name applied to the twelve selected by Jesus to be with him, receive his training, be witnesses of the events of his life, and to preach the gospel (Matt. 4:18–22; 10:2–4; Luke 6:13–16). The original twelve were plain men of humble occupations and without specialized training except that given by Jesus (Acts 1:21–22). Paul was Apostle to the Gentiles.

Apostolical Council—The council held at Jerusalem about A.D. 50. It was an assembly of apostles and elders of the church (Acts 15).

Appaim [Ap'pa·im], *nostrils*—A son of Nadab and the father of Ishi (1 Chron. 2:30–31).

Apphia [Apph'i·a], *fruitful*—A Christian woman addressed by Paul in his letter to Philemon, probably the wife of Philemon (Philem. 2).

Appian Way [Ap'pi·an]—One of the Roman highways, from Brundisium on the Adriatic Sea to Rome. It was built by and named for Appius Claudius. Paul traveled on this road from Puteoli to Rome, on his journey to be tried before Caesar (Acts 28:13–16).

Appiiforum [Ap'pi·i·for'um], *market of Appius*—A station on the Appian Way about forty-three miles from Rome. When the Christians in Rome heard that Paul was coming, they traveled as far as this place to meet him and encourage him as he was being brought into Rome as a prisoner (Acts 28:15).

Aqaba, Gulf of [Aq'a·ba]—See Red Sea.

Aquila [A·quil'a], *eagle*—A Jewish Christian living in Corinth with his wife, Priscilla, at the time of Paul's arrival from Athens (Acts 18:2). Paul stayed with them while he was in the city. Aquila was born in Pontus (located in Asia Minor) but lived in Rome until Claudius commanded that all Jews leave the city. He and Priscilla moved to Corinth, where Aquila took up his trade, tentmaking.

When Paul left Corinth, Aquila and Priscilla traveled with him as far as Ephesus (1 Cor. 16:19), where they met Apollos and instructed him more thoroughly in the Christian faith (Acts 18:24–26). Apparently, they returned to Rome, because Paul sent them greetings in his letter to the Romans (Rom. 16:3).

Ar [Ar], *city*—A chief city of Moab situated in the valley of the Arnon (Num. 21:15; Deut. 2:18). It was later called Areopolis.

Ara [Ar'a], *lion*—A man of Asher (1 Chron. 7:38), one of the three sons of Jether.

Arab [Ar'ab], *ambush*—A town of Judah in the hill country (Josh. 15:52).

Arabah [Ar'a·bah], *plain* or *desert*—A major region of the land of Israel, referring usually to the entire valley region between Mount Hermon in the north to the Red Sea in the south (Num. 22:1; Deut. 1:7). The Arabah is more than 390 kilometers (240 miles) long, varying in width from 10 to 40 kilometers (6 to 25 miles).

The Arabah includes the Sea of Galilee, the Jordan River valley, the Dead Sea, and the area between the Dead Sea and the Red Sea. Much of this region lies below sea level, and the Dead Sea, which lies at approximately 394 meters (1,292 feet) below sea level, is the lowest spot on the earth's surface. The NKJV refers several times to the "Sea of the Arabah," meaning the Salt Sea or the Dead Sea (Deut. 3:17; Josh. 3:16; 2 Kings 14:25).

Before their entry into the promised land, the people of Israel camped in the Arabah, in an area called "the plains of Moab" (Num. 22:1), just north of the Dead Sea. While the Israelites were camped there, God turned Balaam's curses to blessings (Num. 22:1–24:25), Israel committed idolatry and immorality (Num. 25), Moses renewed the covenant, and Joshua sent out spies to prepare for the invasion of Canaan (Josh. 1:1–3:17). Usually rendered *plain* or *wilderness* in the King James Version.

Arabia [A·ra'bi·a]—A vast peninsula lying between the mainlands of Asia and Africa. In the Scriptures only that portion is usually meant which is known as Arabia Petraea, the region comprising the Sinaitic Peninsula and the territory south and east of Palestine. Paul, after his conversion, went to Arabia (Gal. 1:17).

Arad [Ar'ad], *wild ass*—A man and a town in the Old Testament:

1. A Benjamite, son of Beriah who helped expel the inhabitants of Gath (1 Chron. 8:15).

2. A town in the south of Judah belonging to the Canaanites (Num. 21:1; Josh. 12:14; Judg. 1:16).

Aradus [Ar′a·dus]—See Arvad.

Arah [Ar′ah], *wayfarer*—Two Old Testament men:
   1. A son of Ulla of the tribe of Asher (1 Chron. 7:39).
   2. The founder of a family, members of which came to Jerusalem from Babylon in the first expedition (Ezra 2:5; Neh. 7:10).

Aram [Ar′am], *exalted*—Four Old Testament men, and an area:
   1. One of the sons of Shem (Gen. 10:22–23).
   2. The country lying to the northeast of Palestine. It embraced both Syria and northern Mesopotamia. That portion of Aram in which Abraham had lived before coming to Canaan and in which Nahor remained is biblically known as Mesopotamia and Padan-aram (Gen. 24:10; 28:2, 5). It lay east of the Euphrates. It is rendered Padan in Genesis 48:7.
   3. Son of Shamer of the tribe of Asher (1 Chron. 7:34).
   4. Son of Kemuel (Gen. 22:21).
   5. Son of Hezron, the same as Ram, the father of Aminadab (Matt. 1:3–4; Luke 3:33).

Aram Dammesek [Ar′am Dam′me·sek]—Another name for Syria of Damascus (2 Sam. 8:5–6).

Arameans [Ar′a·me·ans]—The people of Aram (see Aram No. 2). Israel and the Arameans sometimes lived peacefully, and sometimes at war. As judgment for their sins, God allowed the Aramean Chushan-rishathaim, king of Mesopotamia, to invade and conquer Israel in the days of the judges (Judg. 3:8–10). Hadadezer of Zobah and Toi of Hamath, whom David subdued, were Aramean rulers (2 Sam. 8:1–13). Rezon the Aramean official, founded the city-state of Damascus, and Israel and Damascus were foes for many years (1 Kings 11:23–24; 15:8–20; 2 Kings 16:5, 7–18).

Aramitess [Ar·am·i′tess]—A woman of Aram. One of Manasseh's concubines is referred to as an Aramitess (1 Chron. 7:14, KJV).

Aram-maacah [Ar′am-ma′a·cah]—See Maacah.

Aram-naharaim [Ar'am-na·ha·ra'im], *Aram of the two rivers*—
The part of Aram which lay east of the great bend of the northern Euphrates, the probable location of Padan–aram (Gen. 28:5); the Aram
of the patriarchs before entering Canaan. Here stood the city of Haran
and at a later date Edessa, the center of Syrian culture. David's war with
this district of Syria is mentioned in the title of Psalm 60.

Aram-zobah [Ar'am-zo'bah], *exalted station* or *exalted conflict*—That part of Aram which lay between Hamath and Damascus
(Ps. 60, title).

Aran [Ar'an], *wild goat*—One of the sons of Dishan and grandson of
Seir, the Horite (Gen. 36:28; 1 Chron. 1:42).

Ararat [Ar'a·rat], *the curse reversed* or *precipitation of curse*—
The mountainous region between the Black Sea and the Caspian Sea
where Noah's ark rested when the Flood subsided (Gen. 8:4). From this
region streams converge to form the Tigris and the Euphrates Rivers.
Originally called Urartu, Ararat referred to the whole mountainous
area; its use, however, has gradually come to be restricted to the huge
volcanic mountain at the borders of Turkey, Iran, and Azerbaijan.

This volcanic mountain includes two peaks, 5,600 meters (17,000
feet) and 4,200 meters (13,000 feet) above sea level. The taller peak,
called Mount Masis by the Armenians and *Kuh-i-Nuh* (mountain
of Noah) by the Persians, rises 920 meters (3,000 feet) above the line
of perpetual snow. Some people believe that Noah's ark still rests on
Mount Ararat, and occasional expeditions have been launched to find
it. However, shifting glaciers, avalanches, hidden crevices, and sudden
storms make the mountain so difficult to climb that it is referred to by
the native inhabitants of that region as "the Painful Mountain."

Araunah, Ornan [A·rau'nah, Or'nan]—A Jebusite from whom
David purchased a threshing floor on Mount Moriah as a site for an
altar (2 Sam. 24:18–25; 2 Chron. 3:1).

Arba [Ar'ba], *fourth*—Father or leading man of Anak and founder
of Kirjath-arba, later called Hebron (Josh. 14:15; 15:13; Judg. 1:10). See
Hebron.

Arbah [Ar'bah], *four*—The city of Hebron (Gen. 35:27).

Arbathite [Ar′ba·thite]—A native of Arabah or Beth-arabah (2 Sam. 23:31; 1 Chron. 11:32).

Arbite [Ar′bite]—A native of Arab in Judah (2 Sam. 23:35).

Archelaus [Ar·che·la′us], *a chief*—Ethnarch of Judea at the time of the return from Egypt of Joseph, Mary, and the child Jesus (Matt. 2:22). He was the elder son of Herod the Great by his fourth wife, Malthace. In A.D. 6 he was charged with tyranny and was banished to Vienne in Gaul where he died. See also Herod.

Archevites [Ar′che·vites], *lengthy*—The inhabitants of Erech, some of whom were placed in Samaria by Asnapper following the overthrow of Israel (Ezra 4:9).

Archi [Ar′chi], *lengthy*—A city on the border of Ephraim (Josh. 16:2).

Archippus [Ar·chip′pus], *master of the horse*—A Christian and officer of the church at Colosse (Col. 4:17; Philem. 2).

Archite [Ar′chite], *lengthy*—The Archites were a Canaanite tribe who settled on the boundary between Ephraim and Benjamin (2 Sam. 15:32; 17:5, 14).

Arcturus [Arc·tu′rus]—A bright red star of the northern sky known as the guard or keeper of the Great Bear (Ursa Major, "The Big Dipper," or "The Plough"). The biblical word *Arcturus* is probably not the guard but the Great Bear itself (Job 9:9; 38:32).

Ard [Ard], *I shall subdue*—Son of Bela and grandson of Benjamin (Gen. 46:21; Num. 26:38, 40). In 1 Chronicles 8:3 he is called Addar.

Ardites [Ard′ites]—Descendants of Ard (Num. 26:40).

Ardon [Ar′don], *subduer*—A man of the family of Hezron, of the house of Caleb, of the tribe of Judah (1 Chron. 2:18).

Areli [A·re′li], *lion of God*—One of the seven sons of Gad, founder of the family of Arelites (Gen. 46:16; Num. 26:17).

Arelites [A·re′lites]—A family descended from Areli (Num. 26:17).

Areopagite [Ar·e·op′a·gite]—A judge of the court of Areopagus (Acts 17:34).

Areopagus [Ar·e·op′a·gus], *hill of Area*—A rocky height in Athens opposite the western end of the Acropolis. It was called Mars' Hill from the supposed fact that Mars, or Area, was here tried for murder by Neptune. Here met the Council of the Areopagus, a tribunal composed of ex-archons. Sixteen steps still lead up to the top of the hill where extends the bench on which the judges sat. Here Paul delivered a notable address (Acts 17:18–34).

Aretas [Ar′e·tas], *graver*—King of Arabia Petraea and father-in-law of Herod Antipas. When Herod desired to divorce his wife and marry Herodias, Aretas made war on him and defeated him. Rome supported Herod and sent Vitellius to punish Aretas but the order was never executed. For a short time Aretas was in possession of Damascus (2 Cor. 11:32).

Argob [Ar′gob], *stony*—A man and a region of the Old Testament:
1. A man slain by Pekah (2 Kings 15:25).
2. A region of Bashan within or near Trachonitis (Deut. 3:4, 13–14; Josh. 13:30; 1 Kings 4:13).

Aridai [Ar′i·dai], *the lion is enough*—Son of Haman who was hanged with his father (Est. 9:9).

Aridatha [Ar·i·da′tha], *the lion of decree*—Son of Haman (Est. 9:8).

Arieh [Ar′i·eh], *lion*—Companion of Argob (2 Kings 15:25).

Ariel [Ar′i·el], *lion of God*—Two men and a city bear this name:
1. A leading man who, with certain others, was directed by Ezra to visit Iddo, the chief at Casiphia (Ezra 8:16–17).
2. A designation of Jerusalem by Isaiah (Isa. 29:1, 2, 7). The significance of the word is obscure, but probably denotes *lion of God* or *altar* or *hearth of God*.
3. A Moabite (2 Sam. 23:20) in the King James Version.

Arimathaea [Ar·im·a·thae′a], *heights*—The native town of Joseph of Arimathaea (Matt. 27:57). It may have been the Ramah of 1 Samuel 1:19.

Arioch [Ar'i·och], *servant of the moon god*—Two men of the Old Testament:
1. A captain of Nebuchadnezzar's guard (Dan. 2:14–15).
2. King of Ellasar (Gen. 14:1, 9).

Arisai [Ar'i·sai], *lion of my banners*—One of the ten sons of Haman. He was slain by the Jews (Est. 9:9).

Aristarchus [Ar·is·tar'chus], *best ruler*—A Macedonian who was with Paul on his third missionary journey. He was of Thessalonica and was with Paul at Ephesus (Acts 19:29). He came with Paul into Asia (Acts 20:4–6), accompanied him to Rome (Acts 27:2), and was afterward his fellow-prisoner (Col. 4:10; Philem. 24).

Aristobulus [A·ris·to·bu'lus], *best counsellor*—A Christian at Rome (Rom. 16:10).

Arkite [Ar'kite], *gnawing*—A family of the Canaanites descended from Ham (Gen. 10:17; 1 Chron. 1:15). They were located in the north of Phoenicia and founded the city of Arks, which is about twelve miles north of Tripolis.

Armenia [Ar·me'ni·a], *land of Aram* or *mountains of Minni*—A region north of Lake Van between the Black and Caspian Seas. It included the district which had earlier been known as Ararat. It is mentioned as the land to which the sons of Sennacherib fled after having slain their father (2 Kings 19:37; Isa. 37:38). See Ararat.

Armoni [Ar·mo'ni], *belonging to the palace*—A son of Saul and Rizpah. He was hanged by the Gibeonites (2 Sam. 21:8–11).

Arnan [Ar'nan], *agile*—A descendant of Zerubbabel (1 Chron. 3:21).

Arni [Ar'ni]—The father of Amminadab, also called Ram (Ruth 4:19; Luke 3:33).

Arnon [Ar'non], *noisy* or *rushing stream*—This river was the boundary between Moab and the Amorites (Num. 21:13–14, 26; Judg. 11:22). After the conquests of Joshua, it separated Moab from the tribe of Reuben (Josh. 12:1–2; 13:9, 16). It empties into the Dead Sea.

Arod, Arodi [Ar'od, A·ro'di], *I shall subdue* or *I shall roam*—A son of Gad (Gen. 46:16; Num. 26:17), ancestor of the Arodites.

Arodites [Ar'o·dites]—See Arod.

Aroer [A·ro'er], *naked*—Three towns of Old Testament Israel:

1. A town in the south of Judah to which David sent booty taken from the Amalekites (1 Sam. 30:28).

2. A city on the northern bank of the Arnon. It was in the southern part of the kingdom of Sihon afterward inhabited by the tribe of Reuben (Deut. 2:36; 3:12; Josh. 12:2). It was captured by King Mesha of Moab and later by King Hazael of Syria (2 Kings 10:33). In the time of Jeremiah Moab possessed it (Jer. 48:19).

3. A town of Gilead belonging to Gad (Num. 32:34; Josh. 13:25).

Aroerite [A·ro'er·ite]—A native or inhabitant of Aroer (1 Chron. 11:44).

Arpachshad [Ar·pach'shad]—See Arphaxad.

Arpad, Arphad [Ar'pad, Ar'phad], *I shall be spread out (or supported)*—A city in Syria near Damascus and Hamath (2 Kings 18:34; 19:13; Isa. 10:9; Jer. 49:23). It was besieged and captured by Tiglath-pileser II in 742–740 B.C. An uprising in 720 B.C. was crushed by Sargon.

Arphaxad, Arpachshad [Ar·phax'ad, Ar·pach'shad], *stronghold of Chaldees*—A son of Shem (Gen. 10:22, 24; 1 Chron. 1:17–18) and an ancestor of Abraham.

Artaxerxes [Ar·ta·xerx'es], *exalted king*—Any one of several Persian kings, as Artaxerxes I, the third son of Xerxes (Ahasuerus). He reigned 464–424 B.C. and was called Artaxerxes Longimanus, which according to some denoted the long length of his hands, but others regard it as a figurative expression indicating the extent of his kingdom. It was probably he who listened to the enemies of the Jews and stopped the work on the second temple (Ezra 4:7); but when the edict of Cyrus was found, the building operations were renewed (Ezra 6:1–4).

In his twentieth year (445 B.C.), he commissioned Nehemiah to go to Jerusalem and rebuild the walls (Neh. 2:1). After an absence of twelve years Nehemiah returned to Persia but in a short time was permitted to return to Jerusalem. During his entire stay in Jerusalem, Nehemiah acted in the capacity of governor (Neh. 13:6). Longimanus did more for the Jews than any other Persian king except Cyrus.

Artemas [Ar'te·mas], *gift of Artemis*—A companion of Paul and, according to tradition, a prominent bishop of Lystra (Titus 3:12).

Artemis [Ar'te·mis]—Greek goddess of hunting, corresponding to the Roman goddess, Diana (Acts 19:24).

Aruboth [A·ru'both], *the lattices*—A city or district of which the son of Hesed was purveyor (1 Kings 4:10).

Arumah [A·ru'mah], *a height*—A town near Shechem. At one time it was the residence of Abimelech (Judg. 9:41) and was possibly the same as Rumah (2 Kings 23:3b).

Arvad [Ar'vad], *wandering*—The most northerly of the Phoenician cities, a sort of second Tyre, built on the rocky island of Aradus. In the time of Ezekiel men of this city defended Tyre (Ezek. 27:8, 11).

Arvadite [Ar'va·dite]—An inhabitant of the island of Aradus or Arvad. They were descendants of the sons of Canaan (Gen. 10:18). See Arvad.

Arza [Ar'za], *delight*—A steward over the house of Elah (1 Kings 16:9).

Asa [A'sa], *physician*—Two Old Testament men:
1. Third king of Judah, the son of Abijam and grandson of Rehoboam. He had a peaceful reign for his first ten years (2 Chron. 14:1). He punished his mother for idolatry (1 Kings 15:9–13).
He defeated Zerah, the Ethiopian, when the latter invaded Judah (2 Chron. 14:9–15) and, aided by Azariah, reformed the people (2 Chron. 15:1–15). He made an alliance with Damascus for which he was reproved by Hanani (1 Kings 15:16–22; 2 Chron. 16:1–10). In his old age Asa was diseased in his feet and was less loyal to the Lord than he had been earlier (1 Kings 15:23; 2 Chron. 16:12).
2. A Levite, son of Elkanah. He lived in one of the Netophathite villages (1 Chron. 9:16).

Asahel [As'a·hel], *God hath made*—Four Old Testament men:
1. The brother of Joab, son of David's sister Zeruiah (1 Chron. 2:16). He is described as being "fleet of foot as a wild gazelle." Abner killed him in self-defense (2 Sam. 2:12–23).

2. One employed by Hezekiah to have charge of offerings and tithes (2 Chron. 31:13).

3. A Levite appointed by Jehoshaphat to instruct the people (2 Chron. 17:8).

4. Father of a certain Jonathan, who opposed Ezra (Ezra 10:15).

Asahiah [A·sahi'ah]—See Asaiah.

Asaiah [A·sai'ah], *the Lord hath made*—Four Old Testament men:

1. A chief of the family of Merari (1 Chron. 6:30; 15:6, 11).

2. A descendant of Simeon (1 Chron. 4:36).

3. An officer sent by Josiah to consult Huldah (2 Kings 22:12, 14).

4. A man of Judah, son of Baruch and head of the family of Shelah (1 Chron. 9:5; Neh. 11:5), also called Maaseiah.

Asaph [A'saph], *gatherer*—Three Old Testament men:

1. A Levite, son of Berachiah, and a leader of David's choir (1 Chron. 6:32, 39). He was appointed to sound the cymbals (1 Chron. 16:4–7), and his family was one of the three families responsible for temple music (1 Chron. 25:1–9). Some of this family were apparently also appointed as gatekeepers (1 Chron. 26:1). The family of Asaph, consisting of 128 or more persons, returned from Babylon (1 Chron. 9:15; Ezra 2:41; Neh. 7:44), and had charge of the music when the foundations of the second temple were laid (Ezra 3:10). Psalm 50 and Psalms 73–83 were written by members of the family of Asaph.

2. The father of the chronicler Joah, in the reign of Hezekiah (2 Kings 18:18, 37).

3. One who had charge of the royal forests in Israel, appointed to the office by the king of Persia (Neh. 2:8).

Asaph, Sons of [A'saph]—See Asaph No 1.

Asaphite [A'saph·ite]—Descendant of Asaph.

Asareel [As'a·reel], *God hath bound*—One of the four sons of Jehaleleel (1 Chron. 4:16) of the tribe of Judah.

Asarelah, Asharelah [As·a·re'lah, Ash·a·re'lah], *right toward God*—A son of Asaph the Levite. Under David he had duties in connection with the temple music (1 Chron. 25:2). In 1 Chronicles 25:14 he is called Jesharelah.

Ascalon [As′ca·lon]—See Ashkelon.

Ascent of Akrabbim [Ak·rab′bim]—See Akrabbim.

Asenath [As′e·nath], *belonging to the goddess Neith*—Daughter of Potiphera, priest of On. She was the wife of Joseph and mother of Manasseh and Ephraim (Gen. 41:45, 50–52; 46:20).

Aser [As′er]—See Asher.

Ashan [Ash′an], *smoke*—This town was allotted to Judah. Later it was assigned to Simeon and then to the Levites (Josh. 15:42; 19:7; 1 Chron. 4:32). The various renderings, Bor-ashan, Chorashan, Corashan, as in 1 Samuel 30:30, may be variants of Ashan.

Asharelah [Ash·a·re′lah]—See Asarelah.

Ashbea [Ash·be′a], *adjuration*—A descendant of Shelah of the tribe of Judah. The members of this family wrought fine linen (1 Chron. 4:21).

Ashbel [Ash′bel], *a man in God* or *a man of Baal* or *I will make a path*—The second son of Benjamin and founder of a tribal family (Gen. 46:21; 1 Chron. 8:1). His descendants were called Ashbelites (Num. 26:38).

Ashbelites [Ash′bel·ites]—Descendants of Ashbel.

Ashchenaz [Ash′che·naz]—See Ashkenaz.

Ashdod [Ash′dod], *fortress*—One of the five principal Philistine cities (1 Sam. 6:17), situated 5 kilometers (3 miles) from the Mediterranean coast and 32 kilometers (20 miles) north of Gaza. The city's military and economic significance was enhanced by its location on the main highway between Egypt and Syria.

Joshua and the Israelites drove the Canaanites out of the hill country of Judah, but the Anakim—a group of Canaanites—remained in Ashdod, Gaza, and Gath (Josh. 11:22). During the time of Eli and Samuel, the ark of the covenant accompanied Israel's army (1 Sam. 4:3). When the Philistines defeated Israel, they took the ark to the temple of Dagon in Ashdod (1 Sam. 5:1–7).

Uzziah, the powerful king of Judah, captured Ashdod (2 Chron. 26:6). The prophet Amos predicted the destruction of the city because of its inhumane treatment of Israelites (Amos 1:8; 3:9). When Sargon II, king of Assyria, destroyed Ashdod in 711 B.C., he fulfilled this prophecy (Isa. 20:1). Psammeticus, king of Egypt, besieged Ashdod for twenty-nine years.

In New Testament times, Ashdod was renamed Azotus. Philip the evangelist preached in all the cities from Azotus to Caesarea (Acts 8:40).

Ashdodites, Ashdothites [Ash′dod·ites, Ash′do·thites]—Inhabitants of Ashdod (Josh. 13:3; Neh. 4:7).

Ashdoth-pisgah [Ash′doth-pis′gah], *slopes of Pisgah*—The slopes, spurs, and ravines of Pisgah, the summit of which is Mount Nebo, east of the Dead Sea (Deut. 3:17; 4:49; Josh. 12:3; 13:20).

Asher [Ash′er], *happy*—The eighth son of Jacob and second by Zilpah, the handmaid of Leah (Gen. 30:13). The tribe of Asher was assigned the district that ran north from Carmel along the sea shore. To the east of it lay the tribes of Zebulun and Naphtali (Josh. 19:24–31).

Asherah [A·she′rah], *groves (for idol worship)*—Name of a Canaanite goddess, frequently associated with Baal. It appears that she was symbolized by sacred poles or trees and that frequently the word does not signify the goddess, but only these symbols. In the King James Version Asherahs are called *groves.*

Asherite [Ash′er·ite]—A member of the tribe of Asher (Judg. 1:32).

Ashhur [Ash′hur]—See Ashur.

Ashima [A·shi′ma], *guiltiness* or *I will make desolate*—The name of a divinity worshipped by the people of Hamath (2 Kings 17:30).

Ashkelon, Askelon [Ash′ke·lon, As′ke·lon]—One of the five principal cities of the Philistines (Josh. 13:3). Situated on the seacoast 19 kilometers (12 miles) north of Gaza, Ashkelon and her sister cities (Ashdod, Gath, Gaza, and Ekron) posed a serious threat to the Israelites during the period of the Judges. Shortly after Joshua's death, Ashkelon was captured and was briefly controlled by the tribe of Judah (Judg. 1:18). A few years later Samson killed 30 men from this city (Judg.

14:19). During most of the Old Testament era, however, Ashkelon remained politically and militarily independent of Israel.

In the eighth century B.C. Ashkelon was denounced by the prophet Amos (Amos 1:8). Shortly before the Babylonian captivity, Zephaniah prophesied that the Jews would return from Babylonia and occupy the ruins of Ashkelon (Zeph. 2:4, 7). Zechariah also prophesied the destruction of Ashkelon (Zech. 9:5).

It was the birthplace of Herod the Great and residence of Salome, his sister. Its inhabitants are called Eshkalonites in Joshua 13:3.

Ashkenaz [Ash·ke′naz], *a man as sprinkled* or *fire as scattered*— The eldest son of Gomer (Gen. 10:3). In 1 Chronicles 1:6 and Jeremiah 51:27 the name is spelled Ashchenaz.

Ashnah [Ash′nah], *strong*—Two towns of Judah:
1. A town in Judah near Zorah (Josh. 15:33).
2. A town farther south in Judah (Josh. 15:43).

Ashpenaz [Ash′pe·naz], *I will make prominent the sprinkled*— Chief of the eunuchs of Nebuchadnezzar who was kind to Daniel and his associates (Dan. 1:3, 7, 11–16).

Ashriel [Ash′ri·el]—See Ashriel.

Ashtaroth [Ash′ta·roth], *star*—
1. A city in Bashan (Deut. 1:4; Josh. 9:10). Named after the goddess Astarte, it was the capital of Og, king of the remnant of the giants (Josh. 12:4; 13:12). Ashtaroth was allotted to Machir, son of Manasseh, but later, having become a Levitical city, it became the residence of the children of Gershom (1 Chron. 6:71).
2. Plural form of the Canaanitish goddess of fertility. See Ashtoreth.

Ashterathite [Ash·te′ra·thite]—Inhabitant of Ashtaroth (1 Chron. 11:44).

Ashteroth-karnaim [Ash′te·roth-kar·na′im], *Ashtaroth of the two horns*—It may be the full name of Ashtaroth or it may have been the place known as Carnaim. In his invasion against the cities of the plain this city was smitten by Chedorlaomer (Gen. 14:5).

Ashtoreth [Ash′to·reth], *a wife*—The principal female divinity of the Phoenicians, called Astarte by the Greeks and Romans and Ishtar by the Assyrians. The worship of this goddess was established at Sidon (1 Kings 11:3, 5; 2 Kings 23:13) and was practiced by the Hebrews in the time of the judges (Judg. 2:13; 10:6). Solomon gave it his support (1 Kings 11:5; 2 Kings 23:13).

Ashur, Ashhur [Ash'ur, Ash'hur], *blackness*—Son of Hezron by his wife, Abiah. He had two wives, Helah and Naarah, and seven children through whom he became ancestor of the inhabitants of Tekoah (1 Chron. 2:24; 4:5–7).

Ashurbanipal [Ash·ur·ban'i·pal], *Ashur is creator of an heir*—The son of the Assyrian king Esarhaddon. He is probably the Osnapper mentioned in Ezra 4:10. See Asnapper.

Ashurites [Ash'u·rites]—Subjects of Ish-bosheth (2 Sam. 2:9), probably the Asherites (Judg. 1:32).

Ashurnasirpal [Ash·ur·nas'ir·pal], *Ashur is guardian of the heir*—The king of Assyria during the reigns of Ahab of Israel and Jehoshaphat of Judah.

Ashvath [Ash'vath], *sleek*—A son of Japhlet and great-grandson of Asher (1 Chron. 7:33).

Asia [A'sia]—The word in modern usage denotes the largest of the continents, but as used biblically it refers only to the western portion of Asia Minor. It was the richest, and except for Africa, the most important of the Roman provinces. Its capital was the large and ancient city of Ephesus.

To the east lay Bithynia, Galatia, Pisidia, and Lycia. Across the strait, now known as the Dardanelles, lay Macedonia. When Paul went on his second missionary journey, he was forbidden by the Holy Spirit to go into Asia (Acts 16:6–10), but later this area, especially the section around Ephesus, was the scene of many of Paul's activities (Acts 19:10, 22, 26; 20:4, 6, 18; 1 Cor. 16:19; 2 Tim. 1:15). In this rich province were located the seven churches of Asia (Rev. 1–3).

Asia Minor [A'sia]—The peninsula which is modern Turkey, the westernmost bit of the continent of Asia. It is bound by the Black Sea on the north, the Aegean Sea on the west, and the Mediterranean Sea on the south.

Asiarchs [A′si·archs], *chiefs of Asia*—A college of ten superintendents of public games and religious rites of proconsular Asia. Among
Paul's friends and supporters were the asiarchs of Ephesus (Acts 19:31).

Asiel [As′i·el], *God hath made*—A Simeonite, ancestor of Jehu
(1 Chron. 4:35).

Askelon [As′ke·lon]—See Ashkelon.

Asnah [As′nah], *a bramble*—The head of a family of Nethinims
(Ezra 2:50).

Asnapper, Osnapper [As·nap′per, Os·nap′per]—An Assyrian
official, a ruler, Esar–haddon or his general or, more probably, Assur-
banipal, son of Esar–haddon. He settled foreign tribes, the Cuthaeans,
in the cities of Samaria after the fall of Israel (Ezra 4:10).

Aspatha [As·pa′tha], *the enticed gathered*—A son of Haman
slain by the Jews (Est. 9:7).

Asriel, Ashriel [As′ri·el, Ash′ri·el], *vow of God*—A son of Gilead
and great-grandson of Manasseh (Num. 26:31; Josh. 17:2).

Asrielites [As′ri·e·lites]—Descendants of Asriel (Num. 26:31).

Asshur [Assh′ur], *a step*—A son of Shem (Gen. 10:22; 1 Chron.
1:17). His descendants inhabited the land of Assyria. See Assyria.

Asshurim [Assh·u′rim]—A people that sprang from Dedan and
more remotely from Abraham by Keturah (Gen. 25:3). According to
one theory, they are the same as the Ashurites mentioned in 2 Samuel
2:9.

Assir [As′sir], *captive*—Three Old Testament men:
  1. Son of Korah (Ex. 6:24). He was born in Egypt.
  2. A descendant of the preceding (1 Chron. 6:23–27).
  3. Son of Jeconiah, the son of Jehoiakim (1 Chron. 3:17).

Assos [As′sos], *approaching*—A seaport of Mysia, a few miles from
Troas (Acts 20:13–14).

Assur [As′sur]—See Assyria.

Assyria, Asshur, Assur [As·syr′i·a, Assh′ur, As′sur], *a step—*
The land lying on the Tigris between Padan-aram, Babylon, Armenia, and Media. The name is derived from Asshur, the son of Shem (Gen. 10:22) who was later worshipped by the Assyrians as a deity. While Moses appears to have known about Assyria (Gen. 2:14; 25:18; Num. 24:22), it did not become important to Jewish history until the reign of Menahem. The Assyrians were a Semitic people who originated in Babylon (Gen. 10:11). They conquered Babylonia about 1300 B.C. and under Tiglath–pileser I became the strongest power in the east.

They are mentioned in the Bible chiefly for their warlike aggressions. During the days of David and Solomon, Assyria had declined under the successors of Tiglath-pileser I, and it was not a serious threat to the expansion of the kingdom of Israel. However, when Tiglath-pileser III came into power, Assyria began to stretch its power and influence. In Scripture, this Assyrian king is also called Pul (2 Kings 15:19). When under pressure from Pekah, king of Israel, and Rezin of Syria, Ahaz, king of Judah gave Tiglath-pileser gifts of treasure in exchange for protection. In consequence of his association with Assyria, Ahaz made the mistake of rearranging the altars and furnishings of the temple; replacing the altar with a copy of one he had seen in Damascus, and offering sacrifices on it himself.

Tiglath-pileser was succeeded by his son Shalmanesar, and Shalmanesar began to put pressure on Israel, demanding tribute. One year, Hoshea refused to pay, and Shalmanesar took swift action. In the year 722 B.C., the nation of Israel was invaded, conquered, and carried captive into Assyria. The nation never recovered from this depredation, and the ten northern tribes were scattered and mixed and forgot their ancestry. Most of the exiles never returned to the land.

Some years later, another Assyrian king, Sennacharib, came up against Jerusalem when Hezekiah was king. This time, however, Judah had a righteous ruler, and God rescued His people from the hands of the Assyrians (2 Kings 18:17–19:37). See Sennacherib.

The Assyrians were a pagan people, whose idol worship was strongly condemned by several Old Testament prophets (Isa. 10:5; Ezek. 16:28; Hos. 8:9). They emphasized the worship of nature, believing that the natural elements were possessed by a spirit. Along with the national deity, Assur, the Assyrian people worshipped Shemach, the sun god;

Sin, the moon god; and Hadad, the god of thunder. The Assyrians were notorious for their savagery in warfare. They burned and looted cities and showed little mercy to their captives. In stone carvings discovered by archeologists, Assyrian soldiers are shown torturing children, blinding warriors, chopping off hands, impaling victims on stakes, and beheading their enemies.

The Hebrew people harbored deep-seated resentment and hostility toward this nation. This attitude is revealed clearly in the book of Jonah. The reluctant prophet Jonah, like the rest of the Israelites, hated and despised the Assyrians. When God told him to go and preach repentance to the Assyrian capital city of Nineveh, Jonah refused. When he finally obeyed God, and the city actually repented, Jonah was angry with God for forgiving such a wicked people, instead of destroying them as he had prophesied.

The entire book of Nahum is a prediction of God's judgment against the Assyrians. Nahum informed the nation that its days as a world power were drawing to a close. In an oracle of woe, the prophet described Nineveh as a "bloody city . . . full of lies and robbery" (Nah. 3:1). But soon the city of Nineveh would be laid waste, and Assyria would crumble before the judgment of God. This happened as Nahum prophesied when the Babylonians and Medians formed a coalition to defeat the Assyrians about 612 B.C.

Astaroth [As′ta·roth]—See Ashtoreth.

Astarte [As·tar′te]—See Ashtoreth.

Asuppim [A·sup′pim], *stores*—A building near the southern gate of the outer court of the temple used as a storehouse (1 Chron. 26:15).

Asyncritus [A·syn′cri·tus], *unlike*—A Christian at Rome to whom Paul sent a salutation (Rom. 16:14).

Atad [A′tad], *thornbush*—A threshing floor of unknown site between Egypt and Hebron where the funeral party bearing Jacob's body halted seven days (Gen. 50:10–11). It is also called Abel–Mizraim.

Atarah [At′a·rah], *a crown*—The second wife of Jerahmeel and mother of Onam (1 Chron. 2:26).

Ataroth [At′a·roth], *crowns*—Three towns and an unknown geographical location:

1. A town in Gilead built by the tribe of Gad and captured by King Mesha of Moab (Num. 32:3, 34).

2. A town of Ephraim near Jericho (Josh. 16:2), possibly the same as Ataroth–addar (Josh. 16:5).

3. A place name, listed among the descendants of Judah (1 Chron. 2:54).

4. A town on the northeast border of Ephraim (Josh. 16:7).

Ataroth-addar [At'a·roth-ad'dar]—See Ataroth.

Ater [A'ter], *shut*—Two men of the Old Testament:

1. A man, probably a descendant of Hezekiah. Ninety-eight of his descendants returned from Babylon (Ezra 2:16; Neh. 7:21; 10:17).

2. A porter of the temple (Ezra 2:42; Neh. 7:45).

Athach [A'thach], *lodging*—To this city of Judah, David gave the spoils taken from the Amalekites (1 Sam. 30:30).

Athaiah [A·thai'ah], *Jehovah has helped*—A son of Uzziah of Judah of the family of Perez (Neh. 11:4).

Athaliah [Ath·a·li'ah], *the Lord is strong*—The name of one woman and two men in the Old Testament:

1. The queen of Judah for six years (2 Kings 11:1–3). Athaliah was the daughter of King Ahab of Israel. Presumably, Jezebel was her mother. Athaliah married Jehoram (or Joram), son of Jehoshaphat, king of Judah. Her marriage was the result of an alliance between Ahab and Jehoshaphat. Jehoram reigned only eight years and was succeeded by his son Ahaziah, who died after reigning only one year. Desiring the throne for herself, Athaliah ruthlessly killed all her grandsons—except the infant Joash, who was hidden by his aunt (2 Kings 11:2).

Athaliah apparently inherited Jezebel's ruthlessness. She was a tyrant whose every whim had to be obeyed. As her mother had done in Israel, Athaliah introduced Baal worship in Judah and in so doing destroyed part of the temple. Joash was hidden in the house of the Lord for six years (2 Kings 11:3), while Athaliah reigned over the land (841–835 B.C.). In the seventh year, the high priest Jehoiada declared Joash the lawful king of Judah. Guards removed Athaliah from the temple before killing her, to avoid defiling the temple with her blood (2 Kings 11:13–16; 2 Chron. 23:12–15).

Athaliah reaped what she sowed. She gained the throne through murder and lost her life in the same way. She also failed to thwart God's promise, because she did not destroy the Davidic line, through which the Messiah was to be born.

2. A son of Jeroham, a Benjamite (1 Chron. 8:26).

3. The father of Jeshaiah (Ezra 8:7).

Athenians [A·the′ni·ans]—The people of the city of Athens (Acts 17:21).

Athens [Ath′ens]—The capital city of the ancient Greek state of Attica, celebrated for the distinction it attained in learning and civilization. It dates to before 3000 B.C., and has a long history of famous and successful military campaigns. Athens was the center of art, architecture, literature, and politics during the "golden age" of the Greeks (fifth century B.C.). Many famous philosophers, playwrights, and other artists lived in Athens during this time. In fact, philosophy, properly considered, began in Athens with the pre-Socratic thinkers and came to its greatest expression in Socrates, Plato, Aristotle. It was destined to leave a deep impression on the Jewish and Christian schools of Alexandria.

The city is recognized even today as the birthplace of Western civilization and culture. Modern visitors to Athens are impressed by the city's ancient glory, with the ruins of the Parthenon and several other massive buildings that were devoted to pagan worship. In ancient days, the city was adorned by the great statue of the Virgin Goddess of the Parthenon and the colossal bronze figure of Athena on the Acropolis, executed by Phidias.

In religious interests, Pausanias says that in the attention paid to the gods, the Athenians surpassed all other states, and the city was filled with sacred buildings, temples, and altars. Paul observed this fact when he visited Athens during his second missionary journey (Acts 17:15–18:1). While waiting in the city for Silas and Timothy to catch up to him, he spent some time sightseeing (Acts 17:23). He noticed the Athenians erected statues to all the gods, and even to "unknown" gods. Paul described Athens as a city "given over to idols" (Acts 17:16).

During his visit, Paul met "certain Epicurean and Stoic philosophers" (Acts 17:18) and preached to them about Jesus. This led them to bring him before the court of Areopagus—an institution revered from the city's earliest times. This court met upon the hill called Areopagus

(Mars' Hill). Its purpose was to decide religious matters. Members of the court were curious about Paul's proclamation of the god they worshipped without knowing (Acts 17:23). Paul's speech to the court (Acts 17:22–31) provides a model for communicating the gospel to a group that has no Bible background. He drew from his surroundings by mentioning the Athenians' love for religion, demonstrated by their many idols. He then made his plea for Christianity by declaring that God does not dwell in man-made temples.

In spite of this approach, most of the Athenians were not responsive to Paul's preaching. They could not accept Paul's statement about the resurrection of Jesus (Acts 17:32). Following apostolic times a Christian church was in Athens. Although not mentioned in the New Testament, it doubtless arose from the labors of the great apostle. Dionysius was converted through that sermon on Mars' Hill. He was a member of the supreme court of Areopagus and is called the Areopagite. According to tradition he was the first bishop of Athens (Acts 17:15–18:1; 1 Thess. 3:1).

Athlai [Ath·la′i], *whom Jehovah afflicts*—An Israelite, son of Bebai, who divorced his foreign wife (Ezra 10:28).

Atroth [At′roth]—See Atroth-shophan.

Atroth-beth-joab [At′roth-beth-jo′ab], *crowns of the house of Joab*—A family or village of Judah (1 Chron. 2:54).

Atroth-shophan [At′roth-sho′phan], *crowns of Shopan*—A Gadite town of unknown site, improperly regarded in the King James Version as two towns (Num. 32:35).

Attai [At′ta·i], *opportune*—Three Old Testament men:

1. A man of Judah whose father was an Egyptian slave but his mother was a descendant of Jerahmeel and Hezron (1 Chron. 2:34–36).

2. A warrior of David, a Gadite, who came to him at Ziklag (1 Chron. 12:11).

3. A son of Rehoboam and Maacah (2 Chron. 11:20).

Attalaia [At·ta′li·a]—A city of Pamphylia. It was built by Attalus Philadelphus, king of Pergamos, and named after him (Acts 14:25).

Augustus [Au·gus′tus], *venerable*—The title of Octavius who succeeded Julius Caesar, his great-uncle. Following the death of Caesar he, Antony, and Lepidus formed a triumvirate. Augustus afterward shared the empire with Antony but by his victory in the battle of Actium (31 B.C.), he was made sole emperor by the senate and had conferred on him the title Augustus (27 B.C.). It was in the reign of Augustus that Jesus was born (Luke 2:1). It was he who issued the decree for the enrollment that brought Joseph and Mary to Bethlehem (Mic. 5:2).

Ava [A′va]—See Avva.

Aven [A′ven], *nothingness* or *vanity*—A geographical and city name:

1. An abbreviation of Beth-aven applied by Hosea to Beth-el. It is no longer the "house of God," as spoken by Jacob, but of idolatry, as here Jeroboam set up his idol (Hos. 10:8).

2. The "plain of Aven" in the kingdom of Damascus, so called doubtless because of the prevalence of idol worship there (Amos 1:5).

3. The city of On in Egypt which the Greeks called Heliopolis (Ezek. 30:17).

Avim [A′vim]—See Avvim.

Avites [A′vites], *perverters*—People of Avvim. Members of a tribe, and the inhabitants of a town:

1. A Canaanite tribe; the early inhabitants of Philistia (Deut. 2:23; Josh. 13:3), also called Avvim.

2. The inhabitants of a town of the tribe of Benjamin (Josh. 18:23), possibly the same as Ai.

Avith [A′vith], *ruins*—A city of the Edomites, the native city of Hadad, king of Edom (Gen. 36:35; 1 Chron. 1:46).

Avva, Ava [Av′va, A′va], possibly *ruin*—An Assyrian city in the northwestern portion of Babylonia. After the fall of Israel, people were brought from Ava to colonize Samaria (2 Kings 17:24).

Avvim, Avim [Av′vim, A′vim]—A tribe and a town:

1. A Canaanite tribe; the early inhabitants of Philistia (Deut. 2:23; Josh. 13:3), also called Avites.

2. A town of the tribe of Benjamin (Josh. 18:23), possibly the same as Ai.

Ayyah [Ay'yah]—A town belonging to Ephraim (1 Chron. 7:28). Possibly Aija (Neh. 11:31), another name for Ai.

Azal [A'zal]—See Azel.

Azaliah [Az·a·li'ah], *Jehovah hath reserved*—Son of Meshullam and father of Shaphan, the scribe (2 Kings 22:3).

Azaniah [Az·a·ni'ah], *Jehovah hath heard*—The father of Jeshua (Neh. 10:9).

Azarael [Az'a·rael]—See Azareel.

Azareel, Azarel [Az'a·reel, Az'a·rel], *God has helped*—Six Old Testament men:

    1. A Korhite who joined David at Ziklag (1 Chron. 12:6).

    2. A musician of the family of Heman in the time of David, also called Uzziel (1 Chron. 25:18).

    3. Prince of the tribe of Dan when David numbered the people (1 Chron. 27:22).

    4. A son of Bani who was induced by Ezra to renounce his foreign wife (Ezra 10:41).

    5. A priest of the family of Immer who returned from Babylon (Neh. 11:13).

    6. A musician of priestly descent, possibly the same as the preceding (Neh. 12:36).

Azarel [Az'a·rel]—See Azareel.

Azariah [Az·a·ri'ah], *Jehovah has helped*—At least twenty-four Old Testament men:

    1. One of Solomon's officials, son of Zadok (1 Kings 4:2).

    2. Son of Nathan and a chief officer of Solomon (1 Kings 4:5).

    3. The tenth king of Judah (2 Kings 14:21; 15:1–7, 32), frequently called Uzziah.

    4. A man of Judah, the son of Ethan (1 Chron. 2:8).

    5. Son of Jehu and father of Helez; a descendent of Judah (1 Chron. 2:38–39).

    6. A high priest, son of Ahimaaz and grandson of Zadok (1 Chron. 6:9).

7. Son of Johanan and grandson of Azariah No. 6. This Azariah ministered in Solomon's temple (1 Chron. 6:10).

8. A high priest, the son of Hilkiah (1 Chron. 6:13–14; 9:11; Ezra 7:1). He served during the time of King Josiah of Judah.

9. An ancestor of Samuel (1 Chron. 6:36).

10. The son of Oded, a prophet who exhorted Asa, king of Judah to follow the Lord (2 Chron. 15:1–8).

11. Two sons of King Jehoshaphat (2 Chron. 21:2), probably of different mothers. The second is also called Azaryahu or Azariahu.

12. The son of Jehoram, king of Judah (2 Chron. 22:6). In the next verse he is called Ahaziah, so calling him Azariah appears to be a copyist's error.

13. A captain who was allied with Jehoiada, the priest who was keeping Joash hidden. He assisted in dethroning Athaliah (2 Chron. 23:1, 14). His father was also named Jehoram.

14. The son of Obed, another officer engaged in the same conspiracy (2 Chron. 23:1).

15. A high priest who rebuked King Uzziah (2 Chron. 26:17–20).

16. A prince of Ephraim (2 Chron. 28:12).

17. A Kohathite, the father of Joel who assisted in the religious reforms of King Hezekiah (2 Chron. 29:12).

18. A Merarite, son of Jehalelel, who assisted in the religious reforms of King Hezekiah (2 Chron. 29:12).

19. Chief priest in the reign of Hezekiah (2 Chron. 31:10–13).

20. Son of Meraioth, ancestor of Ezra (Ezra 7:3). Compare this geneology with 1 Chronicles 6:1–15. Some names appear to be missing from Ezra's list, but this is certainly either Azariah No. 6 or No. 7.

21. The son of Maaseiah, who worked on the walls of Jerusalem in the days of Nehemiah (Neh. 3:23–24).

22. One who returned to Jerusalem with Zerubbabel (Neh. 7:7).

23. A Levite who instructed the people in the law (Neh. 8:7).

24. A priest who sealed the covenant with Nehemiah (Neh. 10:2), and who participated in the dedication of the wall (Neh. 12:33). Azariah No. 23 may be the same person.

25. One who declared that Jeremiah was a false prophet (Jer. 43:2).

26. The Hebrew name of Abed-nego, the contemporary of Daniel (Dan. 1:6–7, 11, 19; 2:17). Abed-nego and his friends were thrown into the fiery furnace by Nebuchadnezzar, but God rescued them.

Azaz [A'zaz], *strong*—A Reubenite, the son of Shema and father of Bela (1 Chron. 5:8).

Azaziah [Az·a·zi'ah], *Jehovah is strong*—Three Old Testament men:

1. A Levite who served as harpist when the ark was brought to Jerusalem (1 Chron. 15:21).

2. Father of a prince of Ephraim (1 Chron. 27:20).

3. An overseer of the temple offerings (2 Chron. 31:13).

Azbuk [Az'buk], *strong devasation*—The father of a certain Nehemiah who labored on the wall (Neh. 3:16).

Azekah [A·ze'kah], *tilled*—A town to which the kings that were besieging Gibeon were driven. It was near Socoh (Josh. 10:10–11). Near it the Philistines encamped when David slew Goliath (1 Sam. 17:1). It was fortified by Rehoboam, the first king of Judah (2 Chron. 11:9). Nebuchadnezzar besieged it (Jer. 34:7).

Azel, Azal [A'zel, A'zal], *proximity* or *he has reserved*—

1. A descendant of Jonathan (1 Chron. 8:37–38; 9:43–44).

2. An unidentified place near Jerusalem (Zech. 14:5).

Azem [A'zem]—See Ezem.

Azgad [Az'gad], *Gad is strong*—An Israelite whose descendants returned with Zerubbabel and with Ezra from Babylon (Ezra 2:12; 8:12; Neh. 7:17).

Aziel [A'zi·el]—See Jaaziel.

Aziza [A·zi'za], *robust*—A descendant of Zattu who, under the influence of Ezra, divorced his foreign wife (Ezra. 10:27).

Azmaveth [Az·ma'veth], *death is strong*—Four men and a town of the Old Testament:

1. A Benjamite whose sons came to David at Ziklag (1 Chron. 12:3).

2. A descendant of Jonathan, son of Saul (1 Chron. 8:36).

3. One of David's treasury officers (1 Chron. 27:25).

4. One of David's mighty men (2 Sam. 23:31).

5. A town near Jerusalem (Ezra 2:24), also called Beth-azmaveth (Neh. 7:28).

Azmon [Az'mon], *robust*—A place on the southern boundary of Palestine near "the river of Egypt" (Num. 34:4–5; Josh. 15:4).

Aznoth-tabor [Az'noth-ta'bor], *peaks of Tabor*—A place near Mount Tabor on the boundary of Naphtali (Josh. 19:34).

Azor [A'zor], *helper*—Son of Eliakim, descendant of Zerubbabel and ancestor of Christ (Matt. 1:13–14).

Azotus [A·zo'tus]—See Ashdod.

Azriel [Az'ri·el], *God is help*—Three Old Testament men:
   1. A chief of Manasseh (1 Chron. 5:24).
   2. A chief of Naphtali (1 Chron. 27:19).
   3. Father of Seraiah (Jer. 36:26).

Azrikam [Az·ri'kam], *help hath arisen*—Four Old Testament men:
   1. A Merarite (1 Chron. 9:14).
   2. Son of Neariah, a descendant of David and of the royal messianic line (1 Chron. 3:23).
   3. Son of Azel, a descendant of Jonathan, son of Saul (1 Chron. 8:38; 9:44).
   4. Governor of the palace of King Ahaz of Judah. He was slain by Zichri when Pekah, king of Israel, invaded Judah (2 Chron. 28:7).

Azubah [A·zu'bah], *forsaken*—Two Old Testament women:
   1. A wife of Caleb (1 Chron. 2:18–19).
   2. The mother of Jehoshaphat, king of Judah (1 Kings 22:42).

Azur [A'zur]—See Azzur.

Azzah [Az'zah]—See Gaza.

Azzan [Az'zan], *strong*—Father of Paltiel, prince of the tribe of Issachar under Moses (Num. 34:26).

Azzur, Azur [Az'zur, A'zur], *helper*—Three Old Testament men:
   1. Father of the false prophet Hananiah (Jer. 28:1).
   2. Father of Jaazaniah, a prince whom Ezekiel denounced (Ezek. 11:1).
   3. One who sealed the covenant with Nehemiah (Neh. 10:17).

B

Baal [Ba'al], *lord* or *master*—A god, two men and a town:

1. The principal male deity of the Canaanites and Phoenicians. He was adopted by other nations and, as early as the time of Moses, was worshipped by the Moabites (Num. 22:41). In the time of the judges altars were built to him by the Israelites (Judg. 2:13; 6:28–32). Jezebel, the wife of King Ahab and a Phoenician by birth, thoroughly established Baalism in Israel. Through Athaliah, the daughter of Jezebel who married King Jehoram of Judah, this false worship took root in that kingdom also (2 Chron. 17:3; 21:6).

On Mount Carmel Elijah proposed a great test which completely discredited Baal and vindicated Jehovah (1 Kings 16:31–32; 18:17–40). Jehu and Hezekiah both checked Baalism during their reigns, but after their deaths it was revived (2 Kings 21:3). The prophets denounced it (Jer. 19:4–5). The worship of Baal was attended by lascivious ceremonies and human sacrifice (1 Kings 14:24; Jer. 19:5).

2. A town of Simeon (1 Chron. 4:33).

3. A Benjamite, son of Jehiel and brother of Kish (1 Chron. 8:30; 9:35–39).

4. A Reubenite (1 Chron. 5:5).

Baalah [Ba'a·lah], *mistress*—Two towns and a hill:

1. A town in the northern section of Judah (Josh. 15:9–10). It is the same as Kirjath-jearim.

2. A town in the south of Judah (Josh. 15:29), probably the same as Balah (Josh. 19:3), also Bilhah (1 Chron. 4:29).

3. A hill on the northern boundary of Judah (Josh. 15:11).

Baalath [Ba'a·lath], *mistress*—A town in the territory of Dan (Josh. 19:44), possibly the place of that name fortified by Solomon (1 Kings 9:18; 2 Chron. 8:6).

Baalath-beer [Ba'a·lath-beer], *mistress of the well*—A city of Simeon, probably the same as Baal (1 Chron. 4:33) and Ramoth of the South (Josh. 19:8).

Baal-berith [Ba'al-be'rith], *covenant of a lord*—A god worshipped in Shechem (Judg. 8:33; 9:4), also called El-berith (Judg. 9:46).

Baale [Ba'a·le], *lords*—A town of Judah, also called Baalah and Kirjath-jearim (Josh. 15:9–10), from which David brought the ark to Jerusalem (2 Sam. 6:2).

Baal-gad [Ba'al-gad], *lord of fortune*—A place in the valley of Lebanon (Josh. 11:17; 12:7; 13:5).

Baal-hamon [Ba'al-ha'mon], *lord of a multitude*—The site of Solomon's vineyard (Song 8:11), perhaps the same as Baal-hermon.

Baal-hanan [Ba'al-ha'nan], *the lord is gracious*—
   1. A king of Edom (Gen. 36:38; 1 Chron. 1:49).
   2. A Gederite who had charge of the olive and sycamore trees of David (1 Chron. 27:28).

Baal-hazor [Ba'al-ha'zor], *lord of a village*—A place in Ephraim where Absalom slew Amnon (2 Sam. 13:23). It was four and a half miles northeast of Beth-el.

Baal-hermon [Ba'al-her'mon], *lord of Hermon*—A place east of Jordan in the northwestern part of the territory of the tribe of Manasseh (Judg. 3:3; 1 Chron. 5:23). It was on or near Mount Hermon.

Baalim [Ba'a·lim]—The plural of Baal.

Baalis [Ba'a·lis], *son of delight*—A king of the Ammonites about the time of the fall of Judah in 586 B.C. Johanan sent word to Gedaliah, appointed as governor of the remnant left in the land, that Baalis sent Ishmael to slay him (Jer. 40:13–14).

Baal-meon [Ba'al-me'on], *lord of dwelling*—An old city of the Amorites on the border of Moab (Num. 32:38). It was rebuilt by the Reubenites. In Jeremiah 48:23 it is called Beth-meon, and in Joshua 13:17 it is Beth-baal-meon.

Baal-peor [Ba'al-pe'or], *lord of Peor*—A deity worshipped by the Moabites with impure rites on Mount Peor. Through the counsel of

Balaam, the Israelites were led to worship this god. For this they were punished by a plague (Num. 25:1–9; Hos. 9:10).

Baal-perazim [Ba'al-per·a'zim], *lord of breaches*—At this place near the valley of Rephaim, David had a signal victory over the Philistines (2 Sam. 5:18–20; 1 Chron. 14:9–11).

Baal-shalishah [Ba'al-shal'i·shah], *lord of Shalisha*—It was from this village that bread and corn were brought to Elisha when he was at Gilgal (2 Kings 4:42–44).

Baal-tamar [Ba'al-ta'mar], *lord of the palm*—At this point in Benjamin the army of the Israelites gathered when about to attack Gibeah (Judg. 20:33).

Baal-zebub [Ba'al-ze'bub], *lord of the fly*—The god of Ekron (2 Kings 1:6, 16). See Beelzebub.

Baal-zephon [Ba'al-ze'phon], *lord of the watchtower*—A place near Pi-hahiroth between Migdol and the sea where the Israelites encamped just before passing through the sea (Ex. 14:2, 9; Num. 33:7).

Baana [Ba'a·na], *in the affliction*—
    1. Two of Solomon's officials (1 Kings 4:12, 16, KJV).
    2. Father of a certain Zadok (Neh. 3:4).

Baanah [Ba'a·nah], *in affliction*—
    1. A Benjamite, the son of Rimmon. He and his brother, Rechab, slew Ish-bosheth, successor of Saul. They carried his head to David at Hebron, thinking they would be rewarded for their deed, but David had them executed as criminals (2 Sam. 4:1–12).
    2. Father of Heled, one of David's warriors, a Netophathite (1 Chron. 11:30).
    3. The son of Hushai and one of Solomon's purveyors in Asher (1 Kings 4:16).
    4. A Babylonian captive who returned with Zerubbabel (Ezra 2:2; Neh. 7:7).

Baara [Ba'a·ra], *brutish*—A wife of Shaharaim of the tribe of Benjamin (1 Chron. 8:8).

Baaseiah [Ba·a·sei'ah], *work of Jehovah*—A descendant of Gershom, a Levite, and ancestor of Asaph, the singer (1 Chron. 6:40).

Baasha [Ba·ash'a], *wicked*—The son of Ahijah, of the tribe of Issachar, and the third king of the northern kingdom of Israel. Baasha
succeeded Nadab, the son of Jeroboam I, as king by assassinating him.
Then he murdered every member of the royal house, removing all who
might claim his throne (1 Kings 15:27–29).

Baasha's twenty-four-year reign (909–885 B.C.) was characterized
by war with Asa, king of Judah (1 Kings 15:32; Jer. 41:9). He fortified
Ramah (2 Chron. 16:1), 6 kilometers (4 miles) north of Jerusalem, to control traffic from the north to Jerusalem during a time of spiritual awak-
ening under Asa (2 Chron. 15:1–10). When the Syrian king, Ben-hadad,
invaded Israel, Baasha withdrew to defend his cities (1 Kings 15:16–21).

Baasha's dynasty ended as it began; his son Elah was murdered by
a servant, and the royal household of Baasha came to an end (1 Kings
16:8–11).

Babel, Tower of [Ba'bel], *confusion (by mixing)*—An ancient
tower symbolizing human pride and rebellion. It was built during the
period after Noah and the Flood.

The narrative of the Tower of Babel appears in Genesis 11:1–9 as
the climax to the account of early mankind found in Genesis 1–11. The
geographical setting is a plain in the land of Shinar (Gen. 11:2). In the
light of information contained in Genesis 10:10, Shinar probably refers
to Babylonia.

The tower was constructed of brick, because there was no stone in
southern Mesopotamia. It corresponds in general to a notable feature of
Babylonian religion, the Ziggurat or temple tower. The one built at Ur
in southern Mesopotamia about 2100 B.C. was a pyramid consisting of
three terraces of diminishing size as the building ascended, topped by
a temple devoted to a pagen god. Converging stairways on one side led
up to the temple. Its surviving lower two terraces were about 21 meters
(70 feet) high. The outside of the structure was built of fired bricks and
bituminous mortar, just like the tower described in Genesis 11:3.

The narrative in Genesis 11 is told with irony and with a negative
attitude toward the people involved. Human beings delight in bricks,
but the narrator and readers know that these are an inferior substitute
for stone (Isa. 9:10). To people the tower is a skyscraper (Deut. 1:28),
but to God it is so small that He must come down from heaven to catch
a glimpse of this tiny effort. The construction of the tower and city

is described as an act of self-glorification by the builders (Gen. 11:4). People seek for their own security in community life and culture, independent of God. This is human initiative apart from God (Ps. 127:1). As such, the activity is evil and sinful.

The account moves from a description of the sin to a narration of the punishment. God has to step in to prevent mankind from seizing yet more power for themselves and going beyond the limits of their creaturehood (Gen. 3:22; 11:5–8). Their communication with one another to advance their efforts is frustrated because they begin to speak different languages. Finally, they abandon the building of the city and go their own way, becoming scattered over the earth.

The climax of the story occurs when the city is identified with Babel, the Hebrew name for Babylonia. This nation's sophisticated culture and power deliberately excluded God. Just as the Old Testament prophets foresaw the future downfall of Babylonia in spite of its glory (Isa. 13:19; Rev. 18), this downfall is anticipated in Genesis 11: The end corresponds to the beginning. Babel derives ultimately from an Akkadian word that means "gateway to God." A similar Hebrew word, *balal*, means "confuse" and provides the author with a useful wordplay that stresses God's confusing of the builders' languages and His scattering of them throughout the earth (Gen. 11:9).

God's rejection of the nations symbolized by the Tower of Babel is reversed in Genesis 12:1–3 by the call of Abraham, through whom all nations would be blessed. Ultimately the sinful and rejected condition of mankind, which is clearly shown by the diversity of human language and territory described in this account, needed Pentecost as its answer. On this day the Holy Spirit was poured out on all people so they understood one another, although they spoke different languages (Acts 2:1–11; Eph. 2:14–18). The barriers that divide people and nations were thus removed.

Babylon, City of [Bab'y·lon], *confusion (by mixing)*—Ancient walled city between the Tigris and Euphrates Rivers and capital of the Babylonian Empire. The leading citizens of the nation of Judah were carried to this city as captives in 586 B.C. after Jerusalem fell to the invading Babylonians. Biblical writers often portrayed this ancient capital of the Babylonian people as the model of paganism and idolatry (Jer. 51:44; Dan. 4:30).

Babylon was situated along the Euphrates River about 485 kilometers (300 miles) northwest of the Persian Gulf and about 49 kilometers (30 miles) southwest of modern Baghdad in Iraq. Its origins are unknown. According to Babylonian tradition, it was built by the god Marduk. The city must have been built some time before 2300 B.C., because it was destroyed about that time by an invading enemy king. This makes Babylon one of the oldest cities of the ancient world. Genesis 10:10 mentions Babel (the Hebrew spelling of Babylon) as part of the empire of Nimrod.

Sometime during its early history, the city of Babylon became a small independent kingdom. Its most famous king was Hammurapi (about 1792–1750 B.C.), who conquered southern Mesopotamia and territory to the north as far as Mari. He was known for his revision of a code of law that showed concern for the welfare of the people under his rule. But the dynasty he established declined under his successors. It came to an end with the conquest of Babylon by the Hittite king Murshilish I about 1595 B.C. Then the Kassites took over for a period, ruling southern Mesopotamia from the city of Babylon as their capital. The Assyrians attacked and plundered Babylon about 1250 B.C., but it recovered and flourished for another century until the Assyrians succeeded in taking over the city with their superior forces about 1100 B.C. After Tiglath-pileser I of Assyria arrived on the scene, the city of Babylon became subject to Assyria by treaty or conquest. Tiglath-pileser III (745–727 B.C.) declared himself king of Babylon with the name Pulu (Pul, 2 Kings 15:19), deporting a number of its citizens to the subdued territory of the northern kingdom of Israel (2 Kings 17:24).

In 721 B.C. a Chaldean prince, Marduk-apal-iddina, (Hebrew, Merodach-baladan), seized control of Babylon and became a thorn in Assyria's side for a number of years. He apparently planned a large-scale rebellion of eastern and western parts of the Assyrian Empire (2 Kings 20:12). In retaliation against this rebellion, Sennacherib of Assyria (704–681 B.C.) attacked Babylon in 689 B.C., totally destroying it, although it was rebuilt by his successor, Esarhaddon (680–669 B.C.). After this, Assyrian power gradually weakened, so the city and kingdom of Babylonia grew stronger once again.

In 626 B.C. Nabopolassar seized the throne of Babylon. He was succeeded by Nebuchadnezzar II (605–562 B.C.), the greatest king of Babylon, who enlarged the capital city to an area of six square miles and beautified it with magnificent buildings. This period of the city's development has been the focal point of all archaeological research done in ancient Babylon.

According to Herodotus and other ancient writers, the city was laid out in the form of a huge square with the Euphrates flowing diagonally through it. The walls were fourteen miles in extent on each side and were approximately 85 feet thick. It was said to have possessed one hundred gates of brass and 250 towers. The city's massive double walls spanned both sides of the Euphrates River. Set into these walls were eight major gates. One of the numerous pagan temples in the city was that of the patron god Marduk, flanked by a Ziggurat or temple-tower. To this temple a sacred processional way led from the main gate, the Ishtar Gate. Both the gate and the walls facing the way were decorated with colored enameled bricks picturing lions, dragons, and bulls.

The city of Babylon also contained a palace complex, or residence for the king. On the northwest side of this palace area, the famous terraced "hanging gardens" may have been situated. They were one of the Seven Wonders of the ancient world. According to tradition, Nebuchadnezzar built these gardens for one of his foreign wives to remind her of the scenery of her homeland. Babylon's glory reflected the king's imperial power. Captured kings and other people were brought to his court at Babylon. These included Jehoiachin (2 Kings 24:15) and Zedekiah (2 Kings 25:7), kings of Judah.

Another of these captives, the prophet Daniel, interpreted a dream for King Nebuchadnezzar, making it clear that God would judge the Babylonians because of their mistreatment of God's people, as well as because of their paganism and idolatry (Dan. 4). Sure enough, during the reign of Nabonidus (555–539 B.C.), while Belshazzar was co-regent (Dan. 5), the city surrendered to the Persians without opposition.

Eventually the balance of power passed from the Persians to Alexander the Great, to whom Babylon willingly submitted in 331 B.C. Alexander planned to refurbish and expand the city and make it his capital, but he died before accomplishing these plans. The city later fell into insignificance because one of Alexander's successors founded a new capital at Seleucia, a short distance away. The city gradually declined and gave place to other cities on the Tigris, of which Baghdad continues to our day.

The books of Isaiah and Jeremiah predicted the downfall of Babylon. This would happen as God's punishment of the Babylonians because of their destruction of Jerusalem and their deportation of the citizens of Judah (Isa. 14:22; 21:9; 43:14; Jer. 50:9; 51:37). Today, the ruins of this city stand as an eloquent testimony to the passing of proud empires and to the providential hand of God.

Babylonia [Bab·y·lo′ni·a]—Babylonia was an ancient pagan empire between the Tigris and Euphrates rivers in southern Mesopotamia. A long narrow country, it was about forty miles wide at its widest point, covering an area of about eight thousand square miles. It was bordered on the north by Assyria, on the south and west by the Arabian Desert, and on the southeast by the Persian Gulf. The region was also called Shinar (Gen. 10:10; 11:2) and the land of the Chaldeans (Jer. 24:5; 25:12; Ezek. 12:13). Some of its ancient cities were Ur (Gen. 11:28, 31; 15:7; Neh. 9:7), Erech, Babel, Accad (Gen. 10:10), and Nippur.

The fortunes of the Babylonians rose and fell during the long sweep of Old Testament history. In its early history Hammurabi (who probably reigned 1792–1750 B.C.) emerged as ruler of the group of city states on the plains of Shinar. He expanded the borders of the empire and organized its laws into a written system. This was about the time that Abraham's family left Ur, one of the ancient states of lower Babylonia (Gen. 11:27–32).

During its long history, Babylonia was constantly at war with Assyria, its neighbor to the north. About 1270 B.C. the Assyrians overpowered Babylonia, reducing its power and influence so effectively that it remained a second-rate nation for the next six or seven centuries. But this began to change dramatically when Nebuchadnezzar became ruler of Babylonia about 605 B.C. During his reign of forty-four years, the Babylonians built an empire, which stretched from north of the Mediterranean Sea to south through Israel along the Red Sea to the Persian Gulf in the east.

Because of his long reign and many military conquests, Nebuchadnezzar is mentioned several times in the Old Testament (2 Kings 24:10–17; Dan. 1:1–3). In 586 B.C. the Babylonian army under Nebuchadnezzar's leadership destroyed Jerusalem and carried Israel's leading citizens to Babylon as captives (2 Chron. 36:6–13). This was a fulfillment of the warning of the prophets Jeremiah and Ezekiel that

God would punish His people unless they turned from their idolatry to worship the one true God (Jer. 27; Ezek. 23:17–21).

The Babylonians had a system of gods, each with a main temple in a particular city. The system included gods of heaven, air, the ocean, sun, moon, storms, love, and war. Their worship included elaborate festivals and many different types of priests, especially the exorcist and the diviner, whose function was to drive away evil spirits. Babylonian literature was dominated by mythology and legends. Among them was a creation legend written to glorify a god known as Marduk, who created heaven and earth on a whim from the corpse of the goddess Tiamat. This is a dramatic contrast to the account of God's creation of the world in the book of Genesis. The biblical writer declares that God created the world from nothing, and He did it with purpose and order in a cycle of six days, resting on the seventh (Gen. 1:1–2:3).

Babylonian dominance of the ancient world came to an end with the fall of their capital city, Babylon, to the Persians about 539 B.C. This was a clear fulfillment of the prophecies of Isaiah and Jeremiah. They predicted God would punish the Babylonians because of their destruction of Jerusalem and their deportation of the citizens of Judah into captivity (Isa. 14:22; 21:9; 43:14; Jer. 50:9; 51:37).

Baca [Ba'ca], *weeping*—In Psalm 84:6 mention is made of the valley of Baca. If an actual valley is intended, it may be so named from the presence there of balsam trees, which, because of their exudations of tearlike drops of resin, suggest weeping.

Bachrites [Bach'rites]—Descendants of Becher, son of Ephraim (Num. 26:35).

Baharumite [Ba·ha·ru'mite]—A native of Bahurim (2 Sam. 23:31; 1 Chron. 11:33).

Bahurim [Ba·hu'rim], *young men's village*—A village on the road from Jerusalem to the Jordan not far from the Mount of Olives (2 Sam. 16:5). It figures in the life of David. Shimei, who cursed him, came from this town and here two of David's men concealed themselves (2 Sam. 3:16; 16:5; 17:18; 1 Kings 2:8).

Bajith [Ba'jith], *house*—A slighting reference to the temple of Moabitish gods (Isa. 15:2).

Bakbakkar [Bak·bak′kar], *searcher*—A Levite (1 Chron. 9:15).

Bakbuk [Bak′buk], *a bottle*—One of the Nethinim, head of one of the families that returned from Babylon under Zerubbabel (Ezra 2:51; Neh. 7:53).

Bakbukiah [Bak·bu·ki′ah], *wasting of Jehovah*—Two Old Testament men:

1. A Levite who occupied a high position in Jerusalem after the Exile (Neh. 11:17).

2. A Levite, perhaps a representative of the family of the preceding. He was employed as a porter of the gates of the temple in the time of Nehemiah (Neh. 12:25).

Balaam [Ba′laam]—A magician or soothsayer (Josh. 13:22), the son of Beor of Pethor, a city of Mesopotamia, who was summoned by the Moabite king Balak to curse the Israelites before they entered Canaan (Num. 22:5–24:25; Deut. 23:4–5). Recently, a plaster inscription concerning Balaam that dates to the eighth century B.C. has been found at Tell Deir Alla in Jordan.

Balaam lived in Aram in the town of Pethor on the Euphrates River. A curious mixture of good and evil, Balaam wavered when he was asked by Balak to curse the Israelites. But he finally agreed to go when the Lord specifically instructed him to go to Balak (Num. 22:20).

The exact meaning of the account of Balaam's "stubborn" donkey is not clear. After telling Balaam it was all right to go, God either tried to forbid him from going or wanted to impress upon him that he should speak only what he was told to say. When the angel of the Lord blocked their way, the donkey balked three times and was beaten by Balaam, who had not seen the angel. Finally, after the third beating, the donkey spoke, reproving Balaam. When the angel told Balaam, "Your way is perverse before Me" (Num. 22:32), Balaam offered to return home. The angel told him to go on, however, and reminded him to speak only the words God gave him to speak.

Balaam and Balak met at the river Arnon and traveled to "the high places of Baal" (Num. 22:41). From there they could see part of the Israelite encampment at Acacia Grove (Num. 25:1). After sacrificing on seven altars, Balaam went off alone. When he heard the word of God, he returned to Balak and blessed the people whom Balak wanted him to curse.

The New Testament mentions Balaam in three passages. Peter speaks of false teachers who "have forsaken the right way and gone astray, following the way of Balaam" (2 Peter 2:15). Jude speaks of back-sliders who "have run greedily in the error of Balaam for profit" (Jude 11). Balaam's error was greed or covetousness; he was well paid to bring a curse upon the people of Israel.

The nature of Balaam's curse is made clear by John in the book of Revelation. It refers to some members of the church in Pergamos who held "the doctrine of Balaam, who taught Balak to put a stumbling block before the children of Israel" (Rev. 2:14).

Before leaving Balak, Balaam apparently told the Moabite leader that Israel could be defeated if its people were seduced to worship Baal, "to eat things sacrificed to idols and to commit sexual immorality" (Rev. 2:14). Indeed, this was exactly what happened: "The people [of Israel] began to commit harlotry with the women of Moab. They invited the people to the sacrifice of their gods, and the people ate and bowed down to their gods. So Israel was joined to Baal of Peor, and the anger of the Lord was aroused against Israel" (Num. 25:1–3).

In condemning "the way of Balaam," the New Testament condemns the greed of all who are well paid to tempt God's people to compromise their moral standards.

Balac [Ba'lac]—Variant of Balak (Rev. 2:14).

Baladan [Bal'a·dan], *a son has been given*—The father (or possibly a more remote ancestor) of Merodach-baladan, also called Berodach-baladan (2 Kings 20:12; Isa. 39:1). The name appears to be an abbreviation of Merodach-baladan.

Balah [Ba'lah], *waxed old*—A town whose location is unknown, in the territory of Simeon (Josh. 19:3), perhaps the Baalah of Joshua 15:29.

Balak [Ba'lak], *empty*—King of the Moabites when the Israelites invaded the plains of Moab. He attempted to influence Balsam to curse the invaders (Num. 22–24).

Bamoth [Ba'moth], *high places*—One of the encampments of the Israelites north of the river Arnon, probably the same as Bamoth-baal (Num. 21:19).

Bamoth-baal [Ba'moth-ba'al], *high places of Baal*—A city of the Reubenites (Josh. 13:17). It is probably to be identified with Bamoth, a camping place of the Israelites north of the Arnon (Num. 21:19–20). It may be the "high places of Baal" from which Balaam viewed Moab (Num. 22:41).

Bani [Ba'ni], *built*—
1. One of David's mighty men of the tribe of Gad (2 Sam. 23:36).
2. A man of Judah of the line of Perez (1 Chron. 9:4).
3. A family that returned with Zerubbabel (Ezra 2:10; Neh. 10:14).
4. A Levite, a Merarite (1 Chron. 6:46).
5. A Levite, the father of Rehum (Neh. 3:17; 10:13).
6. Founder of a family (Ezra 10:34).
7. A Levite of the sons of Asaph, a Gershonite (Neh. 11:22).

Barabbas [Bar·ab'bas], *son of a father*—A prisoner, a robber, who raised an insurrection and committed murder. At the Passover season it was the custom for the procurator to release a prisoner selected by the people. Pilate, anxious to save Jesus, offered the Jews the choice of releasing Him or Barabbas. They were induced by the priests to choose Barabbas, and to demand that Jesus be crucified (Matt. 27:16–26).

Barachel [Ba·ra'chel], *God has blessed*—The father of Elihu, the Buzite (Job 32:2, 6).

Barachiah, Barachias [Bar·a·chi'ah, Bar·a·chi'as], *Jehovah hath blessed*—See Berechiah.

Barak [Bar'ak], *lightning*—A son of Abinoam of the city of Kedesh. Barak was summoned by Deborah, a prophetess who was judging Israel at that time. Deborah told Barak to raise a militia of 10,000 men to fight Jabin, king of Canaan, who had oppressed Israel for 20 years. The commander-in-chief of Jabin's army was Sisera.

Apparently during the battle, the Lord sent a great thunderstorm. The rain swelled the Kishon River and the plain surrounding the battle area, making Sisera's 900 iron chariots useless (Judg. 5:21). The Israelites routed the Canaanites. The victory is described twice: in prose (Judg. 4) and in poetry, the beautiful "Song of Deborah" (Judg. 5). Barak is listed in the New Testament among the heroes of faith (Heb. 11:32).

Barhumite [Bar·hu′mite]—Another form or perhaps misreading of Baharumite (2 Sam. 23:31). See Bahurim.

Bariah [Ba·ri′ah], *fugitive*—A son of Shemaiah, descendant of David (1 Chron. 3:22).

Bar-Jesus [Bar-Je′sus]—See Elymas.

Bar-Jona [Bar-Jo′na], *son of Jona*—The surname of Peter (Matt. 16:17), meaning son of Jonah (John 1:42; 21:15–17).

Barkos [Bar′kos], *painter*—The head of a family of the Nethinim (Ezra 2:53; Neh. 7:55).

Barnabas [Bar′na·bas], *son of encouragement*—An apostle in the early church (Acts 4:36–37; 11:19–26) and Paul's companion on his first missionary journey (Acts 13:1–15:41). A Levite from the island of Cyprus, Barnabas's given name was Joseph, or Joses (Acts 4:36). When he became a Christian, he sold his land and gave the money to the Jerusalem apostles (Acts 4:36–37).

Early in the history of the church, Barnabas went to Antioch to check on the growth of this early group of Christians. Then he journeyed to Tarsus and brought Saul (as Paul was still called) back to minister with him to the Christians in Antioch (Acts 11:25). At this point Barnabas apparently was the leader of the church at Antioch, because his name is repeatedly mentioned before Paul's in the book of Acts. But after Saul's name was changed to Paul, Barnabas's name is always mentioned after Paul's (Acts 13:43).

Because of his good reputation, Barnabas was able to calm the fear of Saul among the Christians in Jerusalem (Acts 9:27). He and Saul also brought money from Antioch to the Jerusalem church when it was suffering a great famine (Acts 11:27–30). Shortly thereafter, the Holy Spirit led the Antioch church to commission Barnabas and Paul, along with John Mark, Barnabas's cousin (Col. 4:10), to make a missionary journey (Acts 13:1–3) to Cyprus and the provinces of Asia Minor. This was known as the first missionary journey.

A rift eventually developed between Barnabas and Paul over John Mark (Col. 4:10). Barnabas wanted to take John Mark on their second missionary journey. Paul, however, felt John Mark should stay behind because he had left the first mission at Cyprus (Acts 13:13). Paul and

Barnabas went their separate ways, and Barnabas took John Mark with him on a second mission to Cyprus (Acts 15:36–39) while Silas accompanied Paul. An epistle named after Barnabas was once falsely attributed to him, but most now believe it was written by an unknown author some time later.

Barsabas [Bar'sa·bas], *son of Saba*—Two New Testament men:

1. Joseph Barsabas was one of two disciples nominated to fill the place of Judas Iscariot, but when the lots were cast, Matthias was chosen (Acts 1:23).

2. Judas Barsabas, with Paul, Barnabas, and Silas, was sent with letters to Antioch (Acts 15:22).

Barsabbas [Bar'sab·bas]—See Barsabas.

Bartholomew [Bar·thol'o·mew], *son of Tolmai*—One of the twelve apostles of Jesus, according to the four lists given in the New Testament (Matt. 10:3; Mark 3:18; Luke 6:14; Acts 1:13). Many scholars equate Bartholomew with Nathanael (John 1:45–49), but no proof of this identification exists, except by inference. According to church tradition, Bartholomew was a missionary to various countries, such as Armenia and India. He is reported to have preached the gospel along with Philip and Thomas. According to another tradition, he was crucified upside down after being flayed alive.

Bartimaeus [Bar·ti·mae·'us], *son of Timaeus*—At Jericho this blind beggar, hearing that Jesus was passing, appealed to Jesus to have mercy upon him and was healed (Mark 10:46).

Bartimeus [Bar·ti·me'us]—See Bartimaeus.

Baruch [Bar'uch], *blessed*—The name of three or four men in the Old Testament:

1. A son of Zabbai. Baruch helped Nehemiah repair the walls of Jerusalem (Neh. 3:20).

2. A man who sealed the covenant with Nehemiah (Neh. 10:6). He may be the same person as No. 1.

3. A son of Col-Hozeh and a returned captive of the tribe of Judah (Neh. 11:5).

4. The scribe or secretary of Jeremiah the prophet (Jer. 32:12–16; 36:1–32; 45:1–5). A son of Neriah, Baruch was a member of a prominent

Jewish family. In the fourth year of the reign of Jehoiakim, king of Judah (605 B.C.), Baruch wrote Jeremiah's prophecies of destruction from the prophet's dictation (Jer. 36:1–8). Baruch read Jeremiah's words publicly on a day of fasting, then read them to the officials of the king's court.

The king burned the texts and ordered the arrest of Baruch and Jeremiah. They escaped (Jer. 36:14–26) and a new copy was made. The enemies of Baruch accused him of influencing Jeremiah in favor of the Chaldeans (Jer. 43:3). After the fall of the city, the remnant at Jerusalem took him and Jeremiah to Egypt (Jer. 43:1–7).

A clay seal inscribed "Baruch son of Neriah the scribe," dating from Jeremiah's time and clearly belonging to his secretary (Jer. 36:32), was recently discovered in a burnt archive in Israel.

Barzillai [Bar·zil·la'i], *made of iron*—Three Old Testament men:

1. A wealthy friend of David, a man of Gilead. When David was at Mahanaim, a fugitive at the time of Absalom's rebellion, he provided David and his people with food (2 Sam. 17:27–29). When David left Mahanaim, Barzillai conducted him across the Jordan. David urged him to become a member of his household, but because of his advanced age he declined and the honor was given to his son, Chimham (2 Sam. 19:31–40).

2. A Meholathite whose son, Adriel, married Michal, Saul's daughter (2 Sam. 21:8).

3. A priest, a son-in-law of Barzillai, the Gileadite, who took the name of his father-in-law (Ezra 2:61; Neh. 7:63).

Basemath [Bas'e·math], *fragrance*—Two or perhaps three Old Testament women:

1. A wife of Esau, the daughter of Elon the Hittite (Gen. 26:34), called Adah in Genesis 36:2.

2. A wife of Esau, daughter of Ishmael (Gen. 36:3–4, 13, 17). Many believe that Esau had but one wife of this name and that the accounts giving her relationships are at variance. She is called Mahalath in Genesis 28:9.

3. A daughter of Solomon. She married the king's tax-gatherer for the district of Naphtali (1 Kings 4:15).

Bashan [Ba'shan], *open* or *smooth* or *fertile land*—The territory east of the Jordan River and the Sea of Galilee.

At the time of the exodus, King Og ruled Bashan. His kingdom included sixty cities (Num. 21:33; Deut. 3:4; 29:7). His capital was at Ashtaroth. When Og was defeated at Edrei (Deut. 3:1–3), the territory was given to the half-tribe of Manasseh (Deut. 3:13), except for the cities of Golan and Be Eshterah, which were given to the Levites (Josh. 21:27). In the days of Jehu, the region was captured by the Aramean king, Hazael (2 Kings 10:32–33).

A rich, fertile tableland about 490 to 700 meters (1600 to 2300 feet) above sea level, with abundant rainfall and volcanic soil, Bashan became the "breadbasket" of the region. Wheat fields, livestock, and oak trees were abundant. But in the Old Testament, the prosperity of Bashan became a symbol of selfish indulgence and arrogant pride. Evil persons who attacked the righteous were compared to "strong bulls of Bashan" (Ps. 22:12). The pampered, pleasure-seeking women of Samaria were called "cows of Bashan" (Amos 4:1).

Bashan-havoth-jair [Ba'shan-ha'voth-ja'ir], *fruitful* (Bashan)— The name Jair gave to the places he conquered in Bashan. The rendering in the King James Version is "and called them, even Bashan, after his own name, Havothjair" (Deut. 3:14). This district contained sixty cities, strongly protected (Josh. 13:30; 1 Kings 4:13).

Bashan, Mountain of [Ba'shan]—Mount Hermon (Ps. 68:15).

Bashemath [Bash'e·math]—See Basemath.

Basmath [Bas'math]—See Basemath.

Bath-rabbim [Bath-rab'bim], *daughter of many*—A gate of Heshbon (Song 7:4).

Bathsheba [Bath·she·ba], *daughter of oath*—A wife of Uriah the Hittite and of King David (2 Sam. 11; 12:24). Standing on the flat roof of his palace in Jerusalem one evening, David saw the beautiful Bathsheba bathing on the roof of a nearby house. With his passion aroused, David committed adultery with Bathsheba. Out of that union Bathsheba conceived a child.

When David discovered her pregnancy, he hurriedly sent for Uriah, who was in battle with the Ammonites. But Uriah refused to engage in marital relations with his wife while his companions were involved in battle. When David's attempt to trick Uriah failed, he sent him back into battle. This time, David ordered that Uriah be placed at the front of the battle and that his fellow soldiers retreat from him, so that he might be killed. After a period of mourning, Bathsheba became David's wife (2 Sam. 11:27). But the child conceived in adultery died.

When Nathan the prophet confronted David with the enormity of his sin, David repented (2 Sam. 12:13). God blessed them with four more children—Shammua (or Shimea), Shobab, Nathan, and Solomon (1 Chron. 3:5). The New Testament mentions Bathsheba indirectly in the genealogy of Jesus (Matt. 1:6). Bathsheba is also called Bathshua (1 Chron. 3:5).

Bath-shua [Bath-shu·a], *daughter of riches*—Two Old Testament women:

1. Daughter of Shua and wife of Judah (1 Chron. 2:3).

2. Variant of Bath-sheba (1 Chron. 3:5).

Bavai, Bavvai [Ba·va'i, Bav·va'i]—A son of Henadad (Neh. 3:18).

Bazlith [Baz'lith], *nakedness*—The head of one of the families of the Nethinim, some of whom returned from the Exile (Ezra 2:52; Neh. 7:54).

Bealiah [Be·a·li'ah], *Jehovah is Lord*—A warrior of the tribe of Benjamin who joined David at Ziklag (1 Chron. 12:5).

Bealoth [Be·a'loth], *mistresses*—

1. A village in the south of Judah. It may be the same as Baalath-beer (Josh. 15:24; 19:8).

2. A place near the territory of Asher (1 Kings 4:16).

Beautiful Gate—One of the gates into the temple area where a lame beggar routinely sat begging. When he asked Peter and John for alms, they healed him instead (Acts 3:10). See Gates of Jerusalem.

Bebai [Be·ba'i]—Two Old Testament men:

1. The head of a family, members of which returned from exile with Zerubbabel and Ezra (Ezra 2:11; 8:11; Neh. 7:16).

2. One who signed the covenant (Neh. 10:15).

Becher [Be'cher], *young camel*—Two Old Testament men:

1. A son of Benjamin (Gen. 46:21; 1 Chron. 7:6).

2. A son of Ephraim (Num. 26:35), called Bered in 1 Chronicles 7:20.

Becherites [Be'cher·ites]—See Bachrites.

Becorath, Bechorath [Be·co'rath, Be·cho'rath], *first-born*—An ancestor of King Saul (1 Sam. 9:1), possibly the same as Becher (1 Chron. 7:6, 8).

Bedad [Be'dad], *separation*—The father of Hadad, king of Edom (Gen. 36:35; 1 Chron. 1:46).

Bedan [Be'dan], *in judging*—A leader mentioned in 1 Samuel 12:11 as being between Jerubbaal (that is Gideon) and Jephthah, hence probably a Hebrew judge. Some have identified him with Jair and some with Abdon (Judg. 10:3; 12:13).

Bedeiah [Be·dei'ah], *servant of Jehovah*—A son of Bani who divorced his foreign wife (Ezra 10:35).

Beeliada [Bee·li'a·da], *whom the Lord knows*—A son of David (1 Chron. 14:7). He is also called Eliada (2 Sam. 5:16; 1 Chron. 3:8).

Beelzebub [Be·el'ze·bub], *lord of the house*—The title of a heathen deity. A slight change in spelling is Baal-zebub, the god of Ekron. To the Jews Beelzebub was the prince of evil spirits (Matt. 10:25; 12:24; Mark 3:22; Luke 11:15–19). Jesus identifies him with Satan (Matt. 12:26; Mark 3:23; Luke 11:18).

Beelzebul [Be·el'ze·bul]—A form of Beelzebub.

Beer [Beer], *a well*—

1. An encampment of the Israelites on the border of Moab (Num. 21:16–18).

2. A place to which Jotham fled (Judg. 9:21).

Beera [Beer'a], *a well*—A son of Zophah (1 Chron. 7:37)

Beerah [Beer'ah], *a well*—The son of Baal, a prince of Reuben (1 Chron. 5:6).

Beer-elim [Beer-e'lim], *well of heroes*—A village of Moab (Isa. 15:8).

Beeri [Beer'i], *man of a well*—Two Old Testament men:
1. A Hittite, father of Judith who was a wife of Esau (Gen. 26:34).
2. The father of Hosea, the prophet (Hos. 1:1).

Beer-lahai-roi, Lahai-roi [Beer-la'hai-roi, La'hai-roi], *the well of him that liveth and seeth me*—A well where Hagar came to realize that she was under the care of the Lord (Gen. 16:7, 14).

Beeroth [Beer'oth], *wells*—Two locations in the Old Testament:
1. A city of the Gibeonites assigned to the tribe of Benjamin (Josh. 9:17; 18:25). This city was one of four which formed a league with Joshua, and it was the native city of Nahari, Joab's armourbearer (2 Sam. 23:37). Following the Exile, persons of this city returned with Zerubbabel (Ezra 2:25).
2. A halting place of the Israelites (Deut. 10:6).

Beeroth-bene-jaakan [Beer'oth-ben'e-ja'a·kan]—See Beeroth No. 2.

Beerothite [Beer'o·thite]—An inhabitant of Beeroth (2 Sam. 4:2; 23:37).

Beersheba [Beer·she'ba], *well of the seven* or *well of the oath*—The chief city of the Negev. Beersheba was situated in the territory of Simeon (Josh. 19:1–2) and was "at the limits of the tribe of the children of Judah, toward the border of Edom in the South" (Josh. 15:21, 28). Midway between the Mediterranean Sea and the southern end of the Dead Sea, Beersheba was considered the southern extremity of the promised land, giving rise to the often-used expression, "from Dan [in the north] to Beersheba" (Judg. 20:1) or "from Beersheba to Dan" (1 Chron. 21:2).

In Beersheba Abraham and Abimelech, king of Gerar (in Philistia), made a covenant and swore an oath of mutual assistance (Gen. 21:31). Abraham pledged to Abimelech seven ewe lambs to bear witness to the sincerity of his oath; from this transaction came the name Beersheba. It was in the wilderness of Beersheba that Hagar wandered as she fled from Sarah (Gen. 21:33). Abraham dug a well and also planted a tamarisk tree here (Gen. 21:33), and he returned to Beersheba after God prevented him from offering Isaac as a sacrifice on Mount Moriah (Gen. 22:19).

At Beersheba a number of important encounters took place between God and various people. Here God appeared to Hagar (Gen. 21:17), Isaac (Gen. 26:23–33), and Jacob, who sacrificed at the well (Gen. 46:1–5). Near it a town arose (Josh. 15:28) which was assigned to Simeon (Josh. 19:1–2). It was at the southern limit of Palestine, hence the famous expression "from Dan to Beersheba." Samuel's sons were judges here (1 Sam. 8:2). Ancient Beersheba has been identified with a large tract known as Tell es-Saba, situated about 3 kilometers (2 miles) east of the modern city.

Beesh-terah [Be·esh-te′rah], *temple of Astarte*—A Levitical city assigned to the Gerahonites (Josh. 21:27; 1 Chron. 6:71), probably the same as Ashtaroth.

Beker [Bek′er]—See Becher.

Bel [Bel], *lord*—The patron or chief god of Babylon (Isa. 46:1; Jer. 50:2; 51:44).

Bela [Be′la], *destruction*—Three Old Testament men and a city:
  1. A king of Edom and son of Beor (Gen. 36:32).
  2. A son of Benjamin, founder of a family (Gen. 46:21; Num. 26:38).
  3. A chief of the Reubenites (1 Chron. 5:8).
  4. One of the cities of the plain—Zoar (Gen. 14:2, 8).

Belah [Be′lah]—See Bela.

Belaites [Be′la·ites]—Descendants of Bela (Num. 26:38).

Belshazzar [Bel·shaz′zar], *Bel protect the king*—The leader in command of the Babylonian forces at the time Babylon was captured by the Persians (Dan. 5:28, 30). He was the son of Nabonidus (last king of the New Babylonian Empire) and coregent with the king in the latter years of the reign. His relationship to Nebuchadnezzar was possibly that of grandson—son of the king's daughter (Dan. 5:11).

Belteshazzar [Bel·te·shazzar], *lord of the straitened's treasure*—When Daniel was taken to Babylon, this was the name given him by the prince of the eunuchs (Dan. 1:7).

Ben [Ben], *son*—

1. A Levite, a porter appointed by David in the service of the ark (1 Chron. 15:18).

2. Hebrew prefix meaning "son of" (Gen. 19:38; 35:18; 1 Sam. 3:6, 16).

Ben-abinadab [Ben-a·bin′a·dab], *son of Abinadab*—Solomon's son-in-law (1 Kings 4:11).

Benaiah [Be·nai′ah], *Jehovah hath built*—Eleven Old Testament men:

1. Son of Jehoiada (2 Sam. 23:20–21) and chief priest (1 Chron. 27:5). He commanded David's bodyguard (2 Sam. 8:18) and held a high position in the army under Solomon (1 Kings 2:35; 4:4).

2. A Levite who played the psaltery when the ark was brought to Jerusalem (1 Chron. 15:18, 20).

3. A Levite of the sons of Asaph (2 Chron. 20:14).

4. An overseer of offerings (2 Chron. 31:13).

5. The father of Pelatiah (1 Chron. 11:31; 27:14; Ezek. 11:1, 13).

7. A prince of Simeon who helped slay the shepherds of Gedor (1 Chron. 4:36–41).

8. Four men who married and divorced foreign wives (Ezra 10:25, 30, 35, 43).

Ben-ammi [Ben-am′mi], *son of my people*—A son of Lot by his younger daughter, ancestor of the Ammonites (Gen. 19:38).

Ben-deker [Ben-de′ker], *son of Deker*—Solomon's purveyor in Beth-shemesh and other places (1 Kings 4:9).

Bene-berak [Ben′e-be′rak], *sons of Berak*—A town of the tribe of Dan, east of Joppa (Josh. 19:45).

Bene-jaakan [Ben′e-ja′a·kan]—See Jaakan.

Bene-kedem [Ben′e-ke′dem], *sons of the east*—A people group mentioned in connection with the Amalekites and Midianites (Gen. 29:1; Judg. 6:3, 33; 7:12; 8:10; Job 1:3). They harassed the Israelites during the days of the judges.

Ben-geber [Ben-ge′ber], *sons of Geber*—A purveyor of Solomon in Ramoth Gilead (1 Kings 4:13).

Ben-hadad [Ben-ha'dad], *son of Hadad*—The name of three kings who ruled at Damascus:

1. The grandson of Hezion. He made an alliance with King Asa of Judah against King Baasha of Israel when the latter was building Ramah. Ben-hadad invaded Israel and captured much territory (1 Kings 15:18–21; 2 Chron. 16:1–6).

2. Son of the preceding who, in the time of Ahab, besieged Samaria but was defeated. The following year the war was renewed, but he was again defeated and peace was made (1 Kings 20:1–34). He was later joined by Ahab and ten other allies in his conflict with the Assyrians whom they met at Karkar on the Orontes in 854 B.C. Though the Assyrian king claimed a great victory, in reality he suffered a severe reverse.

At a later time Ben-hadad besieged Samaria, but a panic in the Syrian camp brought the siege to an end (2 Kings 6:8–7:20). He was murdered and was succeeded by Hazael (2 Kings 8:15).

3. Son of Hazael under whom Damascus lost her conquests in Palestine (2 Kings 13:24).

Ben-hail [Ben-ha'il], *son of strength*—A prince commissioned by Jehoshaphat to teach in the cities of Judah (2 Chron. 17:7).

Ben-hanan [Ben-ha'nan], *sons of a gracious one*—One of the four sons of Shimon of the tribe of Judah (1 Chron. 4:20).

Ben-hayil [Ben-hay'il]—See Ben-hail.

Ben-hesed [Ben-he'sed], *son of Hesed*—The purveyor of Solomon in Aruboth (1 Kings 4:10).

Ben-hur [Ben-hur], *son of Hur*—Solomon's purveyor in Mount Ephraim (1 Kings 4:8).

Beninu [Be·ni'nu], *our son*—A Levite who sealed the covenant with Nehemiah (Neh. 10:13).

Benjamin [Ben'ja·min], *son of the right hand or son of the south*—The name of three or four men in the Old Testament:

1. Jacob's youngest son, born to his favorite wife, Rachel (Gen. 35:18, 24). After giving birth to Benjamin, the dying Rachel named him Ben-oni (Gen. 35:18), which means "son of my pain." But Jacob renamed him Benjamin. When Jacob lost his beloved son Joseph, he became very attached to Benjamin because Benjamin was the only surviving son of Rachel. When his sons went to Egypt in search of food to relieve a famine, Jacob was reluctant to let Benjamin go with them (Gen. 43:1–17).

It is apparent that Joseph also loved Benjamin, his only full brother (Gen. 43:29–34). During this trip Joseph ordered that his silver cup be planted in Benjamin's sack. The reaction of Jacob and Benjamin's brothers shows the great love they had for Benjamin (Gen. 44). Benjamin had five sons and two grandsons, and he became the founder of the tribe that carried his name (Gen. 46:21; Num. 26:38–41; 1 Chron. 7:6–12; 8:1–40).

2. A warrior, son of Bilhan, a Benjamite (1 Chron. 7:10).

3. A son of Harim who lived in Jerusalem following the return from the captivity. Benjamin divorced his pagan wife at Ezra's urging (Ezra 10:31–32).

4. A priest during the time of Nehemiah (Neh. 12:34) who helped repair and dedicate the wall of Jerusalem (Neh. 3:23). He may be the same person as No. 3.

Benjamin, Gate of [Ben'ja·min]—A gate in the north wall of Jerusalem, called also the high gate (2 Chron. 23:20; Jer. 20:2; 37:13; 38:7; Zech. 14:10). See Gates of Jerusalem.

Benjamin, Tribe of [Ben'ja·min,]—When the land was divided, the section allotted to Benjamin was between Judah and Ephraim; its eastern limit was the Jordan (Josh. 18:11–20). Its chief towns were Jerusalem, Jericho, Beth-el, Gibeon, Gibeath, and Mizpeh (Josh. 18:21–28). It was one of the smaller tribes, numbering at the time of the exodus only 35,400.

For protecting the guilty inhabitants of Gibeah (Judg. 19–21) the tribe was nearly annihilated, only 600 escaping. Saul was a Benjamite. When the ten tribes revolted under Jeroboam, a large part of this tribe remained with Judah. Paul, the Great Apostle to the Gentiles, was a descendant of this tribe (Phil. 3:5).

Benjamite [Ben′ja·mite]—A member of the tribe of Benjamin (Judg. 3:15; 19:16; 1 Sam. 9:1, 4, 21).

Beno [Be′no], *his son*—One of the sons of Jaaziah, a Levite of the family of Merari (1 Chron. 24:26–27).

Ben-oni [Ben-o′ni], *son of my sorrow*—The name Rachel gave her child whose birth caused her death. Jacob changed the name to Benjamin (Gen. 35:18).

Ben-zoheth [Ben-zo′heth], *son of Zoheth*—A son or grandson of Ishi (1 Chron. 4:20).

Beon [Be′on], *in the dwelling*—A locality east of Jordan (Num. 32:3), probably a contraction of Baal-meon.

Beor [Be′or], *a torch*—Two Old Testament men:
  1. Father of King Bela of Edom (Gen. 36:32; 1 Chron. 1:43).
  2. Father of Balaam (Num. 22:5) called Bosor in 2 Peter 2:15.

Bera [Be′ra], *son of evil*—A king of Sodom. He was defeated by Chedorlaomer and his allies when they invaded the country (Gen. 14:2).

Beracah [Be·ra′cah], *blessing*—A man and a valley of the Old Testament.
  1. A man of Benjamin who joined David at Ziklag (1 Chron. 12:3).
  2. A valley southwest of Tekoa in Judah. It was here that Jehoshaphat gave thanks after defeating the Moabites, Edomites, and Ammonites (2 Chron. 20:26). Some regard it as the Valley of Jehoshaphat (Joel 3:2, 12).

Berachah [Be·ra′chah]—See Beracah.

Berachiah [Ber·a·chi′ah]—See Berechiah.

Beraiah [Be·rai′ah], *Jehovah has created*—A son of Shimei, a Benjamite of Jerusalem (1 Chron. 8:21).

Berea [Be·re′a], *well watered*—A Macedonian city with a large Jewish population. On his second journey, Paul came to this city and the Bereans searched the Scriptures to confirm the things Paul declared (Acts 17:10–13).

Berechiah [Ber·e·chi′ah], *Jehovah hath blessed*—Seven Old Testament men:

1. The father of Asaph, a Gershonite, also called Berachiah (1 Chron. 6:39; 15:17).

2. A Levite in David's reign, a doorkeeper for the ark (1 Chron. 15:23–24).

3. An Ephraimite in the reign of Pekah. He befriended the captives from Judah (2 Chron. 28:12).

4. Son of Zerubbabel (1 Chron. 3:20).

5. A descendant of Elkanah of Netophah, a Levite (1 Chron. 9:16).

6. Father of Zechariah (Zech. 1:1, 7; Matt. 23:35). He is also called Barachias or Barachiah. See also Jeberechiah (Isa. 8:2).

7. Father of Meshullum (one who repaired the wall of Jerusalem), and son of Meshezabeel (Neh. 3:4, 30; 6:18).

Bered [Bee'red], *hail*—

1. A place in the wilderness of Shur near Kadesh (Gen. 16:7, 14).

2. A son of Shuthelah and grandson of Ephraim (1 Chron. 7:20). Some have identified him with Becher (Num. 26:35).

Berenice [Bereni'ce]—See Bernice.

Beri [Be'ri], *a well*—A son of Zophah (1 Chron. 7:36).

Beriah [Be·ri'ah], *with a friend*—Four Old Testament men:

1. Son of Asher and head of a family (Gen. 46:17; Num. 26:44).

2. Son of Ephraim (1 Chron. 7:23).

3. A Benjamite. He and his brother Shema were ancestors of the people of Aijalon (1 Chron. 8:13).

4. A son of Shimei (1 Chron. 23:10).

Beriites [Be'ri·ites]—Descendants of Beriah, the son of Asher (Num. 26:44).

Berites [Be'rites]—Rendering in 2 Samuel 20:14 for a people visited by Joab in his pursuit of Sheba. They are believed to have been descendants of Bichri.

Berith [Be'rith], *covenant*—A god or idol (Judg. 9:46), called El-berith in the King James Version.

Bernice, Berenice [Ber·ni'ce, Bereni'ce], *victorious*—The eldest daughter of Herod Agrippa I. She was the wife of her uncle, Herod, king of Chalcis. After his death, her relations with her brother, Agrippa II, gave rise to scandal. She married Polemo, king of Cilicia, but soon left him and returned to her brother. She was with Agrippa II when he visited Festus (Acts 25:23; 26:30). Later she became the mistress of both Vespasian and Titus.

Berodach-baladan [Ber·o'dach-bal'a·dan]—See Merodach-baladan.

Beroea [Be·roe'a]—See Berea.

Berothah [Be·ro'thah], *wells*—A town between Hamath and Damascus (2 Sam. 8:8; Ezek. 47:16). In 1 Chronicles 18:8 the King James Version calls it *Chun* and the New Revised Standard Version—*Cun*.

Berothai [Be·ro'thai]—See Berothah.

Berothite [Be·ro'thite]—An inhabitant of Beeroth (1 Chron. 11:39).

Berutha [Be·ru'tha]—See Berothah.

Besai [Be'sai], *my treading*—One of the Nethinim whose descendants returned from the Babylonian exile (Ezra 2:49; Neh. 7:52).

Besodeiah [Bes·o·dei'ah], *in the intimacy of Jehovah*—The father of Meshullam who aided in repairing the gate of Jerusalem (Neh. 3:6).

Besor [Be'sor], *cool*—A brook that flows into the Mediterranean about five miles south of Gaza. Here a large number of David's men encamped while the remainder of his troops pursued the Amalekites (1 Sam. 30:9–10).

Betah [Be'tah], *trust*—A city of Aram-zobah (2 Sam. 8:8), called Tibhath in 1 Chronicles 18:8.

Beten [Be'ten], *valley*—A city on the border of Asher (Josh. 19:25).

Bethabara [Beth·ab'a·ra], *house of the ford*—A place where John the Baptist baptized (John 1:28). Apparently, it was a ford on the Jordan. It corresponds with Bethany No 2.

Beth-acacia [Beth-a·ca'cia]—See Beth-shittah.

Beth-anath [Beth-a'nath], *house of Anath*—A fortified city of Naphtali (Josh. 19:35, 38) from which the Israelites did not drive the Canaanites (Judg. 1:33).

Beth-anoth [Beth-a'noth], *house of Anath*—A town in the mountains of Judah (Josh. 15:59).

Bethany [Beth'a·ny], *house of dates*—The name of two villages in the New Testament:

1. A village on the southeastern slopes of the Mount of Olives about 3 kilometers (2 miles) east of Jerusalem near the road to Jericho (Mark 11:1). Bethany was the scene of some of the most important events of Jesus' life. It was the home of Martha, Mary, and Lazarus and the place where Jesus raised Lazarus from the dead (John 11). During Jesus' final week, He spent at least one night in Bethany (Matt. 21:17). At Bethany Jesus was anointed by Mary in the home of Simon the leper (Matt. 26:6–13). From a site near Bethany, He ascended into heaven (Luke 24:50).

2. A village in Transjordan where John the Baptist was baptizing (John 1:28, NIV; Bethabara, KJV, NKJV).

Beth-aphrah [Beth-aph'rah]—A city of the Philistines (Mic. 1:10). Also called Beth-le-aphrah, Aphrah, and Beth Ophrah.

Beth-arabah [Beth-ar'a·bah], *house of the desert*—A village of Judah on the boundary line between Judah and Benjamin (Josh. 15:6, 61; 18:22). In Joshua 18:18 it is called Arabah.

Beth-aram [Beth-a'ram]—See Beth-haran.

Beth-arbel [Beth-ar'bel], *house of God's ambush*—A place of uncertain site (Hos. 10:14).

Beth-aven [Beth-a'ven], *house of vanity, that is, idols*—

1. A town of Benjamin near Ai (Josh. 7:2) and west of Michmash (1 Sam. 13:5; 14:23).

2. This name was applied by Hosea to Beth-el after Jeroboam made it a center of idolatry (Hos. 4:15; 5:8; 10:5).

Beth-azmaveth [Beth-az·ma'veth]—See Azmaveth.

Beth-azmoth [Beth-az'moth]—See Azmaveth.

Beth-baal-meon [Beth-ba′al-me′on]—See Baal-meon.

Beth-barah [Beth-bar′ah], *house of (the) ford*—A ford of the Jordan near the scene of Gideon's great victory (Judg. 7:24), possibly the same as Beth-abara, the scene of John's baptizing.

Beth-birei [Beth-bir′e·i], *house of a creative one*—A town of Simeon populated by the descendants of Shimei (1 Chron. 4:31). This is probably the Beth-lebaoth of Joshua 19:6. Also called Beth-biri.

Beth-car [Beth-car], *house of a lamb*—The place to which the Philistines were driven by the Israelites after their defeat at Ebenezer (1 Sam. 7:11).

Beth-dagon [Beth-da′gon], *house of Dagon*—Two Old Testament towns:

1. A town in the lowlands of Judah about halfway between Joppa and Lydda (Josh. 15:33, 41).

2. A town of Asher near the border of Zebulun (Josh. 19:27).

Beth-diblathaim [Beth-dib·la·tha′im], *house of fig cakes*]—A city of Moab denounced by Jeremiah (Jer. 48:21–22). It may be the Almon-diblathaim of Numbers 33:46.

Beth-eden [Beth-eden], *house of delight*—A city of Syria. Amos the prophet foretold the exile of the people of this town as a part of the judgment on Damascus (Amos 1:5).

Beth-el [Beth-el], *house of God*—The name of two cities in the Old Testament:

1. A city of Canaan about 19 kilometers (12 miles) north of Jerusalem, west of Ai and southwest of Shiloh (Gen. 12:8; Judg. 21:19). Beth-el is mentioned more often in the Bible than any other city except Jerusalem. It is first mentioned in connection with Abraham, who "pitched his tent with Bethel on the west and . . . built an altar to the Lord" (Gen. 12:8; 13:3). The region around Beth-el is still suitable for grazing by livestock. The Canaanites called the place Luz.

Jacob, Abraham's grandson, had a life-changing experience at this site. He had a vision of a staircase reaching into the heavens with the angels of God "ascending and descending on it" (Gen. 28:12). Jacob called the name of that place Beth-el, "the house of God" (Gen. 28:19).

He erected a pillar at Beth-el to mark the spot of his vision (Gen. 28:22; 31:13). Jacob later built an altar at Beth-el, where he worshipped the Lord (Gen. 35:1–16).

During Israel's war with the Benjamites in later years (Judg. 20), the children of Israel suffered two disastrous defeats (Judg. 20:21, 25). They went to Beth-el (the house of God, NKJV) to inquire of the Lord, for the ark of the covenant was located there (Judg. 20:26–27). At Beth-el they built an altar and offered burnt offerings and peace offerings before the Lord. The third battle ended in disaster for the Benjamites. At the end of the war the Israelites returned to Beth-el (the house of God, NKJV), built an altar, and again offered burnt offerings and peace offerings (Judg. 21:1–4).

After the death of Solomon and the division of his kingdom, Jeroboam, the king of Israel (the Northern Kingdom), set up two calves of gold, one in Beth-el and one in Dan (1 Kings 12:29, 32–33). Thus, Beth-el became a great center of idolatry (1 Kings 13:1–32; 2 Kings 10:29) and the chief sanctuary of Israel (Amos 7:13), rivaling the temple in Jerusalem.

The prophets Jeremiah and Amos denounced Beth-el for its idolatries (Jer. 48:13; Amos 5:5–6). Hosea, deploring its great wickedness (Hos. 10:5, 15), called it Beth Aven ("house of idols"), because of the golden calf set up there. Beth-el, the house of God, had deteriorated into Beth Aven, the house of idols.

In a religious reformation that sought to restore the true worship of God, King Josiah broke down the altar at Beth-el (2 Kings 23:15). Still later in Israel's history, Beth-el was occupied by Jewish people who returned from the captivity in Babylon with Zerubbabel (Ezra 2:28; Neh. 7:32). The place again reverted to the Benjamites (Neh. 11:31). The city was destroyed about 540 B.C. by a great fire. This destruction may have been the work of Nabonidus of Babylon or of the Persians in the period just before Darius. Today the site of Beth-el is occupied by a small village called Beitin.

The New Testament does not refer to Beth-el, but Jesus must have gone through this area on His trips. The city was situated on the main road from Shechem to Jerusalem.

2. A city in the territory of Simeon (1 Sam. 30:27). Scholars believe this Beth-el is a variant reading for Bethul (Josh. 19:4) or Bethuel (1 Chron. 4:30). See Bethuel.

Beth-elite [Beth-el·ite]—A person from Beth-el (1 Kings 16:34).

Beth-emek [Beth-e′mek], *house of the valley*—A town of Asher northwest of the Sea of Galilee (Josh. 19:27).

Bethesda [Beth·es′da], *house of grace*—A pool in the northeastern part of Jerusalem, near the Sheep Gate. At this pool Jesus healed the man "who had an infirmity thirty-eight years" (John 5:5). Archaeologists have discovered two pools in this vicinity, 16 1/2 and 19 1/2 meters (55 and 65 feet) long respectively. The shorter pool had five arches over it with a porch beneath each arch, corresponding to the description given in John 5:2. The Crusaders later built a church on this site to commemorate the healing miracle that took place.

The man who had been lame for 38 years came to the pool hoping to be cured by its miraculous waters; instead he was healed by the word of Jesus (John 5:1–15).

Beth-ezel [Beth-e′zel], *house of narrowing*—A town, probably southwest of Hebron (Mic. 1:11), though some identify it with Azal near Jerusalem (Zech. 14:5).

Beth-gader [Beth-ga′der], *house of a wall*—A town of Judah (1 Chron. 2:51), probably the same as Gedor (Josh. 15:58).

Beth-gamul [Beth-gam′ul], *camel house*—A town of Moab between Medeba and the river Arnon (Jer. 48:23).

Beth-gilgal [Beth-gil′gal], the *house of the wheel*—A proper name used in the Revised Version for the house of Gilgal (Neh. 12:29), perhaps the same as Gilgal.

Beth-haccherem, Beth-haccerem [Beth-hac′che·rem, Beth-hac′ce·rem], *house of the vineyard*—A town of Judah (Neh. 3:14; Jer. 6:1). It is west of Jerusalem.

Beth-haggun [Beth-hagg′un]—*garden house*—(2 Kings 9:27).

Beth-hakkerem [Beth-hak′kerem]—See Beth-haccherem.

Beth-haram [Beth-har′am]—See Beth-haran.

Beth-haran [Beth-har′an], *mountain house*—A town in the valley of the Jordan (Num. 32:36; Josh. 13:27).

Beth-hoglah [Beth-hog'lah], *house of the partridge*—A village of Benjamin on the border between Benjamin and Judah (Josh. 15:6; 18:19, 21).

Beth-horon [Beth-hor'on], *house of the hollow*—Two towns on the road between Gibeon and Azekah. They are about two miles apart and are known as the upper and nether Beth-horon (Josh. 16:3, 5; 18:13–14). One of them was assigned to the Kohathite Levites (Josh. 21:22; 1 Chron. 6:68). They controlled the pass down which the Amorites fled before Joshua (Josh. 10:10). Solomon fortified them (2 Chron. 8:5).

Beth-jeshimoth [Beth-jesh'i·moth], *house of the wastes*—A town near Pisgah east of the Jordan (Josh. 12:3; 13:20). It was the southern limit of the camp of the Israelites at Shittim (Num. 33:49). It was in the territory of the tribe of Reuben (Josh. 13:20) but in the last period of Judah was held by the Moabites (Ezek. 25:9).

Beth-jesimoth [Beth-jes'i·moth]—See Beth-jeshimoth.

Beth-le-aphrah [Beth-le-aph'rah]—See Aphrah.

Beth-lebaoth [Beth-le·ba'oth], *house of lionesses*—A town assigned to the Simeonites in the south of Judah (Josh. 19:6). In Joshua 15:32 it is called Lebaoth. See also Beth-birei.

Bethlehem [Beth'le·hem], *house of bread* or *house of (the god) Lahmu*—The name of two cities and possibly one man in the Bible:

1. The birthplace of Jesus Christ. Bethlehem was situated about 8 kilometers (5 miles) south of Jerusalem in the district known as Ephrathah in Judah (Mic. 5:2), a region known for its fertile hills and valleys.

Bethlehem was the burial place of Rachel, the wife of Jacob (Gen. 35:19). The original home of Naomi and her family, it was also the setting for much of the book of Ruth. Bethlehem also was the ancestral home of David (1 Sam. 17:12) and was rebuilt and fortified by King Rehoboam (2 Chron. 11:6).

The most important Old Testament figure associated with Bethlehem was David, Israel's great king. At Bethlehem Samuel anointed David as Saul's successor (1 Sam. 16:1, 13). Although David made Jerusalem his capital city, he never lost his love for Bethlehem.

Second Samuel 23:14–17 is a warm story about David's longing for a drink of water from the well of Bethlehem, which was a Philistine garrison at the time. But when three of David's mighty men broke through the Philistine lines to draw a drink of water, David refused to drink it because it symbolized "the blood of the men who went in jeopardy of their lives" (2 Sam. 23:17).

The prophet Micah predicted that Bethlehem would be the birthplace of the Messiah (Mic. 5:2), a prophecy quoted in Matthew 2:6. It is significant that the King of kings, who was of the house of David, was born in David's ancestral home. According to Luke 2:11, Jesus was born in "the city of David," Bethlehem. Christ, who is the Bread of Life, was cradled in a town whose name means "house of bread."

The region around Bethlehem today is known for its fertile hills and valleys. Its busy marketplaces and religious shrines continue to attract tourists. The Church of the Nativity, which marks the birthplace of the Savior, is one of the best authenticated sites in the Holy Land. The present structure, built over the cave area that served as a stable for the inn, goes back to the time of the Roman emperor Justinian (sixth century A.D.). This church replaces an earlier building, built in A.D. 330 by Helena, the mother of the Roman emperor Constantine.

Other popular attractions at Bethlehem for Holy Land tourists are the fields of Boaz, where Ruth gleaned grain after the fields had been harvested (Ruth 2:3), and Shepherd's Field, where the angels announced the birth of Jesus to the shepherds (Luke 2:8–18).

2. A town in the land of Zebulun (Josh. 19:15).

3. A son of Salma, a descendant of Caleb (1 Chron. 2:51). As the "father" of Bethlehem, Salma may have been the founder of Bethlehem rather than being the father of a son named "Bethlehem."

Bethlehemite [Beth'le·hem·ite]—One from Bethlehem (1 Sam. 16:1, 18).

Bethlehem-judah [Beth'le·hem-ju'dah]—Another name for Bethlehem.

Beth-maachah [Beth-ma'a·chah], *house of Maacah*—A town near Mount Hermon to which Joab went in search of Sheba, son of Bichri (2 Sam. 20:14–15). See Abel-beth-maachah.

Beth-marcaboth [Beth-mar'ca·both], *house of the chariots*—A town of Simeon (Josh. 19:5; 1 Chron. 4:31).

Beth-meon [Beth-me'on]—See Baal-meon.

Beth-nimrah [Beth-nim'rah], *house of the leopard*—This town in the Jordan Valley, east of Jordan, was assigned to Gad (Num. 32:36; Josh. 13:27). It was once called Nimrah (Num. 32:3).

Beth-ophrah [Beth-oph·rah]—See Beth-aphrah.

Beth-palet [Beth-pa'let]—See Beth-pelet.

Beth-pazzez [Beth-pazzez], *house of dispersion*—A town of Issachar (Josh. 19:21).

Beth-pelet [Beth-pe'let], *house of escape*—A town in the extreme south of Judah (Josh. 15:27). It was assigned to Simeon and mention is made of its inhabitants after the Exile (Neh. 11:26).

Beth-peor [Beth-pe·or], *house of Peor*—A town on the east side of Jordan near Pisgah. It was in the tribe of Reuben (Deut. 3:29; Josh. 13:20). It was near here that Moses was buried (Deut. 34:6).

Bethphage [Beth'pha·ge], *house of figs*—A village on the Mount of Olives, on the road that runs from Jericho to Jerusalem (Mark 11:1; Luke 19:29).

Beth-phelet [Beth-phe'let]—See Beth-pelet.

Beth-rapha [Beth-ra'pha], *house of the giants*—A name appearing in the genealogy of Judah (1 Chron. 4:12).

Beth-rehob [Beth-re'hob], *house of a street*—A town in the north of Palestine, also called Rehob (Num. 13:21; Judg. 18:28). Syrians who were allied with the Ammonites against David inhabited this town (2 Sam. 10:6).

Bethsaida [Beth·sa'i·da], *house of fishing* or *fishing*—The name of one or possibly two cities in the New Testament:

1. Bethsaida, which was later called Julias, was situated 3 kilometers (2 miles) north of the Sea of Galilee and east of the Jordan River. The name Julias was given to it by the tetrarch Philip (Luke 3:1), after Julia,

the daughter of Caesar Augustus. In the wilderness near Bethsaida, Jesus fed the 5,000 and healed the multitudes (Luke 9:10–17). It was also in Bethsaida that He restored sight to a blind man (Mark 8:22).

2. The gospels of Mark, Luke, and John seem to speak of another Bethsaida, which was the home of Philip, Andrew, and Peter (John 1:44) and perhaps of James and John (Luke 5:10). This city was situated northwest of the Sea of Galilee in the fertile plain of Gennesaret (Mark 6:45, 53) near Capernaum (John 6:17) in the province of Galilee (John 12:21). Jesus retired to this town after the death of John the Baptist (Mark 6:31; Luke 9:10).

Some scholars argue that there was only one city called Bethsaida. The Jewish historian Josephus identified the Bethsaida developed by Philip as being near the Jordan in "Lower Gaulanitis." Yet, the Gospels seem to indicate that there was another Bethsaida west of the Jordan River (for example, see Mark 6:45, 53). Philip, Peter, and Andrew were from "Bethsaida of Galilee" (John 12:21). Bethsaida-Julias could not be considered to be "of Galilee." The close connection of Bethsaida with Chorazin (Matt. 11:21) and Capernaum (Matt. 11:23) as the center of Jesus' ministry in Galilee is strong evidence for another Bethsaida situated closer to them.

Beth-shean, Beth-shan [Beth-she'an, Beth-shan], *house of quiet*—A town west of the Jordan about fourteen miles south of the Sea of Galilee. This formidable town, though within the territory of Issachar (Josh. 17:16), was assigned to Manasseh (Josh. 17:11, 16) but this tribe, instead of expelling the Canaanites, made them pay tribute (Josh. 17:12, 16; Judg. 1:27–28). It was here the Philistines fastened the bodies of Saul and his sons to a wall (1 Sam. 31:10–13; 2 Sam. 21:12–14).

Beth-shemesh, Ir-shemesh [Beth-shem'esh, Ir-shem'esh], *house of the sun*—Four towns mentioned in the Old Testament:
1. A town in the vale of the Sorek, on the boundary line of Judah but assigned to Dan (Josh. 15:10; 19:41) and made a city of the Levites (Josh. 21:16; 1 Chron. 6:59). It was to this town the ark was brought when the Philistines wanted to get rid of it. Here many men were struck dead for profanely looking into the ark (1 Sam. 6:19).
2. A city of Naphtali (Josh. 19:38; Judg. 1:33).
3. An unidentified town in Issachar (Josh. 19:22).

4. An Egyptian city, thought to be On or Heliopolis, where the sun was worshipped (Jer. 43:13).

Beth-shemite [Beth-she′mite]—An inhabitant of Beth-shemesh (1 Sam. 6:14).

Beth-shittah [Beth-shit′tah], *house of the acacia*—A town near Abel-meholah in the Jordan Valley (Judg. 7:22).

Beth-tappuah [Beth-tap′pu·ah], *house of apples*—A town in the hill country of Judah (Josh. 15:53) about three miles northwest of Hebron. It is now called Tuffuh.

Bethuel [Be·thu′el], *God destroys* or *man of God* or *dweller in God*—A man and a town of the Old Testament:
    1. Son of Nahor, the father of Rebekah and Laban, and the nephew of Abraham (Gen. 22:20–23; 24:15, 29; 28:2, 5).
    2. A town of Simeon (Josh. 19:4; 1 Chron. 4:30), called Chesil in Joshua 15:30.

Bethul [Beth′ul]—See Bethuel.

Beth-zur [Beth-zur], *house of the rock*—A town in the hill country of Judah fortified by Rehoboam (Josh. 15:58; 2 Chron. 11:7). The people of this city responded to the call of Nehemiah and aided in rebuilding the wall of Jerusalem (Neh. 3:16).

Betonim [Bet′o·nim], *pistachio nuts*—A town in the territory of Gad (Josh. 13:26).

Beulah [Beu′lah], *married*—The name to be given Palestine in its future greatness and when restored to divine favor. It is used figuratively of Israel (Isa. 62:4).

Bezaanannim [Be·za·a·nan′nim]—See Zaanannim.

Bezai [Be·za′i], *conqueror*—The founder of a family, members of which returned from the Babylonion exile (Ezra 2:17; Neh. 7:23; 10:18).

Bezaleel, Bezalel [Bez′a·leel, Bez′a·lel], *in the protection of God*—Two Old Testament men:
    1. A grandson of Hur of the family of Caleb of Judah (1 Chron. 2:20) and a skillful worker in metals and precious stones, Bezaleel was

appointed chief architect for the construction of tabernacle furniture, preparation of the priestly garments, and procurement of oils and incense.

2. A son of Pahath-moab who put away his foreign wife (Ezra 10:30).

Bezek [Be'zek], *lightning*—A town and a place in the Old Testament:

1. A town in the mountains near Jerusalem and the residence of Adoni-bezek (Judg. 1:4–5).

2. A place where Saul numbered his forces before going to the relief of Jabesh-gilead (1 Sam. 11:8).

Bezer [Be'zer], *fortress*—A man and a place in the Old Testament:

1. Son of Zophah (1 Chron. 7:37).

2. A city of Reuben east of the Jordan which was given to the Levites and was designated a city of refuge (Deut. 4:43; Josh. 20:8; 21:36).

Bichri [Bich'ri], *youthful*—A Benjamite whose son Sheba instigated a rebellion (2 Sam. 20:1).

Bidkar [Bit'kar], *with a stab*—The captain of Jehu who threw the body of Jehoram into the field of Naboth (2 Kings 9:25).

Bigtha [Big'tha], *in the wine-press*—A chamberlain in charge of the harem of Ahasuerus (Est. 1:10).

Bigthan, Bigthana [Big'than, Big·tha'na], *in their wine-press*— A keeper of the palace door of Xerxes (Ahasuerus). He and Teresh conspired against the king and were frustrated by Mordecai. They were hanged (Est. 2:21; 6:2).

Bigvai [Big·va'i], *in my bodies*—Two Old Testament men:

1. The head of a family, a leader of the exiles who returned from Babylon under Zerubbabel (Ezra 2:2).

2. A chief of the people, two thousand of whose family returned from Babylon (Ezra 2:14; Neh. 7:19). A large number returned with Ezra about eighty years later (Ezra 8:14).

Bildad [Bil'dad], *confusing (by mingling) love*—One of Job's three friends with whom he debated the question of suffering and affliction.

He is called "the Shuhite," hence was perhaps a descendant of Shuah, Abraham's son by Keturah (Job 2:11; 8:1; 18:1; 25:1).

Bileam [Bi'le·am]—A town in the territory of Manasseh west of the Jordan. It was allotted to the Levitical family of Kohath (1 Chron. 6:70).

Bilgah [Bil'gah], *cheerfulness*—Two Old Testament men:

1. A descendant of Aaron, head of the fifteenth course of the priests (1 Chron. 24:1, 6, 14).

2. A priest who returned from Babylon with Zerubbabel (Neh. 12:5, 7). At a later time this was the name of a priestly house (Neh. 12:18).

Bilgai [Bil·ga'i], *cheerfulness*—A priest who sealed the covenant with Nehemiah (Neh. 10:8), probably the same as Bilgah.

Bilhah [Bil'hah], *bashfulness*—A woman and a town in the Old Testament:

1. Maidservant of Rachel, Jacob's wife. She was the mother of Dan and Naphtali (Gen. 30:1–8; 1 Chron. 7:13).

2. A town of Simeon (1 Chron. 4:29).

Bilhan [Bil'han], *bashful*—Two Old Testament men:

1. A son of Ezer, a Horite (Gen. 36:27; 1 Chron. 1:42).

2. A member of the family of Jediael (1 Chron. 7:10).

Bilshan [Bil'shan], *in slander*—One of the twelve princes of the Jews who returned from Babylon under Zerubbabel (Ezra 2:2; Neh. 7:7).

Bimhal [Bim'hal], *in circumcision*—A great-great-grandson of Asher and son of Japhlet (1 Chron. 7:33).

Binea [Bi'ne·a], *fountain*—A son of Moza (1 Chron. 8:37; 9:43).

Binnui [Bin'nu·i], *building*—Four Old Testament men:

1. Father of Noadiah, a Levite. The son helped to weigh the gold and silver brought from Babylon (Ezra 8:33).

2. A son of Pahath-moab. He relinquished his foreign wife after the return from Babylon (Ezra 10:30).

3. An Israelite, a son of Bani, who put away his foreign wife (Ezra 10:30, 38).

4. The son of Henadad, a Levite (Neh. 10:9). He returned from Babylon with Zerubbabel (Neh. 12:8). Some of his family assisted in

building the wall (Neh. 3:24) and one of them sealed the covenant (Neh. 10:9).

Birsha [Bir'sha], *with iniquity*—A king of Gomorrah, defeated by Chedorlaomer (Gen. 14:2, 8, 10).

Bir-zaith, Bir-zavith [Bir-za'ith, Bit-za'vith], *olive well*—A name in the genealogies of Asher (1 Chron. 7:31).

Bishlam [Bish'lam], *son of peace*—A Persian officer of Artaxerxes (Ezra 4:7).

Bithiah [Bith'i·ah], *daughter, that is, worshipper of Jehovah*—The wife of Mered and daughter of Pharaoh (1 Chron. 4:18).

Bithron [Bith'ron], *devision* or *a cut*—A region north of the Jabbok near Mahanaim (2 Sam. 2:29).

Bithynia [Bi·thyn'ia], *a violent rushing*—A province in northwestern Asia Minor (Acts 16:7; 1 Peter 1:1). When Paul purposed to labor in this region, he was divinely directed not to do so. Its chief town, Nicaea, was the scene of the Council of Nicaea (A.D. 325).

Biziothiah [Biz'i·o·thi·ah]—See Bizjothjah.

Bizjothjah [Biz·joth'jah], *contempt of Jehovah*—A term denoting a place in Judah (Josh. 15:28).

Biztha [Biz'tha], *booty*—A chamberlain in the court of Xerxes (Ahasuerus) in the time of Esther. He was ordered to bring Vashti to the king's banquet (Est. 1:10).

Blastus [Blas'tus], *sprout*—The chamberlain of Herod Agrippa (Acts 12:20).

Boanerges [Bo·an·er'ges], *sons of thunder*—A name Jesus gave to John and James, sons of Zebedee, because of their zeal and impetuosity (Mark 3:17; Luke 9:54).

Boaz [Bo'az], *in him is strength*—The name of a prominent man and an object in the temple:
   1. A wealthy and honorable man of Bethlehem from the tribe of Judah. He was a kinsman of Elimelech, Naomi's husband. He became

the husband of Naomi's widowed daughter-in-law Ruth (Ruth 2–4), and redeemed the estate of her deceased husband. Through their son Obed, Boaz and Ruth became ancestors of King David and of the Lord Jesus Christ (Matt. 1:5; Booz, KJV).

2. One of the two bronze pillars that stood in front of King Solomon's magnificent temple (2 Chron. 3:17), eighteen cubits high. The name of the other was Jachin.

Bocheru [Bo'che·ru], *firstborn*—A son of Azel (1 Chron. 8:38).

Bochim [Bo'chim], *weepers*—At this place near Gilgal Israelites expressed their sorrow when reproved (Judg. 2:1–5).

Bohan [Bo'han], *thumb*—A son of Reuben. A stone which indicated the boundary line between Judah and Benjamin was given his name (Josh. 15:6; 18:17).

Bokeru [Bo'ke·ru]—See Bocheru.

Bokim [Bo'kim]—See Bochim.

Booz [Booz]—Greek. See Boaz.

Bor-ashan [Bor-ash'an]—See Ashan.

Boscath [Bos'cath]—See Bozkath.

Bosor [Bo'sor], *burning* or *torch*—
1. A town of Gilead. It may have been Bezer in the tribe of Reuben (Josh. 20:8).
2. The Grecian form of Beor (2 Peter 2:15).

Bozez [Bo'zez], *shining*—The name of the rock on one side of the pass through which Jonathan tried to reach the Philistines (1 Sam. 14:4–5).

Bozkath, Boscath [Boz'kath, Bos'cath], *elevated* or *stony ground*—A city at the most southern point of Judah (Josh. 15:39); also mentioned as the birthplace of Adaiah, King Josiah's mother (2 Kings 22:1).

Bozrah [Boz'rah], *sheepfold*—Two cities of Old Testament times:
1. An important city of Edom (Gen. 36:33; 1 Chron. 1:44). It is mentioned by Isaiah (Isa. 34:6; 63:1). The judgment that will fall on

it is predicted by Amos (Amos 1:12) and its complete destruction by Jeremiah (Jer. 49:13, 22). It is located twenty-two miles southeast of the Dead Sea.

2. A city of Moab denounced by Jeremiah, perhaps the same as Bezer (Jer. 48:24).

Brazen Sea [Bra'zen]—An enormous bronze bowl which Solomon had made for the new temple. It was approximately fifteen feet in diameter, and seven and a half feet deep. It rested on a base made of twelve cast bronze bulls (1 Kings 7:23–26; 1 Kings 7:13–14; 2 Chron. 4:6; 2 Kings 25:13).

Bronze Sea—See Brazen Sea.

Bukki [Buk'ki], *wasting*—

1. The chief of the tribe of Dan, the son of Jogli, one of the commission appointed by Moses for the division of the land (Num. 34:22).

2. The son of Abishua and descendant of Aaron (1 Chron. 6:5, 51; Ezra 7:4).

Bukkiah [Buk·ki'ah], *tested by Jehovah*—The son of Heman (1 Chron. 25:4, 13).

Bul [Bul], *rain month*—Canaanite name for the eighth month of the sacred and second of the civil year, corresponding to a part of October and November (1 Kings 6:38).

Bunah [Bu'nah]. *discretion*—A descendant of Judah through Jerahmeel (1 Chron. 2:25).

Bunni [Bun'ni], *built*—

1. A Levite. Shemaiah, one of his descendants, was made an overseer of the second temple (Neh. 11:15).

2. A Levite who returned from Babylon and sealed the covenant with Nehemiah (Neh. 9:4; 10:15).

Buz [Buz], *contempt*—Two men and a place in the Old Testament:

1. A tribe descended from a son of Nahor, brother of Abraham (Gen. 22:20–21).

2. A man of the tribe of Gad (1 Chron. 5:14).

3. A place probably in northern Arabia, exact location unknown (Jer. 25:23). Elihu's father came from this area, or possibly was descended from Buz No. 1 (Job 32:2, 6).

Buzi [Bu′zi], *my contempt*—Father of Ezekiel, the prophet (Ezek. 1:3).

Buzite [Bu′zite]—See Buz No. 3.

C

Cabbon [Cab'bon], *a bond*—A place in the lowland of Judah (Josh. 15:40). It may be the same as Machbenah (1 Chron. 2:49).

Cabul [Ca'bul], *sterile*—

1. A town near the southeastern border of Asher, a few miles southeast of Acre (Josh. 19:27).

2. A district of Galilee. It contained twenty towns. These Solomon gave to Hiram, king of Tyre, for service rendered by him in the construction of the temple. Hiram was so displeased with them that he called the region Cabul and returned them to Solomon who fortified there (1 Kings 9:13; 2 Chron. 8:2).

Caesar [Cae'sar]—The surname borne by the Julian family. After the death of the illustrious Gaius Julius Caesar, Augustus adopted the name as an official title, as did practically every other Roman emperor thereafter for some two hundred years. While eleven Caesars (emperors) fall within the scope of New Testament times, only four are mentioned.

Caesar Augustus (31 B.C.–A.D. 14) issued the decree that the world should be taxed (Luke 2:1). It was in the fifteenth year of Tiberius Caesar (A.D. 14–37) that John the Baptist began his ministry (Luke 3:1). In the days of Claudius Caesar (A.D. 41–54) the famine predicted by Agabus came to pass. Claudius also commanded all Jews, including Aquila and Priscilla, to leave Rome (Acts 11:28; 18:2). Finally, Nero Caesar (A.D. 54–68) is called merely Caesar in Philippians 4:22. It was to Nero that Paul made his famous appeal (Acts 25:10–12).

Caesarea [Cae·sa·re'a], *pertaining to Caesar*—An important biblical seaport located south of modern Haifa. Built at enormous expense by Herod the Great between 25 and 13 B.C., and named in honor of Caesar Augustus, the city was sometimes called Caesarea of Palestine to distinguish it from Caesarea Philippi.

Herod spent 12 years building his seaport jewel on the site of an ancient Phoenician city named Strato's Tower. He constructed a huge breakwater. The enormous stones he used in this project were 15.25 meters (50 feet) long, 5.5 meters (18 feet) wide, and 2.75 meters (9 feet) deep. Some of them still can be seen extending 45.75 meters (150 feet) from the shore. Caesarea frequently was the scene of disturbances as cities of mixed Jewish–Gentile population tended to be. When Pilate was prefect (governor) of Judea, he lived in the governor's residence at Caesarea. In 1961, a stone inscribed with his name was found in the ruins of an ancient amphitheater there. Philip the evangelist preached there (Acts 8:40), and Peter was sent there to minister to the Roman centurion Cornelius (Acts 10:1, 24; 11:11). Herod Agrippa I died at Caesarea, being "eaten of worms" (Acts 12:19–23).

Caesarea was prominent in the ministry of the apostle Paul as well. After Paul's conversion, some brethren brought him to the port at Caesarea to escape the Hellenists and sail to his hometown of Tarsus (Acts 9:30). Paul made Caesarea his port of call after both his second and third missionary journeys (Acts 18:22; 21:8). Felix sent Paul to Caesarea for trial (Acts 23:23, 33) and the apostle spent two years in prison before making his celebrated defense before Festus and Agrippa (Acts 26). Paul sailed from the harbor in chains to appeal his case before the emperor in Rome (Acts 25:11; 26:1–13).

Other ruins on the site that demonstrate the splendor of ancient Caesarea are a large amphitheater and sections of an aqueduct, which was used to pipe water from the mountains to the coastal city. Caesarea attained ecclesiastical importance by becoming the seat of a bishop in the second century.

Caesarea Philippi [Cae·sa·re'a Phi·lip'pi], *Caesar's city of Philip*—A city on the southwestern slope of Mount Hermon and at the northernmost extent of Jesus' ministry (Matt. 16:13; Mark 8:27). In New Testament times the city was known as Paneas, although Philip the tetrarch renamed the city Caesarea Philippi, in honor of the Roman emperor Augustus Caesar. Agrippa II later changed its name to Neronias, in honor of Nero. The present-day village of Baniyas is built on the same site. It was near Caesarea Philippi that Jesus asked His disciples who He was and received the inspired answer from Simon Peter: "You are the Christ, the Son of the living God" (Matt. 16:16).

Caiaphas [Cai′a·phas], *depression*—The high priest of Israel appointed about A.D. 18 by the Roman procurator, Valerius Gratus. Caiaphas and his father-in-law, Annas, were high priests when John the Baptist began his preaching (Matt. 26:3, 57; Luke 3:2). Caiaphas also was a member of the Sadducees.

After Jesus raised Lazarus from the dead, the Jewish leaders became alarmed at Jesus' increasing popularity. The Sanhedrin quickly called a meeting, during which Caiaphas called for Jesus' death. As high priest, Caiaphas's words carried great authority, and his counsel was followed (John 11:49–53). Subsequently, Caiaphas plotted the arrest of Jesus (Matt. 26:3–4) and was a participant in the illegal trial of Jesus (Matt. 26:57–68).

The final appearance of Caiaphas in the New Testament was at the trial of Peter and John. He was one of the leaders who questioned the two disciples about the miraculous healing of the lame man "at the gate of the temple which is called Beautiful" (Acts 4:6–7). In 1990, an ornate ossuary bearing the name of Caiaphas and containing the bones of a sixty-year-old man was found outside of Jerusalem. The bones may be those of Caiaphas himself.

Cain [Cain], *metalworker*—The name of a person and a city in the Old Testament:

1. The oldest son of Adam and Eve and the brother of Abel (Gen. 4:1–25). Cain was the first murderer. A farmer by occupation, Cain brought fruits of the ground as a sacrifice to God. His brother Abel, a shepherd, sacrificed a lamb from his flock. Since sin requires death, the vegetable offering was inadequate as a sin offering, and God rejected it. The Lord accepted Abel's offering but rejected Cain's (Gen. 4:7).

Envious of his brother, Cain murdered him. When confronted by God, Cain at first denied his sin, and expressed no repentance. Exiled, he went to Nod where he married; his wife being one of the descendants of Adam. He built a city which he named after his son, Enoch, and became the progenitor of a race distinctive along mechanical lines (Gen. 4:1–25; 1 John 3:12; Jude 11).

The proof of Cain's wrong standing before God is seen in his impulse to kill his own brother Abel when his own offering was rejected (Gen. 4:8). Cain was the ancestor of a clan of metalworkers (Gen. 4:18–19, 22).

The New Testament refers to Cain in three places. Abel's offering to God was "a more excellent sacrifice" than Cain's because Abel was "righteous." His heart was right with God, and Cain's was not (Heb. 11:4). John calls Cain "the wicked one" and asks why he murdered his brother; the answer was "Because his works were evil, and his brother's righteous" (1 John 3:12). Jude warns his readers to beware of those who have "gone in the way of Cain" (Jude 11).

2. A town in the mountains of southern Judah, southeast of Hebron also spelled Kain (Josh. 15:57).

Cainan [Ca·i′nan], *their smith*—
1. Son of Enos (Gen. 5:9–14; Luke 3:37–38). He died at the age of 940 and was of the line of Seth.
2. Son of Arphaxad in the line of the Messiah (Luke 3:36), also called Kenan.

Calah [Ca′lah], *vigor*—One of the four cities of Assyria and one of the most ancient of that country (Gen. 10:11–12). It was rebuilt and adorned by Shalmaneser I (1276–1257 B.C.), and having fallen into decay, was restored by Assurnazipal who made it the king's residence. The ruins, about twenty miles south of Nineveh, are now called Nimrud.

Calcol [Cal′col], *sustenance*—A son of Mahol (1 Kings 4:31; 1 Chron. 2:6).

Caleb [Ca′leb], *dog*—The name of two men in the Old Testament:
1. One of the twelve spies sent by Moses to investigate the land of Canaan from Kadesh (Num. 13:6, 30; 14:6, 24, 30, 38). Ten of the twelve spies frightened the Israelites with reports of fortified cities and gigantic peoples. Compared to the giants in the land, they saw themselves as "grasshoppers" (Num. 13:33). They advised against trying to enter Canaan.

Caleb and Joshua also saw the fortified cities in the land, but they reacted in faith rather than fear. They advised Moses and Aaron and the Israelites to attack Canaan immediately (Num. 13:30). The Israelites listened to the larger group of spies rather than the two, and the Lord viewed their fear as a lack of faith and judged them for their spiritual timidity. Of all the adults alive at that time, only Caleb and Joshua would live to possess the land (Josh. 14:6–15).

Caleb was also part of the group selected by Moses to help divide the land among the tribes. He was eighty-five years old when Canaan was finally conquered. Hebron was given to Caleb as a divine inheritance. His daughter, Achsah, would eventually become the wife of his near relative, Othniel.

2. A son of Hezron of the family of Perez of the tribe of Judah (1 Chron. 2:18–19, 42). Descended from this Caleb were Aaron's associate Hur and Hur's grandson Bezaleel, a skilled craftsman. An alternate spelling of the name is Chelubai (1 Chron. 2:9).

Caleb-ephratah [Ca′leb-eph′ra·tah]—See Caleb-ephrathah.

Caleb-ephrathah [Ca′leb-eph′ra·thah], *dog* or *ash heap*—The place where Hezron died (1 Chron. 2:19, 24). Ephrathah is not infrequently a designation for the district about Bethlehem. The name apparently means that part of Ephrathah which belonged to the clan of Caleb.

Calebite [Ca′leb·ite]—A descendant of Caleb.

Calneh [Cal′neh], *fortress*—

1. A Babylonian city of the kingdom of Nimrod (Gen. 10:10).

2. A city of Syria (Amos 6:2), probably the same as Calno (Isa. 10:9).

Calno [Cal′no], *fortress of Anu*—A city, apparently in Syria, which unsuccessfully resisted Assyria (Isa. 10:9). See Calneh.

Calvary [Cal′va·ry], *the skull*—The name used in the KJV and NKJV for the place outside Jerusalem where the Lord Jesus was crucified (Luke 23:33; the Skull, NIV). No one knows for sure why this place was called "the skull." Some suggest a possible explanation of the name applied to the little hill the fact that unburied skulls may have been there. The most likely reason is that the site was a place of execution; the skull is a widely recognized symbol for death. The site may have been associated with a cemetery, although its location near Jerusalem makes it improbable that skulls could be viewed there. Perhaps the area was an outcropping of rock that in some way resembled a skull.

Mark 15:40 and Luke 23:49 indicate that some people viewed Jesus' crucifixion from a distance. John 19:20 says the place was "near the city" of Jerusalem; and Hebrews 13:12 reports that our Lord "suffered outside the gate," which means outside the city walls. From Matthew's reference to "those who passed by" (27:39), it seems the site was close to a well-traveled road. It also is reasonable to think that Joseph's tomb (John 19:41) was quite close. But the Bible does not clearly indicate exactly where Jesus died.

Sites of the crucifixion have been proposed on every side of Jerusalem. One factor that makes it difficult to pinpoint the site is that Jerusalem was destroyed in A.D. 70 by the Romans, and another Jewish revolt was crushed in a similar manner in A.D. 135. Many geographical features and the location of the city walls were greatly changed because of these and a series of conflicts that continued for centuries.

Except in areas that have been excavated, Jerusalem's present walls date from more recent times. The presence of modern buildings prevents digging to find where the walls were located during New Testament times. Some groups claim to have found the very place where Jesus died, but these complicating factors make it unlikely. At present, Christian opinion is divided over two possible sites for Calvary. One is on the grounds of the Church of the Holy Sepulcher. The other, called "Gordon's Calvary," is about 229 meters (250 yards) northeast of the Damascus Gate in the old city wall. A tradition going back to the fourth century says that a search was initiated by the Christian historian Eusebius and that the site was found by Bishop Macarius. Later the Roman emperor Constantine built a church on the site. Previously the place was the location of a temple to Aphrodite. Tradition also has it that while looking for Jesus' tomb, Constantine's mother, Helena, found part of "the true cross" on which Jesus died. These traditions are very old, but their historical value is uncertain.

The Church of the Holy Sepulcher is now inside what is called "the old city," but supporters claim the location was outside the walls of the city in New Testament times. Following an earlier lead, a British general, Charles Gordon, in 1885 strongly advocated the other major site, which is outside the present existing city walls. The place is a grass-covered rocky knoll that, due to excavations (perhaps mining) some time during the past three centuries, now looks something like a skull when viewed from one direction. Beside the hill is what has been called "Jeremiah's Grotto," where an ancient tomb has been recently landscaped to produce a garden setting. This area is sometimes called the "Garden Tomb."

The site known as "Gordon's Calvary" has commended itself especially to some Protestant groups, while the location at the Church of the Holy Sepulcher is highly regarded by the Roman Catholic and Orthodox churches. For Christians, it is the fact of our Lord's self-sacrifice—"that Christ died for our sins according to the Scriptures, and that He was buried, and that He rose again" (1 Cor. 15:3–4)—not the location, that should concern us. At "Calvary," Golgotha's cross—"the emblem of suffering and shame"—became the symbol of love, blessing, and hope.

The Aramaic name for the place where Jesus was crucified is Golgotha (Matt. 27:33; Mark 15:22; John 19:17), which, like Calvary, also means "the skull."

Camon [Ca'mon]—See Kamon.

Cana [Ca'na], *place of reeds*—A village of upper Galilee, about midway from the Mediterranean to the Sea of Galilee. It was the scene of the first miracle performed by Jesus and His later miracle of healing the nobleman's son (John 2:1–11; 4:46–54). It was the native village of the apostle Nathanael (John 21:2).

Canaan [Ca'na·an], *land of purple*—The name of a man and a land or region in the Old Testament:

1. The fourth son of Ham and the grandson of Noah (Gen. 9:18–27; 10:6, 15). Ham's descendants were dispersed into several distinctive tribes, such as the Jebusites and the Zemarites. These people became known collectively in later years as the Canaanites, pagan inhabitants of the land that God promised to Abraham and his descendants. Under the leadership of Joshua, the people of Israel occupied the land of Canaan and divided it among the twelve tribes. His oldest son, Zidon, founded the city of his name (Sidon) in Phoenicia, and thus he became the progenitor of that nation.

2. The region along the Mediterranean Sea occupied by the Canaanites before it was taken and settled by the Israelite people (Gen. 11:31; Josh. 5:12). The land of Canaan stretched from the Jordan River on the east to the Mediterranean Sea on the west. From south to north, it covered the territory between the Sinai Peninsula and the ancient coastal nation of Phoenicia. Much of this territory was dry, mountainous, and rocky, unfit for cultivation. But it also contained many fertile farmlands, particularly in the river valleys and the coastal plains along

the sea. While leading the people of Israel toward the land of Canaan, Moses sent scouts, or spies, into the territory on a fact-finding mission. They returned with grapes, pomegranates, and figs to verify the fertility of the land (Num. 13:2, 17, 23).

The land of Canaan was ideally situated on the trade routes that stretched from Egypt in the south to Syria and Phoenicia in the north and the ancient Babylonian Empire to the east. This location gave the small region a strategic position in the ancient world. After the Israelites captured the land of Canaan, they developed a thriving commercial system by trading goods with other nations along these routes. The finest royal purple dye was manufactured in Canaan, giving the territory its name. It is called the promised land because it was promised to Abraham; the holy land because it was holy unto the Lord; and Palestine, or Philistia, because it was, in part at least, the land of the Philistines.

Canaanite [Ca'naan·ite]—The Canaanites, an ancient tribe, highly developed in their culture, occupied Palestine long before the Hebrews arrived to drive them out under the leadership of Joshua about 1405 B.C. Archeological evidence indicates the Canaanites must have settled the land of Canaan at least six hundred years before Joshua's time. They had a well-developed system of walled cities, including Jericho, Ai, Lachish, Hebron, Debir, and Hazor.

Under God's leadership, Joshua was successful in taking these cities from the Canaanites (Josh. 6–12). The Canaanites also had their own written language, based upon a unique alphabet, which they apparently developed. Discovery of a number of Canaanite documents at Ras Shamra in northern Palestine has given scholars many insights into Canaanite culture and daily life.

The religion of the Canaanite people posed a peculiar threat to the new inhabitants of Canaan. The Canaanites worshipped many pagan gods that appealed to their animal instincts. Baal, the god who controlled rain and fertility, was their main god. Baal religion was basically a fertility cult. At temples scattered throughout their land, Canaanite worshippers participated in lewd, immoral acts with sacred prostitutes. Bestiality and child sacrifice were other evils associated with this depraved form of religion.

The threat of Baal worship explains why Moses issued a stern warning to the people of Israel about the Canaanites several years before they actually occupied the land of promise. "You shall conquer them and utterly destroy them," Moses commanded. "You shall make no covenant with them nor show mercy to them" (Deut. 7:2). Canaanite religion continued to exert its influence throughout the land for many years after Joshua's conquest. The Hebrew people had to be called back again and again to worship the one true God, who demanded holy and ethical living from His people.

Canaanitess [Ca'naan·it·ess]—A Canaanite woman (1 Chron. 2:3).

Cananaean, Canaanite [Ca·na·nae'an, Ca'naan·ite]—A member of a Jewish patriotic party; equivalent to the Greek word "Zealot" (Matt. 10:4).

Candace [Can'da·ce], *prince of servants*—A queen of Ethiopia. For some time Ethiopia was governed by female rulers who took the name of Candace. The kingdom of this queen was probably in southern Nubia. A eunuch of prominence belonging to her court was returning from Jerusalem when, in the desert of Gaza, he met Philip the evangelist who interpreted to him Isaiah 53. He was converted to Christianity and was baptized (Acts 8:26–39).

Canneh [Can'neh], *to give a flattering title*—A place probably in Mesopotamia (Ezek. 27:23), perhaps the same as Calneh.

Capernaum [Ca·per'na·um], *village of Nahum*—The most important city on the northern shore of the Sea of Galilee in New Testament times and the center of much of Jesus' ministry. Capernaum is not mentioned in the Old Testament, and the Nahum after whom it was named is probably not the prophet Nahum. In all likelihood, Capernaum was founded sometime after the Jews returned from captivity.

By the New Testament era, Capernaum was large enough that it always was called a "city" (Matt. 9:1; Mark 1:33). It had its own synagogue, in which Jesus frequently taught (Mark 1:21; Luke 4:31–38; John 6:59). Apparently the synagogue was built by the Roman soldiers garrisoned in Capernaum (Matt. 8:8; Luke 7:1–10). The synagogue was a center for the Roman system of taxation; for it had a permanent office of taxation (Matt. 9:9; Mark 2:14; Luke 5:27), and itinerant tax collectors operated in the city (Matt. 17:24). Ruins of a later synagogue cover those of the one where Jesus worshiped, although sections of the latter can still be seen today.

After being rejected in His hometown, Nazareth, Jesus made Capernaum the center of His ministry in Galilee. He performed many miracles here, including the healing of the centurion's paralyzed servant (Matt. 8:5–13), a paralytic carried by four friends (Mark 2:1–12), Peter's mother-in-law (Matt. 8:14–15; Mark 1:29–31), and the nobleman's son (John 4:46–54).

As Jesus walked by the Sea of Galilee near Capernaum, He called the fishermen Simon, Andrew, James, and John to be His disciples (Mark 1:16–21, 29). It was also in "His own city" (Capernaum) that Jesus called the tax collector Matthew (Matt. 9:1, 9; Mark 2:13–14). Immediately following the feeding of the five thousand, Jesus delivered His discourse on the Bread of Life near this city (John 6:32).

Although Jesus centered His ministry in Capernaum, the people of that city did not follow Him. Jesus pronounced a curse on the city for its unbelief (Matt. 11:23–24), predicting its ruin (Luke 10:15). So strikingly did this prophecy come true that only recently has Tell Hum been identified confidently as ancient Capernaum.

Caphtor [Caph'tor], *a crown*—An island or seacoast from which the Philistines came (Jer. 47:4; Amos 9:7). Originally the Philistines were apparently Cretans, as were possibly the Cherethites (1 Sam. 30:14; Ezek. 25:16); hence Caphtor was quite probably Crete.

Caphtorim, Caphthorim [Caph'to·rim, Caph'tho·rim], *a crown*—The land of Caphtor (Gen. 10:14; 1 Chron. 1:12); also its people who drove out the Avvim and settled on their land (Deut. 2:23). From them were descended the Philistines (Jer. 47:4; Amos 9:7).

Cappadocia [Cap·pa·do'ci·a], *province of good horses*—A province of Asia Minor, having on its north Pontus, Cilicia on the south, Syria on the east, and Lycaonia and Galatia on the west (Acts 2:9; 1 Peter 1:1).

Carcas [Car'cas], *severe*—One of the seven chamberlains who served King Ahasuerus (Est. 1:10).

Carchemish [Car·che'mish], *fortress of Chemosh*—On the western bank of the upper Euphrates this city occupied a position of great commercial advantage. It was captured by Sargon in 717 B.C. (Isa. 10:9). It was here that Nebuchadnezzar defeated Pharaoh Necho in 605 B.C. (Jer. 46:2).

Careah [Ca·re′ah]—See Kareah.

Carites [Car′ites]—Probably mercenary soldiers from Caria, as Cherethites were probably from Crete (2 Kings 11:4), called captains in Authorized Version.

Carkas [Car′kas]—See Carcas.

Carmel [Car′mel], *garden/orchard of God*—The name of a mountain range and a town in the Old Testament:

1. A town in the hill country of Judah (Josh. 15:55; 1 Sam. 25:2, 5, 7, 40). It has been identified as present-day Khirbet el-Kermel, about 13 kilometers (8 miles) southeast of Hebron. Carmel, near Maon, was the home of a very rich and very foolish man named Nabal. This man was a stubborn, churlish fellow who insulted David by refusing to show hospitality to David's servants. The Lord struck Nabal so that "his heart died within him, and he became like a stone" (1 Sam. 25:37). After Nabal's death, David sent for Abigail the Carmelitess, widow of Nabal, to take her as his wife. Abigail, "a woman of good understanding and beautiful appearance" (1 Sam. 25:3), became one of David's wives. Hezrai (2 Sam. 23:35), or Hezro (1 Chron. 11:37), one of David's mighty men, also came from Carmel.

2. A mountain range stretching about 21 kilometers (13 miles) from the Mediterranean coast southeast to the plain of Dothan. At the Bay of Accho (Acre), near the modern city of Haifa, this mountain range juts out into the Mediterranean Sea in a promontory named Mount Carmel. It rises sharply from the seacoast to a height of 143 meters (470 feet) near Haifa. The mountain range as a whole averages over 1,000 feet above sea level, with 530 meters (1,742 feet) being the summit.

The Canaanites built sanctuaries to pagan deities on this mountain. Thus, Carmel was an appropriate site for a confrontation between Elijah, the prophet of the Lord, and the "prophets of Baal" (1 Kings 18:19–20), the idolatrous Canaanite priests. It was also from the top of Mount Carmel that Elijah saw a sign of the coming storm: "a cloud, as small as a man's hand, rising out of the sea" (1 Kings 18:44), a cloud that signaled the end of a prolonged drought. The prophet Elisha also visited Mount Carmel (2 Kings 2:25; 4:25).

Carmelite [Car'mel·ite]—A native of the town of Carmel. Nabal, the first husband of David's wife Abigail, was described as a Carmelite (1 Sam. 30:5; 2 Sam. 2:2; 3:3). One of David's mighty men, Hezrai, was also a Carmelite (2 Sam. 23:35). He is called Hezro in 1 Chronicles 11:37.

Carmelitess [Car'mel·itess]—A woman from the town of Carmel. Abigail, David's wife, was a Carmelitess (1 Sam. 27:3; 1 Chron. 3:1).

Carmi [Car'mi], *vinedresser*—

1. Son of Reuben, the head of a tribal family (Gen. 46:9; Num. 26:6).

2. The father of Achan (Josh. 7:1).

Carmites [Car'mites]—A Reubenite family descended from Carmi (Num. 26:6).

Carnaim [Car·na'im]—See Ashteroth-karnaim.

Carpus [Car'pus], *fruit*—A man of Troas (2 Tim. 4:13).

Carshena [Car·she'na], *spoiler*—A Persian prince in the court of Ahasuerus (Est. 1:14).

Casiphia [Cas·i·phi'a], *silvery*—A place in the Persian Empire. During the Exile Levites resided here (Ezra 8:17).

Casluhim [Cas·lu'him], *fortified*—A people of Mizraim. In the list of the sons of Mizraim they stand between the Pathrusim and the Caphtorim. It is probable they were settled in upper Egypt (Gen. 10:14; 1 Chron. 1:12).

Castor and Pollux [Cas'tor, Pol'lux], simply names—The twin sons of Jupiter and Leda, Greek and Roman divinities. They appeared in the heavens as the constellation Gemini—Twin Brothers—the protectors of mariners (Acts 28:11).

Cauda [Cau'da]—See Clauda.

Cedron [Ce'dron]—See Kidron.

Cenchrea [Cen·chre'a], *millet*—The eastern harbor of Corinth, about nine miles from the city. It had a Christian church, the deaconess of which was Phebe (Rom. 16:1). It was visited by Paul (Acts 18:18).

Cenchreaa [Cen·chrea'a]—See Cenchrea.

Cephas [Ce'phas], *stone*—Simon Peter. Jesus gave Simon, son of Jonah, the nickname "rock," early on. In Greek, this is Peter; in Aramaic it is Cephas (1 Cor. 1:12; 3:22; 15:5; Gal. 2:9).

Chalcol [Chal'col]—See Calcol.

Chaldea [Chal·de'a], *clod-breakers*—Originally, the lower Tigris and Euphrates Valley, or the southern portion of Babylonia. The term is used for the Hebrew *Kasdim*. In the south were the cities of Ur and Erech and in the north Babylon, Cutha, Sippara.

Later, beginning with the reign of Nebuchadnezzar II (king of Babylonia from 605 to 562 B.C.), the term "Chaldea" came to include practically all of Babylonia and was virtually synonymous with the Neo-Babylonian Empire. In the NKJV the term "Chaldea" is found only in the books of Jeremiah and Ezekiel. Jeremiah prophesied the fall of Babylon by saying, "Chaldea shall become plunder" (Jer. 50:10) and "I will repay Babylon, and all the inhabitants of Chaldea for all the evil they have done" (Jer. 51:24). In a vision, the Spirit of God took Ezekiel into Chaldea to his fellow Jews in captivity (Ezek. 11:24). Ezekiel later referred to "the Babylonians of Chaldea" (Ezek. 16:29; 23:15–16).

Chaldean [Chal·de'an]—A native of Chaldea. At an early day Chaldeans were settled on the shores of the Persian Gulf. They conquered Babylonia but their leader, Merodach-baladan, was defeated by Sennacherib, king of Assyria. Nabo-polassar, a Chaldean, founded the New Babylonian Empire in 625 B.C. and in 605 B.C. was followed on the throne by his illustrious son, Nebuchadnezzar. The magicians, astrologers, and priests—the learned class, were called Chaldeans. It was from Ur of the Chaldees that God called Abraham, the head of the messianic nation (Gen. 11:31; 12:1).

Chaldees [Chal·dees]—See Chaldean.

Champaign [Cham·paign], *open country*—A plain, rendered *Arabah* in the Revised Version (Deut. 11:30).

Chanaan [Cha'na·an]—Form of Canaan (Acts 7:11; 13:19). See Canaan.

Charashim [Cha·ra′shim], *craftsman*—A valley in Judah (1 Chron. 4:14). After the Exile it was occupied by Benjamites (Neh. 11:35). In Nehemiah it is called valley of craftsmen.

Charchemish [Char·che′mish]—See Carchemish.

Charran [Char′ran]—A form of Haran (Acts 7:2, 4). See Haran.

Chebar [Che′bar], *far-off*—A stream of Chaldea where some of the Hebrew captives were settled (Ezek. 1:3) and where Ezekiel received some of his visions (Ezek. 3:15, 23; 10:15, 20). It was a great canal southeast of Babylon.

Chedorlaomer [Ched·or·la·o′mer], *servant of (the Elamite God) Lagamar*—A king of Elam, a country east of Babylonia, in Abraham's day (Gen. 14:1, 4–5, 9, 17; Kedorlaomer, NIV). Allied with three other Mesopotamian kings—Amraphel of Shinar, Arioch of Ellasar, and Tidal of "nations"—Chedorlaomer led a campaign against southern Canaan and defeated the inhabitants in the valley of Siddim near the Dead Sea. The conquered people served Chedorlaomer for twelve years, but in the thirteenth year they rebelled (Gen. 14:4).

Chedorlaomer came again with his allies and conquered the region east of the Jordan River from Bashan southward to the Red Sea as well as the plain around the Dead Sea, thus gaining control of the lucrative caravan routes from Arabia and Egypt through Canaan. In making this conquest, Chedorlaomer captured Lot, Abraham's nephew. Aided by his allies and numerous servants, Abraham launched a night attack on Chedorlaomer at Dan, defeating him and recovering Lot and the spoils. Although Chedorlaomer has not been identified in references outside the Old Testament, the elements of his name are typically Elamite.

Chelal [Che′lal], *perfection*—A son of Pahath-moab. He divorced his Gentile wife after the return from Babylon (Ezra 10:30).

Chelluh [Chel′luh]—See Cheluh.

Chelub [Che′lub], *cage* or *bird trap*—
1. A brother of Shush and father of Mehir of the tribe of Judah (1 Chron. 4:11).
2. The father of Ezri, the officer David placed over his gardeners (1 Chron. 27:26).

Chelubai [Che·lu'bai]—A son of Hezron (1 Chron. 2:9). In verses 18 and 42 of this chapter he is called Caleb.

Cheluh [Che'luh], unknown—A son of Bani who divorced his foreign wife in the time of Ezra (Ezra 10:35).

Cheluhi [Che·lu'hi]—See Cheluh.

Chemarim [Chem'a·rim], *priests*—Idolatrous priests who officiated at Beth-el (2 Kings 23:5; Hos. 10:5) and in the high places of Judah (Zeph. 1:4).

Chemosh [Che'mosh], *fire*—The god worshipped by the Moabites (Num. 21:29; Jer. 48:46). According to Judges 11:24 he seems also to have been the national god of the Ammonites, but Milcom may be intended here, since the latter was the special deity of the Ammonites. Human sacrifices were sometimes offered to Chemosh (2 Kings 3:27). In the days of his apostasy Solomon built a high place for this god, which Josiah destroyed (1 Kings 11:7; 2 Kings 23:13).

Chenaanah [Che·na'a·nah], *trader*—
   1. A Benjamite, the fourth son of Bilhan, a warrior in the time of David (1 Chron. 7:10).
   2. The father of the false prophet Zedekiah (1 Kings 22:11; 2 Chron. 18:10).

Chenani [Che·na'ni], *my station*—A Levite who exercised a beneficent influence on the exiles who returned from Babylon (Neh. 9:4).

Chenaniah [Chen·a·ni'ah], *Jehovah is firm*—A chief of the Levites of the house of Izhar. When the ark was removed from the house of Obed-edom (1 Chron. 15:27), he had charge of the musical services. He and his sons were officers of the sanctuary (1 Chron. 26:29).

Chephar-ammoni [Che'phar-am'mo·ni], *village of the Ammonites*—A town of Benjamin (Josh. 18:24).

Chephar-haamonnai [Che'phar-ha·am'mo·nai]—See Chepharammoni.

Chephirah [Che·phi'rah], *village*—A city of the Gibeonites assigned to the Benjamites (Josh. 9:17; 18:26). After the captivity it was an inhabited city (Ezra 2:25; Neh. 7:29). Its site is identified with the ruin Kefireh about eight miles northwest of Jerusalem.

Cheran [Che'ran], *lyre*—A son of Dishon, a Horite (Gen. 36:26; 1 Chron. 1:41).

Cherethites [Cher'e·thites]—Tribesmen of Philistia, originally probably from Crete (1 Sam. 30:14; Ezek. 25:16; Zeph. 2:5–6). Some served in David's bodyguard (2 Sam. 8:18; 15:18; 1 Kings 1:38, 44). See Caphtor and Carites.

Cherith [Che'rith], *gorge*—The brook where Elijah concealed himself during the time of the drought (1 Kings 17:3, 5). It was "before Jordan," hence doubtless east of Jordan in Gilead.

Chesalon [Ches'a·lon], *trust*—This town was on the northern boundary of Judah (Josh. 15:10), about ten miles west of Jerusalem on Mount Jearim.

Chesed [Ches'ed], *increase*—A son of Nahor and Milcah (Gen. 22:22).

Chesil [Ches'il], *a fool*—A village in the southern section of Judah (Josh. 15:30).

Chesulloth [Che·sul'loth], *loins*—A town of Issachar on the boundary line (Josh. 19:18).

Cheth [Cheth]—See Hittites.

Chezib [Che'zib]—See Achzib.

Chidon [Chi'don], *javelin*—At this threshing floor Uzzah was smitten with death for placing his hand upon the ark to steady it (1 Chron. 13:9). It was near Jerusalem but the exact site is unknown. In 2 Samuel 6:6 it is called Nachon.

Chileab [Chi'le·ab], *like his father*—Son of David by Abigail, born at Hebron (2 Sam. 3:3). In 1 Chronicles 3:1 he is called Daniel.

Chilion [Chi'li·on], *pining*—The younger of the two sons of Elimelech and Naomi. He was the husband of Orpah and brother-in-law of Ruth. He died in Moab (Ruth 1:2, 5).

Chilmad [Chil'mad], *enclosure*—A place spoken of in connection with Sheba and Asshur (Ezek. 27:23).

Chimham [Chim'ham], *longing*—The son of Barzillai, the Gileadite. He was sent to Jerusalem in the place of his father (2 Sam. 19:37–38). He probably resided at Bethlehem where, at a later time, an inn was named for him.

Chinnereth, Chinneroth, Cinneroth [Chin'ne·reth, Chin'ne·roth, Cin'ne·roth], *lute* or *harp*—The name of a lake, a region, and a city in the Bible:

   1. The early name of the Sea of Galilee (Num. 34:11; Josh. 12:3; 13:27; Kinnereth, NIV). It was also called the "Lake of Gennesaret" (Luke 5:1) and the "Sea of Tiberias" (John 6:1; 21:1). The lake is shaped like the outline of a harp. Chinnereth was perhaps an ancient Canaanite name.

   2. A fortified city of Naphtali on the northwest shore of the Sea of Galilee (Deut. 3:17; Josh. 19:35).

   3. A region in or near the territory of Naphtali commonly identified with the plain of Gennesaret (1 Kings 15:20).

Chios [Chi'os], *snowy*—An island in the Greek Archipelago, north of Samos. It lies five miles from the mainland and claims to be the birthplace of Homer. It is named by Paul in his account of his voyage from Troas to Caesarea (Acts 20:15).

Chisleu [Chis'leu]—See Chislev.

Chislev [Chis'lev], possibly *hope* or *positiveness*—The third month of the civil and ninth of the sacred year, corresponding to a part of November and December (Neh. 1:1; Zech. 7:1).

Chislon [Chis'lon], *hope*—The father of Elidad (Num. 34:21).

Chisloth-tabor [Chis'loth-ta'bor], *flanks of Tabor*—A place near Mount Tabor on the boundary line of Zebulun (Josh. 19:12). It is probably the same as Chesuloth (Josh. 19:18).

Chithlish [Chith'lish], *unknown*—A village in the lowland of Judah (Josh. 15:40).

Chittim [Chit'tim], *brusiers*—Descendants of Javan, son of Japheth (Gen. 10:4; 1 Chron. 1:7). They inhabited Cyprus and other

Mediterranean islands and coasts. Balaam predicted that the Assyrians would be afflicted by ships that would proceed from Chittim (Num. 24:24). In Isaiah 23:1, 12 it is spoken of as the resort of the ships of Tyre. Cyprus (Chittim) was the first outport for Phoenician maritime trade. Chittim is frequently mentioned in the Scriptures (Jer. 2:10; Ezek. 27:6; Dan. 11:30).

Chiun [Chi'un], *an image* or *pillar*—Properly Kaiwan, the Babylonian name of the planet Saturn (Amos 5:26).

Chloe [Chlo'e], *green grass*—A Christian woman, possibly residing in Corinth (1 Cor. 1:11).

Chorashan [Chor·ash'an]—See Ashan.

Chorazin [Cho·ra'zin], *a furnace of smoke*—A town about one mile north of the Sea of Galilee, mentioned in connection with its denunciation by Jesus (Matt. 11:21; Luke 10:13).

Chozeba [Cho·ze'ba]—See Cozeba.

Christ [Christ], *anointed*—The Anointed One, the title of the One God promised to send to crush Satan's head (Gen. 3:15), and to restore Israel (Matt. 16:16, 20; Mark 8:29). The word "Christ" is the translation of the Hebrew word *Messiah*. The Messiah, or Anointed One, is so called in the New Testament only twice—once by the early disciples (John 1:41) and once by the woman of Samaria (John 4:25). We begin to feel the impact of the title "Christ" on the original audience if we sometimes substitute the word *Messiah* for "Christ" when we read passages with Jewish connotations. Saying "Jesus Christ" is the same as saying, "Yeshua of Nazareth is the Messiah," anointed by God to be the Savior of the world. See also Jesus and Messiah.

Christian [Chris'tian]—The word signifies a follower of Christ. In the original Greek and in precise translations, "Christian" occurs only three times. We do not often have an authoritative history of the origin of a word. However, in Acts 11:26, we have the inspired record of the people of Antioch coining the term *Christian*. Antiochians were witty, worldly, and rather wicked. There is no reason to believe that they were being complimentary when they used the term *Christian* to describe followers of Jesus. It was no doubt like *Quaker* or *Methodist*—a term of reproach became a badge of honor.

Before Antioch, the disciples were called *brethren* (1 Cor. 7:12), *disciples* (Acts 9:26; 11:29), or *believers* (Acts 5:14). The word "Christian" is also used in an evangelistic context, when Paul witnessed to the Jewish ruler Agrippa (Acts 26:28). Whether "almost persuaded" to be a Christian is a sincere remark (or as many think) a cynical one is not certain.

At any rate, *Christian* was by then becoming the standard word to describe those who follow Jesus as their Messiah. Third, suffering and Christianity were closely related in the early church and still are in many countries. Hence, Peter tells believers that there is no shame in suffering as a Christian, but it is a shame to suffer for wrongdoing (1 Peter 4:16).

Chub [Chub]—See Cub.

Chun [Chun]—See Berothah (1 Chron. 18:8).

Chushan-rishathaim [Chu'shan-rish·a·tha'im]—See Cushan-rishathaim.

Chuza [Chu'za], *the seer*—The steward of Herod Antipas. His wife, Joanna, rendered Jesus service (Luke 8:3).

Cilicia [Ci·lic'i·a], *the land of Celix*—A province in the southeast of Asia Minor, having on the west Pamphylia, Syria on the east, on the north Lycaonia and Cappadocia, and on the south the Mediterranean. Its chief town was Tarsus, the native city of St. Paul (Acts 21:39; 23:34). This province formed part of the kingdom of Syria. Paul labored in this province (Acts 9:30; Gal. 1:21).

Cinneroth [Cin'ne·roth]—See Chinnereth.

Cis [Cis]—See Kish.

Cities of the Plain—A term used for five cities located near the Dead Sea (Gen. 14:2, 8). Because of their great wickedness, four of these cities—Sodom, Gomorrah, Admah, and Zeboiim (Gen. 19:28–29)—were completely destroyed. Only Zoar escaped destruction (Gen. 19:21–22).

Prior to its destruction, this area was well watered and productive; it was compared to the garden of Eden and the rich Nile Delta of Egypt (Gen. 13:10). Today this area is totally barren and supports no life—an eloquent testimony of God's judgment upon the sin of these ancient peoples. Genesis 19 describes the complete destruction of the area; even today earthquakes are common.

Recent archaeological evidence locates the cities of the plain near the entrance to the Lisan, the tongue of land that juts out into the Dead Sea from its eastern shore.

City of Moab [Mo′ab]—See Ar.

City of Salt [Salt]—A city belonging to the territory of Judah (Josh. 15:62).

Clauda [Clau′da], *lame*—A small island southwest of Crete (Acts 27:16).

Claudia [Clau′di·a], *lame*—A Christian woman at Rome (2 Tim. 4:21).

Claudius [Clau′di·us], *lame*—Fourth roman emperor; A.D. 41–54, during which time there were many famines (Acts 11:28–30; 18:2); he was poisoned by his fourth wife, Nero's mother. See Caesar.

Claudius Lysias [Clau′di·us Lys′i·as], *lame* and *releaser*—A Roman officer in Jerusalem, the commander of a thousand men. He protected Paul from the Jewish mob and, when he learned of Paul's Roman citizenship, he unbound him and by night sent him under guard to Caesarea (Acts 22:24–23:35).

Clement [Clem′ent], *kind*—A Christian (Phil. 4:3).

Cleopas [Cle′o·pas], *of a renowned father*—To him and another disciple on their way to Emmaus Jesus appeared on the day of the resurrection (Luke 24:18).

Cleophas [Cle′o·phas]—See Clopas.

Clopas [Clo′pas]—The husband of Mary who stood at the foot of the cross with Mary the mother of Jesus and Mary Magdalene (John 19:25). This Mary is also described as the mother of James the Less (Matt. 10:3) and this James is called the son of Alphaeus (Mark 15:40), so it is supposed that Alphaeus and Clopus are the same person, or possibly that James's father had died and his mother remarried. See Alphaeus. This Clopas should not be confused with Cleopas (Luke 24:18).

Cnidus [Cni'dus]—A city of Caria on the southwest coast of Asia Minor. Paul passed it on his way to Rome (Acts 27:7).

Colhozeh [Col·ho'zeh], *all-seeing one*—The son of Hazaiah and father of Baruch (Neh. 11:5). He is perhaps the same as the father of Shallun who, under Nehemiah, repaired part of the wall of Jerusalem (Neh. 3:15).

Colosse [Co·los'se], *monstrosities*—A city in the Roman province of Asia (western Turkey), situated in the Lycus River Valley about 160 kilometers (100 miles) east of Ephesus. The apostle Paul wrote a letter to the church at Colosse (Col. 1:2; Colossae, NASB, REB, NRSV), though Paul's reference to the Colossian Christians as among those who "have not seen my face in the flesh" (Col. 2:10) seems to indicate that he never visited the church. The Christian community at Colosse apparently grew up under the leadership of Epaphras (Col. 1:7; 4:12) and Archippus (Col. 4:17; Philem. 2). Philemon and Onesimus lived at Colosse (Col. 4:9).

During the fifth century B.C., Colosse was an important trading center on the Lycus River. Under the Romans it remained a free city and was celebrated for its manufacture of wool. Colosse formed a triangle with two other cities of the Lycus Valley, Hierapolis and Laodicea, both of which are mentioned in the New Testament. As early as the fifth century B.C., Colosse was known as a prosperous city; but by the beginning of the Christian era it was eclipsed by its two neighbors. Thereafter its reputation declined to that of a small town.

Shortly after the apostle Paul sent his epistle to Colosse, the cities of the Lycus Valley suffered a devastating earthquake in A.D. 61. They were soon rebuilt, even Laodicea, which had suffered the greatest damage. Although Colosse was increasingly overshadowed by Laodicea and Hierapolis, it retained considerable importance into the second and third centuries A.D. Later, the population of Colosse moved to Chonai (modern Honaz), three miles to the south. The mound that marks the site of Colosse remains uninhabited today.

Conaniah [Con·na·ni'ah], *Jehovah hath sustained*—

1. A Levite in the time of Hezekiah who had charge of the offerings and tithes (2 Chron. 31:12–13).

2. A Levite in the reign of Josiah who held a prominent position and contributed generously to the offerings (2 Chron. 35:9).

Coniah [Co·ni′ah]—See Jehoiachin.

Cononiah [Co·no·ni′ah]—See Conaniah.

Consolation—The Consolation of Israel was a name for the coming Messiah (Luke 2:25).

Coos [Co′os]—(Acts 21:1). See Cos.

Corashan [Cor·a·shan]—See Ashan.

Core [Cor′e]—See Korah.

Corinth [Cor·inth], *satiated*—Ancient Greece's most important trade city (Acts 18:1; 19:1; 1 Cor. 1:2; 2 Cor. 1:1, 23; 2 Tim. 4:20). Ideally situated on the Isthmus of Corinth between the Ionian Sea and the Aegean Sea, Corinth was the connecting link between Rome, the capital of the world, and the east. In Paul's view, Corinth was an ideal city for a church. The constant movement of travelers, merchants, and pilgrims through the city would make it possible for the gospel to influence people from every part of the Roman world.

At Corinth the apostle Paul established a flourishing church, made up of a cross section of the worldly minded people who had flocked to Corinth to participate in the gambling, legalized temple prostitution, business adventures, and amusements available in a first-century navy town (1 Cor. 6:9–11).

Although the apostle Paul did not establish the church in Corinth until about A.D. 51 (Acts 18:1–18), the city's history dates back to prehistoric times, when ancient tribesmen first settled the site. Always a commercial and trade center, Corinth was already prosperous and famous for its bronze, pottery, and shipbuilding more than 800 years before Christ. The Greek poet Homer mentioned "wealthy Corinth" in 850 B.C. In the following centuries Corinth competed for power with Athens, its stronger neighbor across the strait to the north. And in 146 B.C. invading Roman armies destroyed Corinth, killing the men and enslaving the women and children. Only a token settlement remained until 44 B.C., when Julius Caesar ordered the city rebuilt. Not only did he restore it as the capital city of the Roman province of Achaia; he also repopulated it with freed Italians and slaves from every nation. Soon the merchants flocked back to Corinth too.

The city soon became a melting pot for the approximately 500,000 people who lived there at the time of Paul's arrival. Merchants and sailors, eager to work the docks, migrated to Corinth. Professional gamblers and athletes, betting on the Isthmian games, took up residence. Slaves, sometimes freed but with no place to go, roamed the streets day and night. And prostitutes (both male and female) were abundant. People from Rome, the rest of Greece, Egypt, Asia Minor—indeed, all of the Mediterranean world—relished the lack of standards and freedom of thought that prevailed in the city. These were the people who eventually made up the Corinthian church. They had to learn to live together in harmony, although their national, social, economic, and religious backgrounds were very different.

Perched on a narrow strip of land connecting the Peloponnesus, a peninsula of southern Greece, with central Greece and the rest of Europe, Corinth enjoyed a steady flow of trade. The city had two splendid harbor cities—Cenchreae, the eastern port on the Saronic Gulf; and Lechaeum, the western port on the Corinthian Gulf. In the outlying areas around Corinth, farmers tended their grain fields, vineyards, and olive groves. But the pulse of Corinth was the city itself, enclosed by walls 10 kilometers (6 miles) in circumference. Most of the daily business was conducted in the marble-paved agora, or marketplace, in the central part of the city. Although only 1 percent of the ancient city has been excavated by archaeologists, some interesting discoveries give ideas of what the city was like when Paul arrived. A marble lintel or crosspiece of a door was found near the residential section of Corinth. It bore part of the inscription "Synagogue of the Hebrews." This may have been on the same site of the earlier synagogue in which Paul first proclaimed the gospel message to Corinth, accompanied by his new-found Jewish friends, Aquila and Priscilla (Acts 18:2).

Not far from the synagogue excavation site was the magnificent judgment seat, covered with ornate blue and white marble. There, the Roman proconsul of Achaia, Gallio, dismissed Paul's case (Acts 18:12–17). In the pavement of an amphitheater is inscribed the name Erastus, perhaps the official of Corinth mentioned in Romans 16:23 and 2 Timothy 4:20.

South of the marketplace were the butcher stalls (shambles, KJV; meat market, NKJV, NASB, NIV, REB, NRSV) that Paul mentioned in 1 Corinthians 10:25. Corinthians purchased their meat from these stalls. The meat was often dedicated to pagan idols before being sold. This presented a cultural problem for the Christians in Corinth (1 Corinthians 8).

Today the temple of Apollo, partially in ruins, towers above the ancient marketplace. Each fluted Doric column, about 7 meters (almost 24 feet) tall, was cut from a single piece of stone in one of several quarries outside Corinth's walls. Rising 457 meters (1,500 feet) above the city itself and to the south is the Acrocorinth, the acropolis or citadel. From there, the acropolis at Athens, about 73 kilometers (45 miles) away, can be seen. Also, the infamous temple of Aphrodite (or Venus) was located on top of this fortified hill. This pagan temple and its 1,000 "religious" prostitutes poisoned the city's culture and morals. For this reason, the apostle Paul sometimes had to deal harshly with the converts in the Corinthian church. Most of the Corinthians had lived in this godless society all their lives, and the idea of tolerating even incest had not seemed so terrible to them (1 Cor. 5).

In spite of Corinth's notorious reputation, God used the apostle Paul to establish a vigorous church in the city about A.D. 51 (Acts 18:1–18). Later, Paul wrote at least two letters to the church at Corinth. Both deal with divisions in the church, as well as immorality and the abuse of Christian freedom.

The Corinth that Paul knew was partially destroyed by an earthquake in A.D. 521, then totally devastated by another in 1858. Modern Corinth, rebuilt about 4 kilometers (2.5 miles) from the ancient site, is little more than a town. It is certainly not a thriving trade center, but the inhabitants only need to look at the ancient ruins to recall the former glory of their city. The success of the gospel at Corinth—bittersweet though it was—illustrates that the grace of God comes not so much to the noble as to the needy (1 Cor. 1:26–31).

Cornelius [Cor·ne′li·us]—A Roman soldier stationed in Caesarea who was the first recorded Gentile convert to Christianity (Acts 10:1–33).

Cornelius was a God-fearing man strongly attracted to the Jewish teaching of monotheism (the belief in one God), as opposed to pagan idolatry and immorality, and to the concern expressed in the law of

Moses concerning helping the poor and needy (Acts 10:2). He is introduced in the book of Acts as a representative of thousands in the Gentile world who were weary of paganism and who were hungry for the
coming of the Messiah—the Christ who would deliver them from their
sins and lead them into an abundant, Spirit-filled life.

God sent a heavenly vision both to Cornelius and to Simon Peter.
Obeying his vision, Cornelius sent some of his men to Joppa, about 58
kilometers (36 miles) south of Caesarea, to find Peter. Peter, in turn,
obeyed his own vision (which he interpreted to mean that Gentiles were
to be included in Christ's message) and went to Cornelius. While Peter
was still preaching to Cornelius and his household, "the Holy Spirit
fell upon all those who heard the word" (Acts 10:44). And Peter commanded them to be baptized in the name of the Lord.

This incident marked the expansion of the early church to include
Gentiles as well as Jews (Acts 10:34–35; 11:18). Peter alluded to Cornelius's conversion at the Jerusalem Council (Acts 15:7–11).

Cos [Cos], unknown—An island between Miletus and Rhodes (Acts
21:1).

Cosam [Co'sam], *divining*—The son of Elmodam, a descendant of
David through Nathan and ancestor of Zerubbabel and Christ (Luke
3:28).

Court of the Gentiles—The outermost court of Herod's temple.
Gentiles were allowed to enter this court, but could penetrate no further into the temple (Matt. 27:51; Eph. 2:14).

Coz [Coz]—See Hakkoz.

Cozbi [Coz'bi], *false*—A Midianitess slain by Phinehas (Num. 25:6–
8, 14–18).

Cozeba, Chozeba [Co·ze'ba, Cho·ze'ba]—A village of Judah
(1 Chron. 4:22), often identified with Chezib.

Crescens [Cres'cens], *increasing*—A companion of Paul mentioned in 2 Timothy 4:10. He had apparently been with Paul while he
was in prison, and then for reasons which are not stated he left Paul and
went into Galatia.

Cretans [Cre′tans]—Inhabitants of the island of Crete, located in the Mediterranean Sea (Acts 2:11; Titus 1:5, 12).

Crete [Crete], *fleshy*—A large island in the Mediterranean between Syria and Malta, also known as Candia. It is about 160 miles long and 35 miles broad at its widest point. In 66 B.C. it was captured by the Romans and Jews settled there (Acts 2:11). Christianity was established there at an early date by those Cretans who were in Jerusalem at Pentecost. Titus was placed there by Paul (Titus 1:5, 10, 14).

Cretes [Cretes]—See Cretans (Acts 2:11).

Crispus [Cris′pus], *curled*—Ruler of the Jewish synagogue at Corinth. He and his household were brought to faith in Christ through the preaching of Paul (Acts 18:8; 1 Cor. 1:14).

Cub [Cub], unknown—A nation allied with Egypt (Ezek. 30:5).

Cun [Cun]—See Berothah.

Cush [Cush], *black*—The name of two men and two lands in the Old Testament:

1. A land that bordered the Gihon River, one of the four rivers of the garden of Eden (Gen. 2:10–14). Since the Tigris (Hiddekel) and Euphrates are mentioned, this land must have been in or near Mesopotamia. It was named after No. 2.

2. A son of Ham and grandson of Noah. His brothers settled in Egypt and Canaan, and his famous son Nimrod lived in Mesopotamia (Gen. 10:6–12; 1 Chron. 1:8–10; also Mic. 5:6).

3. A man from the tribe of Benjamin who was an enemy of David (see the title of Psalm 7).

4. The land south of Egypt, also called Nubia, which includes part of Sudan. Cush began just beyond Syene (modern Aswan; Ezek. 29:10). The Persian Empire of Ahasuerus (Xerxes, 486–465 B.C.) extended to this point, "from India to Ethiopia" (Est. 1:1; 8:9). Precious stones came from Cush, "the topaz of Ethiopia" (Job 28:19), and the people were tall with smooth skin (Isa. 18:2, 7) that could not be changed (Jer. 13:23). The prophets predicted that the distant land of Cush would be judged by God (Isa. 18:1–6; Zeph. 2:12). Other texts indicate, however, that some from Cush will bring gifts to God and worship Him as their king

(Ps. 68:31; Isa. 11:11; 18:7). Its ancient Greek name was Ethiopia, not to be confused with the modern nation of Ethiopia (Abyssinia).

Cushan-rishathaim, Chushan-rishathaim [Cu'shan-rish·a·-tha'im, Chu'shan-rish·a·tha'im], *twice-wicked Cushan*—A king of Mesopotamia who oppressed the Israelites (Judg. 3:5–11).

Cushi [Cu'shi], *an Ethiopian*—Three Old Testament men:
  1. Father of Zephaniah (Zeph. 1:1).
  2. One of the men who informed David of the defeat of his son, Absalom (2 Sam. 18:21–23, 31–32).
  3. An ancestor of Jehudi (Jer. 36:14).

Cushite [Cush'ite]—A descendant of Cush.

Cuth, Cuthah [Cuth, Cu'thah], *crushing*—One of the cities (probably northeast of Babylon) from which Shalmanezer brought colonists to Samaria (2 Kings 17:24, 30).

Cuza [Cuza]—See Chuza.

Cyprus [Cy'prus]—An island of the Mediterranean about forty miles from the coast of Cilicia, having about 3,584 square miles. It is first mentioned in the New Testament as the native place of Barnabas (Acts 4:36). During the persecution, following the martyrdom of Stephen, Christians went to Cyprus, though it appears that the gospel had already been carried to the island. Paul and Barnabas, on the first missionary journey, visited it (Acts 13:4) and afterward it was visited by Barnabas and Mark (Acts 15:39).

Cyrene [Cy·re'ne], *supremacy of the bridle*—A city of Libya in northern Africa, in the district now known as Tripoli. Simon, who was forced to carry the cross of Jesus, was a native of Cyrene (Matt. 27:32; Mark 15:21; Luke 23:26). Cyrenians had a synagogue in Jerusalem (Acts 6:9). Lucius, prominent member of the church at Antioch, was a Cyrenian (Acts 13:1).

Cyrenian [Cy·re'ni·an]—A native of Cyrene (Mark 15:21; Luke 23:26; Acts 6:9).

Cyrenius [Cy·re'ni·us]—See Quirinius.

Cyrus [Cy'rus], *posses thou the furnace*—The founder of the Persian Empire. Isaiah names him as the divine instrument for the release of the Jews from the Babylonian exile (Isa. 44:28; 45:1–14). In 536 B.C., a few years after the fall of Babylon, Cyrus issued a proclamation which permitted the Jews to return to their own land. He restored the sacred vessels of the temple which had been carried to Babylon by Nebuchadnezzar (Ezra 1:1–11; 5:13–14; 6:3).

D

Dabareh [Dab′a·reh]—See Daberath.

Dabbasheth [Dab′ba·sheth], *hump of a camel*—A town of Zebulun (Josh. 19:11).

Dabbesheth [Dab′be·sheth]—See Dabbasheth.

Daberath [Dab′e·rath], *pasture*—A town of the Levites in Issachar, probably just to the northwest of Mount Tabor (Josh. 19:12; 21:28; 1 Chron. 6:72), also called Dabareh.

Dagon [Da′gon], *a fish*—The national god of the Philistines. Its head, arms, and body had the appearance of a human form, while the lower portion was like the tail of a fish (1 Sam. 5:3–4).

Dalaiah [Da·lai′ah]—See Delaiah.

Dale, The King′s—The valley of Shaveh or King′s Vale near Jerusalem. Here Absalom built a monument, often erroneously called the tomb of Absalom (Gen. 14:17; 2 Sam. 18:18). See Absalom′s Pillar.

Dalmanutha [Dal·ma·nu′tha], *slow firebrand*—A town near the Sea of Galilee, apparently near Magdala (Matt. 15:39; Mark 8:10).

Dalmatia [Dal·ma′tia], *a priestly robe*—The province of Illyricum on the eastern shore of the Adriatic Sea or, as sometimes regarded, its southern half. The province was formed after the tribes were conquered by Augustus Caesar and Tiberius in A.D. 9. In this neighborhood Paul preached (Rom. 15:19) and to this district he sent Titus (2 Tim. 4:10).

Dalphon [Dal′phon], *dripping*—One of the ten sons of Haman slain by the Jews (Est. 9:7).

Damaris [Dam′a·ris], *a heifer*—A woman at Athens who heard Paul preach and was converted to Christianity (Acts 17:34).

Damascene [Dam'as·cene]—An inhabitant of Damascus (2 Cor. 11:32).

Damascus [Da·mas′cus], *silent is the sackcloth weaver*—The oldest continually inhabited city in the world and capital of Syria (Isa. 7:8), located northeast of the Sea of Galilee.

Damascus was situated on the border of the desert at the intersection of some of the most important highways in the ancient Near Eastern world. Three major caravan routes passed through Damascus. Major roads extended from the city to the southwest into Canaan and Egypt, straight south to Edom and the Red Sea, and east to Babylonia. Because of its ideal location, the city became a trade center. Its major exports (Ezek. 27:18) included a patterned cloth called "damask." Egypt, Arabia, and Mesopotamia, as well as Canaan, were some of the trade neighbors that made Damascus the "heart of Syria."

Damascus owed its prosperity to two rivers, the Abana and the Pharpar (2 Kings 5:12). These rivers provided an abundant source of water for agriculture. The Syrian people were so proud of these streams that Naaman the Syrian leper almost passed up his opportunity to be healed when the prophet Elisha asked him to dip himself in the waters of the Jordan River in Israel. He thought of the Jordan as an inferior stream in comparison with these majestic rivers in his homeland (2 Kings 5:9–14).

The Bible first mentions the city as the hometown of Eliezer, Abraham's faithful servant. Early Egyptian texts refer to Egypt's control over Damascus, but this influence did not last long. By the time of David's reign, Syria (Aram) was a powerful state with Damascus as its capital. David defeated the Syrians and stationed his own troops in Damascus (2 Sam. 8:5–6; 1 Chron. 18:5–6). During Solomon's reign, however, God allowed Rezon (1 Kings 11:23–25), Solomon's enemy, to take Syria from Israel's control because of Solomon's sins. Rezon founded a powerful dynasty based in Damascus that lasted more than 200 years.

Shortly after Solomon's death, the king of Damascus formed a powerful league with other Aramean states. This alliance resulted in many years of conflict between Israel and Damascus. First, Ben-hadad I of Damascus defeated King Baasha of Israel (1 Kings 15:16–20; 2 Chron. 16:1–4). Later, God miraculously delivered King Ahab of Israel and his small army from the superior Syrian forces (1 Kings 20:1–30).

Even after this miraculous deliverance, Ahab made a covenant with Ben-hadad II against God's will (1 Kings 20:31–43). Ahab was killed a few years later in a battle with Syria (1 Kings 22:29–38).

In the midst of these wars, the prophet Elijah was instructed by God to anoint Hazael as the new king of Damascus (1 Kings 19:15). King Joram of Israel successfully opposed Hazael for a time (2 Kings 13:4–5), but the situation was eventually reversed. Hazael severely oppressed both Israel and Judah during later years (2 Kings 13:3, 22).

Much later, God sent Rezin, king of Syria, and Pekah, king of Israel, against wicked King Ahaz of Judah (2 Kings 16:1–6). Ahaz called on the Assyrians, who had become a powerful military force, for help (2 Kings 16:7). The Assyrian king Tiglath-pileser responded by conquering Syria, overthrowing the Aramean dynasty, killing Rezin, and destroying Damascus (732 B.C.), just as the prophets Amos and Isaiah had prophesied (Isa. 17:1; Amos 1:4–5). This marked the end of Syria as an independent nation. The city of Damascus was also reduced to a fraction of its former glory.

The exact date of the reconstruction of Damascus is unknown, but such an excellent location could not long remain weak and insignificant. Damascus was the residence of Assyrian and Persian governors for five centuries after its conquest by Tiglath-pileser. Still later, the city was conquered by Alexander the Great, who made it a provincial capital. In 64 B.C. the Romans invaded Syria, making it a province with Damascus as the seat of government.

All references to Damascus in the New Testament are associated with the apostle Paul's conversion and ministry. During this time, the city was part of the kingdom of Aretas (2 Cor. 11:32), an Arabian prince who held his kingdom under the Romans. The New Testament reports that Paul was converted while traveling to Damascus to persecute early Christians who lived in the city (Acts 9:1–8). After his dramatic conversion, Paul went to the house of Judas on "Straight Street," where God sent Ananias, a Christian who lived in Damascus, to heal Paul of his blindness (Acts 9:10–22).

Paul then preached boldly in the Jewish synagogues in Damascus, but eventually he was forced to flee the city because of the wrath of those to whom he preached. The governor of Damascus tried to capture Paul, but the apostle escaped in a large basket through an opening in the city wall (Acts 9:25; 2 Cor. 11:32–33).

Dan [Dan], *a judge*—The name of a man, a people group, and a city in Israel named after him:

1. The fifth son of Jacob and the first born to Rachel's handmaid Bilhah (Gen. 30:1–6). Dan had one son—Hushim (Gen. 46:23), or Shuham (Num. 26:42). Jacob's blessing of Dan predicted:

"Dan shall judge his people as one of the tribes of Israel. Dan shall be a serpent by the way / A viper by the path / That bites the horse's heels / So that its rider shall fall backward" (Gen. 49:16–17). Nothing else is known of Dan himself.

2. The tribe which descended from the above. In the wilderness census the number of Danites was 62,700; second in size to the tribe of Judah. Its territory was in Palestine between Ephraim on the north and east and Judah on the south. Among its towns were Zorah, Ajalon, and Ekron (Josh. 19:40–43; 21:5, 23). Samson was a Danite (Judg. 13:2, 24).

3. A city in the northern territory of the tribe of Dan, identified as the modern ruin or archaeological site known as Tell el-Qadi. This city was located farther north than any other village in Israel during much of the Old Testament period. This explains the phrase "from Dan to Beersheba" (Judg. 20:1), used to describe the entire territory of the Israelites from north to south.

Archaeologists excavating at Dan have uncovered remains that include an intact Middle Bronze Age mud-brick, triple-arch gateway as well as pagan altars dated to the period of Israel's divided monarchy (1 Kings 12:28–30).

Daniel [Dan'iel], *God is my judge*—The name of three or four men in the Bible:

1. A son of David and Abigail (1 Chron. 3:1). He is also called Chileab (2 Sam. 3:3).

2. A priest of the family of Ithamar who returned with Ezra from the captivity (Ezra 8:2). Daniel sealed the covenant in the days of Nehemiah (Neh. 10:6).

3. A wise (Ezek. 28:3) and righteous man (perhaps non-Israelite), mentioned together with Noah and Job (Ezek. 14:14, 20), to be identified with an ancient Canaanite named Daniel. Could be the same Daniel as No. 4.

4. A prophet during the period of the captivity of God's covenant people in Babylon and Persia (Dan. 1:6–12:9; Matt. 24:15). Daniel also wrote the book in the Old Testament that bears his name.

Daniel was a teenager when he was taken from Jerusalem into captivity by the Babylonians in 605 B.C. He was in his 80s when he received the vision of the prophecy of the 70 weeks (Daniel 9). In more than 60 years of his life in Babylon, Daniel faced many challenges. But in all those years, he grew stronger in his commitment to God.

We know very little about Daniel's personal life. His family history is not mentioned, but he was probably from an upper-class family in Jerusalem. It seems unlikely that Nebuchadnezzar, the king of Babylon, would have selected a trainee for his court from the lower classes. Neither do we know whether Daniel married or had a family. As a servant in Nebuchadnezzar's court, he may have been castrated and made into a eunuch, as was common in those days. But the text does not specify that this happened. It does indicate that Daniel was a person of extraordinary abilities.

We tend to think of Daniel as a prophet because of the prophetic dimension of his book. But he also served as an advisor in the courts of foreign kings. Daniel remained in governmental service through the reigns of the kings of Babylon and into the reign of Cyrus of Persia after the Persians became the dominant world power (Dan. 1:21; 10:1).

Daniel was also a person of deep piety. His book is characterized not only by prophecies of the distant future but also by a sense of wonder at the presence of God. From his youth Daniel was determined to live by God's law in a distant land (chap. 1). In moments of crisis, Daniel turned first to God in prayer before turning to the affairs of state (2:14–23). His enemies even used his regularity at prayer to trap him and turn the king against him. But the grace of God protected Daniel (chap. 6).

After one of his stunning prophecies (chap. 9), Daniel prayed a noble prayer of confession for his own sins and the sins of his people. This prayer was based on Daniel's study of the book of Jeremiah (Dan. 9:2). He was a man of true devotion to God.

So the book of Daniel is more than a treasure of prophetic literature. It also paints a beautiful picture of a man of God who lived out his commitment in very troubled times. We should never get so caught up in the meanings of horns and beasts that we forget the human dimension of the book—the intriguing person whose name means "God Is My Judge."

Danite [Dan′ite]—A descendant of Dan or a member of his tribe (Judg. 13:2; 18:1, 11; 1 Chron. 12:35).

Dan-jaan [Dan-ja′an], *purposeful judgment*—A place to which Joab and his officers came when taking the census (2 Sam. 24:6).

Dannah [Dan′nah]—A town in the hill country of Judah (Josh. 15:49), a few miles southwest of Hebron.

Dara [Dar′a]—See Darda.

Darda [Dar′da], *pearl of wisdom*—One who was noted for wisdom, a son of Mahol of the tribe of Judah (1 Kings 4:31; 1 Chron. 2:6).

Darius [Da·ri′us], *lord*—The name of several kings of Media and Persia.

1. *Darius the Mede*, son of Ahasuerus (Dan. 5:31; 6:1; 9:1; 11:1). When Babylon was taken by the army of Cyrus in 538 B.C., he is said to have been made king over Chaldea.

2. *Darius Hystapsis*, called *the Great*. When the rebuilding of the temple at Jerusalem was interrupted by foes of the Jews, Darius had a search instituted for an edict previously issued by Cyrus which permitted the work (Ezra 6:1–12). He extended his kingdom from India to the Grecian archipelago. He was defeated at Marathon in 490 B.C. and died in 484 B.C.

3. *Darius the Persian* (Neh. 12:22), probably Darius Codomannus, king of Persia (336–330 B.C.).

Darkon [Dar′kon], *scatterer*—The founder of a family, descendants of whom returned from Babylon under Zerubbabel (Ezra 2:56; Neh. 7:58).

Dathan [Da′than], *belonging to a fountain*—A Reubenite, the son of Eliab. He and his brother, Abiram, were leaders in the rebellion of Korah (Num. 16:1–35; 26:9; Ps. 106:17).

David [Da′vid], *beloved*—Second king of the united kingdom of Israel, ancestor of Jesus Christ, and writer of numerous psalms. The record of David's life is found in 1 Samuel 16–31; 2 Samuel 1–24; 1 Kings

1–2; and 1 Chronicles 10–29. An Aramaic inscription including the words "house [dynasty] of David" was found in 1993 in the ruins of the city of Dan. It dates to the ninth century B.C. and is the only known mention of David in ancient contemporary writings outside of the Old Testament itself.

David as a Youth: David's youth was spent in Bethlehem. The youngest of eight brothers (1 Sam. 16:10–11; 17:12–14), he was the son of Jesse, a respected citizen of the city. His mother was tenderly remembered for her godliness (Ps. 86:16). As the youngest son, David was the keeper of his father's sheep. In this job he showed courage and faithfulness by killing both a lion and a bear that attacked the flock.

As a lad, he displayed outstanding musical talent with the harp, a fact that figured prominently in his life. When Saul was rejected by God as king, the prophet Samuel went to Bethlehem to anoint David as the future king of Israel. Apparently, there was no public announcement of this event, although David and his father surely must have been aware of it.

David's Service under Saul: King Saul, forsaken by God and troubled by an evil spirit, was subject to moods of depression and insanity. His attendants advised him to secure a harpist, whose music might soothe his spirit. David was recommended for this task. As harpist for Saul, David was exposed to governmental affairs, a situation that prepared him for his later service as king of Israel. Apparently, David did not remain with Saul all the time, since the Bible indicates he returned to Bethlehem to continue caring for his father's sheep.

During one of these visits to his home, the Philistines invaded the country and camped 24 kilometers (15 miles) west of Bethlehem. Saul led the army of Israel to meet the enemy. Three of David's brothers were in Saul's army, and Jesse sent David to the battle area to inquire about their welfare. While on this expedition, David encountered the Philistine giant Goliath.

David as Warrior: Goliath's challenge for an Israelite to do battle with him stirred David's spirit. Weighted with heavy armor, Goliath was equipped to engage in close-range combat. David's strategy was to fight him at a distance. Taking five smooth stones from a brook, David faced Goliath with only a sling and his unflinching faith in God. Goliath fell, struck by a stone from David's sling. For this feat, he became a hero in the eyes of the nation. But it aroused jealousy and animosity in the heart of Saul. Saul's son Jonathan, however, admired David because of his bravery, and they soon became good friends. This friendship lasted until Jonathan's death, in spite of Saul's hostility toward David.

Saul had promised to make the victor in the battle with Goliath his son-in-law, presenting one of his daughters as his wife. He also promised to free the victor's family from taxation. But after the battle, David was no longer allowed to return occasionally to his father's house. He remained at Saul's palace continually. Perhaps Saul realized that Samuel's prediction that the kingdom would be taken from him could reach fulfillment in David. On two occasions, he tried to kill David with a spear; he also gave his daughter, whom he had promised as David's wife, to another man. As David's popularity grew, Saul's fear increased until he could no longer hide his desire to kill him. David was forced to flee with Saul in pursuit.

David as Fugitive Hero: David gathered a handful of fugitives as his followers and fled from Saul. On at least two occasions, David could have killed Saul while the king slept, but he refused to do so. Perhaps David hesitated to kill Saul because he realized that he would be king one day, and he wanted the office to be treated with respect. If he had killed Saul, David also would have entered the office of king through his own personal violence. Perhaps this was a situation he wanted to avoid.

While on the run he took refuge in the cave of Adullam (1 Sam. 22:1) and, gathering a band of six hundred men, defeated the Philistines at Keilah (1 Sam. 23:1–5). King Achish also permitted him to occupy Ziklag for which kindness he protected the Philistines against the raids of desert tribes (1 Sam. 27).

When the Philistines battled Saul and his army at Gilboa, they were victorious, killing Saul and his son Jonathan, whom David loved as a dear friend. When David heard this news, he mourned their fate (2 Sam. 1).

David as King of Judah: At Saul's death the tribe of Judah, to whom David belonged, elected him as king of Judah and placed him on the throne in Hebron. The rest of the tribes of Israel set up Ish-bosheth, Saul's son, as king at Mahanaim. For the next two years civil war raged between these two factions. It ended in the assassination of Ish-bosheth, an event that saddened David.

David as King of All Israel: On the death of Ish-bosheth, David was elected king over all the people of Israel. He immediately began work to establish a united kingdom. One of his first acts as king was to attack the fortified city of Jebus. Although the inhabitants thought it was safe from capture, David and his army took it. He then made it the capital city of his kingdom and erected his palace there. Also known as Jerusalem, the new capital stood on the border of the southern tribe of Judah and the other tribal territories to the north. This location tended to calm the jealousies between the north and the south, contributing greatly to the unity of the kingdom.

After establishing his new political capital, David proceeded to reestablish and strengthen the worship of God. He moved the ark of the covenant from Kirjath-jearim (Josh. 15:9) and placed it within a tabernacle that he pitched in Jerusalem. Next, he organized worship on a magnificent scale and began plans to build a house of worship. But God brought a halt to his plans, informing David that the building of the temple would be entrusted to his successor.

Although David was a righteous king, he was subject to sin, just like other human beings. On one occasion when his army went to battle, David stayed home. This led to his great sin with Bathsheba. While Uriah the Hittite, Bathsheba's husband, was away in battle, David committed adultery with her. Then in an effort to cover his sin, he finally had Uriah killed in battle. David was confronted by the prophet Nathan, who courageously exposed his wrongdoing. Faced with his sin, David repented and asked for God's forgiveness. His prayer for forgiveness is recorded in Psalm 51.

Although God forgave David of this act of adultery, the consequences of the sin continued to plague him. The child born to David and Bathsheba died. The example he set as a father was a bad influence on his sons. One son, Amnon, raped and humiliated his half sister. Another son, Absalom, rebelled against David and tried to take away his kingdom by force.

One of David's deep desires was to build a temple in Jerusalem. But he was prevented from doing so. The prophet Nathan informed David that he would not build the temple because he had been a warrior. David did not build the temple, but he did gather material for the temple to be built later. It was Solomon, David's son and successor, who finally erected the first temple in Jerusalem. David died when he was 71 years old, having been king for a total of over 40 years, including both his reign in Hebron and his kingship over the united kingdom.

David, City of [Da'vid]—The name of two cities in the Bible:

1. The stronghold of Zion, the fortified city of the Jebusites, later known as Jerusalem. King David and his men captured it (2 Sam. 5:7, 9). The Jebusite fortress of Zion was situated on a hill overlooking the Pool of Siloam, at the junction of the Kidron and Tyropoeon valleys (later in southeastern Jerusalem). The account of the capture of Zion implies that David's army entered the fortress by surprise (2 Sam. 5:8). The "water shaft" mentioned in this passage was apparently a tunnel leading from the underground spring of Gihon into the citadel. Joab was the one who went up the shaft first (1 Chron. 11:6); true to his promise, David made him the commander, or "chief," of the armies of Israel.

After the capture of Zion, "David dwelt in the stronghold, and called it the City of David" (2 Sam. 5:9). Not only did David establish his residence here, but he also strengthened the city's fortifications (1 Chron. 11:8). Solomon further strengthened the defenses of the city (1 Kings 11:27). The site of Solomon's temple was on the neighboring Mount Moriah, part of the same strong rock outcropping as Mount Zion.

2. Bethlehem, the birthplace or home of David (1 Sam. 16:1, 13; Luke 2:4, 11; John 7:42) and of Jesus, David's greatest descendant.

David, Tower of [Da'vid]—A fortified tower built by David for an armory or arsenal (Song 4:4, Neh. 3:19).

Daystar—See Lucifer.

Dead Sea—The Dead Sea is a lake about 50 miles long and 10 miles wide in southern Palestine. The Jordan River and other smaller streams flow into it, but because it lies at the lowest point on the earth (about 1,300 feet below the Mediterranean), no water flows out of it. The deepest point of the sea is another 1,300 feet lower yet. Because of its rapid water loss through evaporation, salts and other minerals have become highly concentrated and its saltiness is about four times that of the ocean. This has made the lake unfit for marine life; thus its name "the Dead Sea."

In Abraham's time five cities (see Cities of the Plain) were situated at the south end of the Dead Sea (Gen. 14:2, 8). Because of their great wickedness, four of these cities—Sodom, Gomorrah, Admah, and Zebolim—were destroyed by earthquakes and fire (Gen. 19:28–29; Deut. 29:23). Many scholars believe the remains of these cities were covered in later years by the Dead Sea as the waters shifted when other earthquakes struck the area.

In addition to the destruction of Sodom and Gomorrah, many other biblical events occurred along the shores of the Dead Sea. The springs of En Gedi provided a refuge for David in his flight from King Saul (1 Sam. 24:1). In the Valley of Salt south of the Dead Sea, David was victorious over the Edomites (2 Sam. 8:13; 1 Chron. 18:12–13). The Dead Sea is also famous because of the discovery of ancient biblical manuscripts in the caves on its northwest coast. Known as the Dead Sea Scrolls, these manuscripts include a complete copy of the book of Isaiah and portions of several other books of the Bible, as well as many nonbiblical manuscripts. They are dated to the period between 250 B.C. and A.D. 135.

These manuscripts, some of the earliest copies of biblical texts yet discovered, helped scholars establish dates for several important biblical events and gave helpful information on the development of the Hebrew language. Other names for the Dead Sea used in the Bible are the Salt Sea (Josh. 3:16), the Sea of Arabah (Deut. 3:17), and the eastern sea (Joel 2:20).

Debir [De'bir], *sanctuary*—

1. A king of Eglon who was conquered and slain by Joshua (Josh. 10:3, 27).

2. A city in the hill country of Judah, also known as Kirjath-sepher and Kirjath-sannah (Josh. 15:15, 49; Judg. 1:11). Joshua took it from the Anakim (Josh. 10:38–39; 11:21; 12:13). Caleb offered Achsah, his daughter, to the man who would capture the city. Othniel, Caleb's younger brother, did so and won his niece as his wife (Judg. 1:13; 3:9).

3. Town in Gad, probably the same as Lodebar (Josh. 13:26; 2 Sam. 17:27).

4. A place in Judah between Jerusalem and Jericho (Joel 15:7).

Deborah [Deb'o·ra], *bee*—The name of two women in the Old Testament:

1. A nurse to Rebekah, Isaac's wife (Gen. 24:59; 35:8). Deborah accompanied Rebekah when she left her home in Mesopotamia to become Isaac's wife and lived with Isaac and Rebekah. She probably spent her years caring for their sons, Jacob and Esau. Deborah died at an advanced age. She was buried below Beth-el under a tree that Jacob called Allon-bachuth (literally "oak of weeping")—a fitting name for the burial place of one who had served so long and so faithfully (Gen. 35:8).

2. The fifth judge of Israel, a prophetess and the only female judge (Judg. 4–5). The Bible tells us nothing about her family except that she was the wife of Lapidoth. Deborah's home was in the hill country of Ephraim between Beth-el and Ramah. The palm tree under which she sat and judged Israel was a landmark; it became known as "the palm tree of Deborah" (Judg. 4:5).

Deborah summoned Barak (Judg. 4; 5:1; Heb. 11:32) and told him it was God's will that he lead her forces against the mighty warrior Sisera. Sisera was the commander of the army of Jabin, king of Canaan, who had terrorized Israel for 20 years. Barak accepted on one condition: Deborah must accompany him. Deborah and Barak's army consisted of only 10,000, while Sisera had a multitude of fighters and 900 chariots of iron.

God was on Israel's side, however. When the battle ended, not a single man of Sisera's army survived, except Sisera himself, who fled on foot. When Sisera took refuge in the tent of Heber the Kenite, Jael (the wife of Heber) drove a tent peg through his temple (Judg. 4:21), killing him.

The "Song of Deborah" (Judg. 5) is one of the finest and earliest examples of Hebrew poetry.

Decapolis [De·cap'o·lis], *ten cities*—district, containing ten cities, located southeast of Galilee (Matt. 4:25; Mark 5:20; 7:31). These were built by the followers of Alexander the Great and consisted of Scythop-olis, Damascus, Hippos, Philadelphia, Gadara, Pella, Dion, Gerasa, Kanatha, Raphana.

Decision, Valley of [De·cis'ion]—See Jehoshaphat, Valley of.

Dedan [De'dan], *low country*—
   1. A son of Raamah, the son of Cush (Gen. 10:7).
   2. Son of Jokshan, the son of Abraham and Keturah (Gen. 25:3).
   3. A territory on the southern border of Edom.

Dedanim [De'da·nim]—See Dedanites.

Dedanites [De'dan·ites]—A nomadic Arabian tribe (Isa. 21:13) descended from Abraham and Keturah through Jokshan (Gen. 25:1, 3). They are described as merchants (Ezek. 25:13; 27:15).

Dedication, Feast of [Ded'i·ca'tion], *Chanukah* or *the Feast of Lights*—This festival was instituted in 165 B.C. by Judas Maccabaeus to commemorate the purification of the temple and the restoration of worship after the desecration of the temple by Antiochus Epiphanes. It was somewhat of the nature of the Feast of Tabernacles and continued for eight days. Jesus was present at one of these feasts and spoke to the people (John 10:22).

Dehaites, Dehavites [De·ha'ites, De·ha'vites], *the sickly*—After the fall of the Northern Kingdom (722 B.C.) these and other peoples were brought from the east by the Assyrians to resettle Samaria (Ezra 4:9).

Deker, Dekar [De'ker, De'kar], *piercing*—The father of Ben-deker, Solomon's purveyor (1 Kings 4:9).

Delaiah, Dalaiah [Del·ai'ah, Dal·ai'ah], *delivered by Jehovah*—
    1. A descendant of Aaron and ancestral head of a course of priests (1 Chron. 24:18).
    2. One who advised King Jehoiakim not to destroy the roll prepared by Jeremiah (Jer. 36:12, 25).
    3. Ancestor of a family of servants (Ezra 2:60; Neh. 7:62).
    4. A son of Elioenai (1 Chron. 3:24).

Delilah [De·li'lah], *languishing* or *lustful*—The woman loved by Samson, the mightiest of Israel's judges. She was probably a Philistine. She betrayed Samson to the lords of the Philistines for 1,100 pieces of silver (Judg. 16:5). Deluding Samson into believing she loved him, Delilah persuaded him to tell her the secret of his strength—his long hair, which was the symbol of his Nazirite vow. While Samson slept at her home in the valley of Sorek, the Philistines entered and cut his hair. With his strength gone, Samson was easily captured and imprisoned, then blinded.

    No biblical evidence supports the popular belief that Delilah was deeply repentant over her actions. She even may have been one of the

3,000 Philistines buried beneath the temple of Dagon Samson destroyed when his God-given strength returned (Judg. 16:27–30).

Demas [De'mas], *governor of the people*—A fellow-laborer of Paul (Col. 4:14; Philem. 24). Unwilling to endure privation, he deserted Paul and went to Thessalonica (2 Tim. 4:10).

Demetrius [De·me'tri·us], *belonging to Ceres*—
   1. A silversmith at Ephesus whose business of making silver shrines of the goddess Diana was threatened by Paul's teachings. Demetrius stirred up a riot, whereupon Paul left Ephesus (Acts 19:24–41).
   2. A Christian whom John commends (3 John 12).

Derbe [Der'be], *tanner* or *tanner of skin* or *coverer with skin*—A small town about 35 miles southeast of Lystra in Lycaonia in Asia Minor. After being stoned at Lystra, the home of Timothy, Paul went to Derbe. This was on the first missionary journey (Acts 14:6, 20). He passed through it again on the second journey.

Desire of all Nations—A title of the Messiah (Hag. 2:7; Mal. 3:1).

Destroyer—God's agent for destroying sinners. By placing the blood of the Passover lamb on their doors, the Israelites could be passed over by the destroyer (Ex. 12:23). "The destroyer" brought punishment to the Hebrew people when they complained in the desert as well (1 Cor. 10:10). The enemies of Israel, who were usually sent from God to chastise His disobedient people, are also referred to as destroyers (Isa. 49:17; Jer. 22:7; 50:11).

Destruction—See Abaddon.

Deuel [Deu'el], *known of God*—The father of Eliasaph, of the tribe of Gad (Num. 1:14; 7:42). In Numbers 2:14 he is called Reuel (*friend of God*).

Devil—The KJV translation of the Greek *daimon*, and also *diabolos* (*slanderer, accuser*). The word is used frequently to refer to Satan, the chief of the fallen spirits (Luke 10:18; 2 Peter 2:4; Rev. 12:7–9). It is generally believed that the sin of pride was what caused him to fall from his former state (1 Tim. 3:6). He is the enemy of God and of the divine order (Matt. 13:38–39; Rev. 12:17). He was the tempter of Adam and Eve (Gen. 3:1–15; 2 Cor. 11:3), Jesus (Matt. 4:1–11), and man (John 13:2;

Acts 13:9–10). He is a murderer and liar (John 8:44; Rev. 20:10). Peter represents him as a devouring lion (1 Peter 5:8). He is subtle but can be resisted and put to flight (Eph. 4:27; 6:11–16; James 4:7).

Jesus came to destroy his works (Gen. 3:15; 1 John 3:8). At Christ's coming he will be bound for 1,000 years (Rev. 20:2–3). See Satan.

Dial of Ahaz [Di′al of A·haz]—An instrument, set up by Ahaz for the indication of time and called the dial or sundial of Ahaz (2 Kings 20:11; Isa. 38:8). It was some sort of sun-clock, probably a flight of stairs near an obelisk. The shadow of the obelisk falling upon the steps would indicate the hours or half hours. God set the shadow back ten steps on the sundial as a sign to Hezekiah that he would indeed be healed and that Jerusalem would be delivered from the hand of Assyria.

Diana [Di·an′a], *complete light* or *flow restrained*—The Roman goddess of the moon. According to ancient authorities the image of Diana of the Ephesians was of wood (Acts 19:35). Silver models of it were made by Demetrius and others (Acts 19:24).

Dianites [Di′an·ites]—Assyrian colonists who were settled in Samaria (Ezra 4:9).

Diblah, Diblath [Dib′lah, Dib′lath], *place of the fig cake*—A name occurring only in Ezekiel 6:14. The place intended is generally believed to be Riblah, a town in the far north, on Ezekiel's prophetic border of Palestine.

Diblaim [Dib·la′im]—The father of Gomer, the wife of Hosea (Hos. 1:3).

Diblath [Dib′lath]—See Diblah.

Dibon [Di′bon], *wasting away* or *pining*—Two Old Testament towns:

1. A town east of the Jordan, north of the Arnon. It was taken by the Gadites (Num. 32:3, 34) and was rebuilt by them and called Dibon-gad (Num. 33:45–46). It came into the territory of Reuben (Josh. 13:9, 17). In the time of Isaiah and Jeremiah it was held by Moab (Isa. 15:2; Jer. 48:18, 22).

2. A town of Judah, the residence of members of that tribe after returning from Babylon, probably the same as Dimonah (Neh. 11:25).

Dibon-gad [Di′bon-gad]—See Dibon.

Dibri [Dib'ri], *my word*—Father of Shelomith, a woman whose son was stoned for blasphemy (Lev. 24:11–14).

Didymus [Did'y·mus], *a twin*—See Thomas.

Diklah [Dik'lah], *palm tree*—A son of Joktan (Gen. 10:27; 1 Chron. 1:21).

Dilean [Di'le·an], *gourd*—A town of Judah (Josh. 15:38).

Dimnah [Dim'nah], *dung hill*—Variant of Rimmon.

Dimon [Di'mon], *river bed*—A place east of the Dead Sea, probably the same as Dibon (Isa. 15:9).

Dimonah [Di·mo'nah], *river bed* or *silence*—A town near Edom in the south of Judah, perhaps the same as Dibon (Josh. 15:22; Neh. 11:25).

Dinah [Di'nah], *judged* or *avenged*—Daughter of Jacob and Leah (Gen. 30:21). She was ravished by Shechem. Her brothers, Simeon and Levi, avenged her by slaying all the men of Shechem's city (Gen. 34:1–29).

Dinhabah [Din'ha·bah], *give thou judgement*—A city of Bela, king of Edom (Gen. 36:32; 1 Chron. 1:43).

Dionysius [Di·o·nys'i·us], *of Dionysos*—An Areopagite, a member of the supreme court of Areopagus of Athens. He was converted to Christianity through Paul's sermon on Mars' Hill (Acts 17:34).

Diotrephes [Di·ot're·phes], *Jove-nourished*—A person in 3 John 9–10 who is represented as being inhospitable, resentful of the writer's authority, and as "loving the preeminence." He is supposed by some to have been a presbyter or deacon.

Diphath [Di'phath]—See Riphath.

Dishan [Di'shan], *thresher*—The youngest son of Seir (Gen. 36:21, 28; 1 Chron. 1:38, 42).

Dishon [Di'shon], *antelope*—Two Old Testament men:
   1. The fifth son of Seir (Gen. 36:21, 26; 1 Chron. 1:38).
   2. The grandson of Seir (Gen. 36:25; 1 Chron. 1:41).

Diviner's Terebinth Tree—A particular terebinth tree, probably very large, which could be seen from the gates of Shechem (Judg. 9:37). Some think that it is the same tree mentioned in Genesis 12:6 and 35:4. The reference to "diviners" probably means that the tree was considered sacred by those who practiced magic, probably in very much the same way that the English oak was considered sacred to the druids.

Dizahab [Di'za·hab], *abounding in gold*—A place associated with the last addresses of Moses (Deut. 1:1).

Dodai [Do'dai]—See Dodo.

Dodanim, Rodanim [Do'da·nim, Ro'da·nim], *leaders*—A tribe descended from Javan (Gen. 10:4; 1 Chron. 1:7).

Dodavah [Do'da·vah], *beloved of Jehovah*—A man of Mareshah, the father of Eliezer (2 Chron. 20:37).

Dodo [Do'do], *beloved*—Three Old Testament men:
1. The father of Puah and grandfather of Tola (Judg. 10:1).
2. An Ahohite, father of Eleazar (2 Sam. 23:9), probably the same as Dodai (1 Chron. 27:4).
3. Father of Elhanan (2 Sam. 23:24; 1 Chron. 11:26).

Doeg [Do'eg], *timid*—An Edomite, the chief of Saul's herdsmen. He was at Nob when David fled there from Saul (1 Sam. 21:7; Ps. 52, title). He reported to Saul that Ahimelech, the priest, had befriended David. On orders from King Saul, Doeg slew Ahimelech, the other priests associated with him, and all the inhabitants of Nob (1 Sam. 22:7–23).

Dophkah [Doph'kah], *knocking*—One of the stations of the Israelites on their way to Sinai (Num. 33:12–13).

Dor [Dor], *dwelling*—A town of the Canaanites on the Mediterranean a few miles north of Caesarea (Josh. 11:2). Joshua defeated its king (Josh. 12:23).

Dorcas [Dor'cas], *gazelle*—A charitable Christian woman of Joppa, also called Tabitha, who gave much of her time making garments for the needy. Through the prayer of Peter, she was raised from the dead, a fact which caused many to accept Christianity (Acts 9:36–43).

Dothaim [Do'tha·im]—See Dothan.

Dothan [Do'than], *wells*—An ancient town ten miles north of Samaria on the highway which led through Palestine from Babylonia (Gen. 37:17; 2 Kings 6:13). It was here that Joseph was cast into a pit (Gen. 37:17–28).

Dragon's Well—A well near Jerusalem, possibly the same as En-ro-gel southeast of the city (Neh. 2:13).

Drusilla [Dru·sil'la], *watered by the dew*—The youngest daughter of Herod Agrippa I, and Cypros his wife. She was to become the wife of a certain Epiphanes on the condition that he embraced Judaism. He finally rejected the proposal and the marriage did not occur. When Azizus, king of Emesa, accepted the condition, she became his wife. When Felix, procurator of Judea, became passionately fond of her, Drusilla left her husband and, in defiance of Jewish law, married the foreigner and idolater. It was before Felix and Drusilla that Paul spoke (Acts 24:24–25).

Dumah [Du'mah], *silence*—
1. A son of Ishmael (Gen. 25:14; 1 Chron. 1:30).
2. A town in Judah about eight miles southwest of Hebron (Josh. 15:52).
3. A figurative designation of Edom (Isa. 21:11).

Dura [Du'ra], *dwelling*—A plain in Babylon where the image of Nebuchadnezzar was set up (Dan. 3:1).

Earth [Earth]—The world in which we live as distinguished from the heavens (Gen. 1:1); dry land (Gen. 1:10); and the inhabitants of the world (Gen. 11:1). Mention is made of the foundations of the earth (Ps. 102:25; 104:5–9; Isa. 48:13). The earth is represented as supported by pillars erected by God (1 Sam. 2:8; Job 9:6; Ps. 75:3).

East, Children of the—Tribes of the east country on the border of Ammon and Moab (Ezek. 25:4, 10), the region extending north to Haran, and south into Arabia.

East Country—The region east of Palestine (Zech. 8:7), in particular the Syrian and Arabian deserts (Gen. 25:6).

Easter [East′er]—The Christian festival in celebration of the resurrection of Jesus. Its annual date corresponds roughly to the Jewish Passover. The only appearance of the name in the King James Version (Acts 12:4) is more correctly rendered *Passover* in the Revised Version. Easter is a movable feast, falling on the Sunday after the first full moon following the vernal equinox.

Eastern Sea—The Dead Sea (Ezek. 47:18).

East Gate—See Gates of Jerusalem.

Ebal [E′bal], *stone* or *bare mountain*—

   1. A son of Shobal and descendant of Seir (Gen. 36:23; 1 Chron. 1:40).

   2. The same as Obal (Gen. 10:28; 1 Chron. 1:22).

   3. A mountain on the north side of the valley that separates it from Gerizim (Deut. 27:12–14). Under Joshua some of the Israelites pronounced curses while standing upon Ebal, while the others pronounced blessings as they stood upon Gerizim (Deut. 11:29; 27:9–26; Josh. 8:30–35).

Ebed [E'bed], *servant*—

1. Father of Gaal (Judg. 9:28, 30).

2. Son of Jonathan and head of the descendants of Adin who returned from Babylon with the expedition of Ezra (Ezra 8:6).

Ebed-melech [E'bed-mel'ech], *servant of the king*—An Ethiopian eunuch of King Zedekiah who drew Jeremiah out of the dungeon (Jer. 38:7–13; 39:15–18).

Ebenezer [Eb'en·e'zer], *stone of help*—A stone set up by Samuel to commemorate the Lord's deliverance of the Israelites from the Philistines. This was near Mizpah (1 Sam. 7:10, 12). At this point, twenty years before, the Israelites had been defeated by the Philistines (1 Sam. 4:1).

Eber, Heber [E'ber, He'ber], *the region beyond*—

1. A descendant of Arphaxad, son of Shem (Gen. 10:22, 24) and progenitor of the Hebrews (Gen. 11:16–26), the Joktanide Arabs (Gen. 10:25–30), and the Aramaean tribes descended from Nahor (Gen. 11:29; 22:20–24).

2. A priest in the days of Joiakim (Neh. 12:20).

3. A Gadite chief (1 Chron. 5:13).

4. Son of Elpaal (1 Chron. 8:12).

Ebez [E'bez]—See Abez.

Ebiasaph [E·bi'a·saph]—See Abiasaph.

Ebron [E'bron]—A town on the border of Asher (Josh. 19:28), perhaps the same as Abdon. See Hebron.

Ebronah [Eb·ro'nah]—See Abronah.

Ecbatana [Ec·bat'a·na]—See Achmetha.

Ed [Ed], *witness*—An altar erected by the two and one-half tribes east of the Jordan as a witness to the fact that they were a part of Israel even though they were on the other side of the river (Josh. 22:10, 34).

Edar [E'dar]—See Eder.

Edar, Tower of [Ed'ar]—See Eder.

Eden [E′den], *delight*—The name of a garden, a man, and a region in the Old Testament:

1. The first home of Adam and Eve, the first man and woman. The concept "Garden of Delight" fits perfectly the setting of Genesis 2–3, a place of God's blessing and prosperity.

Suggestions offered as to the location of Eden include Babylonia (in Mesopotamia), Armenia (north of Mesopotamia), and an island in the Indian Ocean. The statement in Genesis 2:10 that four "riverheads" divided from the river that flowed out of the garden of Eden (Gen. 2:10–14) supports a location somewhere in Mesopotamia.

Two of the rivers are clearly identified: the Tigris, which ran along the east side of Asshur (Assyria), and the Euphrates. The Pishon ("Spouter") and Gihon ("Gusher") rivers are hard to identify. The Gihon may have been in Mesopotamia, since Genesis 2:13 says it encompassed the whole land of "Cush" (possibly southeast Mesopotamia). Some think Pishon and Gihon represent the Indus and the Nile, respectively, suggesting that Eden included the whole of the Fertile Crescent from India to Egypt.

A major catastrophe, such as the Flood of Noah's time, may have wiped out all traces of the other two rivers mentioned, but modern space photography has produced evidence that two rivers, now dry beds, could have flowed through the area centuries ago.

The garden of Eden included many kinds of beautiful and fruit-bearing trees, including "the tree of life" and "the tree of the knowledge of good and evil" (Gen. 2:9). Man was to tend and keep the garden (Gen. 2:15), which, in addition to trees, could have contained other vegetation such as grain crops and vegetables (Gen. 1:11–12). The garden was also filled with all kinds of birds and land animals (Gen. 2:19–20), probably including many of the animals created on the sixth day of creation (Gen. 1:24–25). It was well watered (Gen. 2:10), ensuring lush vegetation and pasture.

After Adam and Eve sinned against God (Gen. 3:1–19), the Lord banished them from the garden. Cain, the son of Adam and Eve, is said to have lived "east of Eden" (Gen. 4:16).

God commanded Adam and Eve not to eat of the Tree of Knowledge of Good and Evil (Gen. 2:17). They fell from their original state of innocence when Satan approached Eve through the serpent and tempted her to eat of the forbidden fruit (Gen. 3:1–5). She ate the fruit and also gave it to her husband to eat (Gen. 3:6–7). Their disobedience plunged them and the entire human race into a state of sin and corruption.

Because of their unbelief and rebellion, they were driven from the garden. Other consequences of their sin were loss of their innocence (Gen. 3:7), pain in childbearing and subjection of the wife to her husband (Gen. 3:16), the cursing of the ground and the resultant hard labor for man (Gen. 3:17–19), and separation from God (Gen. 3:23–24).

In several Old Testament passages Eden is used as a symbol of beauty and fruitfulness, the place blessed by God (Isa. 51:3). Revelation 22:1–2 alludes to the garden of Eden by picturing a "river of water of life" and "the tree of life" in the heavenly Jerusalem. The apostle Paul thought of Christ as the Second Adam who would save the old sinful Adam through His plan of redemption and salvation. "As in Adam all die, even so in Christ all shall be made alive" (1 Cor. 15:22).

2. A Levite who lived during the reign of King Hezekiah of Judah. He assisted in the religious reformation under Hezekiah, helping cleanse the temple (2 Chron. 29:12) and overseeing the distribution of the freewill offerings (2 Chron. 31:15).

3. A region or city in Mesopotamia that supplied Tyre with choice items such as beautiful and luxurious clothing (Ezek. 27:23–24). Called Bit-Adini on the Assyrian monuments, the place probably was near Damascus (Beth-eden, Amos 1:5; house of Eden, KJV).

Eder, Edar, Ader [E'der, E'dar, A'der], *tower of the flock*—
1. A tower near which Jacob camped (Gen. 35:21).
2. A town in the south of Judah (Josh. 15:21).
3. A Benjamite, son of Elpaal (1 Chron. 8:15).
4. A Levite, son of Mushi of the family of Merari (1 Chron. 23:23; 24:30).

Edom [E'dom], *red*—The name of a person, a people group, and a region in the Old Testament:
1. An alternate name for Esau, who traded his birthright to his brother Jacob for a meal, which consisted of a red stew (Gen. 25:29–34).
2. Another name for the Edomites (Num. 20:18, 20; Amos 1:6, 11; Mal. 1:4).
3. The land inhabited by the descendants of Edom, or Esau (Gen. 32:3; 36:8). Ancient Edom included the region beginning in the north

at the river Zered, a natural boundary also for southern Moab, and extending southward to the Gulf of Aqabah. At times it included mountain ranges and fertile plateaus on the east and west of the Arabah, the desert valley south of the Dead Sea.

The most significant area of ancient Edom was the mountain-encircled plain on the east of the Arabah. Mount Seir, the highest of this range, rises to an elevation of nearly 1,200 meters (3,500 feet) above the Arabah. Edom's capital during the days of Israel's monarchy was Sela, situated at the southern end of a secluded valley that became the location of the city of Petra in later times. Other important Edomite cities were Bozrah and Teman (Isa. 34:6; Amos 1:12). In New Testament times, Edom was known as Idumea.

From the Conquest until the Division. In dividing the land of Canaan after the conquest, Joshua established Judah's border to the west of the Dead Sea and to the border of Edom (Josh. 15:1, 21). During the reign of Saul, Israel fought against Edom (1 Sam. 14:47). But Edomites at times served in Saul's army (1 Sam. 21:7; 22:9). David conquered Edom, along with a number of other adjacent countries, and stationed troops in the land (2 Sam. 8:13–14). In later years, Solomon promoted the building of a port on the northern coast of the Red Sea in Edomite territory (1 Kings 9:26–27).

After the Division. During the time of the divided kingdom, a number of hostile encounters occurred between the nations of Judah or Israel and Edom. During Jehoshaphat's reign, Edomites raided Judah but were turned back (2 Chron. 20:1, 8). An attempt to reopen the port at Ezion Geber failed (1 Kings 22:48), and the Edomites joined forces with those of Judah in Jehoshaphat's move to put down the rebellion of Mesha of Moab (2 Kings 3:4–5). During the reign of Joram, Edom freed herself from Judah's control (2 Kings 8:20–22), but again became subject to Judah when Amaziah assaulted and captured Sela, their capital city. Edom became a vassal state of Assyria, beginning about 736 B.C. So antagonistic were relationships between Israel and Edom that Edom is pictured as Israel's representative enemy (Isa. 34:5–17). The entire book of Obadiah is a prophecy against Edom.

The Place of the Nabateans. After the downfall of Judah in 586

B.C., Edom rejoiced (Ps. 137:7). Edomites settled in southern Judah as far north as Hebron. Nabateans occupied old Edom beginning in the third century B.C., continuing their civilization well into the first century A.D. Judas Maccabeus subdued the Edomites and John Hyrcanus forced them to be circumcised and then made them a part of the Jewish people. The Herod family of New Testament times was of Idumean (Edomite) stock.

Knowledge of the Edomites comes mainly from the Bible, archaeological excavations of their ancient cities, and references to Edom in Egyptian, Assyrian, and Babylonian sources.

Edomites [E'dom·ites]—The descendants of Edom (Gen. 36:1–19). Their early rulers were called dukes (Gen. 36:15–19, 40–43) and kings (Gen. 36:31–43; 1 Chron. 1:43–51). Because they were descendants of Abraham, the Israelites were not permitted to war against them (Num. 20:14–21). They were the subjects of direful prophecies (Ezek. 35:5–6).

Edrei [Ed're·i], *mighty*—

1. A fortified city of Naphtali (Josh. 19:37).

2. Chief city of Bashan (Deut. 3:10; Josh. 12:4; 13:12, 31). It was here that the Israelites defeated Og (Num. 21:33–35; Deut. 1:4; 3:1, 10).

Eglah [Eg'lah], *heifer*—A wife of David and mother of Ithream (2 Sam. 3:5; 1 Chron. 3:3).

Eglaim [Eg'la·im], *two ponds*—A town of Moab (Isa. 15:8).

Eglath-shelishiyah [Eg'lath-shel'i·shiyah], *third Eglath*—A place in Moab (Isa. 15:5; Jer. 48:34).

Eglon [Eg'lon], *young bull*—The name of a city and a king in the Old Testament:

1. An Amorite city in the western Shephelah (lowlands) that was assigned to Judah. Eglon was one of five allied cities that attacked Gibeon but were conquered by Joshua (Josh. 10:3).

2. An overweight Moabite king who reigned during the period of the judges (Judg. 3:12–25). Allied with the Ammonites and the Amalekites, Eglon invaded the land of Israel. His army captured Jericho, and he exacted tribute from the Israelites.

After eighteen years of Eglon's rule, the Lord raised up Ehud the Benjamite, a left-handed man, to deliver Israel. Ehud stabbed Eglon in the belly with a dagger. Because Eglon was a very fat man, "even the hilt went in after the blade, and the fat closed over the blade, for [Ehud] did not draw the dagger out of his belly" (Judg. 3:22).

Egypt [E'gypt]—The history of Egypt stretches back to about 3000 B.C., at least a thousand years before the time of Abraham. During their formative years as a nation, the Hebrew people spent 430 years as slaves in Egypt (Ex. 12:40) before they were released miraculously through God's power under the leadership of Moses. According to the table of nations in the book of Genesis, Egypt was founded by Mizraim, one of the sons of Ham (Gen. 10:6, 13–14). In the Old Testament, Egypt is referred to in a symbolic way as Mizraim (1 Chron. 1:8, 11).

Soon after arriving in the land of Canaan about 2000 B.C., Abraham migrated into Egypt for a time to escape a famine (Gen. 12:10). Still after, Joseph was sold into Egyptian slavery by his brothers (Gen. 37:12–36). Joseph rose to a position of prominence in the cabinet of the Egyptian pharaoh (Gen. 41:37–46). This led Joseph's family to move to Egypt, and the Hebrew people were eventually enslaved when a new line of pharaohs rose to power (Ex. 1:6–14).

After the exodus of the Hebrews from Egypt, the once powerful Egyptian Empire declined in strength and influence, becoming a second-rate political power. During the time of David and Solomon (about 1000 B.C.), Egypt's weakness and fragmentation contributed to the establishment of Israel as a strong nation. During Isaiah's time, about 730 B.C., the prophet warned the king of Judah about forming an alliance with Egypt against the Assyrians, predicting that "trust in the shadow of Egypt shall be your humiliation" (Isa. 30:3).

The Egyptians worshipped many gods. Many of these were the personification of nature, including the earth, sun, and sky. Even the Nile River was thought to be divine, because its periodic flooding enriched the soil of the Nile delta for a premium agricultural harvest. Several of the plagues God sent upon the Egyptians (Ex. 7–12) affected the Nile, proving the weakness of the entire Egyptian religious system.

Egypt, Brook of [E'gypt]—The Wadi el-Arish, a dry streambed which formed the boundary between Egypt and Canaan (Josh. 15:4; Isa. 27:12).

Egyptian [E'gypt·ian]—A native of the land of Egypt.

Ehi [E'hi], *my brother*—Son of Benjamin (Gen. 46:21); also called Ahiram (Num. 26:38) and Aharah (1 Chron. 8:1).

Ehud [E'hud], *union*—Two Old Testament men:
1. The deliverer of the Israelites from King Eglon of Moab. He went to the king on the pretext that he had a present for him from the children of Israel. When Ehud was left alone with the king, he stabbed him and fled to the hill-country of Ephraim. Ehud was left-handed (Judg. 3:12–30).
2. A Benjamite, son of Bilhan (1 Chron. 7:10).

Eker [E'ker], *offspring*—A son of Ram and the grandson of Jerahmeel (1 Chron. 2:27).

Ekron [Ek'ron], *eradication*—The northernmost of the five chief cities of the Philistines, near the Mediterranean Sea and about 66 kilometers (35 miles) west of Jerusalem (1 Sam. 6:16–17). Ekron was apportioned first to the tribe of Judah (Josh. 15:45–46), then given to the tribe of Dan (Josh. 19:40–43).

It was recaptured by the Philistines. When the ark was taken from the Israelites in the time of Eli, it was sent to Ekron and then returned to Israel (1 Sam. 5:10). After David killed Goliath, the Israelites pursued the Philistines to the very gates of Ekron, their fortified stronghold (1 Sam. 17:52).

The prophets pronounced God's judgment upon Ekron, along with her sister cities (Amos 1:8).

Ekronite [Ek'ron·ite]—An inhabitant of Ekron (Josh. 13:3; 1 Sam. 5:10).

El [el], *God*—See God, Names of.

Eladah, Eleadah [El'a·dah, El'e·a·dah], *God has adorned*—A descendant of Ephraim (1 Chron. 7:20).

Elah [E'lah], *an oak*—Six Old Testament men:
1. The father of Shimei (1 Kings 4:18).
2. A duke of Edom (Gen. 36:41; 1 Chron. 1:52).
3. A son of Caleb (1 Chron. 4:15).
4. A Benjamite, son of Uzzi (1 Chron. 9:8).

5. Son and successor of Baasha, king of Israel. He reigned less than two years. He was slain by Zimri (1 Kings 16:6, 8–10).

6. The father of Hoshea (2 Kings 15:30; 17:1; 18:1).

Elah, The Valley of [El'ah]—The valley in which the Israelites were fighting the Philistines when the shepherd boy David was pitted against the Philistine champion, Goliath (1 Sam. 17:2, 19).

Elam [E'lam], *eternity*—Six Old Testament men and a country:

1. A son of Shem (Gen. 10:22; 1 Chron. 1:17) and ancestor of the Elamites (Ezra 4:9).

2. An important country of western Asia. Its southern boundary was the Persian Gulf; its territory was in the area that is now part of Iran, including a part of the Karun River. It was bounded on the east and southeast by Persia (Iran), and on the north by Assyria and Media (now parts of Iraq and Syria). "Chedorlaomer, king of Elam" held dominion over three other kings in the time of Abraham (Gen. 14:1–9). Elam was one of the places to which God's people were exiled (Isa. 1:11), they were a warlike people (Isa. 22:6), who would one day experience the wrath of God (Jer. 25:15, 25; Ezek. 32:24–25). After the Assyrians had taken over the northern kingdom of Israel, they relocated several foreign peoples, including the Elamites, to Samaria (Ezra 4:9).

Daniel and Esther refer to Shushan, the capital of Elam (Est. 1:2; 8:14–15; Dan. 8:2), during the time that this area was under Babylonian domination. Centuries later, Elamites were among those present in Jerusalem when the Holy Spirit came upon the believers at Pentecost (Acts 2:9).

3. A Benjamite, son of Shashak (1 Chron. 8:24).

4. A Korhite, fifth son of Meshelemiah who was a porter of the tabernacle in the time of David (1 Chron. 26:3).

5. The head of a family which returned from Babylon (Ezra 2:1, 2, 7; Neh. 7:12)

6. The head of another family which returned from Babylon with Zerubbabel (Ezra 2:31; Neh. 7:34).

7. The ancestor of Jeshaiah son of Athaliah, who returned to Israel with Ezra (Ezra 8:7).

8. The grandfather (or more distant ancestor) of Shecaniah, who confessed to having taken a pagan wife, and suggested that he and all who had done so should "put them away" (Ezra 10:3).

9. One of the leaders of the people who signed the covenant to follow the God of Israel (Neh. 10:14).

10. A priest who participated in the dedication of the walls (Neh. 12:42).

Several of these entries may actually be the same person, such as No. 5, 6, 7 or 8, and 9 and 10.

Elamites [E'lam·ites]—Inhabitants of Elam (Ezra 4:9). See Elam No. 2.

Elasah [El·a'sah], *God has made*—

1. A son of Shaphan. He and another were sent by Zedekiah on a mission to Nebuchadnezzar, and at the same time they carried a letter from Jeremiah to the captives in Babylon (Jer. 29:3).

2. A son of Pashur. He was led by Ezra to renounce his pagan wife (Ezra 10:22).

Elath, Eloth [E'lath, E'loth], *grove of lofty trees*—An Edomite town on the northeast arm of the Red Sea. The Israelites passed it in their wanderings (Deut. 2:8). It appears that Elath was destroyed, for in 2 Kings 14:22 it is spoken of as being rebuilt by Judah.

El-berith [El-be'rith]—See Baal-berith.

El-bethel [El-beth'el], *God of Beth-el*—Jacob gave this name to an altar he set up at Beth-el when he returned from Padan-aram. It commemorated God's previous appearance to him there in a dream (Gen. 35:7).

Eldaah [El·da'ah], *God hath called*—One of the sons of Midian, the son of Abraham and Keturah (Gen. 25:4; 1 Chron. 1:33).

Eldad [El'dad], *God has loved*—One of the seventy whom Moses selected to aid him in the government of the people. For some reason Eldad and Medad remained in the camp when Moses gathered the elders of the people together to hear from the Lord, but nevertheless, the divine Spirit rested on them as upon the others and they prophesied in the camp. A young man ran to tell Moses what was happening; when Joshua asked Moses to forbid this, Moses rebuked him, declaring he wished the Lord would endow all the people with His Spirit (Num. 11:26–29).

Elead [El'e·ad], *God has testified*—A descendant of Ephraim. In attempting to drive away the cattle from Gath, a city of the Philistines, he and his brother were killed by the people (1 Chron. 7:20–22).

Eleadah [El'e·a'dah]—See Eladah.

Elealeh [El·e·a'leh], *God is ascending*—A town near Heshbon in Moab rebuilt by the Reubenites (Num. 32:3, 37). It was later retaken by the Moabites (Isa. 15:4; 16:9; Jer. 48:34).

Eleasah [El·e·a'sah], *God hath made*—
1. A Judahite (1 Chron. 2:39).
2. Son of Rapha (1 Chron. 8:37).

Eleazar [El·e·a'zar], *God is helper*—The name of seven men in the Bible:
1. Aaron's third son by his wife, Elisheba (Ex. 6:23). Eleazar was the father of Phinehas (Ex. 6:25). Consecrated a priest along with his brothers Nadab, Abihu, and Ithamar, he was made chief of the Levites after his elder brothers, Nadab and Abihu, were killed for offering unholy fire (Lev. 10:1–7). Before Aaron died, Eleazar ascended Mount Hor with him and was invested with Aaron's high priestly garments (Num. 20:25–28). Eleazar served as high priest during the remainder of Moses' life and throughout Joshua's leadership. He helped in the allotment of Canaan among the twelve tribes of Israel (Josh. 14:1), and was buried "in a hill that belonged to Phinehas his son . . . in the mountains of Ephraim" (Josh. 24:33). Phinehas succeeded him as high priest (Judg. 20:28). Upon their return from Babylon, the Zadokite priests traced their descent from Aaron through Eleazar, ignoring the house of Eli (1 Chron. 6:3–8).
2. The son of Abinadab who was charged with keeping watch over the ark while it stayed in Abinadab's house in Kirjath-jearim (1 Sam. 7:1) after it was returned by the Philistines.
3. The son of Dodo the Ahohite (1 Chron. 11:12). He was one of David's three mighty men (2 Sam. 23:9).
4. A man from the tribe of Levi, the family of Merari, and the house of Mahli (1 Chron. 23:21–22).
5. The Levite son of Phinehas (Ezra 8:33). He assisted the high priest in taking care of the sacred vessels.

6. A son of Parosh who divorced his foreign wife (Ezra 10:25).

7. A priest who acted as a musician when the rebuilt walls of Jerusalem were dedicated (Neh. 12:27, 42).

8. Eliud's son and one of the ancestors of Jesus (Matt. 1:15).

Elect Lady—The unknown recipient of John's second epistle (2 John 1). Some believe that she was an actual woman, others think that this is a euphemism for the church in general.

El-elohe-israel [El-el'o·he-is'ra·el], *God, the God of Israel*—The name Jacob gave an altar which he erected not far from Shechem (Gen. 33:20).

Eleph [El'eph], *thousand*—A town belonging to Benjamin (Josh. 18:28).

Elhanan, Elthanan [El·ha'nan, El·tha'nan], *God is gracious*—

1. A son of Dodo, a Bethlehemite, one of David's thirty heroes (2 Sam. 23:24; 1 Chron. 11:26).

2. A son of Jair, a Bethlehemite. In the original of 2 Samuel 21:19 it says that he killed Goliath, the Gittite. But the Authorized Version says that he killed the brother of Goliath, thus bringing the passage into agreement with 1 Chronicles 20:5.

Eli [E'li], *the Lord is high*—A judge and high priest at the temple of Shiloh during the eleventh century B.C., with whom the prophet Samuel lived during his childhood (1 Sam. 1–4; 14:3).

The first mention of Eli occurs when the childless Hannah poured out to him her unhappiness over her barren condition. Later, her prayers for a son were answered when Samuel was born. True to her word, she brought her son to the tabernacle and dedicated him to God. There the future prophet lived with the high priest Eli. Eli was a deeply pious man whose service to the Lord was unblemished. However, he was a lax father who had no control over his two sons. Phinehas and Hophni took meat from sacrificial animals before they were dedicated to God. They also "lay with the women that assembled at the door of the tabernacle" (1 Sam. 2:22). God pronounced judgment on Eli because of his failure to discipline his sons.

God's judgment was carried out through the Philistines. Hophni and Phinehas carried the ark of the covenant into battle to help the

Israelites. Both were killed, and the ark was captured. When Eli, ninety-eight years old and nearly blind, heard the news, he fell backward and broke his neck. God's final judgment against Eli and his descendants occurred when Solomon removed Abiathar, Eli's descendant, and put Zadok in his place as high priest of the nation (1 Kings 2:35).

Eliab [E·li′ab], *God is father*—Six Old Testament men:

1. Son of Pallu, a Reubenite and father of Dathan and Abiram (Num. 16:1, 12; 26:8–9).

2. An ancestor of Samuel, a Levite (1 Chron. 6:27–28).

3. Chief of the family of Zebulun in the wilderness, the son of Helon (Num. 1:9; 2:7; 7:24, 29; 10:16).

4. The oldest son of Jesse and brother of David. From his fine appearance Samuel was sure he was the one to be king of Israel but the Lord showed Samuel that he was deceived by appearances (1 Sam. 16:6–7; 17:13).

5. A Gadite who allied himself with David at Ziklag (1 Chron. 12:9).

6. A Levite, one of David's musicians, who accompanied the ark to Jerusalem (1 Chron. 15:20).

Eliada [E·li′a·da], *God knows*—Three Old Testament men:

1. Father of Rezon of Zobah (1 Kings 11:23).

2. A son of David, also called Beeliada, born after David captured Jerusalem (2 Sam. 5:16; 1 Chron. 3:8).

3. A chief captain of Jehoshaphat, a Benjamite (2 Chron. 17:17).

Eliadah [E·li′a·dah]—See Eliada.

Eliah [E·li′ah]—See Elijah.

Eliahba [E·li·ah′ba], *God will hide*—A Shaalbonite (2 Sam. 23:32; 1 Chron. 11:33).

Eliakim [E·li′a·kim], *God will establish*—Five Old Testament men:

1. A son of Hilkiah who was one of three sent by King Hezekiah to confer with the commander of Sennacherib when the Assyrians threatened Jerusalem (2 Kings 18:18, 26, 37; Isa. 36:3, 11, 22). Eliakim was commended by Isaiah (Isa. 22:20–25).

2. A son of Josiah who was placed on the throne by Pharaoh Necho and whose name was changed to Jehoiakim (2 Kings 23:34; 2 Chron. 36:4).

3. A priest who participated in the dedication of the wall (Neh. 12:41).

4. An ancestor of the family of Christ (Luke 3:30–31).

5. An ancestor of the family of Christ (Matt. 1:13).

Eliam [E·li'am], *people's God*—Two Old Testament men:

1. Father of Bath-sheba whose first husband was Uriah and whose second husband was David (2 Sam. 11:3). In 1 Chronicles 3:5 Eliam's name is changed to Ammiel and Bathsheba's to Bath-shua.

2. The son of Ahithophel (2 Sam. 23:34).

Elias [E·li'a·s]—Greek for Elijah (Mark 9:5). See Elijah.

Eliasaph [E·li'a·saph], *God has added*—Two Old Testament men:

1. The son of Lael, a Levite. During the wilderness period he was the prince of the Gerahonites (Num. 3:24).

2. The head of the Gadites in the wilderness (Num. 1:14; 2:14; 7:42).

Eliashib [E·li·ash'ib], *God restores*—Six Old Testament men:

1. A son of Elioenai, a descendant of the royal family of Judah (1 Chron. 3:24).

2. A priest in the time of David (1 Chron. 24:12).

3. Father of Jehohanan (Johanan), the head of a house of Levi (Ezra 10:6; Neh. 12:22–23).

4. A Levite, a singer who renounced his foreign wife (Ezra 10:24).

5. A son of Zattu who renounced his foreign wife (Ezra 10:27).

6. A son of Bani who renounced his foreign wife (Ezra 10:36).

7. The high priest in the time of Nehemiah. He and the priests built the sheep gate in Jerusalem (Neh. 3:1, 20–21). Possibly No. 3.

Eliathah [E·li'a·thah], *God has come*—A musician, son of Heman (1 Chron. 25:4, 27).

Elidad [E·li'dad], *my God has loved*—A Benjamite, the son of Chislon, who was assigned to help divide up the land (Num. 34:21).

Eliehoenai [El·ieh·o·e'nai]—See Elioenai.

Eliel [E·li'el], *my God is God*—Nine Old Testament men:

1. A Levite of the Kohath family. He was an ancestor of Samuel (1 Chron. 6:34). See Elihu.

2. A Gadite who joined David at Ziklag (1 Chron. 12:11).

3. A Mahavite who was one of David's warriors (1 Chron. 11:46).

4. One of David's heroes (1 Chron. 11:47).

5. Son of Shimhi, a Benjamite (1 Chron. 8:20).

6. Son of Shashak, a Benjamite (1 Chron. 8:22).

7. Son of Hebron, a Levite living at the time of David (1 Chron. 15:9, 11). He helped move the ark to Jerusalem.

8. A leader in eastern Manasseh; also a warrior (1 Chron. 5:24).

9. A Levite appointed by Hezekiah to take charge of the offerings of the temple (2 Chron. 31:13).

Elienai [E·lie′na·i], *unto God are my eyes*—A Benjamite, son of Shimei (1 Chron. 8:20).

Eliezer [El·i·e′zer], *God is help*—Eleven Old Testament men:

1. The servant of Abraham, a man of Damascus. He was sent to Mesopotamia to secure a wife for Isaac (Gen. 15:2).

2. A son of Moses and Zipporah (Ex. 18:4; 1 Chron. 23:15, 17).

3. Son of Becher, grandson of Benjamin (1 Chron. 7:8).

4. One of the priests who blew the trumpet before the ark (1 Chron. 15:24).

5. A son of Zichri. In David's reign he was captain of the Reubenites (1 Chron. 27:16).

6. Son of Dodavah of Mareshah. He was the prophet who predicted that the vessels of Jehoshaphat would be wrecked because of his league with the family of Ahab (2 Chron. 20:37).

7. One of those sent by Ezra to Casiphia to get Levites for the temples (Ezra 8:16–17).

8, 9, 10. Three men of this name—a priest, a Levite, and a son of Harim—renounced their foreign wives (Ezra 10:18, 23, 31).

11. An ancestor of the family of Christ (Luke 3:29).

Elihoenai [Eli·hoe′nai], *unto Jehovah are my eyes*—Son of Zerahiah and descendant of Pahath-moab (Ezra 8:4).

Elihoreph [E·li·hor′eph], *God of winter (harvest time)*—Son of Shisha. He and his brother, Ahijah, were appointed royal scribes by Solomon (1 Kings 4:3).

Elihu [E·li′hu], *he is my God*—Five Old Testament men:

1. Son of Tohu and an ancestor of Samuel (1 Sam. 1:1). He was also known as Eliab or Eliel (1 Chron. 6:27, 34).

2. David's eldest brother, also called Eliab (1 Sam. 16:6; 1 Chron. 27:18).

3. A captain of Manasseh who joined David at Ziklag (1 Chron. 12:20).

4. A member of the family of Obed-edom who was a porter of the temple (1 Chron. 26:7).

5. The son of Barachel the Buzite who reproved Job (Job 32–37).

Elijah [E·li′jah], *the Lord is my God*—The name of three or four men in the Old Testament:

1. A Benjamite, the son of Jeroham, who resided at Jerusalem (1 Chron. 8:27).

2. An influential prophet who lived in the ninth century B.C. during the reigns of Ahab and Ahaziah in the northern kingdom of Israel. Elijah shaped the history of his day and dominated Israelite thinking for centuries afterward.

Elijah's prophetic activities emphasized the unconditional loyalty to God required of the nation of Israel. His strange dress and appearance (2 Kings 1:8), his fleetness of foot (1 Kings 18:46), his rugged constitution that resisted famine (1 Kings 19:8), and his cave-dwelling habits (1 Kings 17:3; 19:9) all suggest that he was a robust, outdoors-type person.

Elijah was opposed to the accepted standards of his day, when belief in many gods was normal. He appears in the role of God's instrument of judgment upon a wayward Israel because of the nation's widespread idolatry. The miracles that Elijah performed occurred during the period when a life-or-death struggle took place between the religion of the Lord and Baal worship.

Elijah's views were in conflict with those of King Ahab, who had attempted to cultivate economic ties with Israel's neighbors, especially Tyre. One of the consequences was that he had married Jezebel, a daughter of Ethbaal, king of Tyre. Ahab saw no harm in participating in the religion of his neighbors, particularly the religion of his wife. Therefore, he established a center of Baal worship at Samaria. Influenced by Jezebel, Ahab gave himself to the worship of Baal. Suddenly Elijah appeared on the scene.

Contest on Mount Carmel: After the drought had lasted three years, the Lord instructed Elijah to present himself before Ahab with the message that the Lord would provide rain. Elijah then challenged the 850 prophets of Baal and Asherah to a contest on Mount Carmel (1 Kings 18:21). Each side would offer sacrifices to their God without building a fire. The ignition of the fire was left to the strongest god, who would thereby reveal himself as the true God.

The best efforts of the pagan prophets through the better part of a day failed to evoke a response from Baal. Elijah poured water over his sacrifice to remove any possibility of fraud or misunderstanding about the offering. After Elijah prayed briefly to the Lord, his sacrifice was consumed by fire from heaven. The people of Israel responded strongly in favor of God (1 Kings 18:39). Then the prophets of Baal were slaughtered at Elijah's command (1 Kings 18:40), and God sent rain to end the drought (1 Kings 18:41–46).

Flight from Jezebel: Queen Jezebel was furious over the fate of her prophets. She vowed that she would take revenge on Elijah. He was forced to flee to Mount Horeb—the mountain where Moses had received the Ten Commandments. Like Moses, Elijah was sustained for forty days and nights in the wilderness.

While Elijah was at Mount Horeb, the Lord revealed Himself in a low, murmuring sound. The prophet received a revelation of the coming doom on Ahab and Israel (1 Kings 19:14). Then Elijah was given a threefold charge: He was instructed to anoint Hazael as king of Syria, Jehu as the future king of Israel, and Elisha as the prophet who would take his place (1 Kings 19:16). These changes would bring to power those who would reform Israel in the coming years.

Naboth's Vineyard and the Challenge of Ahaziah: In the years of war that followed between Ahab and Ben-hadad of Syria, Elijah did not appear (1 Kings 20). But he did appear after Jezebel acquired a family-owned vineyard for Ahab by having its owner, Naboth, falsely accused and executed (1 Kings 21:1–29). Elijah met the king in the vineyard and rebuked him for the act (1 Kings 21:1–24). Ahab repented, and Elijah brought him word from the Lord that the prophesied ruin on his house would not come during his lifetime, but would occur in the days of his son.

Shortly after Ahaziah, the son of Ahab, took the throne from his father, he was involved in a serious accident. He sent messengers to inquire of Baal-zebub ("Lord of Flies"), the god of Ekron, whether he would recover. Elijah intercepted the messengers and predicted his death because of his belief in other gods (2 Kings 1:1–17). This event would also be a fulfillment of the doom pronounced earlier upon Ahab's house.

Twice King Ahaziah sent a detachment of soldiers to capture Elijah. But both times they were consumed by fire from heaven. The third group sent by the king begged for mercy, and an angel of God directed Elijah to go with the commander to see the king. Elijah repeated his message of doom to Ahaziah, who soon died (2 Kings 1:9–17). Elijah's prophecy that Jezebel would meet a violent death was also fulfilled (2 Kings 9:36).

Ascension to Heaven: The prophet Elijah did not die. He was carried bodily to heaven in a whirlwind (2 Kings 2:1–11). This was an honor previously bestowed only upon Enoch (Gen. 5:24). Elisha, the only witness to this event, picked up Elijah's mantle, which fell from him as he ascended. He carried it during his ministry as a token of his continuation of Elijah's ministry (2 Kings 2:13–14).

Elijah's influence continued even after he ascended into heaven. King Jehoram of Israel received a letter from the prophet seven years after his ascension, indicating that the king would be punished severely for his sins (2 Chron. 21:12–15).

Elijah's Contribution: The prophet Elijah understood that the nation of Israel had a mission to preserve its religious system—the worship of the one true God—in a pure form without any mixture with idol worship. Elijah was strongly opposed to the worship of pagan gods such as Baal and Asherah. This uncompromising stand often endangered his life by bringing him into conflict with those in positions of power, especially Queen Jezebel and her followers.

Elijah's impact on the prophetic movement among the Hebrew people was extensive. He stands as the transitional figure between Samuel (the adviser and anointer of kings) and the later writing prophets. Like the prophets who followed him, Elijah emphasized Israel's responsibility for total commitment to their God and the covenant responsibilities that God and His people had sworn to each other. Both ideas are more fully developed in later prophets, such as Amos and Hosea. In later

Jewish thought, the messianic age was frequently associated with Elijah's return. The Old Testament spoke of the reappearance of Elijah. The prophet Malachi prophesied that the Lord would send Elijah before the day of the Lord arrived. This prophecy was fulfilled in the coming of John the Baptist (Matt. 11:4; 17:10–13; Luke 1:17). John the Baptist was similar to Elijah in his preaching as well as his dress and physical appearance (Matt. 11:7–8; Luke 7:24–28). During Jesus' earthly ministry, some identified him with Elijah (Matt. 16:14; Luke 9:8).

The New Testament also mentions the reappearance of Elijah in person. Along with Moses, he appeared with Jesus on the Mount of Transfiguration (Matt. 17:3).

3. A son of Harim (Ezra 10:21). Elijah divorced his foreign wife following the captivity in Babylon.

4. An Israelite who divorced his foreign wife (Ezra 10:26). He may be the same as No. 3.

Elika [El'ika], *my God rejects*—A Harodite, one of David's mighty men (2 Sam. 23:25).

Elim [E'lim]—Oasis of seventy palm trees and twelve springs of water (Ex. 15:27; 16:1; Num. 33:9–10).

Elimelech [E·lim'e·lech], *my God is king*—Husband of Naomi (Ruth 1).

Elioenai [El·i·o·e'nai]—Seven Old Testament men:
1. A Benjamite of the Becher family (1 Chron. 7:8).
2. A Simeonite (1 Chron. 4:36).
3. Son of Neariah, a descendant of Zerubbabel (1 Chron. 3:23–24).
4. A son of Meshelemiah, a Korhite porter of the temple (1 Chron. 26:3).
5. A priest, son of Pashur, who divorced his foreign wife (Ezra 10:22).
6. A priest at the dedication of the wall of Jerusalem (Neh. 12:41).
7. A son of Zattu who renounced his foreign wife (Ezra 10:27).

Eliphal [E·li'phal], *God has judged*—A son of Ur and one of David's warriors (1 Chron. 11:35).

Eliphalet [E·liph'alet]—(2 Sam. 5:15; 1 Chron. 14:7). See Eliphelet.

Eliphaz [E·li′phaz], *God is strong*—Two Old Testament men:

    1. Son of Esau and Adah (Gen. 36:4).

    2. One of the friends of Job, a Temanite (Job 2:11; 4:1; 15:1; 22:1; 42:7, 9).

Elipheleh [E·liph′e·leh], *my God sets him apart*—One of the gate-keepers who played the harp when the ark was brought from the home of Obed-edom (1 Chron. 15:18, 21).

Eliphelehu [E·li·phe·le′hu]—See Elipheleh.

Eliphelet [E·liph′e·let], *God is deliverance*—Six Old Testament men:

    1. Son of Eshek and a descendant of Jonathan (1 Chron. 8:39).

    2. A son of David, born in Jerusalem (1 Chron. 3:6; 14:5).

    3. Another son of David, probably born after the death of the first son of that name (1 Chron. 3:6, 8).

    4. One of David's warriors, son of Ahasbai (2 Sam. 23:34). He was also called Eliphal (1 Chron. 11:35).

    5. Son of Hashum. He renounced his foreign wife (Ezra 10:33).

    6. One of those who accompanied Ezra to Jerusalem, son of Adonikam (Ezra 8:13).

Elisabeth [E·lis′a·beth]—See Elizabeth.

Elisha [E·li′sha], *my God saves*—An early Hebrew prophet who succeeded the prophet Elijah when Elijah's time on earth was finished (1 Kings 19:16). Elisha ministered for about fifty years in the northern kingdom of Israel, serving God during the reigns of Jehoram, Jehu, Jehoahaz, and Joash. The period of his ministry dates from about 850 to 800 B.C. Elisha's work consisted of presenting the Word of God through prophecy, advising kings, anointing kings, helping the needy, and performing several miracles.

    Elisha was the son of Shaphat of Abel Meholah, a town on the western side of the Jordan River. Elijah found Elisha plowing with a team of oxen. As Elijah walked past Elisha, he threw his mantle over the younger man's shoulders. Elisha "arose and followed Elijah, and became his servant" (1 Kings 19:21), but Elisha is not mentioned again until 2 Kings 2:1, shortly before Elijah ascended to heaven in a chariot of fire. Before taking his leave, Elijah fulfilled the final request of

Elisha by providing him with a double portion of his prophetic spirit (2 Kings 2:9–10), making him his spiritual firstborn. Upon receiving Elijah's mantle, Elisha demonstrated this gift by parting the waters of the Jordan River, allowing him to cross on dry land (2 Kings 2:14). In this way, Elisha demonstrated that he had received God's blessings on his ministry as Elijah's successor.

Elisha cultivated a different image from his predecessor. Instead of following Elijah's example as a loner and an outsider, Elisha chose to work within the established system. He assumed his rightful place as the head of the "official" prophetic order in Israel, where his counsel and advice were sought out by kings. In contrast to Elijah's strained relationship with the king and his officials, Elisha enjoyed the harmonious role of trusted advisor. This is not to say that Elisha never had a word of criticism for the government, as for example in the part he played in the overthrow of Jezebel and the dynasty of Ahab (2 Kings 9:1–3).

Elisha's appearance was much more typical and average than Elijah's. He was bald (2 Kings 2:23), while Elijah had been an extremely hairy man (2 Kings 1:8). Elisha did not wander as extensively as Elijah. Instead, he had a house in Samaria (2 Kings 6:32). Much tension had existed between Elijah and his audience. Elisha's ministry provided a strong contrast as he was welcomed into virtually all levels of society.

In perhaps the most important part of his ministry, however, Elisha followed in Elijah's footsteps. This consisted of his performance of miracles, which answered a wide variety of needs in every level of society. He had a reputation for sympathizing with the poor and the oppressed. Elisha's activities and miracles as a prophet were often focused on those who were abused by officials in positions of power. One of Elisha's "community service" miracles was his purification of an unhealthy spring near Jericho. After learning that the spring was bad, Elisha threw a bowl of salt into it, making it pure (2 Kings 2:19–21). The Bible reports that "the water remains healed to this day" (2 Kings 2:22).

In another miracle, Elisha helped the widow of one of the sons of the prophets. To help her pay off creditors who intended to take the widow's two sons, Elisha multiplied the amount of oil in one jar to fill all available containers. This brought in enough money to pay off the debts and provided a surplus on which the widow and her sons could live (2 Kings 4:1–7).

Elisha became a friend of a wealthy family in Shunem. The Shunammite woman displayed hospitality toward the prophet by regularly feeding him and building a room onto her home where he could lodge. Elisha repaid the childless couple by promising them a son (2 Kings 4:8–17). Later, when tragedy struck the child, Elisha raised him from the dead (2 Kings 4:18–37). When Elisha learned that a famine would strike Israel, he warned the family to flee the land. When the family returned seven years later, the king restored their property because of their relationship with Elisha (2 Kings 8:1–6).

Elisha also advised kings and performed miracles for them. He helped Jehoram, king of Israel, and Jehoshaphat, king of Judah. He also helped the king of Edom defeat Mesha, king of Moab (2 Kings 3:1–19).

Elisha ministered to all people, regardless of their nationalities. He cured Naaman, the commander of the Syrian army (2 Kings 5:1–14), of leprosy, but he also advised the king of Israel of the plans (2 Kings 6:8–10) of their Assyrian enemies. Even the bones of the dead Elisha had miraculous powers. When a corpse was hidden in Elisha's tomb, it came back to life as it touched the prophet's bones (2 Kings 13:21).

Other notable acts of Elisha include the death of the children who mocked his bald head (2 Kings 2:23–25) and the feeding of the hundred men (2 Kings 4:42–44).

Elishah [E·li′shah], *God of the coming (one)*—Eldest son of Javan (Gen. 10:4; 1 Chron. 1:7). He seems to have given the name to the "isles of Elishah" (Ezek. 27:7).

Elishama [E·li′sha·ma], *God has heard*—Six Old Testament men:

1. Son of Jekamiah. a descendant of Judah (1 Chron. 2:41).

2. The son of Ammihud, chief of the Ephraimites at the time of the sojourn in the wilderness (Num. 1:10; 2:18). He was an ancestor of Joshua (1 Chron. 7:26).

3. A son of David (2 Sam. 5:16). Elishua (2 Sam. 5:15; 1 Chron. 14:5) is probably the more exact name.

4. Another son of David (1 Chron. 3:8; 14:7).

5. The father of Nethaniah and grandfather of Ishmael (2 Kings 25:25; Jer. 41:1).

6. A priest commissioned by Jehoshaphat to teach the law to the people of Judah (2 Chron. 17:8).

7. A scribe to Jehoiakim (Jer. 36:12, 20–21).

Elishaphat [E·li'sha'phat], *God has judged*—A captain who led a revolt against Athaliah (2 Chron. 23:1).

Elisheba [E·li'she·ba], *God is an oath*—Daughter of Amminadab and sister of Naashon. She became the wife of Aaron. Their four sons were Nadab, Abihu, Eleazar, and Ithamar (Ex. 6:23).

Elishua [E·li'shu·a], *God is salvation*—A son of David (2 Sam. 5:15; 1 Chron. 14:5). In 1 Chronicles 3:6, David's son Elishua is called Elishama.

Eliud [E·li'ud], *God his Praise*—The son of Achim and father of Eleazar in Christ's genealogy (Matt. 1:14–15).

Elizabeth [E·liz'a·beth], *God is my oath*—The mother of John the Baptist (Luke 1). Of the priestly line of Aaron, Elizabeth was the wife of the priest Zacharias. Although both "were . . . righteous before God, they had no child, because Elizabeth was barren" (Luke 1:6–7). But God performed a miracle, and Elizabeth conceived the child who was to be the forerunner of the Messiah.

Elizabeth was privileged in another way. When her cousin Mary visited her, Elizabeth, six months pregnant, felt the child move as if to welcome the child whom Mary was carrying. Elizabeth recognized the significance of this action and acknowledged the Messiah before He had been born.

Elizaphan [E·li·za'phan], *my God has protected*—Two Old Testament men:

1. The son of Uzziel. He was the chief of the Kohathites in the wilderness (Ex. 6:18, 22; Num. 3:30). He and his brother, Mishael, removed the bodies of Nadab and Abihu when they were burned to death for their sacrilegious offering to the Lord. In the reign of David his family helped bring the ark to Jerusalem (1 Chron. 15:8).

2. Son of Parnach and chief of the tribe of Zebulun. He assisted in dividing the land (Num. 34:25).

Elizur [E·li'zur], *my God is a rock*—Son of Shedeur and prince of the tribe of Reuben (Num. 1:5; 2:10; 7:30; 10:18).

Elkanah [El·ka'nah], *God has possessed*—Eight Old Testament men:

1. A son of Korah and brother of Assir and Abiasaph (Ex. 6:24).

2. The husband of Hannah and father of Samuel (1 Sam. 1:1; 2:11, 20; 1 Chron. 6:27, 34).

3. The father of Zophai and a descendant of Assir (1 Chron. 6:23).

4. Son of Joel and father of Amasai (1 Chron. 6:25–26).

5. The head of a Levite family who lived in the village of the Netophathites (1 Chron. 9:16).

6. A Korite who lived in Benjamin. He joined David at Ziklag (1 Chron. 12:6).

7. A doorkeeper for the ark during the reign of David (1 Chron. 15:23).

8. A chief officer in the court of Ahaz of Judah. He was slain by Zichri when Pekah of Israel invaded Judah (2 Chron. 28:7).

Elkosh [El'kosh], *God the ensnarer*—The residence and probably birthplace of the prophet Nahum (Nah. 1:1).

Ellasar [El·la'sar], *God is chastener*—A Mesopotamian nation, whose king was Arioch (Gen. 14:1). Together with the kings of Elam and Shinar, he made war on the kings of Sodom and Gommorah, Admah, Zeboiim, and Bela.

Elmodam [El·mo'dam], *measure*—Son of Er and father of Cosam, an ancestor of Christ (Luke 3:28).

Elnaam [El·na'am], *God is delight*—Father of two of David's warriors (1 Chron. 11:46).

Elnathan [El·na'than], *God has given*—Three Old Testament men:

1. The father of Nehushta, mother of Jehoiachin, king of Judah (2 Kings 24:8).

2. The son of Achbor who was among those sent by King Jehoiakim to bring Urijah, the prophet, from Egypt (Jer. 26:22). The prophet failed to persuade Jehoiakim not to destroy the written prophesy of Jeremiah (Jer. 36:12, 25)

3. Three men sent by Ezra to secure Levites for the temple (Ezra 8:16).

Elohim [El·o'him], *mighty*—The plural of Eloah, sometimes used in the sense of gods, true or false (Ex. 12:12; 35:2, 4). See God, Names of.

Elon [E'lon], *an oak*—Three Old Testament men and a town:

1. A Hittite and father of Adah who was the wife of Esau (Gen. 36:2). Adah is also called Bashemath (Gen. 26:34).

2. A son of Zebulun, the head of the family of Elonites (Num. 26:26).

3. A member of the Zebulunite family who was a judge of Israel for ten years (Judg. 12:11–12).

4. A town on the border of Dan (Josh. 19:43).

Elon-beth-hanan [E'lon-beth-ha'nan], *oak of the house of grace*—Probably the same as Elon, a town in Dan (1 Kings 4:9).

Elonites [E'lon·ites]—Descendants of Elon, a son of Zebulun (Gen. 46:14; Num. 26:26).

Eloth [El'oth]—See Elath.

Elpaal [El·pa'al], *God is maker*—A Benjamite, son of Shaharaim and his wife Hushim (1 Chron. 8:11).

Elpalet [El·pa'let]—See Elpelet.

Elparan [El·par'an]—(Gen. 14:6). See Paran.

Elpelet [El·pe'let], *God is deliverance*—A son of David born in Jerusalem (1 Chron. 14:5).

Eltekeh [El'te·keh], *God is its fear*—A town of Dan (Josh. 19:44; 21:23). It was the scene of the defeat of the Egyptians by Sennacherib in 701 B.C.

Eltekon [El'te·kon], *God is straight*—A town of Judah (Josh. 15:59).

Eltolad [El·to'lad], *God's generations*—A town in the southern part of Judah (Josh. 15:30) which was allotted to Simeon (Josh. 19:4). It is probably the Tolad of 1 Chronicles 4:29.

Elul [E'lul], *nothingness*—Sixth month of the sacred, and twelfth of the civil year (Neh. 6:15), corresponding roughly with the end of August/beginning of September.

Eluzai [El·u'zai], *God is my strength*—A warrior of Benjamin who joined David (1 Chron. 12:5).

Elymas [El′y·mas], *a wise man*—A Jew, Bar-jesus (Son of Joshua), an imposter, who claimed to be able to tell future events. Paul met him at Paphos where he attempted to prevent the conversion of Sergius Paulus, the Roman deputy. Paul denounced him and he was smitten with blindness for a time. The deputy immediately accepted Christianity (Acts 13:6–12).

Elzabad [El·za′bad], *God has given*—

1. A Gadite warrior who allied himself with David at Ziklag (1 Chron. 12:12).

2. A Levite, son of Shemaiah, of the family of Obed-edom (1 Chron. 26:7).

Elzaphan [El′za·phan], *my God has protected*—A Levite, son of Uzziel (Ex. 6:22).

Emek-keziz [E′mek-ke′ziz], *cut off*—A town of Benjamin, apparently near Jericho and Beth-hoglah. It is referred to as the valley of Keziz in the King James Version (Josh. 18:21).

Emim [E′mim], *terror*—The early inhabitants of Moab. They were a powerful people (Deut. 2:9–11).

Emmanuel [Em·man′u·el]—See Immanuel.

Emmaus [Em·ma′us], *warm wells*—A village in Judea where Jesus revealed Himself to two disciples after His resurrection. The disciples, Cleopas and an unidentified companion, encountered Jesus on the road to Emmaus, but they did not recognize Him. Jesus accompanied them to Emmaus, and they invited Him to stay there with them. As He blessed and broke bread at the evening meal, the disciples' "eyes were opened and they knew Him" (Luke 24:31). The modern location of ancient Emmaus is uncertain. Luke reported the village was 11 kilometers (7 miles) from Jerusalem, but he did not specify in which direction.

Emmor [Em·mor]—(Acts 7:16). See Hamor.

Enaim [E′naim]—See Enam.

Enam [E′nam], *fountains*—A town in the lowland of Judah (Josh. 15:34).

Enan [E'nan], *having eyes*—Father of Ahira (Num. 1:15; 2:29).

Endor [En'dor], *fountain of Dor*—A town in Manasseh about four miles from Mount Tabor (Josh. 17:11). It was here the witch lived whom Saul consulted the night before his death (1 Sam. 28:7).

En-eglaim [En-eg'la·im], *fountain of two calves*—This place is mentioned by Ezekiel (Ezek. 47:10) in the vision of holy waters.

En-gannim [En-gan'nim], *fountain of gardens*—
   1. A town of Issachar (Josh. 19:21) allotted to the Levites (Josh. 21:29).
   2. A town in Judah (Josh. 15:34).

En-gedi [En-ge'di], *fount of the kid*—A town, also called Hazazon-tamar, located on the edge of the wilderness on the west shore of the Dead Sea (Josh. 15:62). Its inhabitants, the Amorites, were attacked by Chedorlaomer (Gen. 14:7). In one of its many caves David found refuge after fleeing from Saul (1 Sam. 23:29). Here he cut off a piece of Saul's robe instead of killing him (1 Sam. 24:1–22).

En-haddah [En-had'dah], *swift fountain*—A border town of Issachar (Josh. 19:21).

En-hakkore [En-hak·kor'e], *spring of One calling*—The name of a fountain at Lehi (Judg. 15:15, 18, 19).

En-hazor [En-ha'zor], *fountain of the village*—A fenced city of Naphtali (Josh. 19:37).

En-mishpat [En-mish'pat], *fountain of judgment*—The earlier name of Kadesh-barnea (Gen. 14:7).

Enoch [E'noch], *dedicated*—Two Old Testament men:
   1. The eldest son of Cain (Gen. 4:17–18).
   2. Son of Jared and father of Methuselah; he belonged to the Seth line, "the antediluvian line of the Messiah" (Gen. 5:18–24). Enoch was a righteous man. He did not die, but instead "he was not for the Lord took him." A prophecy of Enoch is found in the epistle of Jude (Jude 14–15).

Enos [E'nos]—See Enosh.

Enosh [E'nosh], *man*—Son of Seth, the grandson of Adam (Gen. 5:6–11; Luke 3:38).

En-rimmon [En-rim'mon], *fountain of the pomegranate*—A town in southern Judah (Neh. 11:29), called Ain in Joshua 15:32, and Remmon in Joshua 19:7.

En-rogel [En-ro'gel], *fountain of the fuller*—A fountain near Jerusalem (Josh. 15:7; 18:16; 2 Sam. 17:17).

En-shemesh [En-she'mesh], *fountain of the sun*—A fountain and town on the road from Jerusalem to Jericho (Josh. 15:7; 18:17).

Entappuah [En·tap'pu·ah]—(Josh. 17:7). See Tappuah.

Ep-aenetus, Ep-enetus [Ep-ae'ne·tus, Ep-e'ne·tus], *praiseworthy*—A convert to Christianity in Achaia (Rom. 16:5).

Epaphras [Ep'a·phras], *lovely*—A member of the Colossian church and possibly the founder of it. He came to Paul at Rome during his first imprisonment. In Paul's epistle to that church he joined the apostle in sending salutations (Col. 1:7–8; 4:12). Paul speaks of him as "my fellow prisoner" (Philem. 23).

Epaphroditus [Ep·aph·ro·di'tus]—A Christian sent with gifts from the church at Philippi to Paul, then a prisoner at Rome. Epaphroditus became ill while there but, upon recovery, he returned to Philippi taking with him Paul's epistle to that church (Phil. 2:15–30; 4:18).

Ep-enetus [Ep-e'ne·tus]—See Ep-aenetus.

Ephah [E'phah], *gloom*—Two men and a woman:
1. One of the five sons of Midian (Gen. 25:4; 1 Chron. 1:33). His descendants formed a branch of the Midianites and lived in the northeastern part of Arabia (Isa. 60:6).
2. A concubine of Caleb of the tribe of Judah (1 Chron. 2:46).
3. The son of Jahdai of Judah (1 Chron. 2:47).
4. Also a unit of dry measure equal to one-tenth of an omer or about 0.65 bushels (Ex. 16:36), used for measuring commodities such as grain (Ruth 2:17).

Ephai [E′phai], *gloomy*—A Netophathite. When Jerusalem fell in 586 B.C., his sons came to Gedaliah, the governor placed over the remnant left in the city, and were assured of protection. They were slain with Gedaliah by Ishmael (Jer. 40:8; 41:3).

Epher [E′pher], *gazelle*—Three Old Testament men:

1. A son of Midian who was the son of Abraham and Keturah (Gen. 25:4; 1 Chron. 1:33).
2. A son of Ezra (1 Chron. 4:17).
3. A leader of a family of Manasseh (1 Chron. 5:24).

Ephes-dammim [E′phes-dam′mim], *edge of blood*—A place in Judah between Shochoh and Azekah where the Philistines were encamped when David killed Goliath (1 Sam. 17:1). In 1 Chronicles 11:13 it is called Pas-dammim.

Ephesian [E·phe′sian]—The inhabitants of the city of Ephesus. Paul's friend Trophimus was an Ephesian (Acts 21:29).

Ephesus [Eph′es·us], *permitted*—A large and important city on the west coast of Asia Minor where the apostle Paul founded a church. A number of factors contributed to the prominence that Ephesus enjoyed.

The first factor was economics. Situated at the mouth of the river Cayster, Ephesus was the most favorable seaport in the province of Asia and the most important trade center west of Tarsus. Today, because of silting from the river, the ruins of the city lie in a swamp 8 to 11 kilometers (5 to 7 miles) inland. Another factor was size. Although Pergamum was the capital of the province of Asia in Roman times, Ephesus was the largest city in the province, having a population of perhaps 300,000 people. A third factor was culture. Ephesus contained a theater that seated an estimated 25,000 people. A main thoroughfare, some 35 meters (105 feet) wide, ran from the theater to the harbor, at each end of which stood an impressive gate. The thoroughfare was flanked on each side by rows of columns 15 meters (50 feet) deep. Behind these columns were baths, gymnasiums, and impressive buildings. The fourth, and perhaps most significant, reason for the prominence of Ephesus was religion. The temple of Artemis (or Diana, according to her Roman name) at Ephesus ranked as one of the Seven Wonders of the Ancient World. As the twin sister of Apollo and the daughter of Zeus, Artemis was known variously as the moon goddess, the goddess of hunting, and the patroness of young girls. The temple at Ephesus housed the image of Artemis that was reputed to have come directly from Zeus (Acts 19:35).

The temple of Artemis in Paul's day was supported by 127 columns, each of them 60 meters (197 feet) high. The Ephesians took great pride in this grand edifice. During the Roman period, they promoted the worship of Artemis by minting coins with the inscription "Diana of Ephesus." The history of Christianity at Ephesus began about A.D. 50, perhaps as a result of the efforts of Priscilla and Aquila (Acts 18:18). Paul came to Ephesus in about A.D. 52, establishing a resident ministry for the better part of three years (Acts 20:31). During his Ephesian ministry, Paul wrote 1 Corinthians (1 Cor. 16:8).

The book of Acts reports that "all who dwelt in Asia heard the word of the Lord Jesus" (Acts 19:10), while Paul taught during the hot midday hours in the lecture hall of Tyrannus (Acts 19:9). Influence from his ministry undoubtedly resulted in the founding of churches in the Lycus River valley at Laodicea, Hierapolis, and Colossae.

So influential, in fact, was Paul's ministry at Ephesus that the silversmiths' league, which fashioned souvenirs of the temple, feared that the preaching of the gospel would undermine the great temple of Artemis (Acts 19:27). As a result, one of the silversmiths, a man named Demetrius, stirred up a riot against Paul.

During his stay in Ephesus, Paul encountered both great opportunities and great dangers. He baptized believers who apparently came to know the gospel through disciples of John the Baptist (Acts 19:1-5), and he countered the strong influence of magic in Ephesus (Acts 19:11-20).

After Paul departed from Ephesus, Timothy remained to combat false teaching (1 Tim. 1:3; 2 Tim. 4:3; Acts 20:29). Many traditions testify that the apostle John lived in Ephesus toward the end of the first century. In his vision from the island of Patmos off the coast of Asia Minor, John addressed the book of Revelation to the seven churches of Asia Minor, which included the congregation at Ephesus and described the church of Ephesus as flourishing, although it was troubled with false teachers and had lost its first love (Rev. 1:11; 2:1-7). The traditional tomb of John is located at the Church of St. John in Ephesus.

Ephlal [Eph'lal], *intercessor*—Son of Zabad and father of Obed, in the genealogy of the sons of Judah (1 Chron. 2:37).

Ephod [E'phod], *a covering*—

1. Father of Hanniel, a leader of the tribe of Manasseh in the wilderness (Num. 34:23).

2. An official garment of the Jewish high priest which he was required to wear when engaged in religious duties (Ex. 28:4). Suspended from the shoulders it covered both back and front. On the shoulders were two onyx stones on which the names of the tribes were engraved (Ex. 28:9; 39:6–7). Attached to the ephod was the breastplate (Ex. 28:25–28; 9:19–21).

Ephraim [E'phra·im], *doubly fruitful*—The second son of Joseph by Asenath, who was the daughter of Potipherah, priest of On.

When Ephraim was born to Joseph in Egypt, he gave him his name meaning "fruitful" because "God has caused me to be fruitful in the land of my affliction" (Gen. 41:52). Even though Joseph was a foreigner (a Hebrew) in Egypt, he had been blessed by God as he rose to a high position in the Egyptian government and fathered two sons. Later this same theme of fruitfulness and blessing was echoed by Joseph's father, Jacob, as he accepted Ephraim as his grandson (Gen. 48:5) by placing his hand on his head. He explained to Joseph that Ephraim would be greater than his brother and would be the ancestor of a multitude of peoples. The descendants of the two sons were to be regarded as two tribes (Gen. 48:8–20).

Eventually Ephraim's thousands of descendants settled in the land of Canaan as one of the most numerous of the tribes of Israel (Gen. 48:19; Num. 1:10).

Ephraim, City of [E'phra·im]—A city of Judea to which Jesus fled after restoring Lazarus (John 11:54).

Ephraim, Forest of [E'phra·im]—The Forest or Wood of Ephraim was the scene of the decisive battle between the armies of David and his rebellious son Absalom (2 Sam. 18:6–17). The area was given to Ephraim because the sons of Joseph were so numerous (Josh. 17:14–18).

Ephraim, Gate of [E′phra·im]—A gate of Jerusalem, probably in the northeast portion of the wall (2 Kings 14:13; 2 Chron. 25:23; Neh. 8:16; 12:39). See Gates of Jerusalem.

Ephraimite [E′phra·im·ite]—See Ephrathite.

Ephraim, Mountains of [E′phra·im]—A mountain ridge in central Palestine within the territories of Ephraim and the western half-tribe of Manasseh. Samuel's parents were from Mount Ephraim (1 Sam. 1:1). Joshua's inheritance was in the mountains of Ephraim (Josh. 19:50).

Ephraim, Tribe of [E′phra·im]—The descendants of Joseph's younger son (Josh. 16:4, 10; Judg. 5:14). A year after the exodus, when the census was taken, the tribe numbered 40,500. At the close of the wandering, in the second census, they numbered 32,500 (Num. 26:37). Joshua was an Ephraimite (Josh. 19:50; 24:30). In the division of the land, on the south of Ephraim was Benjamin, on the north Manasseh, and on the west Dan. Strongest of the northern tribes, Ephraim was resentful of Judean supremacy and was critical of the undertakings of other tribes, such as those led by Gideon and Jephthah (Judg. 8:1–33; 12:1–6).

Ephrain [E′phra·in], unknown—A town of Israel, taken in battle by Abijah, king of Israel, in the days of Jeroboam king of Israel (2 Chron. 13:19).

Ephratah [Eph′ra·tah]—A town and a woman:
   1. The name by which Bethlehem was originally known; the place where Rachel was buried (Gen. 35:19; 48:7; Ruth 4:11). The city was also called Bethlehem Ephratah (Mic. 5:2). See Bethlehem.
   2. The wife of Caleb and mother of Hur (1 Chron. 2:19, 50; 4:4).

Ephrath [E′phrath]—See Ephratah.

Ephrathah [Eph′ra·thah]—See Ephratah.

Ephrathite [Eph′ra·thite]—
   1. A native of Ephrath, that is, Bethlehem (1 Sam. 17:12; Ruth 1:2).
   2. One belonging to the tribe of Ephraim (1 Sam. 1:1; 1 Kings 11:26).

Ephron [E′phron], *fawn-like*—A town, a man, and a mountain:
   1. The son of Zohar, a Hittite, who lived at Hebron. He owned the cave of Machpelah and sold it to Abraham (Gen. 23:8; 25:9).

2. A city captured by Abijah from Jeroboam (2 Chron. 13:19). In the KJV the city is called Ephrain.

3. A mountain on the border between Benjamin and Judah (Josh. 15:9).

Epicureans [Ep·i·cu·re'ans]—A philosophical sect of Greece and Rome. The name is derived from the philosopher Epicurus, born about 341 B.C. on the island of Samos. He was the founder of a school in Athens in which he taught until his death in 270 B.C. According to his ethical ideas, pleasure should be sought and pain avoided. The Epicureans were present when Paul preached Christianity in Athens (Acts 17:18–20).

Er [Er], *watchful*—Three Old Testament men:

1. The eldest son of Judah. His mother was Shua, a Canaanite. His wickedness caused the Lord to kill him (Gen. 38:1–7; 46:12; 1 Chron. 2:3).

2. Son of Shelah of Judah (1 Chron. 4:21).

3. Son of Jose, an ancestor of Joseph, husband of Mary (Luke 3:28–29).

Eran [E'ran], *watcher*—Son of Shuthelah, a descendant of Ephraim (Num. 26:36).

Eranites [E'ran·ites]—The clan or family descended from Eran, the Ephraimite (Num. 26:36).

Erastus [E·ras'tus], *beloved*—A Christian whom Paul sent with Timothy from Ephesus (Acts 19:22). He is probably the same as the chamberlain of Corinth (Rom. 16:23).

Erech [E·rech]—A city of the kingdom of Nimrod, the mighty hunter descended from Ham (Gen. 10:10).

Eri [E'ri], *watching*—The fifth son of Gad and founder of a tribal family (Gen. 46:16; Num. 26:16).

Esarhaddon [E·sar·had'don], *Ashur has given a brother*—Son of Sennacherib, king of Assyria. His being favored by his father so angered two of his brothers that they assassinated their father and fled into Armenia (2 Kings 19:36–37; 2 Chron. 32:21; Isa. 37:37–38). At that time, Esarhaddon was conducting a campaign in Armenia. When he heard of this foul deed, he returned with his army to Nineveh but on the way encountered the rebel forces and defeated them. In 680 B.C., he succeeded to the throne.

Esau [E'sau], *hairy*—A son of Isaac and Rebekah and the twin brother of Jacob. Also known as Edom, Esau was the ancestor of the Edomites (Gen. 25:24–28; Deut. 2:4–8).

Most of the biblical narratives about Esau draw a great contrast between him and his brother, Jacob. Esau was a hunter and outdoorsman who was favored by his father, while Jacob was not an outdoors type and was favored by Rebekah (Gen. 25:27–28).

Even though he was a twin, Esau was considered the oldest son because he was born first. By Old Testament custom, he would have inherited most of his father's property and the right to succeed him as family patriarch. But in a foolish, impulsive moment, he sold his birthright to Jacob in exchange for a meal (Gen. 25:29–34). This determined that Jacob would carry on the family name in a direct line of descent from Abraham and Isaac, his grandfather and father.

The loss of Esau's rights as firstborn is further revealed in Genesis 27. Jacob deceived his blind father by disguising himself as Esau in order to receive his father's highest blessing. Esau was therefore the recipient of a lesser blessing (Gen. 27:25–29, 38–40; Heb. 11:20). He was so enraged by Jacob's actions that he determined to kill him once his father died. But Jacob fled to his uncle Laban in Haran in Mesopotamia and remained there for twenty years. Upon Jacob's return to Canaan, Esau forgave him and set aside their old feuds (Gen. 32:1–33:17). Years later, the two brothers together buried their father in the cave at Machpelah without a trace of their old hostilities (Gen. 35:29).

Esau in many ways was more honest and dependable than his scheming brother, Jacob. But he sinned greatly by treating his birthright so casually and selling it for a meal (Heb. 12:16–17). To the ancient Hebrews, one's birthright actually represented a high spiritual value. But Esau did not have the faith and farsightedness to accept his privileges and responsibilities. Thus, the right passed to his younger brother.

Esau's Wives [E'sau]—Esau was married to two Hittite women, Judith and Adah (also called Basemath). This greatly displeased his parents (Gen. 26:34, 46). When Esau realized that they were unhappy with his foreign wives, he took another wife, one of Ishmael's daughters (Gen. 28:8–9). Seeing Isaac send Jacob back to Rebekah's relatives to find a wife probably gave him the idea that one of Abraham's family would be more acceptable to his parents.

Esdraelon, Plain of [Es'dra-e'lon]—See Megiddo.

Esek [E'sek], *contention*—A well dug by Isaac and claimed by the Philistines (Gen. 26:20).

Eshan, Eshean [E'shan, Esh'e·an], *support*—A town in the mountains of Judah (Josh. 15:52).

Eshbaal [Esh·ba'al]—See Ish-bosheth.

Eshban [Esh'ban], *fire of discernment*—A son of Dishon, the Horite (Gen. 36:26; 1 Chron. 1:41).

Eshcol [Esh'col], *a cluster*—A man and a valley:

1. A valley near Hebron (Num. 13:22–23; Deut. 1:24) which is renowned for its great clusters of grapes. From here the scouts sent out by Moses brought back to the Israelites at Kadesh-barnea a cluster of grapes so large that it took two men to carry it (Num. 13:24).

2. The Amorite brother of Mamre (Gen. 14:13, 24).

Eshean [Esh'e·an]—See Eshan.

Eshek [E'shek], *oppression*—A descendant of Saul (1 Chron. 8:39).

Eshkalonite [Esh'ka·lon·ite]—See Ashkelon.

Eshtaol [Esh'ta·ol], *entreaty*—A town between Judah and Dan which was eventually assigned to Dan (Josh. 15:33; 19:41). Samson was born near here (Judg. 13:24–25).

Eshtaulite [Esh·ta·u'lite]—An inhabitant of Eshtaol (1 Chron. 2:53).

Eshtemoa [Esh·te·mo'a], *I will make myself heard*—A man and a town:

1. A son of Hodiah (1 Chron. 4:19).

2. A town of Judah assigned to the priests (Josh. 15:50; 21:14). When David captured Ziklag, he sent to this town some of the spoils (1 Sam. 30:28).

Eshtemoah [Esh·te·mo'ah]—See Eshtemoa.

Eshton [Esh'ton], *effeminate*—A Judahite (1 Chron. 4:11–12).

Esli [Es'li], *reserved of Jehovah*—An ancestor of Jesus (Luke 3:25).

Esrom [Es'rom]—See Hezron.

Essenes [Es·senes]—A sect of Judaism noted for their separatism and strict religious discipline. They practiced communal living, and strove for simplicity in dress and lifestyle. They were flourishing at the time of Christ, and one community of them lived at Qumran, near the Dead Sea, a few miles from Jericho. It was this community which stored copies of the Scriptures and other religious manuscripts in clay jars in the nearby caves. These were rediscovered in the 1940s and proved to be of great interest. While it is speculated that some of John's early disciples were from the Essene communities, as a whole the Essenes rejected Jesus and continued to wait for the Messiah.

Esther [Es'ther], *star*—The Jewish queen of the Persian king Ahasuerus (Xerxes). Esther saved her people, the Jews, from a plot to eliminate them. A daughter of Abihail (Est. 2:15; 9:29) and a cousin of Mordecai (Est. 2:7, 15), Esther was raised by Mordecai as his own daughter after her mother and father died. Esther was a member of a family carried into captivity in Babylon that later chose to stay in Persia rather than return to Jerusalem. Her Jewish name was Hadassah, which means "myrtle" (Est. 2:7).

The story of Esther's rise from an unknown Jewish girl to become the queen of a mighty empire illustrates how God used events and people as instruments to fulfill His promise to His chosen people. Following several days of revelry, the drunken king Ahasuerus—identified with Xerxes I (reigned 486–465 B.C.)—asked his queen, Vashti, to display herself to his guests. When Vashti courageously refused, she was banished from the palace. Ahasuerus then had "all the beautiful young virgins" (Est. 2:3) of his kingdom brought to his palace in order to choose from among them Vashti's replacement.

Scripture records that "the young woman [Esther] was lovely and beautiful" (Est. 2:7). The king loved Esther more than all the other women. He appointed her queen to replace Vashti (Est. 2:17).

At the time, Haman was Ahasuerus's most trusted advisor. An egotistical and ambitious man, Haman demanded that people bow to him as he passed—something that Mordecai, a devout Jew, could not do in good conscience. In rage, Haman sought revenge not only on Mordecai but also on the entire Jewish population of the empire. He persuaded the king to issue an edict permitting him to kill all the Jews and seize their property.

With great tact and skill, Esther exposed Haman's plot and true character to the king. As a result, Ahasuerus granted the Jews the right to defend themselves and to destroy their enemies. With ironic justice, "they hanged Haman on the gallows that he had prepared for Mordecai (Est. 7:10).

Even today Jews celebrate their deliverance from Ahasuerus's edict at the Feast of Purim (Est. 9:26–32), celebrated on the fourteenth and fifteenth days of the month of Adar.

Etam [E'tam], *hawk ground*—

1. A place in the lowland of Judah, later transferred to the territory of Simeon (1 Chron. 4:32). For a time Samson dwelt in a rock near here (Judg. 15:8, 11).

2. A town near Bethlehem (1 Chron. 4:3; 2 Chron. 11:6).

Etham [E'tham], *with them* or *their plowshare*—The location of the first encampment of the Israelites (Ex. 13:20; Num. 33:6).

Ethan [E'than], *perpetuity*—Three Old Testament men:

1. A Levite of the family of Gershom (1 Chron. 6:42–43).

2. A Levite of the family of Merari, a singer in the time of David (1 Chron. 6:44, 47; 15:17, 19).

3. A descendant of Judah, of the family of Zerah (1 Chron. 2:6), probably the one who was renowned for his wisdom (1 Kings 4:31; Ps. 89, title).

Ethanim [Eth'a·nim], *enduring*—The seventh month of the sacred and first month of the civil year, also called Tishri.

Ethbaal [Eth·ba'al], *with Baal*—King of Tyre and Sidon and father of Jezebel (1 Kings 16:31).

Ether [E'ther], *abundance*—A village in the lowland of Judah assigned to Simeon (Josh. 15:42; 19:7).

Ethiopia [E·thi·o'pi·a]—A country in the upper Nile Valley called Cush by the Hebrews (2 Chron. 16:8; Ps. 68:31; Isa. 20:3–5; Ezek. 30:4–5; Dan. 11:43; Nah. 3:9). The people were tall and dark skinned. Its topaz was celebrated (Job 28:19). The inhabitants traded with other countries (Isa. 45:14) and prospered (Isa. 43:3). They were defeated by Asa of Judah (2 Chron. 14:9–15; 16:8). The twenty-fifth dynasty of Egypt was Ethiopian. The modern nation of Ethiopia is far from the biblical land of Cush, separated from upper Egypt by the country of Sudan.

Ethiopian [E·thi·o'pi·an]—A native of Ethiopia, a Cushite (Jer. 13:23; 2 Chron. 14:9; Jer. 38:7, 10, 12; 39:16).

Ethiopian Eunuch [E·thi·o'pi·an Eu·nuch]—A person baptized by Philip who held a responsible position as the royal treasurer in the court of Candace, queen of Ethiopia (Acts 8:26–40). The word *eunuch* refers to an emasculated servant who could rise to positions of power and influence in ancient times. The Ethiopian eunuch had apparently been a convert to Judaism. A keen student of the Bible, he was probably a proselyte who had come to Jerusalem to participate in worship at the temple. On his return to his own country, he encountered Philip. On Philip's explanation of Isaiah 53, he confessed his faith in Christ and was baptized.

Eth-kazin [Eth-ka'zin], *time of the judge*—A place on the boundary of Zebulun (Josh. 19:13).

Ethnan [Eth'nan], *gift*—A son of Helah (1 Chron. 4:7).

Ethnarch [Eth'narch]—Governor or ruler of a province or people.

Ethni [Eth'ni], *munificent*—A Levite of the family of Gerahom (1 Chron. 6:41). In 1 Chronicles 6:21 he is called Jeaterai.

Eubulus [Eu·bu'lus], *prudent*—A Christian in Rome (2 Tim. 4:21).

Eunice [Eu·ni'ce], *good victory*—The mother of Timothy (Acts 16:1; 2 Tim. 1:5).

Euodias [Eu·o′di·as], *fragrant*—A member of the church of Philippi, whose quarrel with Syntyche, another member of the church, Paul tried to end (Phil. 4:2–3).

Euphrates [Eu·phra′tes], *the good and abounding river*—The longest river of Western Asia and one of two major rivers in Mesopotamia. The river begins in the mountains of Armenia in modern-day Turkey. It then heads west toward the Mediterranean Sea, turns to the south, swings in a wide bow through Syria, and then flows some 1,000 miles southeast to join the Tigris River before it empties into the Persian Gulf.

The Euphrates is about 2,890 kilometers (1,780 miles) long and is navigable for smaller vessels for about 1,950 kilometers (1,200 miles). The ruins of many ancient cities are located along the river in Iraq. Among them are Babylon, Eridu, Kish, Larsa, Nippur, Sippar, and Ur. In the Bible the Euphrates is referred to as "the River Euphrates," "the great river, the River Euphrates," or simply as "the River." It was one of the four rivers that flowed from the garden of Eden (Gen. 2:14). The Euphrates formed the northern boundary of the territories promised by God to Israel (Gen. 15:18; Josh. 1:4).

The biblical writer declared that the fathers of Israel had lived on "the other side of the River" (Josh. 1:2–3, 14–15; "beside the Euphrates," REB), where they served other gods. But God took Abraham "from the other side of the River" (v. 3) and brought him to the land of Canaan. David attempted to expand the boundaries of his kingdom to this river (2 Sam. 8:3). The Euphrates also was the site of the great battle at Carchemish (605 B.C.) that led to the death of King Josiah (2 Chron. 35:20–24). "The great river Euphrates" is also mentioned in Revelation 9:14 and 16:12.

Euraquilo [Eu·raq′ui·lo]—See Euroclydon.

Euroclydon [Eu·roc′ly·don], *a violent agitation*—A violent wind from the northeast. This wind caught Paul's ship as it sailed along the coast of Crete, blew it to the open sea, then wrecked it on the island of Melita (Acts 27:14–44).

Eutychus [Eu′ty·chus], *good fortune*—A young man of Troas who, while sleeping, fell from a window. Paul restored him to life (Acts 20:9–10).

Eve [Eve], *life-giving*—The first woman and mother of all living (Gen. 3:20; 4:1), created from one of Adam's ribs to be "a helper comparable to him" (Gen. 2:18–22).

Adam and Eve lived together in innocence and happiness, enjoying sexual union ("one flesh") without guilt and sin (Gen. 2:25). However, the serpent tempted Eve to eat the forbidden fruit (Gen. 2:17).

Eve succumbed to the serpent's temptation and ate the fruit. Then "she also gave to her husband with her, and he ate" (Gen. 3:6). The result of this disobedience was losing innocence and receiving the disturbing knowledge of sin and evil. "Then the eyes of both of them were opened, and they knew that they were naked; and they sewed fig leaves together and made themselves coverings" (Gen. 3:7) to conceal their shame.

In falling into temptation (Gen. 3:6), Eve learned about sin and death (Gen. 2:17). She and her descendants experienced the animosity between Satan and Christ—the "offspring of the serpent" and "the seed of the woman" (Gen. 3:15). Her pain in childbirth and Adam's authority over her were other results of her sin (Gen. 3:16).

The apostle Paul referred to Eve twice. By saying "the serpent deceived Eve by his craftiness," Paul gave an example of how easily a person can be led into temptation and sin, with disastrous consequences (2 Cor. 11:3; 1 Tim. 2:12–14).

Evi [E'vi], *my desire*—A king of Midian (Num. 31:8; Josh. 13:21).

Evil-merodach [E'vil-mer'o·dach], *man of Merodach*—A Babylonian king, son of Nebuchadnezzar (2 Kings 25:27–30; Jer. 52:31–34).

Evil One—See Devil; Satan.

Ezar [E'zar]—See Ezer.

Ezbai [Ez'bai], *my humblings*—Father of Naarai (1 Chron. 11:37).

Ezbon [Ez'bon], *hasting to discern*—Two Old Testament men:
1. A Benjamite, head of a house of the family of Bela (1 Chron. 7:7).
2. A son of Gad (Gen. 46:16), also called Ozni (Num. 26:16).

Ezekias [E·zek'i·as]—(Matt. 1:9–10). See Hezekiah.

Ezekiel [E·zek'i·el], *God will strengthen*—A prophet of a priestly family carried captive to Babylon in 597 B.C. when he was about twenty-five years old. His call to the prophetic ministry came five years later. Ezekiel prophesied to the captives who dwelled by the river Chebar at Tel Abib. He is the author of the book of Ezekiel.

In his book, Ezekiel identifies himself as a Zadokite priest, the son of Buzi (1:3). He was married to a woman who was "the desire of his eyes" (24:16). One of the saddest events of his life was the death of his wife. The prophet was told that on the very day he received this revelation, his wife would die as the armies of Babylon laid siege against the holy city of Jerusalem. Ezekiel's sadness at the death of his wife was to match the grief of the people at the destruction of Jerusalem. Ezekiel was commanded not to grieve her death; he was to steel himself for this tragedy even as God's people were to prepare themselves for the death of their beloved city (24:15–22). Perhaps no other event in the lives of the Old Testament prophets is as touching as this.

During the captivity, he was consulted by the elders on several important matters (Ezek. 8:1; 14:1; 20:1).

Ezel [E′zel], *departure*—The hiding place of David where he received Jonathan's report (1 Sam. 20:19).

Ezem, Azem [E′zem, A′zem], *a bone*—A village allotted to the tribe of Judah near the border of Edom. It was afterward assigned to Simeon (Josh. 15:29; 19:3; 1 Chron. 4:29).

Ezer, Ezar [E′zer, E′zar], *treasure*—Six Old Testament men:

1. A Horite tribe (Gen. 36:21, 30; 1 Chron. 1:38).

2. The father of Hushah of Judah, a descendant of Hur (1 Chron. 4:4).

3. A son of Ephraim who was killed by the men of Gath (1 Chron. 7:21).

4. A Gadite who allied himself with David at Ziklag (1 Chron. 12:9).

5. A priest who participated in the dedication of Nehemiah's wall (Neh. 12:42).

6. Son of Jeshua (Neh. 3:19).

Ezion-gaber [E′zi·on-ga′ber]—See Ezion-geber.

Ezion-geber [E′zi·on-ge′ber], *backbone of a man*—A town on the coast of the Gulf of Akaba (Deut. 2:8) used as a port by Solomon

(1 Kings 9:26). It was one of the camps of Israelites during their wanderings (Num. 33:35).

Eznite [Ez'nite]—Josheb-Basshebeth the Tachmonite, the "chief of the captains" and one of David's mighty men, was given the nickname "Adino the Eznite," "because he had killed 800 men at one time" (2 Sam. 23:8). The definition of this nickname is not known. He is also called Jashobeam, the son of a Hachmonite (1 Chron. 11:11).

Ezra [Ez'ra], *(God is) a help*—The name of three men in the Old Testament:

1. A descendant of Judah (1 Chron. 4:17; Ezrah, NIV, NRSV; perhaps Ezer, 1 Chron. 4:4).

2. A scribe and priest who led the returned captives in Jerusalem to make a new commitment to God's law. A descendant of Aaron through Eleazar, Ezra was trained in the knowledge of the law while living in captivity in Babylon with other citizens of the nation of Judah. Ezra gained favor during the reign of Artaxerxes, king of Persia. This king commissioned him to return to Jerusalem about 458 B.C. to bring order among the people of the new community. Artaxerxes even gave Ezra a royal letter (Ezra 7:11–16), granting him civil as well as religious authority, along with the finances to furnish the temple, which had been rebuilt by the returned captives.

Ezra was a skilled scribe and teacher with extensive training in the Books of the Law (Genesis, Exodus, Leviticus, Numbers, and Deuteronomy). After his return to Jerusalem, he apparently did a lot of work on the Hebrew Bible of that time, modernizing the language, correcting irregularities in the transmitted text, and updating and standardizing expressions in certain passages. References to this work by Ezra are found in 2 Esdras, one of the apocryphal books of the Old Testament. He also refers to himself in his own book as a skilled scribe (Ezra 7:6, 12), whose task was to copy, interpret, and transmit the Books of the Law.

When he arrived in Jerusalem, Ezra discovered that many of the Hebrew men had married foreign wives from the surrounding nations (Ezra 9:1, 2). After a period of fasting and prayer (Ezra 9:3, 15), he insisted that these men divorce their wives (Ezra 10:1, 17). He feared that intermarriage with pagans would lead to worship of pagan gods in the restored community of Judah.

In addition to these marriage reforms, Ezra also led his country-men to give attention to the reading of the law. Several priests helped Ezra read the law given by Moses, translating and interpreting it for the people's clear understanding in their new language (Aramaic). This reading process went on for seven days as the people focused on God's commands (Neh. 7:73–8:18).

During this period, they also celebrated one of their great religious festivals, the Feast of Tabernacles, to commemorate their sustenance by God in the wilderness following their miraculous escape from Egyptian bondage (Neh. 8). The result of this week of concentration on their heritage was a religious revival. The people confessed their sins and renewed their covenant with God (Neh. 9–10).

Ezra must have been a competent scribe and priest, since he found favor with the ruling Persians. But he was also devoted to his God and the high standards of holiness and righteousness that the Lord demanded of His people. As he communicated God's requirements to the captives in Jerusalem, Ezra also proved he was a capable leader who could point out shortcomings while leading the people to a higher commitment to God's law at the same time. Through it all, Ezra worked with a keen sense of divine guidance, "according to the good hand of his God upon him" (Ezra 7:9).

3. One of the priests who returned from the captivity with Zerubbabel (Neh. 12:1, 13).

Ezrah [Ez'rah]—See Ezra.

Ezrahite, Ezrarite [Ez'ra·hite, Ez'ra·rite]—The family name of Ethan and Heman (1 Kings 4:31; Ps. 88, title; Ps. 89, title).

Ezri [Ez'ri], *my help*—Son of Chelub (1 Chron. 27:26).

F

Fair Havens—This harbor in the island of Crete is near the city of Lasea (Acts 27:8).

False Prophet, The—In the last days, a "beast" and a false prophet will arise, who will rule the earth, persecuting believers and demanding worship for the beast (Rev. 13:1–12). They will prophesy falsely and perform miraculous signs by the aid of demons (Rev. 16:13), but when Christ returns they will be thrown alive into a lake of fire where Satan will later be also thrown (Rev. 19:20; 20:10).

Father, God the—See God, Names of.

Felix [Fe'lix], *happy*—A Roman official, procurator of Judea. He was liberated from slavery by Claudius, who appointed him to his high position. Felix had a reputation for being very corrupt. When Paul was arrested in Jerusalem, he was sent to Caesarea to be tried before Felix (Acts 23:24, 34). When Paul spoke before Felix and his wife, Drusilla, who was a Jewess, Felix was deeply affected by the story of Paul's conversion. He continued to call Paul back again, hoping to be bribed into letting him go. However, failing to receive a bribe from Paul and to placate the Jews, he left Paul in prison (Acts 24:24–27).

Festus, Porcius [Fes'tus, Por'ci·us]—The successor of Felix as procurator of Judea (Acts 24:10, 27) about A.D. 60. He listened to Paul's defense in the presence of Agrippa II. Festus was satisfied as to Paul's innocence but proposed that he be tried in Jerusalem. This was unwise and Paul asserted his right to appeal to Caesar (Acts 25:1–26:32).

Field of Sharp Swords—The site of a universally fatal hand-to-hand combat between David's men and Ish-bosheth's men, and the ensuing battle in which Abner (Ish-bosheth's general) and his men were beaten (2 Sam. 2:16).

Fire, Lake of—See Hinnom, Valley of.

First Gate—A gate of Jerusalem (Zech. 14:10).

Fish Gate—One of the gates of Jerusalem (2 Chron. 33:14; Neh. 3:3; 12:39).

Former Gate—A gate of Jerusalem, also called the First Gate (Zech. 14:10).

Fortunatus [For·tun·na'tus], *fortunate*—A Roman and a member of the church at Corinth. With two others he came to Paul at Ephesus (1 Cor. 16:17).

Foundation Gate—A gate of Jerusalem (Neh. 3:15; 12:37).

Fuller's Field [Full'er]—A field mentioned several times, apparently quite near Jerusalem, where fullers spread their cloth to bleach in the sun (2 Kings 18:17, 26; Isa. 7:3; 36:2).

Furnaces, Tower of the—See Ovens, Tower of the.

G

Gaal [Ga′al], *loathing*—The son of Ebed. He helped the Shechemites in their revolt against Abimelech but was unsuccessful (Judg. 9:26–41).

Gaash [Ga′ash], *quaking*—A hill in the district of Mount Ephraim whose brooks and streams are occasionally mentioned (Josh. 24:30; Judg. 2:9; 2 Sam. 23:30; 1 Chron. 11:32).

Gaba [Ga′ba]—See Geba.

Gabbai [Gab·ba′i], *tax gatherer*—A Benjamite who dwelt at Jerusalem (Neh. 11:8).

Gabriel [Ga′bri·el], *man of God*—A heavenly messenger high in rank among the angels. He was sent to Daniel to interpret a vision received by the prophet (Dan. 8:16–27). The same occurred in connection with the prophecy of the seventy weeks (Dan. 9:21–27). Centuries afterward he appeared to Zacharias to announce the birth of John the Baptist (Luke 1:11–22), and at Nazareth he declared to Mary her great distinction and honor (Luke 1:26–31). Gabriel's special job seems to have been the announcing of things concerning the Messiah.

Gad [Gad], *good fortune*—The name of the founder of a tribe in Israel, the tribe itself, a prophet, and a pagan god:
    1. The seventh of Jacob's twelve sons. Gad was the firstborn of Zilpah (Leah's maid) and a brother of Asher (Gen. 30:11). Moses praised Gad for his bravery and faithfulness to duty (Deut. 33:20–21). With the possible exception of Ezbon, Gad's seven sons all founded tribal families (Num. 26:15–18).
    2. The tribe of Gad (Num. 1:14; Deut. 27:13). In the first numbering it had 45,650 men (Num. 1:25), but in the second census the number was 40,500 (Num. 26:15–18). The tribe was assigned territory east of the Jordan. It was required to assist the other tribes in the conquest of

the country (Num. 32:6–34). The territory of Reuben was south of that of Gad and the half-tribe of Manasseh was on the north. It was rich pastureland (Num. 32:1–4). Ramoth, a city of refuge, was in this territory (Josh. 20:8).

3. A prophet described as David's "seer" (1 Chron. 21:9). Gad commanded David to buy the threshing floor of Araunah the Jebusite, which became the site of the temple. Gad the prophet also helped arrange the tabernacle music (2 Chron. 29:25) and is credited with writing an account of David's reign (1 Chron. 29:29).

4. The name of a pagan god (Isa. 65:11, NKJV; Fortune, NIV). The name "Gad" appears in compound names, such as Baal-gad (Josh. 11:17) and Migdal-gad (Josh. 15:37).

Gad, Ravine of—One of the places Joab and his men camped when they went out to take a census of the fighting men at David's command (2 Sam. 24:5). Also called "river of Gad," it probably refers to the River Arnon, east of the Dead Sea.

Gadara [Gad′a·ra], unknown—A city of the Decapolis. It is not mentioned in the Bible, but the "country of the Gadarenes" which is "opposite Galilee" is mentioned. Some versions say "Gerasenes" (Luke 8:26–37). See Gadarenes.

Gadarenes [Gad′a·renes]—Residents of Gadara and the surrounding area. The "country of the Gadarenes" was an area south and east of the Sea of Galilee, related to the area of the Decapolis. It was near here that Jesus cured a demoniac by permitting the outcast demons to enter a herd of swine which in turn plunged into the sea (Luke 8:26–37). The word *Gergesenes* is used in Matthew 8:28 and the word *Geresenes* is used in the King James Version (Mark 5:1; Luke 8:26).

Gaddi [Gad′di], *fortunate*—One of the spies, or scouts, representing the tribe of Manasseh (Num. 13:11).

Gaddiel [Gad′di·el], *fortune of God*—One of the twelve spies, or scouts, sent to Canaan (Num. 13:10).

Gadi [Ga′di], *a Gadite*—Father of Menahem, king of Israel (2 Kings 15:14).

Gadites [Gad·ites]—The people of the tribe of Gad (Deut. 3:12; Josh. 1:12).

Gaham [Ga'ham], *burning*—A son of Nahor (Gen. 22:24).

Gahar [Ga'har], *hiding place*—The head of the family of Nethinim (Ezra 2:47; Neh. 7:49).

Gai [Ga'i], unknown—A name used in the Revised Version for valley (1 Sam. 17:52). It may be Gath.

Gaius [Gai'us]—A Roman name sometimes written Caius. Four men of the New Testament:

1. Gaius of Macedonia was a traveling companion of Paul. In the riot in Ephesus he was seized by the Ephesians (Acts 19:29).

2. Gaius of Derbe accompanied Paul on his last journey to Asia (Acts 20:4).

3. Gaius of Corinth, Paul's host, was baptized by Paul (Rom. 16:23; 1 Cor. 1:14). He was probably the same as Gaius of Derbe.

4. The Gaius to whom John addressed his third epistle (3 John 1).

Galaad [Gal'a·ad]—See Gilead.

Galal [Ga'lal]—Two Old Testament men:

1. A Levite, the son of Jeduthun, and father of Shemaiah (1 Chron. 9:16; Neh. 11:17).

2. Another Levite (1 Chron. 9:15).

Galatia [Ga·la'tia], *land of the Galli or Gauls*—A region in central Asia Minor (modern Turkey) bounded on the east by Cappadocia, on the west by Asia, on the south by Pamphylia and Cilicia, and on the north by Bithynia and Pontus. The northern part of the region was settled in the third century B.C. by Celtic tribes that had been driven out of Gaul (France). These tribes were given the territory by Nicomedes, king of Bithynia, in return for military service (Acts 16:6; 18:23; Gal. 1:2). From these tribes, the region derived its name, Galatia.

In 64 B.C. the Roman general Pompey defeated the king of Pontus, Mithradates VI, and established a foothold for Rome in the region. When the last Galatian king, Amyntas, died in 25 B.C., the Romans inherited the kingdom. Caesar Augustus then created the Roman province of Galatia, making Ancyra the capital and annexing a number of districts to the south and west, including Pisidia, Isauria, Phrygia, and Lycaonia. The term "Galatia," consequently, is somewhat ambiguous. It may refer to the older ethnic region in north-central Asia Minor (north Galatia), or to the later and larger Roman province (including south Galatia).

On his first missionary journey (about A.D. 46–48), the apostle Paul and Barnabas evangelized the Galatian cities of Pisidian Antioch, Iconium, Lystra, and Derbe (Acts 13–14). Paul revisited the area on his second and third missionary journeys.

Although the point is debated, it appears that Paul's epistle to the Galatians (Gal. 1:2; 3:1) was addressed to the churches founded by him in the southern part of the province of Galatia (south Galatian theory). No evidence exists to show that Paul visited the region of Galatia in north-central Asia Minor. Although Acts 16:6 and 18:23 are sometimes thought to refer to this more remote northern region, the context of these passages seems to point to southern Galatia (Acts 13–14).

Galeed [Ga′leed], *heap of witness*—This was the name given by Jacob to a pile of stones in Gilead, north of the river Jabbok. It was a memorial of the covenant between Laban and Jacob, under which each agreed not to pass the pillar (Gen. 31:45–54). See Mizpah.

Galilaean, Galilean [Gal·i·lae′an, Gal·i·le′an]—A native or inhabitant of Galilee (Matt. 26:69; Mark 14:70; Luke 13:1; John 4:45).

Galilee [Gal′i·lee], *circle* or *circuit*—A Roman province of Palestine during the time of Jesus. Measuring roughly 80 kilometers (50 miles) north to south and about 58 kilometers (30 miles) east to west, Galilee was the most northerly of the three provinces of Palestine—Galilee, Samaria, and Judea. Covering more than a third of Palestine's territory, Galilee extended from the base of Mount Hermon in the north to the Carmel and Gilboa ranges in the south. The Mediterranean Sea and the Jordan River valley were its western and eastern borders, respectively.

Originally a district in the hill country of Naphtali (2 Kings 15:29; 1 Chron. 6:76), Galilee was inhabited by a "mixed race" of Jews and heathen. In the Old Testament it was considered to be roughly the territories of Asher, Naphtali, Zebulun, and Issachar. The Canaanites continued to dominate Galilee for many years after Joshua's invasion (Judg. 1:30–33; 4:2). It was historically known among the Jews as "Galilee of the Gentiles" (Isa. 9:1; Matt. 4:15).

Galilee had such a mixed population that Solomon could award unashamedly to Hiram, king of Tyre, twenty of its cities in payment for timber from Lebanon (1 Kings 9:11). After conquest by Tiglath-pileser, king of Assyria (about 732 B.C.), Galilee was repopulated by a colony of heathen immigrants (2 Kings 15:29; 17:24). Thus the Galilean accent and dialect were very distinct (Matt. 26:69, 73). For this and other reasons, the pure-blooded Jews of Judea, who were more orthodox in tradition, despised the Galileans (John 7:52). Rather contemptuously Nathanael asked, "Can anything good come out of Nazareth?" (John 1:46).

Galilee consisted essentially of an upland area of forests and farmlands. An imaginary line from the plain of Acco (Acre) to the north end of the Sea of Galilee divided the country into Upper and Lower Galilee. Since this area was actually the foothills of the Lebanon mountains, Upper and Lower Galilee had two different elevations. The higher of the elevations, Upper Galilee, was more than 1,000 meters (3,000 feet) above sea level; and in the days of the New Testament it was densely forested and thinly inhabited. The lower elevation, Lower Galilee, averaged between 500 to 700 meters (1,500 to 2,000 feet) above sea level; it was less hilly and enjoyed a milder climate than Upper Galilee. This area included the rich plain of Esdraelon and was a "pleasant" land (Gen. 49:15). Chief exports of the region were olive oil, grains, and fish.

Galilee was the boyhood home of Jesus Christ. He was a lad of Nazareth, as it was prophesied: "He shall be called a Nazarene" (Matt. 2:23). Here He attempted to begin His public ministry, but was rejected by His own people (Luke 4:16–30).

All the disciples of Jesus, with the exception of Judas Iscariot, came from Galilee (Matt. 4:18; John 1:43–44; Acts 1:11; 2:7). In Cana of Galilee He performed His first miracle (John 2:11); in fact, most of His thirty-three great miracles were performed in Galilee. Capernaum in Galilee became the headquarters of His ministry (Matt. 4:13; 9:1). Of His thirty-two parables, nineteen were spoken in Galilee. The first three Gospels concern themselves largely with Christ's Galilean ministry. Most of the events of our Lord's life and ministry are set against the backdrop of the Galilean hills.

When Herod the Great died in 4 B.C., Galilee fell to the authority of Herod Antipas, who governed until A.D. 39. He built his capital city at Tiberias on the Sea of Galilee and was succeeded by Herod I who took the title of "king." After Agrippa's death in A.D. 44 (Acts 12:23), Galilee became a Zealot stronghold until the Romans crushed Jewish resistance in Palestine between A.D. 66 and 73.

Galilee, Sea of [Gal′i·lee]—A freshwater lake, fed by the Jordan River, which was closely connected with the earthly ministry of Jesus. This "sea" is called by four different names in the Bible: the "Sea of Chinnereth" [or "Chinneroth"] (the Hebrew word for "harp-shaped," the general outline of the lake; Num. 34:11; Josh. 12:3; 13:27); the "Lake of Gennesaret" (Luke 5:1), taking the name from the fertile plain of Gennesaret that lies on the northwest (Matt. 14:34); the "Sea of Tiberias" (John 6:1; 21:1), because of its association with the capital of Herod Antipas; and the "Sea of Galilee" (Matt. 4:18; Mark 1:16).

One of the lowest points on earth, standing 680 feet below sea level, The Sea of Galilee is situated some 98 kilometers (60 miles) north of Jerusalem. It contains fresh water since it is fed by the Jordan River. The lake itself is the deepest part of the northern Jordan Rift and thus the water collects there before it flows on its way. The surface of Galilee is about 230 meters (700 feet) below the Mediterranean Sea. The floor of the lake is another 25 to 50 meters (80 to 160 feet) lower. The lake itself is nearly 21 kilometers (13 miles) long and 13 kilometers (8 miles) wide at Magdala, the point of its greatest width. The lake is surrounded, except on the southern side, by steep cliffs and sharply rising mountains. On the east these mountains rise to the fertile Golan Heights as high as 900 meters (2,700 feet). As a result of this formation, cool winds frequently rush down these slopes and unexpectedly stir up violent storms on the warm surface of the lake. Waves such as these were easily calmed at the command of Jesus (Mark 4:35–41).

The region around the Sea of Galilee in the upper Jordan River Valley in northern Palestine is a lush garden, with an abundance of fertile soil, water, fish, and a hot climate. About 200,000 people, mostly Gentiles, were scattered in the many towns along the shores of the lake and throughout the upper Jordan Valley when Jesus taught and healed in Palestine.

Because of their openness to new ideas, Jesus appealed to the common people of Galilee, and many of them "heard Him gladly" (Mark 12:37). Jesus recruited eleven of His disciples from this area, including His first disciples—Peter, Andrew, James, and John—from the thriving fishing industry that existed (1:16–20).

In spite of the steep hillsides around the lake, nine cities of 15,000 population or more thrived in the first century as part of an almost continuous belt of settlements around the lake. Of these cities, Bethsaida, Tiberias, and Capernaum were the most important. On and around the Sea of Galilee Jesus performed most of His thirty-three recorded miracles and issued most of His teachings to His disciples and the multitudes that followed Him.

Gallim [Gal'lim], *heaps*—A village south of Jerusalem. Here lived Phalti (Phaltiel) to whom Saul gave Michal, the wife of David (1 Sam. 25:44; 2 Sam. 3:15).

Gallio [Gal'li·o], *one who lives on milk*—The proconsul of Achaia under Claudius. He was the brother of Seneca, the Roman philosopher, to whom he probably owed much of his political advancement. When the labors of Paul at Corinth aroused opposition, the Jews brought him before Gallio to be tried for breaking the Mosaic law. Gallio refused to hear the case, declaring that matters involving religious laws or customs were not in his jurisdiction. Likewise when the Greeks beat Sosthenes, the ruler of the synagogue, he again refused the case (Acts 18:12–17).

Gamaliel [Ga·ma'li·el], *God is my recompense*—The name of two men in the Bible:

1. Son of Pedahzur, a leader of the tribe of Manasseh chosen to help take the census during Israel's wandering in the wilderness (Num. 1:10).

2. A famous member of the Jewish Sanhedrin and a teacher of the law. Gamaliel, who had taught the apostle Paul (Acts 22:3), advised the Sanhedrin to treat the apostles of the young Christian church with moderation. Gamaliel's argument was simple. If Jesus was a false prophet, as many others had been, the movement would soon fade into obscurity. If, however, the work was "of God," he pointed out, "you cannot overthrow it" (Acts 5:39). He died about A.D. 50.

Gammad [Gam'mad], *brave men* or *valorous men* or *warriors*—A group of people who defended Tyre (Ezek. 27:11).

Gammadim [Gam'ma·dim]—See Gammad.

Gamul [Gam'ul], *weaned*—An Aaronite. In the reign of David his family was appointed as the twenty-second course of priests (1 Chron. 24:17).

Garden of Eden—See Eden.

Gareb [Gar'eb], *scabby*—
   1. One of David's warriors (2 Sam. 23:38).
   2. The name of a hill near Jerusalem (Jer. 31:39).

Garmite [Gar'mite], *bony*—An epithet of obscure meaning apparently denoting the family or the residents of Keilah (1 Chron. 4:19).

Gashmu [Gash'mu]—See Geshem.

Gatam [Ga'tam], *puny*—A son of Eliphaz and grandson of Esau (Gen. 36:11).

Gates of Jerusalem—Many different gates for the city of Jerusalem and for the temple are mentioned in Scripture. It is difficult to identify all of these exactly—there are so many that probably some of the names overlap one another. Listed in alphabetical order with references, gates named in the NKJV:

   Beautiful Gate (Acts 3:10)
   Benjamin's Gate (Jer. 38:7; Zech. 14:10)
   Corner Gate (2 Kings 14:13; 2 Chron. 25:23; 26:9; Jer. 31:38; Zech. 14:10)
   East Gate (1 Chron. 26:14; 2 Chron. 31:14)
   Ephraim, Gate of (2 Kings 14:13; 2 Chron. 25:23; Neh. 8:16; 12:39)
   First Gate (Zech. 14:10) also called Forme Gate
   Fish Gate (2 Chron. 33:14; Neh. 3:3; 12:39; Zech. 1:10)
   Foundation Gate (Neh. 3:15; 12:37)
   Horse Gate (2 Chron. 23:15; Neh. 3:28; Jer. 31:40)
   Joshua, Gate of (2 Kings 23:8)
   King's Gate (1 Chron. 9:18)
   Middle Gate (Jer. 39:3)
   Miphkad Gate (Neh. 3:31) also called Inspection Gate or Muster Gate
   New Gate (Jer. 36:10)
   North Gate (1 Chron. 26:14)
   Old Gate (Neh. 3:6; 12:39) also called Jeshanah Gate
   Potsherd Gate (Jer. 19:2)

Prison, Gate of the (Neh. 12:39) also called Guard Gate

Refuse Gate (Neh. 2:13; 3:13–14; 12:31) also called Dung Gate, or Dung Port

Shallecheth Gate (1 Chron. 26:16)

Sheep Gate (Neh. 3:1, 32; 12:39; John 5:2) also called Sheep Market

South Gate (1 Chron. 26:15)

Upper Gate (2 Kings 15:35; 2 Chron. 23:20; 27:3

Valley Gate (2 Chron. 26:9; Neh. 2:13, 15; 3:13)

Water Gate (Neh. 3:26; 8:1, 3, 16; 12:37)

West Gate (1 Chron. 26:16).

Gath [Gath], *wine press*—One of the five chief cities of the Philistines (Judg. 3:3). Although Gath is frequently used as a prefix in combination with a proper name to refer to other cities—for example, Gath-hepher (Josh. 19:13) and Gath-rimmon (Josh. 19:45)—when it appears alone it refers to the great Philistine city.

Gath was known as the residence of the Anakim, men of great stature (Josh. 11:22). Goliath and other giants belonged to this race and the city of Gath (1 Sam. 17:4). David captured Gath during his reign (1 Chron. 13:1). The residents of Gath, known as Gittites, were still subject to Israel during Solomon's reign, although they still had their own king (1 Kings 2:39, 42).

Solomon's son Rehoboam later fortified Gath (2 Chron. 11:8), but the city returned to the hands of the Philistines. Later, it was recaptured by Hazael (2 Kings 12:17), and Uzziah broke down its walls (2 Chron. 26:6).

Gath-hepher [Gath-he'pher], *wine press of the well*—A town of Zebulun near Nazareth, the native city of Jonah (2 Kings 14:25). It is once called Gittah-hepher (Josh. 19:13).

Gath-rimmon [Gath-rim'mon], *wine press of the pomegranate*—The name of two towns, one of Dan (Josh. 19:45), the other of Manasseh, west of the Jordan (Josh. 21:25).

Gaulanitus [Gaul·an·it'us], *unknown*—An area east of the Sea of Galilee, named after the city of Golon (Deut. 4:43).

Gaza [Ga'za], *stronghold*—One of the five principal cities of the Philistines. The southernmost city of Canaan, Gaza was situated on the great caravan route between Mesopotamia and Egypt, at the junction of the trade route from Arabia. This location made Gaza an ideal rest stop and a commercial center for merchants and travelers.

Gaza was originally inhabited by the Avvim, a people who were replaced by the Caphtorim (Deut. 2:23). Gaza was allotted to the tribe of Judah by Joshua (Josh. 15:47), but it was not immediately occupied (Judg. 1:18), because the Anakim were still present in the city (Josh. 11:22; 13:3). Soon afterward the Philistines recovered Gaza (Judg. 13:1). Here the mighty Samson was humiliated by being forced to grind grain as a blinded prisoner (Judg. 16:21). In a final victorious performance, Samson brought down the house of the pagan god Dagon, destroying many Philistines (Judg. 16:23–31).

Although Solomon ruled over Gaza, not until the reign of Hezekiah, king of Judah, was the decisive blow dealt to the Philistines (2 Kings 18:8). Through the prophet Amos, God threatened Gaza with destruction by fire for its sins (Amos 1:6–7). This prophecy was fulfilled by the army of Alexander the Great in 332 B.C., when Gaza was destroyed and her inhabitants massacred (Zeph. 2:4; Zech. 9:5).

In the New Testament the evangelist Philip was directed by God to preach the gospel along the road from Jerusalem to Gaza (Acts 8:26). On this road the Ethiopian eunuch professed faith in Jesus and was baptized. Gaza is referred to as Azzah three times in the King James Version.

Gazathite [Ga′za·thite]—See Gazite.

Gazer [Ga′zer]—A variant form of Gezer. See Gezer.

Gazez [Ga′zez], *shearer*—Two Old Testament men:
1. A son of Caleb of Judah. His mother, Ephah, was Caleb's concubine (1 Chron. 2:46).
2. A grandson of Caleb (1 Chron. 2:46).

Gazite [Ga′zite]—An inhabitant of Gaza (Judg. 16:2).

Gazzam [Gaz′zam], *devouring*—Progenitor of a family of Nethinim (Ezra 2:48).

Geba, Gaba [Ge′ba, Ga′ba], *a hill*—A frontier city of Benjamin near the border of Judah, assigned to the Levites (Josh. 18:24; 21:17).

David drove the Philistines from Geba to Gezer (2 Sam. 5:25). Asa rebuilt the city (1 Kings 15:22).

Gebal [Ge'bal], *mountain*—The name of a city and a region:

1. A mountainous region between Petra and the southern end of the Dead Sea. Inhabited by the Edomites, Gebal was one of the areas allied against Israel (Ps. 83:7).

2. An ancient and thriving seaport situated on a bluff in the foothills of Lebanon that overlooked the Mediterranean Sea. Gebal was about 32 kilometers (20 miles) north of Beirut between Sidon and Tripoli (Ezek. 27:9). One of the most important seaports of Phoenicia, Gebal imported so much papyrus from Egypt that its Greek name, *Byblos*, ultimately gave rise to words like "Bible" and "bibliography."

Gebalites [Ge'bal·ites]—Inhabitants of Gebal (John 13:5; 1 Kings 5:18; Ezek. 27:9).

Geber [Ge'ber], *man*—Two Old Testament men:

1. The father of one of Solomon's twelve food officers in Ramoth Gilead. Each of these twelve officers was responsible for providing food for the king's household for one month of the year (1 Kings 4:7, 13).

2. Son of Uri and purveyor of food for Solomon in Gilead (1 Kings 4:19).

Gebim [Ge'bim], *trenches*—A town of Benjamin north of Jerusalem (Isa. 10:31).

Gedaliah [Ged·a·li'ah], *the Lord is great*—The name of five Old Testament men:

1. Son of Ahikam, a person of high birth appointed governor of Judah by Nebuchadnezzar (2 Kings 25:22–25). Gedaliah governed Judah from Mizpah, where after ruling for only two or three months he was assassinated by Jewish nationalists led by Ishmael. Gedaliah's father had protected the prophet Jeremiah, and Gedaliah probably did the same.

2. A Levite musician of David's time. Gedaliah was one of the six sons of Jeduthun (1 Chron. 25:3, 9). He was a member of the Levitical choir and of the second course, or order, of priests appointed by David for the sanctuary.

3. A priest who divorced his pagan wife after the captivity (Ezra 10:18).

4. A son of Pashhur, a jewish prince who called for the death and imprisonment of the prophet Jeremiah (Jer. 38:1, 4).

5. An ancestor of the prophet Zephaniah (Zeph. 1:1).

Gedeon [Ged′e·on]—See Gideon.

Geder [Ge′der], *a wall*—A town in the south of Judah taken by Joshua (Josh. 12:13).

Gederah [Ge·de′rah], *sheepfold*—A town of Judah (Josh. 15:36).

Gederathite [Ge′der·a·thite]—A man of Gederah. Jozabad, one of David's mighty men, was a Gederathite (1 Chron. 12:4).

Gederite [Ge·de′rite]—A man of Geder or Gederah (1 Chron. 27:28).

Gederoth [Ge·de′roth], *enclosures*—A town of Judah (Josh. 15:41).

Gederothaim [Ge·de·ro·tha′im], *two enclosures*—A place listed as one of the cities of Judah (Josh. 15:36).

Gedor [Ge′dor], *wall*—

1. A hill town of Judah near Hebron (Josh. 15:58), probably the place from which a number of warriors joined David at Ziklag (1 Chron. 12:7).

2. A district from which the Simeonites drove out the Hamite settlers (1 Chron. 4:39–40).

3. An ancestor of Saul (1 Chron. 8:31; 9:37).

4. Ancestors of two Judahite families (1 Chron. 4:4, 18).

Geharashim [Ge·ha·ra′shim]—See Charashim.

Gehazi [Ge·ha′zi], *valley of vision*—The servant of Elisha (2 Kings 4:8–37; 5:20–27).

Gehenna [Ge·hen′na], *Valley of Hinnom*—The Valley of Hinnom south of Jerusalem became notorious as a place of child sacrifice to Molech (2 Chron. 28:3; 33:6). King Josiah wiped out this dreadful practice (2 Kings 23:10), and the place later became a garbage dump with its continually burning fires. The place name was already beginning to take on the New Testament meaning of the place of judgment for sinners in Jeremiah 7:32 and 19:6.

Three terms are combined in both verses: "the valley of the son of Hinnom," "Tophet," and "the valley of slaughter." In the New Testament, James uses *Gehenna* once for "hell" (3:6), and Christ Himself uses it eleven times in the Synoptic Gospels with the same meaning. Since hell is a fearful place, it is a comfort to know that the One who talked the most about it also made a way to escape its torments. See Hell.

Geliloth [Ge·li′loth], *circles*—A place in Benjamin, probably Gilgal (Josh. 18:17).

Gemalli [Ge·mal′li], *camel driver*—The father of Ammiel (Num. 13:12).

Gemariah [Gem·a·ri′ah], *Jehovah has perfected*—

1. Son of Shaphan, the scribe. From Gemariah's chamber in the temple Baruch read to the people the prophecies of Jeremiah. Gemariah was among those who vainly sought to deter Jehoiakim from burning the written record of the prophecy (Jer. 36:10–12, 25).

2. Son of Hilkiah (Jer. 29:3).

Gennesaret [Gen·nes′a·ret], *a harp*—The land of Gennesaret is mentioned in connection with the crossing of the Sea of Galilee by Jesus and His disciples (Matt. 14:34; Mark 6:53). See Galilee, Sea of.

Gentiles [Gen′tiles]—All non-Jews. In the Old Testament, the word *goy* ("nation," "people," "heathen," "Gentile") has several usages and is hard to define. Basically, it refers to a defined group of people or a large subdivision of people.

Genesis 10's "table of nations" uses *goy* without labeling the mentioned nations as "heathen" or by other pejorative terms. Unsurprisingly, *goy* is used for Egypt and Syria, but in view of the tendency to associate the word with Gentiles, it is interesting to note how the Hebrew Old Testament used *goy* for Israel. God promised to make Abraham "a great nation [*goy*]" (Gen. 17:20). Moses reminded God to "consider that this nation [*goy*] is Your people" (Ex. 33:13).

While the plural form is used for ethnic groups that would be descendants of Abraham (Gen. 17:16), as time passed the term more and more came to be used for the Gentiles. Even the concept of their being pagan or heathen is evident in some texts (Judg. 4:2, 13, 16). The "uncircumcised" were idolaters, usually wicked, and often enemies of

Israel. Nevertheless, the Old Testament does predict a bright future for the Gentiles when they come to know the Messiah (Isa. 11:10; 42:6). The shortest chapter in the Bible, Psalm 117 (perhaps made short to draw attention to a truth that was unpopular in Israel), calls on all the Gentiles (*goyim*) and all the peoples to praise the Lord. In the New Testament the term is used for the word *nations* (Matt. 24:7; Acts 2:5) and for the word *Greek* (Rom. 2:9; 1 Cor. 12:13).

Gentiles, Court of—See Court of the Gentiles.

Genubath [Ge·nu′bath], *robbery*—Son of Hadad (1 Kings 11:20).

Gera [Ge′ra], *a grain*—Son of Bela (1 Chron. 8:3) and grandson of Benjamin (Gen. 46:21).

Gerar [Ge′rar], *a lodging place*—An ancient city south of Gaza (Gen. 10:19; 20:1; 26:26). At an early time it was held by the Philistines (Gen. 26:1). Abimelech was its ruler (Gen. 20:2; 26:16–17).

Gerasa [Ger′a·sa]—One of the ten cities of the Decapolis. It is not mentioned in the Bible, but the Gospels record Jesus healing a man from "the country of the [Gerasenes]" (Mark 5:1; Luke 8:26, 37). Many versions say "Gadarenes." Gadara was also a city of the Decapolis, exactly which one is meant is unclear. The Decapolis was south and east of the Sea of Galilee. See Gadarenes.

Gerasenes [Ger′a·senes]—See Gadarenes.

Gergesenes [Ger′ge·senes]—See Gadarenes.

Gerizim [Ge·ri′zim], *a piece or a portion (as cut off)*—A mountain in the district of Samaria. Mount Gerizim is located southwest of Mount Ebal. The main north–south road through central Palestine ran between these two mountains. Thus, Gerizim was of strategic military importance.

When the Hebrew people reached the promised land, Moses directed them to climb Mount Gerizim and Mount Ebal. Six tribes stood on each mountain (Deut. 27:11–14). Then Moses pronounced the blessings for keeping the law from Mount Gerizim and the curses for not keeping it from Mount Ebal (Deut. 11:29; 27:4–26). A ledge halfway to the top of Gerizim is called "Jotham's pulpit" (see Judg. 9:7). The characteristics of the two mountains make it possible to speak from either mountain and be heard easily in the valley below.

When the Israelites returned from their years of captivity in Babylon, they refused to allow the Samaritans, the residents of this mountain region, to assist in rebuilding Jerusalem (Ezra 4:1–4; Neh. 2:19–20; 13:28). In the days of Alexander the Great, a Samaritan temple was built on Mount Gerizim. Although it was destroyed by the Hasmonean king John Hyrcanus in 128 B.C., the Samaritans still worshipped on Mount Gerizim in Jesus' day (John 4:20–21). The small Samaritan community in Israel continues to celebrate the Passover on Mount Gerizim to this day.

Jacob's Well is situated at the foot of Mount Gerizim, today called Jebel et-Tor. This is the well where Jesus met the woman of Samaria, discussed Samaritan worship practices on Mount Gerizim, and told her of Himself—"a fountain of water springing up into everlasting life" (John 4:14). A little to the north is the tomb of Joespeh (Josh. 24:32). It was also on Mount Gerizim that Abraham was directed to sacrifice Isaac, according to the Samaritans.

Gerizites [Ge·ri′zites]—See Gerzites.

Gershom [Ger′shom], *explusion*—

1. The firstborn of Moses by his wife, Zipporah, daughter of Jethro (Ex. 2:22; 18:3). He was circumcised by his mother. Gershom's descendants through his son, Jonathan, worshipped graven images (Judg. 18:30–31).

2. The eldest son of Levi, the name being spelled Gershon in several passages (1 Chron. 6:16–17, 20, 43; 15:7).

3. The head of the family of Phinehas (Ezra 8:2).

Gershomites [Ger′shom·ites]—Family descended from Gershom (1 Chron. 6:62, 71, NRSV). Other versions say Gershon.

Gershon [Ger′shon], *explusion*—The oldest of the three sons of Levi; his brothers were Kohath and Merari (Gen. 46:11; Num. 3:17). He is also called Gershom (1 Chron. 15:7). Gershon was founder of the family called the Gershonites (Num. 26:57), one of three main divisions of the Levitical priesthood whose sons had charge of the coverings, curtains, and hangings of the tabernacle (Num. 3:21–26; 4:22–28). Gershon was apparently born to Levi before Jacob's family moved to

Egypt to escape a famine (Ex. 6:16). Although Gershon was the oldest of Levi's sons, it was through the line of Gershon's younger brother, Kohath, that the priestly line of Aaron sprang years later after the exodus of the Hebrew people from Egypt.

Gershonites [Ger'shon·ites]—The descendants of Gershon, son of Levi. See Gershon.

Geruth Kimham [Ger'uth Kim'ham]—See Chimham.

Gerzites [Ger·zites], unknown—A Canaanite nation which had inhabited the land "from of old" (1 Sam. 27:8). David and his men raided this group during the time he was running from Saul.

Gesham [Ge'sham]—See Geshan.

Geshan [Ge'shan], lump—A son of Jahdai of the family of Caleb of Judah (1 Chron. 2:47).

Geshem [Ge'shem], rain—An Arabian, and probably the chief of an Arabian tribe (Neh. 2:19; 6:1, 2, 6).

Geshur [Ge'shur], proud behavior—A district in Bashan. It joined Argob (Deut. 3:14) and Aram (2 Sam. 15:8). It was an Aramaean kingdom. One of David's wives was of this district and to it Absalom fled after slaying Amnon (2 Sam. 3:3; 13:37).

Geshurites [Ge·shu'rites]—
  1. Inhabitants of Geshur (Deut. 3:14; Josh. 12:5; 13:11).
  2. A tribe between Arabia and Philistia (Josh. 13:2; 1 Sam. 27:8).

Gether [Ge'ther], fear—A son of Aram (Gen. 10:23).

Gethsemane [Geth·sem'a·ne], olive press—The garden where Jesus often went alone or with His disciples for prayer, rest, or fellowship, and the site where He was betrayed by Judas on the night before His crucifixion (Luke 21:37; John 18:1–2).

Gethsemane was situated on the Mount of Olives (or Mount Olivet) just east of Jerusalem, across the Kidron Valley and opposite the temple (Mark 13:3; John 18:1). From its name scholars conclude that the garden was situated in an olive grove that contained an olive press. Attempts to locate the exact site of the garden have been unsuccessful. Many Christians have agreed on one site—the place that Constantine's mother

Helena designated about A.D. 325. But at least two other sites are also defended by tradition and have their supporters. The gospel accounts do not provide enough details to show the exact site of the garden. At the time of Christ, it contained many olive trees but these were probably cut down in the first Christian century by Titus.

The four gospel writers focus special attention on Jesus' final visit to Gethsemane just before His arrest and crucifixion. After the Last Supper, Jesus returned there with His disciples for final instructions and a period of soul-searching prayer. All the disciples were instructed; but only Peter, James, and John went to Gethsemane with Jesus to pray (Mark 14:26–32). Jesus urged them to stand watch while He prayed. Then He pleaded with God to deliver Him from the coming events (Mark 14:32–42). But His prayer was not an arrogant attempt to resist God's will or even to change God's plan. His pleas clearly acknowledged His obedience to the will of the Father: "O My Father, if this cup cannot pass away from Me unless I drink it, Your will be done" (Matt. 26:42).

Geuel [Geu′el], *majesty of God*—The son of Machi (Num. 13:15).

Gezer [Ge′zer], *portion*—An ancient city of Canaan. It was taken by Joshua and its inhabitants were slain (Josh. 10:33; 12:12). It was on the southern boundary of Ephraim (Josh. 16:3) and was allotted to the Levites (Josh. 21:21; 1 Chron. 6:67).

Gezrite [Gez′rite]—See Girzite.

Ghost, Holy—See Holy Spirit.

Giah [Gi′ah], *fountain*—A place indicating the position of the hill Ammah (2 Sam. 2:24).

Giants, Valley of—See Rephaim.

Gibbar [Gib′bar], *hero*—Ninety-five children of Gibbar returned with Zerubbabel (Ezra 2:20).

Gibbethon [Gib′be·thon], *a height*—A town of Dan (Josh. 19:44), later given to the Kohathite branch of the Levites (Josh. 21:23).

Gibea [Gib′e·a], *hill*—One of the grandsons of Caleb (1 Chron. 2:49).

Gibeah, Gibeath [Gib′e·ah, Gib′e·ath], *hill*—The name of three or four different places in the Old Testament:

1. Gibeath-Haaraloth, "the hill of the foreskins" (Josh. 5:3), a place in Canaan where male Israelites were circumcised.

2. A small, unidentified city in a mountainous territory of Judah (Josh. 15:57). It was probably south of Hebron.

3. A city belonging to Benjamin (Judg. 19:14). Scholars disagree over whether this is the same city called Gibeath in Joshua 18:28. Gibeah has been excavated at the modern site of Tell el-Ful, 5 kilometers (3 miles) north of Jerusalem. This city figured prominently in two separate periods of Old Testament history. It first appeared in Judges 19–20 as the site of a crime of lewdness and obscenity. All the children of Israel came together to punish Gibeah for its crimes. After a prolonged and mostly unsuccessful war against the Benjamites, the Israelites completely destroyed Gibeah (Judg. 20:40). The Tel el-Ful excavations have uncovered the remains of a village completely destroyed by fire.

Gibeah was apparently rebuilt after the fire. The birthplace of Saul, it became the capital of his kingdom (1 Sam. 14:16; 15:34). In many passages, it is even called "Gibeah of Saul" (1 Sam. 11:4; Isa. 10:29). It is likely that this is the same place where the ark of the covenant was kept (2 Sam. 6:3–4). At Tell el-Ful, the remains of Saul's fortress, built around 1015 B.C., have been found. The fortress walls, 2.5 to 3.5 meters (8 to 10 feet) thick, enclosed an area of 52 x 47 meters (170 x 155 feet). The stronghold was made up of two stories joined by a stone staircase.

4. The KJV uses "Gibeah" instead of "hill" in some passages, such as "the house of Abinadab that was in Gibeah" (2 Sam. 6:4).

Gibeath [Gib′e·ath]—See Gibeah.

Gibeath Elohim [Gib′e·ath El·ohim′], *hill of God*—The hill where Samuel told Saul that the Spirit of the Lord would come upon him as a sign that his anointing was really from God (1 Sam. 10:5).

Gibeathite [Gib′e·a·thite]—A native of Gibeah (1 Chron. 12:3).

Gibeon [Gib′e·on], *pertaining to a hill*—A city in the territory of Benjamin about 10 kilometers (6 miles) northwest of Jerusalem. It was the chief city of the Hivites. Though in the territory of Benjamin it was assigned to the priests (Josh. 21:17). The first reference to Gibeon in the

Bible is Joshua 9:3. After the Israelites destroyed the cities of Jericho and Ai (Joshua 6–8), Gibeon's inhabitants, fearing the same fate, made a covenant with the Israelites. Although they established the treaty by deceit and thus were made slaves by the Israelites, the Gibeonites were still protected from the alliance of five Amorite kings. In a battle over Gibeon between Joshua and the Amorite alliance (Josh. 10:1–11), the sun stood still for a day and hailstones rained down on the fleeing Amorites.

Gibeon does not appear again in Scripture until about 1000 B.C. Then, in a gruesome contest of strength, twelve of David's men and twelve of the men of Ish-bosheth (Saul's son) killed one another with their swords. The place was named "the Field of the Sharp Swords" (2 Sam. 2:16) because of this event. There followed a great battle in which David's forces were victorious (2 Sam. 2:12–17).

The prophet Jeremiah mentioned a "great pool that is in Gibeon" (Jer. 41:12). This pool was discovered in an excavation of the site, beginning in 1956. Archaeologists discovered a large open pit about 11 meters (35 feet) deep that had been dug into the solid rock. A large stone stairway descended into the pit, then continued another 11 meters down to a water chamber. Gibeon was the center of a winemaking industry during the seventh century B.C. The lower chamber of the "great pool" provided water for the wine and also served as the city's main water supply.

Gibeon, Pool of [Gib′e·on]—A battle between David's forces and Saul's son Ish-bosheth began with a meeting "by the pool of Gibeon" (2 Sam. 2:13). The book of the prophet Jeremiah, written hundreds of years after David's time, also referred to as "the great pool that is in Gibeon" (Jer. 41:12). This "great pool" was obviously an impressive feature of the city.

Archeologists have discovered a huge well dug through solid limestone at the site of the Old Testament city of Gibeon, located about seven miles north of Jerusalem. About 40 feet in diameter and 80 feet deep, this giant well apparently provided water for the Canaanite city of Gibeon as early as Joshua's time about 1400 B.C. (Josh. 9). It must have still been in use about eight centuries later during the ministry of the prophet Jeremiah, when the citizens of Judah occupied the site.

Digging a well like this with hand tools was a massive undertaking. But a dependable water supply was essential for ancient cities of Bible times. Access to the precious water was provided by a spiraling stairway cut into the rock around the edge of the shaft. The women of Gibeon made the long climb every day to bring up fresh water for their households. In addition to this well at Gibeon, the wells dug by Isaac (Gen. 26:18–22) and Uzziah (2 Chron. 26:10) are also mentioned in the Bible. David longed for water from the well in his hometown of Bethlehem (2 Sam. 23:15–16), and Jesus spoke about His free gift of unfailing water to the woman at the well in Samaria (John 4:1–26).

Gibeonites [Gib'e·on·ites]—A Canaanite tribe which deceived Israel into making a contract with them, promising to protect them and not wipe them out (Josh. 9:17, 23, 27; 2 Sam. 21:1–2, 5–6, 9).

Giblite [Gib'lite], unknown—An inhabitant of Gebal, a town in Phoenicia. Mention is made of their work on Solomon's temple. In the Revised Version the word *Gebalite* is used (Josh. 13:5; 1 Kings 5:18).

Giddalti [Gid·dal'ti], *I have magnified*—A son of Heman, the king's seer (1 Chron. 25:4, 29).

Giddel [Gid'del], *gigantic*—The children of Giddel returned with Zerubbabel from Babylon and were included both among the Nethinim (Ezra 2:47; Neh. 7:49) and among the children of Solomon's servants (Ezra 2:56; Neh. 7:58).

Gideon [Gid'e·on], *feller of trees*—A military hero and spiritual leader who delivered Israel from the oppression of the Midianites.

As a young lad, Gideon had seen the land oppressed by the Midianites and Amalekites for seven years (Judg. 6:1). Like invading locusts, the roving bands camped on the land of the Israelites. At harvest time, they destroyed the crops and animals and plundered the farmers' houses. Israel's misfortune was apparently caused by their spiritual relapse into Baal worship (Judg. 6:1).

As young Gideon was threshing wheat, the angel of the Lord appeared with strong words of encouragement: "The Lord is with you, you mighty man of valor. . . . Surely, I will be with you, and you shall defeat the Midianites as one man" (Judg. 6:12, 16).

Gideon then asked the messenger for a sign that God had selected him for divine service. He prepared an offering and placed it on an altar. The angel touched the offering with his staff, and fire consumed it (6:19–21). Gideon then recognized his personal call to serve God.

Gideon's first assignment was to destroy his father's altar of Baal in the family's backyard (Judg. 6:25). This act required great courage, for Gideon feared his father's house and the men of the city who must have worshipped at the altar. For this reason, Gideon and ten servants destroyed the altar of Baal and a wood idol by night and erected an altar to the Lord. Gideon immediately presented an offering to the Lord on the altar (6:27–28). When Gideon's fellow citizens discovered that the altar to Baal had been destroyed, they were outraged. When it was learned that "Gideon the son of Joash has done this thing" (6:29), Joash was called to account for his son's behavior. To his credit, Joash defended Gideon by implying that an authentic god should require no defense. "If he [Baal] is a god, let him plead for himself" (6:31). So that day Gideon was called Jerubbaal, meaning "Let Baal plead" (6:25–32).

As the oppression of the Midianites intensified, Gideon sent out messengers to all Manasseh and the surrounding tribes to rally volunteers to Israel's cause (Judg. 6:35). When Gideon's volunteers assembled, about 32,000 citizen soldiers stood in the ranks (Judg. 7:1). Although there were 135,000 Midianites camped in a nearby valley, God directed Gideon to thin out the ranks. After dismissing the fearful and afraid, only 10,000 remained. Gideon's band was now outnumbered about 13 to 1.

"There are still too many," God told Gideon. "Bring them down to the water, and I will test them for you there" (7:4). Those who scooped up the water with their hands, never taking their eyes from the horizon, were retained in Gideon's army; those who got down on their knees to drink, forgetting to keep watch for the enemy, were dismissed. Now only 300 soldiers remained (Judg. 7:5–7). The Midianites outnumbered Gideon's band 450 to 1. But God and Gideon had a secret plan.

Gideon divided the army into three companies. Then he gave each man a trumpet, a pitcher, and a torch. At the appointed time, 300 trumpets blasted the air, 300 hands raised their pitchers and smashed them to bits, 300 burning torches pierced the darkness, and 300 warriors cried, "The sword of the LORD and of Gideon" (Judg. 7:19–21).

The Midianites were thrown into panic. In the confusion, some committed suicide or killed their comrades. The remaining soldiers fled. The enemies of Israel were completely routed, and Israel's homeland was secure (Judg. 7:22; 8:10). It was a glorious victory for God and for Gideon, who became an instant hero (8:22).

Gideon and his men pursued the fleeing enemy. Many of them were killed or captured by Gideon's allies. Two Midianite kings, Zebah and Zalmunna, were captured and killed for their murderous deeds (Judg. 8).

As a conquering warrior, Gideon was invited to become king (Judg. 8:22), but he declined. Modest and devout, he was careful not to grasp at the power and glory that belonged to God. After he retired to his home, Israel was blessed with forty years of peace (Judg. 8:28).

Through the life and exploits of Gideon, God reveals much about Himself and the preparation that His leaders need for divine service. Gideon shows that God calls leaders from unlikely situations. Gideon was a poor farmer's son who worked with his hands, and his father was an idol worshiper (Judg. 6:15, 25). Still, Gideon was an effective leader in God's service.

The story of Gideon also reminds us that God prefers a few dedicated and disciplined disciples to throngs of uncommitted workers. God can win victories with a fully committed minority (Judg. 7:2, 4, 7).

Another leadership lesson from Gideon's life is that a leader's spiritual life is sustained by regular worship. Devout Gideon appears to have worshipped frequently—in times of personal crisis as well as celebration (Judg. 6:18-21; 7:15).

Gideoni [Gid·e·o′ni], *cutting down*—Father of Abidan (Num. 1:11; 2:22; 7:60, 65).

Gidom [Gi′dom], *a cutting down*—A place near Gibeah to which the Benjamites fled (Judg. 20:45).

Gihon [Gi′hon], *gusher*—The name of a river and a spring in the Old Testament:

1. One of the four rivers of the garden of Eden (Gen. 2:13). Some scholars believe the name refers to the Nile River. Others, however, believe it refers to a smaller river in the Euphrates Valley system—perhaps a major irrigation ditch or canal.

2. A spring outside the walls of Jerusalem where the city obtained part of its water supply (2 Chron. 32:30). The Canaanite inhabitants of ancient Jerusalem, or Jebus, had used and protected the spring in their fortifications too. When David and his soldiers conquered Jebus, they entered it through the water shaft that led from the spring into the city (2 Sam. 5:8). Israel continued to use Gihon and its water channel. King Hezekiah channeled the water more elaborately when he constructed the famous Siloam tunnel in 701 B.C. as part of the city's preparation against the siege of the Assyrians (2 Kings 20:20).

Gihon was the site where Solomon was anointed and proclaimed king (1 Kings 1:33, 38, 45). Some scholars believe it later became customary for the new king to drink from the waters of Gihon during his coronation ceremony (Ps. 110:7).

Gilalal [Gil′a·lal], unknown—The son of a priest who was present when the wall was dedicated (Neh. 12:36).

Gilboa [Gil·bo′a], *bubbling fountain*—A mountain near the city of Jezreel on the eastern side of the plain of Esdraelon (1 Sam. 28:4). Here the forces of Israel under Saul were defeated by the Philistines. The sons of Saul were killed in the battle and Saul committed suicide by falling on his sword (1 Sam. 31:1; 2 Sam. 1:6; 21:12).

Gilead [Gil′e·ad], *rocky region*—The name of three men, two mountains, and one city in the Old Testament:

1. A son of Machir and grandson of Manasseh (Josh. 17:1). He founded a tribal family, the Gileadites.

2. A mountain region east of the Jordan River 915 meters (3,000 feet) above sea level. Extending about 97 kilometers (60 miles) from near the south end of the Sea of Galilee to the north end of the Dead Sea, Gilead is about 32 kilometers (20 miles) wide. It is bounded on the west by the Jordan River, on the south by the land of Moab, on the north by the Yarmuk River, and on the east by the desert. It is sometimes called Mount Gilead (Gen. 31:25) and sometimes the land of Gilead (Num. 32:1).

The Jabbok River divides Gilead into two parts: northern Gilead, the land between the Jabbok and the Yarmuk, and southern Gilead, the land between the Jabbok and the Arnon (Josh. 12:2). The term "Gilead," however, came to be applied to the entire region of Israelite Transjordan (Deut. 34:1).

This lush region receives an annual rainfall of from 71 to 81 centimeters (28 to 32 inches). Thus, much of it is thickly wooded today, as it was in Absalom's day (2 Sam. 18:6–9). Many fugitives fled to this region for safety. Jacob fled to Gilead from Laban, his father-in-law (Gen. 31:21). The Israelites who feared the Philistines in King Saul's day fled here (1 Sam. 13:7), as did Ish-bosheth (2 Sam. 2:8–9) and David (2 Sam. 17:22, 26) during Absalom's revolt. Gilead also contains rich grazing land (1 Chron. 5:9–10).

The Balm of Gilead, an aromatic resin used for medical purposes (Jer. 8:22), was exported to Tyre and elsewhere (Ezek. 27:17). The Ishmaelites who carried Joseph into Egyptian bondage also traded in Gilead's balm (Gen. 37:25).

When Canaan was being allocated to the Israelite tribes, Gilead fell to the Reubenites and Gadites because of its suitability for grazing cattle (Deut. 3:12–17). The half-tribe of Manasseh also shared in the land of Gilead.

3. A mountain on the edge of the Jezreel Valley (Judg. 7:3). Gideon and his men were camped here when Gideon ordered a reduction in his troops before he fought the Midianites.

4. The father of Jephthah, a judge of Israel (Judg. 11:1–12:7).

5. A chief of the family of Gad (1 Chron. 5:14).

6. A city in the region of Gilead condemned by the prophet Hosea (Hos. 6:8). The name "Gilead" in this passage is probably a poetic shortening of Ramoth Gilead or Jabesh-gilead, two of the cities of Gilead.

Gileadites [Gil′e·ad·ites]—Descendants of Gilead, grandson of Manasseh (Num. 26:29).

Gilgal [Gil′gal], *circle or rolling*—The name of a campsite and two cities in the Old Testament:

1. A village from which the prophet Elijah ascended into heaven (2 Kings 2:1). Gilgal was perhaps in the hill country of Ephraim, about 13 kilometers (8 miles) northwest of Beth-el.

2. The first campsite of the people of Israel after they crossed the Jordan River and entered the promised land (Josh. 4:19–20). They took stones from the Jordan and set them up at Gilgal as a memorial to

God's deliverance. Many important events in Israel's history are associated with this city. The first Passover in Canaan was held at Gilgal (Josh. 5:9–10). It also became the base of military operations for Israel during the conquest of Canaan. From Gilgal Joshua led Israel against the city of Jericho (Josh. 6:11, 14) and conducted his southern campaign (Josh. 10). It was there that he began allotting the promised land to the tribes.

In later years, Gilgal was the site of King Saul's coronation as well as his rejection by God as king (1 Sam. 11:15; 13:4–12; 15:12–33). After Absalom's revolt, the people of Judah gathered at Gilgal to welcome David back as their king (2 Sam. 19:15, 40). But during the days of later kings, Gilgal became a center of idolatry. Like Beth-el, it was condemned by the prophets (Hos. 4:15; Amos 5:5). The presumed site of Gilgal is about 2 kilometers (1 mile) northeast of Old Testament Jericho (Josh. 4:19).

3. A town between Dor and Tirzah (Josh. 12:23), probably Jiljulieh, a little town north of the brook Kanah and 8 kilometers (5 miles) northeast of Antipatris.

4. A place on the northern border of Judah (Josh. 15:7).

Giloh [Gi'loh], *exile*—A mountain town of Judah (Josh. 15:51). It was the native place of David's counselor, Ahithophel (2 Sam. 15:12; 17:23).

Gilonite [Gi'lo·nite]—A native of Giloh, specifically Ahithophel (2 Sam. 15:12; 23:34).

Gimzo [Gim'zo], *full of sycomores*—A town of Judah (2 Chron. 28:18).

Ginath [Gi'nath], *protection*—Father of Tibni (1 Kings 16:21–22).

Ginnetho [Gin'ne·tho], *gardener*—A priest who returned with Zerubbabel from Babylon (Neh. 12:4).

Ginnethoi [Gin'ne·thoi]—See Ginnethon.

Ginnethon [Gin'ne·thon], *gardener*—A priest who sealed the covenant with Nehemiah (Neh. 10:6), probably the same as Ginnetho.

Girgashites [Gir'ga·shites], unknown—One of the tribes living in Canaan before the land was taken by Joshua and the Israelites (Gen.

10:16; Deut. 7:1; Josh. 24:11; Neh. 9:8). They probably lived west of the Jordan.

Girzite [Gir′zite], unknown—A people who occupied a district south of the Philistines (1 Sam. 27:8).

Gishpa [Gish′pa], *caress*—An overseer of the Nethinim after the return from Babylon (Neh. 11:21).

Gispa [Gis′pa]—See Gishpa.

Gittah-hepher [Git′tah-he′pher]—See Gath-hepher.

Gittaim [Git·ta′im], *two wine presses*—A village of Benjamin (Neh. 11:31, 33). To escape the cruelty of Saul the people of Beeroth fled to this city (2 Sam. 4:3).

Gittite [Git′tite], *belonging to Gath*—A native of the city of Gath (Josh. 13:3). The six hundred members of the "bodyguard" of David, under the command of Ittai, were called Gittites (2 Sam. 15:18–19).

Gizonite [Gi′zon·ite], *shearer* or *quarryman*—The designation of Hashem, the Gizonite, the ancestor of two members of David's warrior band (1 Chron. 11:34).

Gizrites [Giz′rites]—See Girzite.

Glass, Sea of—See Sea of Glass.

Goah [Go′ah]—See Goath.

Goath [Go′ath], *lowing*—A place near Jerusalem (Jer. 31:39).

Gob [Gob], *a pit*—The place where the brother of Goliath was killed by El-hanan (2 Sam. 21:18–19).

God—The Bible opens with the fact of God—"In the beginning God." The Bible is the record of the revelation of God. It is because man "by searching" cannot "find out the Almighty unto perfection," cannot know God as he has revealed himself, that such a revelation of God is necessary—the fact grounded in the need. The Greek philosopher worked from the world and its phenomena up to God, but the Bible works in exactly the opposite direction. The writers did not reason from the world to God; they began with God as the source, and the world and all things followed.

I. *Unity of God.* There is but one self-existing being. The Bible reveals God to us as the one, and the only God. There cannot be more than one God for eternity; infinity, omnipresence, and so forth, cannot apply to more than one such being. Two such beings would limit and exclude each other and thus render impossible the being of God. God makes Himself known in the Scriptures as Father, Son, and Holy Spirit, three separate personalities: three persons in one Godhead, but not three Gods. It is the Trinity and not tri-theism (Deut. 6:4; 1 Kings 8:60; Isa. 44:6; Mark 12:29; John 10:30; 1 Cor. 8:4; Eph. 4:6).

II. *God the Creator.* God is the creator of the heavens and the earth (Gen. 1:1; Ex. 20:11; Ps. 8:3; 19:1; John 1:3; Acts 14:15; Rom. 11:36; Heb. 1:2), and the creator of man (Gen. 1:26; 5:1; Ex. 4:11; Job 10:8–12; Ps. 33:15; Eccl. 12:1; Isa. 43:1; Acts 17:25–29; 1 Cor. 15:38).

III. *Natural Attributes.* Properties or qualities of the Divine Being. The true representations of God as revealed by Himself in His Word. They are inseparable from His nature. Being God He must be what He is in these essential attributes or perfections.

1. *Infinity.* His infinitude expressed in all things. In no manner limited. He is unconditioned (1 Kings 8:27; Ps. 139:8; Acts 15:18; Heb. 4:13).

2. *Eternity.* He is infinite, not finite in the duration of His being. He is not only without beginning, always was, but in the nature of that perfection is timeless. Time has no place in His eternal nature. There can be no progression, advancing from point to point, in His being (Gen. 21:23; Ex. 3:14–15; Ps. 90:2; 2 Peter 3:8).

3. *Omnipotence.* Unlimited in might and power. It is sometimes superficially asked, "If He can do all things can He make two hills without a valley between?" This is not a *thing* but an absurdity. He is not less than omnipotent because He does not do what involves an absurdity or contradiction (Gen. 1:1, 3; 18:14; Deut. 32:39; Ps. 66:3; Isa. 40:12; Dan. 4:35; Matt. 19:26; Rom. 1:20).

4. *Omniscience.* All-knowing. God is infinite in understanding just as He is in power. There can be no advance or progression in knowledge. He already knows everything that has happened, that will happen, and every possible combination of "what ifs" (Job 37:16; Ps. 33:13; 119:168; Jer. 23:24; Matt. 10:29; Acts 1:24; 15:18).

5. *Omnipresence.* Simultaneously present everywhere, always. His presence as His power extends over all His works. There is no place we can go where we are out of His reach (Job 34:21–22; Ps. 139:7–12; Isa. 66:1; Acts 17:27).

6. *Immutability.* Unchangeable. God is no more subject to change than to any other limitation (Ps. 33:11; Isa. 46:10; Mal. 3:6; Heb. 1:12; 6:17–18; James 1:17).

7. *Wisdom.* God's wisdom is perfect, and beyond our understanding (Job 36:5; Ps. 104:24; Isa. 28:29; Rom. 16:27; 1 Tim. 1:17).

IV. *Moral Perfections of God.* As the natural attributes appear in the statements relative to His own nature, and in relation to His acts of power, His relations to the universe and His creatures, so the Scriptures reveal His moral attributes in His dealings with man in His moral constitution and conduct, and His relation to the moral order. In a marvelous manner the Bible sets forth the ethical God.

1. *Holiness.* God is as essentially and infinitely holy as He is essentially omnipotent, and requires holiness of the beings made in His image (Lev. 19:2; Josh. 24:19; 1 Sam. 2:2; Job 36:2–3; Ps. 89:35; Isa. 5:16; 6:3; Hos. 11:9; 1 Peter 1:15).

2. *Justice.* In the Scriptures justice and righteousness are used synonymously. In the being of God, it is a necessary outflow from His holiness, the manifestation of that holiness in the moral government of the world. He is perfectly just as the righteous governor of the world, and His perfect righteousness appears in the penalties pronounced and rewards bestowed (Gen. 18:25; Deut. 10:17; Job 8:3, 20; Ps. 9:8; 119:142; Jer. 11:20; Dan. 9:7; Rom. 2:11; Rev. 15:3).

3. *Mercy.* The divine goodness and compassion exercised toward the guilty and wretched in harmony with truth and justice, the ministry of love for the relief of those unworthy of it (Ex.

34:7; Deut. 4:31; Ps. 51:1; 117:2; Isa. 55:7; Jer. 3:12; Luke 1:50; 6:36; Eph. 2:4; Titus 3:5; Heb. 4:16).

4. *Faithfulness.* This divine attribute is noted especially in the Psalms. By it we are assured that God will fulfill His promises regarding temporal necessities (Ps. 84:11; Isa. 33:16; 1 Tim. 4:8); support in temptation and persecution (Isa. 41:10; 1 Cor. 10:13; 1 Peter 4:12–13); comfort in afflictions (Heb. 12:4–12); guidance in trouble (2 Chron. 32:22; Ps. 32:8), power to persevere (Jer. 32:40); and spiritual blessings and final glory (1 Cor. 1:9; 1 John 2:25).

5. *Love.* Our conceptions of God must be derived from the revelation of Himself in His Word, and in that revelation He declares this attribute of love. Not only so, but it is the only attribute by which His being as such is defined—"God is love." In no instance is another attribute so employed, as "God is power," or "God is omniscience." Love is the distinctive characteristic of God in which all others harmoniously blend. In both the Old and New Testaments God's gracious love to men is so strongly and frequently declared it would take considerable space to set down the passages (Ex. 34:6; Isa. 63:9; Jer. 31:3; John 3:16; 1 John 4:10). The highest expression of divine love is in redemption—God in Christ reconciling the world to Himself (Rom. 5:8; 8:32–39; 1 John 4:9–10).

V. *The Triune God—Father, Son, Holy Spirit.* The Scriptures set forth the Godhead in this distinction of persons with absolute unity of essence. At the beginning of our Lord's ministry, the three persons are exhibited at His baptism; the Holy Spirit rested on Him as a dove, and the Father spoke acknowledging the Son. In the formula of baptism the doctrine of Trinity is established by the resurrected Lord (Matt. 28:19).

1. *The Father is God* (Matt. 11:25; John 6:27; 8:41; Rom. 15:6; 1 Cor. 8:6; Eph. 4:6; James 1:27).

2. *The Son is God* (John 1:1, 18; 20:28; Rom. 9:5; Phil. 2:6; Col. 2:9; Heb. 1:8; 2 Peter 1:1).

3. *The Spirit is God* (Acts 5:3–4; 1 Cor. 2:10–11; Eph. 2:22).

4. The distinctness of the three from one another (John 15:26; 16:13–14; 17:1–8, 18–23).

God, Children of—See Sons of God.

Godhead [God·head]—A term which emphasizes the supremacy of God; deity (Rom. 1:20; Col. 2:9).

God, Names of—The one true God is addressed by numerous names in the Old and New Testaments. Each of these names emphasizes one aspect of God's nature and character.

> *Adonai*—This name means "my Lord," or "master." When reading the Scriptures aloud, it became customary to replace the name Yahweh with Adonai, as a precaution against possible disrespect. Moses addressed God as "Adonai" when he talked with Him at the burning bush (Ex. 4:10, 13).
>
> *YHWH (Jehovah, Yahweh, I AM)*—When Moses spoke with God at the burning bush, asking Him what to say when the Israelites inquired who sent him, God replied, "I AM WHO I AM." The name Yahweh or Jehovah comes from the Hebrew state of being verb. This name emphasizes God's exclusive and unique nature: He is defined only by Himself. In Hebrew, the name is written YHWH. Because of the custom of reading "Adonai" when reading aloud, the original pronunciation has been lost. Jehovah and Yahweh are the most used forms, though most Bible translations follow the tradition and translate it LORD (all capital letters). This name could reasonably be called the most important name of God. It is used some 6,800 times in Scripture. Several compound names of God are based on this name.
>
> *Jehovah-Jireh*—The LORD Who Provides. When Abraham was about to sacrifice Isaac, God provided a substitute (Gen. 22:14).
>
> *Jehovah-Nissi*—The LORD Is My Banner. This name celebrated the victory God gave the Israelites over the Amalekites (Ex. 17:15).
>
> *Jehovah-Shalom*—The LORD Is My Peace. Gideon gave this name to the altar he built after the Lord told him that he would defeat the Midianites (Judg. 6:24).
>
> *Jehovah-Shammah*—The LORD Is There (Ezek. 48:35).
>
> *Jehovah-Saboath (Jehovah-tsebaoth)*—The LORD of Hosts, signifying that God is surrounded by hosts of angels who obey Him (1 Sam. 1:3).

Jehovah Elohe Yisrael—The LORD God of Israel; this name appears many times throughout the Old Testament.

El—Simply, God (Deut. 5:9).

El Elohe Israel—God, the God of Israel (Gen. 32:28–30).

El Olam—The Everlasting God (Gen. 21:33).

El Shaddai—God Almighty (Ex. 6:3).

Elohim—Plural form of El. This is the name used in the creation story (Gen. 1:1–3).

God-Who-Forgives—A title that shows God's great mercy (Ps. 99:8).

Branch of Righteousness—A title used to describe the coming Messiah, Jesus (Jer. 23:5–6).

Shepherd—The most popular and well-known psalm begins with the words "The Lord is my shepherd" (Ps. 23:1). The image of God as a shepherd is one that is repeated over and over in Scripture (Isa. 40:11; Jer. 31:10; Ezek. 34:11–16; Luke 15:4–7; John 10:11–16).

Servant—The coming Messiah is described as a servant (Isa. 42:1–4; 49:1–7; 53:1–12) Jesus fulfilled this as He "put on the form of a servant and came in the likeness of men" (Phil. 2:7).

God, Sons of—See Sons of God.

Gods, Pagan—Numerous pagan gods and goddesses are mentioned in the pages of Scripture. God strictly forbade His people from worshipping or bowing down to any of these and commanded them to destroy the idolatrous pagan Canaanites so that they would not be ensnared in their evil practices. The worship of pagan deities was often accompanied by gross sexual immorality, self-disfigurement, and in some cases, human sacrifice. Following is a list of the false deities mentioned in the Bible:

Adrammelech (2 Kings 17:31, also called Annamelech)

Asherah (1 Kings 18:19)

Ashima(2 Kings 17:30)

Ashtoreth (2 Kings 23:13)

Baal (Num. 22:41)

Baal-berith (Judg. 9:4)

Baal of Peor (Ps. 106:28)

Baal-zebub (2 Kings 1:2–3; Mark 3:22)

Bel (Isa. 46:1)

Chemosh (Jer. 48:7, 13)

Chiun (Amos 5:26)

Dagon (1 Sam. 5:2–7)

Diana (Acts 19:24, 27–28)

Gad (Isa. 65:11)

Golden Calf (Ex. 32)

Hermes (Acts 14:12)

Mammon (Luke 16:13)

Meni (Isa. 65:11, also called Fate)

Merodach (Jer. 50:2)

Molech (Lev. 18:21; Zeph. 1:5; Acts 7:43, also called Milcom and Moloch)

Nebo (Isa. 46:1)

Nehushtan (2 Kings 18:4)

Nergai (2 Kings 17:30)

Nisroch (Isa. 37:38)

Remphan (Acts 7:43)

Rimmon (2 Kings 5:18)

Sikkuth (Amos 5:26)

Succoth-benoth (2 Kings 17:30)

Tammuz (Ezek. 8:14)

Tartak (2 Kings 17:31)

Twin Brothers, Castor and Pollux (Acts 28:11)

Zeus (Acts 14:12–13), also called Jupiter.

Gog [Gog], *mountain*—The name of two men in the Bible:

1. A descendant of Joel and son of Shemaiah, of the tribe of Reuben (1 Chron. 5:4).

2. The leader of a confederacy of armies that attacked the land of Israel. Described as "the prince of Rosh, Meshech, and Tubal," Gog is also depicted as being "of the land of Magog" (Ezek. 38:2–3), a "place out of the far north" of Israel. Ezekiel prophetically describes Gog and his allies striking at Israel with a fierce and sudden invasion (Ezek. 38–39). According to Ezekiel's prophecy, Gog will be crushed on the mountains of Israel in a slaughter so great it will take seven months to bury the dead (Ezek. 39:12).

3. Figuratively, the terms Gog and Magog are used to represent the nations Satan will gather about him to attack the forces of the Messiah (Rev. 20:8–15). See Magog.

Goiim [Go·i'im]. *nations* or *Gentiles*—The word is used to describe the "nations" who battled the kings of Sodom and Gomorrah (Gen. 14:1, 9) as well as a tribe Joshua conquered (Josh. 12:23). See Gentiles.

Golan [Go'lan]—A city of Bashan (Josh. 20:8).

Golgotha [Gol'go·tha]—See Calvary.

Goliath [Go·li'ath], *exile*—A Philistine giant whom David felled with a stone from his sling (1 Sam. 17:4–51). Goliath, who lived in the Philistine city of Gath, was probably a descendant of a tribe of giants known as the Anakim, or descendants of Anak (Num. 13:33). These giants probably served in a capacity similar to that of a foreign mercenary or soldier of fortune.

Based on the figures in the Bible (1 Sam. 17:4), Goliath was over 9 feet tall. The magnificence of Goliath's armor and weapons—his bronze coat of mail, bronze greaves, bronze javelin, spear with an iron spearhead, and huge sword—must have made him appear invincible.

For forty days this enormous man challenged Saul's army to find one man willing to engage in hand-to-hand combat. The winner of that one battle would determine the outcome of the war. The young David, chosen by God as Israel's next king, accepted the challenge, felling Goliath with a single stone to the forehead from his sling. When David beheaded the fallen giant, the Philistines fled in panic.

Gomer [Go'mer], *complete*—the name of a man, a people, and a woman:

1. The oldest son of Japheth (Gen. 10:2–3). He was included by Ezekiel in the army of Gog (Ezek. 38:3, 6). He represents the people known as Cimmerians whose original home was north of the Black Sea and who later migrated to Asia Minor.

2. The people descended from Gomer, son of Japheth. Apparently they lived to the far north, beyond the Black Sea (Ezek. 38:6). They were probably the Cimmerians of classical history.

3. Daughter of Diblaim, a prostitute who became the wife of the prophet Hosea (Hos. 1:1–11). When Gomer left Hosea and became the slave of one of her lovers, Hosea bought her back at God's command for the price of a slave. Gomer's unfaithfulness and Hosea's forgiveness symbolized God's forgiving love for unfaithful Israel.

Gomorrah [Go·mor′rah], *submersion*—One of the five Cities of the Plain located in the valley of Siddim (Salt Sea or Dead Sea). The other cities were Sodom, Admah, Zeboiim, and Zoar (Gen. 14:2–3). Gomorrah is associated closely with its twin city, Sodom. Because these cities became the site of intolerable wickedness, they were destroyed by fire (Gen. 19:24, 28). The destruction of Sodom and Gomorrah is often referred to in the Bible as a clear example of divine judgment against the vilest of sinners (Isa. 13:19; Jer. 49:18; Amos 4:11; Matt. 10:15; 2 Peter 2:6; Jude 7).

The exact location of the "cities of the plain" has been a subject of much debate. The current consensus, however, places them near Bab edh-Dhra, the entrance to the "tongue" (Lisan) of land that juts out into the Dead Sea on its eastern shore.

Goshen [Go′shen], *drawing near*—The name of two areas and one city in the Old Testament:

1. The northeastern territory of the Nile Delta in Egypt, known today as the area of the Wadi Tumilat. Jacob and his family were granted permission to settle in this fertile section during Joseph's rule as prime minister of Egypt (Gen. 46:28).

During the time of the exodus, Goshen was protected from the plagues of flies (Ex. 8:22) and hail (Ex. 9:26) that engulfed the rest of Egypt. The district was not large, containing perhaps 900 square miles, and it had two principal cities: Rameses and Pithom. It was near the frontier of Canaan and was rich in pastureland.

2. A district of southern Palestine between Gaza and Gibeon and the hill country and the Negeb, which was taken by Josuah (Josh. 10:41).

3. A town in the mountains of southwest Judah (Josh. 15:51).

Gozan [Go′zan], *a cutting off*—A district in Mesopotamia on the river Habor (2 Kings 17:6; 18:11; 19:12; 1 Chron. 5:26; Isa. 37:12).

Captives were transported to it from Israel after the fall of Samaria (722–721 B.C.).

Grecians [Gre'cians]—This word is used to describe not only the people who lived in Greece (Joel 3:6), but Greek-speaking Jews as distinguished from those who spoke Aramaic (Acts 6:1; 9:29). See Greece.

Greece [Greece], *unstable* or *the miry ones*—The Anglicized Roman term for lands called Hellas by the inhabitants. The name is derived from a small tribe, the Graeci, who lived along the Adriatic coast. The Old Testament word for Greece is Javan (Gen. 10:4–5; Isa. 66:19).

Greece was a nation of the ancient world, which rose to the status of a world power near the end of the Old Testament era. The Greeks exerted great influence on the Jewish people, particularly during the period between the Old and New Testaments. Greek culture also paved the way for the expansion of Christianity in the first century A.D.

Under the leadership of the great military conqueror Alexander the Great (ruled 336–323 B.C.), the Greek Empire was extended through Asia Minor to Egypt and the borders of India. The rule of Greece was foretold by the prophet Daniel (Dan. 11:3–35). Alexander's conquests and his passion to spread Greek culture contributed to the advancement of Greek ideas throughout the ancient world. This adoption of Greek ideas by the rest of the world was known as Hellenism.

So thoroughly did Greek ideas penetrate the other nations that the Greek language became the dominant language of the ancient world. The Greece of New Testament times consisted of two Roman provinces: Macedonia and Achaia, with Corinth as the chief city and seat of the pro-consul. Athens was the great center of learning.

Since Greek was the universal language, the apostle Paul could communicate easily with the various nations and provinces he visited during his missionary journeys to spread the gospel. Paul visited such major cities as Philippi, Thessalonica, Athens, and Corinth, all of which retained distinct Greek cultural ideas, although they were ruled by the Romans. He showed a deep understanding of Greek thought and was able to communicate the gospel so the Greek mind could understand (Acts 17).

In the New Testament, the word "Greeks" refers to all people who have been influenced by Greek culture and who are not Jews (Mark 7:26). But the term "Hellenists" refers to Greek-speaking Jews (Acts

9:29) who lived in areas outside Palestine. Converts to Christianity included people from both these groups.

Greek [Greek]—After the east was conquered by the Macedonians, the name *Greek* was applied to all those who spoke Greek or who settled in the lands conquered by Alexander. In the New Testament Greek commonly means a foreigner or stranger (Rom. 1:14, 16; 10:12). The New Testament was written in Greek.

Greeks [Greeks]—People born in Greece, or with Greek ancestors; also in the New Testament this word is used as a general term for Gentiles (non-Jews). In Mark 7:26, the Syro-Phoenician woman is called a "Greek."

Guard, Gate of the—One of the gates of Jerusalem, in the new wall built by Nehemiah and the Israelites (Neh. 12:39).

Guni [Gu'ni], *colored*—

1. A Gadite, father of Abdiel, and grandfather of the chief of the Gadites (1 Chron. 5:15).

2. A son of Naphtali. He founded a tribal family. His descendants were called Gunites (Gen. 46:24; Num. 26:48; 1 Chron. 7:13).

Gur, Ascent to [Gur], *a lion's whelp*—A place near Ibleam (2 Kings 9:27).

Gur-baal [Gur-ba'al], *sojourn of Baal*—A place of undetermined site mentioned as a residence of Arabians (2 Chron. 26:7).

Haahashtari [Ha′a·hash′tari], unknown—A Judahite and son of Ashur and Naarah (1 Chron. 4:6).

Habaiah [Ha·bai′ah], *Jehovah hath hidden*—A priest whose descendants returned from Babylon (Ezra 2:61; Neh. 7:63).

Habakkuk [Ha·bak′kuk], *embrace*—A courageous Old Testament prophet and author of the book of Habakkuk. The Scriptures say nothing of his ancestry or place of birth. A man of deep emotional strength, Habakkuk was both a poet and a prophet. His hatred of sin compelled him to cry out to God for judgment (Hab. 1:2–4). His sense of justice also led him to challenge God's plan to judge the nation of Judah by the pagan Babylonians (Hab. 1:12–2:1). His deep faith led him to write a beautiful poem of praise in response to the mysterious ways of God (Hab. 3).

Habaziniah [Ha·baz·i·ni′ah]—Variant spelling of Habazziniah.

Habazziniah [Ha·baz·zi·ni′ah], unknown—The father of one Jeremiah (not the prophet) and grandfather of Jaazaniah, a Rechabite (Jer. 35:3).

Habor [Ha′bor], *joining together*—A river of Mesopotamia (2 Kings 17:6; 18:11; 1 Chron. 5:26).

Hacaliah [Hac·a·li′ah]—See Hachaliah.

Hachaliah [Hach·a·li′ah], *darkness of Jehovah*—Father of Nehemiah (Neh. 1:1).

Hachilah [Ha·chi′lah], *dark*—A hill not far from Maon in the wilderness of Ziph (1 Sam. 26:1–3).

Hachmoni [Hach·mo′ni], *wise*—The father of Jehiel, and founder of the family of Hachmonites (1 Chron. 11:11; 27:32).

Hacmoni [Hac·mo′ni]—See Hachmoni.

Hadad [Ha′dad]—Four Old Testament men:
1. Son of Ishmael (1 Chron. 1:30).
2. An Edomite king, son of Bedad (Gen. 36:35–36).
3. An Edomite king of the city of Pai (1 Chron. 1:50) who is called Hadar in Genesis 36:39.
4. A prince of Edom who as a child escaped to Egypt when Joab and the Israelites began to slay the males of Edom (1 Kings 11:14–22).

Hadadezer [Had·a·de′zer], *Hadad is helper*—Son of Rehob and king of Zobah in Syria (2 Sam. 8:3). He is also called Hadarezer. He was king in the time of David and fought many battles against David and the Israelites before he was finally beaten decisively (2 Sam. 10:6–19; 1 Chron. 19:16–19).

Hadadrimmon [Ha·dad·rim′mon], possibly *mighty pomegranate of the breach*—A city in the valley of Megiddo in the plain of Jezreel (Zech. 12:11). It was near here that Josiah was slain in his conflict with Pharaoh Necho (2 Chron. 35:22–25).

Hadar [Ha′dar]—See Hadad.

Hadarezer [Had·a·re′zer]—See Hadadezer.

Hadashah [Ha·dash′ah], *new*—A village of Judah in the lowland (Josh. 15:37).

Hadassah [Ha·das′sah], *a myrtle*—The Jewish name of Esther (Est. 2:7). See Esther.

Hades [Ha′des]—See Hell.

Hadid [Ha′did], *sharp*—A town inhabited by Benjamites (Ezra 2:33; Neh. 11:34).

Hadlai [Had·la′i], *rest of God*—The father of Amasa (2 Chron. 28:12).

Hadoram [Ha·dor′am], *noble honour*—Three Old Testament men:
1. One of the sons of Joktan from whom an Arabian tribe was descended (Gen. 10:27; 1 Chron. 1:21).

2. A son of Tou, king of Hamath (1 Chron. 18:10). He was sent by his father to congratulate David on his victory over Hadadezer.

3. An officer of the tribute appointed by Rehoboam of Judah (2 Chron. 10:18), probably the same as Adoniram of 1 Kings 4:6; 5:14.

Hadrach [Ha'drach], *dwelling*—A country or region of Syria mentioned in Zechariah 9:1.

Hagab [Ha'gab], *a locust*—Head of a family of Nethinim (Ezra 2:46).

Hagaba [Hag'a·ba], *locust*—Head of a family of Nethinim (Ezra 2:45; Neh. 7:48).

Hagabah [Hag'a·bah]—See Hagaba.

Hagar [Ha'gar], *flight*—The Egyptian bondwoman of Sarah who bore a son, Ishmael, to Abraham (Gen. 16:1–16). After waiting ten years for God to fulfill His promise to give them a son, Sarah presented Hagar to Abraham so he could father a child by her, according to the custom of the day. Sarah's plan and Abraham's compliance demonstrated a lack of faith in God.

When Hagar became pregnant, she mocked Sarah, who dealt with her harshly. Hagar then fled into the wilderness, where, at a well on the way to Shur, she encountered an angel of the Lord. The angel revealed Ishmael's future to Hagar—that his descendants would be a great multitude. Tradition has it that Hagar is the ancestress of all the Arab peoples and of the prophet Muhammad. Hagar called the well Beer-lahai-roi, "The well of the Living One who sees me." When Hagar returned to Abraham's camp, Ishmael was born and accepted by Abraham as his son. But when Ishmael was fourteen, Isaac, the promised son, was born. The next year Ishmael mocked Isaac at the festival of Isaac's weaning. At Sarah's insistence and with Abraham's approval, Hagar and Ishmael were expelled from Abraham's family. Abraham grieved for Ishmael, but God comforted him by revealing that a great nation would come out of Ishmael. Hagar and Ishmael wandered in the wilderness until their water was gone. When Hagar laid her son under the shade of a bush to die, the angel of the Lord appeared to Hagar and showed her a well. This is a beautiful picture of God's concern for the outcast and helpless. In Paul's allegory in Galatians 4, Hagar stands for Mount Sinai and corresponds to the earthly Jerusalem, while Isaac stands for the children of promise who are free in Christ.

Hagarene [Hag'a·rene]—See Hagarite.

Hagarite [Hag'a·rite]—A people inhabiting the region east of Gilead. They were defeated by the Reubenites in the time of Saul (1 Chron. 5:10), and are listed as enemies of Israel in Psalm 83:6.

Hagerite [Hag'e·rite]—See Hagarite.

Haggai [Hag'gai], *festive*—An Old Testament prophet and author of the book of Haggai. As God's spokesman, he encouraged the captives who had returned to Jerusalem to complete the reconstruction of the temple. This work had started shortly after the first exiles returned from Babylon with Zerubbabel in 538 B.C. But the building activity was soon abandoned because of discouragement and oppression. Beginning in 520 B.C., the second year of Darius Hystaspis, Haggai and his fellow prophet, Zechariah, urged the people to resume the task. The temple was completed five years later, about 515 B.C. (Ezra 5:1). He was the tenth of the minor prophets.

Haggedolim [Hag'ge·do·lim]—The father of Zabdiel who was chief officer of the priests who returned to live in Jerusalem (Neh. 11:14). In some translations, Zabdiel is called "the son of one of the great men."

Haggeri [Hag·ge'ri]—The father of Mibhar, one of David's warriors (1 Chron. 11:38).

Haggi [Hag'gi], *festive*—One of the sons of Gad and the founder of the family of Haggites (Gen. 46:16; Num. 26:15).

Haggiah [Hag·gi'ah], *festival of Jehovah*—A Levite of the family of Merari (1 Chron. 6:30).

Haggites [Hag'gites]—The tribal family descended from Haggi the son of Gad (Num. 26:15).

Haggith [Hag'gith], *festal*—A wife of David and mother of Adonijah (2 Sam. 3:4; 1 Kings 1:5).

Hagri [Hag'ri]—See Haggeri.

Hagrite [Ha'grite]—See Hagarite.

Hahiroth [Ha·hir'oth]—See Pi-hahiroth.

Hai [Ha'i]—See Ai.

Haines [Ha′ines], unknown—An Egyptian city, probably in middle Egypt (Isa. 30:4).

Hakilah [Hak′i·lah]—See Hachilah.

Hakkatan [Hak′ka·tan], *little* or *junior*—Father of Johanan (Ezra 8:12).

Hakkoz [Hak′koz], *a thorn*—Two Old Testament men:

    1. A descendant of Aaron. In the time of David his family was made the seventh course, or order, of priests (1 Chron. 24:10). When members of this family first returned from Babylon they were unable to establish their genealogy and thus lost their place in the priesthood (Ezra 2:61–62; Neh. 7:63–64).

    2. A man of Judah (1 Chron. 4:8).

Hakupha [Ha·ku′pha], *crooked*—The ancestor of certain Nethinim (Ezra 2:51; Neh. 7:5, 53).

Halah [Ha′lah], *painful*—A place in Assyria to which Israelite captives were deported after the fall of Samaria (2 Kings 17:6; 18:11; 1 Chron. 5:26).

Halak [Ha′lak], *bare*—A mountain mentioned in connection with Joshua's conquests (Josh. 11:17; 12:7). It was in the south of Palestine.

Half-Tribe—When the Israelites began to settle the promised land, the tribe of Manasseh was divided in two. Half of Manasseh, along with Gad and Reuben, wanted to settle on the east side of the Jordan while the other half chose to enter the land with the rest of the tribes (Num. 32:33–42; Deut. 3:12–13; Josh. 1:12–18).

Halhul [Hal′hul], *trembling*—A village in the hill country of Judah (Josh. 15:58) about three miles north of Hebron.

Hali [Ha′li], *necklace*—A town of the tribe of Asher (Josh. 19:25).

Hallohesh, Halohesh [Hal·lo′hesh, Ha·lo′hesh], *whisperer*—The father of Shallum (Neh. 3:12; 10:24).

Halohesh [Ha·lo′hesh]—See Hallohesh.

Ham [Ham], *hot* or *sunburnt*—The name of a person and two places in the Old Testament:

1. The youngest of Noah's three sons (Gen. 9:18, 24), born when Noah was five hundred years old. Ham, along with the rest of Noah's household, was saved from the great Flood by entering the ark (Gen. 7:7). After the waters went down and Noah's household left the ark, Ham found his father, naked and drunk, asleep in his tent. Ham told his brothers, Shem and Japheth, who covered their father without looking on his nakedness. Noah was furious because Ham had seen him naked, and he placed a prophetic curse on Canaan, the son of Ham (Gen. 9:18, 25). The Canaanites were to serve the descendants of Shem and Japheth (Gen. 9:26–27; Josh. 9:16–27).

Ham had four sons: Cush, Mizraim, Put, and Canaan (Gen. 10:6). The tribe of Mizraim settled in Egypt, while the tribes of Cush and Put settled in other parts of Africa. The tribe of Canaan populated Phoenicia and Palestine.

2. A city east of the Jordan River during the time of Abraham ruled by the Zuzim. It was attacked by Chedorlaomer and other allied kings (Gen. 14:5). The modern city of Ham lies 6 kilometers (4 miles) south of Irbid.

3. Another name for Egypt, used in poetry (Pss. 78:51; 105:23, 27).

4. Some of the inhabitants of Gedor were men of Ham (1 Chron. 4:40).

Haman [Ha′man], *magnificent*—The evil and scheming prime minister of Ahasuerus (Xerxes I), king of Persia (485–464 B.C.). He was called an Agagite (Est. 3:1; 9:24), based on his real or alleged descent from Agag whom Samuel cut to pieces (1 Sam. 15:33). When Mordecai refused to bow to Haman, Haman plotted to destroy Mordecai and his family, as well as all of the Jews in the Persian Empire. But Esther intervened and saved her people. When his intrigue against the Jews was exposed by Esther, Haman was hanged on the very gallows he had constructed for Mordecai (Est. 3:1–9:25).

Hamath, Hemath [Ha′math, He′math], *fortress*—
1. A city on the Orontes north of Damascus where the Canaanites settled (Gen. 10:18). Its King Toi sent his son to congratulate David on his victory over Hadadezer (2 Sam. 8:9–10). It was taken by Solomon (2 Chron. 8:3–4), but shortly afterward came again into the hands of the former inhabitants. It was captured by Jeroboam II of Israel (2 Kings 14:28) and later was taken by the Assyrians (2 Kings 18:34; 19:13).

2. The district under the government of the city. One of its towns was Riblah (2 Kings 23:33). It was regarded as the northern border of Israel (Num. 13:21; 34:8; 1 Kings 8:65).

Hamathites [Ha'math·ites]—The people of Hamath (Gen. 10:18).

Hamath-zobah [Ha'math-zo'bah], *fortress of Zobah*—A city mentioned in 2 Chronicles 8:3, possibly Hamath on the Orontes.

Hamites [Ham·ites]—Descendants of Ham.

Hammath [Ham'math], *warm springs*—

    1. The founder of the house of Rechab, a Kenite family (1 Chron. 2:55).

    2. A fenced city of Naphtali (Josh. 19:35). It was probably the same as Hammoth-dor and Hammon (Josh. 21:32; 1 Chron. 6:76).

Hammedatha [Ham·me·da'tha], *double*—Father of Haman, an Agagite (Est. 3:1).

Hammelech [Ham'me·lech], *the king*—Father of Jerahmeel (Jer. 36:26).

Hammolecheth [Ham·mo'le·cheth]—See Hammoleketh.

Hammoleketh [Ham·mo'le·keth], *the queen*—The daughter of Machir and the sister of Gilead (1 Chron. 7:17–18). Through her son, Abiezer, Gideon was descended (Judg. 6:11).

Hammon [Ham'mon], *warm*—

    1. A town of Naphtali. See Hammath.

    2. A town of Asher (Josh. 19:28), a few miles south of Tyre.

Hammoth-dor [Ham'moth-dor], *hot springs of Dor*—See Hammath.

Hammuel [Ham·mu'el], *warmth of God*—A son of Mishma of Simeon (1 Chron. 4:26).

Hammurabi [Ham·mu·ra'bi], possibly *Hammu (the god) is great*—An ancient king of Babylon, who ruled between approximately 1792 and 1750, about 300 years after Abraham. While he is not mentioned in the Bible, he is interesting to Bible students because of his famous law code, called the Code of Hammurabi. This code, which Hammurabi claimed to have received from Shamash, the god of justice, bears striking resemblance to many of the laws of Moses, providing regulations for dealing with crimes, marriage, selling property, the rights of the firstborn, and many other social issues. The seven-foot stone pillar containing Hammurabi's code was discovered in 1901–02 at Susa.

Hamonah [Ha·mo'nah], *multitude*—A city to be built in commemoration of the anticipated defeat of Gog (Ezek. 39:16).

Hamon-gog [Ha'mon-gog], *multitude of Gog*—The name Ezekiel gives to the valley where Gog and his forces were to be destroyed (Ezek. 39:11, 15).

Hamor [Ha'mor], *he-ass*—Prince of the Shechemites (Gen. 34:20; Josh. 24:32). After his son, Shechem, defiled Dinah, daughter of Jacob, he and his son were killed by Dinah's brothers, Simeon and Levi (Gen. 34:1–31).

Hamran [Ham'ran]—See Hemdan.

Hamuel [Ham·u'el]—See Hammuel.

Hamul [Ham'ul], *pitied* or *spared*—The younger of the two sons of Pharez and founder of a tribal family of Judah (Gen. 46:12; Num. 26:21; 1 Chron. 2:5).

Hamulites [Ham'ul·ites]—A clan of descendants of Hamul (Num. 26:21).

Hamurapi [Ham·u·ra'pi]—See Hammurabi.

Hamutal [Ha·mu'tal], *kin to the dew*—Daughter of Jeremiah of Libnah, wife of Josiah, king of Judah, and mother of Jehoahaz and Zedekiah (2 Kings 23:31; 24:18; Jer. 52:1).

Hanameel [Han'a·meel], *God is gracious*—Son of Shallum and cousin of Jeremiah (Jer. 32:6–12).

Hanamel [Han'a·mel]—See Hanameel.

Hanan [Ha'nan], *merciful*—Nine Old Testament men:
1. Son of Shashak, a Benjamite (1 Chron. 8:23).
2. Son of Azel, a descendant of Jonathan (1 Chron. 8:38; 9:44).
3. One of David's mighty men and son of Maachah (1 Chron. 11:43).
4. Chief of a family of Nethinim, some of which came with Zerubbabel from Babylon (Ezra 2:46; Neh. 7:49).
5. One who assisted Ezra in reading and teaching the law (Neh. 8:7).

6. A Levite who sealed the covenant with Nehemiah (Neh. 10:10).

7. Two chiefs of the people. They sealed the covenant (Neh. 10:22, 26).

8. A Levite who was appointed as treasurer over the storehouse of tithes. He was the son of Zaccur (Neh. 13:13).

9. Son of Igdaliah, a prophet (Jer. 35:4). His sons occupied a chamber in the temple.

Hananeel [Han'a·neel], *God has favored*—A tower near the sheepgate at Jerusalem and possibly another name for the tower of Meah (Neh. 3:1; 12:39; Jer. 31:38; Zech. 14:10).

Hananel [Han'a·nel]—See Hananeel.

Hanani [Ha·na'ni], *gracious*—Five Old Testament men:

1. Father of Jehu, the prophet (1 Kings 16:1). He denounced Asa, king of Judah, and was imprisoned (2 Chron. 16:7).

2. Son of Heman. He was the head of the eighteenth course of musicians appointed by David for the sanctuary (1 Chron. 25:4, 25).

3. Son of Immer, a priest. He rejected his foreign wife (Ezra 10:20).

4. Nehemiah's brother (Neh. 1:2; 7:2).

5. A Levite musician who officiated at the dedication of the wall of Jerusalem (Neh. 12:36).

Hananiah [Han·a·ni'ah], *Jehovah has been gracious*—

1. Son of Zerubbabel and father of Pelatiah and Jeshaiah (1 Chron. 3:19, 21).

2. Son of Shashak, a Benjamite (1 Chron. 8:24).

3. A son of Heman and head of the sixteenth course of musicians appointed by David for the sanctuary (1 Chron. 25:4, 23).

4. A captain of Uzziah, king of Judah (2 Chron. 26:11).

5. One of the family of Bebai who divorced his foreign wife (Ezra 10:28).

6. A perfumer who labored on the wall of Jerusalem (Neh. 3:8).

7. Son of Shelemiah and a laborer on the wall of Jerusalem (Neh. 3:30).

8. One associated with the brother of Nehemiah as governor of the castle at Jerusalem (Neh. 7:2).

9. One of the leaders of the people who, with Nehemiah, sealed the covenant (Neh. 10:23).

10. A priest of the house of the father of Jeremiah after the Exile (Neh. 12:12).

11. A priest who participated in the dedication of the wall of Jerusalem (Neh. 12:41).

12. Son of Azur, a prophet of Gibeon. He prophesied that the captives would return after two years' captivity. His false prophecy brought upon him the penalty of death (Jer. 28:1–17).

13. The father of Zedekiah (Jer. 36:12).

14. The grandfather of Irijah (Jer. 37:13–15).

15. The original name of Shadrach, one of Daniel's three companions (Dan. 1:6–7, 11; 2:17).

Haniel [Han'i·el], *grace of God*—Two Old Testament men:

1. Son of Ulla, of Asher (1 Chron. 7:39).

2. Son of Ephod, prince of Manasseh (Num. 34:23).

Hannah [Han'nah], *grace*—One of the two wives of Elkanah; the mother of Samuel. She was especially favored by her husband which aroused the hostility of the other wife who subjected her to annoyances. Hannah was childless, but vowed that if she became the mother of a son, she would dedicate him to the Lord's service. Samuel was born and Hannah kept her vow (1 Sam. 1:1–28). Her triumphant song (1 Sam. 2:1–10) may have been in the mind of Mary (Luke 1:26–55).

Hannathon [Han'na·thon], *favored*—A town of Zebulun near the border of Asher (Josh. 19:14).

Hanniel [Han'ni·el]—See Haniel.

Hanoch [Ha'noch], *dedicated*—Two Old Testament men:

1. A son of Midian and grandson of Abraham and Keturah (Gen. 25:4; 1 Chron. 1:33).

2. Son of Reuben (Gen. 46:9; Ex. 6:14; Num. 26:5; 1 Chron. 5:3).

Hanochites [Ha'noch·ites]—Descendants of Hanoch, son of Reuben (Num. 26:5).

Hanun [Ha'nun], *favored*—

1. Two Jews of that name labored on the wall of Jerusalem under Nehemiah (Neh. 3:13, 30).

2. A king of the Ammonites. When Hanun's father, Nahash, died, David sent his condolence. His motives were misjudged and it was believed that David's messengers were spies to gather facts that would aid David to capture the capital. They were ill-treated and humiliated. Knowing David would resent this, Hanun secured an alliance with the Syrians but was defeated (2 Sam. 10:1–11:1; 1 Chron. 19:1–20:3).

Hapharaim [Haph′a·ra·im]—See Haphraim.

Haphraim [Haph′ra·im], *two pits*—A border town of Issachar (Josh. 19:19).

Happizzez [Hap′piz·zez], *the shattered one*—An Aaronite (1 Chron. 24:15).

Hara [Ha′ra], *mountainous*—Captives of Israel were taken to this place in Assyria (1 Chron. 5:26).

Haradah [Ha·ra′dah], *terror*—An encampment of the Israelites (Num. 33:24).

Haran [Har′an], *crossroads*—A city and three men of the Old Testament:

1. A city of northern Mesopotamia. Abraham and his father, Terah, lived there for a time (Gen. 11:31–32; 12:4–5). He remained there until after the death of his father, Terah, and then he started for Canaan. A commercial center, the family of Abraham's brother Nahor also lived in this city for a time, as did Jacob and his wife Rachel (Gen. 28:10; 29:4–5). The city was on the Balikh, a tributary of the Euphrates River, 386 kilometers (240 miles) northwest of Nineveh and 450 kilometers (280 miles) northeast of Damascus. Haran lay on one of the main trade routes between Babylonia and the Mediterranean Sea. Like the inhabitants of Ur of the Chaldeans, Haran's inhabitants worshipped Sin, the moon-god. Second Kings 19:12 records that the city was captured by the Assyrians.

Today Haran is a small Arab village, Harran, a spelling that preserves the two *r*'s of the original place name and helps to distinguish it from the personal name Haran. The city name is also spelled Charran (Acts 7:2, 4, KJV).

2. A son of Terah and brother of Abraham who died in Ur. Lot was his son and Milcah and Iscah, his daughters (Gen. 11:29).

3. A son of Caleb and Ephah (1 Chron. 2:46).

4. A Gershonite Levite of the family of Shimei (1 Chron. 23:9).

Hararite [Har′a·rite]—Probably the inhabitant of a place called Harar (2 Sam. 23:11, 33).

Harbona [Har·bo′na], *ass-driver*—A chamberlain in the court of Ahasuerus (Est. 1:10; 7:9).

Harbonah [Har·bo′nah]—See Harbona.

Hareph [Har′eph], *a plucking off*—Son of Caleb (1 Chron. 2:51).

Hareth, The Forest of [Har′eth], *forest*—A forest in the land of Judah where David hid from Saul (1 Sam. 22:5).

Harhaiah [Har·hai′ah], *fear of Jehovah*—Father of Uzziel, the goldsmith (Neh. 3:8).

Harhas [Har′has], *very poor*—An ancestor of Shallum, husband of the prophetess Huldah (2 Kings 22:14). In 2 Chronicles 34:22 he is called Hasrah.

Harhur [Har′hur], *fever*—Ancestor of certain Nethinim (Ezra 2:51; Neh. 7:53).

Harim [Har′im], *flat-nosed*—Several Old Testament men:
1. A name connected with certain priestly families. Of the children of Harim, 1,017 returned from Babylon with Zerubbabel (Ezra 2:39; Neh. 7:42). Certain of the sons of Harim took foreign wives (Ezra 10:21). One bearing the name sealed the covenant (Neh. 10:5). Another was head of the third order of priests (1 Chron. 24:8). Adna represented the family as a priest in the time of Joiakim (Neh. 12:12, 15). Malchijah, son of Harim, labored on the wall of Jerusalem (Neh. 3:11). Once the name appears as Rehum (Neh. 12:3).
2. A lay family, representatives of which returned from Babylon with the same caravan as the priests of this name (Ezra 2:32; Neh. 7:35), married foreign women (Ezra 10:31), and signed the covenant (Neh. 10:27).

Hariph [Har′iph], *autumnal*—Founder of a family, many members of which came to Jerusalem from Babylon with Zerubbabel (Neh. 7:24). A prince of this name sealed the covenant (Neh. 10:19). It is rendered Jorah in Ezra 2:18.

Harmon [Har'mon], *high fortress*—The location of this place is not known, but God warned the people of Samaria that they would be cast into Harmon because of their disobedience (Amos 4:3).

Harnepher [Har'ne·pher], *panting*—A son of Zophah, a chief of Asher (1 Chron. 7:36).

Harod [Har'od], *fear*—It was at the well of Harod that the Israelites under Gideon gathered, preparing to fight the Midianites who were in the nearby valley by the hill of Moreh. Here Gideon carried out his famous test which reduced his army to the 300 men required by the Lord (Judg. 7:1–7).

Harodite [Har'od'ite]—A native or resident of the town of Harod (2 Sam. 23:25).

Haroeh [Har·o'eh], *vision*—A descendant of Shobal, one of the tribe of Judah (1 Chron. 2:52).

Harorite [Har'o·rite]—Shammoth, one of David's mighty men, is described as a Harorite (1 Chron. 11:27).

Harosheth Hagoyim [Ha·ro'sheth Ha·goy'im], *woodland*—A city called Harosheth of the Gentiles. It is now identified with a village on the northern bank of the Kishon. Here Sisera lived (Judg. 4:2, 13, 16).

Harsha [Har'sha], *enchanter*—The ancestor of certain Nethinim (Ezra 2:52; Neh. 7:54).

Harum [Har'um], *exalted*—The father of Aharhel of Judah (1 Chron. 4:8).

Harumaph [Ha·ru'maph], *flat-nose*—Father of Jedaiah (Neh. 3:10).

Haruphite [Ha·ru'phite]—A member of the family of Hariph (1 Chron. 12:5).

Haruz [Har'uz], *active*—The father-in-law of Manasseh, king of Judah (2 Kings 21:19).

Hasadiah [Has·a·di'ah], *kindness of Jeovah*—Son of Zerubbabel (1 Chron. 3:20).

Hasenuah [Has·e·nu'ah]—See Hassenuah.

Hashabiah [Hash·a·bi′ah], *Jehovah regards*—Nine Old Testament men:

1. A Levite of the family of Merari (1 Chron. 6:45).

2. Son of Jeduthun, a Merarite Levite. He was appointed by David to be head of a company of musicians for the sanctuary (1 Chron. 25:3, 19).

3. A Levite of the family of Hebron (1 Chron. 26:30).

4. Son of Kemuel, a Levite. He was a captain during the reign of David (1 Chron. 27:17).

5. A chief of the Levites during the reign of Josiah (2 Chron. 35:9).

6. A Levite of the family of Merari who came with Ezra from Babylon and who, with others, had charge of the treasure and the temple music (Ezra 8:19, 24; Neh. 10:11; 12:24).

7. A ruler of Keilah in the time of Nehemiah. He worked on the wall of Jerusalem (Neh. 3:17).

8. Grandfather of Uzzi, the overseer of the Levites (Neh. 11:22).

9. A priest of the house of Hilkiah (Neh. 12:21).

Hashabnah [Ha·shab′nah], *Jehovah has considered*—One who sealed the covenant with Nehemiah (Neh. 10:25).

Hashabneiah [Hash·ab·ne·i′ah]—See Hashabniah.

Hashabniah [Hash·ab·ni′ah], *whom Jehovah regards*—

1. A Levite who, with others, exhorted the people regarding the sealing of the covenant (Neh. 9:5).

2. Father of Hattush. The son labored on the wall of Jerusalem (Neh. 3:10).

Hashbadana [Hash·ba·da′na], *considerate judge*—One who stood at Ezra's left as the law was read (Neh. 8:4).

Hashbaddana [Hash·bad·da′na]—Variant of Hashbadana.

Hashem [Hash′em], *fat*—One of those listed among David's warriors; a Gizonite (1 Chron. 11:34). See Jashen.

Hashmonah [Hash·mo′nah], *fertility*—A place where the Israelites encamped (Num. 33:29–30).

Hashub [Hash′ub]—See Hasshub.

Hashubah [Ha·shu′bah], *esteemed*—A son of Zerubbabel (1 Chron. 3:20).

Hashum [Hash′um], *wealthy*—The head of a family, members of which came with Zerubbabel from Babylonia (Ezra 2:19; 10:33; Neh. 7:22).

Hashupha [Ha·shu′pha]—See Hasupha.

Hasmonean [Has·mo·ne′an], *unknown*—The family dynasty which ruled Israel during the years from 135 to 63 B.C. When Antiochus Epiphanes defiled the temple in an attempt to subdue the Jews, Judas Maccabeus led the revolt which brought independence to the nation. Judas Maccabeus's brother was appointed as high priest, and this brother's son, John, was the first Hasmonean ruler. The Hasmoneans ruled Israel until 63 B.C. when Rome took over.

Hasrah [Has′rah], *lack*—The grandfather of the husband of Huldah the prophetess. He is also described as "the keeper of the wardrobe" (2 Chron. 34:22; in 2 Kings 22:14 he is called Harhas).

Hassenaah [Has·se·na′ah], *thorny*—Father of the men who built the fish-gate of Jerusalem (Neh. 3:3). Without the article the name is *Senaah*. About 3,000 of his descendants returned from Babylon with Zerubbabel (Ezra 2:35; Neh. 3:3; 7:38).

Hassenuah, Hasenuah [Has·se·nu′ah, Has·e·nu′ah], *thorny*—
    1. Father of Hodaviah, a Benjamite (1 Chron. 9:7).
    2. Father of Judah, a Benjamite overseer of Jerusalem (Neh. 11:9). The name is rendered *Senuah* in the KJV.

Hasshub, Hashub [Has′shub, Hash′ub], *considerate*—
    1. A Levite; father of Shemaiah (1 Chron. 9:14; Neh. 11:15).
    2. Laborers on the wall of Jerusalem (Neh. 3:11, 23).
    3. A signer of the covenant (Neh. 10:23).

Hassophereth [Has·so′phe·reth]—See Sophereth.

Hasupha, Hashupha [Ha·su′pha, Ha·shu′pha], *stripped*—Head of a family of Nethinim, some of the members of which returned from Babylon (Ezra 2:43; Neh. 7:46).

Hatach [Ha'tach], *verily*—A chamberlain in the court of Ahasuerus. He served Esther (Est. 4:5, 10).

Hathach [Ha'thach]—See Hatach.

Hathath [Ha'thath], *terror*—A son of Othniel of Judah (1 Chron. 4:13).

Hatipha [Ha·ti'pha], *seized*—Founder of a family of Nethinim, some of the members of which returned with Zerubbabel from Babylon (Ezra 2:54; Neh. 7:56).

Hatita [Ha·ti'ta], *dug*—Ancestor of a family of porters, or gatekeepers. Some of this family returned from Babylon with Zerubbabel (Ezra 2:42; Neh. 7:45).

Hattil [Hat'til], *vacillating*—A servant of Solomon. Members of his family were of the company of Zerubbabel (Ezra 2:57; Neh. 7:59).

Hattush [Hat'tush], *assembled*—Five Old Testament men:
   1. A descendant of David who came with Ezra to Jerusalem (Ezra 8:2).
   2. Son of Shemaiah of Judah (1 Chron. 3:22).
   3. A priest who came with Zerubbabel to Jerusalem (Neh. 12:2, 7).
   4. A son of Hashabniah. He helped to build the wall of Jerusalem (Neh. 3:10).
   5. A priest who sealed the covenant with Nehemiah (Neh. 10:4).

Hauran [Hau'ran], *cave land*—This district, south of Damascus, was known to the Greeks and Romans as Auranitis. On the north and northwest were Trachonitis and Batanea (Ezek. 47:16, 18). This district was given to Herod the Great by Augustus but later, in the division of his kingdom, these sections fell to the tetrarchy of Philip (Luke 3:1).

Havilah [Hav'i·lah], *circle*—
   1. A son of Cush or of Joktan (Gen. 10:7, 29).
   2. A district probably in central or southwestern Arabia, famous for its gold and precious stones (Gen. 2:11). It bordered the territory of the Ishmaelites and was bounded by the Pison River (Gen. 2:10–12).

Havoth-jair [Ha'voth-ja'ir], *hamlets of Jair*—A group of towns east of the Jordan in Gilead (Num. 32:40–41; Judg. 10:3–4) or in Bashan (Deut. 3:13–14; Josh. 13:30).

Havvoth-jair [Hav'voth-ja'ir]—See Havoth-jair.

Hazael [Ha·za'el], *God has seen*—A Syrian whom Jehovah directed Elijah to anoint king over Syria (1 Kings 19:15, 17). Ben-hadad was then king; his capital being at Damascus. Elisha came to the city. The king was seriously ill and he sent Hazael to Israel's prophet to inquire the issue of his sickness. When Hazael was informed that the king would die and that he would take the throne, he returned to Ben-hadad and falsely stated that the king would recover, and the following day assassinated him (2 Kings 8:7–15). Shortly after he ascended the throne, Shalmaneser, king of Assyria, came into conflict with him and demanded that he pay tribute.

In the reign of Jehu, king of Israel, Hazael attacked the tribes east of the Jordan (2 Kings 10:32). In the reign of Jehoahaz he severely oppressed the Israelites (2 Kings 13:4–7), captured Gath, the city of the Philistines, and would have attacked Jerusalem had not the treasures of the temple been given to him (2 Kings 12:17–18).

Hazaiah [Ha·zai'ah], *Jehovah has seen*—Son of Adaiah, a descendant of Perez (Neh. 11:5).

Hazar-addar [Ha'zar-ad'dar]—See Addar.

Hazar-enan [Ha'zar-e'nan], *village of fountains*—A village of Palestine near Damascus (Num. 34:9; Ezek. 47:17; 48:1).

Hazar-enon [Ha'zar-e'non]—See Hazar-enan.

Hazar-gaddah [Ha'zar-gad'dah], *village of fortune*—A town in Judah (Josh. 15:27).

Hazar-hatticon [Ha'zar-hat'ti·con]—See Hazer-hatticon.

Hazarmaveth [Ha·zar·ma'veth], *village of death*—The son of Joktan (Gen. 10:26; 1 Chron. 1:20).

Hazar-shual [Ha'zar-shu'al], *fox village*—Town in the south of Judah (Josh. 15:28; 19:3; 1 Chron. 4:28).

Hazar-susah [Ha'zar-su'sah], *village of horses*—A village of Simeon in southern Judah (Josh. 19:5; 1 Chron. 4:31).

Hazar-susim [Ha'zar-su'sim]—See Hazar-susah.

Hazazon-tamar [Haz'a·zon-ta'mar]—See En-gedi.

Hazelel-poni [Haz·el·el-po'ni], *unknown*—A woman of Judah, daughter of Etam (1 Chron. 4:3).

Hazer-hatticon [Ha'zer-hat'ti·con], *middle court*—A border town of the Hauran (Ezek. 47:16).

Hazerim [Ha·ze'rim], *villages*—The towns peopled by the Avvim (Deut. 2:23).

Hazeroth [Ha·ze'roth], *settlement*—A place in the wilderness where the Israelites camped after leaving Sinai (Num. 11:35; 12:16; 33:17; Deut. 1:1); the scene of the sedition of Miriam and Aaron (Num. 11:35–12:16).

Hazezon-tamar [Ha·ze'zon-ta'mar]—See En-gedi.

Haziel [Ha'zi·el], *vision of God*—Son of Shimei, a Levite of the family of Gershon (1 Chron. 23:9).

Hazo [Ha'zo], *vision*—The son of Nahor (Gen. 22:22).

Hazor [Ha'zor], *enclosure*—The name of four cities and one district in the Bible:

1. An ancient Canaanite fortress city in northern Palestine, situated about 16 kilometers (10 miles) northwest of the Sea of Galilee. When Joshua and the Israelites invaded Palestine, Hazor was one of the most important fortresses in the land (Josh. 11:10). This was due to its enormous size, its large population, and its strategic location on the main road between Egypt and Mesopotamia.

When the Israelites approached Palestine, Jabin, the king of Hazor, and several other kings formed an alliance against them. Through God's power the Israelites defeated these armies, killed all the people of Hazor, and burned the city (Josh. 11:1–14). The city regained its strength during the time of the Judges and was ruled by another person named Jabin. Because of Israel's sinfulness, God allowed the armies of Hazor to oppress the Israelites for 20 years (Judg. 4:1–3). Sisera, the captain of the armies of Hazor, and his 900 chariots were miraculously defeated by God through the efforts of Deborah and Barak (Judg. 4:4–24). Solomon later chose Hazor as one of his military outposts

(1 Kings 9:15). The rebuilt city continued to play an important part in the northern defenses of Israel until it was destroyed by the Assyrian king Tiglath-pileser (2 Kings 15:29), about ten years before the collapse of the Northern Kingdom in 722 B.C.

2. A city in the southern desert of Judah (Josh. 15:23).

3. Hazor-hadattah ("New Hazor") and Kerioth-hazor ("City of Hazor"), which may be identical sites in southern Judea (Josh. 15:25).

4. A nomadic district or kingdom of villages in the Arabian desert (Jer. 49:28).

5. A district in the Arabian desert (Jer. 49:28–33).

Hazor-hadattah [Ha′zor-ha·dat′tah], *new Hazor*—A town of Judah (Josh. 15:25). The KJV translates this as two towns, Hazor and Hadattah.

Hazzelel-poni [Haz·zel·el-po′ni]—See Hazelel-poni.

Heaven, The Heavens [Heav′en]—

1. The region about the earth—the heavens and the earth (Gen. 1:1), comprising the universe (Gen. 14:19; Jer. 23:24). The mass beyond the visible firmament (Gen. 1:7; Ps. 108:4). To the Jews the highest, or seventh heaven, was God's dwelling place. Paul relates a personal experience in which he was carried into the third heaven, but whether he was bodily transported to it, or it was a vision, he did not know (2 Cor. 12:1–4).

2. The place of God's presence from whence Christ came and to which he returned (Ps. 80:14; Isa. 66:1; Matt. 5:16, 45, 48; John 3:13; Acts 1:11). It is from here he will come in his return to the earth (Matt. 24:30; Rom. 8:33–34; 1 Thess. 4:16; Heb. 6:20). Heaven is the dwelling place of angels (Matt. 28:2; Luke 22:43) and the future home of the redeemed (Eph. 3:15; 1 Peter 1:4; Rev. 19:1–4).

Heavenly City—The city which will be the dwelling place of God and His saints after the end of the world; also called the New Jerusalem (Heb. 11:10, 16; 12:22; 13:14; Rev. 21–22).

Heber [He′ber], *comrade*—Seven Old Testament men:

1. A Benjamite, son of Elpaal, a descendant from Shaharaim (1 Chron. 8:17).

2. Son of Beriah and grandson of Asher (Gen. 46:17). His descendants were called Heberites (Num. 26:45).

3. A descendant of Hobab, a Kenite. It was his wife, Jael, who slew Sisera (Judg. 4:11–24).

4. A Judahite descendant of Ezra and ancestor of the men of Socoh (1 Chron. 4:18).

5. One of the chiefs of the Gadites in Bashan (1 Chron. 5:13).

6. A Benjamite, son of Shashak (1 Chron. 8:22).

7. The son of Sala and father of Phalec (Luke 3:35).

Heberites [He′ber·ites]—Descendants of Heber, the grandson of Asher (Num. 26:45; Gen. 46:17).

Hebrew [He′brew], *pertaining to Eber*—A designation first applied to Abraham, a descendant of Eber (Gen. 14:13). It was applied by foreigners to the Israelites (Gen. 39:14, 17; 41:12; Ex. 1:16; 1 Sam. 4:6, 9), and the Israelites used the word in regard to themselves (Gen. 40:15; Ex. 1:19) In the New Testament it is used to describe those whose speech was Aramaic to distinguish them from Greek-speaking Jews (Acts 6:1). Paul called himself a Hebrew of the Hebrews, indicating that his parents were of Hebrew stock (Phil. 3:5).

Hebron [He′bron], *alliance*—The name of two cities and two men in the Bible:

1. A city situated 31 kilometers (19 miles) southwest of Jerusalem on the road to Beersheba. Although it lies in a slight valley, the city is 927 meters (3,040 feet) above sea level, which makes it the highest town in Palestine. It is also one of the oldest cities in the world. In fact, it preceeded Zoan in Egypt by seven years (Num. 13:22). Originally Hebron was called Kirjath-arba (Gen. 23:2). Numbers 13:22 speaks of Hebron being built seven years before Zoan in Egypt. This probably refers to the rebuilding of the city by the Hyksos rulers of Egypt. The twelve Hebrew spies viewed Hebron on their mission to explore the promised land.

The area surrounding Hebron is rich in biblical history. Abram spent much of his time in Mamre in the area of Hebron (Gen. 13:18). He was living in Mamre when the confederacy of kings overthrew the cities of the plain and captured Lot (Gen. 14:1–13). Here, too, Abram's name was changed to Abraham (Gen. 17:5). At Hebron the angels revealed to Abraham that he would have a son who would be called

Isaac (Gen. 18:1–15). Later, Sarah died at Hebron (Gen. 23:2); Abraham bought the cave of Machpelah as her burial place (Gen. 23:9). The present mosque built over the cave is called Haran el-Khalil, "the sacred precinct of the friend (of God)," reminiscent of a title given to Abraham in 2 Chronicles 20:7; Isaiah 41:8; James 2:23.

During the period of the conquest of the land of Canaan, Joshua killed the king of Hebron (Josh. 10:3–27). Later, Caleb drove out the Anakim and claimed Hebron for his inheritance (Josh. 14:12–15). Hebron was also designated as one of the cities of refuge (Josh. 20:7). David ruled from Hebron the first seven years of his reign (2 Sam. 2:11), after which he established Jerusalem as his capital.

When Absalom rebelled against his father, David, he made Hebron his headquarters (2 Sam. 15:7–12). King Rehoboam fortified the city to protect his southern border (2 Chron. 11:10–12). The discovery of five jar handles stamped with the royal seal dating from the eighth century B.C. testifies that Hebron was a key storage city, perhaps for rations of Uzziah's army (2 Chron. 26:10).

2. The third son of Kohath, the grandson of Levi (Ex. 6:18). Hebron was an uncle of Moses, Aaron, and Miriam. He founded a tribal family. His descendants were called Hebronites (Num. 3:27).

3. The son of Mareshah, a descendant of Caleb (1 Chron. 2:42–43).

4. A town in Asher (Josh. 19:28, KJV; Ebron, NRSV, NKJV). This may be the same town as Abdon (Josh. 21:30).

Hebronites [He'bron·ites]—Descendants of Hebron, the Kohathite (Num. 3:27).

Hegai [He'gai], *eunuch*—A chamberlain of Ahasuerus (Est. 2:3, 8, 15).

Hege [He'ge]—See Hegai.

Helah [He'lah], *rust*—One of the two wives of Ashur (1 Chron. 4:5, 7).

Helam [He'lam], *stronghold*—A place east of the Jordan where David defeated Hadarezer (2 Sam. 10:16–19).

Helbah [Hel'bah], *fatness*—A town of Asher in which the Canaanites were allowed to remain (Judg. 1:31).

Helbon [Hel'bon], *fertile*—This town of Syria, north of Damascus (Ezek. 27:18), was famous for its wines.

Heldai [Hel'dai], *worldly*—Two Old Testament men:

1. A descendant of Othniel. He was a captain in David's army and commanded 24,000 men (1 Chron. 27:15).

2. One who returned from Babylon. With the gold and silver he carried with him, Zechariah made crowns for Joshua (Zech. 6:10–14).

Heleb [He'leb], *fatness*—One of David's mighty men (2 Sam. 23:29), elsewhere called Heled.

Helech [He'lech], *your army*—The NIV and NRSV translate Ezekiel 27:11 as "men of Arvad and Helech," while the NKJV and KJV say, "men of Arvad with your army."

Heled [He'led], *endurance*—Son of Baanah, one of David's warriors (1 Chron. 11:30).

Helek [He'lek], *a portion*—Son of Gilead of Manasseh (Num. 26:30; Josh. 17:2).

Helekites [He'lek·ites]—Descendants of Helek, grandson of Manasseh (Num. 26:30).

Helem [He'lem], *strength*—Two Old Testament men:

1. Brother of Shomer and Japhlet, one of the leaders of the Asher family (1 Chron. 7:32, 35), probably the same as Hotham.

2. One of those who assisted Zechariah in crowning Joshua, the high priest. He was probably the same as Heldai (Zech. 6:10, 14).

Heleph [He'leph], *exchange*—A town of Naphtali (Josh. 19:33).

Helez [He'lez], *he saved me*—Two Old Testament men:

1. An Ephraimite, one of David's warriors (2 Sam. 23:26; 1 Chron. 11:27).

2. Son of Azariah of Judah, descended from Hezron (1 Chron. 2:39).

Heli [He'li], *Greek form of Eli*—Father of Joseph who was the husband of Mary, the mother of Jesus (Luke 3:23).

Heliopolis [He'li·op'o'lis]—See On.

Helkai [Hel·ka'i], *my portion is Jehovah*—A priest in the time of Joiakim (Neh. 12:15).

Helkath [Hel'kath], *field*—A town on the eastern border of Asher (Josh. 19:25), assigned to the Levites (Josh. 21:31). In 1 Chronicles 6:75 it is called Hukok.

Helkath-hazzurim [Hel'kath-haz·zu'rim], *full of sharp edges*—The name given to the place near the pool of Gibeon (2 Sam. 2:16). See Field of Sharp Swords.

Hell [Hell]—A word meaning the place of the dead. It is a frequent translation of the Hebrew word *sheol* and the Greek words *hades* and *gehenna*. The early Hebrews regarded it merely as the place to which the dead go but later the word came to mean a place of punishment.

1. *Sheol* in Hebrew meant the realm of the dead. But the Semitic conception of it was vague. They thought of it as beneath the earth (Ezek. 31:17; Amos 9:2), entered by gates (Isa. 38:10). In Sheol the sinful and the righteous were either punished or rewarded. See Sheol.

2. *Hades,* a Greek term used in the New Testament. According to a parable told by Jesus it was a place where good and evil people lived close together, but were separated by a chasm. Those who had led a good life on earth were comforted; those who had not were punished.

3. *Gehenna,* the place of eternal punishment, the antithesis of heaven, to which the wicked were cast after the last judgment. It is depicted as a fiery furnace (Matt. 13:42), and as a lake of fire (Rev. 19:20; 20:10, 14–15; 21:8). See Gehenna.

Helon [He'lon], *strong*—Father of Eliab, prince of Zebulun (Num. 1:9; 2:7; 7:24, 29; 10:16).

Hemam [He'mam]—See Homam.

Heman [He'man], *faithful*—Three Old Testament men:

1. Son of Joel and grandson of Samuel, the Kohathite prophet (1 Chron. 6:33; 15:17), a singer in the time of David.

2. One who was distinguished for his wisdom in the time of Solomon (1 Kings 4:31).

3. A son (or clan) of the Judahite Zerah (1 Chron. 2:6), probably alluded to in the title of Psalm 88 as Heman the Ezrahite.

Hemath [He'math]—See Hamath.

Hemdan [Hem'dan], *pleasant*—Son of Dishon (Gen. 36:26). He is called Amram (Hamran in the Revised Version) in 1 Chronicles 1:41.

Hena [He'na], *troubling*—A town which fell to the Assyrians (2 Kings 18:34; 19:13; Isa. 37:13).

Henadad [Hen·a'dad], *favor of Hadad*—A Levite (Ezra 3:9; Neh. 3:18).

Henoch [He'noch]—See Enoch and Hanoch.

Hepher [He'pher], *pit* or *well*—Three men and a town of the Old Testament:
　　1. Son of Gilead and great-grandson of Manasseh (Num. 27:1; Josh. 17:2). His descendants were called Hepherites (Num. 26:32).
　　2. Son of Ashur of Tekoa, a Judahite (1 Chron. 4:6).
　　3. One of David's heroes, a Mecherathite (1 Chron. 11:36).
　　4. A town west of the Jordan taken by Joshua (Josh. 12:17).

Hepherites [He'pher·ites]—Descendants of Hepher, the grandson of Manasseh (Num. 26:32).

Hephzibah [Heph'zi·bah], *my delight is in her*—
　　1. Wife of Hezekiah of Judah and mother of Manasseh (2 Kings 21:1).
　　2. A symbolic name given Zion by Isaiah. Once Zion had been called "Forsaken," but this name was changed to Hephzi-bah when it found favor with the Lord (Isa. 62:4).

Heres [He'res], *sun*—A mountain in Aijalon to which the children of Dan were forced by the Amorites (Judg. 1:34–35).

Heresh [He'resh], *artificer*—A Levite (1 Chron. 9:15).

Hereth [Her'eth]—See Hareth, The Forest of.

Hermas [Her'mas], *Mercury*—A Christian who lived in Rome; one of those to whom Paul sent greetings in his epistle to the Romans (Rom. 16:14).

Hermes [Her'mes], *herald of the gods*—
　　1. The messenger of the gods. The Greek Hermes corresponds to the Roman Mercury with his swift winged feet (Acts 14:12).
　　2. A Christian at Rome, to whom Paul sent greetings (Rom. 16:14).

Hermogenes [Her·mog′e·nes], *sprung from Hermes*—One of those who abandoned Paul. He lived in the Roman province of Asia (2 Tim. 1:15).

Hermon [Her′mon], *sacred place*—The northern boundary of the land east of the Jordan River that Israel took from the Amorites (Deut. 3:8; Josh. 12:1). The mountain is the southern end of the Anti-Lebanon range and is about 32 kilometers (20 miles) long. It has three peaks (Ps. 42:6), two of which rise over 2,750 meters (9,000 feet) above sea level.

Hermon was regarded as a sacred place by the Canaanites who inhabited the land before the Israelites (Judg. 3:3). Snow covers the mountain during most of the year. Patches of snow remain even through the summer in shaded ravines. The beautiful snow-covered peaks of Mount Hermon can be seen from the region of the Dead Sea, over 196 kilometers (120 miles) distant as well as from most parts of Palestine. The glaciers of Mount Hermon are a major source of the Jordan River, and water from its slopes ultimately flows into the Dead Sea.

The psalmist speaks of the "dew of Hermon" (Ps. 133:3). The snow condenses to vapor during the summer, so that a heavy dew descends on the mountain while the areas surrounding Hermon are parched.

Mount Hermon probably was the site of our Lord's transfiguration (Matt. 17:1–9; Mark 9:2–9; Luke 9:28–37). Jesus traveled with His disciples from Bethsaida, on the Sea of Galilee, to the area of Caesarea Philippi to the north and from there to a "high mountain." There, in the presence of His disciples, Jesus was transfigured. A late tradition identifies the "high mountain" as Mount Tabor, but Mount Hermon is nearer Caesarea Philippi.

Hermonites [Her′mo·nites]—Natives of Mount Hermon (Ps. 42:6).

Herod [Her′od], *heroic*—The name of several Roman rulers in the Palestine region during Jesus' earthly ministry and the periods shortly before His birth and after His resurrection.

The Herodian dynasty made its way into Palestine through Antipater, an Idumean by descent. The Idumeans were of Edomite stock as descendants of Esau. Antipater was installed as procurator of Judea by Julius Caesar, the emperor of Rome, in 47 B.C. He appointed two of his sons to ruling positions. One of these was Herod, known as "Herod the Great," who was appointed governor of Judea.

Herod the Great (37–4 B.C.). The title "Herod the Great" refers not so much to Herod's greatness as to the fact that he was the eldest son of Antipater. Nevertheless, Herod did show some unusual abilities. He was a ruthless fighter, a cunning negotiator, and a subtle diplomat. The Romans appreciated the way he subdued opposition and maintained order among the Jewish people. These qualities, combined with an intense loyalty to the emperor, made him an important figure in the life of Rome and the Jews of Palestine.

After Herod became governor of Galilee, he quickly established himself in the entire region. For thirty-three years he remained a loyal friend and ally of Rome. He was appointed king of Judea, where he was in direct control of the Jewish people. This required careful diplomacy because he was always suspect by the Jews as an outsider (Idumean) and thus a threat to their national right to rule. At first Herod was conscious of Jewish national and religious feelings. He moved slowly on such issues as taxation, Hellenism, and religion. He did much to improve his relationship with the Jews when he prevented the temple in Jerusalem from being raided and defiled by invading Romans.

Herod the Great established his authority and influence through a centralized bureaucracy, well-built fortresses, and foreign soldiers. To assure his continued rule, he slaughtered all male infants who could possibly be considered legal heirs to the throne. His wife, Mariamne, also became a victim. The territories under Herod's rule experienced economic and cultural growth. His business and organizational ability led to the erection of many important buildings. Hellenistic (Greek) ideas were introduced into Palestine through literature, art, and athletic contests. His major building project was the temple complex in Jerusalem, which, according to John 2:20, had taken forty-six years to build up to that time. From the Jewish perspective, this was his greatest achievement.

He also rebuilt and enlarged the city of Caesarea into a port city on the Mediterranean Sea. Caesarea served as the Roman provincial capital for Palestine during the New Testament era. The magnificent aqueducts that he built at this city are still visible today.

At times Herod implemented his policies with force and cruelty. His increasing fear of Jewish revolt led to suppression of any opposition. His personal problems also increased, and by 14 B.C. his kingdom began to decline. This decline was brought on mainly by his personal and domestic problems.

Herod's murder of his wife, Mariamne, apparently haunted him. This was compounded when his two sons from that marriage, Alexander and Aristobulus, realized that their father was responsible for their mother's death. By 7 B.C., Herod had both of these sons put to death. Of Herod it was said, "It is better to be Herod's pig (*hys*) than to be his son (*huios*)."

As Herod became increasingly ill, an intense struggle for succession to his throne emerged within the family. His ten marriages and fifteen children virtually guaranteed such a struggle. One son, Antipater, poisoned Herod's mind against two other eligible sons, Archelaus and Philip. This resulted in his initial choice of a younger son, Antipas, as sole successor. However, he later changed his will and made Archelaus king. Antipas and Philip received lesser positions as Tetrarchs, or rulers, over small territories.

After Herod died, his will was contested in Rome. Finally Archelaus was made ethnarch over Idumea, Judea, and Samaria—with a promise to be appointed king if he proved himself as a leader. Antipas became tetrarch over Galilee and Perea. Philip was made tetrarch over Gaulanitis, Trachonitis, Batanea, and Paneas in the northern regions. Jesus was born in Bethlehem during the reign of Herod the Great. The wise men came asking, "Where is He who has been born King of the Jews?" This aroused Herod's jealous spirit. According to Matthew's account, Herod tried to eliminate Jesus by having all the male infants of the Bethlehem region put to death (Matt. 2:13–16). But this despicable act failed. Joseph and Mary were warned by God in a dream to take their child and flee to Egypt. Here they hid safely until Herod died (Matt. 2:13–15).

Herod Archelaus (4 B.C.–A.D. 6). Archelaus inherited his father Herod's vices without his abilities. He was responsible for much bloodshed in Judea and Samaria. Jewish revolts, particularly those led by the Zealots, were brutally crushed. Antipas and Philip did not approve of Archelaus's methods, so they complained to Rome. Their complaints were followed by a Jewish delegation that finally succeeded in having Archelaus stripped of power and banished to Rome.

The only biblical reference to Archelaus occurs in Matthew 2:22. Matthew recorded the fear that Mary and Joseph had about going through Judea on their way from Egypt to Galilee because Archelaus was the ruler.

Herod Antipas (4 B.C.–A.D. 39). Antipas, another of Herod the Great's sons, began as tetrarch over Galilee and Perea. He was the ruling Herod during Jesus' life and ministry. Herod Antipas was first married to the daughter of Aretas, a Nabatean king. But he became infatuated with Herodias, the wife of his half brother, Philip I. The two eloped, although both were married at the time. This scandalous affair was condemned severely by John the Baptist (Matt. 14:4; Mark 6:17–18; Luke 3:19).

Although Antipas apparently had some respect for John the Baptist, he had John arrested and imprisoned for his outspokenness. Later, at a royal birthday party, Antipas granted Salome, the daughter of Herod Philip, a wish. Probably at the prodding of Herodias (Mark 6:19), Salome requested the head of John the Baptist (Matt. 14:6–12; Mark 6:21–29). Since he was under oath and did not want to lose face before his guests, Herod ordered John's execution.

Antipas's contacts with Jesus occurred at the same time as the ministry of John the Baptist. Because of Jesus' popularity and miraculous powers, Antipas may have been haunted by the possibility that Jesus was John the Baptist come back to life. The New Testament record shows that the relationship between Jesus and Antipas must have been strained. Jesus' popularity and teachings may have threatened Antipas, who, according to the Pharisees, sought to kill Him (Luke 13:31). By calling Herod a fox ("Go, tell that fox," Luke 13:32), Jesus showed His disapproval of his cunning and deceitful ways.

The next encounter between Antipas and Jesus occurred at the trial of Jesus (Luke 23:6–12). Luke indicated that Herod could not find anything in the charges against Jesus that deserved death, so he sent Jesus back to Pilate for a final decision.

During this time of his rule, Antipas was experiencing political problems of his own. Aretas, the Nabatean king whose daughter had been Antipas's wife before he became involved with Herodias, returned to avenge this insult. Antipas's troops were defeated. This, together with some other problems, led to his political downfall. Antipas was finally banished by the Roman emperor to an obscure section of France.

Herod Agrippa I (A.D. 37–44). Agrippa took over Antipas's territory after Antipas fell from favor, given to him by Emperor Caligula. Agrippa's power and responsibilities extended far beyond his ability. As a young person growing up in the imperial court, he developed an undisciplined and extravagant lifestyle. But Agrippa had enough charm and intelligence to stay on the good side of Rome.

After the Roman emperor Caligula was murdered, Agrippa helped Claudius gain the throne. His loyalty was rewarded. Claudius confirmed Agrippa in his present position and added the territories of Judea and Samaria. This made Agrippa ruler of a kingdom as large as that of his grandfather, Herod the Great. Very little about Agrippa I is recorded in Scripture. He had James put to death and had Peter arrested. Beyond that, from the comments in Acts 12:1–23, we know that Agrippa sought to win the favor of his Jewish subjects by opposing the early Christian church and its leaders. The record of his death as recorded in Acts 12:20–23 shows the humiliating way he died, slain by an angel of the Lord. After his death, Palestine struggled through a number of chaotic years before Rome was able to establish order.

Herod Agrippa II (A.D. 50–100). Agrippa II was judged to be too young to assume leadership over all the territory of his father, Agrippa I. Thus, Emperor Claudius appointed Cuspius Fadus procurator of Palestine. But in A.D. 53, Agrippa II was appointed as the legitimate ruler over part of this territory including Abilene, Trachonitis, Acra, and important parts of Galilee and Perea.

The only reference to Agrippa II in the New Testament occurs in Acts 25:13–26:32, which deals with Paul's imprisonment in Caesarea. Agrippa listened to Paul's defense, but the apostle appealed to Rome. Agrippa had no power to set him free.

Agrippa was caught in the Jewish revolts that preceded the destruction of Jerusalem in A.D. 70 under the Roman emperor Titus. He continued to rule by appointment of Vespasian until his death in A.D. 100. His death marked the end of the Herodian dynasty in the affairs of the Jewish people in Palestine.

The other two Herods mentioned in the New Testament are Herod Archelaus (Matt. 2:22) and Herod Philip (Luke 3:1). Both of these rulers were sons of Herod the Great; they ruled parts of the territory administered by their father.

Herodians [He·ro′di·ans]—An influential group, probably a Jewish political party which is thrice mentioned in the New Testament (Matt. 22:16; Mark 3:6; 12:13).

Herodias [heh ROE dee uhs], *heroic*—Granddaughter of Herod the Great and sister of King Herod Agrippa, the queen who demanded John the Baptist's head on a platter (Matt. 14:1–12). The granddaughter of Herod the Great, Herodias first married her father's brother, Herod Philip I. One child was born to this union. Philip's half brother, the tetrarch Herod Antipas, wanted Herodias for his own wife, so he divorced his wife and married Herodias while Philip was still living.

When John the Baptist denounced their immorality, Herodias plotted John's death. She had her daughter Salome gain Herod's favor by dancing seductively for him at a banquet. As a result, Herod promised her anything she wanted. Following her mother's wishes, Salome asked for the head of John the Baptist.

Herodion [He·ro'di·on], *heroic*—A Christian at Rome to whom Paul sent his greeting (Rom. 16:11).

Hesed [He'sed], *son of faithfulness*—Father of one of Solomon's officers of provisions (1 Kings 4:10).

Heshbon [Hesh'bon], *stronghold*—An ancient city of Moab about 20 miles east of the Dead Sea, taken by Sihon, king of the Amorites, who made it his capital. It and the surrounding cities were allotted by Moses to Gad and Reuben (Num. 32:1–3; 31–37; Josh. 13:10). Eventually it became a Levitical city (Josh. 13:26; 21:39). The pools of Heshbon are mentioned in Song of Solomon 7:4.

Heshmon [Hesh'mon], *fatness*—A town in the south of Judah (Josh. 15:27).

Hesron [Hes'ron]—See Hezron.

Heth [Heth]—See Hittites.

Hethlon [Heth'lon], *hiding place*—A city on the ideal boundary of Palestine (Ezek. 47:15; 48:1).

Hezeki [Hez'e·ki]—See Hizki.

Hezekiah [Hez·e·ki'ah], *the Lord is my strength*—The name of three or four men in the Old Testament:

1. The thirteenth king of Judah. Born the son of Ahaz by Abi, daughter of Zechariah, Hezekiah became known as one of Judah's godly kings. That an ungodly man like Ahaz could have such a godly son can only be attributed to the grace of God. Hezekiah's father had given the kingdom over to idolatry; but upon his accession to the throne, Hezekiah decisively and courageously initiated religious reforms (2 Kings 18:4).

In the first month of his reign, Hezekiah reopened the temple doors that his father had closed. He also assembled the priests and Levites and commissioned them to sanctify themselves for service and to cleanse the temple. Appropriate sacrifices were then offered with much rejoicing (2 Chron. 29:3–36).

Hezekiah faced a golden opportunity to reunite the tribes spiritually. In the north Israel had fallen to Assyria in 722 B.C. Hezekiah invited the remnant of the people to come to Jerusalem to participate in the celebration of the Passover. Although some northern tribes scorned the invitation, most responded favorably (2 Chron. 30:1–27).

Hezekiah's reformation reached beyond Jerusalem to include the cleansing of the land, extending even to the tribes of Benjamin, Ephraim, and Manasseh. High places, images, and pagan altars were destroyed. The bronze serpent that Moses had made in the wilderness centuries earlier (Num. 21:5–9) had been preserved, and people were worshipping it. Hezekiah had it destroyed also (2 Kings 18:4; 2 Chron. 31:1). The land had never undergone such a thorough reform.

When Hezekiah experienced a serious illness, the prophet Isaiah informed the king that he would die. In response to Hezekiah's prayer for recovery, God promised him fifteen additional years of life. God also provided a sign for Hezekiah as evidence that the promise would be fulfilled. The sign, one of the most remarkable miracles of the Old Testament, consisted of the sun's shadow moving backward ten degrees on the sundial of Ahaz (Isa. 38:1–8).

Shortly after he recovered from his illness (Isa. 39:1), Hezekiah received visitors from the Babylonian king Merodach-baladan (2 Kings 20:12). They came with letters to congratulate Hezekiah on his recovery and to inquire about the sign (2 Chron. 32:31) in the land. But their real reason for visiting may have been to gain an ally in their revolt against Assyria. When they lavished gifts upon Hezekiah, he in turn showed them his wealth—an action that brought stiff rebuke from Isaiah (2 Kings 20:13–18).

There is no evidence to indicate that Hezekiah formed an alliance with Babylon. Neither is there any indication that he joined the rebellion in 711 B.C. led by Ashdod, the leading Philistine city. However, Scripture does reveal that he finally did rebel. Sargon II had died in 705 B.C., and his successor, Sennacherib, was preoccupied with trying to consolidate the kingdom when Hezekiah rebelled. With that accomplished, however, Sennacherib was ready to crush Hezekiah's revolt.

Anticipating the Assyrian aggression, Hezekiah made extensive military preparations. He strengthened the fortifications of Jerusalem, produced weapons and shields for his army, and organized his fighting forces under trained combat commanders. Realizing the importance of an adequate water supply, Hezekiah constructed a tunnel that channeled water from the Spring of Gihon outside the city walls to the Pool of Siloam inside the walls (2 Kings 20:20). This waterway (now known as Hezekiah's Tunnel) was cut through solid rock, extending more than 520 meters (1,700 feet).

As Sennacherib captured the fortified cities of Judah, Hezekiah realized that his revolt was a lost cause and he attempted to appease the Assyrian king. To send an apology and tribute, he emptied the palace treasuries and the temple, even stripping the gold from the doors and pillars. But this failed to appease Sennacherib's anger. At the height of the Assyrian siege, the angel of the Lord struck the Assyrian camp, leaving 185,000 dead (2 Kings 19:35). In humiliation and defeat, Sennacherib withdrew to his capital city of Nineveh.

Little more is said about Hezekiah's remaining years as king, but his achievements are recorded in 2 Chronicles 32:27–30. When he died, after reigning for 29 years, the people of Jerusalem "buried him in the upper tombs of the sons of David" (2 Chron. 32:33), a place of honor.

2. A descendant of David's royal line, a son of Neariah (1 Chron. 3:23).

3. A head of a family who returned from the captivity in Babylon (Neh. 7:21).

4. The great-great-grandfather of the prophet Zephaniah (Zeph. 1:1; Hizkiah, KJV, perhaps the same as No. 1).

Hezekiah's Water Tunnel [Hez·e·ki'ah]—The long underground shaft known as Hezekiah's water tunnel, or the Siloam tunnel, was dug through solid rock under the city wall of Jerusalem by King Hezekiah of Judah in the eighth century B.C. (2 Kings 20:20). The tunnel linked the Gihon Springs outside the city walls to the water reservoir known as the Pool of Siloam inside the city walls. It was dug to provide water to the city in case of a prolonged siege by Assyrian forces.

Built around 700 B.C., the crooked shaft is 1,750 feet long, often running 60 feet below the surface of the earth. It was rediscovered in 1838, but little scientific exploration and excavation work was done on the channel until 1866. Not until 1910 was it cleared of debris left by the destruction of Jerusalem in 586 B.C. A walk through Hezekiah's tunnel is a popular activity for modern tourists while visiting Jerusalem. An inscription in Hebrew found in the tunnel near the Pool of Siloam describes the construction project.

Two separate crews worked from opposite ends and eventually met in the middle of the shaft. Digging far below the earth's surface in bedrock, they labored for months in semidarkness with crude hand tools under difficult breathing conditions. But their hard work was rewarded when the Pool of Siloam began to fill with precious water that would spell the difference between life and death for Jerusalem if the Assyrians should attack the city.

A tactic used by besieging armies against walled cities was to cut off food and water supplies to the people inside (2 Kings 6:26–29). Hezekiah's tunnel and pool was more than a marvel of ancient engineering; it was a brilliant survival strategy. Hezekiah's tunnel may not have been the first water shaft dug at Jerusalem.

There is some evidence that when David captured the city from the Jebusites, about three hundred years before Hezekiah's time, his men gained entrance to the walled city through some sort of water shaft.

Hezion [He′zi·on], *vision*—Father of Tabrimmon and grandfather of Ben-hadad (1 Kings 15:18).

Hezir [He′zir], *swine*—Two Old Testament men:

1. A descendant of Aaron. In the time of David his family became the seventeenth course of the priests (1 Chron. 24:15).

2. One of the chief men with Nehemiah (Neh. 10:20).

Hezrai [Hez′ra·i], *walled in*—One of David's mighty men, a Carmelite (2 Sam. 23:35).

Hezro [Hez′ro]—See Hezrai.

Hezron [Hez'ron], *surrounded by a wall*—

1. A son of Reuben. His descendants were called Hezronites (Gen. 46:9; Ex. 6:14; Num. 26:6; 1 Chron. 5:3).

2. A Judahite whose descendants were also called Hezronites (Gen. 46:12; Num. 26:21; Ruth 4:18).

3. A place on the southern boundary of Judah (Josh. 15:3). It is identified with Hazor in Joshua 15:25.

Hiddai [Hid·da'i], *for the rejoicing of Jehovah*—One of David's mighty men (2 Sam. 23:30).

Hiddekel [Hid'de·kel]—One of the four rivers of Eden (Gen. 2:14), usually identified with the Tigris.

Hiel [Hi'el], *God liveth*—A native of Beth-el. In the reign of Ahab he rebuilt Jericho (1 Kings 16:34), thus bringing upon himself the curse pronounced by Joshua (Josh. 6:26).

Hierapolis [Hi·er·a'po·lis], *sacred city*—A town of Asia Minor in the valley of the Lycos (Col. 4:13).

High Gate—A gate of Jerusalem (2 Chron. 23:20; 27:3), also called the Upper Gate.

Hilen [Hi'len]—See Holon.

Hilkiah [Hil·ki'ah], *the Lord is my portion*—The name of seven or eight Old Testament men:

1. The father of Eliakim in the reign of Hezekiah (2 Kings 18:18, 26, 37).

2. A high priest during the reign of King Josiah of Judah (2 Kings 22:4–14). Hilkiah found the Book of the Law assisted Josiah in reforming Judah's backslidden people.

3. A Levite and a son of Amzi of the Merari family (1 Chron. 6:45–46).

4. A son of Hosah of the Merari branch (1 Chron. 26:11) and a tabernacle gatekeeper.

5. A priest who helped Ezra read the Book of the Law to the people (Neh. 8:4; 11:11). He may be the same person as No. 6.

6. A chief priest who returned from the captivity with Zerubbabel from Babylon (Neh. 12:7).

7. Father of Jeremiah the prophet (Jer. 1:1).

8. Father of Gemariah, a contemporary of Jeremiah (Jer. 29:3).

Hillel [Hil′lel], *he has praised—*

1. Father of Abdon, the judge; a Pirathonite (Judg. 12:13, 15).

2. A famous Jewish rabbi who flourished from about 30 B.C. to A.D. 9.

Hill of Foreskins, *Gibeath-harroloth*—The place where Joshua circumcised all the Israelites who had been born during the forty years in the wilderness (John 5:3, 9).

Hill of God—A hill where a high place was set up for worshipping God. Saul was filled with the Spirit here, and prophesied (1 Sam. 10:5).

Hinnom, Valley of [Hin′nom], *lamentation*—A deep, narrow ravine west and south of Jerusalem. At the high places of Baal in the Valley of Hinnom, parents sacrificed their children as a burnt offering to Molech by making them walk through fire (2 Kings 23:10). Ahaz and Manasseh, kings of Judah, were both guilty of this awful wickedness (2 Chron. 28:3; 33:6). But good King Josiah destroyed the pagan altars to remove this temptation from the people of Judah.

The prophet Jeremiah foretold that God would judge this awful abomination of human sacrifice and would cause such a destruction that "the Valley of the Son of Hinnom" would become known as "the Valley of Slaughter" (Jer. 7:31–32; 19:2, 6; 32:35). The place was also called "Tophet."

Apparently, the Valley of Hinnom was used as the garbage dump for the city of Jerusalem. Refuse, waste materials, and dead animals were burned here. Fires continually smoldered, and smoke from the burning debris rose day and night. Hinnom thus became a graphic symbol of woe and judgment and of the place of eternal punishment called hell.

Translated into Greek, the Hebrew "Valley of Hinnom" becomes gehenna, which is used twelve times in the New Testament (eleven times by Jesus and once by James), each time translated as "hell" (Matt. 5:22; Mark 9:43, 45, 47; Luke 12:5; James 3:6).

Hirah [Hi′rah], *nobility*—An Adullamite who became a friend of Judah (Gen. 38:1, 12).

Hiram, Huram [Hi'ram, Hu'ram], *noble*—

1. A king of Tyre who greatly enlarged his city. When David captured Jerusalem, Hiram sent to him an embassy and later furnished the timber and workmen for David's house (2 Sam. 5:11). He was also a friend of Solomon and contracted with him to furnish timber and workmen for the building of the temple (1 Kings 5:1–12; 2 Chron. 2:3–16). He assisted Solomon in securing from Ophir precious metals (1 Kings 9:26–28). Solomon offered him twenty towns in Galilee which he did not accept (1 Kings 9:10–12; 2 Chron. 8:1–2).

2. One whose mother was a widow of either the tribe of Naphtali or of Dan. His father was from Tyre (1 Kings 7:13–14). Hiram was a workman on Solomon's temple (1 Kings 7:13–46; 2 Chron. 2:13–14).

Hittites [Hit'tites], unknown—The Hittites were a people of the ancient world who flourished in Asia Minor and surrounding regions between about 1900 B.C. and 1200 B.C. While the Hittites are mentioned prominently in the Bible, some scholars questioned the existence of these people for many years because there was little physical evidence of their empire. But recent discoveries of Hittite culture by archeologists have confirmed the accuracy of the biblical accounts. The Hittite nation, with Hattusa as capital, eventually spread into northern Syria, then into the land of Canaan. Hittites are mentioned in the Bible during the earliest time of Israel's history.

When Sarah died, Abraham bought a burial cave from Ephron the Hittite (Gen. 23:10–20). Isaac's son Esau took two Hittite women as wives (Gen. 26:34). Several centuries later, the Hittites were included among the groups that would have to be driven out of Canaan before Israel could possess the land (Ex. 3:8; Deut. 7:1). In David's time, Ahimelech the Hittite was a trusted companion of David during his flight from Saul (1 Sam. 26:6). Uriah the Hittite, Bathsheba's husband, was sent to his death by David to cover up David's adultery with Bathsheba (2 Sam. 11:14–15). Since Uriah was a brave soldier in David's army, this shows that at least some of the Hittites had been assimilated into Israelite culture by this time in their history.

In Solomon's time, Solomon disobeyed God's instructions and married a Hittite woman to seal an alliance with these ancient people (1 Kings 11:1–2). This shows how objectionable the Hittite religious system was in God's eyes. The Hittites worshipped many different pagan gods, including several adopted from the Egyptians and the Babylonians. Solomon's marriages became a corrupting influence that pulled the nation of Israel away from worship of the one true God (1 Kings 11:9–13).

Hittite, Uriah the—See Uriah.

Hivites [Hi'vites], unknown—One of the nations of Canaan prior to the conquest of the land by Joshua (Gen. 10:17; Ex. 3:17; Josh. 9:1). Some Hivites were in Shechem when Jacob returned from Padan-aram (Gen. 34:2). Later, fearing that Joshua's army would destroy them, a number of them disguised themselves as distant tribesmen and by this ruse succeeded in forming a treaty with Joshua (Josh. 9). One section of them was settled in the extreme north even as late as David's time (Josh. 11:3). Some became bond-servants of Solomon (1 Kings 9:20–22).

Hizki [Hiz'ki], *my strength*—Son of Elpaal, a Benjamite (1 Chron. 8:17).

Hizkiah [Hiz·ki'ah]—See Hezekiah.

Hizkijah [Hiz·ki'jah], *Jehovah is my strength*—A signer of the covenant (Neh. 10:17).

Hobab [Ho'bab], *beloved*—The son of Reuel and a relative of Moses. He joined Moses and the Israelites at Rephidim (Ex. 18:1, 5, 27), at which time the Scripture refers to him as Jethro, the father-in-law of Moses (Num. 10:29, 32).

Hobah [Ho'bah], *hiding place*—A town north of Damascus (Gen. 14:15).

Hobaiah [Ho·bai'ah]—See Habaiah.

Hod [Hod], *splendour*—Son of Zophah, a descendant of Asher (1 Chron. 7:37).

Hodaiah [Ho·dai'ah]—See Hodaviah.

Hodaviah [Ho·da·vi'ah], *praise ye Jehovah*—Four Old Testament men:

    1. A Benjamite (1 Chron. 9:7).
    2. A leader of the half-tribe of Manasseh east of the Jordan (1 Chron. 5:24).

3. A son of Elioenai, descended from David through Shechaniah (1 Chron. 3:24).

4. Head of a Levitical family (Ezra 2:40).

Hodesh [Ho'desh], *new moon*—A wife of Shaharaim of Benjamin (1 Chron. 8:9).

Hodevah [Ho'de·vah]—See Hodaviah.

Hodiah [Ho·di'ah], *majesty of Jehovah*—The husband of the sister of Naham (1 Chron. 4:19).

Hodijah [Ho·di'jah], *my majesty is Jehovah*—

1. A Levite who assisted Ezra (Neh. 8:7; 9:5).

2. One who ratified the covenant along with Nehemiah (Neh. 10:18).

Hoglah [Hog'lah], *a partridge*—A daughter of Zelophehad (Num. 26:33).

Hoham [Ho'ham], *whom Jehovah impels*—A king of Hebron (Josh. 10:1–27).

Holon [Ho'lon], *sandy*—

1. A town of Moab (Jer. 48:21), perhaps Horon.

2. A town of Judah (Josh. 15:51). It was assigned to the priests (Josh. 21:15). In 1 Chronicles 6:58 it is called Hilen.

Holy of Holies—See Holy Place.

Holy Place—The innermost sanctuary of the tabernacle, where the ark of God rested, with His presence between the wings of the cherubim. The Holy of Holies could only be entered by the high priest, after sacrifices had been made to atone for his sin (Ex. 25:10–22; Lev. 16).

Holy Spirit—The third person of the Trinity, frequently "the Spirit" or "the Spirit of the Lord" or "the Holy Spirit." He is designated in the Old Testament only three times as "Holy Spirit" (Ps. 51:11; Isa. 63:10–11), though His work is frequently mentioned.

The Person of the Holy Spirit: One of the most serious errors in the minds of many people concerning the Holy Spirit is that He is simply a principle or an influence. On the contrary, the Holy Spirit is as much a person (individual existence of a conscious being) as the Father and the Son. He is the third person of the Trinity, thus not simply a divine energy or influence proceeding from God. As a person, He possesses intelligence, self-consciousness, and self-determination. His personality is explicitly described (Matt. 3:16–17; 28:19; John 14:16–17; 15:26).

Personal pronouns are used of Him (John 16:13–14; Acts 13:2). The Bible speaks of the mind (Rom. 8:27) and will (1 Cor. 12:11) of the Holy Spirit. He is often described as speaking directly to men in the book of Acts. During Paul's second missionary journey the apostle was forbidden by the Spirit to visit a certain mission field (Acts 16:6–7) and then was instructed to proceed toward another field of service (Acts 16:10). It was God's Spirit who spoke directly to Christian leaders in the Antioch church, commanding them to send Paul and Barnabas on their first missionary journey (Acts 13:2).

Divinity: When the personality of the Holy Spirit is admitted there is little disputation as to His divinity. He is distinctly addressed as God and designations are used that belong only to God (Acts 5:3–4; 2 Cor. 3:17–18; Heb. 10:15). Having the divine attributes of eternity, knowledge, sovereignty (1 Cor. 2:11; 12:11; Heb. 9:14). Operations ascribed to Him are of a divine nature, as creation (Gen. 1:2; Job 26:13), and regeneration (John 3:5–8). The unpardonable sin is the sin against the Holy Spirit (Matt. 12:31–32), and sin is not committed against an influence or an energy. It is committed against God alone. In His relation to Father and Son, He is the same as they in divine substance, in power and glory.

He proceeds from the Father and Son and in this relation is subordinate (not inferior) to them as they operate through Him (John 15:26; 16:13; Phil. 1:19). As is God the Father, the Holy Spirit is everywhere at once (Ps. 139:7). As the Son is eternal, the Holy Spirit has also existed forever (Heb. 9:14). He is often referred to as God in the Bible (Matt. 3:16–17; Acts 5:3–4) and is mentioned by Jesus Himself just prior to His ascension from the Mount of Olives (Matt. 28:19–20).

O.T. Teaching. The Holy Spirit is described as brooding over the surface of the deep during the creation (Gen. 1:2; Ps. 139:7). The Holy Spirit is the giver of life: physical, mental, and moral (Gen. 6:3; Job 32:8; 33:4; 34:14; Ps. 104:30). The prophets were inspired by the Holy Spirit (1 Sam. 10:6; Hos. 9:7; Mic. 3:8; Zech. 7:12), and they predicted the effusion of the Spirit in messianic times (Isa. 44:3; Ezek. 36:26; Joel 2:28; Zech. 12:10).

Beginning of the Christian Age: The Holy Spirit was directly involved in the conception of Jesus (Matt. 1:18–20). At Jesus's baptism, the Holy Spirit came down in the form of a dove and rested on Him while the Father voiced His approval (Matt. 3:16; Mark 1:10; John 1:32). The effusion of the Spirit which the prophets had foretold occurred at Pentecost (Acts 2:4), when the disciples were waiting in the upper room in Jerusalem. A sound came like a mighty rushing wind and tongues of fire appeared resting on each believer. They were filled with the Spirit, and spoke boldly for Christ in different languages.

Homam [Ho'mam], *destruction*—A son of Lotan (1 Chron. 1:39). In Genesis 36:22 it is Hemam.

Hophni [Hoph'ni], *tadpole*—A son of Eli the high priest who, along with his brother Phinehas, proved unworthy of priestly duties (1 Sam. 1:3; 2:34; 4:4–17). Their behavior was characterized by greed (1 Sam. 2:13–16) and lust (1 Sam. 2:22). Eli made only a halfhearted attempt to control his sons' scandalous behavior. Consequently, God's judgment was pronounced upon Eli and his household. Hophni and Phinehas were killed in a battle, and the ark of the covenant was captured by the Philistines (1 Sam. 4:1–11). When Eli heard the news, he fell backward and died of a broken neck (1 Sam. 4:12–18).

Hophra [Hoph'ra], *the great house* or *covering evil*—One of the Egyptian pharaohs, whose overthrow was prophesied by Jeremiah (Jer. 44:30).

Hor, Mount [Hor]—The name of two mountains in the Old Testament:

1. The mountain on the border of the Edomites where Aaron died and was buried (Num. 20:22–29; Deut. 32:50). Numbers 20:23 indicates that Mount Hor was situated by the border of the land of Edom. This was the place where the Hebrew people stopped after they left Kadesh (Num. 20:22; 33:37).

Early tradition established Jebel Harun, meaning "Aaron's Mountain," as the site of Mount Hor. It is a conspicuous mountain about 1,440 meters (4,800 feet) high on the eastern side of the Arabah, midway between the southern tip of the Dead Sea and the northern end of the Gulf of Aqaba. However, this peak is far from Kadesh. In recent years Jebel Madurah northeast of Kadesh on the northwest border of Edom has been suggested as the more likely site for Mount Hor.

2. A mountain in northern Palestine between the Mediterranean Sea and the approach to Hamath (Num. 34:7–8).

Horam [Hor'am], *lofty*—A king of Gezer. He was defeated and slain by Joshua (Josh. 10:33).

Horeb [Hor'eb], *desert*—See Sinai.

Horem [Hor'em], *sacred*—A city of Naphtali (Josh. 19:38).

Horesh [Hor'esh], *forest*—A place where David hid from the pursuing Saul (1 Sam. 23:15).

Hor-haggidgad [Hor-hag·gid'gad], possibly *hill of crickets*—One of the encampments of the Israelites in the wilderness (Num. 33:32), probably the same as Gudgodah (Deut. 10:6–7).

Hor-hagidgad [Hor-ha·gid'gad]—See Hor-haggidgad.

Hori [Hor'i], *cave dweller*—Two Old Testament men:

1. The son of Lotan and grandson of Seir (Gen. 36:22; 1 Chron. 1:39).

2. The father of the Simeonite spy Shaphat (Num. 13:5).

Horims [Hor'ims]—See Horites.

Horites [Hor'ites], unknown—The original inhabitants of Seir (Gen. 36:20, 29–30).

Hormah [Hor'mah], *devoted to destruction*—A city of uncertain site in southern Palestine where the Israelites were defeated by the Amalekites and the Canaanites (Num. 14:45). Later, however, the Israelites defeated the Canaanites here and thereupon named the place Hormah (Num. 21:1–3).

Horonaim [Hor·o·na'im], *two caverns*—A city of the Moabites (Isa. 15:5; Jer. 48:3, 5, 34).

Horonite [Hor'on·ite]—A native of Horonaim, or more probably of Beth-horon (Neh. 2:10, 19).

Horse Gate—A gate of Jerusalem, apparently leading into the royal palace (2 Chron. 23:15; Neh. 3:28; Jer. 31:40).

Hosah [Ho'sah], *refuge*—
1. A town on the border of Asher near Tyre (Josh. 19:29).
2. A Levite of the family of Merari (1 Chron. 16:38; 26:10).

Hosea [Ho·se'a], *deliverance*—An Old Testament prophet and author of the book of Hosea. The son of Beeri (Hos. 1:1), Hosea ministered in the northern kingdom of Israel during the chaotic period just before the fall of this nation in 722 B.C. The literary features within Hosea's book suggest he was a member of the upper class. The tone and contents of the book also show he was a man of deep compassion, strong loyalty, and keen awareness of the political events taking place in the world at that time. As a prophet, he was also deeply committed to God and His will as it was being revealed to His covenant people.

Hosea is one of the most unusual prophets of the Old Testament, since he was commanded by God to marry a prostitute (Hos. 1:2–9). His wife, Gomer, eventually returned to her life of sin, but Hosea bought her back from the slave market and restored her as his wife (Hos. 3:1–5). His unhappy family experience was an object lesson of the sin or "harlotry" of the nation of Israel in rejecting the one true God and serving pagan gods. Although the people deserved to be rejected because they had turned their backs on God, Hosea emphasized that God would continue to love them and use them as His special people.

In his unquestioning obedience of God, Hosea demonstrated he was a prophet who would follow his Lord's will, no matter what the cost. He was a sensitive, compassionate spokesman for righteousness whose own life echoed the message that God is love.

Hoshaiah [Ho·shai'ah], *Hehovah has saved*—Two Old Testament men:
1. Father of Jezaniah (Jer. 42:1) or Azariah (Jer. 43:2). The son accused Jeremiah of prophesying falsely.
2. A man who participated in the dedication of the wall of Jerusalem (Neh. 12:32).

Hoshama [Ho'sha·ma], *Jehovah has heard*—A son of Jehoiachin (1 Chron. 3:18).

Hoshea [Ho'she'a]—
1. The former name of Joshua, changed to Joshua by Moses (Num. 13:8, 16). In the King James Version of this passage it is Oshea (*save*).

2. Son of Azaziah. He was the prince of the tribe of Ephraim in the reign of David (1 Chron. 27:20).

3. Israel's last king, son of Elah. He slew Pekah and seized the throne (2 Kings 15:30; 17:3).

4. One who sealed the covenant (Neh. 10:23).

Hosts, Lord of—See God, Names of.

Hotham [Ho'tham], *a seal* or *a ring*—Two Old Testament men:
    1. An Aroerite. Two of his sons were warriors of David (1 Chron. 11:44).
    2. Son of Heber (1 Chron. 7:32).

Hothan [Ho'than]—See Hotham.

Hothir [Ho'thir], *abundance*—A son of Heman (1 Chron. 25:4).

Hozai [Ho'za·i], *seer*—Probably the proper name for the one who wrote a history about Manasseh, king of Judah. The expression "history of Hozai" is rendered "sayings of the seers" (2 Chron. 33:19, KJV).

Hukkok [Huk'kok], *decreed*—A town a few miles west of Capernaum (Josh. 19:34).

Hukok [Hu'kok]—See Helkath.

Hul [hul], *circle*—Second son of Aram (Gen. 10:23; 1 Chron. 1:17).

Huldah [Hul'dah], *weasel*—A prophetess, the wife of Shallum, in the time of King Josiah. She assured this godly king that the judgment against Jerusalem would not be fulfilled in his day (2 Kings 22:12–20; 2 Chron. 34:20–28).

Humtah [Hum'tah], *place of lizards*—A town of Judah (Josh. 15:54).

Hundred, Tower of the—A part of the wall of Jerusalem (Neh. 3:1; 12:39).

Hupham [Hu'pham], *coast-man*—A son or more remote descendant of Benjamin and founder of a tribal family (Num. 26:39); called Huppim in Genesis 46:21. In 1 Chronicles 7:12 he is called son of Ir, also a Benjamite.

Huphamites [Hu'pha·mites]—The descendants of Benjamin's offspring Hupham (Num. 26:39).

Huppah [Hup'pah], *a covering*—A priest, a descendant of Aaron (1 Chron. 24:13).

Huppim [Hup'pim]—See Hupham.

Hur [Hur], *hole*—Four Old Testament men:

1. A king of Midian whom Moses killed when the Israelites were in the plain of Moab (Num. 31:8; Josh. 13:21).

2. The grandfather of Bezaleel of the family of Hezron and house of Caleb (Ex. 31:1–2; 1 Chron. 2:18–20).

3. One who, with Aaron, during the battle with the Amalekites supported the arms of Moses while he prayed (Ex. 17:10–12). While Moses was in Mount Sinai, Hur aided Aaron in the management of things (Ex. 24:14).

4. Father of Ben-hur (1 Kings 4:8).

5. Father of Rephaiah (Neh. 3:9).

Hurai [Hu·ra'i], *linen-weaver*—One of David's warriors (1 Chron. 11:32). He is called Hiddai in 2 Samuel 23:30.

Huram [Hu'ram], *noble*—

1. A Benjamite, son of Bela (1 Chron. 8:5).

2. A king of Tyre who assisted in the building of Solomon's temple (2 Chron. 2:3). See Hiram.

3. An artificer of Tyre (2 Chron. 4:11, 16). See Hiram.

Huri [Hu'ri], *linen worker*—Father of Abihail of the tribe of Gad (1 Chron. 5:14).

Hurrians [Hur'ri·ans]—See Horites.

Hushah [Hu'shah], *haste*—The son of Ezer, a descendant of Hur (1 Chron. 4:4).

Hushai [Hu'shai], *hasty*—An Archite, one of the two chief counselors of David (2 Sam. 15:32–37; 17:5–16).

Husham [Hu'sham], *haste*—A Temanite king of Edom (Gen. 36:34–35; 1 Chron. 1:45–46).

Hushathite [Hu'sha·thite]—An inhabitant of Hushah (2 Sam. 21:18; 23:27).

Hushim [Hu′shim], *who makes haste—*

1. The sons of Aher, a Benjamite family (1 Chron. 7:12).

2. One of the wives of Shaharaim, a Benjamite in the land of Moab (1 Chron. 8:8, 11).

3. Son of Dan (Gen. 46:23). In Numbers 26:42 he is called Shuham, possibly the same as in 1 Chronicles 7:12.

Huz [Huz]—(Gen. 22:21). See Uz.

Hymenaeus [Hy·me·nae′us], *pertaining to Hymen* or *the god of marriage—*A man of Ephesus (1 Tim. 1:20).

I

I Am, I am that I Am—The name by which God revealed Himself to Moses at the bush (Ex. 3:14). It represents God as the self-existent one. He is defined by Himself, not by comparison with something higher, or something that we know. Jesus electrified His Jewish audience by claiming this title for Himself, thereby clearly identifying Himself as God (John 8:58–59). See God, Names of.

Ibhar [Ib'har], *chosen of God*—A son of David born in Jerusalem (2 Sam. 5:15; 1 Chron. 14:5).

Ibleam [Ib'le·am], *devouring the people*—A city belonging to the territory of Issachar. It was given to the half-tribe of Manasseh, on the west side of the Jordan River, about ten miles southeast of Megiddo (Josh. 17:11–12). The tribe of Manasseh failed to drive out the inhabitants and the Canaanites living there were allowed to remain (Judg. 1:27). The town of Bileam, mentioned in 1 Chronicles 6:70, is probably the same as Ibleam.

Ibneiah [Ib·nei'ah], *built of Jehovah*—Son of Jeroham, a Benjamite; the head of one of the families returning from captivity (1 Chron. 9:8).

Ibnijah [Ib·ni'jah], *built by Jehovah*—Father of Reuel, a Benjamite (1 Chron. 9:8).

Ibri [Ib'ri], *Hebrew*—A Levite, he lived during the reign of King David (1 Chron. 24:27).

Ibsam, Jibsam [Ib'sam, Jib'sam], *pleasant*—A man of Issachar of the family of Tola (1 Chron. 7:2).

Ibzan [Ib'zan], *active*—A judge over Israel for seven years; Ibzan was the father of thirty sons and thirty daughters (Judg. 12:8–10).

Ichabod [I'cha·bod], *inglorious*—Son of Phinehas and grandson of Eli, the high priest who mentored the young Samuel. His mother, dying after a difficult premature labor brought on by the news of her husband's death, her father-in-law's death, and the Philistine capture of the ark of the Lord, gave Ichabod this name as a symbol of what she believed was happening to Israel (1 Sam. 4:19–22).

Iconium [I·co'ni'um], *little image*—An important city of Asia Minor, in the fertile plain of Lycaonia. On his first missionary journey with Barnabas Paul visited the city (Acts 13:51–52; 14:1–6, 19–22; 16:1–2; 2 Tim. 3:11). Today, Iconium is known as Konya or Konia.

Idalah [I'da·lah]—A city of Zebulun (Josh. 19:15). Located near Nazareth, it is called Khirbet el-Hawarah today.

Idbash [Id'bash], *honeyed*—A man of the tribe of Judah, one of the sons of Etam (1 Chron. 4:3).

Iddo [Id'do], *I will praise him*—The name of at least six men in the Old Testament:

1. Father of Ahinadab, purveyor of food for Solomon at Mahanaim (1 Kings 4:14).

2. A descendant of Gershom, son of Levi (1 Chron. 6:21); also called Adaiah (1 Chron. 6:41).

3. Son of Zechariah, ruler of the half-tribe of Manasseh east of the Jordan in the time of King David (1 Chron. 27:21).

4. A seer who wrote a book about events in the reign of Solomon (2 Chron. 9:29), a book of genealogies recording deeds of Rehoboam (2 Chron. 12:15), and a history concerning Abijah (2 Chron. 13:22). These books are lost, but they may have formed a part of the foundation of the books of Chronicles.

5. Grandfather of Zechariah the prophet (Zech. 1:1, 7), probably a chief of the priests who was of the company of Zerubbabel (Neh. 12:4, 16).

6. A chief of the Jews, living in Casiphia in Babylon (Ezra 8:17–20).

Idumaea [I·du·mae'a], *unknown*—The name the Greeks and Romans gave to Edom (Isa. 34:5–6; Ezek. 35:15; 36:5; Mark 3:8). Herod the Great was an Edomite, or Idumean.

Idumea [I·du·me'a]—See Idumaea.

Iezer [I-e'zer]—See Abiezer.

Igal [I′gal], *the Lord redeems*—Three Old Testament men:

　1. The Issacharite spy sent by Moses with other scouts to Canaan (Num. 13:7).

　2. Son of Nathan of Zobah; one of David's mighty men (2 Sam. 23:36).

　3. Son of Shemaiah; a descendant of Jehoiachin, also called Igeal or Igar (1 Chron. 3:22).

Igdaliah [Ig·da·li′ah], *great is the Lord*—Father of Hanan (Jer. 35:4).

Igeal [I′ge·al]—See Igal.

Iim [I′im], *ruins*—

　1. A town in the extreme south of Judah (Josh. 15:28–29).

　2. A town east of the Jordan (Num. 33:45). See Iye-abarim.

Ije-abarim [I′je-ab′a·rim]—See Iye-abarim.

Ijim [I′jim]—See Ijon.

Ijon [I′jon], *ruins*—A town of Naphtali. At the suggestion of Asa, king of Judah, it was captured from King Baasha of Israel by Ben-hadad of Syria (1 Kings 15:20; 2 Chron. 16:4). Later, the inhabitants of this town were carried into captivity in Assyria (2 Kings 15:29).

Ikkesh [Ik′kesh], *preverse*—Father of Ira, a Tekoite and a captain of David's troops (2 Sam. 23:26; 1 Chron. 11:28; 27:9).

Ilai [I′la·i], *supreme*—One of David's mighty men (1 Chron. 11:29). He is also called Zalmon (2 Sam. 23:28).

Illyricum [Il·lyr′i·cum], *the lyric band*—A district lying along the eastern coast of the Adriatic Sea. It is mentioned only once in the New Testament, as the territorial limit to Paul's preaching (Rom. 15:19). Its people were wild mountaineers whose acts of piracy brought them into conflict with the Romans. By Paul's time, the area had become a Roman province. The northern half was called Liburnia, the southern half, Dalmatia (2 Tim. 4:10). Later, the whole district was called Dalmatia. Today, this area includes Albania and former Yugoslavia. See Dalmatia.

Imla [Im'la], *full*—Father of the prophet Micaiah (1 Kings 22:8–9; 2 Chron. 18:7–8). Micaiah was a prophet during the reign of Ahab, the king of Israel and husband of Jezebel.

Imlah [Im'lah]—See Imla.

Immanuel, Emmanuel [Im·man'u·el, Em·man'u·el], *God is with us*—The symbolic name of the child whose birth Isaiah promised as a sign of deliverance and safety to King Ahaz (Isa. 7:14). The name is repeated in Isaiah 8:8. This prophecy was made at a time of national crisis (735 B.C.) when the kingdom of Ahaz was threatened with defeat by the combined armies of Syria and Ephraim. In addition to its immediate significance as a sign to Ahaz, this prophecy has always been regarded as a forewarning of the Messiah. Matthew specifically tells us that it was fulfilled in the birth of Christ (Matt. 1:23). The ultimate fulfillment of "God with us" will be found in the New Jerusalem, where we will be finally in God's presence forever (Rev. 21:2–4).

Immer [Im'mer], *he hath said*—This is both the name of a town, and the name of several men in the Old Testament.

1. A descendant of Aaron, Immer was a priest in the time of David. His family was made the sixteenth course of priests of the twenty-four divisions who served in the tabernacle (1 Chron. 24:1, 6, 14).

2. Apparently the name of a town in Babylon, Immer was the exile home of certain priestly families who could not establish their descent from Israel (Ezra 2:59; Neh. 7:61).

3. Father of Pashur. Pashur was the priest who had Jeremiah beaten and put in the stocks (Jer. 20:1–2).

4. A priest and the father of Meshillemith (1 Chron. 9:12; Neh. 11:13). Over one thousand of Immer's descendants accompanied Zerubbabel to Jerusalem (Ezra 2:37; Neh. 7:40).

5. Father of Zadok, who labored on the wall of Jerusalem under Nehemiah (Neh. 3:29).

Imna [Im'na], *he will restrain*—A son of Helem, a descendant of Asher (1 Chron. 7:35).

Imnah [Im'nah], *right hand*—Two Old Testament men:
1. A son of Asher, founder of a tribal family (Gen. 46:17; Num. 26:44; 1 Chron. 7:30).

2. The father of Kore, a Levite (2 Chron. 31:14). Kore lived during the reign of Hezekiah, king of Judah.

Imrah [Im′rah], *stubborn*—A son of Zophah of the tribe of Asher (1 Chron. 7:36).

Imri [Im′ri], *eloquent*—

1. Son of Bani and descendant of Perez (1 Chron. 9:4). This Imri may possibly be the same person as Amariah (Neh. 11:4).

2. Father of Zaccur, who labored on the wall (Neh. 3:2).

India [In′di·a]—The India mentioned in the Old Testament probably included approximately the same area which today makes up the nations of India and Pakistan. India is part of the continent of Asia, south of the Himalaya Mountains. Its name comes from the Indus River, which rises in Tibet, and flows southward to the Arabian Sea. India is named in Scripture as the easternmost boundary of the Persian Empire under Ahasuerus, who reigned over 127 provinces from India to Ethiopia (Est. 1:1; 8:9). Solomon's fleets may have gone as far as India on their voyages in search of treasures for Solomon's court (1 Kings 10:22).

Inspection Gate—See Gates of Jerusalem.

Iob [I′ob]—A form of Jashub.

Iphdeiah [Iph·dei′ah], *Jehovah delivers*—A son of Shashak (1 Chron. 8:25).

Iphedeiah [Iph·e·dei′ah]—See Iphdeiah.

Iphtah [Iph′tah]—A town of Judah (Josh. 15:43).

Iphtahel [Iph′tah·el], *God opens*—A valley that lies between Zebulun and Asher (Josh. 19:14, 27).

Ir [Ir], *belonging to a city*—The father of Shuppim and Huppim, a descendant of Benjamin (1 Chron. 7:12). Maybe the same person as Iri.

Ira [I′ra], *watchful*—Two or three of David's entourage.

1. Son of Ikkesh, a Tekoite, one of David's mighty men (2 Sam. 23:26; 1 Chron. 11:28).

2. An Ithrite, one of David's mighty men, and possibly the same as Ira I (2 Sam. 23:38; 1 Chron. 11:40).

3. A Jairite, "chief minister" under David (2 Sam. 20:26).

Irad [I'rad], *smitten by God*—Son of Enoch (Gen. 4:18).

Iram [I'ram], *belonging to a city*—A chief of Edom (Gen. 36:43; 1 Chron. 1:54).

Ir Ha-heres [Ir Ha-he'res], *city of destruction*—Some versions translate this as City of the Sun, that is, Heliopolis (Isa. 19:18). See also On.

Iri [I'ri], *belonging to a city*—A son of Bela (1 Chron. 7:7), possibly the same as Ir.

Irijah [I·ri'jah], *Jehovah sees me*—A captain of the guard at the time the Chaldeans besieged Jerusalem (Jer. 37:13).

Ir-nahash [Ir-na'hash], *city of a serpent*—A town of Judah (1 Chron. 4:12).

Irpeel [Ir'peel], *God heals*—A town of Benjamin, not far from Jerusalem (Josh. 18:27).

Ir-shemesh [Ir'she'mesh], *city of the sun*—A town in the territory of Dan (Josh. 19:41); it appears to be the same as Beth-shemesh (Josh. 15:10; 21:16; Judg. 1:33).

Iru [I'ru], *citizen*—A son of Caleb. His father was sent with Joshua to spy in the land of Canaan (1 Chron. 4:15).

Isaac [I'saac], (God) *laughs*—The only son of Abraham by his wife, Sarah; father of Jacob and Esau. God promised to make Abraham's descendants a great nation that would become God's chosen people. But the promised son was a long time in coming. Isaac was born when Abraham was one hundred years old and Sarah was ninety (Gen. 17:17; 21:5). Both Abraham and Sarah laughed when they heard they would have a son in their old age (Gen. 17:17–19; 18:9–15). This partially explains why they named their son Isaac.

Abraham believed that God would one day send him children to fulfill the promise, but before Isaac was born Sarah became anxious about her barrenness. She arranged for Abraham to have children with her Egyptian servant, Hagar. Through this Ishmael was born. While God promised that Ishmael would also be the father of many descendants, he was not the son of the promise. It was thirteen more years before God again addressed the problem of Abraham and Sarah's childlessness and Isaac was born.

On the eighth day after his birth, Isaac was circumcised (Gen. 21:4). As he grew, his presence as Abraham's rightful heir brought him into conflict with Ishmael, Abraham's son by Sarah's handmaid Hagar. The strained relationship caused Sarah to send away Hagar and Ishmael (Gen. 21:9–21). God comforted Abraham by telling him that Ishmael would also become the father of a great nation (Gen. 21:13).

Isaac, the son of promise, had reached young manhood (Gen. 22:6) when his father was commanded to offer him as a burnt offering. When the Lord was convinced that Abraham passed this test of faith, He spared Isaac's life (Gen. 22:12). Isaac was in a special position in terms of his birthright. While Abraham provided materially for his other sons (Ishmael, and the sons of his second wife, Keturah, and of his concubines), Isaac received not only the birthright of an oldest son, but he also inherited the blessings and responsibility of the covenant with God.

Birthright: Isaac's birthright was an important part of his life. The blessings that God gave to Abraham were also given to his descendants. Thus, to inherit this covenant with God was of far greater value than to inherit property or material goods.

Isaac's life gave evidence of God's favor. His circumcision was a sign of the covenant with God. God's favor toward him was also evident in Ishmael's disinheritance. The dismissal of the sons of Abraham's concubines to the "country of the east" is associated with the statement that Isaac inherited all that Abraham had, including God's blessing. Isaac was in a unique position historically because he would carry on the covenant. When Isaac was a young man, God tested Abraham's faith by commanding him to sacrifice Isaac as an offering. But when Abraham placed Isaac upon the altar, an angel appeared and stopped the sacrifice, providing a ram instead (Gen. 22). This showed clearly that Isaac was God's choice to carry on the covenant.

Marriage: Abraham arranged for Isaac to marry Rebekah, sister of Laban and granddaughter of Nahor (Gen. 24), when he was forty years old. She became Isaac's wife when God directed one of Abraham's servants to her. The Bible reveals that Isaac loved Rebekah and that she was a comfort to him after his mother Sarah's death (Gen. 24:67). Isaac and Rebekah had twin sons, Jacob and Esau, who were born when Isaac was sixty years old (Gen. 25:20–26).

After Abraham's death, famine prompted the family to move to Gerar, where God appeared to Isaac and reaffirmed the covenant. Moving through the valley of Gerar, where he reopened the wells that Abraham had dug (Gen. 26:23; 28:10), Isaac made a camp at Beersheba. This place became his permanent home. There he built an altar just as his father had done (Gen. 26:24–25).

Jacob and Esau: The older twin, Esau, was Isaac's favorite son, although God had declared that the older should serve the younger (Gen. 25:23). Jacob was Rebekah's favorite. Disagreement arose over which of the twins would receive the birthright and carry on the covenant that God had made with Abraham. Rebekah conspired with Jacob to trick the aging, blind Isaac into giving his blessing to Jacob rather than Esau.

Shortly thereafter, Isaac sent Jacob to Laban in Padan-aram to find a wife and to escape Esau's wrath. Esau soon left his father's household. Many years passed before the two brothers were at peace with each other. But they were united at last in paying last respects to their father after his death. Isaac lived in Hebron until his death at 180 years old. He was buried alongside Abraham, Sarah, and Rebekah in the cave of Machpelah (Gen. 35:28–29; 49:30–31).

Isaiah [I·sa'ah], *the Lord has saved*—Also Esaius (Greek form). A famous Old Testament prophet who predicted the coming of the Messiah; the author of the book of Isaiah. Isaiah is called the "messianic prophet," because so much of the prophecy concerning Christ is in his book. Besides the book of Isaiah, he also wrote biographies of Uzziah and Hezekiah, which have been lost (2 Chron. 26:22; 32:32).

Isaiah was probably born in Jerusalem of a family that was related to the royal house of Judah. He recorded the events of the reign of King Uzziah of Judah (2 Chron. 26:22). When Uzziah died (740 B.C.), Isaiah received his prophetic calling from God in a stirring vision of God in the temple (Isa. 6). The king of Judah had died; now Isaiah had seen the everlasting King in whose service he would spend the rest of his life. He continued to prophesy during the reigns of Jotham, Ahaz, and Hezekiah in Jerusalem (Isa. 1:1).

Isaiah was married to a woman described as "the prophetess" (Isa. 8:3). They had two sons whom they named Shear-Jashub, "A Remnant

Shall Return" (Isa. 7:3), and Maher-Shalal-Hash-Baz, "Speed the Spoil, Hasten the Booty" (Isa. 8:3). These strange names portray two basic themes of the book of Isaiah: God is about to bring judgment upon His people, hence Maher-Shalal-Hash-Baz, but after that there will be an outpouring of God's mercy and grace to the remnant of people who will remain faithful to God, hence Shear-Jashub.

After God called Isaiah to proclaim His message, He told Isaiah that most of his work would be a ministry of judgment. Even though the prophet would speak the truth, the people would reject his words (Isa. 6:10). Jesus found in these words of Isaiah's call a prediction of the rejection of his message by many of the people (Matt. 13:14–15).

Isaiah's response to this revelation from the Lord was a lament: "Lord, how long?" (Isa. 6:11). The Lord answered that Isaiah's ministry would prepare the people for judgment, but one day God's promises would be realized. For forty years, Isaiah faithfully prophesied the doom and destruction which would fall upon an unrepentant nation, as well as the future deliverance of Israel and the glorious future that would be theirs when they turned again to their God. In Isaiah's lifetime, Israel did not listen, just as God had said. When the Messiah came, God's words to Isaiah were further fulfilled (Matt. 13:14–15).

Judah was to experience utter devastation, to be fulfilled with the destruction of the city of Jerusalem by the Babylonians in 586 B.C. (Isa. 6:11). This destruction would be followed by the deportation of the people to Babylon (Isa. 6:12). But although the tree of the house of David would be cut down, there would still be life in the stump (Isa. 6:13). Out of the lineage of David would come a Messiah who would establish His eternal rule among His people.

Isaiah was a writer of considerable literary skill. The poetry of his book is magnificent in its sweep. A person of strong emotion and deep feelings, Isaiah also was a man of steadfast devotion to the Lord. His vision of God and His holiness in the temple influenced his messages during his long ministry. Isaiah's ministry extended from about 740 B.C. until at least 701 B.C. (Isa. 37–39). His forty years of preaching doom and promise did not turn the nation of Judah from its headlong rush toward destruction. But he faithfully preached the message God gave him until the very end.

According to a popular Jewish tradition, Isaiah met his death by being sawn in half during the reign of the evil king Manasseh of Judah.

This tradition seems to be supported by the writer of Hebrews (Heb. 11:37). Certainly Isaiah is one of the heroes of the faith "of whom the world was not worthy" (Heb. 11:38).

Iscah [Is'cah], *watchful*—A daughter of Abraham's brother Haran, and sister of Milcah who married Abraham's other brother Nahor (Gen. 11:27, 29).

Iscariot [Is·car'i·ot], *man of Kerioth*—Judas, the apostle who betrayed his Lord (Matt. 10:4; Luke 6:16). Judas is called Iscariot to differentiate him from the other apostle named Judas, and also from the Lord's brother (Mark 6:3; Luke 6:16; Acts 1:13, 16). It probably denotes that he was a native of Kerioth (Josh. 15:25).

Ishbah [Ish'bah], *he praises*—A descendant of Judah; son of Mered and father of Eshtemoa (1 Chron. 4:17).

Ishbak [Ish'bak], *relinquish*—Son of Abraham and his second wife, Keturah (Gen. 25:2).

Ishbi-benob [Ish'bi-be'nob], *my seat is at Nob*—A Philistine giant slain by Abishai, son of Zeruiah, in the days of David the king (2 Sam. 21:16–17).

Ish-bosheth [Ish-bo'sheth], *man of shame*—A son of Saul whom Abner, Saul's captain, proclaimed king after Saul's death (2 Sam. 2:8–10). He escaped being slain in Saul's last battle, where both Saul and Jonathan died. The tribe of Judah proclaimed David king after the death of Saul and Jonathan at Gilboa, but the eleven other tribes remained loyal to Saul's family. Ish-bosheth reigned two turbulent years from Mahanaim, east of the Jordan River, while David ruled Judah from Hebron. Throughout the period, each side attempted unsuccessfully to gain control of the entire kingdom (2 Sam. 2:12–3:1).

Ish-bosheth made a grave error in charging Abner with having relations with Saul's concubine, Rizpah. In anger, Abner changed his allegiance to David (2 Sam. 3:6–21). When Joab murdered Abner in Hebron (2 Sam. 3:27), Ish-bosheth became discouraged (2 Sam. 4:1). Two captains of his guard, Baanah and Rechab, assassinated Ish-bosheth as he lay napping. They carried Ish-bosheth's severed head to David, who ordered it buried in the tomb of Abner in Hebron. Then

David put the assassins to death (2 Sam. 4:5–12). Saul's dynasty ended with Ish-bosheth's death.

Ishhod, Ishod [Ish'hod, I'shod], *man of renown*—A man of the tribe of Manasseh, son of Gilead's sister Hammoloketh (1 Chron. 7:18).

Ishi [Ish'i], *salutary*—

1. Son of Appaim of the house of Jerahmeel (1 Chron. 2:31).

2. Father of Zoheth of Judah, a descendant of Caleb (1 Chron. 4:20).

3. A Simeonite whose sons led a force to mount Seir, overcame the Amalekites, and seized their territory (1 Chron. 4:42).

4. A chief of the half-tribe of Manasseh (1 Chron. 5:24).

5. A special name which Israel will use after the restoration, as a symbol of the close relationship that will come about between God and His people (Hos. 2:16–17).

Ishiah [Ish·i'ah]—See Isshiah.

Ishijah [Ish·i'jah], *Jehovah will lend*—A son of Harim, one of those who had taken a foreign wife (Ezra 10:31).

Ishma [Ish'ma], *desolate*—A man of Judah. He is a son of the father (founder) of Etam (1 Chron. 4:3).

Ishmael [Ish'ma·el], *God hears*—The name of six men in the Old Testament:

1. The first son of Abraham, by his wife's Egyptian maidservant, Hagar. Although God had promised Abraham an heir (Gen. 15:4), Abraham's wife Sarah had been unable to bear a child. When Abraham was eighty-five, Sarah offered her maid to him in order to help fulfill God's promise (Gen. 16:1–2). Ishmael was about fourteen years of age when Isaac was born, the child of promise and heir to the covenant promises (Gen. 21:5).

After Hagar learned that she was pregnant, she grew proud and began to despise Sarah. Sarah complained to Abraham, who allowed her to discipline Hagar. Sarah's harsh treatment of Hagar caused her to flee into the wilderness. There she met the angel of God, who told her to return to Sarah and submit to her authority. As an encouragement, the angel promised Hagar that her son, who would be named Ishmael, would have uncounted descendants. Hagar then returned to Abraham and Sarah and bore her son (Gen. 16:4–15).

When Ishmael was thirteen, God appeared to Abraham to tell him that Ishmael was not the promised heir. God made a covenant with Abraham that was to be passed down to the descendants of Isaac—a son who would be conceived by Sarah the following year. Because Abraham loved Ishmael, God promised to bless Ishmael and make him a great nation (Gen. 17:19–20).

At the customary feast to celebrate Isaac's weaning, Sarah saw sixteen-year-old Ishmael making fun of Isaac. She was furious and demanded that Abraham disown Ishmael and his mother so Ishmael could not share Isaac's inheritance. Abraham was reluctant to cast out Ishmael and Hagar, but he did so when instructed by God (Gen. 21:8–13).

Hagar and Ishmael wandered in the wilderness of Beersheba. When their water was gone and Ishmael grew weary, Hagar placed him under a shrub to await death. The angel of God again contacted Hagar and showed her a well. After drawing water, she returned to Ishmael. Ishmael grew up in the wilderness of Paran and gained fame as an archer. Hagar arranged his marriage to an Egyptian wife (Gen. 21:14–21).

When Abraham died, Ishmael returned from exile to help Isaac with the burial (Gen. 25:9). As God promised, Ishmael became the father of twelve princes (Gen. 25:16), as well as a daughter, Mahalath, who later married Esau, son of Isaac (Gen. 28:9). Ishmael died at the age of 137 (Gen. 25:17).

Ishmael was the father of the Ishmaelites, a nomadic nation that lived in northern Arabia. Modern-day Arabs claim descent from Ishmael.

2. The son of Nethaniah and a member of the house of David. After the Babylonian conquest of Judah, King Nebuchadnezzar appointed a Jewish captive, Gedaliah, as governor. Gedaliah promised to welcome all Jews who came under his protection. Ishmael and several others accepted Gedaliah's offer with the intent of killing him (2 Kings 25:22–24). Gedaliah was warned that Ishmael was allied with the Ammonite king in plotting to kill him, but he refused to believe it (Jer. 40:14–16). When Gedaliah invited Ishmael and ten others to a banquet, they murdered everyone in attendance. The killers fled toward the Ammonite country with several hostages, but they were overtaken by pursuers in Gibeon. The hostages were rescued, but Ishmael and eight men escaped to the Ammonites (Jer. 41:1–15).

3. A descendant of Jonathan, son of Saul (1 Chron. 8:38; 9:44).

4. The father of Zebadiah, ruler of the house of Judah and the highest civil authority under King Jehoshaphat (2 Chron. 19:11).

5. A son of Jehohanan. Ishmael was one of five army officers recruited by Jehoiada to help overthrow Queen Athaliah of Judah in favor of the rightful heir, Joash (2 Chron. 23:1).

6. A priest of the clan of Pashhur who divorced his foreign wife after the Babylonian captivity (Ezra 10:22).

Ishmaelite [Ish'mae·lite]—A descendant of Ishmael. There were twelve Ishmaelite princes (Gen. 17:20; 25:12–16) who settled in northern Arabia. Modern-day Arabs consider themselves to be descendants of Ishmael.

Ishmaiah [Ish·mai'ah], *Jehovah will hear*—

1. A Gibeonite. During David's outlawry he allied himself with David at Ziklag (1 Chron. 12:4).

2. Son of Obadiah, ruler of the tribe of Zebulun (1 Chron. 27:19).

Ishmeelite [Ish'mee·lite]—See Ishmaelite.

Ishmerai [Ish'me·rai], *He keeps me*—Son of Elpaal, a descendant of Benjamin (1 Chron. 8:18).

Ishod [I'shod]—See Ishhod.

Ishpah [Ish'pah], *baldhead*—Son of Beriah, a descendant of Benjamin (1 Chron. 8:16).

Ishpan [Ish·pan], *he hides*—Son of Shashak, a descendant of Benjamin (1 Chron. 8:22).

Ishtar [Ish·tar]—See Gods, Pagan.

Ishtob [Ish'tob], *man of Tob*—See Tob (2 Sam. 10:6, 8).

Ishuah [Ish'u·ah]—See Ishvah.

Ishuai [Ish'u·ai]—See Ishvi.

Ishui [Ish'u·i]—See Ishvi.

Ishvah [Ish'vah], *he is equal*—A son of Asher (Gen. 46:17; 1 Chron. 7:30).

Ishvi [Ish'vi], *he is equal*—Two Old Testament men:

1. A son of Asher and head of a tribal family (Gen. 46:17; Num. 26:44; 1 Chron. 7:30).

2. A son of Saul (1 Sam. 14:49).

Ishyo [Ish·yo]—A form of Ishvi.

Ismachiah [Is·ma·chi'ah], *Jehovah sustains*—A Levite who was a temple overseer in the days of Hezekiah, king of Judah (2 Chron. 31:12–13).

Ismaiah [Is·mai'ah]—See Ishmaiah.

Ispah [Is'pah]—See Ishpah.

Israel [Is'ra·el], *he strives with God*—

1. The name given to Jacob after his great struggle with God at Peniel near the brook Jabbok, on his way to Canaan (Gen. 32:28; 35:10). This night, where he wrestled with the Lord and saw the ladder up to heaven, was a turning point in his life (Gen. 32:22–30). The name "Israel" has been interpreted by different scholars as "prince with God," "he strives with God," "let God rule," or "God strives." The name was later applied to the descendants of Jacob. The twelve tribes were called "Israelites," "children of Israel," and "house of Israel," identifying them as the descendants of Israel through his sons and grandsons.

2. The covenant people, descendants of Jacob. Dating from the change of his name, Jacob's descendants were called "the children of Israel" (Gen. 32:32). The name was often used during the period in the wilderness (Ex. 32:4; Deut. 4:1; 27:9). While the name referred to the Hebrew people as a whole, a separation began to exist between Judah and the other tribes prior to the actual disruption of the kingdom (1 Sam. 11:8; 17:52; 18:16).

3. The designation of the Northern Kingdom after the disruption of the united kingdom. Division took place when the already rebellious northern tribes were confronted with the fact that Rehoboam, Solomon's son and successor, would not reduce the taxes and other burdens imposed by Solomon (1 Kings 12:9–17). When the northern tribes broke away from Judah, their king, Jeroboam feared that loyalty to the temple in Jerusalem would undermine the solidarity of his new kingdom. To combat this possibility, he set up new worship

centers, including two golden calves for the people to worship (1 Kings 12:26–33).

While he initially presented these as means for worshipping the true God, eventually they became centers of pagan worship, particularly of Baal. Idolatry was especially strong during the reign of Ahab because of the encouragement given it by Ahab's wife, Jezebel (1 Kings 16:30–33). Elijah labored in vain to destroy the idolatry. The kingdom of Israel ended with the fall of Samaria (721 B.C.), at which time many of the people were carried away to Assyria (2 Kings 17:3–6).

Israel, God's Covenant People—

Selection of Israel: The selection of Israel as a special nation to God was part of God's plan (Rom. 11:2). Historically, the selection of Israel began with the Lord's promise to Abraham, "I will make you a great nation" (Gen. 12:2). The name *Israel* actually is from the new name which God gave to Abraham's grandson Jacob. It was occasioned by Jacob's spiritual victory at the ford of Jabbock (Gen. 32:28). This fact explains why his descendants are often called the children of Israel. The motivation for the Lord's choice of Israel as His select nation did not lie in any special attraction it possessed. Its people were, in fact, the least in number among all the nations (Deut. 7:6–8). Rather, the Lord chose them because of His love for them and because of His covenant with Abraham. This fact does not mean that God did not love other nations, because it was through Israel that He intended to bring forth the Savior and to bless the entire world (Gen. 12:8).

History of Israel: The biblical history of Israel covers 1,800 years and represents a marvelous panorama of God's gracious working through promise, miracle, blessing, and judgment. Israel began as only a promise to Abraham (Gen. 12:2). For over four hundred years the people of Israel relied on that promise, especially during the period of bondage to Egypt. Finally, in God's perfect timing, He brought the nation out of Egypt with the greatest series of miracles known in the entire Old Testament (Ex. 7–15). This event is called the exodus, meaning *a going out.* Since it constitutes the miraculous birth of the nation, it is to this great act of redemption that the nation always looks back as the foremost example of God's care for His people (Ps. 77:14–20; 78:12–55; Hos. 11:1).

Once God had redeemed Israel He established His covenant with them at Mount Sinai (Ex. 19:5–8). From that point forward the nation was truly the Lord's possession, and He was their God. The covenant foretold gracious blessings for obedience and severe judgments for disobedience. The rest of Israel's history demonstrates the certainty of that prophecy. Through the periods of conquest, judges, monarchy, exile, restoration, and Gentile domination, Israel was blessed when she obeyed and judged when she disobeyed. The nation was finally destroyed in A.D. 70, although this event is not described in the New Testament. Many prophecies, however, promise a future redemption for Israel (Rom. 11:26).

The practical value of studying Israel's history is threefold:

a. It sets forth examples to be followed or avoided (1 Cor. 10:6).

b. It shows God's control of all historical events, in that He was able to deal with Israel as He chose (Ps. 78).

c. It serves as a model for all ages of God's kindness and mercy toward His people (Ps. 103:14).

Purpose of Israel. The modern-day student of the Bible may well ask why so much of Scripture is taken up with the history of a single nation. Certainly many Christians wonder why one nation should be called "God's chosen people." The answer to this question is bound up in God's purpose for Israel. When God promised Abraham that he would become the father of a great nation, He also promised that He would bless all peoples through that nation (Gen. 12:1–3). Therefore Israel was to be a channel of blessing as well as a recipient. Even their deliverance from Egypt was partially designed to show other nations that Israel's God was the only true God (Ex. 7:5; 14:18; Josh. 2:9–11). It was further prophesied by Isaiah that the Messiah would bring salvation to the Gentiles (Isa. 49:6). Also in the Psalms there are many invitations to other nations to come and worship the Lord in Israel (Pss. 2:10–12; 117:1). Ruth the Moabitess is an example of a foreigner who believed in Israel's God.

It is clear that God's promise to Abraham to bless the whole world through him is still being fulfilled. The life, ministry, and death of Jesus Christ, and the existence and influence of the church today, all came about through God's choice of Israel. All whom the church wins to Christ, whether Jew or Gentile, enter into those great blessings channeled through Israel.

The Government of Israel. The government of Israel may be considered under two important headings: the laws, and the leaders.

The Laws:

a. The "Commandments," especially the Ten Commandments, revealed God's holiness and set up a divine standard of righteousness for the people to follow (Ex. 20:1–17).

b. The judgments governed the social life of the people and concerned masters and servants (Ex. 21:1–11), physical injuries (Ex. 21:12–36), protection of property rights (Ex. 22:1–15), among others.

c. The ordinances included the sacrifices that showed that blood must be shed for sinners to be forgiven (Lev. 1–17).

The Leaders: At first Moses was the sole leader; then he was replaced by Joshua. After Joshua's death the nation was governed for many years by judges, who were usually raised up by God to oppose a specific enemy. Finally, at the people's request, God granted them a king, thus establishing the monarchy (1 Sam. 8:5, 22). Under the monarchy there were four key leaders:

a. The *king* was the Lord's representative who ruled the people, but only as the Lord's servant. He led in war (1 Sam. 8:20) and made judicial decisions (2 Sam. 15:2), but he could not make law, since he himself was under the law (Deut. 17:19). His relationship was so close to the Lord that he was adopted by the Lord (2 Sam. 7:14; Ps. 2:7).

b. The *priest* taught the Lord's laws and officiated at the offering of the sacrifices (Lev. 1:5; Jer. 18:18).

c. The *prophet* was the man of God who spoke for God and gave divine pronouncements for the present (forthtelling) or for the future (foretelling).

d. The *wise man* produced literary works stressing practical wisdom (Prov. 1:1), taught discipline of character to the young (Prov. 22:17), and gave counsel to the king (2 Sam. 16:20). The choice of these men indicates an important biblical principle: God uses people to reach other people, a principle that is also evident in the Great Commission given to Christians (Matt. 28:19–20).

Worship by Israel: The central aspect of Israel's worship was the object of their worship, the Lord. While other nations paid homage to many gods (Deut. 29:18), only Israel worshipped the one true God (Ex. 20:3). This worship could be private (Ex. 34:8), as a family (Gen. 22:5), or corporate (1 Chron. 29:20). The first place of worship for the people of Israel was the tabernacle constructed by Moses (Ex. 25–27; 30–31; 35–40) and later the magnificent temple constructed by Solomon (1 Chron. 22:5). The structures served to localize the worship of the entire nation. This geographic limitation stands in bold contrast to the privilege of immediate and direct access to God now available to the new Testament believer who himself is the temple of God (1 Cor. 6:19; Heb. 4:16).

Israelite [Is′rael·ite]—A descendant of Israel, who was previously called Jacob (Lev. 23:42–43).

Issachar [Is′sa·char], *there is hire* or *reward*—The name of two men in the Old Testament:

1. The ninth son of Jacob; the fifth child by his first wife, Leah (Gen. 30:17–18; 35:23). He fathered four sons: Tola, Puvah or Puah, Job or Jashub, and Shimron. He and his sons went with their father, Jacob, to Egypt to escape the famine (Gen. 46:13; Ex. 1:3; Num. 26:23–24; 1 Chron. 2:1; 7:1). Before his death, Jacob described Issachar as "a strong donkey lying down between two burdens" (Gen. 49:15). In other words, Jacob saw that Issachar could be a strong fighter but that his love of comfort could also cause him to settle for the easy way out.

2. A Levite gatekeeper in David's time (1 Chron. 26:5).

Issachar, Tribe of [Is′sa·char]—The descendants of Jacob and Leah's son Issachar. It consisted of four tribal families, the descendants of Issachar's four sons (Num. 26:23–24). When the land was divided, the territory of Issachar was south of Zebulun and Naphtali; north of Manasseh and bound on the east by the Jordan.

Isshiah [Is·shi′ah], *let Yahweh forget*—

1. A great-grandson of Moses and head of the house of Rehabiah (1 Chron. 24:21).

2. A man of Issachar, of the posterity of Tola (1 Chron. 7:3).

3. Son of Uzziel; a descendant of Levi's son Kohath (1 Chron. 23:20; 24:25).

4. One who allied himself with David at Ziklag (1 Chron. 12:6).

Isshijah [Is·shi′jah]—A form of Ishijah.

Isuah [Is′u·ah]—See Ishvah.

Isui [Is′u·i]—See Ishvi.

Italy [It′a·ly], *calf-like*—The long, boot-shaped peninsula extending from the European continent into the Mediterranean Sea. It is bound on three sides by the sea, and on the north by the Alps. Its most important city is Rome, the New Testament era capital of the Roman Empire (Acts 18:2; 27:1, 6; Heb. 13:24).

Ithai [I′thai]—See Ittai.

Ithamar [Ith′a·mar], *palm coast*—The youngest son of Aaron (Ex. 6:23; 1 Chron. 6:3; 24:1). Along with his brothers, he was consecrated to the priesthood (Ex. 28:1; 1 Chron. 24:2).

Ithiel [I′thi·el], *God with me*—
   1. Son of Jesaiah, a Benjamite. One of his descendants returned from Babylon (Neh. 11:7).
   2. One of the two persons to whom Agur, writer of a portion of the book of Proverbs, addressed his confession and instructions (Prov. 30:1).

Ithlah [Ith′lah], possibly *he hangs*—A town of Dan (Josh. 19:42).

Ithmah [Ith′mah], *bereavement*—A Moabite, part of David's bodyguard (1 Chron. 11:46).

Ithnan [Ith′nan], *hire*—A town in Judah (Josh. 15:23).

Ithra [Ith′ra], *excellence*—An Israelite, but more correctly an Ishmaelite, who married David's sister, Abigail. His son was Amass (2 Sam. 17:25; 1 Kings 2:5, 32). He is also called Jether.

Ithran [Ith′ran], *abundance*—
   1. Son of Dishon, a Horite, grandson of Seir (Gen. 36:26; 1 Chron. 1:41).
   2. Son of Zophah of Asher (1 Chron. 7:37).

Ithream [Ith′re·am], *abundance of people*—A son of David and his sixth wife, Eglah (2 Sam. 3:5; 1 Chron. 3:3).

Ithrite [Ith′rite], *a remnant*—A family who lived at Kirjath-jearim, the descendants of Ithra (1 Chron. 2:53).

Ittah-kazin [It'tah-ka'zin]—See Eth-kazin.

Ittai [It·tai], *with me*—

1. A Gittite, and native of Gath. When David fled from Absalom's rebellion, Ittai and six hundred men joined David's entourage. Ittai became one of the commanders of David's army during the struggle with Absalom (2 Sam. 15:18–22; 18:2, 5).

2. Son of Ribai of Gibeah, one of David's warriors (2 Sam. 23:29), called Ithai in 1 Chronicles 11:31.

Ituraea [I·tu·rae'a], *past the limits*—A province on the northeastern border of Palestine (Gen. 25:15; 1 Chron. 1:31).

Ivah [I'vah]—See Ivvah.

Ivvah [Iv'vah], *ruin*—A city of Samaria, captured by the Assyrians. Sennacherib attempted to intimidate Hezekiah by boasting of the ease with which he was able to take over Ivvah, in spite of the local gods, intimating that the God of Israel would be just as powerless before him (2 Kings 18:34; 19:13; Isa. 37:13). Possibly the same as Ava (2 Kings 17:24).

Iye-abarim, Ije-abarim [I'ye-ab'a·rim, I'je-ab'a·rim], *ruins of Abarim*—One of the encampments of the Israelites on the border of Moab (Num. 21:11; 33:44). It is also called Iyim (Num. 33:45), and Iim in the King James Version.

Iyim [I'yim]—A form of Ijim.

Izhari, Izehar [Iz'har, I'ze·har], *unknown*—

1. Son of Kohath, a Levite and head of a tribal family (Ex. 6:18, 21; Num. 3:19, 27; 1 Chron. 6:18, 38). Izhar's son, Korah, started an insurrection against Moses in the wilderness (Num. 16:1).

2. Son of Ashur of the family of Hezron (1 Chron. 4:5–7). He is called Jezoar in the King James Version.

Izliah, Jezliah [Iz·li'ah, Jez·li'ah], *long-lived* or *Yahweh delivers*—Son of Elpaal, descended from Shaharaim (1 Chron. 8:18).

Izrahiah [Iz·ra·hi'ah], *Jehovah will shine*—Son of Uzzi, of the family of Tola of Issachar (1 Chron. 7:3). Possibly the Jezrahiah mentioned in Nehemiah is the same person (12:42).

Izrahite [Iz′ra·hite]—A resident of the town of Izrah. Shamhuth, one of David's captains, was so designated (1 Chron. 27:8).

Izri [Iz′ri], *my fashioner*—Also Jizri. Son of Jeduthun, leader of the fourth course of the Levitical musicians for the sanctuary in the time of David (1 Chron. 25:11), also called Zeri (1 Chron. 25:3).

Izziah, Jeziah [Iz·zi′ah, Je·zi′ah], *Jehovah sprinkles*—A son of Parosh, one of those who gave up his foreign wife (Ezra 10:25).

J

Jaakan [Ja′a·kan], *to be fast*—Grandson of Seir (1 Chron. 1:38, 42).

Jaakobah [Ja·a·ko′bah], *supplanting*—A descendant of Simeon (1 Chron. 4:36).

Jaala [Ja′a·la], *doe*—A servant of Solomon whose family came back from the Exile with Zerubbabel (Ezra 2:56; Neh. 7:58).

Jaalah [Ja′a·lah]—See Jaala.

Jaalam [Ja′a·lam]—See Jalam.

Jaanai [Ja′a·nai], *The Lord answers*—A chief of Gad (1 Chron. 5:12).

Jaar [Ja′a·r], *forest*—The wooded area where the ark of the covenant was kept for some years (Ps. 132:6).

Jaare-oregim [Ja′a·re-or′e·gim]—See Jair.

Jaareshiah [Ja·ar·e·shi′ah], *Yahweh plants*—Son of Jeroham, a Benjamite (1 Chron. 8:27).

Jaasai [Ja′a·sai], unknown—Son of Bani. He renounced his foreign wife (Ezra 10:37).

Jaasau [Ja′a·sau]—See Jaasai.

Jaasiel [Ja·as′i·el], *God is maker*—Two men of the Old Testament:
  1. One of David's mighty men (1 Chron. 11:47).
  2. Son of Abner (1 Chron. 27:21).

Jaasu [Ja′a·su]—See Jaasai.

Jaazaniah, Jezaniah [Ja·az·a·ni′ah, Jez·a·ni′ah], *Jehovah hears*—Four Old Testament men:
  1. A Rechabite and one of those successfully tested by Jeremiah (Jer. 35:3).

2. A Maachatite and a military commander (2 Kings 25:23; Jer. 40:8). After Gedaliah was slain, he was among those who asked advice of Jeremiah as to where the remaining Israelites should go next. Disregarding the prophet's advice, he went with the remnant into Egypt (Jer. 42:1; 43:4–5).

3. Son of Azur and a prince of Judah. He appeared in Ezekiel's vision (Ezek. 11:1).

4. A son of Shaphan (Ezek. 8:11).

Jaazer [Ja'a·zer]—See Jazer.

Jaaziah [Ja·a·zi'ah], *God consoles*—A Levite of the family of Merari (1 Chron. 24:26–27).

Jaaziel, Aziel [Ja·a'zi·el, A'·zi·el], *God consoles*—A Levite musician (1 Chron. 15:18, 20).

Jabal [Ja'bal], *a stream*—Son of Lamech (Gen. 4:20).

Jabbok [Jab'bok], *effusion*—One of the principal eastern tributaries of the Jordan. It was the western boundary of the Ammonites (Num. 21:24; Deut. 2:36–37; Josh. 12:2–6).

Jabesh [Ja'besh], *dry*—
1. A town. See Jabesh-gilead.
2. Father of Shallum (2 Kings 15:10).

Jabesh-gilead [Ja'besh-gil'e·ad] (*Jabesh of Gilead*)—a town of Gilead (1 Sam. 31:11; 2 Sam. 2:4), situated about 16 kilometers (10 miles) southeast of Beth Shan and about 3 kilometers (2 miles) east of the Jordan River. It was within the territory assigned to the half-tribe of Manasseh (Num. 32:29, 40).

Jabesh-gilead refused to join in the punishment of the Benjamites (Judg. 21:8–14), an offense for which every man was put to the sword. Four hundred young virgins of Jabesh were given to the Benjamites as wives.

During King Saul's reign, the king of Ammon besieged the city of Jabesh. He promised to spare the lives of those who lived in Jabesh if each of the men would submit to having his right eye put out. A seven-day truce was called and appeal was made to Saul, who mustered an army and defeated the Ammonites (1 Sam. 11).

The people of Jabesh-gilead never forgot this act of Saul. When Saul and his sons were slain at Gilboa, the men of Jabesh-gilead rescued their bodies, cremated them, and buried the ashes near Jabesh (1 Sam. 31:1–13).

Jabesh (1 Chron. 10:12) is the abbreviated name of Jabesh-gilead.

Jabez [Ja'bez], *sorrowful*—A man and a place:

1. A man of Judah, who was considered more honorable than his brethren (1 Chron. 4:9–10).

2. A place, probably in Judah where the families of scribes lived (1 Chron. 2:55).

Jabin [Ja'bin], *discerner*—Two kings of Hazor:

1. A king of Hazor in Galilee, the head of a confederacy of kings defeated by Joshua at the waters of Merom. The king was slain in the battle (Josh. 11:1–14).

2. Another Canaanite king of Hazor, probably a descendant of the preceding (Judg. 4:2).

Jabneel [Jab'neel], *built by God*—

1. A town of Naphtali (Josh. 19:33).

2. A town on the northern border of Judah (Josh. 15:5, 11), probably the same as Jabneh (2 Chron. 26:6).

Jabneh [Jab'neh]—See Jabneel.

Jacan [Ja'can]—See Jachan.

Jachan [Ja'chan], *troublous*—A chief of the tribe of Gad (1 Chron. 5:13).

Jachin [Ja'chin], *he establishes*—

1. A son of Simeon (Gen. 46:10; Ex. 6:15; Num. 26:12). In 1 Chronicles 4:24 he is called Jarib.

2. A priest, whose family in the time of David was the twenty-first course in the service of the sanctuary (1 Chron. 24:17).

3. A priest who lived in Jerusalem after the captivity (1 Chron. 9:10; Neh. 11:10).

Jachin and Boaz [Ja'chin, Bo'az]—The names of the two pillars Solomon set up in front of the temple. Each pillar was approximately sixty feet tall; the pillar on the right was called Jachin and the pillar on the left was called Boaz (2 Chron. 3:17; 2 Kings 25:13).

Jachinites [Ja'chin·ites]—The descendants of Simeon's son Jachin (Num. 26:12).

Jackal's Well—See Serpent Well.

Jacob [Ja'cob], *he supplants*—One of the twin sons of Isaac and Rebekah. The brother of Esau, he was known also as Israel (Gen. 32:28).

Jacob was born in answer to his father's prayer (Gen. 25:21), but he became the favorite son of his mother, whereas Esau became the favorite of Isaac (25:28). He was named Jacob because, at the birth of the twins, "his hand took hold of Esau's heel" (25:26). According to the accounts in Genesis, Jacob continued to "take hold of" the possessions of others. In his youth Jacob tricked Esau into giving up his birthright (25:29–34) and his father's blessing, originally belonging to Esau (27:1–29), and his father-in-law's flocks and herds (30:25–43; 31:1). Some time later he married Laban's daughters, Leah and Rachel, in Haran. The latter, his favorite, gave birth to Joseph, his favored son. Later he returned, had a reconciliation with Esau, and settled in Canaan.

The pattern of Jacob's life is found in his journeys, much like the travels of his grandfather Abraham. Leaving his home in Beersheba, he traveled to Beth-el (28:10–22); later he returned to Shechem (33:18–20), Beth-el (35:6–7), and Hebron (35:27). At Shechem and Beth-el he built altars, as Abraham had done (12:6–7, 8). Near the end of his life Jacob migrated to Egypt; he died there at an advanced age (Gen. 46–49).

The most dramatic moments in Jacob's life occurred at Beth-el (Gen. 28:10–22), at the ford of the river Jabbok (32:22–32), and on his deathbed (49:1–33).

The experience at Beth-el occurred when he left the family home at Beersheba to travel to Haran (a city in Mesopotamia), the residence of his uncle Laban (28:10). On the way, as he stopped for the night at Beth-el, he had a dream of a staircase reaching from earth to heaven with angels upon it and the Lord above it. He was impressed by the words of the Lord, promising Jacob inheritance of the land, descendants "as the dust of the earth" in number, and His divine presence. Jacob dedicated the site as a place of worship, calling it Beth-el (literally, "house of God"). More than twenty years later, Jacob returned to this spot, built an altar, called the place El Bethel (literally, "God of the house of God"), and received the divine blessing (35:6–15).

The experience at the ford of the river Jabbok occurred as Jacob returned from his long stay at Haran. While preparing for a reunion with his brother, Esau, of whom he was still afraid (32:7), he had a profound experience that left him changed in both body and spirit.

At the ford of the Jabbok, "Jacob was left alone" (32:24). It was night, and he found himself suddenly engaged in a wrestling match in the darkness. This match lasted until the breaking of the dawn. The socket of Jacob's hip was put out of joint as he struggled with this mysterious stranger, but he refused to release his grip until he was given a blessing. For the first time in the narrative of Genesis, Jacob had been unable to defeat an opponent. When asked to identify himself in the darkness, he confessed he was Jacob—the "heel-grabber."

But Jacob's struggling earned him a new name. For his struggle "with God and with men" in which he had prevailed, his name was changed to Israel (literally, "he struggles with God") [see Hos. 12:3]. In return, he gave a name to the spot that marked the change; it would be called Peniel—"For I have seen God face to face, and my life is preserved" (32:30).

In these first two instances, a deep spiritual sensitivity is evident in Jacob. He appears outwardly brash and grasping, always enriching himself and securing his future. Yet he responded readily to these night experiences—the dream and the wrestling contest—because he apparently sensed "the presence of the holy" in each of them. He also proved to be a man of his word in his dealings with Laban (Gen. 31:6), and in the fulfillment of his vow to return to Beth-el (35:1–3).

At the end of his life, Jacob—now an aged man (47:28)—gathered his twelve sons about his bed to tell them what should befall them "in the last days" (49:1).

The harshest language came against Reuben, the firstborn, who was rejected by his father for his sin (49:3–4), and Simeon and Levi, who were cursed for their anger and cruelty (49:5–7). The loftiest language was applied to Judah, who would be praised by his brothers and whose tribe would be the source of royalty, even the ruler of the people (49:8–12).

Words of warning were addressed to Dan, called "a serpent" and "a viper," a life that would be marked by violence (49:16–17). The two longest speeches were addressed to Judah and to Joseph, Jacob's favorite son (49:22–26).

Following this scene, Jacob died and was embalmed by the physicians (Gen. 49:33; 50:2). By his own request Jacob was carried back to the land of Canaan and was buried in the family burial ground in the cave of the field of Machpelah (Gen. 49:29–32; 50:13).

Jacob's Well—A well ostensibly dug by Jacob in the Samaritan city of Sychar. Jesus sat by this well and talked to the Samaritan woman about living water and eternal life (John 4:1–26). The well is not mentioned specifically in the Old Testament.

Jada [Ja′da], *wise*—Son of Onam, of the tribe of Judah (1 Chron. 2:28, 32).

Jadai [Ja′dai], unknown—A son of Nebo who had married a foreign wife (Ezra 10:43). Also called Iddo.

Jaddua [Jad′du·a], *knowing*—

1. A high priest, the son of Jonathan, a descendant of Jeshua, the high priest who returned with Zerubbabel from Babylon (Neh. 12:11, 22). He was probably high priest when the Persian Empire was overthrown by Alexander the Great in 331 B.C.

2. A Levite chief of the people who sealed the covenant (Neh. 10:21).

Jadon [Ja′don], *he judgeth*—A Meronothite. He labored on the wall of Jerusalem (Neh. 3:7).

Jael [Ja′el], *wild goat*—The wife of Heber the Kenite (Judg. 4:17). When Sisera, Jabin's captain, was defeated by Barak, he (Sisera) fled to the tent of Heber. While asleep she drove a tent peg (probably a wooden pin) into his head (Judg. 4:11–22).

Jagur [Ja′gur], *a lodging*—A town in the south of Judah (Josh. 15:21).

Jah [Jah]—A contraction for Jehovah (Ps. 68:4).

Jahaleleel [Ja·ha′le·leel]—See Jehaleleel.

Jahath [Ja′hath], *He will snatch up*—Four Old Testament men:

1. A descendant of Shobal, of the family of Hezron (1 Chron. 4:2).

2. Son of Libni, a Levite of Gershom (1 Chron. 6:20).

3. A Levite of the branch of Gershom and one of the heads of the house of Shimei (1 Chron. 23:10).

4. A Levite of the family of Kohath (1 Chron. 24:22).

5. A Levite of the family of Merari (2 Chron. 34:12).

Jahaz [Ja'haz], *trodden down*—The place in the plain of Moab where the Israelites defeated the Amorites (Num. 21:23; Deut. 2:32; Judg. 11:20). It was in the territory of Reuben and became a Levitical city (Josh. 21:36).

Jahaza [Ja·ha'za]—See Jahaz.

Jahazah [Ja·ha'zah]—See Jahaz.

Jahaziah [Ja·ha·zi'ah], *the Lord sees*—A son of Tikvah (Ezra 10:15).

Jahaziel [Ja·ha'zi·el], *God sees*—Five Old Testament men:

1. Son of Hebron; a Levite of the family of Kohath (1 Chron. 23:19).

2. A Benjamite, a warrior who joined David at Ziklag (1 Chron. 12:4).

3. A priest who sounded the trumpet when the ark was brought to Jerusalem in David's reign (1 Chron. 16:6).

4. Son of Zechariah (2 Chron. 20:14).

5. Ancestor of a family which returned with Ezra from Babylon (Ezra 8:5).

Jahdai [Jah'da·i], *whom he will place*—A Calebite (1 Chron. 2:47).

Jahdiel [Jah'di·el], *my unity is God*—A chief of the half-tribe of Manasseh (1 Chron. 5:24).

Jahdo [Jah'do], *union*—Son of Buz (1 Chron. 5:14).

Jahleel [Jah'leel], *God waits*—Son of Zebulun, head of a tribal family (Gen. 46:14; Num. 26:26).

Jahleelites [Jah'le·e·lites]—Descendants of Zebulun's son Jahleel (Num. 26:26).

Jahmai [Jah'ma·i], *who Jehovah guards*—A son of Tola (1 Chron. 7:2).

Jahzah [Jah'zah]—See Jahaz.

Jahzeel [Jah'zeel], *God distributes*—Son of Naphtali (Gen. 46:24; Num. 26:48; 1 Chron. 7:13).

Jahzeelites [Jah'ze·e·lites]—Descendants of Naphtali's son Jazeel (Num. 26:48).

Jahzeiah [Jah·zei'ah]—See Jahaziah.

Jahzerah [Jah'ze·rah], *led back by God*—The son of Meshullam, a priest (1 Chron. 9:12). Maybe the same as Ahzai (Neh. 11:13).

Jahziel [Jah'zi·el]—See Jahzeel.

Jair [Ja'ir], *he enlightens*—Three Old Testament men:
　1. A son of Segub and grandson of Hezron of Judah. His wife was of the tribe of Manasseh, of the family of Machir (1 Chron. 2:21–22). He captured villages in the Argob which bordered on Gilead and named them Havoth-jair. He was probably the judge mentioned in Judges 10:3–5.
　2. Father of El-hanan who killed Lahmi, the brother of Goliath (1 Chron. 20:5). He is called Jaareoregim in 2 Samuel 21:19.
　3. A Benjamite, father of Mordecai (Est. 2:5).

Jairite [Ja'ir·ite]—A descendant of Jair (2 Sam. 20:26).

Jairus [Ja·i'rus], *whom God enlightens*—A ruler of the synagogue, probably at Capernaum. His daughter was raised from the dead by Jesus (Mark 5:35–43; Luke 8:49–56).

Jakan [Ja'kan]—See Jaakan.

Jakeh [Ja'keh], *pious*—The father of Agur (Prov. 30:1).

Jakim [Ja'kim], *God raises up*—Two Old Testament men:
　1. A descendant of Aaron (1 Chron. 24:12).
　2. A Benjamite, son of Shimhi (1 Chron. 8:19).

Jalam [Ja'lam], *their ibex* or *mountain goat*—A son of Esau, a chief of the Edomites (Gen. 36:5, 18; 1 Chron. 1:35).

Jalon [Ja'lon], *Jehovah lodges*—A son of Ezra (1 Chron. 4:17).

Jambres [Jam'bres]—See Jannes and Jambres.

James [James], *supplanter*—Five men in the New Testament:

1. James, the son of Zebedee, one of Jesus' twelve apostles. James's father was a fisherman; his mother, Salome (Mary's sister), often cared for Jesus' daily needs (Matt. 27:56; Mark 15:40–41). In lists of the twelve apostles, James and his brother John always form a group of four with two other brothers, Peter and Andrew. The four were fishermen on the Sea of Galilee. Their call to follow Jesus is the first recorded event after the beginning of Jesus' public ministry (Matt. 4:18–22; Mark 1:16–20).

James is never mentioned apart from his brother John in the New Testament, even at his death (Acts 12:2). When the brothers are mentioned, James is always mentioned first, probably because he was the older. After the resurrection, however, John became the more prominent, probably because of his association with Peter (Acts 3:1; 8:14). James was killed by Herod Agrippa I, the grandson of Herod the Great, sometime between A.D. 42–44. He was the first of the twelve apostles to be put to death and the only one whose martyrdom is mentioned in the New Testament (Acts 12:2).

James and John must have contributed a spirited and headstrong element to Jesus' band of followers, because Jesus nicknamed them "Sons of Thunder" (Mark 3:17). On one occasion (Luke 9:51–56), when a Samaritan village refused to accept Jesus, the two asked Jesus to call down fire in revenge, as Elijah had done (2 Kings 1:10, 12). On another occasion, they earned the anger of their fellow disciples by asking if they could sit on Jesus' right and left hands in glory (Matt. 20:20–28; Mark 10:35–45).

James was one of three disciples—Peter, James, and John—whom Jesus took along privately on three special occasions. The three accompanied Him when He healed the daughter of Jairus (Mark 5:37; Luke 8:51); they witnessed His transfiguration (Matt. 17:1; Mark 9:2; Luke 9:28); and they were also with Him in His agony in Gethsemane (Matt. 26:37; Mark 14:33).

2. James, the son of Alphaeus. This James was also one of the twelve apostles. In each list of the apostles he is mentioned in ninth position (Matt. 10:3; Mark 3:18; Luke 6:15; Acts 1:13).

3. James the Less. This James is called the son of Mary (not the mother of Jesus), and the brother of Joses (Matt. 27:56; Mark 16:1; Luke 24:10). Mark 15:40 refers to him as "James the Less." The Greek word

mikros can mean either "small" or "less." It could, therefore, mean James the smaller (in size), or younger (NIV), or James the less (well-known). Assuming that the James of Matthew 27:56; Mark 15:40; 16:1; and Luke 24:10 is this James, it may be assumed that his mother was called Mary, that she may be identified with the Mary, wife of Cleopas of John 19:25.

4. James, the father of Judas (not Iscariot). Two passages in the New Testament refer to a James, the father of Judas (Luke 6:16; Acts 1:13). Judas was one of the twelve apostles; he was the last to be listed before his more infamous namesake, Judas Iscariot.

5. James, the brother of Jesus. James is first mentioned as the oldest of Jesus' four younger brothers (Matt. 13:55; Mark 6:3).

In the third and fourth centuries A.D., when the idea of the perpetual virginity of Mary gained ground, a number of church fathers argued that James was either a step-brother to Jesus (by a former marriage of Joseph) or a cousin. But both options are forced. The New Testament seems to indicate that Mary and Joseph bore children after Jesus (Matt. 1:25; 12:47; Luke 2:7; John 2:12; Acts 1:14), and that the second oldest was James (Matt. 13:55–56; Mark 6:3). The Gospels reveal that Jesus' family adopted a skeptical attitude toward His ministry (Matt. 12:46–50; Mark 3:31–35; Luke 8:19–21; John 7:5). James apparently held the same attitude, because his name appears in no lists of the apostles, nor is he mentioned elsewhere in the Gospels.

After Jesus' crucifixion, however, James became a believer. Paul indicated that James was a witness to the resurrection of Jesus (1 Cor. 15:7). He called James an apostle (Gal. 1:19), though, like himself, not one of the original Twelve (1 Cor. 15:5, 7).

In the book of Acts, James emerges as the leader of the church in Jerusalem. His brothers also became believers and undertook missionary travels (1 Cor. 9:5). But James considered it his calling to oversee the church in Jerusalem (Gal. 2:9). He advocated respect for the Jewish law (Acts 21:18–25), but he did not use it as a weapon against Gentiles. Paul indicated that James endorsed his ministry to the Gentiles (Gal. 2:1–10).

The decree of the Council of Jerusalem (Acts 15:12–21) cleared the way for Christianity to become a universal religion. Gentiles were asked only "to abstain from things polluted by idols, from sexual immorality, from things strangled, and from blood" (Acts 15:20). The intent of this decree was practical rather than theological. It asked the Gentiles to observe certain practices that otherwise would offend their Jewish brothers in the Lord and jeopardize Christian fellowship with them.

Both Paul and Acts portray a James who was personally devoted to Jewish tradition but flexible enough to modify it to admit non-Jews into Christian fellowship. This James is probably the author of the epistle of James in the New Testament.

James the Less—See James No. 2.

Jamin [Ja'min], *right hand*—Three Old Testament men:

1. A son of Ram, of the family of Jerahmeel of Judah (1 Chron. 2:27)

2. A son of Simeon, the head of a tribal family (Gen. 46:10; Ex. 6:15; Num. 26:12).

3. A Levite who assisted Ezra (Neh. 8:7–8).

Jaminites [Ja'min·ites]—Descendants of Simeon's son Jamin (Num. 26:12).

Jamlech [Jam'lech], *whom God makes a king*—A chief of the tribe of Simeon (1 Chron. 4:34, 41).

Jamnia [Jam'nia]—See Jabneel.

Janai [Ja'nai]—See Jaanai.

Janim [Ja'nim]—See Janum.

Janna [Jan'na], *flourishing*—The father of Melchi, ancestor of Jesus (Luke 3:24).

Jannai [Jan'nai]—See Janna.

Jannes and Jambres [Jan'nes, Jam'bres], both unknown—Two men who, according to the apostle Paul, "resisted Moses" (2 Tim. 3:8). Although Jannes and Jambres are not named in the Old Testament, they are common figures in late Jewish tradition. According to legend, they were two Egyptian magicians who opposed Moses' demand that the Israelites be freed. They sought to duplicate the miracles of Moses in an attempt to discredit him before Pharaoh "so the magicians of Egypt, they also did in like manner with their enhancement" (Ex. 7:11–12, 22).

Janoah, Janohah [Ja·no'ah, Ja·no'hah], *quiet*—Two Israelite towns:

    1. A town on the border of Ephraim (Josh. 16:6–7).

    2. A town of Naphtali (2 Kings 15:29).

Janum [Ja'num], *sleep*—A town of Judah near Hebron (Josh. 15:53).

Japheth [Ja'pheth], *let him enlarge*—One of the three sons of Noah, born when Noah was about five hundred years old (Gen. 5:32; 6:10; 10:21).

Japhia [Ja'phi·a], *bright*—

    1. A king of Lachish. He was defeated and executed by Joshua (Josh. 10:3–27).

    2. A border town of Zebulun (Josh. 19:12).

    3. A son of David born at Jerusalem (2 Sam. 5:15).

Japhlet [Japh'let], *he will deliver*—A son of Heber and grandson of Asher (1 Chron. 7:32–33).

Japhleti [Japh'le·ti]—See Japhletite.

Japhletite [Japh'le·tite], *unknown*—An unidentified tribe (Josh. 16:3). They lived near Ephraim's southern border.

Japho [Ja'pho]—See Joppa.

Jarah [Jar'ah], *honey*—A descendant of King Saul (1 Chron. 9:42), called Jehoadah in 1 Chronicles 8:36.

Jareb [Jar'eb], *adversary*—A king of Assyria who has not been identified, but who was spoken of as a person in Hosea 5:13; 10:6. Possibly it is a nickname for Sargon II; the NIV and NRSV translate this word as "the great king."

Jared [Jar'ed], *descent*—Son of Mahalaleel and father of Enoch (Gen. 5:15–20; 1 Chron. 1:2; Luke 3:37).

Jaresiah [Jar·e·si'ah]—See Jaareshiah.

Jarha [Jar'ha], *the month of sweeping away*—The Egyptian slave of Sheshan who married his master's daughter (1 Chron. 2:34–41).

Jarib [Jar'ib], *an adversary*—Three Old Testament men:

1. A son of Simeon (1 Chron. 4:24). See Jachin.

2. A man sent by Ezra to Casiphia in search of Levites and Nethinim (Ezra 8:16–17).

3. A priest who divorced his foreign wife in the time of Ezra (Ezra 10:18).

Jarmuth [Jar'muth], *a height*—Two Old Testament towns:

1. A town in the lowland of Judah where the Canaanite king Piram dwelt. He was one of the confederacy of kings who combined to punish the Gibeonites because of their alliance with Joshua (Josh. 10:3, 5). He was defeated and put to death by Joshua (Josh. 10:3–27; 12:11). The town was assigned to Judah (Josh. 15:35)

2. A town of Issachar, a Levitical city of the Gershonites (Josh. 21:28–29), called Ramoth (1 Chron. 6:73) and Remeth (Josh. 19:21).

Jaroah [Ja·ro'ah], *new moon*—A man of Gad (1 Chron. 5:14).

Jashar [Jash'ar]—See Jasher.

Jashen [Jash'en], *sleeping*—Several of his sons belonged to David's bodyguard (2 Sam. 23:32). He is called Hashem in 1 Chronicles 11:34.

Jasher [Jash'er], unknown—In Joshua 10:13 and 2 Samuel 1:18 the book of Jashar is quoted. It has been inferred that it was a collection of poems.

Jashobeam [Ja·shob'e·am], *people returning to God*—Three Old Testament men:

1. A warrior of David of the family of Hachmoni (1 Chron. 11:11). He was the military captain over the course for the first month (1 Chron. 27:2–3). In 2 Samuel 23:8 he is called Josheb-basshebeth.

2. A Benjamite of the Korahites. He joined David at Ziklag (1 Chron. 12:1–2, 6).

3. A commander of David's army (1 Chron. 27:2).

Jashub [Jash'ub], *he returns*—Two Old Testament men:

1. A son of Issachar and founder of a tribal family (Num. 26:24; 1 Chron. 7:1). In Genesis 46:13 he is called Job, probably the error of a copyist.

2. A son of Bani (Ezra 10:29).

Jashubi-lehem [Ja·shu'bi-le'hem], *returner of bread*—It is not certain if this is the name of a person or a place. It has to do with the descendants of Shelah (1 Chron. 4:22).

Jashubites [Ja'shub·ites]—The descendants of Issachar's son Jashub (Num. 26:24).

Jasiel [Jas'i·el]—See Jaasiel.

Jason [Ja'son], *to curve*—A kinsman of Paul, a Christian (Rom. 16:21), probably the same as the Jason who lived at Thessalonica (Acts 17:5–9).

Jathniel [Jath'ni·el], *gifts bestowed by God*—The son of Meshel-emiah (1 Chron. 26:2).

Jattir [Jat'tir], *excellence*—A Levitical town in the mountain district of Judah (Josh. 15:48; 21:14).

Javan [Ja'van], *Ionia* or *Greece*—

1. A son of Japheth (Gen. 10:2). The name was given to Greece by the Hebrews because the region was settled by Javan's descendants.

2. A people or town of Arabia (Ezek. 27:19).

Jazer, Jaazer [Ja'zer, Ja·a'zer], *helpful*—A city of Gilead east of the Jordan (2 Sam. 24:5; 1 Chron. 26:31) from which the Amorites were driven by the Israelites (Num. 21:32).

Jaziz [Ja'ziz], *He makes prominent*—A Hagerite who had charge of David's flocks (1 Chron. 27:31).

Jearim [Je'a·rim], *forests*—A mountain marking the northern boundary of Judah (Josh. 15:10). See Chesalon.

Jeaterai [Je·at'e·rai]—See Ethni.

Jeatherai [Je·ath'e·rai]—See Ethni.

Jeberechiah [Je·ber·e·chi'ah], *Jehovah blesses*—Father of Zechariah (not the prophet). He was a witness to Isaiah's marriage (Isa. 8:2).

Jebus [Je'bus], *threshing place*—A name for Jerusalem, in use when the city was in possession of the Jebusites (Josh. 15:63; Judg. 19:10; 1 Chron. 11:4).

Jebusi [Jeb'u·si]—See Jebusite.

Jebusite [Jeb'u·site], *descendants of Jebus*—A member of the mountain tribe which was encountered by the Israelites on their conquest of Canaan (Num. 13:29). After the Jebusite king was slain by Joshua, their territory was assigned to Benjamin (Josh. 10:23–26; 18:28). The tribe was small, and as it was not exterminated by the Hebrews, the Jebusites lived on among their conquerors. King Adoni-zedek and Araunah are the only two Jebusites specifically named (Josh. 10:1, 23; 2 Sam. 24:21–25).

Jecamiah [Jec·a·mi'ah]—See Jekamiah.

Jechiliah [Jech·i·li'ah]—See Jecoliah.

Jecholiah [Jech·o·li'ah]—See Jecoliah.

Jechoniah [Jech·o·ni'ah]—See Jeconiah.

Jechonias [Jech·o·ni'as]—See Jeconiah.

Jecoliah [Jec·o·li'ah], *Jehovah is able*—The mother of Uzziah, king of Judah (2 Kings 15:2; 2 Chron. 26:3).

Jeconiah [Jec·o·ni'ah], *whom Jehovah establishes*—An altered form of Jehoiachin, son and successor of Jehoiakim, king of Judah (1 Chron. 3:16–17; Jer. 24:1; 27:20; 28:4; 29:2).

Jedaiah [Je·dai'ah], *praised of Jehovah*—Five Old Testament men:

1. The son of Shimri of the tribe of Simeon (1 Chron. 4:37).
2. Ancestor of a family appointed by David as the second division of priests (1 Chron. 24:1, 6–7).
3. Son of Harumaph; he labored on the wall of Jerusalem (Neh. 3:10).
4. Two priests who returned with Zerubbabel to Jerusalem (Neh. 12:6–7).
5. One who came from Babylon with gifts (Zech. 6:10, 14).

Jediael [Jed·i·a'el], *known of God*—Four Old Testament men:

1. A son of Benjamin, and ancestor of a Benjamite tribe (1 Chron. 7:6, 10–11), usually regarded as another name of Ashbel (Num. 26:38).

2. Son of Shimri, a warrior of David (1 Chron. 11:45).

3. A man of Manasseh who allied himself with David at Ziklag (1 Chron. 12:20).

4. A Korahite. In the reign of David, he was a doorkeeper (1 Chron. 26:1–2).

Jedidah [Je·di′dah], *beloved*—Wife of Amon, mother of Josiah, king of Judah (2 Kings 22:1).

Jedidiah [Jed·i·di′ah], *beloved of Jehovah*—A name given Solomon by Nathan (2 Sam. 12:25).

Jeduthun [Je·du′thun], *praising*—Two Old Testament men:

　1. Father of Obed-edom, probably a Kohathite (1 Chron. 16:38). Some hold that he was the singer of the family of Merari.

　2. A Levite, a chief musician of the time of David and founder of a musical family (1 Chron. 16:41; 25:1, 6; Neh. 11:17). He was known earlier as Ethan.

Jeezer [Je·e′zer]—See Abiezer.

Jeezerite [Je·e′zer·ite]—See Abiezrite.

Jegar-sahadutha [Je′gar-sa·ha·du′tha], *heap of testimony*—The name Laban gave the memorial made of stones (Gen. 31:47). See Galeed.

Jehaleleel [Je·hal′e·leel]—See Jehalelel.

Jehalelel [Je·hal′e·lel], *he praises God*—Two Old Testament men:

　1. A man of Judah whose parentage is unknown (1 Chron. 4:16).

　2. A Levite (2 Chron. 29:12).

Jehallelel [Je·hal′le·lel]—See Jehalelel.

Jehdeiah [Jeh·dei′ah], *Jehovah is unity*—Two Old Testament men:

　1. A Levite (1 Chron. 24:20).

　2. A Meronothite (1 Chron. 27:30).

Jehezekel [Je·hez′ek·el], *God strengthens*—A descendant of Aaron (1 Chron. 24:16).

Jehezkel [Je·hez'kel]—See Jehezekel.

Jehiah [Je·hi'ah]. *Jehovah liveth*—In David's reign he was a door-keeper for the ark (1 Chron. 15:24).

Jehiel [Je·hi'el], *God lives*—

1. A Levite who played a psaltery when the ark was brought to Jerusalem (1 Chron. 15:18, 20; 16:5).

2. A Levite of the family of Gershon. He lived in David's reign (1 Chron. 23:8). He is also called Jehieli (1 Chron. 26:21–22).

3. Son of Hachmoni in the reign of David (1 Chron. 27:32).

4. Son of Jehoshaphat, placed by his father over the fortified cities of Judah. He was slain by Jehoram (2 Chron. 21:2–4).

5. A Levite of Kohath and son of the singer Heman (2 Chron. 29:14).

6. One who labored under Hezekiah in aiding the latter's reforms (2 Chron. 31:13).

7. A temple ruler who aided Josiah in his work of reform (2 Chron. 35:8).

8. Father of Obadiah (not the prophet) in the time of Ezra (Ezra 8:9).

9. Son of Elam (Ezra 10:2).

10. A priest of the family of Harim (Ezra 10:21).

11. One who divorced his foreign wife (Ezra 10:26), possibly the same as No. 8.

Jehieli [Je·hi·e'li]—See Jehiel No. 2.

Jehizkiah [Je·hiz·ki'ah], *Jehovah strengthens*—A son of Shallum, king of Israel (2 Chron. 28:12).

Jehoadah [Je·ho'a·dah]—See Jehoaddah.

Jehoaddah [Je·ho'ad·dah], *Jehovah adorns*—Son of Ahaz and a descendant of Jonathan, the son of Saul (1 Chron. 8:36). In 1 Chronicles 9:42 he is called Jarah.

Jehoaddan, Jehoaddin [Je·ho·ad'dan, Je·ho·ad'din], *Jehovah delights*—Mother of Amaziah (2 Kings 14:2; 2 Chron. 25:1).

Jehoahaz [Je·ho′a·haz], *Jehovah has seized*—Three Old Testament men:

1. Son of Jehu. He followed his father on the throne of Israel and reigned seventeen years (2 Kings 10:35; 13:1).

2. Son of Josiah; he followed his father on the throne of Judah. He reigned three months, was deposed by Pharaoh Necho and taken to Egypt (2 Kings 23:30–34; 2 Chron. 36:1–4). He is called Shallum in Jeremiah 22:11.

3. Another name of Ahaziah (2 Chron. 21:17).

Jehoash [Je·ho′ash]—See Joash.

Jehohanan [Je·ho·ha′nan], *Jehovah is gracious*—Seven Old Testament men:

1. A Levite in the time of David; a Korahite. The head of the sixth division of temple porters (1 Chron. 26:3).

2. A captain of Jehoshaphat having command of 280,000 men (2 Chron. 17:15).

3. Father of Ishmael who was allied with Jehoiada in removing Athaliah from the throne of Judah (2 Chron. 23:1).

4. Son of Bebai. He renounced his pagan wife (Ezra 10:28).

5. Son of Tobiah (Neh. 6:18).

6. A priest, descendant of Amariah. He lived in the days of the high priest Joiakim (Neh. 12:13).

7. A priest (Neh. 12:42).

Jehoiachin [Je·hoi′a·chin], *the Lord establishes*—The son and successor of Jehoiakim as king of Judah, about 598 or 597 B.C. (2 Chron. 36:8–9; Ezek. 1:2). Jehoiachin did evil in the sight of the Lord, like his father. But he had little opportunity to influence affairs of state, since he reigned only three months. His brief reign ended when the armies of Nebuchadnezzar of Babylon besieged Jerusalem. When the city surrendered, Jehoiachin (along with many others including Ezekiel) was exiled to Babylonia (2 Kings 24:6–15).

Nebuchadnezzar then made Mattaniah, Jehoiachin's uncle, king in his place and changed Mattaniah's name to Zedekiah (v. 17). Zedekiah was destined to rule over a powerless land containing only poor farmers and laborers, while Jehoiachin was held a prisoner in Babylon.

In the 37th year of his captivity, Jehoiachin was finally released by a new Babylonian king, Evil-Merodach (Amel-Marduk). He must have been awarded a place of prominence in the king's court, since he ate his meals regularly in the presence of the king himself (2 Kings 25:27–30).

Jehoiachin is also called Jeconiah (1 Chron. 3:16–17) and Coniah (Jer. 22:24). In the New Testament he is listed by Matthew as an ancestor of Jesus (Matt. 1:11–12).

Jehoiada [Je·hoi'a·da], *Jehovah knows*—

1. The father of Benaiah, a military officer under David and Solomon (2 Sam. 23:22; 1 Kings 4:4).

2. A son of Benaiah and a counselor of David following Ahithophel (1 Chron. 27:34).

3. A high priest who organized a revolt against Queen Athaliah which resulted in her death. Joash, son of Ahaziah, was then crowned king of Judah. Under the influence of Jehoiada, Joash ruled well (2 Kings 11:1–12:16; 2 Chron. 22:10–24:14), but he abandoned the worship of Jehovah for idolatry after Jehoiada's death (2 Chron. 24:17–22).

4. A son of Paseah who lived at the time of Nehemiah (Neh. 3:6).

5. A priest in Jeremiah's time. He was deposed and succeeded by Zephaniah (Jer. 29:26).

Jehoiakim [Je·hoi'a·kim], *the Lord raises up*—An evil king of Judah whose downfall was predicted by the prophet Jeremiah.

A son of the good king Josiah, Jehoiakim was twenty-five years old when he succeeded to the throne. His original name was Eliakim. He was placed on the throne by Pharaoh Necho who deposed his brother, Jehoahaz, and carried him to Egypt. He reigned eleven years in Jerusalem, from 609 B.C. to 598 B.C. During his reign Pharaoh Necho of Egypt exacted heavy tribute from the people of Judah (2 Chron. 36:3, 5). Jehoiakim was forced to levy a burdensome tax upon his people to pay this tribute.

The prophet Jeremiah described the arrogance of Jehoiakim in great detail (Jer. 1:3; 24:1; 27:1, 20; 37:1; 52:2). He censured Jehoiakim for exploiting the people to build his own splendid house with expensive furnishings (Jer. 22:13–23). Unlike his father, Josiah, Jehoiakim ignored justice and righteousness. Jehoiakim had no intention of obeying the Lord; he "did evil in the sight of the Lord" (2 Kings 23:37). His eleven-year reign was filled with abominable acts against God (2 Chron. 36:8).

Because of this evil, Jeremiah predicted that no one would lament the death of Jehoiakim.

Jeremiah also told of Jehoiakim's execution of Urijah, a prophet of the Lord (Jer. 26:20–23). Perhaps Jehoiakim's most cynical act was his burning of Jeremiah's prophecies (Jer. 36:22–23). Jeremiah wrote a scroll of judgment against the king, but as this scroll was read, Jehoiakim sliced it into pieces and threw them into the fire.

Jehoiakim could burn the Word of God, but he could not destroy its power. Neither could he avoid Jeremiah's prophecy of his approaching destruction. Recognizing the power of the Babylonians, he made an agreement with Nebuchadnezzar to serve as his vassal king on the throne of Judah. After three years of subjection, he led a foolish rebellion to regain his nation's independence. The rebellion failed and Jerusalem was destroyed by the Babylonians. Jehoiakim was bound and carried away as a captive (2 Chron. 36:6). Ultimately, he reigned eleven years and was succeeded by his son Jehoiachin (2 Kings 23:36; 24:6).

Jehoiarib [Je·hoi'a·rib], *Jehovah will contend*—A descendant of Aaron (1 Chron. 24:1, 6–7). See Joiarib.

Jehonadab [Je·hon'a·dab]—See Jonadab.

Jehonathan [Je·hon'a·than], *Jehovah hath given*—Three Old Testament men:

1. Son of Uzziah, overseer of the storehouses under David (1 Chron. 27:25).

2. A Levite appointed by King Jehoshaphat to teach in the cities of Judah (2 Chron. 17:8).

3. A priest of the family of Shemaiah (Neh. 12:18).

Jehoram [Je·hor'am], *exalted by Jehovah*—

1. Son and successor of Jehoshaphat of Judah (2 Kings 8:16). His wife was Athaliah, daughter of Ahab and Jezebel of Israel. See Joram.

2. Son of Ahab and king of Israel (2 Kings 3:1). See Joram.

3. A priest appointed by Jehoshaphat to teach the people (2 Chron. 17:8).

Jehoshabeath [Je·ho·shab'e·ath]—See Jehosheba.

Jehoshaphat [Je·hosh'a·phat], *the Lord is judge*—The name of five men in the Old Testament:

1. Son of Ahihud. A recorder in the court of David and Solomon (2 Sam. 8:16).

2. A son of Paruah and an official responsible for supplying food for King Solomon's table (1 Kings 4:17).

3. A son of Asa who succeeded his father as king of Judah (1 Kings 15:24). Jehoshaphat was thirty-five years old when he became king. Conjointly with Asa, then alone, he reigned twenty-five years in Jerusalem (2 Chron. 20:31), from about 873 B.C. to about 848 B.C. Jehoshaphat received an excellent heritage from his father, Asa, who in the earlier years of his reign showed a reforming spirit in seeking God (2 Chron. 15:1–19). Jehoshaphat's faith in God led him to "delight in the ways of the LORD" (2 Chron. 17:6). He attacked pagan idolatry and he sent teachers to the people to teach them more about God (2 Chron. 17:6–9). In affairs of state, Jehoshaphat also showed a willingness to rely on the Lord. In a time of danger he prayed for God's help (2 Chron. 20:6–12). He also brought an end to the conflicts between Israel and Judah.

Jehoshaphat showed a high regard for justice in his dealings (2 Chron. 19:4–11). He reminded the judges whom he appointed that their ultimate loyalty was to God. His attitude toward impartial justice is reflected in these words: "Behave courageously, and the LORD will be with the good" (2 Chron. 19:11).

But in his dealings with Ahab, king of Israel, Jehoshaphat made some serious mistakes. Through the marriage of his son, Jehoram, to Ahab's daughter, Jehoshaphat allied himself with Ahab (2 Chron. 21:5–6). This alliance led to even further dealings with the wicked king of Israel (2 Chron. 18:1–34), which the prophet Jehu rebuked (2 Chron. 19:1–3).

Through his alliance with Ahab, he fought with him against the Syrians at Ramoth Gilead. Ahab was slain but Jehoshaphat escaped (1 Kings 22:1–38; 2 Chron. 18:1–34). After his death he was succeeded by his son, Jehoram (1 Kings 22:50).

Jehoshaphat and his father, Asa, are bright lights against the dark paganism that existed during their time. Both father and son had certain weaknesses, but their faith in the Lord brought good to themselves as well as God's people during their reigns.

4. A son of Nimshi and father of Jehu, king of Israel (2 Kings 9:2, 14).

5. A priest who helped move the ark of the covenant from the house of Obed-edom to Jerusalem. He was a trumpet player (1 Chron. 15:24; Joshaphat, NIV, NRSV).

Jehoshaphat, Valley of [Je·hosh'a·phat]—The valley between Jerusalem and Mount of Olives, also called the valley of the Kidron and the Valley of Decision. Here Jehoshaphat defeated the enemies of Israel (2 Chron. 20:26).

Jehosheba [Je·hosh'e·ba], *Jehovah an oath*—Daughter of Jehoram, son of Jehoshaphat, and sister of Ahaziah. She was the wife of Jehoiada, the high priest, and hid Joash, son of Ahaziah when his grandmother Athaliah planned to murder him (2 Kings 11:2; 2 Chron. 22:11).

Jehoshua [Je·ho·shu·a]—See Joshua.

Jehoshuah [Je·ho·shu·ah]—See Joshua.

Jehovah [Je·ho'vah], *Yaweh* or *I Am*—One of the names of God (Ex. 17:15). The later Hebrews and translators of the Septuagint substituted the word *Lord*. What it denotes is essentially different from El-shaddai and Elohim. The latter signifies God the Creator, the Sustainer and Moral Governor of the Universe, Mightiness. El-shaddai is the covenant God of the patriarchs, their strength and hope, God Almighty. Jehovah is the God of grace dwelling with His people, guiding them, manifesting His grace, the covenant-keeping God (1 Kings 8:43; Pss. 9:10; 91:14; Isa. 52:6; Jer. 16:21). See God, Names of.

Jehovah-jireh [Je·ho'vah-ji'reh], *Jehovah will provide*—The name given by Abraham to the place where he was commanded to sacrifice his son Isaac (Gen. 22:14).

Jehovah-nissi [Je·ho'vah-nis'si], *Jehovah my banner*—The name Moses gave the altar which he built at Rephidim (Ex. 17:15–16).

Jehovah-shalom [Je·ho'vah-sha'lom], *Jehovah is peace*—The name given by Gideon to an altar erected by him in Ophrah (Judg. 6:23–24).

Jehozabad [Je·ho'za·bad], *Jehovah endowed*—Three Old Testament men:

1. Son of a Moabitess. He was a servant of Joash and one of his master's assassins. He was put to death (2 Kings 12:21; 2 Chron. 24:26).

2. Son of Obed-edom, a Korhite Levite, a porter at a gate of the temple (1 Chron. 26:4).

3. A Benjamite, one of Jehoshaphat's generals (2 Chron. 17:18).

Jehozadak [Je·ho′za·dak], *Jehovah is righteous*—The great-grandson of Hilkiah the high priest; Jehozadak went into captivity with Judah when Nebuchadnezzar carried the people into Babylon (1 Chron. 6:14–15).

Jehu [Je′hu], *the Lord is He*—The name of five men in the Old Testament:

1. A prophet, son of Hanani, who announced a message of doom against Baasha, king of Israel for his idolatry (1 Kings 16:12). Jehu also rebuked Jehoshaphat, king of Judah for the alliance he made with Ahab (2 Chron. 19:2). He was the author of a book which recorded the acts of Jehoshaphat (2 Chron. 20:34).

2. The eleventh king of Israel (2 Chron. 22:7–9), son of Jehoshaphat and grandson of Nimshi (1 Kings 19:16; 2 Kings 9:2). Divinely directed to annoint him as king (1 Kings 19:16–17), Jehu was actually anointed king by Elisha the prophet. He later overthrew Joram (Jehoram) to take the throne. He reigned for twenty-eight years (841–813 B.C.), establishing the fifth, and longest, dynasty of the kingdom of Israel. His corrupt leadership weakened the nation. He is known for his violence against all members of the "house of Ahab" as he established his rule throughout the nation.

At Jehu's command, Jezebel, the notorious wife of Ahab, was thrown out of the window of the palace to her death, as prophesied by Elijah (1 Kings 21:23). Ahab's murder of Naboth and the subversion of the religion of Israel had brought terrible vengeance, but more blood was to be shed by Jehu. Next to feel the new king's wrath were the seventy sons of Ahab who lived in Samaria (2 Kings 10). Jehu ordered them killed by the elders of Samaria. Jehu's zeal extended even further, commanding the death of Ahab's advisors and close acquaintances. This excessive violence led the prophet Hosea to denounce Jehu's bloodthirstiness (Hos. 1:4).

Jehu continued his slaughter against the family of Ahaziah, king of Judah (2 Kings 10:12–14). Then he made an alliance with Jehonadab, the chief of the Rechabites, to destroy the followers of Baal. Jehu and

Jehonadab plotted to conduct a massive assembly in honor of Baal. After assuring the Baal worshipers of their sincerity and gathering them into the temple of Baal, Jehu had them all killed (2 Kings 10:18–28). So complete was this destruction that Baalism was wiped out in Israel, and the temple of Baal was torn down and made into a garbage dump.

Although Jehu proclaimed his zeal for the Lord (2 Kings 10:16), he failed to follow the Lord's will completely (2 Kings 10:31). He did not completely eliminate worship of the golden calves at Dan and Beth-el, and his disobedience led to the conquest of many parts of Israel by the Syrians (2 Kings 10:32–33).

3. A son of Obed and a descendant of Hezron (1 Chron. 2:38). Jehu was descended from the family of Jerahmeel and the tribe of Judah. This Jehu fathered Azariah of Judah.

4. A son of Joshibiah, of the tribe of Simeon in the time of Hezekiah (1 Chron. 4:35). He was with those who captured the valley of Gedor.

5. A Benjamite of Anathoth (1 Chron. 12:3) who joined David's army at Ziklag.

Jehubbah [Je·hub′bah], *hidden*—Son of Shamer of the tribe of Asher (1 Chron. 7:34).

Jehucal [Je·hu′cal], *able*—Son of Shelemiah (Jer. 37:3).

Jehud [Je′hud], *beauty*—A town of Dan (Josh. 19:45).

Jehudi [Je·hu′di], *a Jew*—The man sent by Jehoiakim, king of Judah to Baruch for Jeremiah's roll of prophecies (Jer. 36:14, 21, 23).

Jehudijah [Je·hu·di′jah], *Jewess*—A wife of Mered (1 Chron. 4:18).

Jehush [Je′hush]—(1 Chron. 8:39) See Jeush.

Jeiel [Je·i′el], *God sweeps away*—Several Old Testament men:

1. A Reubenite chief (1 Chron. 5:7–8).

2. One of the ancestors of Saul, the first king of Israel (1 Chron. 9:35).

3. One of David's mighty men, a son of Hotham the Aroerite (1 Chron. 11:44).

4. A Levite porter, a harpist when the ark was brought to Jerusalem and afterward appointed to serve regularly in the tent (1 Chron. 15:18, 21; 16:5).

5. A Levite of the Merari family, a musician who participated in bringing the ark to Jerusalem (1 Chron. 16:5). See Jaaziel.

6. A Levite of the sons of Asaph (2 Chron. 20:14).

7. A scribe who, with others, recorded the number of troops of Uzziah, king of Judah (2 Chron. 26:11).

8. A Levite in the time of Hezekiah who assisted in the restoration of the temple service (2 Chron. 29:13).

9. A Levite in the time of Josiah (2 Chron. 35:9).

10. One of the company of Ezra who returned from Babylon (Ezra 8:13).

11. A Hebrew in the time of Ezra (Ezra 10:43); one who divorced his foreign wife.

Jekameam [Je·kam′e·am], *the people will come together*—A Levite of Kohath (1 Chron. 23:19; 24:23).

Jekamiah, Jecamiah [Jek·a·mi′ah, Je·ca·mi′ah], *Jehovah raises*—Two Old Testament men:

1. A son of Shallum, descendant of Sheshan, of Judah (1 Chron. 2:41)

2. A son of Jeconiah (Jehoiachin), king of Judah (1 Chron. 3:18).

Jekuthiel [Je·ku′thi·el], *reverence for God*—A man of Judah (1 Chron. 4:18).

Jemima [Je·mi′ma]—See Jemimah.

Jemimah [Je·mi′mah], *dove*—One of Job's daughters (Job 42:14).

Jemuel [Je·mu′el], *day of God*—Son of Simeon and founder of a tribal family (Gen. 46:10; Ex. 6:15). He is called Nemuel in Numbers 26:12 and 1 Chronicles 4:24.

Jephthae [Jeph′thae]—See Jephthah.

Jephthah [Jeph′thah], *he opens*—A son of Gilead; he was expelled from his home by his brothers because of his illegitimate birth (Judg. 11:1–2). He went to Tob where he became a famous hunter. At this time the Ammonites were holding the tribes east of the Jordan in subjection. Those who had driven Jephthah away now urged him to be their chief and deliver them from this oppression. A very religious man, Jephthah made a vow that if he were victorious he would sacrifice to God the first person who came from his house on his return. It was his daughter. Some believe that he actually did sacrifice her, for in Judges 11:39 it says that he "did with her according to his vow." Others believe that because of what God says about human sacrifice, Jephthah simply prevented his daughter from marrying, as a way of consecrating her to the Lord. He judged Israel six years (Judg. 10:6–12:7; 1 Sam. 12:11). He is one of the heroes of faith (Heb. 11:32).

Jephunneh [Je·phun′neh], *He will be facing*—Two Old Testament men:

1. Father of Caleb. His son represented Judah as a spy when the Israelites were scouting the land of Canaan (Num. 13:6).

2. A son of Jether (1 Chron. 7:38).

Jerah [Je′rah], *moon*—A son of Joktan (Gen. 10:26; 1 Chron. 1:20).

Jerahmeel [Je·rah′meel], *may God have compassion*—Three Old Testament men:

1. A great-grandson of Judah and Tamar (descended through Perez and Hezron); the husband of two wives and the progenitor of many descendants (1 Chron. 2:9, 25–41).

2. The son of Kish who was a Merarite Levite, not the father of Saul (1 Chron. 24:29).

3. One of the three men Jehoiakim ordered to arrest Jeremiah and Baruch (Jer. 36:26).

Jerahmeelites [Je·rah′meel·ites]—Probably the descendants of Jerahmeel, the descendant of Perez (1 Sam. 27:10; 30:29; 1 Chron. 2:9, 25–41).

Jered [Je′red], *descent*—Two Old Testament men:

1. Son of Mahalaleel of the line of Seth in the antediluvian period (1 Chron. 1:2); also called Jared (Gen. 5:15–20, KJV).

2. A man of Judah and the founder of Gedor (1 Chron. 4:18).

Jeremai [Jer·e·ma′i], *high*—A son of Hashum in the time of Ezra (Ezra 10:33).

Jeremiah [Jer·e·mi′ah], *the Lord hurls*—The name of nine men in the Old Testament:

1. The father of Hamutal, the wife of Josiah, king of Judah (2 Kings 23:31; 24:18; Jer. 52:1). He lived in Libnah.

2. The head of a family of the tribe of east Manasseh (1 Chron. 5:23–24).

3. A Benjamite warrior who joined David at Ziklag (1 Chron. 12:4).

4. A Gadite who joined David at Ziklag (1 Chron. 12:10).

5. Another Gadite who joined David at Ziklag (1 Chron. 12:13).

6. A priest who sealed Nehemiah's covenant after the captivity (Neh. 10:2).

7. A priest who returned from the Babylonian captivity with Zerubbabel (Neh. 12:1, 12, 34).

8. A son of Habazziniah and father of Jaazaniah, of the house of the Rechabites (Jer. 35:3).

9. The major prophet during the decline and fall of the southern kingdom of Judah and author of the book of Jeremiah. Son of Hilkiah, he prophesied during the reigns of the last five kings of Judah. Jeremiah was born in Anathoth, situated north of Jerusalem in the territory of Benjamin (Jer. 1:1–2). It is believed that the family was descended from Abiathar who was expelled to Anathoth by King Solomon (1 Kings 2:26–27).

He was called to the prophetic ministry in the thirteenth year of Josiah's reign, about 627 B.C. He must have been a young man at the time, since his ministry lasted for about forty years—through the very last days (and beyond) of the nation of Judah when the capital city of Jerusalem was destroyed in 586 B.C. Jeremiah's call is one of the most instructive passages in his book. God declared that he had sanctioned him as a prophet even before he was born (Jer. 1:5). But the young man responded with words of inadequacy: "Ah, Lord GOD!" (Jer. 1:6). These words actually mean "No, Lord GOD!" Jeremiah pleaded that he was a youth and that he lacked the ability to speak. But God replied that he was being called not because of age or ability but because God had chosen him.

Immediately Jeremiah saw the hand of God reaching out and touching his mouth. "Behold, I have put My words in your mouth," God declared (Jer. 1:9). From that moment, the words of the prophet were to be the words of God. And his ministry was to consist of tearing down and rebuilding, uprooting and replanting: "See, I have this day set you over the kingdoms, to root out and to pull down, to destroy and to throw down, to build and to plant" (Jer. 1:10).

Because of the negative nature of Jeremiah's ministry, judgmental texts abound in his book. Jeremiah was destined from the very beginning to be a prophet of doom. He was even forbidden to marry so he could devote himself fully to the task of preaching God's judgment (Jer. 16:1–13). A prophet of doom cannot be a happy man. All of Jeremiah's life was wrapped up in the knowledge that God was about to bring an end to the holy city and cast off His covenant people.

Jeremiah is often called "the weeping prophet" because he wept openly about the sins of his nation (Jer. 9:1). He was also depressed at times about the futility of his message. As the years passed and his words of judgment went unheeded, he lamented his unfortunate state: "O LORD, You induced me, and I was persuaded; You are stronger than I, and have prevailed. I am in derision daily; everyone mocks me" (Jer. 20:7).

At times Jeremiah tried to hold back from his prophetic proclamation. But he found that the word of the Lord was "like a burning fire shut up in my bones" (Jer. 20:9). He had no choice but to proclaim the harsh message of God's judgment.

Jeremiah did not weep and lament because of weakness, nor did he proclaim evil because of a dark and gloomy personality. He cried out because of his love for his people and his God. This characteristic of the prophet is actually a tribute to his sensitivity and deep concern. Jeremiah's laments remind us of the weeping of the Savior (Matt. 23:37–39).

As Jeremiah predicted, the nation of Judah was eventually punished by God because of its sin and disobedience. In 586 B.C. Jerusalem was destroyed and the leading citizens were deported to Babylonia. Jeremiah remained in Jerusalem with a group of his fellow citizens under the authority of a ruling governor appointed by the Babylonians. But he was forced to seek safety in Egypt after the people of Jerusalem revolted against Babylonian rule. He continued his preaching in Egypt (Jer. 43–44). This is the last we hear of Jeremiah. There is no record of what happened to the prophet during these years of his ministry.

In the New Testament (KJV) Jeremiah was referred to as Jeremy (Matt. 2:17; 27:9) and Jeremias (Matt. 16:14).

Jeremias [Jer·e·mi′as]—The Greek form of the name Jeremiah (Matt. 16:14).

Jeremoth [Jer′e·moth], *heights*—Eight Old Testament men:
1. A Benjamite of the family of Becher (1 Chron. 7:8).
2. A son of the house of Beriah of Elpaal, of the tribe of Benjamin

(1 Chron. 8:14). Mushi (1 Chron. 23:23), called Jerimoth in 1 Chronicles 24:30.

3. A Levite of the family of Merari; son of Mushi (1 Chron. 23:23), called Jerimoth in 1 Chronicles 24:30.

4. Son of Heman; head of the fifteenth course of musicians in David's reign (1 Chron. 25:4, 22).

5. Son of Azriel of Naphtali in the reign of David (1 Chron. 27:19).

6. A "son of Elam." He renounced his foreign wife (Ezra 10:26).

7. A descendant of Zattu who renounced his foreign wife (Ezra 10:27).

8. Also called Ramoth (Ezra 10:29).

Jeremy [Jer′e·my]—(Matt. 2:17; 27:9) The Greek form of Jeremiah.

Jeriah [Je·ri′ah], *taught by Jehovah*—A Levite of the family of Kohath (1 Chron. 23:19; 24:23; 26:31).

Jeribai [Jer·i·ba′i], *the Lord contends*—Son of Elnaam; one of David's warriors (1 Chron. 11:46).

Jericho [Jer′i·cho], *fragrant*—One of the oldest inhabited cities in the world. Situated in the wide plain of the Jordan Valley (Deut. 34:1, 3) at the foot of the ascent to the Judean mountains, Jericho lies about 13 kilometers (8 miles) northwest of the site where the Jordan River flows into the Dead Sea, some 8 kilometers (5 miles) west of the Jordan.

Since it is approximately 244 meters (800 feet) below sea level, Jericho has a climate that is tropical and at times is very hot. Only a few inches of rainfall are recorded at Jericho each year, but the city is a wonderful oasis, known as "the city of palm trees" (Deut. 34:3) or "the city of palms" (Judg. 3:13). Jericho flourishes with date palms, banana trees, balsams, sycamores, and henna (Song 1:14; Luke 19:4).

There have been three different Jerichos throughout its long history. Old Testament Jericho is identified with the mound of Tell es-Sultan, about 2 kilometers (a little more than a mile) from the village of er-Riha. This village is modern Jericho, located about 27 kilometers (17 miles) northeast of Jerusalem. New Testament Jericho is identified with the mounds of Tulul Abu el-'Alayiq, about 2 kilometers west of modern Jericho and south of Old Testament Jericho. By far the most imposing site of the three is Old Testament Jericho, a pear-shaped mound about 366 meters (400 yards) long, north to south, 183 meters (200 yards) wide at the north end, and some 67 meters (70 yards) high. It has been the site of numerous archaeological diggings and is a favorite stop for Holy Land tourists.

Old Testament Jericho: Jericho first appears in the biblical record when the Israelites encamped at Shittim on the east side of the Jordan River (Num. 22:1; 26:3). Joshua sent spies to examine the city (Josh. 2:1–24) and later took the city by perhaps the most unorthodox method in the history of warfare. Under orders from the Lord, the Israelites marched around the massive walls at the fortified city for six days. On the seventh day the priests blew their trumpets and all the warriors let out a loud shout. The walls came tumbling down, leaving the city exposed to the invaders (Josh. 6). Joshua placed a curse on anyone who would attempt to rebuild Jericho (Josh. 6:26).

As the Israelites settled into the land, Jericho was awarded to the tribe of Benjamin, although it was on the border between Ephraim and Benjamin (Josh. 16:1, 7). Jericho is only incidentally mentioned in the reign of David (2 Sam. 10:5) and does not figure prominently again in Old Testament history until the reign of King Ahab (about 850 B.C.; 1 Kings 16:34), when Hiel the Bethelite attempted to fortify the city and Joshua's curse was realized. During the days of Elijah and Elisha, Jericho was a community of the prophets (2 Kings 2:5) and was mentioned on other occasions as well (Ezra 2:34; Neh. 3:2; Jer. 39:5).

Excavations of Old Testament Jericho indicate that the site had been occupied for thousands of years before Joshua captured the city. Unfortunately, extensive archeological excavations there have failed to uncover conclusive evidence of Joshua's conquest, because there are few remains from this period. This lack of evidence is most often attributed to centuries of erosion on the ruin.

New Testament Jericho: In the early years of Herod the Great, the Romans plundered Jericho. But Herod later beautified the city and ultimately died there. Jesus passed through Jericho on numerous occasions. Near there He was baptized in the Jordan River (Matt. 3:13–17), and on the adjacent mountain range He was tempted (Matt. 4:1–11). At Jericho Jesus healed blind Bartimaeus (Mark 10:46–52). Here, too, Zacchaeus was converted (Luke 19:1–10). And Jesus' parable of the good Samaritan has the road from Jerusalem to Jericho as its setting (Luke 10:30–37).

Jeriel [Jer′i·el], *founded by God*—A descendant of Tola of Issachar (1 Chron. 7:2).

Jerijah [Je·ri′jah]—See Jeriah.

Jerimoth [Jer′i·moth], *heights*—Several Old Testament men:

1. A son of Bela who was son of Benjamin (1 Chron. 7:7).

2. A Benjamite who joined David at Ziklag, an archer (1 Chron. 12:5).

3. A son of Becher and head of a house of Benjamin (1 Chron. 7:8).

4. A son of Heman and head of the fifteenth course of musicians, also called Jeremoth (1 Chron. 25:4, 22).

5. A son of David. His daughter, Mahalath, was the wife of Rehoboam, grandson of David (2 Chron. 11:18).

6. A Levite (2 Chron. 31:13). See Jeremoth.

Jerioth [Jer′i·oth], *curtains*—A wife of Caleb (1 Chron. 2:18).

Jeroboam [Jer·o·bo′am], *let the kinsman plead*—The name of two kings of the northern kingdom of Israel:

1. Jeroboam I, the first king of Israel (the ten northern tribes, or the Northern Kingdom), a state established after the death of Solomon (1 Kings 11:26–14:20). The son of Nebat and Zeruah, Jeroboam reigned over Israel for twenty-two years (1 Kings 14:20), from 931/30 to 910/09 B.C. Jeroboam I first appears in the biblical record as Solomon's servant: "the officer over all the labor force of the house of Joseph" (1 Kings 11:28). One day as Jeroboam went out of Jerusalem, the prophet Ahijah the Shilonite met him on the road and confronted him with an enacted parable. Ahijah, who was wearing a new garment, took hold of the garment and tore it into twelve pieces. He then said to Jeroboam, "Take for yourself ten pieces, for thus says the Lord, the God of Israel: 'Behold, I will tear the kingdom out of the hand of Solomon and will give ten tribes to you' " (1 Kings 11:31).

When Solomon learned of Ahijah's words, he sought to kill Jeroboam. But Jeroboam fled to Egypt, where he was granted political asylum by Shishak I, the king of Egypt. Only after the death of Solomon did Jeroboam risk returning to his native Palestine (1 Kings 11:40; 12:2–3).

Solomon's kingdom was outwardly rich, prosperous, and thriving. But the great building projects he undertook were accomplished by forced labor, high taxes, and other oppressive measures. Discontent and unrest existed throughout Solomon's kingdom. When the great king died, the kingdom was like a powder keg awaiting a spark. The occasion for the explosion, the tearing of the ten northern tribes from Solomon's successor, came because of the foolish insensitivity of Solomon's son Rehoboam. Rehoboam had gone to Shechem to be anointed as the new king. A delegation led by Jeroboam, who had returned from Egypt following Solomon's death, said to Rehoboam, "Your father made our yoke heavy; now therefore, lighten the burdensome service of your father, and his heavy yoke which he put on us, and we will serve" (1 Kings 12:4).

But Rehoboam followed the advice of his inexperienced companions and replied, "Whereas my father laid a heavy yoke on you, I will add to your yoke; my father chastised you with whips, but I will chastise you with scourges!" (1 Kings 12:11). After this show of Rehoboam's foolishness, the ten northern tribes revolted against Rehoboam and appointed Jeroboam as their king (1 Kings 12:16–20).

Jeroboam was concerned that the people of Israel might return to the house of David if they continued to journey to Jerusalem for the festivals and observances at the temple of Solomon. So he proposed an alternative form of worship that was idolatrous. He made two calves of gold that bore a close resemblance to the mounts of the Canaanite pagan god Baal. The king told his countrymen: "It is too much for you to go up to Jerusalem. Here are your gods, O Israel, which brought you up from the land of Egypt!" (1 Kings 12:28). One calf was erected in Beth-el and one in Dan.

Once committed to this sinful direction, Jeroboam's progress was downhill. He next appointed priests from tribes other than Levi. He offered sacrifices to these images and gradually polluted the worship of Israel. The Lord confronted Jeroboam by sending him an unnamed prophet who predicted God's judgment on the king and the nation. Although outwardly he appeared to be repentant, Jeroboam would not change his disastrous idolatry. His rebellious, arrogant attitude set the pattern for rulers of Israel for generations to come. Eighteen kings sat on the throne of Israel after his death, but not one of them gave up his pagan worship.

2. Jeroboam II, the fourteenth king of Israel, who reigned for forty-one years (793–753 B.C.). Jeroboam, of the fifth dynasty of Israel, was the son and successor of Joash (or Jehoash); he was the grandson of Jehoahaz and the great-grandson of Jehu (2 Kings 13:1, 13; 1 Chron. 5:17). The Bible declares that Jeroboam "did evil in the sight of the LORD" (2 Kings 14:24).

Jeroboam was successful in his military adventures. His aggressive campaigns "recaptured for Israel, from Damascus and Hamath, what had belonged to Judah" (2 Kings 14:28). The boundaries of Israel expanded to their greatest extent since the days of David and Solomon: "He restored the territory of Israel from the entrance of Hamath to the Sea of the Arabah" (2 Kings 14:25).

Jeroboam II was king during the prosperous interval between the economic reverses of other rulers. Hosea, Amos, and Jonah lived during his reign (2 Kings 14:25; Hos. 1:1; Amos 1:1–2). During this time of superficial prosperity, the prophet Amos especially spoke out against the many social abuses in Israel. A severe oppression of the poor had been instituted by the newly prosperous class. Justice was in the hands of lawless judges, dishonest merchants falsified the balances by deceit, and worship was little more than a pious smokescreen that covered the terrible abuses of the poor. Amos prophesied that the destructive fury of God would fall upon the house of Jeroboam (Amos 7:9).

After Jeroboam's death, his son Zechariah succeeded him on the throne of Israel (2 Kings 14:29). Zechariah reigned in Samaria only six months before he was assassinated by Shallum (2 Kings 15:10).

Jeroham [Je·ro′ham], *compassionate*—Seven Old Testament men:

1. The father of Elkanah, the father of Samuel, a Levite (1 Sam. 1:1; 1 Chron. 6:27, 34).

2. The father of several chiefs of Benjamin who lived at Jerusalem (1 Chron. 8:27).

3. Father of Ibneiah, a Benjamite (1 Chron. 9:8).

4. An inhabitant of Gedor, a Benjamite. His sons allied themselves to David at Ziklag (1 Chron. 12:7).

5. A priest, father of Adaiah. The son was a priest at Jerusalem (1 Chron. 9:12; Neh. 11:12).

6. Father of the chief of the tribe of Dan in the reign of David (1 Chron. 27:22).

7. Father of Azariah (2 Chron. 23:1).

Jerubbaal [Jer·ub·ba′al], *let Baal contend*—A name given to Gideon by his father after Gideon had destroyed the altars to Baal (Judg. 6:32; 9:1–2, 5, 16, 19, 24, 28, 57).

Jerubbesheth [Je·rub′be·sheth], *shame will contend*—A name of Gideon (2 Sam. 11:21), given to supplant his previous name, Jerubbaal (Judg. 6:32).

Jeruel [Je·ru′el], *founded of God*—A wilderness west of the Dead Sea (2 Chron. 20:16).

Jerusalem [Je·ru′sa·lem], *city of peace*—Sacred city and well-known capital of Palestine during Bible times. The earliest known name for Jerusalem was Urushalem. Salem, of which Melchizedek was king (Gen. 14:18), was a natural abbreviation for Jerusalem. Thus, Jerusalem appears in the Bible as early as the time of Abraham, although the city had probably been inhabited for centuries before that time.

The city of Jerusalem is mentioned directly in the Bible for the first time during the struggle of Joshua and the Israelites to take the land of Canaan (Josh. 10:1–4). Their efforts to take the city were unsuccessful, although the areas surrounding it were taken and the land was given to the tribe of Judah. Still remaining in the fortress of the city itself were the Jebusites. Thus, the city was called Jebus.

Jerusalem under David: After the death of Saul, the first king of the united kingdom of the Hebrew people, David was named the new king of Israel. One of his first efforts was to unite the tribes of the north and south by capturing Jerusalem from the Jebusites, making the city the political and religious capital of the kingdom (1 Chron. 11:4–9). Because it was captured during his reign, Jerusalem also came to be known as the "City of David." The city is often referred to by this title in the Bible.

David built a palace in the section of Jerusalem that served previously as the Jebusite stronghold. This section, situated in the highest part of the city, frequently is referred to as Mount Zion. The location was probably selected because it was easily defended from invaders. Jerusalem has little to recommend it as a capital city, when compared to other major cities of the ancient world. It was an inland city not situated near a seaport. Moreover, it was not near the major trade routes used during that time. Why, then, did David select Jerusalem as the capital of his nation? The reasons are twofold. First, Jerusalem was centrally located between the northern and southern tribes. Thus, it was geographically convenient for the nation. The central location of the capital city tended to unite the people into one kingdom. Second, the topography of the city made it easy to defend. Jerusalem was situated on a hill. The eastern and western sides of the city consisted of valleys that made invasion by opposing forces difficult. The southern portion consisted of ravines that made an attack from this position unwise. The best point from which to attack Jerusalem was the north, which had the highest elevation of any portion of the city. It was from this position that attacks on the city were made in the centuries following the establishment of Jerusalem as the capital. David also made Jerusalem the religious capital of the nation. He moved the ark of the covenant, which had been kept at Kirjath-jearim (Josh. 15:9), to Jerusalem. One of his desires was to build a temple in the capital city, but he was prevented from completing this task. The prophet Nathan instructed him that God did not want him to build the temple because his hands had been involved in so much bloodshed (1 Chron. 17). David did make preparation for the building of the temple, however, leaving the actual building task to Solomon, his son and successor.

During the reign of David, Jerusalem was firmly established politically and religiously as the capital city of the Israelite nation. The selection of this site resulted in the unification of the nation as David had hoped. But the selection of Jerusalem as the capital was more than a choice by a human king. Divine providence was also involved. Jerusalem was referred to as "the place which the Lord your God shall choose out of all your tribes to put His name there" (see Deut. 12:5, 11, 14, 18, 21).

Jerusalem under Solomon: The glory of Jerusalem, begun under David, reached its greatest heights under Solomon. Solomon proceeded to construct the temple about which David had dreamed (2 Chron. 3–4). He also extended the borders of the city to new limits. Because surrounding nations were engaged in internal strife, Jerusalem was spared from invasions from opposing forces during Solomon's administration.

After completing the temple, Solomon built the palace complex, a series of five structures. These other buildings were the "house of the Forest of Lebanon," an assembly hall and a storage place for arms; an anteroom for the throne, where distinguished guests were received; the throne room, an ornately carved enclosure that contained the throne, which was made of carved ivory inlaid with gold; the king's palace, which was very large so as to hold the king's family; and the residence for Solomon's Egyptian wives, which adjoined the king's palace. Solomon also planted vineyards, orchards, and gardens that contained all types of trees and shrubs. These were watered by streams and pools that flowed through the complex. Unfortunately, this splendor came to an end with the death of Solomon about 931 B.C. The division of the kingdom into two separate nations after Solomon's reign resulted in the relapse of Jerusalem to the status of a minor city.

Jerusalem under Siege: After the death of Solomon, the division that occurred in the kingdom resulted in the ten northern tribes establishing their own capital, first at Shechem and later at Samaria. The southern tribes, consisting of Judah and Benjamin, retained Jerusalem as the capital. Although separated politically from Jerusalem, the northern tribes continued their allegiance to the "holy city" by occasionally coming there for worship.

In 722 B.C., the northern tribes were conquered by the Assyrians. Many of the citizens of the northern kingdom of Israel were deported to the Assyrian nation, never to return to the "promised land." But the Southern Kingdom, with Jerusalem as its capital, continued to exist as an independent nation. Although occasionally threatened and plundered by surrounding nations, Jerusalem remained intact until 586 B.C. At that time, Nebuchadnezzar, king of Babylonia, ravaged the city and carried the inhabitants into captivity. During the siege of the city, Jerusalem's beautiful temple was destroyed and the walls around the city were torn down. While a few inhabitants remained in the city, the glory of Jerusalem was gone.

The memory of Jerusalem among the Jewish people, however, would not die. They continued to grieve and to remember the City of David with affection. Psalm 137 is a good example of their expression of grief: "By the rivers of Babylon, there we sat down, yea, we wept, when we remembered Zion. We hanged our harps upon the willows in the midst thereof. For there they that carried us away captive required of us a song; and they that wasted us required of us mirth, saying, Sing us one of the songs of Zion. How shall we sing the LORD's song in a strange land? If I forget thee, O Jerusalem, let my right hand forget her cunning. If I do not remember thee, let my tongue cleave to the roof of my mouth; if I prefer not Jerusalem above my chief joy."

The Restoration: For more than half a century the Jews remained captives in Babylonia, and their beloved Jerusalem lay in ruins. But this changed when Cyrus, king of Persia, defeated the Babylonians. He allowed the Jewish captives to return to Jerusalem to restore the city. Zerubbabel was the leader of a group that left Babylon in 538 B.C. to return to Jerusalem to rebuild the temple. After a period of over twenty years, the temple was restored, although it was not as lavish as Solomon's original temple had been.

Under the leadership of Nehemiah, a second group of Jewish exiles returned to the holy city to restore the wall around the city. Through a masterful strategy of organization and determination, "the wall was finished on the twenty-fifth day of the month of Elul, in fifty-two days" (Neh. 6:15).

During the succeeding years of domination by the Persian Empire, Jerusalem apparently enjoyed peace and prosperity. When Alexander the Great conquered Persia, the Jews were reluctant to pledge loyalty to the Greek ruler, preferring instead to remain under Persian rule. Only by tactful concessions of religious privileges was Alexander able to win the loyalty of the Jews.

Jerusalem during the Period between the Testaments: The years that followed the death of Alexander brought many contending armies into conflict in the territory that surrounded Jerusalem. But the greatest threat to the Jews was the onslaught of Greek or Hellenistic culture, which threatened to erode the Jewish way of life. When the Jews resisted Greek cultural influence, the Greek leader Antiochus IV Epiphanes attacked the city and destroyed the temple. Many of the inhabitants fled the city, taking refuge in the surrounding hills.

Led by Judas, these inhabitants later recaptured Jerusalem and restored the temple. The successors to Judas Maccabeus were able to gain independence and to set up Jerusalem as the capital of a newly independent Judea—a position the city had not enjoyed since its defeat by the Babylonians four centuries before. This situation prevailed until the Roman Empire conquered Judea and reduced Jerusalem to a city-state under Roman domination. This was the situation that prevailed during New Testament times.

Jerusalem in the New Testament: The wise men who sought Jesus after His birth came to Jerusalem because this was considered the city of the king (Matt. 2:1–2). Although Jesus was born in Bethlehem, Jerusalem played a significant role in His life and ministry. It was to Jerusalem that He went when He was twelve years old. Here He amazed the temple leaders with His knowledge and wisdom (Luke 2:47). In Jerusalem He cleansed the temple, chasing away the moneychangers who desecrated the holy place with their selfish practices. And, finally, it was outside Jerusalem where He was crucified, buried, and resurrected.

The record of the New Testament church indicates that Jerusalem continued to play a significant role in the early spread of Christianity. After the martyrdom of Stephen, the early believers scattered from Jerusalem to various parts of the Mediterranean world (Acts 8:1). But Jerusalem always was the place to which they returned for significant events. For example, Acts 15 records that when the early church leaders sought to reconcile their differences about the acceptance of Gentile believers, they met in Jerusalem. Thus, the city became a holy city for Christians as well as Jews.

The Jerusalem of New Testament times contained a temple that had been built by Herod, the Roman leader. Although the main portion of the temple was completed in eighteen months, other areas of this building were still under construction during Jesus' ministry. In fact, the temple was not completed until A.D. 67—only three years before it was finally destroyed by the Roman leader Titus and the Roman army.

As Jesus had prophesied in Matthew 24, the city of Jerusalem was completely destroyed in A.D. 70. The temple was destroyed, and the high priesthood and the Sanhedrin were abolished. Eventually, a Roman city was erected on the site, and Jerusalem was regarded as forbidden ground for the Jews.

Topography: Unlike many other ancient cities, Jerusalem is neither a harbor city nor a city situated on trade routes. It sits about 800 meters (2,500 feet) above sea level in mountainous country about 60 kilometers (37 miles) from the Mediterranean Sea and 23 kilometers (14 miles) from the northern end of the Dead Sea. The site seems unattractive because it lacks an adequate supply of water, is surrounded by relatively infertile land, and is hemmed in by deep valleys and difficult roads.

But these disadvantages were probably the major factors that led to its establishment as a capital city. Its location made the city a fortress that could be easily defended against attack—a very important consideration in Old Testament times. Topographically, Jerusalem was built on two triangle-shaped ridges that converge to the south. On the east lay the ravine known as the Kidron Valley. On the west lay the deep gorge known as the Valley of Hinnom. At the southern border of the city, the two valleys converged. Only on the northern border was the city vulnerable to attack.

The lack of a water supply was solved by using a natural spring that flowed from the Kidron Valley. During the reign of Hezekiah in the Old Testament period, this spring was diverted underground so that it flowed into the city. Thus, the inhabitants of the city had water, while invading armies did not. According to 2 Chronicles 32:30, "Hezekiah ... stopped the upper watercourse of Gihon, and brought it straight down to the west side of the City of David." Hezekiah's new water supply helped save the city when it was attacked by the Assyrians a short time later (701 B.C.).

Jerusalem is considered a holy city not only by Jews and Christians but also by Muslims. The book of Revelation speaks of a "new Jerusalem" (Rev. 21:2), a heavenly city fashioned by God Himself for those who are known as His people.

Jerusalem Council, The—The council was called together to discuss the question of the necessity of Gentile believers following the law (Acts 15). Did a Gentile believer have to be circumcised and keep the law of Moses in order to accept Christ? Some believers from Judea had been teaching just that, and when Paul heard it he argued strongly to the contrary. The church decided that this important issue should be discussed without delay, and Paul and Barnabas set off toward Jerusalem to meet with the elders and apostles there. Paul, Barnabas, and Simon Peter testified at the meeting of their experiences with Gentile conversions. They had all seen obvious manifestations of God's power and approval upon uncircumcised Gentiles who turned to the Lord, and Peter said, "Now therefore, why do you test God by putting a yoke on the neck of the disciples which neither our fathers nor we were able to bear? But we believe that through the grace of the Lord Jesus Christ we shall be saved in the same manner as they" (Acts 15:10–11).

After listening to the testimony of Paul and Barnabas, James joined in, pointing out that the Scriptures taught that Gentiles would be saved

(Amos 9:11–12). The council agreed that the Gentile believers should be taught to abstain from sexual immorality, from idols, from strangled meat, and from blood. Therefore, they wrote an encouraging letter to the believers in Antioch, telling them that they were not required to be under the burden of keeping the Mosaic law. They should abstain from the things mentioned, but were not asked to be circumcised or to follow the strict dietary rules.

Jerusalem, New—The holy city that John the apostle describes in Revelation 21–22. The New Jerusalem is described as coming down from heaven "prepared as a bride adorned for her husband" (Rev. 21:2). The New Jerusalem is where God and the Lamb reign, *Immanuel,* "God with us" (Rev. 21:3). There will be no need for the sun's light because God's presence will be all its light. Sorrow, sin, and the curse will all pass away. Those who are saved by the blood of the Lamb shall walk here, but nothing defiling and no one whose name is not in the Lamb's book of life will enter the city (Rev. 21:24, 27).

Jerusha [Je·ru′sha], *possession*—Wife of Uzziah (2 Kings 15:33; 2 Chron. 27:1).

Jerushah [Je·ru′shah]—See Jerusha.

Jesaiah [Je·sai′ah]—See Jeshaiah.

Jeshaiah [Je·shai′ah], *Yahweh delivered*—

1. Son of Jeduthun, a harpist at the head of the eighth division of musicians in the reign of David (1 Chron. 25:3).

2. A son of Hananiah and grandson of Zerubbabel (1 Chron. 3:21). Another form is Jesaiah.

3. A son of Rehabiah, a Levite, in the reign of David. He was of the Levitical branch of Eliezer (1 Chron. 26:25).

4. Son of Athaliah and head of the house of Elam. With seventy males he returned from Babylon with Ezra (Ezra 8:7).

5. A Levite of the Merari branch. He came to Jerusalem with Ezra (Ezra 8:19).

6. The father of Ithiel, a Benjamite (Neh. 11:7).

Jeshanah [Je·sha′nah], *old*—A city of Ephraim (2 Chron. 13:19).

Jeshanah Gate [Je·sha′nah]—One of the gates of Jerusalem (Neh. 3:6; 12:39). Also called "Old Gate" (NKJV).

Jesharelah [Jesh·a·re'lah]—See Asharelah.

Jeshebeab [Je·sheb'e·ab], *father's dwelling*—A descendant of Aaron (1 Chron. 24:13).

Jesher [Je'sher], *uprightness*—A son of Caleb, the son of Hezron (1 Chron. 2:18).

Jeshiah [Je'shi·ah]—See Jesshiah.

Jeshimon [Je·shi'mon], *a waste*—A desolate stretch of wasteland in Judah to the west and near the middle of the Dead Sea (1 Sam. 23:19, 24; 26:1, 3).

Jeshishai [Je·shish'ai], *aged*—Son of Jahdo, a Gadite of Gilead (1 Chron. 5:14).

Jeshohaiah [Jesh·o·hai'ah], *Jehovah humbles*—A prince of Simeon. He went to Gedor (1 Chron. 4:36).

Jeshua [Jesh'u·a], *he is saved*—Eight Old Testament men:

    1. A form of Joshua, son of Nun (Neh. 8:17).

    2. A descendant of Aaron. In the time of David, his family was the ninth course of priests (1 Chron. 24:1, 6, 11).

    3. A Levite in the reign of Hezekiah. He was one of those in charge of the temple offerings (2 Chron. 31:15).

    4. A high priest who came from Babylon with Zerubbabel (Ezra 2:2; Neh. 7:7). He labored on the altar and urged the people to build the second temple (Ezra 3:2–9). He is called Joshua in Zechariah 3:1–10; 6:11–13.

    5. The head of a Levitical family who returned from Babylon with Zerubbabel (Ezra 2:40; Neh. 7:43; 12:8). He took an active part in stimulating the people to rebuild the temple.

    6. A man of Pahath-moab. His descendants numbering 2,812 returned with Zerubbabel from Babylon to Jerusalem (Ezra 2:6; Neh. 7:11).

    7. A Levite who assisted Ezra in teaching the people the law (Neh. 8:7; 9:4–5).

    8. A village in the southern section of Judah (Neh. 11:26).

Jeshurun, Jesurun [Je·shu′run, Jes·u′run], *upright one*—A term meaning righteous nation (Deut. 32:15; 33:5, 26; Isa. 44:2).

Jesiah [Je·si′ah]—See Isshiah.

Jesimiel [Je·sim′i·el], *God sets up*—A Simeonite who lived in the time of Hezekiah (1 Chron. 4:36).

Jesse [Jes′se], *wealthy* or *I possess*—Son of Obed and grandson of Ruth and Boaz, the father of King David (1 Sam. 16:18–19) and an ancestor of Jesus. He was descended from Nahshon, who in the days of Moses was the chief of the tribe of Judah (Ruth 4:18–22). Jesse was the father of eight sons—Eliab, Abinadab, Shimea (Shammah), Nethanel, Raddai, Ozem, Elihu, and David—and two daughters, Zeruiah and Abigail (1 Chron. 2:13–16). He is called a "Bethlehemite" (1 Sam. 16:1, 18).

On instructions from the Lord, the prophet Samuel went to Bethlehem to select a new king from among Jesse's eight sons. After the first seven were rejected, David was anointed by Samuel to replace Saul as king of Israel (1 Sam. 16:1–13). Later King Saul asked Jesse to allow David to visit his court and play soothing music on the harp. Jesse gave his permission and sent Saul a present (1 Sam. 16:20).

The title "son of Jesse" soon became attached to David. It was sometimes used in a spirit of insult and ridicule, mocking David's humble origins (1 Sam. 20:27; 1 Kings 12:16). But the prophet Isaiah spoke of "a Rod from the stem of Jesse" (Isa. 11:1) and of "a Root of Jesse" (Isa. 11:10)—prophecies of the Messiah to come. For the apostle Paul, the "root of Jesse" (Rom. 15:12) was a prophecy fulfilled in Jesus Christ.

Jesshiah [Jes·shi′ah], *unknown*—A Kohathite, the son of Uzziel (1 Chron. 23:20); also called Isshiah (1 Chron. 24:25).

Jesui [Jes′u·i], *he resembles me*—The third of Asher's sons (Num. 26:44); also called Isui (Gen. 46:17) or Ishvi (1 Chron. 7:30).

Jesuites [Jes′u·ites]—The descendants of Asher's son Jesui (Num. 26:44).

Jesurun [Jes′u·run]—See Jeshurun.

Jesus [Je′sus], *the Lord is salvation*—The name of five men in the Bible:

1. Jesus Barabbas, a prisoner released by the Roman governor Pontius Pilate before Jesus was crucified (Matt. 27:16–17, REB; some manuscripts omit the word *Jesus* and have simply *Barabbas*).

2. An ancestor of Christ, also called Jose (Luke 3:29; Jose, KJV, NKJV; Joshua, NASB, REB, NIV).

3. The KJV rendering of Joshua, the son of Nun, in the New Testament (Acts 7:45; Heb. 4:8). He was a military leader of the Israelites.

4. Jesus Justus, a Jewish Christian who, with the apostle Paul, sent greetings to the Colossians (Col. 4:11).

5. Jesus, the son of Mary. See Jesus Christ.

Jesus Christ [Je′sus Christ]—The human-divine Son of God born of the Virgin Mary; the great High Priest who intercedes for His people at the right hand of God; founder of the Christian church and central figure of the human race.

To understand who Jesus was and what He accomplished, students of the New Testament must study: (1) His life, (2) His teachings, (3) His person, and (4) His work.

The Life of Jesus: The twofold designation Jesus Christ combines the personal name "Jesus" and the title "Christ," meaning "anointed" or "Messiah." The significance of this title became clear during the scope of His life and ministry. The name *Jesus*, announced by the angel as that divinely selected for Mary's son (Matt. 1:21; Luke 1:31–33), signifies *the Lord is salvation*. The word *Christ* (the Anointed One) is essentially an official title borne by Jesus as the Messiah (John 1:41) and as the Son of the living God (Matt. 16:16).

Political Situation: The political situation in Palestine in the time of Jesus was complicated and seething with discontent. The country, since the Exile, had been successively under Persian, Greek, Egyptian, and Syrian domination. Foreign rule was followed by about a century of independence under the Maccabees, which ended near the middle of the first century B.C. when the country was incorporated into the Roman Empire as part of the province of Syria. Jewish reaction to Roman rule ranged from mildly critical to hostile but was usually tempered with the spirit of opportunism.

Religious Situation: The religious life of Judaism in Jesus's time was at a low ebb. Formal religion was dominated by two powerful sects— the Pharisees and the Sadducees. The former were the more influential, but to the word of God they added much religious tradition and theological subtleties. The latter, while rejecting the traditions of the Pharisees, were more interested in politics than religion. Sadducees controlled the Sanhedrin and limited the high priests to members of their own families. Both sects were denounced by John the Baptist, and Jesus warned against them (Matt. 3:7; 16:6; Luke 11:42–52). It was to the common people that the gospel of Jesus was destined to appeal (Mark 12:37; Luke 19:47–48).

Birth and Upbringing: Jesus was born in Bethlehem, a town about 10 kilometers (6 miles) south of Jerusalem, toward the end of Herod the Great's reign as king of the Jews, in 4 B.C. (some scholars say late 5 B.C.). The Roman abbot who (prior to A.D. 550) devised the Christian calendar fixed the year 1, the year intended to mark Christ's birth, too late. Early in His life He was taken to Nazareth, a town of Galilee. There He was brought up by His mother, Mary, and her husband, Joseph, a carpenter by trade. Hence He was known as "Jesus of Nazareth" or, more fully, "Jesus of Nazareth, the son of Joseph" (John 1:45).

Jesus was His mother's firstborn child; He had four brothers (James, Joses, Judas, and Simon) and an unspecified number of sisters (Mark 6:3). Joseph apparently died before Jesus began His public ministry. Mary, with the rest of the family, lived on and became a member of the church of Jerusalem after Jesus' death and resurrection.

The only incident preserved from Jesus' first 30 years (after His infancy) was His trip to Jerusalem with Joseph and Mary when He was 12 years old (Luke 2:41–52). Since He was known in Nazareth as "the carpenter" (Mark 6:3), He may have taken Joseph's place as the family breadwinner at an early age.

The little village of Nazareth overlooked the main highway linking Damascus to the Mediterranean coast and Egypt. News of the world outside Galilee probably reached Nazareth quickly. During His boyhood Jesus probably heard of the revolt led by Judas the Galilean against the Roman authorities. This happened when Judea, to the south, became a Roman province in A.D. 6 and its inhabitants had to pay tribute to Caesar. Jews probably heard also of the severity with which the revolt was crushed.

Galilee, the province in which Jesus lived, was ruled by Herod Antipas, youngest son of Herod the Great. So the area where He lived was not directly involved in this revolt. But the sympathies of many Galileans were probably stirred. No doubt the boys of Nazareth discussed this issue, which they heard their elders debating. There is no indication of what Jesus thought about this event at the time. But we do know what He said about it in Jerusalem 24 years later (Mark 12:13–17).

Sepphoris, about 6 kilometers (4 miles) northwest of Nazareth, had been the center of an anti-Roman revolt during Jesus' infancy. The village was destroyed by the Romans, but it was soon rebuilt by Herod Antipas. Antipas lived there as tetrarch of Galilee and Perea until he founded a new capital for his principality at Tiberias, on the western shore of the Lake of Galilee (A.D. 22). Reports of happenings at his court, while he lived in Sepphoris, were probably carried to Nazareth. A royal court formed the setting for several of Jesus' parables.

Scenes from Israel's history could be seen from the rising ground above Nazareth. To the south stretched the valley of Jezreel, where great battles had been fought in earlier days. Beyond the valley of Jezreel was Mount Gilboa, where King Saul fell in battle with the Philistines. To the east Mount Tabor rose to 562 meters (1,843 feet), the highest elevation in that part of the country. A growing boy would readily find his mind moving back and forth between the stirring events of former days and the realities of the contemporary situation: the all-pervasive presence of the Romans.

Beginnings of Jesus' Ministry: Jesus began His public ministry when He sought baptism at the hands of John the Baptist. John preached between A.D. 27 and 28 in the lower Jordan Valley and baptized those who wished to give expression to their repentance (Matt. 3:13–17; Mark 1:9–11; Luke 3:21–22; John 1:29–34). The descent of the dove as Jesus came up out of the water was a sign that He was the One anointed by the Spirit of God as the Servant-Messiah of His people (Isa. 11:2; 42:1; 61:1).

A voice from heaven declared, "You are My beloved Son; in You I am well pleased" (Luke 3:22). This indicated that He was Israel's anointed King, destined to fulfill His kingship as the Servant of the Lord described centuries earlier by the prophet Isaiah (Isa. 42:1; 52:13).

In the gospels of Matthew, Mark, and Luke, Jesus' baptism is followed immediately by His temptation in the wilderness (Matt. 4:1–11;

Mark 1:12–13; Luke 4:1–13). This testing confirmed His understanding of the heavenly voice and His acceptance of the path that it marked out for Him. He refused to use His power as God's Son to fulfill His personal desires, to amaze the people, or to dominate the world by political and military force.

Apparently, Jesus ministered for a short time in southern and central Palestine, while John the Baptist was still preaching (John 3:22–4:42). But the main phase of Jesus' ministry began in Galilee after John's imprisonment by Herod Antipas. This was the signal, according to Mark 1:14–15, for Jesus to proclaim God's good news in Galilee: "The time is fulfilled, and the kingdom of God is at hand. Repent, and believe in the gospel." What is the character of this kingdom? How was it to be established?

A popular view was that the kingdom of God meant throwing off the oppressive yoke of Rome and establishing an independent state of Israel. Judas and his brothers and followers had won independence for the Jewish people in the second century B.C. by guerrilla warfare and diplomatic skill. Many of the Jewish people believed that with God's help, the same thing could happen again. Other efforts had failed, but the spirit of revolt remained. If Jesus had consented to become the military leader, which the people wanted, many would gladly have followed Him. But in spite of His temptation, Jesus resisted taking this path.

Jesus' proclamation of the kingdom of God was accompanied by works of mercy and power, including the healing of the sick, particularly those who were demon-possessed. These works also proclaimed the arrival of the kingdom of God. The demons that caused such distress to men and women were signs of the kingdom of Satan. When they were cast out, this proved the superior strength of the kingdom of God. For a time, Jesus' healing aroused great popular enthusiasm throughout Galilee. But the religious leaders and teachers found much of Jesus' activity disturbing. He refused to be bound by their religious ideas. He befriended social outcasts. He insisted on understanding and applying the law of God in the light of its original intention, not according to the popular interpretation of the religious establishment. He insisted on healing sick people on the Sabbath day. He believed that healing people did not profane the Sabbath but honored it, because it was established by God for the rest and relief of human beings (Luke 6:6–11).

This attitude brought Jesus into conflict with the scribes, the official teachers of the law. Because of their influence, He was soon barred from preaching in the synagogues. But this was no great inconvenience. He simply gathered larger congregations to listen to Him on the hillside or by the lakeshore. He regularly illustrated the main themes of His preaching by parables. These were simple stories from daily life that would drive home some special point and make it stick in the hearer's understanding.

The Mission of the Twelve and Its Sequel: From among the large number of His followers, Jesus selected 12 men to remain in His company for training that would enable them to share His preaching and healing ministry. When He judged the time to be ripe, Jesus sent them out two by two to proclaim the kingdom of God throughout the Jewish districts of Galilee. In many places, they found an enthusiastic hearing.

Probably some who heard these disciples misunderstood the nature of the kingdom they proclaimed. Perhaps the disciples themselves used language that could be interpreted as stirring political unrest. News of their activity reached Herod Antipas, ruler of Galilee, arousing his suspicion. He had recently murdered John the Baptist. Now he began to wonder if he faced another serious problem in Jesus. On the return of His 12 apostles, they withdrew under Jesus' leadership from the publicity that surrounded them in Galilee to the quieter territory east of the Lake of Galilee. This territory was ruled by Antipas's brother Philip—"Philip the tetrarch"—who had only a few Jews among his subjects. Philip was not as likely to be troubled by Messianic excitement. But even here Jesus and His disciples found themselves pursued by enthusiastic crowds from Galilee. He recognized them for what they were, "sheep without a shepherd," aimless people who were in danger of being led to disaster under the wrong kind of leadership. Jesus gave these people further teaching, feeding them also with loaves and fishes. But this only stimulated them to try to compel Him to be the king for whom they were looking. He would not be the kind of king they wanted, and they had no use for the only kind of king He was prepared to be. From then on, His popularity in Galilee began to decline. Many of His disciples no longer followed Him. He took the Twelve further north, into Gentile territory. Here He gave them special training to prepare them for the crisis they would have to meet shortly in Jerusalem. He knew the time was approaching when He would present His challenging message to the people of the capital and to the Jewish leaders. At the city of Caesarea Philippi, Jesus decided the time was ripe to encourage the Twelve to state their convictions about His identity and His mission. When Peter declared that He was the Messiah, this showed that He and the other apostles had given up most of the traditional ideas about the kind of person the Messiah would be. But the thought that Jesus would have to suffer and die was something they could not accept. Jesus recognized that He could now make a beginning with the creation of a new community. In this new community of God's people, the ideals of the kingdom He proclaimed would be realized. These ideals that Jesus taught were more revolutionary in many ways than the insurgent spirit that survived the overthrow of Judas the Galilean. The Jewish rebels against the rule of Rome developed into a party known as the Zealots. They had no better policy than to counter force with force, which, in Jesus' view, was like invoking Satan to drive out Satan. The way of nonresistance that He urged upon the people seemed impractical. But it eventually proved to be more effective against the might of Rome than armed rebellion.

Jerusalem: The Last Phase: At the Feast of Tabernacles in the fall of A.D. 29, Jesus went to Jerusalem with the Twelve. He apparently spent the next six months in the southern part of Palestine. Jerusalem, like Galilee, needed to hear the message of the kingdom. But Jerusalem was more resistant to it even than Galilee. The spirit of revolt was in the air; Jesus' way of peace was not accepted. This is why He wept over the city. He realized the way that so many of its citizens preferred was bound to lead to their destruction. Even the magnificent temple, so recently rebuilt by Herod the Great, would be involved in the general overthrow.

During the week before Passover in A.D. 30, Jesus taught each day in the temple area, debating with other teachers of differing beliefs. He was invited to state His opinion on a number of issues, including the question of paying taxes to the Roman emperor. This was a test question with the Zealots. In their eyes, to acknowledge the rule of a pagan king was high treason against God, Israel's true King.

Jesus replied that the coinage in which these taxes had to be paid belonged to the Roman emperor because his face and name were stamped on it. Let the emperor have what so obviously belonged to him, Jesus declared; it was more important to make sure that God received what was due Him. This answer disappointed those patriots who followed the Zealot line. Neither did it make Jesus popular with the priestly authorities. They were terrified by the rebellious spirit in the land. Their favored position depended on maintaining good relations with the ruling Romans. If revolt broke out, the Romans would hold them responsible for not keeping the people under control. They were afraid that Jesus might provoke an outburst that would bring the heavy hand of Rome upon the city. The enthusiasm of the people when Jesus entered Jerusalem on a donkey alarmed the religious leaders. So did His show of authority when He cleared the temple of traders and moneychangers. This was a "prophetic action" in the tradition of the great prophets of Israel. Its message to the priestly establishment came through loud and clear. The prophets' vision of the temple—"My house shall be called a house of prayer for all nations" (Isa. 56:7)—was a fine ideal. But any attempt to make it measure up to reality would be a threat to the priestly privileges. Jesus' action was as disturbing as Jeremiah's speech foretelling the destruction of Solomon's temple had been to the religious leaders six centuries earlier (Jer. 26:1–6).

To block the possibility of an uprising among the people, the priestly party decided to arrest Jesus as soon as possible. The opportunity came earlier than they expected when one of the Twelve, Judas Iscariot, offered to deliver Jesus into their power without the risk of a public disturbance. Arrested on Passover Eve, Jesus was brought first before a Jewish court of inquiry, over which the high priest Caiaphas presided. The Jewish leaders attempted first to convict Him of being a threat to the temple. Protection of the sanctity of the temple was the one area in which the Romans still allowed the Jewish authorities to exercise authority. But this attempt failed. Then Jesus accepted their charge that He claimed to be the Messiah. This gave the religious leaders an occasion to hand Him over to Pilate on a charge of treason and sedition. While "Messiah" was primarily a religious title, it could be translated into political terms as "king of the Jews." Anyone who claimed to be king of the Jews, as Jesus admitted He did, presented a challenge to the Roman emperor's rule in Judea. On this charge Pilate, the Roman governor, finally convicted Jesus. This was the charge spelled out in the inscription fixed above His head on the cross. Death by crucifixion was the penalty for sedition by one who was not a Roman citizen. With the death and burial of Jesus, the narrative of His earthly career came to an end. But with His resurrection on the third day, He lives and works forever as the exalted Lord. His appearances to His disciples after His resurrection assured them He was "alive after His suffering" (Acts 1:3). These appearances also enabled them to make the transition in their experience from the form in which they had known Him earlier to the new way in which they would be related to Him by the Holy Spirit.

The Teachings of Jesus: Just as Jesus' life was unique, so His teachings are known for their fresh and new approach. Jesus taught several distinctive spiritual truths that set Him apart from any other religious leader who ever lived.

The Kingdom of God: The message Jesus began to proclaim in Galilee after John the Baptist's imprisonment was the good news of the kingdom of God. When He appeared to His disciples after the resurrection, He continued "speaking of the things pertaining to the kingdom of God" (Acts 1:3). What did Jesus mean by the kingdom of God?

When Jesus announced that the kingdom of God was drawing near, many of His hearers must have recognized an echo of those visions recorded in the book of Daniel. These prophecies declared that one day "the God of heaven will set up a kingdom which shall never be destroyed" (Dan. 2:44). Jesus' announcement indicated the time had come when the authority of this kingdom would be exercised.

The nature of this kingdom is determined by the character of the God whose kingdom it is. The revelation of God lay at the heart of Jesus' teaching. Jesus called Him "Father" and taught His disciples to do the same. But the term that He used when He called God "Father" was "Abba" (Mark 14:36), the term of affection that children used when they addressed their father at home or spoke about him to others. It was not unusual for God to be addressed in prayer as "my Father" or "our Father." But it was most unusual for Him to be called Abba. By using this term, Jesus expressed His sense of nearness to God and His total trust in Him. He taught His followers to look to God with the trust that children show when they expect their earthly fathers to provide them with food, clothes, and shelter.

This attitude is especially expressed in the Lord's Prayer, which may be regarded as a brief summary of Jesus' teaching. In this prayer the disciples were taught to pray for the fulfillment of God's eternal purpose (the coming of His kingdom) and to ask Him for daily bread, forgiveness of sins, and deliverance from temptation. In Jesus' healing of the sick and proclamation of good news to the poor, the kingdom of

God was visibly present, although it was not yet fully realized. Otherwise, it would not have been necessary for Him to tell His disciples to pray, "Your kingdom come" (Matt. 6:10). One day, He taught, it would come "with power" (Mark 9:1), and some of them would live to see that day.

In the kingdom of God the way to honor is the way of service. In this respect, Jesus set a worthy example, choosing to give service instead of receive it. The death and resurrection of Jesus unleashed the kingdom of God in full power. Through proclamation of the kingdom, liberation and blessing were brought to many more than could be touched by Jesus' brief ministry in Galilee and Judea.

The Way of the Kingdom: The ethical teaching of Jesus was part of His proclamation of the kingdom of God. Only by His death and resurrection could the divine rule be established. But even while the kingdom of God was in the process of inauguration during His ministry, its principles could be translated into action in the lives of His followers. The most familiar presentation of these principles is found in the Sermon on the Mount (Matt. 5–7), which was addressed to His disciples. These principles showed how those who were already children of the kingdom ought to live.

Jesus and the Law of Moses: The people whom Jesus taught already had a large body of ethical teaching in the Old Testament law. But a further body of oral interpretation and application had grown up around the law of Moses over the centuries. Jesus declared that He had come to fulfill the law, not to destroy it (Matt. 5:17). But He emphasized its ethical quality by summarizing it in terms of what He called the two great commandments: "You shall love the Lord your God" (Deut. 6:5) and "You shall love your neighbor as yourself" (Lev. 19:18). "On these two commandments," He said, "hang all the Law and the Prophets" (Matt. 22:40).

Jesus did not claim uniqueness or originality for His ethical teaching. One of His purposes was to explain the ancient law of God. Yet there was a distinctiveness and freshness about His teaching, as He declared His authority: "You have heard that it was said . . . But I say to you" (Matt. 5:21–22). Only in listening to His words and doing them could people build a secure foundation for their lives (Matt. 7:24–27; Luke 6:46–49).

In His interpretation of specific commandments, Jesus did not use the methods of the Jewish rabbis. He dared to criticize their rulings, which had been handed down by word of mouth through successive generations of scribes. He even declared that these interpretations sometimes obscured the original purpose of the commandments. In appealing to that original purpose, He declared that a commandment was most faithfully obeyed when God's purpose in giving it was fulfilled. His treatment of the Sabbath law is an example of this approach. In a similar way, Jesus settled the question of divorce by an appeal to the original marriage ordinance (Gen. 1:26–27; 2:24–25). Since husband and wife were made one by the Creator's decree, Jesus pointed out, divorce was an attempt to undo the work of God. If the law later allowed for divorce in certain situations (Deut. 24:1–4), that was a concession to people's inability to keep the commandment. But it was not so in the beginning, He declared, and it should not be so for those who belong to the kingdom of God.

Jesus actually injected new life into the ethical principles of the law of Moses. But He did not impose a new set of laws that could be enforced by external sanctions; He prescribed a way of life for His followers. The act of murder, forbidden in the sixth commandment, was punishable by death. Conduct or language likely to provoke a breach of the peace could also bring on legal penalties. No human law can detect or punish the angry thought; yet it is here, Jesus taught, that the process that leads to murder begins. Therefore, "whoever is angry with his brother . . . shall be in danger of the judgment" (Matt. 5:22). But He was careful to point out that the judgment is God's, not man's.

The law could also punish a person for breaking the seventh commandment, which forbade adultery. But Jesus maintained that the act itself was the outcome of a person's internal thought. Therefore, "whoever looks at a woman to lust for her has already committed adultery with her in his heart" (Matt. 5:28).

Jesus' attitude and teaching also made many laws about property irrelevant for His followers. They should be known as people who give, not as people who get. If someone demands your cloak (outer garment), Jesus said, give it to him, and give him your tunic (undergarment) as well (Luke 6:29). There is more to life than abundance of possessions (Luke 12:15); in fact, He pointed out, material wealth is a hindrance to one's spiritual life. The wise man therefore will get rid of it: "It is easier for a camel to go through the eye of a needle than for a rich man to enter the kingdom of God" (Mark 10:25). In no area have Jesus' followers struggled more to avoid the uncompromising rigor of His words than in His teaching about the danger of possessions.

Jesus insisted that more is expected of His followers than the ordinary morality of decent people. Their ethical behavior should exceed "the righteousness of the scribes and Pharisees" (Matt. 5:20). "If you love [only] those who love you," He asked, "what credit is that to you? For even sinners love those who love them" (Luke 6:32). The higher standard of the kingdom of God called for acts of love to enemies and words of blessing and goodwill to persecutors. The children of the kingdom should not insist on their legal rights but cheerfully give them up in response to the supreme law of love.

The Way of Nonviolence: The principle of nonviolence is deeply ingrained in Jesus' teaching. In His references to the "men of violence" who tried to bring in the kingdom of God by force, Jesus gave no sign that He approved of their ideals or methods. The course He called for was the way of peace and submission. He urged His hearers not to strike back against injustice or oppression but to turn the other cheek, to go a second mile when their services were demanded for one mile, and to take the initiative in returning good for evil.

But the way of nonviolence did not appeal to the people. The crowd chose the militant Barabbas when they were given the opportunity to have either Jesus or Barabbas set free. But the attitude expressed in the shout, "Not this man, but Barabbas!" (Matt. 27:15–26) was the spirit that would one day level Jerusalem and bring misery and suffering to the Jewish nation.

The Supreme Example: In the teaching of Jesus, the highest of all incentives is the example of God. This was no new principle. The central section of Leviticus is called "the law of holiness" because of its recurring theme: "I am the Lord your God. . . . Be holy; for I am holy" (Lev. 11:44). This bears a close resemblance to Jesus' words in Luke 6:36, "Be merciful, just as your Father also is merciful." The children of God should reproduce their Father's character. He does not discriminate between the good and the evil in bestowing rain and sunshine; likewise, His followers should not discriminate in showing kindness to all. He delights in forgiving sinners; His children should also be marked by a forgiving spirit.

The example of the heavenly Father and the example shown by Jesus on earth are one and the same, since Jesus came to reveal the Father. Jesus' life was the practical demonstration of His ethical teaching. To His disciples He declared, "I have given you an example, that you should do as I have done to you" (John 13:15).

This theme of the imitation of Christ pervades the New Testament letters. It is especially evident in the writings of Paul, who was not personally acquainted with Jesus before he met Him on the Damascus Road. Paul instructed his converts to follow "the meekness and gentleness of Christ" (2 Cor. 10:1). He also encouraged them to imitate him as he himself imitated Christ (1 Cor. 11:1). When he recommended to them the practice of all the Christian graces, he declared, "Put on the Lord Jesus Christ" (Rom. 13:14). Throughout the New Testament, Jesus is presented as the One who left us an example, that we should follow in His steps (1 Peter 2:21).

The Person of Christ: The doctrine of the person of Christ, or christology, is one of the most important concerns of Christian theology. The various aspects of the person of Christ are best seen by reviewing the titles that are applied to Him in the Bible.

Son of Man: The title "Son of Man" was Jesus' favorite way of referring to Himself. He may have done this because this was not a recognized title already known by the people and associated with popular ideas. This title means essentially "The Man." But as Jesus used it, it took on new significance.

Jesus applied this title to Himself in three distinct ways: First, He used the title in a general way, almost as a substitute for the pronoun "I." A good example of this usage occurred in the saying where Jesus contrasted John the Baptist, who "came neither eating bread nor drinking wine," with the Son of Man, who "has come eating and drinking" (Luke 7:33–34). Another probable example is the statement that "the Son of Man has nowhere to lay His head" (Luke 9:58). In this instance He warned a would-be disciple that those who wanted to follow Him must expect to share His homeless existence.

Second, Jesus used the title to emphasize that "the Son of Man must suffer" (Mark 8:31). The word *must* implies that His suffering was foretold by the prophets. It was, indeed, "written concerning the Son of Man, that He must suffer many things and be treated with contempt" (Mark 9:12). So when Jesus announced the presence of the betrayer at the Last Supper, He declared, "The Son of Man indeed goes just as it is written of Him" (Mark 14:21). Later the same evening He submitted to His captors with the words "The Scriptures must be fulfilled" (Mark 14:49).

Finally, Jesus used the title "Son of Man" to refer to Himself as the one who exercised exceptional authority—authority delegated to Him by God. "The Son of Man has power [authority] on earth to forgive sins" He declared (Mark 2:10). He exercised this authority in a way that made some people criticize Him for acting with the authority of God: "The Son of Man is also Lord of the Sabbath" (Mark 2:28).

The Son of Man appeared to speak and act in these cases as the representative human being. If God had given people dominion over all the works of His hands, then He who was the Son of Man in this special representative sense was in a position to exercise that dominion. Near the end of His ministry, Jesus spoke of His authority as the Son of Man at the end of time. Men and women "will see the Son of Man coming in the clouds with great power and glory," He declared (Mark 13:26). He also stated to the high priest and other members of the supreme court of Israel: "You will see the Son of Man sitting at the right hand of Power, and coming with the clouds of heaven" (Mark 14:62). He seemed deserted and humiliated as He stood there awaiting their verdict. But the tables would be turned when they saw Him vindicated by God as Ruler and Judge of all the world.

Only once was Jesus referred to as the Son of Man by anyone other than Himself. This occurred when Stephen, condemned by the Jewish Sanhedrin, saw "the Son of Man standing at the right hand of God" (Acts 7:56). In Stephen's vision the Son of Man stood as his heavenly advocate, in fulfillment of Jesus' words: "Whoever confesses Me before men, him the Son of Man also will confess before the angels of God" (Luke 12:8).

Messiah: When Jesus made His declaration before the high priest and his colleagues, He did so in response to the question: "Are You the Christ, the Son of the Blessed?" (Mark 14:61). He replied, "I am" (Mark 14:62). "It is as you said" (Matt. 26:64).

The Christ was the Messiah, the Son of David—a member of the royal family of David. For centuries the Jewish people had expected a Messiah who would restore the fortunes of Israel, liberating the nation from foreign oppression and extending His rule over Gentile nations.

Jesus belonged to the family of David. He was proclaimed as the Messiah of David's line, both before His birth and after His resurrection. But He Himself was slow to make messianic claims. The reason for this is that the ideas associated with the Messiah in the minds of the Jewish people were quite different from the character and purpose of His ministry. Thus, He refused to give them any encouragement. When, at Caesarea Philippi, Peter confessed Jesus to be the Messiah, Jesus directed him and his fellow disciples to tell no one that He was the Christ. After His death and resurrection, however, the concept of messiahship among His followers was transformed by what He was and did. Then He could safely be proclaimed as Messiah, God's Anointed King, resurrected in glory to occupy the throne of the universe.

Son of God: Jesus was acclaimed as the Son of God at His baptism (Mark 1:11). But He was also given this title by the angel Gabriel at the annunciation: "That Holy One who is to be born will be called the Son of God" (Luke 1:35). The gospel of John especially makes it clear that the Father-Son relationship belongs to eternity—that the Son is supremely qualified to reveal the Father because He has His eternal being "in the bosom of the Father" (John 1:18).

At one level the title "Son of God" belonged officially to the Messiah, who personified the nation of Israel. "Israel is My son, My firstborn," said God to Pharaoh (Ex. 4:22). Of the promised prince of the house of David, God declared, "I will make him My firstborn" (Ps. 89:27).

But there was nothing merely official about Jesus' consciousness of being the Son of God. He taught His disciples to think of God and to speak to Him as their Father. But He did not link them with Himself in this relationship and speak to them of "our Father"—yours and mine. The truth expressed in His words in John 20:17 is implied throughout His teaching: "My Father and your Father . . . My God and your God."

As the Son of God in a special sense, Jesus made Himself known to the apostle Paul on the Damascus Road. Paul said, "It pleased God . . . to reveal His Son in me" (Gal. 1:15–16). The proclamation of Jesus as the Son of God was central to Paul's preaching (Acts 9:20; 2 Cor. 1:19).

When Jesus is presented as the Son of God in the New Testament, two aspects of His person are emphasized: His eternal relation to God as His Father and His perfect revelation of the Father to the human race.

Word and Wisdom: Jesus' perfect revelation of the Father is also expressed when He is described as the Word (*logos*) of God (John 1:1–18). The Word is the self-expression of God; that self-expression has personal status, existing eternally with God. The Word by which God created the world (Ps. 33:6) and by which He spoke through the prophets "became flesh" in the fullness of time (John 1:14), living among men and women as Jesus of Nazareth.

Much that is said in the Old Testament about the Word of God is paralleled by what is said of the Wisdom of God: "The Lord by wisdom founded the earth" (Prov. 3:19). In the New Testament Christ is portrayed as the personal Wisdom of God (1 Cor. 1:24, 30)—the one through whom all things were created (1 Cor. 8:6; Col. 1:16; Heb. 1:2).

The Holy One of God: This title was given to Jesus by Peter (John 6:69, NIV, NRSV) and, remarkably, by a demon-possessed man (Mark 1:24). In their preaching, the apostles called Jesus "the Holy One and the Just" (Acts 3:14). This was a name belonging to Him as the Messiah, indicating He was especially set apart for God. This title also emphasized His positive goodness and His complete dedication to the doing of His Father's will. Mere "sinlessness," in the sense of the absence of any fault, is a pale quality in comparison to the unsurpassed power for righteousness that filled His life and teaching.

The Lord: "Jesus is Lord" is the ultimate Christian creed. "No one can say that Jesus is Lord except by the Holy Spirit" (1 Cor. 12:3). A Christian, therefore, is a person who confesses Jesus as Lord.

Several words denoting lordship were used of Jesus in the New Testament. The most frequent, and the most important in relation to the doctrine of His person, was the Greek word *kyrios*. It was frequently given to Him as a polite term of address, meaning "Sir." Sometimes the title was used of Him in the third person, when the disciples and others spoke of Him as "The Lord" or "The Master."

After His resurrection and exaltation, however, Jesus was given the title "Lord" in its full, christological sense. Peter, concluding his address to the crowd in Jerusalem on the Day of Pentecost, declared, "Let all the house of Israel know assuredly that God has made this Jesus, whom you crucified, both Lord and Christ" (Acts 2:36).

The title "Lord" in the christological sense must have been given to Jesus before the church moved out into the Gentile world. The evidence for this is the invocation "Maranatha" (KJV) or "O Lord, come!"

(1 Cor. 16:22). The apostle Paul, writing to a Gentile church in the Greek-speaking world, assumed that its members were familiar with this Aramaic phrase. It was an early Christian title for Jesus that was taken over untranslated. It bears witness to the fact that from the earliest days of the church, the One who had been exalted as Lord was expected to return as Lord.

Another key New Testament text that shows the sense in which Jesus was acknowledged as Lord is Philippians 2:5–11. In these verses Paul may be quoting an early confession of faith. If so, he endorsed it and made it his own. This passage tells how Jesus did not regard equality with God as something that He should exploit to His own advantage. Instead, He humbled Himself to become a man, displaying "the form of God" in "the form of a servant." He became "obedient to the point of death, even the death of the cross. Therefore God also has highly exalted Him and given Him the name which is above every name, that at the name of Jesus every knee should bow, . . . and that every tongue should confess that Jesus Christ is Lord" (Phil. 2:8–11).

The "name which is above every name" is probably the title "Lord" in the highest sense that it can bear. The words echo Isaiah 45:23, where the God of Israel swears, "To Me every knee shall bow, every tongue shall take an oath [or, make confession]." In the Old Testament passage the God of Israel denies to any other being the right to receive the worship that belongs to Him alone. But in the passage from Philippians He readily shares that worship with the humiliated and exalted Jesus. More than that, He shares His own name with Him. When human beings honor Jesus as Lord, God is glorified.

God: If Jesus is called "Lord" in this supreme sense, it is not surprising that He occasionally is called "God" in the New Testament. Thomas, convinced that the risen Christ stood before him, abandoned his doubts with the confession, "My Lord and my God!" (John 20:28).

But the classic text is John 1:1. John declared that the Word existed not only "in the beginning," where He was "with God," but also actually "was God." This is the Word that became incarnate as real man in Jesus Christ, without ceasing to be what He had been from eternity. The Word was God in the sense that the Father shared with Him the fullness of His own nature. The Father remained, in a technical phrase of traditional theology, "the fountain of deity." But from that fountain the Son drew in unlimited measure.

The Bible thus presents Christ as altogether God and altogether man—the perfect mediator between God and mankind because He partakes fully of the nature of both.

The Work of Christ: The work of Christ has often been stated in relation to His threefold office of prophet, priest, and king. As prophet, He is the perfect spokesman of God to the world, fully revealing God's character and will. As priest, Jesus has offered to God by His death a sufficient sacrifice for the sins of the world. Now, on the basis of that sacrifice, He exercises a ministry of intercession on behalf of His people. As king, He is "the ruler over the kings of the earth" (Rev. 1:5)—the One to whose rule the whole world is subject.

The work of Jesus can be discussed in terms of past, present, and future.

The Finished Work of Christ: By the "finished" work of Christ is meant the work of atonement or redemption for the human race that He completed by His death on the cross. This work is so perfect in itself that it requires neither repetition nor addition. Because of this work, He is called "Savior of the world" (1 John 4:14) and "the Lamb of God who takes away the sin of the world" (John 1:29).

In the Bible sin is viewed in several ways: as an offense against God, which requires a pardon; as defilement, which requires cleansing; as slavery, which cries out for emancipation; as a debt, which must be canceled; as defeat, which must be reversed by victory; and as estrangement, which must be set right by reconciliation. However sin is viewed, it is through the work of Christ that the remedy is provided. He has procured the pardon, the cleansing, the emancipation, the cancellation, the victory, and the reconciliation. When sin is viewed as an offense against God, it is also interpreted as a breach of His law. The law of God, like law in general, involves penalties against the lawbreaker. So strict are these penalties that they appear to leave no avenue of escape for the lawbreaker. The apostle Paul, conducting his argument along these lines, quoted one uncompromising declaration from the Old Testament: "Cursed is everyone who does not continue in all things which are written in the book of the law, to do them" (Deut. 27:26; Gal. 3:10).

But Paul goes on to say that Christ, by enduring the form of death on which a divine curse was expressly pronounced in the law, absorbed in His own person the curse invoked on the lawbreaker: "Christ has redeemed us from the curse of the law, having become a curse for us (for it is written, 'Cursed is everyone who hangs on a tree')" (Deut. 21:23; Gal. 3:13).

Since Christ partakes of the nature of both God and humanity, He occupies a unique status with regard to them. He represents God to humanity, and He also represents humanity to God. God is both Lawgiver and Judge; Christ represents Him. The human family has put itself in the position of the lawbreaker; Christ has voluntarily undertaken to represent us. The Judge has made Himself one with the guilty in order to bear our guilt. It is ordinarily out of the question for one person to bear the guilt of others. But when the one person is the representative human being, Jesus Christ, bearing the guilt of those whom He represents, the case is different. In the hour of His death, Christ offered His life to God on behalf of mankind. The perfect life that He offered was acceptable to God. The salvation secured through the giving up of that life is God's free gift to mankind in Christ. When the situation is viewed in terms of a law court, one might speak of the accused party as being acquitted. But the term preferred in the New Testament, especially in the apostle Paul's writings, is the more positive word *justified*. Paul goes on to the limit of daring in speaking of God as "Him who justifies the ungodly" (Rom. 4:5). God can be so described because "Christ died for the ungodly" (Rom. 5:6). Those who are united by faith to Him are "justified" in Him. As Paul explained elsewhere, "He made Him who knew no sin to be sin for us, that we might become the righteousness of God in Him" (2 Cor. 5:21). The work of Christ, seen from this point of view, is to set humanity in a right relationship with God.

When sin is considered as defilement that requires cleansing, the most straightforward affirmation is that "the blood of Jesus Christ His Son cleanses us from all sin" (1 John 1:7). The effect of His death is to purify a conscience that has been polluted by sin. The same thought is expressed by the writer of the book of Hebrews. He speaks of various materials that were prescribed by Israel's ceremonial law to deal with forms of ritual pollution, which was an external matter. Then he asks, "How much more shall the blood of Christ, who through the eternal Spirit offered Himself without spot to God, purge your conscience from dead works to serve the living God?" (Heb. 9:14). Spiritual defilement calls for spiritual cleansing, and this is what the death of Christ has accomplished.

When sin is considered as slavery from which the slave must be set free, then the death of Christ is spoken of as a ransom or a means of redemption. Jesus Himself declared that He came "to give His life a ransom for many" (Mark 10:45). Paul not only spoke of sin as slavery; he also personified sin as a slaveowner who compels his slaves to obey his evil orders. When they are set free from his control by the death of Christ to enter the service of God, they find this service, by contrast, to be perfect freedom.

The idea of sin as a debt that must be canceled is based on the teaching of Jesus. In Jesus' parable of the creditor and the two debtors (Luke 7:40–43), the creditor forgave them both when they could make no repayment. But the debtor who owed the larger sum, and therefore had more cause to love the forgiving creditor, represented the woman whose "sins, which are many, are forgiven" (Luke 7:47). This is similar to Paul's reference to God as "having canceled the bond which stood against us with its legal demands" (Col. 2:14, NRSV).

Paul's words in Colossians 2:15 speak of the "principalities and powers" as a personification of the hostile forces in the world that have conquered men and women and held them as prisoners of war. There was no hope of successful resistance against them until Christ confronted them. It looked as if they had conquered Him too, but on the cross He conquered death itself, along with all other hostile forces. In His victory all who believe in Him have a share: "Thanks be to God, who gives us the victory through our Lord Jesus Christ" (1 Cor. 15:57).

Sin is also viewed as estrangement, or alienation, from God. In this case, the saving work of Christ includes the reconciliation of sinners to God. The initiative in this reconciling work is taken by God: "God was in Christ reconciling the world to Himself" (2 Cor. 5:19). God desires the well-being of sinners; so He sends Christ as the agent of His reconciling grace to them (Col. 1:20).

Those who are separated from God by sin are also estranged from one another. Accordingly, the work of Christ that reconciles sinners to God also brings them together as human beings. Hostile divisions of humanity have peace with one another through Him. Paul celebrated the way in which the work of Christ overcame the mutual estrangement of Jews and Gentiles: "For He Himself is our peace, who has made both one, and has broken down the middle wall of division between us" (Eph. 2:14).

When the work of Christ is pictured in terms of an atoning sacrifice, it is God who takes the initiative. The word *propitiation*, used in this connection in older English versions of the Bible (Rom. 3:25; 1 John 2:2; 4:10), does not mean that sinful men and women have to do something to appease God or turn away His anger; neither does it mean that Christ died on the cross to persuade God to be merciful to sinners. It is the nature of God to be a pardoning God. He has revealed His pardoning nature above all in the person and work of Christ. This saving initiative is equally and eagerly shared by Christ: He gladly cooperates with the Father's purpose for the redemption of the world.

Jesus Justus [Je'sus Jus'tus]—(Col. 4:11) See Justus.

Jether [Je'ther], *abundance*—Five Old Testament men:

1. A descendant of Judah; son of Ezra (1 Chron. 4:17).

2. Gideon's first son. He was commanded by Gideon to slay two kings of Midian, but he could not bring himself to do it because of youthful fears (Judg. 8:20–21).

3. Son of Zophah of Asher; probably the same as Ithran (1 Chron. 7:37).

4. Son of Jada and a descendant of Hezron of Judah (1 Chron. 2:32).

5. Father of Amasa (1 Kings 2:5).

Jetheth [Je'theth], *a nail*—A chief of Edom (Gen. 36:40; 1 Chron. 1:51).

Jethlah [Jeth'lah]—See Ithlah.

Jethro [Jeth'ro], *his excellency*—A priest of Midian, the father-in-law of Moses (Ex. 3:1), also called Reuel (Ex. 2:18), Hobab (Judg. 4:11), and Raguel (Num. 10:29; Reuel, NIV).

After Moses fled from Egypt into the region of the Sinai Peninsula, he married one of Jethro's daughters, Zipporah (Ex. 2:21). Then Moses tended Jethro's sheep for forty years (Acts 7:30) before his experience at the burning bush (Ex. 3), when he was called to lead the Israelites from bondage in Egypt.

During the exodus, Jethro and the rest of Moses' family joined Moses in the wilderness near Mount Sinai (Ex. 18:5). During this visit, Jethro taught Moses to delegate his responsibilities. He noted that Moses was doing all the work himself and advised Moses to decide the difficult cases and to secure able men to make decisions in lesser matters (Ex. 18:13–23). Following this meeting, Jethro departed from the Israelites.

Jetur [Je'tur], *enclosed*—A son of Ishmael (Gen. 25:15). The name also signifies his descendants, the Ituraeans (1 Chron. 1:31; 5:19). See Ituraea.

Jeuel [Jeu'el], *God sweeps away*—Three Old Testament men:

1. A Levite who assisted Hezekiah, king of Judah in his work of reform (2 Chron. 29:13); also called Jeiel.

2. A descendant of Zerah of Judah. After the Exile, he and 690 of his people lived in Jerusalem (1 Chron. 9:6).

3. One of those who returned with Ezra (Ezra 8:13); also called Jeiel (KJV).

Jeush, Jehush [Je'ush, Je'hush], *assembler*—Five Old Testament men:

1. A son of Esau and Aholibamah and a chief in Edom (Gen. 36:5, 18).

2. Son of Shimei, a Levite of the family of Gershon (1 Chron. 23:10–11).

3. Son of Bilhan of Benjamin (1 Chron. 7:10).

4. A descendant of Jonathan (1 Chron. 8:39), also called Jehush.

5. Son of Rehoboam (2 Chron. 11:19).

Jeuz [Je'uz], *counsellor*—Son of Shaharaim and Hodesh of Benjamin (1 Chron. 8:10).

Jew [Jew]—A descendant of Judah, of the tribe of Judah, and later of the kingdom of Judah (2 Kings 16:6; 25:25). The word came into use after the captivity of Judah and denoted anyone returned from the captivity (Est. 2:5; Matt. 2:2).

Jewess [Jew'ess]—A female of the tribe of Judah (1 Chron. 4:18) or of the Hebrew race (Acts 16:1; 24:24). See Jehudijah.

Jewish [Jew'ish]—(Titus 1:14) See Jew.

Jewry [Jew'ry], *archaic, Norman French origin, Old English*— The land of Judea (Dan. 5:13).

Jezaniah [Jez·a·ni′ah], *Jehovah has listened*—In 2 Kings 25:23 he is called Jaazaniah, son of Hoshaiah, a Maacathite (Jer. 40:8; 42:1). After the fall of Jerusalem, he and his men offered allegiance to Gedaliah.

Jezebel [Jez′e·bel], *there is no prince*—The name of two women in the Bible:

1. The wife of Ahab, king of Israel, daughter of Eth-baal and mother of Ahaziah, Jehoram, and Athaliah (1 Kings 16:31). Jezebel was a tyrant who corrupted her husband, as well as the nation, by promoting pagan worship.

She was reared in Sidon, a commercial city on the coast of the Mediterranean Sea, known for its idolatry and vice. When she married Ahab and moved to Jezreel, a city that served the Lord, she decided to turn it into a city that worshipped Baal, a Phoenician god.

The wicked, idolatrous queen soon became the power behind the throne. Obedient to her wishes, Ahab erected a sanctuary for Baal and supported hundreds of pagan prophets (1 Kings 18:19).

When the prophets of the Lord opposed Jezebel, she had them "massacred" (1 Kings 18:4, 13). After Elijah defeated her prophets on Mount Carmel, she swore revenge. She was such a fearsome figure that the great prophet was afraid and "ran for his life" (1 Kings 19:3).

After her husband, Ahab, was killed in battle, Jezebel reigned for 10 years through her sons Ahaziah and Joram (or Jehoram). These sons were killed by Jehu, who also disposed of Jezebel by having her thrown from the palace window. In fulfillment of the prediction of the prophet Elijah, Jezebel was trampled by the horses and eaten by the dogs (1 Kings 21:19). Only Jezebel's skull, feet, and the palms of her hands were left to bury when the dogs were finished (2 Kings 9:30–37).

2. A prophetess of Thyatira who enticed the Christians in that church "to commit sexual immorality and to eat things sacrificed to idols" (Rev. 2:20). John probably called this woman "Jezebel" because of her similarity to Ahab's idolatrous wicked queen.

Jezer [Je′zer], *formation*—Son of Naphtali (Gen. 46:24; Num. 26:49; 1 Chron. 7:13).

Jezerites [Je′zer·ites]—The descendants of Jezer, son of Naphtali (Num. 26:49).

Jeziah [Je·zi'ah]—See Izziah.

Jeziel [Je'zi·el], *assembly of God*—Son of Azmaveth a Benjamite (1 Chron. 12:3).

Jezliah [Jez·li'ah]—See Izliah.

Jezrahiah [Jez·ra·hi'ah], *Jehovah will shine*—One who was placed over the singers (Neh. 12:42).

Jezreel [Jez'reel], *God scatters*—The name of two people, two cities, and a valley or plain in the Old Testament:

1. A man of the tribe of Judah, descendant of Hur (1 Chron. 4:3).

2. A symbolic name given by the prophet Hosea to his oldest son (Hos. 1:4). The name Jezreel signified the great slaughter that God would bring on the house of Jehu because of the violent acts he had committed (2 Kings 9).

3. A city in the hill country of Judah, near Jokdeam and Zanoah (Josh. 15:56). Apparently David obtained one of his wives, Ahinoam, from this place (1 Sam. 25:43). The site is probably present-day Khirbet Terrama on the plain of Dibleh.

4. A city in northern Israel, on the plain of Jezreel about 90 kilometers (56 miles) north of Jerusalem. The city was in the territory of Issachar, but it belonged to the tribe of Manasseh (Josh. 19:18). It was between Megiddo and Beth-shean (1 Kings 4:12) and between Mount Carmel and Mount Gilboa. It was the camping place of the forces of the Israelites in Saul's last battle with the Philistines (1 Sam. 29:1). Later, the palace of King Ahab of Israel was situated in Jezreel. Here Jezebel and all the others associated with Ahab's reign were assassinated by the followers of Jehu (2 Kings 9–10). The city of Jezreel has been identified with modern Zer'in.

5. The Old Testament name of the entire valley that separates Samaria from Galilee (Josh. 17:16). Some authors now refer to the western part of this valley as Esdraelon (Greek for "Jezreel"), while the name Jezreel is restricted to the eastern part of the valley.

The entire valley is the major corridor through the rugged Palestinian hills. It was a crossroads of two major routes: one leading from the Mediterranean Sea on the west to the Jordan River valley on the east, the other leading from Syria, Phoenicia, and Galilee in the north to the hill country of Judah and to the land of Egypt on the south. Throughout history, the valley of Jezreel has been a major battlefield of nations.

Jezreelite [Jez′reel·ite]—An inhabitant of Jezreel. Naboth, who had a vineyard in the valley of Jezreel, is called a Jezreelite (1 Kings 21:1, 4, 6–7, 15–16). Jezebel, Ahab's wicked wife, arranged to have Naboth killed in order to gratify Ahab's desire to own the vineyard.

Jezreelitess [Jez′reel·it·ess]—A woman of Jezreel. Ahinoam, one of David's wives, was a Jezreelitess (1 Sam. 27:3; 30:5; 2 Sam. 2:2; 3:2; 1 Chron. 3:1).

Jibsam [Jib′sam], *pleasant*—One of the sons of Tola, a descendant of Issachar (1 Chron. 7:2).

Jidlaph [Jid′laph], *tearful*—Son of Nahor and Milcah (Gen. 22:22) and nephew of Abraham.

Jimna [Jim′na]—See Imnah.

Jimnah [Jim′nah]—See Imnah.

Jiphtah [Jiph′tah]—See Iphtah.

Jiphthah-el [Jiph′thah-el]—See Iphtah-el.

Jishui [Jish′u·i]—See Ishui.

Jisshiah [Jis·shi′ah]—See Isshiah.

Jithlah [Jith′lah]—See Ithlah.

Jithra [Jith′ra]—See Ithra.

Jithran [Jith′ran]—See Ithran.

Jizliah [Jiz′li·ah]—See Izliah.

Jizri [Jiz′ri]—See Izri.

Joab [Jo′ab], *the Lord is father*—The name of three men and one village in the Old Testament:

1. One of the three sons of Zeruiah (2 Sam. 2:13; 8:16; 14:1; 17:25; 23:18, 37; 1 Kings 1:7; 2:5, 22; 1 Chron. 11:6, 39; 18:15; 26:28; 27:24) who

was David's sister (or half sister). Joab was the "general" or commander-in-chief of David's army (2 Sam. 5:8; 1 Chron. 11:6; 27:34).

Joab's father is not mentioned by name, but his tomb was at Bethlehem (2 Sam. 2:32). Joab's two brothers were Abishai and Asahel. When Asahel was killed by Abner (2 Sam. 2:18–23), Joab got revenge by killing Abner (2 Sam. 3:22–27).

When David and his army went to Jerusalem, in an attempt to capture that city (then called Jebus), he said, "Whoever attacks the Jebusites first shall be chief and captain" (1 Chron. 11:6). Joab led the assault at the storming of the Jebusite stronghold on Mount Zion, apparently climbing up into the city by way of a water shaft. The city was captured and Joab was made the general of David's army (2 Sam. 5:8).

Other military exploits by Joab were achieved against the Edomites (2 Sam. 8:13–14; 1 Kings 11:15) and the Ammonites (2 Sam. 10:6–14; 11:1–27; 1 Chron. 19:6–15; 20:1–3). His character was deeply stained, as was David's, by his participation in the death of Uriah the Hittite (2 Sam. 11:14–25). In putting Absalom to death (2 Sam. 18:1–14), he apparently acted from a sense of duty.

When Absalom revolted against David, Joab remained loyal to David. Soon afterward, however, David gave command of his army to Amasa, Joab's cousin (2 Sam. 19:13; 20:1–13). Overcome by jealous hate, Joab killed Amasa (2 Sam. 20:8–13).

Another of David's sons, Adonijah, aspired to the throne, refusing to accept the fact that Solomon was not only David's choice but also the Lord's choice as the new king. Joab joined the cause of Adonijah against Solomon. Joab was killed by Benaiah, in accordance with Solomon's command and David's wishes. Joab fled to the tabernacle of the Lord, where he grasped the horns of the altar. Benaiah then struck him down with a sword. Joab was buried "in his own house in the wilderness" (1 Kings 2:34).

2. A village apparently situated in Judah near Bethlehem (1 Chron. 2:54). The KJV translation, "Ataroth, the house of Joab," is better rendered by the NKJV, "Atroth Beth Joab."

3. A son of Seraiah and grandson of Kenaz (1 Chron. 4:13–14). He was the "father of Ge-Harashim" (1 Chron. 4:14), or the founder of a place in Judah called the "Valley of Craftsmen."

4. A man of the house of Pahath-moab, some of whose descendants returned from the Exile with Zerubbabel (Ezra 2:6; 8:9; Neh. 7:11).

Joah [Jo'ah], *Jehovah is brother*—Four Old Testament men:

1. Son of Zimmah, a Levite of the family of Gershom (1 Chron. 6:21). It may have been he who aided Hezekiah in his reformation (2 Chron. 29:12).

2. Son of Obed-edom, a porter of the sanctuary in the time of David (1 Chron. 26:4).

3. A son of Asaph, the recorder of Hezekiah, king of Judah (2 Kings 18:18, 26; Isa. 36:3, 11, 22).

4. Son of Joahaz. He was recorder under Josiah (2 Chron. 34:8).

Joahaz [Jo'a·haz], *Jehovah holds*—Father of Joah, the recorder of King Josiah (2 Chron. 34:8).

Joanan [Jo·a'nan]—See Joannas.

Joanna [Jo·an'na], *Jehovah is a gracious giver* or *gift of God* or *grace*—

1. The wife of Chuza, Herod's steward (Luke 8:3; 24:10).

2. Variant of Joannas.

Joannas [Jo·an'nas]—Son of Rhesa, an ancestor of Christ (Luke 3:27).

Joash, Jehoash [Jo'ash, Je·ho'ash], *the Lord supports*—The name of eight men in the Old Testament:

1. The father of Gideon of the family of Abiezer of the tribe of Manasseh (Judg. 6:11). Apparently Joash was an idolater who built an altar to Baal on his land. Gideon pulled down his father's altar, and the men of the city of Ophrah demanded that Joash put his son to death. But Joash refused, saying, "If he [Baal] is a god, let him plead for himself" (Judg. 6:31). After this event, Joash called his son Jerubbaal, which means "Let Baal plead" (Judg. 6:32).

2. A man who was commanded by Ahab, king of Israel, to imprison the prophet Micaiah because Micaiah had advised aginst the plan to seize Ramoth Gilead (1 Kings 22:26).

3. The eighth king of Judah; he was a son of King Ahaziah (2 Kings 11:2) by Zibiah of Beersheba (2 Kings 12:1). Joash was seven years old when he became king, and he reigned forty years in Jerusalem (2 Chron. 24:1), from about 835 B.C. until 796 B.C. He is also called Jehoash (2 Kings 11:21).

After Ahaziah died, his grandmother, Athaliah, killed all the royal heirs to the throne. But God spared Joash through his aunt, Jehosheba, who hid him for six years in the house of the Lord (2 Kings 11:2-3). When Joash reached the age of seven, Jehoiada the priest arranged for his coronation as king (2 Kings 11:4-16).

Early in his reign, Joash repaired the temple and restored true religion to Judah, destroying Baal worship (2 Kings 11:18-21). But the king who began so well faltered upon the loss of his advisor, Jehoiada. After Jehoiada died, Joash allowed idolatry to grow (2 Chron. 24:18). He even went so far as to have Zechariah, the son of Jehoiada, stoned to death for rebuking him (2 Chron. 24:20-22). God's judgment came quickly in the form of a Syrian invasion, which resulted in the wounding of Joash (2 Chron. 24:23-24). He was then killed by his own servants.

4. The thirteenth king of Israel; he was the son and successor of Jehoahaz, king of Israel, and was the grandson of Jehu, king of Israel. He is also called Jehoash (2 Kings 13:10, 25; 14:8-17). Joash reigned in Samaria for sixteen years (2 Kings 13:9-10), from about 798 B.C. to 782/81 B.C. Israel was revived during the reign of Joash (2 Kings 13:7), following a long period of suffering at the hands of the Syrians. But while achieving political success, Joash suffered spiritual bankruptcy: "He did evil in the sight of the LORD; he did not depart from all the sins of Jeroboam the son of Nebat, who had made Israel sin; but he walked in them" (2 Kings 13:11). He was succeeded by his son Jeroboam II, whose reign was the most brilliant of the kingdom of Israel.

5. A descendant of Shelah, of the family of Judah (1 Chron. 4:22).

6. A descendant of Becher, of the family of Benjamin (1 Chron. 7:8).

7. Son of Shemaah, a Benjamite of Gibeah. A commander of the warriors who left Saul and joined David's army at Ziklag (1 Chron. 12:3).

8. An officer in charge of David's olive oil supplies (1 Chron. 27:28).

Joatham [Jo·ath′am]—See Jotham.

Job [Job], *hated*—The name of two men in the Old Testament:

1. The third son of Issachar, and founder of a tribal family, the Jashubites (Gen. 46:13). He is also called Jashub (Num. 26:24; 1 Chron. 7:1).

2. The central personality of the book of Job. He was noted for his perseverance (James 5:11) and unwavering faith in God, in spite of his suffering and moments of frustration and doubt. All the facts known about Job are contained in the Old Testament book that bears his name. He is described as "a man in the land of Uz" (Job 1:1) and "the greatest of all the people of the East" (Job 1:3). Uz is probably a name for a region in Edom (Jer. 25:20; Lam. 4:21).

A prosperous man, Job had 7,000 sheep, 3,000 camels, 500 yoke of oxen, 500 female donkeys, and a large household, consisting of seven sons and three daughters. He was also "blameless and upright, and one who feared God and shunned evil" (Job 1:1).

Satan suggested to God that Job would remain righteous as long as it was financially profitable for him to do so. Then the Lord permitted Satan to test Job's faith in God. Blow after blow fell upon Job: his children, his servants, and his livestock were taken from him and he was left penniless. Nevertheless, "In all this Job did not sin nor charge God with wrong" (Job 1:22).

Satan continued his assault by sneering, "Touch his bone and his flesh, and he will surely curse You to Your face!" (Job 2:5). The Lord allowed Satan to afflict Job with painful boils from the soles of his feet to the crown of his head, so that Job sat in the midst of ashes and scraped his sores with a piece of pottery. "Do you still hold fast to your integrity?" his wife asked him. "Curse God and die!" (Job 2:9). But Job refused to curse God. "Shall we indeed accept good from God," he replied, "and shall we not accept adversity?" (Job 2:10).

Job's faith eventually triumphed over all adversity, and he was finally restored to more than his former prosperity. He had 14,000 sheep, 6,000 camels, 1,000 yoke of oxen, and 1,000 female donkeys. He also had seven sons and three daughters. He died at a ripe old age (Job 42:12–13, 16–17). He is later mentioned by Ezekiel (Ezek. 14:14, 16, 20).

Jobab [Jo'bab], *howling*—Four Old Testament men:

1. A tribe of Arabia descended from Joktan (Gen. 10:29; 1 Chron. 1:23).

2. Son of Zerah of Bozrah, a king of Edom (Gen. 36:33; 1 Chron. 1:44–45).

3. One of the kings that formed the northern confederacy against Joshua. He was defeated in the battle of Merom (Josh. 11:1; 12:19).

4. A son of Shaharaim of Benjamin (1 Chron. 8:9, 18).

Jochebed [Joch'e·bed], *Jehovah is glorious*—A daughter of Levi. She married Amram, her nephew, and was the mother of Miriam, Aaron, and Moses (Ex. 6:20; Num. 26:59).

Joda [Jo'da]—See Judah.

Joed [Jo'ed], *Jehovah is witness*—Son of Pedaiah (Neh. 11:7).

Joel [Jo'el], *the Lord is God*—The name of fourteen men in the Old Testament:

1. The oldest son of Samuel the prophet (1 Sam. 8:2; 1 Chron. 6:28; Vashni, KJV) and the father of Heman the singer (1 Chron. 6:33). He is called Vashni in 1 Chronicles 6:28.

2. A prince of the tribe of Simeon, one of those who settled in a valley of Gedor (1 Chron. 4:35).

3. The father of Shemaiah, of the tribe of Reuben (1 Chron. 5:4).

4. A chief of the tribe of Gad and a chief in the land of Bashan (1 Chron. 5:12).

5. A Levite of the family of Kohath, ancestor of Samuel the prophet (1 Chron. 6:36).

6. A chief of the tribe of Issachar, son of Izrahiah (1 Chron. 7:3).

7. Brother of Nathan and one of David's mighty men (1 Chron. 11:38).

8. A Levite, chief of the family of Gershom. At the head of 130 of his brethren he helped bring the ark of the covenant from the house of Obed-edom to Jerusalem (1 Chron. 15:7). He was probably the son of Laadan (1 Chron. 23:8).

9. A keeper of the temple treasuries in David's time (1 Chron. 26:22).

10. A son of Pedaiah and chief of the half-tribe of Manasseh, who lived during the time of David (1 Chron. 27:20).

11. Son of Azariah, a Levite of the family of Kohath, who helped cleanse the temple during the reign of King Hezekiah of Judah (2 Chron. 29:12).

12. A son of Nebo who divorced his pagan wife after the captivity (Ezra 10:43).

13. Son of Zichri, an overseer of the Benjamites in Jerusalem in Nehemiah's government (Neh. 11:9).

14. Son of Pethuel, an Old Testament prophet and author of the book of Joel. A citizen of Jerusalem, he spoke often of the priests and their duties (Joel 1:9, 13–14, 16). For this reason, many scholars believe he may have been a temple prophet. He also had an ear for nature (Joel 1:4–7), and included imagery from agriculture and the natural world in his messages.

Joelah [Jo·e′lah], *may he avail*—Son of Jeroham (1 Chron. 12:7).

Joezer [Jo·e′zer], *Jehovah is help*—A Korahite who joined David at Ziklag (1 Chron. 12:6).

Jogbehah [Jog′be·hah], *lofty*—A city of the tribe of Gad (Num. 32:35).

Jogli [Jog′li], *exiled*—Father of Bukki (Num. 34:22).

Joha [Jo′ha], *Jehovah gives life*—Two Old Testament men:
  1. A son of Beriah of Benjamin, and a tribal chief (1 Chron. 8:16).
  2. Son of Shimri, a Tizite; one of David's soldiers (1 Chron. 11:45).

Johanan [Jo·ha′nan], *Jehovah is gracious*—Several men of the Old Testament:
  1. Son of Kareah, a captain (2 Kings 25:22–23; Jer. 40:8–9).
  2. King Josiah's eldest son (1 Chron. 3:15).
  3. A son of Elioenai (1 Chron. 3:24).
  4. A man who executed the high priest's office (1 Chron. 6:10).
  5. A Benjamite who joined David at Ziklag (1 Chron. 12:4).
  6. A Gadite captain of David's forces (1 Chron. 12:12, 14).
  7. Father of Azariah, of Ephraim; he demanded that those taken from Judah be returned (2 Chron. 28:12).
  8. Son of Hakkatan. He and 110 others were of the company of Ezra that returned from Babylon (Ezra 8:12).
  9. Son of Eliashib (Ezra 10:6).
  10. Son of Tobiah, enemy of Nehemiah; he married a Jewess (Neh. 6:18).
  11. Grandson of Eliashib, a high priest (Neh. 12:22). In verse 11 he is called Jonathan.

John [John], *Jehovah is gracious*—
  1. John Mark, writer of the second gospel (Acts 12:12, 25). See Mark, John.

2. A Jewish official who opposed Peter and John in association with Caiaphas, Annas, and Alexander (Acts 4:6).

3. John the apostle.

4. John the Baptist.

John Mark [John Mark]—The author of the gospel of Mark.

John the Apostle—One of Jesus' disciples, the son of Zebedee, and the brother of James. Before his call by Jesus, John was a fisherman, along with his father and brother (Matt. 4:18–22; Mark 1:16–20). His mother was probably Salome (Matt. 27:56; Mark 15:40), who may have been a sister of Mary (John 19:25), the mother of Jesus.

Although it is not certain that Salome and Mary were sisters, if it were so it would make James and John cousins of Jesus. This would help explain Salome's forward request of Jesus on behalf of her sons (Matt. 20:20–28). The Zebedee family apparently lived in Capernaum on the north shore of the Sea of Galilee (Mark 1:21). The family must have been prosperous, because the father owned a boat and hired servants (Mark 1:19–20). Salome the mother provided for Jesus out of her substance (Mark 15:40–41; Luke 8:3). John must have been the younger of the two brothers, for he is always mentioned second to James in the gospels of Matthew, Mark, and Luke.

The brothers Zebedee were called by Jesus after His baptism (Mark 1:19–20). This happened immediately after the call of two other brothers, Simon Peter and Andrew (Mark 1:16–18), with whom they may have been in partnership (Luke 5:10). Three of the four—Peter, James, and John—eventually became Jesus' most intimate disciples. They were present when Jesus healed the daughter of Jairus (Mark 5:37; Luke 8:51). They witnessed His transfiguration (Matt. 17:1–2; Mark 9:2; Luke 9:28–29), as well as His agony in Gethsemane (Matt. 26:37; Mark 14:33). Along with Peter, John was entrusted by Jesus with preparations for the Passover supper (Luke 22:8).

James and John must have contributed a headstrong element to Jesus' band of followers, because Jesus nicknamed them "Sons of Thunder" (Mark 3:17). On one occasion (Luke 9:51–56), when a Samaritan village refused to accept Jesus, the two offered to call down fire in revenge, as the prophet Elijah had once done (2 Kings 1:10, 12). On another occasion, they earned the anger of their fellow disciples by asking if they could sit on Jesus' right and left hands in glory (Mark 10:35–45).

Following the ascension of Jesus, John continued in a prominent position of leadership among the disciples (Acts 1:13). He was present when Peter healed the lame man in the temple. Together with Peter he bore witness before the Sanhedrin to his faith in Jesus Christ. The boldness of their testimony brought the hostility of the Sanhedrin (Acts 3–4). When the apostles in Jerusalem received word of the evangelization of Samaria, they sent Peter and John to investigate whether the conversions were genuine (Acts 8:14–25). This was a curious thing to do. The Samaritans had long been suspect in the eyes of the Jews (John 4:9). John himself had once favored the destruction of a Samaritan village (Luke 9:51–56). That he was present on this mission suggests he had experienced a remarkable change.

In these episodes Peter appears as the leader and spokesman for the pair, but John's presence on such errands indicates his esteem by the growing circle of disciples. After the execution of his brother James by Herod Agrippa I, between A.D. 42–44 (Acts 12:1–2), John is not heard of again in Acts. Paul's testimony to John as one of the "pillars," along with Peter and James (the Lord's brother, Gal. 2:9), however, reveals that John continued to hold a position of respect and leadership in the early church.

As might be expected of one of Jesus' three closest disciples, John became the subject of an active and varied church tradition. Tertullian (about A.D. 160–220) said that John ended up in Rome, where he was "plunged, unhurt, into boiling oil." A much later tradition believed that both James and John were martyred. The dominant tradition, however, was that the apostle John moved to Ephesus in Asia Minor, and that from there he was banished to the island of Patmos (during Domitian's reign, A.D. 81–96). Tradition also held that he returned later to Ephesus, where he died some time after Trajan became emperor in A.D. 98.

Stories that John reclaimed a juvenile delinquent, raised a dead man, and opposed the Gnostic heretic Cerinthus survive from this era in his life. It was also the general opinion of the time that from Ephesus John composed the five writings that bear his name in the New Testament (gospel of John; 1, 2, and 3 John; and Revelation).

Only the Revelation identifies its author as John (1:1, 9). The second and third epistles of John identify the author as "the elder" (2 John 1; 3 John 1). Although 1 John and the gospel of John do not name their author, he can be none other than "the elder," because style and content in these writings are unmistakably related. It may be, as tradition asserts, that the apostle John wrote all five documents. It appears more likely, however, that four of the five writings were actually penned not by John the apostle but by John the elder, a disciple and friend of John's who relied directly on the apostle's testimony as he wrote the documents. This would explain those passages in the gospel that speak about the beloved disciple (who presumably is John the apostle; John 19:35; 21:24), as well as the reference to "the elder" in 2 and 3 John. The Revelation, however, was probably written directly by the apostle John himself.

John the Baptist—Forerunner of Jesus; a moral reformer and preacher of messianic hope. According to Luke 1:36, Elizabeth and Mary, the mothers of John and Jesus, were either blood relatives or close kinswomen. Luke adds that both John and Jesus were announced, set apart, and named by the angel Gabriel even before their birth.

The son of Zacharias. His mother, Elizabeth, was a descendant of Aaron (Luke 1:5) and a cousin of the Virgin Mary. His parents lived in the hill country of Judea. When the angel informed Zacharias that a son was to be born to them, he instructed him to name the baby John (Luke 1:8–17).

As is true of Jesus, practically nothing is known of John's boyhood, except that he "grew and became strong in spirit" (Luke 1:80). The silence of his early years, however, was broken by his thundering call to repentance some time around A.D. 28–29, shortly before Jesus began His ministry. Matthew reports that the place where John preached was the wilderness of Judea (3:1). It is likely that he also preached in Perea, east of the Jordan River. Perea, like Galilee, lay within the jurisdiction of Herod Antipas, under whom John was later arrested.

The four Gospels are unanimous in their report that John lived "in the wilderness." There he was raised (Luke 1:80) and was called by God (Luke 3:2), and there he preached (Mark 1:4) until his execution. The wilderness—a vast badland of crags, wind, and heat—was the place where God had dwelled with His people after the exodus. Ever since, it had been the place of religious hope for Israel. John called the people away from the comforts of their homes and cities and out into the wilderness, where they might meet God.

The conviction that God was about to begin a new work among this unprepared people broke upon John with the force of a desert storm. He was called to put on the prophet's hairy mantle with the resolve and urgency of Elijah himself. Not only did he dress like Elijah, in camel's hair and leather belt (2 Kings 1:8; Mark 1:6), he understood his ministry to be one of reform and preparation, just as Elijah did (Luke 1:17). In the popular belief of the time, it was believed that Elijah would return from heaven to prepare the way for the Messiah (Mal. 4:5–6). John reminded the people of Elijah because of his dress and behavior (Matt. 11:14; Mark 9:12–13).

John was no doubt as rugged as the desert itself. Nevertheless, his commanding righteousness drew large crowds to hear him. What they encountered from this "voice . . . crying in the wilderness" (Mark 1:3) was a call to moral renewal, baptism, and a messianic hope.

The bite of John's moral challenge is hard for us to appreciate today. His command to share clothing and food (Luke 3:11) was a painful jab at a society that was hungry to acquire material objects. When he warned the tax collectors not to take more money than they had coming to them (Luke 3:12–13), he exposed the greed that had drawn persons to such positions in the first place. And the soldiers, whom he told to be content with their wages, must have winced at the thought of not using their power to take advantage of the common people (Luke 3:14).

John's baptism was a washing, symbolizing moral regeneration, administered to each candidate only once. He criticized the people for presuming to be righteous and secure with God because they were children of Abraham (Matt. 3:9). John laid an ax to the root of this presumption. He warned that they, the Jews, would be purged and rejected unless they demonstrated fruits of repentance (Matt. 3:7–12).

John's effort at moral reform, symbolized by baptism, was his way of preparing Israel to meet God. He began his preaching with the words "Prepare the way of the Lord, make His paths straight" (Mark 1:3). He had a burning awareness of one who was to come after him who would baptize in fire and Spirit (Mark 1:7–8). John was a forerunner of this mightier one, a herald of the messianic hope that would dawn in Jesus.

John was a forerunner of Jesus not only in his ministry and message (Matt. 3:1; 4:17) but also in his death. Not until John's arrest did Jesus begin His ministry (Mark 1:14), and John's execution foreshadowed Jesus' similar fate. Imprisoned by Antipas in the fortress of Machaerus on the lonely hills east of the Dead Sea, John must have grown disillusioned by his own failure and the developing failure he sensed in Jesus' mission. He sent messengers to ask Jesus, "Are You the Coming One, or do we look for another?" (Matt. 11:3). John was eventually killed by a functionary of a puppet king who allowed himself to be swayed by a scheming wife, a loose daughter-in-law, and the people around him (Mark 6:14–29).

Josephus records that Herod arrested and executed John because he feared his popularity might lead to a revolt. The Gospels reveal it was because John spoke out against Herod's immoral marriage to Herodias, the wife of his brother Philip (Mark 6:17–19). The accounts are complementary, because John's moral righteousness must have fanned many a smoldering political hope to life.

Jesus said of John, "Among those born of women there has not risen one greater than John the Baptist" (Matt. 11:11). He was the last and greatest of the prophets (Matt. 11:13–14). Nevertheless, he stood, like Moses, on the threshold of the promised land. He did not enter the kingdom of God proclaimed by Jesus; and consequently, "he who is least in the kingdom of heaven is greater than he" (Matt. 11:11).

John's influence continued to live on after his death. When Paul went to Ephesus nearly thirty years later, he found a group of John's disciples (Acts 19:1–7). Some of his disciples must have thought of John in messianic terms. This compelled the author of the gospel of John, writing also from Ephesus some sixty years after the Baptist's death, to emphasize Jesus' superiority (John 1:19–27; 3:30).

Joiada [Joi′a·da], *Jehovah knows*—A high priest and the great-grandson of Jeshua (Neh. 12:10; 13:28).

Joiakim [Joi′a·kim], *Jehovah raises up*—A high priest, son of Jeshua and father of Eliashib (Neh. 12:10, 12, 21–26).

Joiarib, Jehoiarib [Joi′a·rib, Je·hoi′a·rib], *Jehovah defends*—Five Old Testament men:

1. A chief priest of the company of Zerubbabel that returned to Jerusalem from Babylon (Neh. 12:6–7).

2. One in Ezra's company returning to Jerusalem from Babylon who was sent to secure Levites and Nethinim for temple service (Ezra 8:16–17).

3. Son of Zechariah and father of Adaiah, a descendant of Judah (Neh. 11:5).

4. An Aaronite (1 Chron. 24:7).

5. Father of Jedaiah (Neh. 11:10).

Jokdeam [Jok′de·am], *burning of a people*—A town south of Hebron in the mountain region of Judah (Josh. 15:56).

Jokim [Jo′kim], *Jehovah raises up*—A descendant of Shelah of Judah (1 Chron. 4:22).

Jokmeam [Jok′me·am], *gathered by the people*—A town of Ephraim given to the Levites of the Kohath family (1 Chron. 6:66, 68). Kibzaim of Joshua 21:22 is thought to be its other name.

Jokneam [Jok′ne·am], *the people lament*—A city on the border of the territory of Zebulun (Josh. 12:22; 19:11).

Jokshan [Jok′shan], *a fowler*—Second son of Abraham and Keturah (Gen. 25:1–3).

Joktan [Jok′tan], *small*—He and Peleg were the two sons of Eber (Gen. 10:25, 29; 1 Chron. 1:19–23).

Joktheel [Jok′theel], *the blessedness of God*—

1. A town in the lowlands of Judah (Josh. 15:33, 38).

2. A name given to the town of Sela by Amaziah (2 Kings 14:7).

Jona [Jo′na]—Variant of Jonah.

Jonadab, Jehonadab [Jon′a·dab, Je·hon′a·dab], *Jehovah is bounteous*—

1. Son of Shimeah, David's brother (2 Sam. 13:3).

2. Son of Rechab (Jer. 35:6–7).

Jonah [Jo′nah], *a dove*—Two men in the Old Testament:

1. Father of Peter the apostle (Matt. 16:17; John 1:42; 21:15). See Bar-Jona.

2. The prophet who was first swallowed by a great fish before he obeyed God's command to preach repentance to the Assyrian city of Nineveh. Jonah was not always a reluctant spokesman for the Lord. He is the same prophet who predicted the remarkable expansion of Israel's territory during the reign of Jeroboam II (ruled about 793–753 B.C.;

2 Kings 14:25). This passage indicates that Jonah, the son of Amittai, was from Gath Hepher, a town in Zebulun in the northern kingdom of Israel.

While Jonah is described as a servant of the Lord in 2 Kings 14:25, he is a sad and somewhat tragic figure in the book bearing his name. It is a mark of the integrity and reliability of the Bible that a prophet like Jonah is described in such a candid manner. The natural tendency of human writers would be to obscure and hide such a character. But the Spirit of God presents valiant heroes along with petty people to illustrate truth, no matter how weak and unpleasant these characters may have been. We know nothing of Jonah after he returned to Israel from his preaching venture in Nineveh.

Jonam, Jonan [Jo'nam, Jo'nan], *Jehovah is a gracious giver*— Son of Eliakim and ancestor of Joseph (Luke 3:30).

Jonas [Jo'nas]—Variant of Jonah.

Jonathan [Jon'a·than], *the Lord has given*—The name of fourteen men in the Old Testament:

1. A Levite from Bethlehem in Judah (Judg. 17:7–9) who was employed by an Ephraimite named Micah. Jonathan became the priest at Micah's idol shrine in the mountains of Ephraim, which he was happy to do, for he paid well. When the tribe of the Danites took Micah's graven image, ephod, household idols, and molded image (Judg. 18:18), Jonathan went with them. They inquired of the Lord at the house of the priest, and then when the priest gave them a positive answer they were pleased. Upon returning from a successful raid, they stopped at Micah's house a second time, to make off with his valuable silver images. The priest at first protested, but when they invited him to return with them and continue as their priest, he was happy to accompany the idols and the Danites. Jonathan and the Danites settled in the newly captured city of Dan (formerly Laish), and he became their priest (Judg. 17–18).

2. The oldest son of King Saul and a close friend of David. The first time Jonathan is mentioned in Scripture he is described as a commander of 1,000 men (1 Sam. 13:2). When Jonathan attacked the Philistine garrison at Geba, his action brought swift retaliation by the Philistines, who subdued and humiliated the Israelites. But Jonathan and his armorbearer courageously attacked the Philistine garrison at Michmash and were successful. This action inspired the Israelites to overthrow their oppressors (1 Sam. 14:1–23). When Saul's army arrived he found the Philistines confused and demoralized (1 Sam. 14:1–14).

Perhaps the best-known fact about Jonathan is his close friendship with David, which began when David slew Goliath. It continued in the face of Saul's persecution of David (1 Sam. 18:1–4). He made a covenant with David (1 Sam. 18:3–4) and warned David of Saul's plot against his life (1 Sam. 19:1–2). When Saul sought David's life, Jonathan interceded on behalf of David, and Saul reinstated David to his good favor (1 Sam. 19:1–7). Jonathan's loyalty to David was proven time after time as he warned David of Saul's threats of vengeance (1 Sam. 20) and encouraged David in times of danger (1 Sam. 23:16, 18).

The tragic end for Jonathan came at Mount Gilboa when he, his father Saul, and two of his brothers were slain by the Philistines (1 Sam. 31:1–2; 1 Chron. 10:1–6). When David heard of this, he mourned and fasted (2 Sam. 1:12). He then composed a lamentation, the "Song of the Bow," in which he poured out his grief over the death of Saul and Jonathan (2 Sam. 1:17–27).

Because David loved Jonathan, he treated Jonathan's lame son, Mephibosheth, kindly (2 Sam. 9:1–13). As a final act of love and respect, David brought the bones of Saul and Jonathan from Jabesh-gilead and buried them "in the country of Benjamin in Zelah, in the tomb of Kish his father" (2 Sam. 21:12–14). In this way David honored God's anointed king, Saul, and recognized the loyal, unselfish love of his friend. The story of David and Jonathan is a good example of the unselfish nature of love.

3. A son of Abiathar, a high priest in David's time (2 Sam. 15:27, 36; 17:17, 20). During Absalom's rebellion, when David and his supporters were forced to flee from Jerusalem, Jonathan relayed messages to David about developments in Jerusalem. He brought the news that Solomon had been proclaimed king to Adonijah (1 Kings 1:41–49).

4. A son of Shimeah (2 Sam. 21:21), or Shimea (1 Chron. 20:7), one of David's brothers. He slew a Philistine giant.

5. Son of Shage and one of David's mighty men (1 Chron. 11:34).

6. A son of Jada, grandson of Jerahmeel of Judah (1 Chron. 2:32).

7. An uncle of David. Jonathan was "a counselor, a wise man, and a scribe" (1 Chron. 27:32).

8. The father of Ebed, a descendant of Adin (Ezra 8:6).

9. A son of Asahel who opposed Ezra's proposal that pagan wives should be divorced (Ezra 10:15).

10. Son of Joiada, a descendant of Jeshua the high priest (Neh. 12:10–11), also called Johanan (Neh. 12:22).

11. A priest descended from Melichu in the days of the high priest Johanan (Neh. 12:14).

12. A priest descended from Shemaiah (Neh. 12:35), also called Jehonathan (Neh. 12:18).

13. A scribe in whose house Jeremiah the prophet was imprisoned (Jer. 37:15; 38:26).

14. A son of Kareah. He placed himself under the protection of Gedaliah whom Nebuchadnezzar appointed governor of Jerusalem (Jer. 40:8).

Joppa [Jop'pa], *beautiful*—An ancient seaport city on the Mediterranean Sea, about 56 kilometers (35 miles) northwest of Jerusalem. Today, Joppa is the modern city of Jaffa, a suburb of Tel Aviv, Israel.

A walled city, Joppa was built about 35 meters (116 feet) high on a rocky ledge overlooking the Mediterranean. It supposedly received its name "beautiful" from the sunlight that its buildings reflected. The first mention of Joppa in the Bible indicates it was part of the territory inherited by the tribe of Dan (Josh. 19:46; Japho, KJV). In later years, the prophet Jonah tried to escape his call to preach to the city of Nineveh by going to Joppa to catch a ship bound for Tarshish (Jonah 1:3).

The only natural harbor on the Mediterranean between Egypt and Acco, it was the seaport for the city of Jerusalem and the site of significant shipping in both Old and New Testament times. Rafts of cedar logs from the forests of Lebanon were floated from Tyre and Sidon to Joppa and then transported overland to Jerusalem to be used in building Solomon's temple (2 Chron. 2:16).

In New Testament times Joppa was the home of a Christian disciple, Tabitha (or Dorcas), a woman "full of good works and charitable deeds" (Acts 9:36). After she became sick and died, she was raised to life by Simon Peter. As a result, many believed on the Lord (Acts 9:36–42).

Joppa was also the home of Simon the tanner (Acts 10:32). Simon Peter stayed many days in Joppa with Simon. On the roof of Simon's house, Peter received his vision of a great sheet descending from heaven (Acts 10:9–16)—a vision that indicated that all who believe in Christ, Gentiles as well as Jews, are accepted by God.

Jorah [Jor'ah]—See Hariph.

Jorai [Jo'ra·i], *Jehovah has taught me*—One of seven Gadite chieftains (1 Chron. 5:13).

Joram, Jehoram [Jor'am, Je·hor'am], *Jehovah is exalted*—

1. Son of Toi, king of Hamath. His father sent him to congratulate David on his victory over Hadadezer (2 Sam. 8:9–10). In 1 Chronicles 18:10 he is called Hadoram.

2. A Levite, the descendant of Eliezer, son of Moses (1 Chron. 26:25).

3. A priest sent by Jehoshaphat to instruct the people (2 Chron. 17:8).

4. Son of Jehoshaphat. He followed his father on the throne and murdered his brothers (2 Chron. 21:1–4). His wife was Athaliah, daughter of Ahab and Jezebel of Israel. She introduced Phoenician idolatry as did her mother (2 Kings 8:18; 2 Chron. 21:6, 11). The Edomites and Libnah rebelled during his reign (2 Kings 8:20–22; 2 Chron. 21:8–10).

Later the palace was plundered by Philistines and Arabs who carried off the wives and children of the king with the exception of Ahaziah, also called Jehoahaz, who succeeded Joram (2 Chron. 21:16–17; 22:1–4). Joram was the wicked son of a pious father.

5. Son of Ahab, king of Israel. He followed his brother, Ahaziah, on the throne and reigned for eleven years (2 Kings 3:1–27; 9:14–26).

Jordan [Jor'dan], *the descender*—The Jordan River has such an important role in biblical history that many visitors to the Holy Land ask to be baptized in its waters, near Jericho, where Jesus was baptized by John (Matt. 3:13). This famous river begins as a small stream in the foothills of Mount Hermon near Caesarea Philippi (now called Banias). Popularly, the name *Jordan* is thought to mean "descender" or "the river that rushes down," which it does at the rate of 25 feet per mile along its twisting 100-mile journey. Its descent ranges from about 1,200 feet above sea level to about 1,286 feet below sea level.

The course of the river is almost directly south. At Lake Huleh it is only a few feet above sea level. From this marshy region it continues to the Sea of Galilee where it is almost 700 feet below the level of the Mediterranean. Ninety miles farther south, where it empties into the Dead Sea, is the lowest point on earth. In its course the river receives two tributaries from the east, the Yarmuk and the Jabbok. The Jordan's tributaries from the west are unimportant. The river is small in normal times but becomes a torrent in the rainy season (Josh. 3:15). It is not navigable though small craft have been known to descend it. At several points between the Sea of Galilee and the Dead Sea the river can be forded.

Through the centuries, the Jordan has served as a natural boundary between Palestine and other nations. In the period between the Old Testament and the New Testament, the Jordan River formed the main eastern boundary of the Persian and Greek province of Judea. The Decapolis, a federation of ten Greek cities, was formed on the eastern side of the Jordan in the Greek period.

The Old Testament speaks of the Jordan as the site of the land favored by Lot (Gen. 13:10–11); the place where Israel would cross into the land of Canaan in Joshua's time (Deut. 3:20, 25, 27); and the scene of events in Elijah's and Elisha's lives (1 Kings 17:2–5; 2 Kings 2:13–15). Because the Jordan is a short and rather shallow river, it was compared unfavorably by Naaman the leper to the two larger rivers in his homeland of Syria. When the prophet Elisha directed him to dip in the Jordan to be healed of his leprosy, he replied, "Are not the Abanah and the Pharpar, the rivers of Damascus, better than all the waters of Israel? Could I not wash in them and be clean?" (2 Kings 5:12). But his servants persuaded him to do as Elisha asked, and Naaman was healed.

Jorim [Jo′rim], *whom Jehvoah has exalted*—Son of Matthat and ancestor of Jesus (Luke 3:29).

Jorkeam [Jor′ke·am]—See Jorkoam.

Jorkoam [Jor′ko·am], *the people empty*—The name of a man of Judah (1 Chron. 2:44).

Josabad [Jos′a·bad]—See Jozabad.

Josaphat [Jos′a·phat]—See Jehoshaphat.

Jose [Jo′se]—A form of Joses (Luke 3:29).

Josech [Jo'sech], unknown—A name in the genealogy of Jesus (Luke 3:26 NIV), also Joseph (NKJV, KJV, NASB).

Josedech [Jos'e·dech]—See Jozadak.

Joseph [Jo'seph], *may he add*—The name of several men in the Bible:

1. The eleventh son of Jacob (Gen. 30:24). Joseph was sold into slavery and later rose to an important position in the Egyptian government. The account of Joseph's life is found in Genesis 37–50.

Joseph was the first child of Rachel (30:24) and his father's favorite son (37:31). This is most clearly shown by the special coat that Jacob gave to Joseph. This favoritism eventually brought serious trouble for the whole family. Joseph's ten older brothers hated him because he was Jacob's favorite and because Joseph had dreams that he interpreted to his brothers in a conceited way. It is no surprise that Joseph's brothers hated him enough to kill him (37:4).

Joseph's brothers were shepherds in the land of Canaan. One day Jacob sent Joseph to search for his brothers, who were tending the flocks in the fields. When Joseph found them, they seized upon the chance to kill him. The only opposing voice was Reuben's, but they finally sold Joseph into slavery to passing merchants. To hide the deed from their father, Jacob, Joseph's brothers took his coat and dipped it in animal blood. When Jacob saw the coat, he was convinced that Joseph had been killed by a wild animal (37:34–35).

Joseph was taken to Egypt, where he was sold to Potiphar, an officer of the ruling pharaoh of the nation. His good conduct soon earned him the highest position in the household. Potiphar's wife became infatuated with Joseph and tempted him to commit adultery with her. When he refused, she accused him of the crime and Joseph was sent to prison.

While in prison, Joseph's behavior earned him a position of responsibility over the other prisoners. Among the prisoners Joseph met were the pharaoh's baker and his butler. When each of them had a dream, Joseph interpreted their dreams. When the butler left prison, he failed to intercede on Joseph's behalf, and Joseph spent two more years in prison. When the pharaoh had dreams that none of his counselors could interpret, the butler remembered Joseph and mentioned him to the pharaoh. Then Joseph was called to appear before the pharaoh. He interpreted the pharaoh's dreams, predicting seven years of plentiful food, followed by seven years of famine. He also advised the pharaoh to appoint a commissioner to store up supplies during the plentiful years. To Joseph's surprise, the pharaoh appointed him as food commissioner. This was a position of great prestige. Under Joseph's care, many supplies were stored and the land prospered (41:37–57). Joseph was given many comforts, including servants and a wife. He was called Zaphenath-paneah. When the famine struck, Joseph was second only to the pharaoh in power. People from all surrounding lands came to buy food from him.

Many years passed between Joseph's arrival in Egypt as a slave and his rise to power in the nation during the famine. The famine also struck Canaan, and Joseph's brothers eventually came to Egypt to buy grain. When they met Joseph, they did not recognize him. He recognized them, however, and decided to test them to see if they had changed. He accused them of being spies. Then he sold them grain only on the condition that Simeon stay as a hostage until they brought Benjamin, the youngest brother, to Egypt with them. Upon returning to Canaan, the brothers told Jacob of their experiences. He vowed not to send Benjamin to Egypt. But the continuing famine forced him to change his mind. On the next trip Benjamin went with his brothers to Egypt. When they arrived, Joseph treated them royally, weeping openly at the sight of his youngest brother. Simeon was returned to them. After purchasing their grain, they started home. On their way home, however, they were stopped by one of Joseph's servants, who accused them of stealing Joseph's silver cup. The cup was found in Benjamin's bag, where Joseph had placed it. The brothers returned to face Joseph, who declared that Benjamin must stay in Egypt. At this point Judah pleaded with Joseph, saying that it would break their father Jacob's heart if Benjamin failed to return with them. Judah's offer to stay in Benjamin's place is one of the most moving passages in the Old Testament. Joseph was overcome with emotion. He revealed himself to them as their brother, whom they had sold into slavery years earlier. At first Joseph's brothers were afraid that Joseph would take revenge against them, but soon they were convinced that Joseph's forgiveness was genuine. Judah's plea on Benjamin's behalf was evidence of the change that Joseph had hoped to find in his brothers. He sent them back to Canaan with gifts for his father and invited the family to come live in Egypt. The grace of God working in the family of Jacob is evident in the way Joseph dealt with his brothers. Joseph did not want revenge against them. He realized that his personal suffering had preserved the family as an instrument of God's will. Joseph also was aware that his rise to power was for the good of his family, not for his own glory (45:7–8).

2. The father Igal, one of the spies sent into Canaan (Num. 13:7).

3. A son of Asaph (1 Chron. 25:2, 9).

4. A son of Bani, one who married a foreign wife during the Exile (Ezra 10:42) and put her away in the time of Ezra.

5. A priest, head of the family of Shebaniah (Neh. 12:14).

6. The husband of Mary, mother of Jesus (Matt. 1:16–24; 2:13; Luke 1:27; 2:4). When Augustus issued his decree that all should be enrolled, or taxed, Joseph and Mary went to Bethlehem. At that time Jesus was born (Mic. 5:2; Luke 2:4, 16). After the death of Herod, they returned to Nazareth from Egypt (Matt. 2:22–23). He was a carpenter (Matt. 13:55), as was Jesus (Mark 6:3). At the beginning of our Lord's work Joseph was evidently alive (Matt. 13:55) but probably died prior to the crucifixion since, on the cross, Jesus committed His mother to the care of John (John 19:26–27).

7. Joseph of Arimathaea. He was a member of the Sanhedrin and, like Nicodemus, was a secret disciple of Jesus. He took a positive stand regarding his Lord by going boldly to Pilate and asking for the body of Jesus. His request was granted and he had the body placed in a new tomb which belonged to him (Matt. 27:58–60; Mark 15:43–46).

8. Son of Mattathias, an ancestor of Jesus (Luke 3:24–25).

9. The father of Semei who lived after the Exile; an ancestor of Jesus (Luke 3:26).

10. An ancestor of Christ (Luke 3:30).

11. A disciple (known also as Barsabas and Justus) considered to take the place of Judas Iscariot (Acts 1:23).

12. The personal name of Barnabas; called Joses in the King James Version (Acts 4:36).

Joses [Jo'ses], *a Greek form of Joseph*—

1. The son of Mary and Cleopas, one of the brethren of the Lord (Matt. 13:55; Mark 6:3).

2. The personal name of Barnabas, a Levite of Cyprus, and Paul's companion (Acts 4:36).

Joshah [Jo'shah], *Jehovah makes equal*—Son of Amaziah of the tribe of Simeon (1 Chron. 4:34).

Joshaphat [Josh'a·phat], *Jehovah has judged*—
1. A Mithnite who was one of David's warriors (1 Chron. 11:43).
2. A priest who served as a trumpeter at the time the ark was brought to Jerusalem (1 Chron. 15:24). He is called Jehoshaphat in the King James Version.

Joshaviah [Josh·a·vi'ah], *Jehovah makes equal*—A warrior of David, son of Elnaam (1 Chron. 11:46).

Joshbekashah [Josh·be·ka'shah], *seated in hardness*—Son of Heman and head of the seventeenth course of singers (1 Chron. 25:4, 24).

Josheb-basshebeth [Jo'sheb-bas·she'beth], *dwelling in rest*—A Tachmonite who was chief of David's captains (2 Sam. 23:8). He is called Jashobeam in 1 Chronicles 11:11.

Joshibiah, Josibiah [Josh·i·bi'ah, Jos·i·bi'ah], *Jehovah causes to dwell*—A Simeonite of the family of Asiel (1 Chron. 4:35).

Joshua [Josh'u·a], *the Lord is salvation*—Four Old Testament men:
1. The successor to Moses and the man who led the nation of Israel to conquer and settle the promised land.

Son of Nun, Joshua was born in Egypt. His original name was Oshea. He went through the great events of the Passover and the exodus with Moses and all the Hebrew people who escaped from slavery in Egypt at the hand of their Redeemer God. In the wilderness of Sinai, Moses took his assistant Joshua with him when he went into the mountains to talk with God (Ex. 24:13). Moses also gave Joshua a prominent place at the tabernacle. As Moses' servant, Joshua would remain at the tabernacle as his representative while the great leader left the camp to fellowship with the Lord (Ex. 33:11). He was also the commander of the Israelites in their first battle and defeated the Amalekites at Rephidim (Ex. 17:8–16).

When Moses sent spies to scout out the land of Canaan, Joshua was selected as the representative of the tribe of Ephraim (Num. 13:8). Only Joshua and Caleb returned to the camp with a report that they could conquer the land with God's help. The other ten spies complained that they were "like grasshoppers" in comparison to the Canaanites (Num. 13:33). Because of their show of faith, Joshua and Caleb were allowed to enter the land at the end of their years of wandering in the wilderness. But all the other Israelites who lived at that time died before the nation entered the promised land (Num. 14:30).

At Moses' death, Joshua was chosen as his successor (Josh. 1:1–2). He led the Israelites to conquer the land (Josh. 1–2), supervised the division of the territory among the twelve tribes, and led the people to renew their covenant with God (Josh. 13–22).

When Joshua died at the age of 110, he was buried in the land of his inheritance at Timnath-serah (Josh. 24:30). As Moses' successor, Joshua completed the work that this great leader had begun. Moses led Israel out of Egypt; Joshua led Israel into Canaan. Joshua's name, an Old Testament form of Jesus, means "the Lord is salvation." By his name and by his life, he demonstrated the salvation that comes from God.

2. A native of Beth-shemesh. He owned the field through which was driven the cart that carried the ark from the land of the Philistines (1 Sam. 6:14).

3. The governor of Jerusalem at the time King Josiah was engaged in his reform work (2 Kings 23:8).

4. The high priest during Zerubbabel's governorship of Judah. In Ezra and Nehemiah he is called Jeshua (Ezra 3:2, 8–9; Neh. 12:1, 7, 10, 26; Hag. 1:1, 12, 14; 2:2–4; Zech. 3:1–9).

Joshua, Gate of—A gate of Jerusalem (2 Kings 23:8).

Josiah [Jo·si'ah], *Jehovah heals*—The name of two men in the Old Testament:

1. The sixteenth king of Judah, the son of Amon, and the grandson of Manasseh (2 Kings 21:23–23:30). The three decades of Josiah's reign were characterized by peace, prosperity, and reform. Hence, they were among the happiest years experienced by Judah. King Josiah devoted himself to pleasing God and reinstituting Israel's observance of the Mosaic law. That a wicked king like Amon could have such a godly son and successor is a tribute to the grace of God. The Bible focuses almost exclusively on Josiah's spiritual reform, which climaxed in the eighteenth year of his reign with the discovery of the Book of the Law.

Josiah's reform actually occurred in three stages. Ascending to the throne at age eight, he apparently was blessed with God-fearing advisors who resisted the idolatrous influence of his father. More important, however, at the age of sixteen (stage one), Josiah personally "began to seek the God of his father David" (2 Chron. 34:3).

At the age of twenty (stage two), Josiah began to cleanse Jerusalem and the land of Judah of idolatrous objects (2 Chron. 34:3–7). His reform was even more extensive than that of his predecessor, Hezekiah (2 Kings 18:4; 2 Chron. 29:3–36). Josiah extended his cleansing of the land into the territory of fallen Israel; at the time Israel was nominally controlled by Assyria. Josiah personally supervised the destruction of the altars of the Baals, the incense altars, the wooden images, the carved images, and the molded images as far north as the cities of Naphtali. Josiah's efforts were aided by the death of the great Assyrian king, Ashurbanipal, which brought about a serious decline in Assyria's power and allowed Josiah freedom to pursue his reforms.

At the age of twenty-six (stage three), Josiah ordered that the temple be repaired under the supervision of Hilkiah, the high priest. In the process, a copy of the Book of the Law was discovered (2 Chron. 34:14–15). When it was read to Josiah, he was horrified to learn how far Judah had departed from the law of God. This discovery provided a new momentum for the reformation that was already in progress.

In 609 B.C. Josiah attempted to block Pharaoh Necho II of Egypt as he marched north to assist Assyria in her fight with Babylon for world supremacy. Despite the pharaoh's assurance to the contrary, Josiah saw Necho's northern campaign as a threat to Judah's security. When he engaged Necho in battle at Megiddo, Josiah was seriously injured. He was returned to Jerusalem, where he died after reigning thirty-one years. His death was followed by widespread lamentation (2 Chron. 35:20–27). In the New Testament, Josiah is referred to as Josias (Matt. 1:10, KJV).

2. A son of Zephaniah, a captive who returned to Jerusalem from Babylon in Zechariah's day (Zech. 6:10), also called Hen (Zech. 6:14).

Josias [Jo·si′as]—See Josiah.

Josibiah [Jos·i·bi′ah]—See Joshibiah.

Josiphiah [Jos·i·phi′ah], *increased by Jehovah*—Head of the house of Shelomith (Ezra 8:10).

Jotbah [Jot'bah], *pleasantness*—The town where Haruz lived. He was the maternal grandfather of Amon, king of Judah (2 Kings 21:19).

Jotbath [Jot'bath], *pleasantness*—One of the encampments of the Israelites (Num. 33:33–34).

Jotbathah [Jot'ba·thah]—Variant of Jotbath.

Jotham [Jo'tham], *Jehovah is upright*—Two Old Testament men:
   1. The youngest son of Gideon, who escaped the massacre of his seventy brothers ordered by Abimelech. After Abimelech became king of Shechem, Jotham, on Mount Gerizim, spoke the parable to the Shechemites of the trees anointing a king (Judg. 9:1–21).
   2. King of Judah, son of Uzziah (Azariah). Jotham became king after his father contracted leprosy. He was twenty-five years old at the time (2 Kings 15:5, 32–33). Near the end of his rule, Pekah of Israel and Rezin of Syria began their invasion of Judah (2 Kings 15:32–38; 2 Chron. 27:1–9).

Jozabad [Joz'a·bad], *Jehovah has endowed*—Several Old Testament men:
   1. An inhabitant of Gederah. He allied himself with David at Ziklag (1 Chron. 12:4).
   2. Two men of Manasseh had this name. They assisted David in his conflict with the Amalekites (1 Chron. 12:20).
   3. A Levite, an overseer of the tithes in the reign of Hezekiah (2 Chron. 31:13).
   4. A Levite prince in the reign of Josiah (2 Chron. 35:9).
   5. Son of Jeshua (Ezra 8:33).
   6. A son of Pashur (Ezra 10:22). Also see Jozachar.

Jozacar [Jo'za·car]—Variant of Jozachar.

Jozachar [Jo'za·char], *remembered by Jehovah*—One of the assassins of Joash, king of Judah, who was slain in Millo (2 Kings 12:21). He is also called Jozabad (NIV).

Jozadak [Jo'za·dak], *Jehovah is just*—Father of Jeshua, the high priest of Zerubbabel's time (Ezra 3:2, 8; Hag. 1:12, 14; Zech. 6:11). Jozadak was carried into captivity by Nebuchadnezzar.

Jubal [Ju'bal], *stream*—The son of Lamech. He is described as "the father of all those who play the harp and flute" (Gen. 4:21).

Jubilee [Ju'bi·lee], *ram's horn* or *trumpet*—The Jubilee year, also known as the "year of liberty" (Ezek. 46:17), was proclaimed on the fiftieth year after seven cycles of seven years. This fiftieth year was a time when specific instructions about property and slavery outlined in the Jewish law took effect (Lev. 25:8–55).

The word *jubilee* comes from a Hebrew word meaning "ram's horn," or "trumpet." The Jubilee year was launched with a blast from a ram's horn on the Day of Atonement, signifying a call to celebration, liberation, and the beginning of a year for "doing justice" and "loving mercy." The fiftieth year was a special year in which to "proclaim liberty throughout all the land" (Lev. 25:10). Individuals who had sold themselves as slaves or servants indentured because of indebtedness were released from their debts and set free. If a family's land had been taken away because of indebtedness, this land was returned to the original owners in the Jubilee year.

God apparently established the Jubilee year to prevent the Israelites from oppressing and cheating one another (Lev. 25:17). This law prevented a permanent system of classes from developing; it gave everyone the opportunity to start over, economically and socially. The Jubilee year reminds us of God's concern for human liberty. God wants people to be free (Luke 4:18–19). Calling into question any social practice that leads to permanent bondage and loss of economic opportunity, it also stands as a witness to God's desire for justice on earth.

Jucal [Ju'cal]—See Jehucal.

Juda [Ju'da]—Variant of Judah.

Judaea [Ju·dae'a]—Variant of Judea.

Judah [Ju'dah], *praise*—The name of seven men and a place in the Old Testament:

1. The fourth son of Jacob and Leah and the founder of the family out of which the messianic line came (Gen. 29:35; Num. 26:19–21; Matt. 1:2).

Judah was one of the most prominent of the twelve sons of Jacob. He saved Joseph's life by suggesting that his brothers sell Joseph to

Ishmaelite merchants rather than kill him (Gen. 37:26–28). In Egypt it was Judah who begged Joseph to detain him rather than Benjamin, Jacob's beloved son. In an eloquent speech Judah confessed what he and his brothers had done to Joseph; shortly thereafter, Joseph identified himself to his brothers (Gen. 44:14–45:1).

It appears that Judah was the leader of Jacob's sons who remained at home. Even though he was not the oldest son, Judah was sent by Jacob to precede him to Egypt (Gen. 46:28). Also Judah, rather than his older brothers, received Jacob's blessing (Gen. 49:3–10). In that blessing, Jacob foretold the rise of Judah: "Your father's children shall bow down before you. . . . The scepter shall not depart from Judah . . . until Shiloh comes" (Gen. 49:8, 10).

Judah had three sons: Er, Onan, and Shelah (Gen. 38:3–5). Er and Onan were killed by divine judgment because of their sins (Gen. 38:7–10). Judah also fathered twin sons, Perez and Zerah, by Tamar, Er's widow (Gen. 38:29–30). The line of Judah ran through Perez to David and thus became the messianic line (Luke 3:30; Judas, KJV). In Jacob's dying prophetical vision Judah was selected as the tribe of the Messiah. It is called the "Shiloh Prophecy" (Gen. 49:10).

2. Tribe of Judah. It consisted of five tribal families (Num. 26:19–21; 1 Chron. 2:3–6). In the early period of the wandering Nahahon, son of Amminadab, was the prince of the tribe (Num. 1:7; 2:3; 7:12–17; 10:14). The tribe occupied the large part of southern Palestine. Its western boundary was the Mediterranean, and the eastern the Dead Sea. From north to south the length of its territory was about fifty miles.

3. An ancestor of certain Israelites who helped rebuild the temple after the captivity (Ezra 3:9).

4. A Levite who divorced his pagan wife after returning from the captivity (Ezra 10:23).

5. A son of Senuah (also called Hassenuah), a Benjamite (Neh. 11:9).

6. A Levite who returned from the captivity with Zerubbabel (Neh. 12:8).

7. A leader of Judah who officiated in the dedication of the Jerusalem wall (Neh. 12:34).

8. A musician and son of a priest (Neh. 12:36).

9. A place on the border of Naphtali (Josh. 19:34).

Judah, Kingdom of—The division of the kingdom of Israel occurred in 931 B.C., after the death of Solomon, son of David. Due to Rehoboam's foolish political moves, the ten northern tribes revolted under Jeroboam and formed the kingdom of Israel. The kingdom of Judah in the south included Judah and Benjamin. David's descendants continued to sit on the throne of Judah; many of them were wicked, but every once in a while a good king rose up who tried to turn the nation back to worshipping God. The Northern Kingdom existed from 931 to 722 B.C.; Judah continued until 586 B.C. when Nebuchadnezzar carried the people into captivity.

Judaizers—Those who were teaching that it is necessary to follow the Mosaic law in order to be saved (Acts 15:1). The Jerusalem Council was held to discuss and refute this way of thinking, but this did not put an end to the idea. Paul's letter to the Galatians deals extensively with the problem of the Judaizers.

Judas [Ju′das], *praise*—The name of five men in the New Testament:

1. Judah, son of Jacob (Matt. 1:2–3), in the genealogy of Jesus.

2. An ancestor of Jesus, who lived prior to the Exile (Luke 3:30).

3. One of the four brothers of Jesus (Matt. 13:55; Mark 6:3; Juda, KJV). Some scholars believe he was the author of the epistle of Jude.

4. One of the twelve apostles of Jesus. John is careful to distinguish him from Judas Iscariot (John 14:22). He is called "Judas the son of James" (Luke 6:16; Acts 1:13). In the list of the Twelve given in Mark, instead of "Judas . . . of James" a Thaddaeus is mentioned (Mark 3:18). Matthew has Lebbaeus, whose surname was Thaddaeus (Matt. 10:3). He was also called Judas the Zealot. Tradition says he preached in Assyria and Persia and died a martyr in Persia.

5. Judas of Galilee (Acts 5:37). In the days of the census (Luke 2:2), he led a revolt against Rome. He was killed, and his followers were scattered. According to the Jewish historian Josephus, Judas founded a sect whose main belief was that their only ruler and lord was God.

6. A man with whom the apostle Paul stayed in Damascus after his conversion (Acts 9:11).

7. A disciple surnamed Barsabas who belonged to the church in Jerusalem. The apostles and elders of that church chose Judas and Silas

to accompany Paul and Barnabas to Antioch; together they conveyed to the church in that city the decree of the Jerusalem Council about circumcision (Acts 15:22, 27, 32).

Judas Iscariot [Ju′das Isa′car·i·ot]—The disciple who betrayed Jesus. Judas was the son of Simon (John 6:71), or of Simon Iscariot (NRSV). The term "Iscariot," which is used to distinguish Judas from the other disciple named Judas (Luke 6:16; John 14:22; Acts 1:13), refers to his hometown of Kerioth, in southern Judah (Josh. 15:25). Thus, Judas was a Judean, the only one of the Twelve who was not from Galilee.

The details of Judas's life are sketchy. Because of his betrayal of Jesus, Judas, however, is even more of a mystery. It must be assumed that Jesus saw promise in Judas, or He would not have called him to be a disciple. Judas's name appears in three of the lists of the disciples (Matt. 10:2–4; Mark 3:16–19; Luke 6:14–16), although it always appears last. His name is missing from the list of the eleven disciples in Acts 1:13; by that time Judas had already committed suicide. Judas must have been an important disciple, because he served as their treasurer (John 12:6; 13:29).

During the week of the Passover festival, Judas went to the chief priests and offered to betray Jesus for a reward (Matt. 26:14–16; Mark 14:10–11). At the Passover supper, Jesus announced that He would be betrayed and that He knew who His betrayer was—one who dipped his hand with him in the dish (Mark 14:20), the one to whom He would give the piece of bread used in eating (John 13:26–27). Jesus was saying that a friend, one who dipped out of the same dish as He, was His betrayer. These verses in John indicate that Judas probably was reclining beside Jesus, evidence that Judas was an important disciple.

Jesus said to Judas, "What you do, do quickly" (John 13:27). Judas left immediately after he ate (John 13:30). The first observance of the Lord's Supper was probably celebrated afterward, without Judas (Matt. 26:26–29).

Judas carried out his betrayal in the Garden of Gethsemane. By a prearranged sign, Judas singled out Jesus for the soldiers by kissing him. The Gospels do not tell us why Judas was needed to point out Jesus, who had become a well-known figure. It is possible that Judas disclosed where Jesus would be that night, so that He could be arrested secretly without the knowledge of His many supporters (Matt. 26:47–50).

Matthew reports that, realizing what he had done, Judas attempted to return the money to the priests. When the priests refused to take it, Judas threw the money on the temple floor, went out, and hanged himself. Unwilling to use "blood money" for the temple, the priests bought a potter's field, which became known as the "Field of Blood" (Matt. 27:3–10). This field is traditionally located at the point where the Kidron, Tyropoeon, and Hinnom valleys come together.

It is difficult to understand why Judas betrayed Jesus. Since he had access to the disciples' treasury, it seems unlikely that he did it for the money only; thirty pieces of silver is a relatively small amount. Some have suggested that Judas thought that his betrayal would force Jesus into asserting His true power and overthrowing the Romans. Others have suggested that Judas might have become convinced that Jesus was a false messiah, and that the true Messiah was yet to come, or that he was upset over Jesus' apparent indifference to the law and His association with sinners and his violation of the Sabbath. Whatever the reason, Judas's motive remains shrouded in mystery. Acts 1:20 quotes Psalm 109:8 as the basis for electing another person to fill the place vacated by Judas: "Let another take his office." When the eleven remaining apostles cast lots for Judas's replacement, "the lot fell on Matthias. And he was numbered with the eleven apostles" (Acts 1:26).

Judas Maccabaeus—See Maccabees, The.

Jude [Jude], *praise*—The author of the epistle of Jude, in which he is described as "a servant of Jesus Christ, and brother of James" (Jude 1). Jude is an English form of the name Judas. Many scholars believe that the James mentioned in this passage is James the brother of Jesus. In Matthew 13:55 the people said concerning Jesus, "Is this not the carpenter's son? Is not His mother called Mary? And His brothers James, Joses, Simon, and Judas?" (Mark 6:3).

If Jude (Judas) was the brother of James and of Jesus, Jude did not believe in Him (John 7:5) until after Jesus' resurrection (Acts 1:14).

Judea [Ju·de'a], *Jewish*—The Greek and Roman name for the land which was once the kingdom of Judah. Its northern boundary extended from Joppa on the Mediteranean to a point on the Jordan about ten miles north of the Dead Sea. Its southern boundary extended from about seven miles southwest of Gaza to the southern portion of the Dead Sea. The name "Judea" is first mentioned in Scripture in Ezra 5:8.

Judge—A civil magistrate invested with authority to hear and decide disputes. Moses originally acted as the only leader of Israel (Ex. 18:13–26), and he appointed Joshua as his successor. After the death of Joshua, the nation of Israel was ruled by judges, or heroic military deliverers, for about three hundred years until the united monarchy was established under King Saul.

The era of the judges was a time of instability and moral depravity, a dark period when everyone "did what was right in his own eyes" (Judg. 17:6). The judges tried to rally the people against their enemies, but many of the judges were morally weak and the people often turned to idolatry. Along with the well-known judges, there were several minor judges whose battles are not recorded in the Bible: Abimelech, Tola, Jair, Ibzan, Elon, and Abdon. When the monarchy was established, the king became the supreme judge in civil affairs (2 Sam. 15:2; 1 Kings 3:9, 28; 7:7). Six thousand officers and judges were appointed by David (1 Chron. 23:4; 26:29).

Judith [Ju′dith], *Jewess*—The daughter of Beeri, the Hittite, and one of the wives of Esau (Gen. 26:34). In Genesis 36:2 she is called Aholibamah.

Julia [Ju′li·a], *the feminine of Julius*—A Christian woman at Rome (Rom. 16:15).

Julius [Ju′li·us], *soft-haired*—The Centurion who took Paul as a prisoner to Rome (Acts 27:1, 42–43).

Junias, Junia [Ju′ni·as, Ju′ni·a]—A Christian Jew at Rome, a kinsman of Paul (Rom. 16:7).

Jupiter [Ju′pi·ter], *a father of helps*—Chief god of the Romans, corresponding to the Grecian god Zeus (Acts 14:12–13).

Jushab-hesed [Ju′shab-he′sed], *kindness returned*—A son of Zerubbabel (1 Chron. 3:20).

Justus [Jus′tus], *just*—Three New Testament men:
1. The surname of Joseph, also called Barsabas, one of two persons considered by the apostles to fill the place of Judas Iscariot (Acts 1:23).

2. A disciple at Corinth with whom Paul lodged and in whose house Paul preached (Acts 18:7).

3. A Jewish Christian, also called Jesus (Col. 4:11).

Jutah [Ju'tah]—Variant of Juttah.

Juttah [Jut'tah], *stretched out*—A Levitical city in the hill country of Judah (Josh. 15:55; 21:16).

K

Kabzeel [Kab'zeel], *God gathers*—A city in the south of Judah (Josh. 15:21), also called Jekabzeel.

Kadesh [Ka'desh]—See Kadesh-barnea.

Kadesh, Kadesh-barnea [Ka'desh, Ka'desh-bar'ne·a], *consecrated*—A wilderness region between Egypt and the land of Canaan where the Hebrew people camped after the exodus. Kadesh-barnea (the modern oasis of Ain el-Qudeirat) was situated on the edge of Edom (Num. 20:16) about 114 kilometers (70 miles) from Hebron and 61 kilometers (50 miles) from Beersheba in the wilderness of Zin. Kadesh-barnea is also said to be in the wilderness of Paran (Num. 13:26). Paran was probably the general name for the larger wilderness area, while Zin may have been the specific name for a smaller portion of the wilderness territory.

The first mention of Kadesh-barnea occurred during the time of Abraham. Chedorlaomer, king of Elam, and his allied armies waged war against the Amalekites and Amorites from Kadesh (Gen. 14:7). When Hagar was forced by Sarah to flee from Abraham's home, she was protected by the angel of the Lord, who brought her to the well Beer-lahai-roi, between Kadesh and Bered (16:14). Later Abraham moved to Gerar, situated between Kadesh and Shur (20:1).

The most important contacts of the Israelites with Kadesh-barnea occurred during the years of the wilderness wanderings. During the second year after the exodus from Egypt, the Israelites camped around Mount Horeb, or Sinai. God told them to leave Sinai and take an eleven-day journey to Kadesh-barnea (Num. 10:11–12; Deut. 1:2). From here the people would have direct entry into the land of Canaan. Moses selected one man from each tribe as a spy and sent them to "spy out the land" (Num. 13:2). After forty days they returned with grapes and other fruits, proving Canaan to be a fertile, plentiful land.

Ten of these spies reported giants in the land, implying that Israel was too weak to enter Canaan (Num. 13:33). But two of the spies, Joshua and Caleb, said, "Do not fear" (Num. 14:9). The people wanted to stone the two for their report (Num. 14:10), and they went so far as to ask for another leader to take them back to Egypt.

Because of their fear and rebellion at Kadesh (Deut. 9:23), the Israelites were forced to wander in the wilderness of Paran for thirty-eight years. Kadesh apparently was their headquarters while they moved about during these years. In the first month of the fortieth year of the exodus, the people again assembled at Kadesh for their final march to the promised land.

While they were still camped at Kadesh, a number of the leaders of the people rebelled against Moses and Aaron (Num. 16:1–3). They were killed in an earthquake (16:31, 32). Miriam, Moses' sister, also died and was buried (20:1). At Kadesh, Moses also disobeyed God by striking the rock to bring forth water (20:8–11). He had been told to speak, not strike the rock. Soon after Moses and the people began to move from Kadesh toward Canaan, Aaron died and was buried (20:23–29).

Kadmiel [Kad'mi·el], *God's presence*—Two Old Testament men:

    1. A Levite who returned with Zerubbabel (Ezra 2:40; Neh. 7:43; 12:8) and was placed over the workmen in the erection of the temple (Ezra 3:9).

    2. A Levite who assisted in the religious instruction and devotions of the people (Neh. 9:4–5; 10:9).

Kadmonites [Kad'mo·nites], *people of the east*—A tribe mentioned in Genesis 15:19.

Kain [Kain]—

    1. The tribal name from which Kenite is derived (Num. 24:22).

    2. A town in Judah. Also spelled Cain (Josh. 15:57).

Kalai [Ka·la'i]—Variant spelling of Kallai.

Kallai [Kal·la'i], *swift*—Son of Sallai (Neh. 12:20).

Kamon [Ka'mon], unknown—A place, the location of which is unknown. Jair, the Gileadite who judged Israel for twenty-two years, was buried here (Judg. 10:5). Also spelled Camon.

Kanah [Ka'nah], *place of reeds—*

1. A stream that marked, in part, the boundary between Ephraim and Manasseh (Josh. 16:8; 17:9).

2. A town on the northern border of Asher (Josh. 19:28).

Kareah [Ka·re'ah], *bald—*His sons, Johanan and Jonathan, came for protection to Gedaliah (2 Kings 25:23; Jer. 40:8). Also spelled Careah.

Karka [Kar'ka]—Variant spelling of Karkaa.

Karkaa [Kar'ka·a], *ravine—*A place in the extreme south of Judah (Josh. 15:3).

Karkor [Kar'kor], *foundation—*A place east of the Jordan (Judg. 8:10).

Kartah [Kar'tah], *city—*A town of the Levites in Zebulun (Josh. 21:34).

Kartan [Kar'tan], *two cities—*A town of Naphtali assigned to the Gershonite Levites (Josh. 21:32). In 1 Chronicles 6:76, it is called Kirjathaim.

Kattath [Kat'tath], *small—*A town of Zebulun (Josh. 19:15), identified by some with Kitron (Judg. 1:30).

Kedar [Ke'dar], *dark—*Descendants of Ishmael (Gen. 25:13).

Kedemah [Ke·de'mah], *eastward—*An Ishmaelite tribe (Gen. 25:15; 1 Chron. 1:31).

Kedemoth [Ke'de·moth], *beginnings—*A city east of the Jordan in the territory of Reuben (Deut. 2:26; Josh. 13:18) and assigned to the Levites of the Merari branch (Josh. 21:37; 1 Chron. 6:79).

Kedesh [Ke'desh], *sanctuary—*Three Israelite towns:

1. A town on the southern border of Judah (Josh. 15:23); possibly the same as Kadesh-barnea.

2. A town of Naphtali (Josh. 12:22; 19:37) and called Kedeshnaphtali (Judg. 4:6). It was a city of refuge, the residence of Gershonite Levites (Josh. 21:32), and the home of Barak (Judg. 4:6).

3. A Levitical city of Issachar (1 Chron. 6:72). In Joshua 21:28 it is called Kishon.

Kedron [Ked'ron]—See Kidron.

Kefr Kenna [Kefr Ken'na]—See Cana.

Kehelathah [Ke·he·la'thah], *assembly*—One of the encampments of the Israelites (Num. 33:22–23).

Keilah [Ke·i'lah], *fortress*—A town of Judah delivered from the Philistines by David (Josh. 15:44; 1 Chron. 4:19).

Keilah the Garmite [Ke·i'lah the Gar·mite]—A man of the tribe of Judah, a descendant of Hodiah (1 Chron. 4:19).

Kelaiah [Ke·lai'ah]—See Kelita.

Kelita [Ke·li'ta], *dwarf*—A Levite who renounced his foreign wife (Ezra 10:23), assisted Ezra in instructing the people (Neh. 8:7), and sealed the covenant (Neh. 10:10).

Kemuel [Ke·mu'el], *assembly of God*—Three Old Testament men:
1. A prince of Ephraim who assisted in the division of the land (Num. 34:24).
2. Son of Nahor and Milcah and father of Aram (Gen. 22:20–21).
3. Father of Hashabiah, a Levite (1 Chron. 27:17).

Kenan [Ke'nan]—See Cainan.

Kenath [Ke'nath], *possession*—The most easterly of the ten cities of the Decapolis (Num. 32:42).

Kenaz [Ke'naz], *hunter*—Two Old Testament men:
1. A son of Eliphaz who was the son of Esau (Gen. 36:11). He was a chieftain of a tribe of Edom (Gen. 36:40–43).
2. Son of Jephunneh (Josh. 15:17; 1 Chron. 4:15).

Kenezite [Ke'nez·ite]—See Kenizzite.

Kenite [Ke'nite], *smiths*—A member of a nomadic tribe. In the time of Abraham, a branch of the tribe dwelt in Canaan (Gen. 15:19); another branch in Midian (Judg. 1:16; 4:11). Hobab, the brother-in-law of Moses, was a Kenite (Num. 10:29–32).

Kenizzite [Ke·niz'zite], *unknown*—A member of an Edomite clan of southern Judah (Gen. 15:19; Num. 32:12; Josh. 14:6, 14).

Keren-happuch [Ker'en-hap'puch], *paint horn*—One of Job's daughters born after his affliction (Job 42:14).

Kerioth [Ker'i·oth]—

1. A border town in the south of Judah (Josh. 15:25). It is quite possible it was the birthplace of Judas Iscariot.

2. A town of Moab (Jer. 48:24; Amos 2:2).

Kerioth-hezron [Ker'i·oth-hez'ron]—A place in southern Judah (Josh. 15:25, Revised Version). See Kerioth and Hazor.

Keros [Ke'ros], *curved*—A Nethinim. Members of his family returned to Jerusalem (Ezra 2:44; Neh. 7:47).

Keturah [Ke·tu'rah], *incense*—A wife of Abraham (Gen. 25:1, 4), also called Abraham's concubine (1 Chron. 1:32–33). Some suggest that Keturah had been Abraham's "concubine-wife," before the death of Sarah. After Sarah died, Keturah was then elevated to the full status of Abraham's wife. Keturah bore to Abraham six sons: Zimran, Jokshan, Medan, Midian, Ishbak, and Shuah (Gen. 25:1–4). These men were the founders or ancestors of six Arabian tribes in southern and eastern Palestine. Late Arabian genealogies mention a tribe by the name of Katura dwelling near Mecca.

Keturah's sons were not on the same level as Abraham's promised son, Isaac. Through Isaac God would carry out His promise to Abraham to make of his descendants a chosen people. While he was still alive, therefore, Abraham gave Keturah's sons gifts and sent them to "the country of the east" (Gen. 25:6).

Abraham was already advanced in years when he married Keturah. She brought him both companionship and children in his old age. Keturah apparently outlived Abraham (Gen. 25:7).

Kezia [Ke·zi'a]—Variant of Keziah.

Keziah [Ke·zi'ah], *cassia* or *cinnammon*—Job's second daughter, born after his affliction (Job 42:14).

Keziz [Ke'ziz]—See Emek-keziz.

Kibroth-hattaavah [Kib'roth-hat·ta'a·vah], *graves of lust*—A place between Mount Sinai and Hazeroth (Num. 11:33–35; 33:16–17; Deut. 9:22).

Kibzaim [Kib·za'im], *two gatherings*—One of the cities given to the Levites (Josh. 21:22), called Jokmeam in 1 Chronicles 6:68.

Kidron [Ki'dron], *gloomy* or *dark*—A valley on the eastern slope of Jerusalem through which a seasonal brook of the same name runs. The meaning of the name is fitting, in view of the great strife that has surrounded the Kidron throughout Bible times. A torrent in the winter rains, it contains little water in the summer months.

The ravine of the Kidron Valley begins north of Jerusalem, running past the temple, Calvary, the Garden of Gethsemane, and the Mount of Olives to form a well-defined limit to Jerusalem on its eastern side. From there the valley and the brook reach into the Judean wilderness, where the land is so dry that the brook takes the name of Wady en-Nar or "fire wady." Finally its dreary course brings it to the Dead Sea. Kidron was the brook crossed by David while fleeing from Absalom (2 Sam. 15:23, 30). While the brook is not large, the deep ravine is a significant geographical obstacle. When David crossed the Kidron and turned east to retreat from Absalom to the safety of Hebron, he signaled his abandonment of Jerusalem (2 Sam. 15:23).

On the west side of the Kidron is the spring of Gihon, which King Hezekiah tapped for city water before the Assyrians besieged Jerusalem. Hezekiah also blocked the Kidron and lesser springs in the valley to deny water to the besieging Assyrians.

Asa, Hezekiah, and Josiah, the great reforming kings of Judah, burned the idols and objects of worship of the pagan cults that they suppressed in the Kidron Valley (1 Kings 15:13). Beside the brook King Asa destroyed and burned his mother's idol of Asherah (1 Kings 15:13). After this, the valley became the regular receptacle for the impurities and abominations of idol worship when they were removed from the temple and destroyed (2 Kings 23:4, 6, 12; 2 Chron. 29:16; 30:14).

From the Kidron Valley Nehemiah inspected the walls of Jerusalem at night, probably because the walls were clearly visible along that side (Neh. 2:15). In the time of Josiah, this valley was the common cemetery of Jerusalem (2 Kings 23:6; Jer. 26:23). When Jesus left Jerusalem for the Garden of Gethsemane on the night of His arrest, He crossed the Kidron along the way.

Kinah [Ki'nah], *lamentation*—A village in the extreme south of Judah (Josh. 15:22).

Kir [Kir], *fortress*—The place is not certainly identified. Tiglath-pileser took the people of Damascus here as captives (2 Kings 16:9; Amos 1:3–5; 9:7).

Kir-haraseth [Kir-har'a·seth]—A fortified city of Moab (2 Kings 3:25), also spelled Kir Hareseth (Isa. 16:7), Kir Heres (Isa. 16:11; Jer. 48:31, 36), and Kirharesh (Isa. 16:11, KJV). Kir of Moab (Isa. 15:1) is also thought to be identical with Kir-haraseth.

Mesha, king of Moab, fled to Kir-haraseth after he was defeated by Jehoram, king of Israel, and Jehoshaphat, king of Judah. Accompanied by the king of Edom, these two rulers crushed the rebellion Mesha had started (2 Kings 3:4). Because Kir-haraseth was the only city of Moab that could not be overthrown, it was the last refuge of Mesha (2 Kings 3:25).

The prophets foretold God's certain destruction of Kir-haraseth, a seemingly invincible city (Isa. 16:7). Many commentators identify Kir-haraseth with present-day el-Kerak, about 80 kilometers (50 miles) southeast of Jerusalem.

Kir-haresh [Kir-har'esh]—Variant spelling of Kir-heres.

Kir-heres [Kir-he'res]—Variant spelling of Kir-haresh.

Kiriath [Kir'i·ath]—Variant spelling of Kirjath.

Kiriathaim [Kir·i·a·tha'im], *twin cities*—

1. An ancient town east of the Jordan, a city of the Emim conquered by the Moabites (Gen. 14:5).

2. A city of Naphtali (1 Chron. 6:76).

Kiriath-arba [Kir'i·ath-ar'ba]—Variant spelling of Kirjath-arba.

Kiriath-baal [Kir'i·ath-ba'al], *city of Baal*—See Kirjath-jearim.

Kiriath-huzoth [Kir'i·ath-hu'zoth]—Variant spelling of Kirjath-huzoth.

Kiriath-jearim [Kir'i·ath-je'a·rim]—Variant spelling of Kirjath-jearim.

Kiriath-sannah [Kir'i·ath-san'nah]—See Debir.

Kiriath-sepher [Kir'i·ath-se'pher]—See Debir.

Kirjath [Kir′jath], *city*—A town of Benjamin (Josh. 18:28). The identification of Kirjath-jearim is disputed.

Kirjath-arba [Kir′jath-ar′ba], *city of Arba*—An ancient name for Hebron (Gen. 23:2; Josh. 14:15; 20:7; Judg. 1:10; Neh. 11:25).

Kirjath-huzoth [Kir′jath-hu′zoth], *city of streets*—town of Moab near Bamoth-baal (Num. 22:39).

Kirjath-jearim [Kir′jath-je′a·rim], *city of forests*—A fortified city that originally belonged to the Gibeonites. Kirjath-jearim is first mentioned as a member of a Gibeonite confederation of four fortress cities, which also included Gibeon, Chephirah, and Beeroth (Josh. 9:17). Kirjath-jearim was also known as Baalah (Josh. 15:9), Baale Judah (2 Sam. 6:2), and Kirjath-baal (Josh. 15:60), and Kirjath (Josh. 18:28, NKJV, KJV). These names suggest that perhaps it was an old Canaanite "high place," a place of idolatrous worship.

Originally assigned to the tribe of Judah (Josh. 15:60), and later assigned to Benjamin (Josh. 18:14–15, 28), Kirjath-jearim was on the western part of the boundary line between Judah and Benjamin (Josh. 15:9). When the ark of the covenant was returned to the Israelites by the Philistines, it was brought from Beth-shemesh to Kirjath-jearim and entrusted to a man named Eleazar (1 Sam. 7:1–2). The ark remained in Kirjath-jearim, in the house of Abinadab, the father of Eleazar, for twenty years. It was from here that David transported the ark to Jerusalem (2 Sam. 6:2–3).

Kirjath-sannah [Kir′jath-san′nah]—See Debir.

Kirjath-sepher [Kir′jath-se′pher]—See Debir.

Kir of Moab [Kir of Mo′ab], *wall of Moab*—This city and Ar were the two fortified cities of Moab (Isa. 15:1). It is believed to be the same as Kir-hareseth (2 Kings 3:25; Isa. 16:7, 11; Jer. 48:31, 36).

Kiroth [Kir′oth]—See Kerioth.

Kish [Kish], *bent*—The name of five men in the Old Testament:

1. A son of Jeiel and Maachah. He was a Benjamite who lived in Jerusalem (1 Chron. 8:30; 9:35–36).

2. The father of King Saul of Benjamin, and a descendant of Abiel (1 Sam. 9:1; 10:11, 21; 14:51). He sent his son, Saul, after the straying asses (1 Sam. 9:3).

3. A Levite who lived in David's time (1 Chron. 23:21–22; 24:29). He was a son of Mahli and a grandson of Merari.

4. A Levite, son of Abdi of the Merari family, who helped cleanse the temple during the reign of King Hezekiah of Judah (2 Chron. 29:12).

5. A Benjamite ancestor of Mordecai (Est. 2:5).

Kishi [Kish'i]—See Kushaiah.

Kishion [Kish'i·on], *hardness*—A town of Issachar, a Gershonite Levitical city (Josh. 21:28). The town of Kedesh in 1 Chronicles 6:72 is probably the same place. Also called Kishon (KJV).

Kishon [Ki'shon], *bending* or *tortuous*—A river in Palestine, next to the Jordan in importance, which flows from sources on Mount Tabor and Mount Gilboa westward through the plain of Esdraelon and the valley of Jezreel, then empties into the Mediterranean Sea near the northern base of Mount Carmel. Because the Kishon falls slightly as it crosses the level plain, it often becomes swollen and floods much of the valley during the season of heavy rains.

At the river Kishon the Israelites won a celebrated victory over Sisera under the leadership of Deborah and Barak (Judg. 4:7). Fully armed with nine hundred chariots of iron (Judg. 4:13), the forces of Sisera became bogged down in the overflow of the Kishon (Judg. 5:21), and the Israelites defeated them. It was at the brook Kishon, also, that the prophets of Baal were executed following their contest with Elijah on Mount Carmel (1 Kings 18:40).

Kison [Ki'son]—Variant of Kishon.

Kithlish [Kith'lish], *unknown*—A town in the valley of Judah (Josh. 15:40).

Kitron [Kit'ron], *incense*—A town in Zebulun (Judg. 1:30).

Kittim [Kit'tim], *bruisers*—Islands west of Palestine, particularly the island of Cyprus (Gen. 10:4; 1 Chron. 1:7; Isa. 23:1–12; Ezek. 27:6).

Koa [Ko'a], *he-camel*—Apparently a people from east of the Tigris River (Ezek. 23:23).

Kohath [Ko'hath], *assembly*—A son of Levi and head of the Ko-hathite family (Gen. 46:11; Ex. 6:16, 18).

Kohathites [Ko'hath·ites]—Descendants of Kohath, son of Levi (Ex. 6:20).

Kolaiah [Ko·lai'ah], *voice of Jehovah*—Two Old Testament men:
1. Father of Ahab, the false prophet (Jer. 29:21).
2. A Benjamite (Neh. 11:7).

Korah [Kor'ah], *ice*—Four Old Testament men:
1. A son of Esau. His mother was Aholibamah (Gen. 36:5, 14).
2. A son of Eliphaz and grandson of Esau (Gen. 36:16).
3. A Levite of the family of Kohath, of the house of Izhar (Num. 16:1). He, with Abiram, Dathan, and On, conspired against Moses and Aaron. Moses ordered the people to leave the locality where Korah, Dathan, and Abiram had their tents. At that spot the earth opened and swallowed the conspirators (Num. 16; 26:10). Fire then destroyed those that offered incense (Num. 16:35).
4. Son of Hebron of the family of Caleb (1 Chron. 2:43).

Korahite [Kor'a·hite]—A descendant of the Korah. Samuel was a Korahite (1 Sam. 1:1; 1 Chron. 6:26), also the singer Heman (1 Chron. 6:33–38; 9:31–32).

Korathite [Kor'a·thite]—See Korahite.

Kore [Kor'e], *a partridge*—Two Old Testament men:
1. A Levite (1 Chron. 9:19; 26:1), father of two of the gatekeepers of the tabernacle.
2. Son of Immah, a Levite (2 Chron. 31:14), who kept the East Gate of the temple.

Korhite [Kor'hite]—See Korahite.

Koz [Koz], *thorn*—See Hakkoz (Ezra 2:61; Neh. 3:4).

Kushaiah [Ku·sha'iah], *bow of Jehovah*—A Levite of the Merarite family of the house of Mushi (1 Chron. 15:17). His son was Ethan who was appointed the assistant of Heman by David. In 1 Chronicles 6:44 he is called Kishi.

L

Laadah [La′a·dah], *order*—Son of Shelah of Judah and founder of Mareshah (1 Chron. 4:21).

Laadan [La′a·dan], *order*—Two Old Testament men:
1. An Ephramite, son of Tahan (1 Chron. 7:26).
2. A son of Gershom (1 Chron. 23:7–9; 26:21).

Laban [La′ban], *white*—Son of Bethuel and grandson of Nahor (the brother of Abraham). He is the father-in-law of Jacob. Laban lived in the city of Haran in Padan-aram where Abraham sent his servant to find a wife for Isaac. Laban, brother of Rebekah, is introduced when he heard of the servant's presence, saw the golden jewelry given Rebekah, and eagerly invited Abraham's emissary into their home (Gen. 24:29–60). Laban played an important role in the marriage arrangements. His stubbornness and greed characterized his later dealings with Rebekah's son Jacob.

Many years later, Jacob left home to escape Esau's wrath. At the well of Haran he met Rachel, Laban's daughter. Laban promised her to his nephew Jacob in return for seven years of labor from Jacob. Laban consequently dealt with Jacob with deception and greed; he gave him the wrong wife and then forced him to work seven more years for Rachel. Then he persuaded Jacob to stay longer, but the wages he promised were changed ten times in six years (Gen. 29–30).

When family situations became tense, Jacob quietly left with his wives, children, and possessions, only to be pursued by Laban (Gen. 31). Laban and Jacob eventually parted on peaceful terms, but they heaped up stones as a mutual testimony that they would have no further dealings with each other. On Mount Gilead they called upon God as their witness that they would not impose upon each other again (Gen. 31:43–55).

Also the name of a place in the Sinaitic peninsula (Deut. 1:1), thought by some to be the same as Libnah (Num. 33:20).

Lachish [La'chish], *impregnable*—A city in the lowland of Judah (Josh. 15:33, 39) which was taken by Joshua (Josh. 10:3–35; 12:11). Amaziah, king of Judah, fled to this city and was slain by conspirators (2 Kings 14:19; 2 Chron. 25:27). It was besieged by Sennacherib (2 Kings 18:14, 17) and by Nebuchadnezzar (Jer. 34:7). Excavations have restored the wall of the ancient city and other things that belong to the period of Judah from Rehoboam to Manasseh.

Ladan [La'dan]—Variant of Laadan.

Lael [La'el], *devoted to God*—Father of Eliasaph of the family of Gershom (Num. 3:24).

Lahad [La'had], *oppression*—Son of Jahath of Judah (1 Chron. 4:2).

Lahai-roi [La'hai-roi]—See Beer-lahai-roi.

Lahmas [Lah·mas], possibly *violence* or *provisions*—A village in the plain of Judah (Josh. 15:40).

Lahmi [Lah'mi], *my bread*—The brother of Goliath who was slain by Elhanan (1 Chron. 20:5).

Laish [La'ish], *a lion*—

1. A city in the north of Palestine, also called Leshem. When the land was divided, this city was given to the tribe of Dan, and they renamed the city after their progenitor, Dan (Josh. 19:47; Judg. 18:7–29).

2. The father of Paltiel, to whom Saul gave David's wife Michal (1 Sam. 25:44; 2 Sam. 3:15).

3. A city of Benjamin near Anathoth (Isa. 10:30); sometimes called Laishah (NRSV).

Laishah [La'i·shah]—See Laish.

Lake of Gennesaret [Gen·nes'a·ret]—See Galilee, Sea of.

Lakkum [Lak'kum], *obstruction*—A town of Naphtali (Josh. 19:33).

Lakum [La'kum]—See Lakkum.

Lamech [La'mech], *vigorous*—Two antediluvian men:

1. Son of Methusael of the line of Cain. His wives were Adah and Zillah. He was father of Jabal, Jubal, and Tubal-cain (Gen. 4:18–24).

2. Son of Methuselah and father of Noah of the line of Seth (Gen. 5:25, 28–31).

Laodicea [La·od·i·ce′a], *justice of the people*—A city in the Lycus Valley of the province of Phrygia where one of the seven churches of Asia Minor was situated (Rev. 3:14). In New Testament times, Laodicea was the most important city in the Roman province of Phrygia in central Asia Minor. About 65 kilometers (40 miles) east of Ephesus and about 16 kilometers (10 miles) west of Colossae, Laodicea was built on the banks of the river Lycus, a tributary of the Maeander River.

The words of the risen Christ to Laodicea in Revelation 3:14–22 contain allusions to the economic prosperity and social prominence of the city. Founded by the Seleucids and named for Laodice, the wife of Antiochus II (261–247 B.C.), Laodicea became extremely wealthy during the Roman period. For example, in 62 B.C. Flaccus seized the annual contribution of the Jews of Laodicea for Jerusalem amounting to twenty pounds of gold. Moreover, when the city was destroyed by an earthquake in A.D. 60 (along with Colossae and Hierapolis), it alone refused aid from Rome for rebuilding (compare the self-sufficient attitude of the church of Laodicea in Revelation 3:17). Laodicea was known for its black wool industry; it manufactured garments from the raven-black wool produced by the sheep of the surrounding area.

Although it had many natural advantages, Laodicea had one serious shortcoming—lack of good drinking water. Nearly all the streams in the area come from hot springs, which are filled with impurities. When the apostle John addressed the Christians at Laodicea, he referred to them as "lukewarm," and "neither cold nor hot" (Rev. 3:16). Many have guessed that this is a reference to Laodicea's thermal springs. John's statement "I will spew you out of My mouth" (Rev. 3:16) also brings to mind a mouthful of warm water, which is not a pleasant way to quench one's thirst!

The apostle Paul does not seem to have visited Laodicea at the time he wrote Colossians 2:1. Epaphras, Tychicus, Onesimus, and Mark seem to have been the early messengers of the gospel there (Col. 1:7; 4:7–15). A letter addressed to the Laodiceans by Paul (Col. 4:16) has apparently been lost; some consider it to be a copy of the Ephesian letter. A church council was supposedly held at Laodicea (A.D. 344–363), but all that has come down to us are statements from other councils.

The site of Laodicea is now a deserted heap of ruins that the Turks call Eski Hisar, or "old castle." Excavations at Laodicea have revealed that the city apparently tried to solve its water supply problem by bringing water in through stone pipes from an outside source. But these pipes contain limestone deposits, a sign that this water was not much better than the supply from Laodicea's hot springs.

According to the comments about the church at Laodicea in the book of Revelation, this congregation consisted of lukewarm Christians (Rev. 3:14–22). The living Lord demands enthusiasm and total commitment from those who worship Him.

Lapidoth [Lap'i·doth], *torches*—The husband of Deborah (Judg. 4:4).

Lappidoth [Lap'pi·doth]—Variant of Lapidoth.

Lasea [La·se'a], *shaggy*—A seaport of Crete (Acts 27:8).

Lasha [La'sha], *spring*—A city of Canaan, near the Dead Sea (Gen. 10:19). It is listed with Sodom and Gomorrah and other Cities of the Plain.

Lasharon [La·shar'on], *belonging to Sharon*—A city of unknown location, whose king Joshua defeated (Josh. 12:18).

Lazarus [Laz'a·rus], *God has helped*—The name of two men in the New Testament:

1. The beggar in Jesus' story about a rich man and a poor man (Luke 16:19–25). The wealthy man despised the beggar, paying no attention to his needs when he passed him each day. After the death of Lazarus, the poor man, he was carried by angels to Abraham's bosom, where he found comfort. But the rich man at death found himself in hades, in eternal torment.

This story was not intended to praise the poor and condemn the rich. It shows the dangers of turning away from the needs of others. It teaches that our attitude on earth will result in an eternal destiny that parallels our attitude. This note is sounded frequently in the teaching of Jesus (Matt. 7:24–27; Luke 16:9).

2. The brother of Martha and Mary of Bethany (John 11:1). One long account in the gospel of John tells about his death and resurrection at the command of Jesus (John 11). A second account in the same gospel describes him as sitting with Jesus in the family home after the resurrection miracle (John 12:1–2). Because of the publicity surrounding this event, the chief priest plotted to kill Lazarus (John 12:9–11).

Twice John's gospel records Jesus' love for Lazarus (John 11:3, 5). Yet, upon hearing of the sickness of his friend, Jesus delayed in returning to Bethany. When He finally arrived, both Martha and Mary rebuked Jesus for not coming sooner. Jesus showed His impatience at their unbelief (11:33) as well as His personal sorrow ("Jesus wept"). Then He brought Lazarus back to life (11:43).

Leah [Le′ah], *weary*—The older daughter of Laban, who deceitfully gave her in marriage to Jacob instead of her younger sister Rachel (Gen. 29:16–30). Although Rachel was the more beautiful of the two daughters of Laban and obviously was Jacob's favorite wife, the Lord blessed Leah and Jacob with six sons—Reuben, Simeon, Levi, Judah (Gen. 29:31–35), Issachar, and Zebulun (Gen. 30:17–20)—and a daughter, Dinah (Gen. 30:21). Leah's maid, Zilpah, added two more sons: Gad and Asher (Gen. 30:9–13).

Leah was the less favored of the two wives of Jacob, and she must have been painfully conscious of this during all the years of her marriage. But it was Leah rather than Rachel who gave birth to Judah, through whose line Jesus the Messiah was eventually born. Apparently Leah died in the land of Canaan before the migration to Egypt (Gen. 46:6). She was buried in the cave of Machpelah in Hebron (Gen. 49:31).

Lebana [Le·ba′na]—Variant of Lebanah.

Lebanah [Le·ba′nah], *white* or the poetic word for *moon*—One of the Nethinim. His descendants returned from Babylon in the first expedition (Ezra 2:45; Neh. 7:48).

Lebanon [Leb′a·non], *white*—A mountain range along the northwestern boundary of the promised land (Deut. 11:24; Josh. 1:4; 12:7; 13:5). It consists of two ranges with hills running from it (Hos. 14:5). The nation of Lebanon took its name from these mountains, which hem the beautiful valley of Lebanon (Josh. 11:17). The country covers much of the territory that was once Phoenicia. The beauties of Lebanon are often mentioned in Scripture, especially its richness and fertility (Pss. 72:16; 92:12; Song 4:15; 5:15). The famed cedars of Lebanon were used in the construction of the temple, as well as in construction of various kinds by many other nations. Eventually, the cedars were almost gone, and this wanton destruction is used as a figurative illustration of what would happen to Israel (Jer. 22:7; Ezek. 27:5; Zech. 11:2).

Lebaoth [Le·ba'oth], *lioness*—A town in the south of Judah (Josh. 15:32). See Beth-lebaoth.

Lebbaeus [Leb·bae'us], *a man of heart*—See Thaddaeus.

Leb Kamai [Leb Kam'ai], unknown—This word is thought to be a cryptic reference to Chaldea (Jer. 51:1).

Lebonah [Le·bo'nah], *incense*—A town north of Shiloh (Judg. 21:19).

Lecah [Le'cah], *a journey* or *progress*—A town of Judah (1 Chron. 4:21).

Lehabim [Le'ha·bim], *flaming* or *fiery*—A tribe of the Egyptians (Gen. 10:13; 1 Chron. 1:11). Quite possibly the Lehabim were the ancestors from which Libya and the Libyans derived their name.

Lehi [Le'hi], *cheek* or *jawbone*—In this place in Judah, Samson slew one thousand Philistines with the jawbone of an ass (Judg. 15:9, 14, 16).

Lemuel [Lem'u·el], *devoted to God*—An unknown king whose mother taught him the lessons of chastity and temperance (Prov. 31).

Leshem [Le'shem], *precious stone*—A city in the north of Palestine (Josh. 19:47), also called Laish.

Letushim [Le·tu'shim], *hammered*—Second son of Dedan son of Jokshan, and great-grandson of Abraham by Keturah (Gen. 25:3).

Leummim [Le·um'mim], *nations*—The last of the sons of Dedan (Gen. 25:3).

Levi [Le′vi], *joined*—The name of four men and one tribe in the Bible:

1. The third son of Jacob and Leah (Gen. 29:34). Together with his brother, Simeon, he massacred Shechem and the males of his city to punish Shechem for violating Levi's sister, Dinah (Gen. 34:25–31). His three sons (Gershon, Kohath, and Merari) were ancestors of the three main divisions of the Levitical priesthood: the Gershonites, the Kohathites, and the Merarites (Gen. 46:11). Levi participated in the plot against Joseph (Gen. 37:4) and later took his family to Egypt with Jacob. On his deathbed Jacob cursed Simeon and Levi because of their "cruelty" and "wrath," and foretold that their descendants would be divided and scattered (Gen. 49:5–7). Levi died in Egypt at the age of 137 (Ex. 6:16).

2. A tribe descended from Levi (Ex. 6:19).

3. Another name for Matthew, one of the twelve apostles (Mark 2:14). Levi was formerly a tax collector.

4. An ancestor of Jesus Christ (Luke 3:24). Levi was a son of Melchi and the father of Matthat.

5. Another ancestor of Jesus Christ (Luke 3:29). This Levi was a son of Simeon and the father of Matthat.

Leviathan [Le·vi′a·than], *coiled one*—This word occurs only six times in the Old Testament but the term has stirred up great interest and controversy. *Leviathan* has become a word for anything of enormous size and power. The word is thought to be derived from a verb meaning "to twist." Job 41 is devoted to a detailed description of Leviathan, with God challenging Job to master him.

Some scholars believe that in Job the word poetically describes the Nile crocodile with his scaly hide, terrible teeth, and fast swimming. They feel that this fits in with the overthrow of Egypt in the Red Sea, since "Leviathan" is used for Egyptian troops in Psalm 74:13–14. But in Psalm 104:25–26, some envision a dolphin or a whale. However, the description in Job 41:33–34 seems too majestic for a crocodile or dolphin, or even for a whale: "On earth there is nothing like him, which is made without fear. He beholds every high thing; he is king over all the children of pride." Since we really do not know for certain what a Leviathan was (or is), the best we can say is "great sea animal whose identity we do not know."

Levites [Le'vites]—Descendants of Levi, son of Jacob. His sons, Gershon or Gershom, Kohath, and Merari, were each the founder of a tribal family (Gen. 46:11; Ex. 6:16; Num. 3:17; 1 Chron. 6:16–48). Moses and Aaron were of the line of Kohath of the house of Amram.

The Levites at Sinai remained true to Jehovah, and were chosen for religious services (Ex. 32:26–29; Num. 3:9, 11–13, 40–41; 8:16–18). When the census was taken the firstborn of Israel, exclusive of Levites, numbered 22,273 (Num. 3:43, 46). There were 22,000 Levites. The first-born belonged to God, but He arranged that, instead of the firstborn from each family, He would choose one family to serve before Him. The 22,000 Levites took the place of 22,000 firstborn of Israel, and the remaining 273 firstborn of the other tribes were redeemed by paying five shekels apiece (Num. 3:46–51). At thirty years of age the Levites were eligible to full service in connection with the sanctuary (Num. 4:3; 1 Chron. 23:3–5), although they began to assist in these duties at the age of twenty (1 Chron. 23:24, 28–31). Luke notes that Jesus entered upon His public ministry, inaugurated by baptism, when thirty years of age (Luke 3:23).

Levitical Cities—Instead of being given a portion of the land as an inheritance, along with the other tribes, the tribe of Levi was allotted forty-eight cities scattered throughout the territories of the other eleven tribes (Num. 35:1–8; Josh. 20–21). Among these were the six cities of refuge.

Libanus [Lib·an'us]—See Lebanon.

Libertines [Lib'er·tines], *freedmen*—The word occurs in Acts 6:9. They were Jews made captive by the Romans under Pompey and later set free. They built a synagogue at Jerusalem. They joined the foes of Stephen the first martyr.

Libnah [Lib'nah], *whiteness*—Two geographical locations:
1. A place in the wilderness where the Israelites camped (Num. 33:20).
2. A city near Lachish in the territory of Judah (Josh. 10:29–31), which was taken by Joshua (Josh. 10:30, 39; 12:15). It revolted against Judah in the reign of Jehoram (2 Kings 8:22). Libnah was the birthplace of the father-in-law of Josiah (2 Kings 23:31; 24:18).

Libni [Lib′ni], *white*—

1. Son of Gershon, grandson of Levi and founder of the Libnites (Ex. 6:17; Num. 3:18–21; 26:58).

2. A Levite (1 Chron. 6:29).

Libnites [Lib·nites]—Descendants of Levi's grandson Libni (Num. 3:21; 26:58; Ex. 6:17)

Libya [Lib′y·a], *afflicted* or *weeping*—Country of the Libyans on the Mediterranean, west of lower Egypt (Ezek. 27:10; 30:5); also called Put (NIV, NRSV) or Phut (KJV). One of its cities was Cyrene (Acts 2:10), and Libyans were present in Jerusalem at Pentecost. Simon, who carried Jesus's cross, was from Cyrene (Matt. 27:32). Libya is mentioned in the Prophets (Jer. 46:9; Nah. 3:9), called Lubim in the KJV.

Likhi [Lik′hi], *learning*—Ancestor of a Manassite family (1 Chron. 7:19).

Linus [Li′nus], *a net*—This Christian at Rome sent greetings to Timothy (2 Tim. 4:21).

Lo-ammi [Lo-am′mi], *not my people*—The figurative name Hosea gave his second son (Hos. 1:8–9).

Lod [Lod], *travail*—A town of Benjamin (1 Chron. 8:12). It is now called Lydda (Ezra 2:33; Neh. 7:37).

Lodebar [Lo·de′bar], *no pasture*—Probably the same as Debir (Josh. 13:26), a place in Gilead near Mahanaim (2 Sam. 9:4–5; 17:27). See Debir.

Lois [Lo′is]—The grandmother of Timothy. She was commended by Paul for her godliness and devotion (2 Tim. 1:5; 3:15).

Lord [Lord]—The most used name of God in the Bible. Exodus 3 records one of the greatest revelations in the Old Testament: the personal name of God. (The words translated *God* in our Bible [′El, ′Elohim, ′Eloah] are not names, but the standard vocabulary for the Deity and even for false gods.)

God had told Moses His plan to use him in delivering the Israelites from Egyptian bondage, and Moses had asked whom he should tell the people had sent him. God answered Moses: "I AM WHO I AM." He told Moses to tell them that "I AM" had sent him, "the LORD God." "I AM" and "LORD" are both probably derived from the Hebrew verb *to be (hayah)* because God is the ever-present One, "the Eternal."

Many people are puzzled that in this and many other passages (over six thousand) some Bibles read *LORD* in all capitals (KJV, NKJV, NIV), some read "Jehovah" (ASV, Darby), and some read "Yahweh" (Jerusalem Bible). Because the name of God is so important—Jews devoutly refer to Him as "the Name" (*ha Shem*)—it is well worth exploring this revelation in some detail. It is merely a question of a Jewish tradition and how various Christian scholars handle that tradition.

In the Ten Commandments, God forbids us to take His name "in vain." We must not treat the name of God carelessly, as though it means nothing. In their great fear of violating this command, devout Hebrews went beyond the law, and when they read the Hebrew Scriptures aloud they would read the word *Lord* (*'Adonai*) whenever they saw the four letters (YHWH, or traditionally JHVH in Latin pronunciation) that spelled out God's revealed covenant name. This was the sacred name by which He had committed Himself to Israel as a nation.

The most ancient copies of the Hebrew text were written in consonants only. As the language became less and less used, scholars (called Masoretes) added little dots and dashes called "vowel points" to indicate how the text was to be pronounced. Oddly enough, they put the vowels that go with the word *'Adonai* together with the sacred four-letter name (called "tetragrammaton") to guide the readers to say *'Adonai* aloud in synagogue services.

This is the origin of the name "Jehovah." It is actually a hybrid name, combining the vowels of *'Adonai* with the consonants of YHWH into JeHoVaH or YeHoWah. The people who produced this name were medieval Christian Hebrew scholars; the Jews never acknowledged such a name. The defense of this Christian hybrid is the same as the defense of the Jewish avoidance of pronouncing the name—tradition. There are many lovely hymns and paraphrases of the Psalms that use this name, so it would be a loss to eliminate it from our Christian vocabulary. The poetical form of Jehovah is *Jah*. It is very likely that the name was actually pronounced very much like "Yahweh." Comparisons with transliterations of the name into other alphabets from very ancient times confirm this.

The best argument for this spelling is that it is probably historically accurate. However, it is less familiar than Jehovah, and it seems to many to be an unnecessary striving to try and change to the form, which is probably more correct. Actually, all the names which begin with "J" in our English Bibles were pronounced in their original language with a "Y" sound, as in "hallelu-Yah." Most recent major English Bibles, dissatisfied with both *Jehovah* and *Yahweh*, have retained the KJV's *LORD*. The NASB, which is an updating of the ASV, actually restored *LORD* (the 1901 text read *Jehovah*).

The word "Lord" also often appears with only a capital "L." In these passages, "Lord" is the translation of *'Adon* which means "Master" or "Lord." For example, if one looks closely at Psalm 8, one will notice the capitalization. "O LORD, our Lord" means "O Jehovah [Yahweh] our Lord [Master]." In Psalm 136:3, we are told to "give thanks to the Lord of lords," in other words, the One Master over all masters. When the personal suffix for "my" in Hebrew is put on *'adon,* it is generally *'adoni* (singular) for men and *'adonai* (plural) for God. We use lowercase letters in the English Bible when the word *lord* refers to a mortal man. We have already noticed that David was called "lord." Pharaoh (Gen. 40:1) and Saul (1 Sam. 16:16) are referred to as "lord." Other important leaders called *'adon* include Joseph (Gen. 42:10), Eli the priest (1 Sam. 1:15), David's commander Joab (2 Sam. 11:9), and the prophet Elijah (1 Kings 18:7). Even ordinary people were called by this title of respect: Abraham was addressed as "lord" by Sarah (Gen. 18:12) and by his servant Eliezer (Gen. 24). Ruth also called Boaz "my lord" in Ruth 2:13.

Lord, Jesus is—*Lord* or *Master (Kyrios)* is a most important New Testament word. In secular usage, the word meant "master," "guardian," or "trustee." This ancient usage still occurs in New Testament passages, such as Ephesians 6:5 and Colossians 4:1, regarding masters and servants. In the Septuagint, *Kyrios* was chosen as the translation of the Hebrew *Adonai* ("Lord"), as well as *Yahweh.*

Kyrios can also mean "Sir," therefore we cannot always be sure how the speaker was using the title. When Thomas, after seeing the risen Lord, exclaimed, "My Lord and my God!" (John 20:28), there can be no doubt he recognized Christ's lordship. When the Samaritan woman in John 4 addressed Him as an unknown traveler from a rival ethnic group, the KJV translation "sir" is no doubt correct. There are also several doubtful passages. For example, in Matthew 8:2, 6, were the leper and the centurion aware of who Jesus was, or were they just being polite?

Jesus is Lord of His church and Lord of lords (1 Tim. 6:15; Rev. 11:15); He should receive the service and homage He deserves. We who know Him as Savior and Lord do well to address Him as "Lord Jesus."

Lord of Hosts—An important title of God, used frequently in the Old Testament. The Hebrew word for "hosts" is used by both Paul and James, transliterated into Greek as *Sabaoth*. Paul quotes the LXX Isaiah, which along with the LXX 1 Samuel, includes this transliterated (rather than translated) form. Even though *Sabaoth* looks like *Sabbath* in English letters, the two words are totally unrelated. *Sabbath* comes from the word meaning "to cease" or "rest," and *Sabaoth* is from the Hebrew word meaning "host" or "army." The word "hosts" can refer to the host of heaven (singular) or hosts of soldiers, that is, armies. The term first occurs in 1 Samuel 1:3. Elkanah "went up from his city yearly to worship and sacrifice to the LORD of hosts in Shiloh."

God was the head of the forces of Israel (1 Sam. 17:45); and not merely of Israel's armies, but of all hosts, celestial and terrestrial— angelic and human. God can and does rule all the armies of the whole world. Also, perhaps as a warning against joining the heathen in worshipping the host of heaven (sun, moon, and stars) God stresses that He controls all the heavenly host.

One of the most familiar passages using this regal title is Psalm 24: "Who is the King of glory? The LORD of hosts, He is the King of glory" (v. 10). The title is not always military: "Even the sparrow has found a home, and the swallow a nest for herself, where she may lay her young—even Your altars, O LORD of hosts" (Ps. 84:3). The prophets Jeremiah, Isaiah, Zechariah, and Malachi used this title of God numerous times in their books.

Lo-ruhamah [Lo-ru·ha′mah], *not favored*—The symbolic name given to the daughter of Hosea the prophet and his wife, Gomer (Hos. 1:6–8).

Lot [Lot], *a covering*—A Shemite, who was the son of Haran and Abraham's nephew. Lot accompanied Abraham from Mesopotamia to Canaan and to and from Egypt (Gen. 11:27–31; 12:4–5; 13:1). Both Lot and Abraham had large herds of cattle, and their herdsmen quarreled over their pasturelands. At Abraham's suggestion, the two decided to separate.

Abraham gave Lot his choice of land; and Lot chose the more fertile, well-watered site—the Jordan River valley—as opposed to the rocky hill country. Failing to take into account the character of the inhabitants, Lot "pitched his tent toward Sodom" (Gen. 13:12, KJV).

When the Elamite king Chedorlaomer invaded Canaan with his allies, Lot was taken captive. Abraham attacked Chedorlaomer's forces by night and rescued his nephew (Gen. 13:1–14:16).

When two angels were sent to warn Lot that God intended to destroy Sodom, Lot could not control the Sodomites, who wished to abuse the two visitors carnally. The angels struck the Sodomites blind to save Lot (Gen. 19:1–11), and Lot and his family fled the doomed city. Lot's wife, however, did not follow the angels' orders and looked back at Sodom. Because of her disobedience she was turned into a "pillar of salt" (Gen. 19:26). Our Lord Jesus warned, "Remember Lot's wife" (Luke 17:32), as a reminder of the disastrous results of disobedience.

Following his escape from Sodom, Lot lived in a cave near Zoar (Gen. 19:30–38). His two daughters served their father wine and enticed him into incest. They did this because "there is no man on the earth to come in to us as is the custom of all the earth" (Gen. 19:31). Out of that union came two sons, Moab and Ben-ammi, the ancestors of the Moabites and the Ammonites respectively.

Lotan [Lo'tan], *covering*—Son of Seir (Gen. 36:20, 29; 1 Chron. 1:38).

Lowland—The low area between Philistia and the Mediterranean Sea, including the cities of Lachish and Beth-shemesh. These lowlands are to the east of Hebron and Debir (1 Kings 10:27).

Lubim [Lu'bim], *unknown*—An African people mentioned in connection with the Egyptians and Ethiopians (2 Chron. 12:3; 16:8). See Libya.

Lucas [Lu'cas]—Another form of the name Luke (Philem. 24).

Lucifer [Lu'ci·fer], *brightness*—The "bright star," or "morning star." This name often refers to Venus; though Jupiter, Mars, Mercury, and Saturn may also be seen with the naked eye if they are in the morning sky before sunrise. Isaiah likens the glory of the king of Babylon to Lucifer, whom he calls the "son of the morning" (Isa. 14:12). Isaiah speaks of Lucifer "fallen from heaven" because of his pride and desire to be like the Most High (Isa. 14:12–15). At least from the time of Jerome the name has been applied to Satan. It is assumed by many that Jesus' statement, "I saw Satan fall like lightning from heaven" (Luke 10:18) is a reference to Isaiah 14:12–15, and probably Ezekiel 28:12–19 as well. The prophecies of Isaiah and Ezekiel specifically refer to the kings of Babylon and Tyre, but these nations are often used as symbolic references to evil governments (as in the book of Revelation). If these passages do refer to Satan, it seems that the name "Lucifer" or "morning star" is not a name or a title, but rather a description of the original beauty of this angel. In Revelation 22:16 Jesus describes Himself as the bright, the morning star; this is clearly a description of beauty and majesty, not an identifying name.

Lucius [Lu′ci·us], *light* or *bright* or *white*—A Christian of Cyrene. He was a teacher in the church at Antioch (Acts 13:1).

Lud [Lud], *strife*—Lud was the fourth son of Shem (Gen. 10:22; 1 Chron. 1:17).

Ludim [Lu′dim], *to the firebrands* or *travailings*—The Ludim (Gen. 10:13; 1 Chron. 1:11) were the descendants of Mizraim.

Luhith [Lu′hith], *made of planks* or *floored*—A town of Moab (Isa. 15:5; Jer. 48:5).

Luke [Luke], *light-giving*—A "fellow laborer" of the apostle Paul (Philem. 24) and the author of the gospel of Luke and the Acts of the Apostles. A Greek, by profession he was a physician (Col. 4:14) and is often referred to as the beloved physician. During one of Paul's imprisonments, probably in Rome, Luke's faithfulness was recorded by Paul when he declared, "Only Luke is with me" (2 Tim. 4:11). These three references are our only direct knowledge of Luke in the New Testament.

A bit more of Luke's life and personality can be pieced together with the aid of his writings (Luke and Acts) and some outside sources. Tradition records that he came from Antioch in Syria. This is possible, because Antioch played a significant role in the early Gentile mission that Luke described in Acts (Acts 11; 13; 14; 15; 18). Luke was a Gentile (Col. 4:10–17) and the only non-Jewish author of a New Testament book. A comparison of 2 Corinthians 8:18 and 12:18 has led some to suppose that Luke and Titus were brothers, but this is a guess.

Luke accompanied Paul on parts of his second, third, and final missionary journeys. At three places in Acts, the narrative changes to the first person ("we"). This probably indicates that Luke was personally present during those episodes. On the second journey (A.D. 49–53), Luke accompanied Paul on the short voyage from Troas to Philippi (Acts 16:10–17). On the third journey (A.D. 54–58), Luke was present on the voyage from Philippi to Jerusalem (Acts 20:5–21:18). Whether Luke had spent the intervening time in Philippi is uncertain, but his connection with Philippi has led some to favor it (rather than Antioch) as Luke's home.

Once in Palestine, Luke probably remained close by Paul during his two-year imprisonment in Caesarea. During this time, Luke probably drew together material, both oral and written, which he later used in the composition of his gospel (Luke 1:1–4). A third "we" passage describes in masterful suspense the shipwreck during Paul's voyage to Rome for his trial before Caesar. Each of the "we" passages involves Luke on a voyage, and the description of the journey from Jerusalem to Rome is full of observations and knowledge of nautical matters (Acts 27).

Luke apparently was a humble man, with no desire to sound his own horn. More than one-fourth of the New Testament comes from his pen, but not once does he mention himself by name. He had a greater command of the Greek language and was probably more broad-minded and urbane than any other New Testament writer. He was a careful historian, both by his own admission (Luke 1:1–4) and by the judgment of later history.

Luke's gospel reveals his concern for the poor, sick, and outcast, thus offering a clue to why Paul called him "the beloved physician" (Col. 4:14). He was faithful not only to Paul, but to the greater cause he served—the publication of "good tidings of great joy" (Luke 2:10).

Luz [Luz], *nut tree*—Two towns:

1. An ancient town of the Canaanites which was later called Beth-el (Gen. 28:19; 35:6; 48:3; Josh. 18:13).

2. A town of the Hittites, built by an inhabitant of the former Luz. This man betrayed the first town to the Israelites (Judg. 1:22–26).

Lycaonia [Ly·ca·o'ni·a], *wolf land*—A district of Asia Minor, adapted to pasturage. Paul preached in three of its cities, Iconium, Derbe, Lystra (Acts 13:51–14:1–23). Timothy came from this area (Acts 16:1).

Lycia [Lyc'i·a], *wolfish*—A Roman province in the southwest of Asia Minor. On his voyage to Jerusalem Paul stopped at Patara in this district (Acts 21:1–2). He landed at Myra, another of its cities, on the way to Rome (Acts 27:5–6).

Lydda [Lyd'da], *strife*—A village near Joppa, or Jaffa (Acts 9:32, 38).

Lydia [Lyd'i·a], *travail*—

1. A woman of Thyatira, a town of Asia. This city was noted for the art of dyeing and when Lydia settled in Philippi, she sold the dyed garments of Thyatira. She was a pious woman, a true worshipper of God. When she heard Paul she accepted the gospel. It was in Philippi the gospel was first preached in Europe. Paul and Silas lodged in her home (Acts 16:14–15, 40).

2. *(land of Lydus)*. A region on the western coast of Asia Minor. Its capital was Sardis and Philadelphia and Thyatira were within its bounds (Rev. 1:11).

Lydians [Lyd'i·ans]—Soldiers, also referred to as "men of Lydia" (NIV) or "men of Ludim" (NRSV), who fought at the Battle of Carchemish with the Egyptians (Jer. 46:9). They may have come from Lydia (in modern Turkey), or an African people. See Ludim.

Lysanias [Ly·sa'ni·as], *sadness ended*—The tetrarch of Abilene during the time of John the Baptist and Jesus (Luke 3:1).

Lysias Claudius [Lys'i·as Clau'di·us], *releaser* and *lame*—The commander of the Roman troops in Jerusalem. He rescued Paul from an angry mob, and sent him by night to Caesarea for safekeeping (Acts 21:31–38; 22:24–30; 23:17–30; 24:7, 22). He was a tribune, the commander of a cohort (600 to 1,000 men).

Lystra [Lys'tra], *ransoming*—A city of Lycaonia. Paul visited this city on his first missionary journey. After he healed a lame man, the people insisted that he and Barnabas be worshipped as gods. As soon as they figured out what was happening, they managed to prevent the sacrifices, but it was only with great difficulty that the crowds were restrained. Only a short time later, the same crowds were enthusiastically stoning Paul, at the instigation of the hostile Jews from the neighboring town. Paul survived this ordeal, and continued on his way the next day (Acts 14:6–21; 2 Tim. 3:11). Timothy came from this town, the son of a believing Jewish woman and her Gentile husband (Acts 16:1–2).

M

Maacah, Maachah [Ma'a·cah, Ma'a·chah], *oppression*—Six women, three men, and a kingdom:

1. The son of Reumah, the concubine of Nahor, the brother of Abraham (Gen. 22:24).

2. A wife of David, the mother of Absalom. She was the daughter of Talmai, king of Geshur (2 Sam. 3:3; 1 Chron. 3:2).

3. An Aramean kingdom, also called Syrian Maachah, from whose king the Ammonites hired 1,000 soldiers to fight against David (2 Sam. 10:6, 8; 1 Chron. 19:6–7).

4. Father of Achish and king of Gath in the time of Solomon (1 Kings 2:39).

5. Granddaughter of Abishalom and wife of Rehoboam, king of Judah, and mother of Abijah (1 Kings 15:2). Because she encouraged idolatry, her grandson, Asa, removed her from the throne (1 Kings 15:10–13; 2 Chron. 15:16).

6. Concubine of Caleb, mother of Sheber and Tirhanah (1 Chron. 2:48).

7. Wife of Machir, the son of Manasseh (1 Chron. 7:15–16).

8. Wife of Jehiel, who was the father of Gibeon. Maacah was an ancestress of King Saul (1 Chron. 8:29; 9:35).

9. Father of Hanan, one of David's mighty men (1 Chron. 11:43).

10. Father of Shephatiah, ruler of the Simeonites in David's reign (1 Chron. 27:16).

Maachathite, Maacathite [Ma·ach'a·thite, Ma·ac'a·thite]—Inhabitants of Maacah, probably the descendants of Maacah the son of Nahor (see Maacah No. 1; Deut. 3:14; Josh. 12:5; 11:13; 2 Sam. 23:34; 2 Kings 25:23; Jer. 40:8).

Maadai [Ma·a·da'i], *ornament of Jehovah*—A son of Bani, one of the group who had married foreign wives (Ezra 10:34).

Maadiah [Ma·a·di'ah], *ornament of Jehovah*—A priest who returned from Babylon (Neh. 12:5, 7), perhaps the same as Moadiah (Neh. 12:17).

Maai [Ma·a'i], *compassionate*—A priest who blew a trumpet at the dedication of the rebuilt wall of Jerusalem (Neh. 12:36).

Maaleh-acrabbim [Ma'a·leh-ac·rab'bim], *ascent of scorpions*—(Josh. 15:3) See Akrabbim.

Maarath [Ma'a·rath], *desolation*—A town in the mountains of Judah (Josh. 15:59). Its present-day location is uncertain, but other towns mentioned in conjunction with it are located a few miles to the north of Hebron.

Maasai [Ma'a·sai], *work of Jehovah*—A priest of the family of Immer (1 Chron. 9:12; Maasiai, KJV).

Maaseiah [Ma·a·sei'ah], *work of Jehovah*—Possibly as many as twenty-one Old Testament men:

1. A Levite who played a psaltery as the ark was brought to Jerusalem (1 Chron. 15:18, 20).

2. A captain of a force which assisted Jehoiada in the removal of Athaliah from the throne of Judah (2 Chron. 23:1).

3. An officer in the reign of Uzziah (2 Chron. 26:11).

4. A son of Ahaz, king of Judah, slain by Zichri, the mighty man of Ephraim (2 Chron. 28:7).

5. Governor of Jerusalem during the days of Josiah, king of Judah (2 Chron. 34:8).

6. A priest of the descendants of Jeshua (Ezra 10:18).

7. A priest of the sons of Harim (Ezra 10:21).

8. A priest of the house of Pashur (Ezra 10:22).

9. A descendant of the house of Pahath-moab (Ezra 10:30).

10. Father of Azariah (Neh. 3:23).

11. One who was with Ezra when he instructed the people (Neh. 8:4).

12. A priest who explained the law (Neh. 8:7).

13. A chief of the people, one who sealed the covenant (Neh. 10:25).

14. A man of Judah who resided in Jerusalem at the time of Nehemiah (Neh. 11:5).

15. Son of Ithiel, a Benjamite (Neh. 11:7).

16. A priest who participated in the dedication of the wall, one of the trumpeters (Neh. 12:41).

17. Another priest who participated in the dedication of the wall, a singer (Neh. 12:42).

18. Father of Zephaniah, who was a priest during the time of King Zedekiah of Judah (Jer. 21:1; 29:25).

19. Father of the false prophet Zedekiah (Jer. 29:21).

20. Ancestor of Seraiah, quartermaster to King Zedekiah; and Baruch, Jeremiah's scribe (Jer. 32:12; 51:59).

21. Son of Shallum and doorkeeper of the temple during the time of Jehoiakim, king of Judah (Jer. 35:4).

Maasiai [Ma·as·i'ai]—See Maasai.

Maath [Ma'ath], *small*—An ancestor of Jesus (Luke 3:26).

Maaz [Ma'az], *anger*—A son of Ram (1 Chron. 2:27).

Maaziah [Ma·a·zi'ah], *consolation of Jehovah*—Two Old Testament men:

1. A descendant of Aaron (1 Chron. 24:18).

2. A priest who signed the covenant with Nehemiah (Neh. 10:8). Possibly another name for Maadiah (Neh. 12:5).

Macbannai [Mac'ban·nai]—See Machbanai.

Maccabees, The [Mac'ca·bees], *hammer*—A family of Jewish patriots also known as the Asmonaeans, or Hasmonaeans. The name is derived from one of the family's most prominent members, Judas, whose surname was Maccabaeus. Judas Maccabaeus led the revolt against the rule of the defiler Antiochus Epiphanes. See Hasmonean.

Macedonia [Mac·e·do'ni·a], *extended land*—A country north of Greece. It rose to worldwide power under Philip of Macedon (359–336 B.C.) and his celebrated son Alexander the Great (336–323 B.C.). Macedonia is first mentioned in Acts 16:6–10; Paul received a vision of a Macedonian man begging for someone to come and explain the gospel to them. Luke describes Paul's journey through Macedonia in chapters 16:6–17:14. Paul later returned to Macedonia to encourage the churches there (Acts 20:1). See Philippi, and Thessalonica.

Macedonians [Mac·e·do′ni·ans]—Inhabitants of Macedonia. Two of Paul's traveling companions, Gaius and Aristarchus, were Macedonians (Acts 19:29). Paul also mentions the Macedonian believers in his letter to the Corinthian church (2 Cor. 9:2).

Machaerus [Mach·aer′us], unknown—According to Josephus, the place where John the Baptist was imprisoned and beheaded.

Machbanai [Mach·ba′nai], *bond of the Lord*—A Gadite hero who joined David at Ziklag (1 Chron. 12:13).

Machbena [Mach·be′na]—See Machbenah.

Machbenah [Mach·be′nah], *bond*—A name, probably of a town, mentioned in a genealogical list (1 Chron. 2:49).

Machi [Ma′chi], *decrease*—Father of Geuel (Num. 13:15).

Machir [Ma′chir], *sold*—Two Old Testament men:
1. The son of Manasseh, son of Joseph. He was the founder of the Machirites (Gen. 50:23; Num. 26:29; Josh. 17:1) who were given the district taken from the Amorites, east of the Jordan (Num. 32:39–40; Deut. 3:15).
2. A son of Ammiel in Lodebar (2 Sam. 9:4–5; 17:27–29).

Machirites [Ma′chir·ites]—Descendants of Machir, son of Manasseh, son of Joseph (Num. 26:29).

Machnadebai [Mach·nad′e·bai], *he brought low my willing ones*—A son of Bani. He renounced his foreign wife (Ezra 10:40).

Machpelah [Mach·pe′lah], *double*—A field, a cave, and the surrounding land purchased by Abraham as a burial place for his wife Sarah. The cave was to the east of Mamre, or Hebron (Gen. 23:19). At an earlier time, Abraham pitched his tent "and went and dwelt by the terebinth trees of Mamre, which are in Hebron, and built an altar there to the LORD" (Gen. 13:18). He also received three visitors who spoke of a child of promise to be born to Sarah (Gen. 18:1–15).

Abraham purchased the field of Machpelah from Ephron the Hittite for four hundred shekels of silver. Abraham, Sarah, Isaac, Rebekah, Jacob, and Leah were all buried here (Gen. 49:31; 50:13).

Today the modern city of el-Khalil (Hebron) is built up around the site of Machpelah. The site of the cave was once protected by a Christian church but is now marked by a Muslim mosque. The Muslims held this site so sacred that for centuries Christians were forbidden to enter the ancient shrine. It is open to the public today.

Madaba [Ma'da·ba]—See Medeba.

Madai [Ma'dai], *middle land*—The son of Japheth, from whom the Medes probably descended (Gen. 10:2; 1 Chron. 1:5).

Madian [Mad'i·an]—See Midian (Acts 7:29).

Madmannah [Mad·man'nah], *dunghill*—A town in the extreme south of Judah (Josh. 15:31; 1 Chron. 2:49).

Madmen [Mad'men], *dunghill*—A town in Moab (Jer. 48:2).

Madmenah [Mad·me'nah], *dunghill*—A town north of Jerusalem near Gibeah (Isa. 10:31).

Madon [Ma'don], *strife*—A city of the Canaanites in the north of Palestine (Josh. 11:1–12; 12:19).

Magadan [Mag'a·dan], *a tower*—A place probably on the western shore of the Sea of Galilee (Matt. 15:39). A variant of Magdala.

Magbish [Mag'bish], *congregating*—A name listed with those who returned to Jerusalem with Zerubbabel (Ezra 2:30); apparently the town these families originally came from.

Magdala [Mag'da·la], *tower*—A place on the Sea of Galilee, perhaps on the west shore, about 5 kilometers (3 miles) northwest of Tiberias. Jesus and His disciples withdrew to this place after the feeding of the 4,000 (Matt. 15:39; Magadan, NIV, NASB, REB, NRSV). The parallel passage (Mark 8:10) says they went to Dalmanutha. Magdala was either the birthplace or the home of Mary Magdalene.

Magdalene [Mag'da·lene], *from Magdala*—The designation given to a woman named Mary, one of Jesus' most prominent Galilean female disciples, to distinguish her from the other Marys. The first appearance of Mary Magdalene in the Gospels is in Luke 8:2, which mentions her among those who were ministering to Jesus. Mary Magdalene has sometimes mistakenly been described as a woman of bad character and loose morals, simply because Mark 16:9 states that Jesus had cast seven demons out of her. Nor is there any reason to conclude that she was the same person as the sinful woman whom Simon the Pharisee treated with such disdain and contempt (Luke 7:36–50).

Mary Magdalene was among the "many women who followed Jesus from Galilee, ministering to Him" (Matt. 27:55). She was one of the women at Calvary who were "looking on from afar" (Mark 15:40) when Jesus died on the cross (John 19:25). She was at Joseph's tomb when the body of Jesus was wrapped in a fine linen cloth and a large stone was rolled against the door of the tomb (Matt. 27:61; Mark 15:47). And she was a witness of the risen Christ (Matt. 28:1; Mark 16:1; Luke 24:10; John 20:1). In fact, she was the first of any of Jesus' followers to see Him after His resurrection (Mark 16:9; John 20:11–18).

Apparently Mary is called "Magdalene" because she was a native or inhabitant of Magdala.

Magdiel [Mag'di·el], *honor of God*—An Edomite chief descended from Esau (Gen. 36:43; 1 Chron. 1:54).

Magog [Ma'gog], *land of Gog*—The name of a man and a people in the Bible:

1. The second son of Japheth and a grandson of Noah (Gen. 10:2).

2. The descendants of Magog (Ezek. 38:2), possibly a people who lived in northern Asia and Europe. The Jewish historian Josephus identified these people as the Scythians, known for their destructive warfare. Magog may be a comprehensive term meaning "northern barbarians." The people of Magog are described as skilled horsemen (Ezek. 38:15) and experts in the use of the bow and arrow (Ezek. 39:3, 9). The book of Revelation uses Ezekiel's prophetic imagery to portray the final, apocalyptic encounter between good and evil at the end of this age. It was prophesied that their ruler, Gog, would fail in his expedition against the restored Israel. "Gog and Magog" (Rev. 20:8–9) symbolize the anti-Christian forces of the world.

Magor-missabib [Ma'gor-mis'sa·bib], *fear round about*—A name given to Pashur by Jeremiah (Jer. 20:3).

Magpiash [Mag'pi·ash], *moth killer*—A chief of the people who sealed the covenant (Neh. 10:20).

Mahalab [Ma·ha'lab]—A town of Asher (Josh. 19:29, NRSV). Also translated "at the sea" (NKJV).

Mahalah [Mah'a·lah]—See Mahlah.

Mahalaleel [Ma·hal'a·leel], *praise of God*—Two Old Testament men:
  1. Grandson of Seth (Gen. 5:12–17; Luke 3:37).
  2. A man of Judah of the family of Perez who lived in Jerusalem after the Exile (Neh. 11:4).

Mahalath [Ma'ha·lath], *sickness*—Two Old Testament women:
  1. Wife of Esau and daughter of Ishmael also called Bashemath (Gen. 28:9).
  2. A wife of Rehoboam (2 Chron. 11:18).

Mahali [Ma'ha·li]—See Mahli.

Mahanaim [Ma·ha·na'im], *two armies*—An ancient town in Gilead, east of the Jordan River in the vicinity of the river Jabbok. Located on the border between the tribes of Manasseh and Gad (Josh. 13:26, 30), Mahanaim was later assigned to the Merarite Levites (Josh. 21:38).

On his way home after an absence of twenty years, Jacob was met by angels of God at this site. "When Jacob saw them, he said, 'This is God's camp.'" He named the place Mahanaim, meaning "two armies." This was a significant moment for Jacob, who was about to meet his estranged brother Esau. The knowledge that he was being accompanied by an angelic band undoubtedly brought him the confidence and assurance he needed. Following the slaying of King Saul by the Philistines, his son Ish-bosheth reigned for two years at Mahanaim (2 Sam. 2:8, 12, 29). Later, Mahanaim became the headquarters for David during the rebellion of his son Absalom (2 Sam. 17:24). Solomon also made Mahanaim the capital of one of his twelve districts (1 Kings 4:14).

Mahaneh-dan [Ma'ha·neh-dan], *camp of Dan*—An encampment of the Danites (Judg. 13:25; 18:12).

Maharai [Ma'ha·rai], *hasty*—One of David's warriors, a Netophathite (2 Sam. 23:28; 1 Chron. 11:30; 27:13).

Mahath [Ma'hath], *gasping*—Two Old Testament Levites:

1. A Levite of the family of Kohath and an ancestor of Samuel (1 Chron. 6:33–35).

2. A Levite who lived during the days of Hezekiah, an overseer of priests who assisted in Hezekiah's reforms (2 Chron. 29:12; 31:13).

Mahavite [Ma'ha·vite], *propagators*—The designation of Eliel, one of David's mighty men (1 Chron. 11:46).

Mahazioth [Ma·ha'zi·oth], *visions*—A descendant of Heman, a Levite (1 Chron. 25:4).

Maher-shalal-hash-baz [Ma·her-shal'al-hash'-baz], *hasten the booty* or *speed the plunder*—These were the words Isaiah wrote upon a scroll that became the symbolic name of the second son of the prophet Isaiah (Isa. 8:1, 3), signifying the doom of Damascus and Samaria and the destruction of Syria and Israel, who had formed a military alliance against Jerusalem (Isa. 7:1).

Mahlah [Mah'lah], *disease*—Two Old Testament women:

1. Daughter of Zelophehad of Manasseh (Num. 26:33; 27:1).
2. The daughter of Gilead's sister Hammoleketh (1 Chron. 7:18).

Mahli [Mah'li], *weak*—Two Old Testament men:

1. A son of Merari and brother of Mushi, a Levite. He was founder of a tribal house (Ex. 6:19; Num. 3:20, 33; 26:58).

2. A Levite (1 Chron. 6:47; 23:23; 24:30).

Mahlites [Mah'lites]—The descendants of Mahli, son of Merari, a Levite (Num. 3:33; 26:58).

Mahlon [Mah'lon], *sickly*—Son of Elimelech and Naomi and the first husband of Ruth (Ruth 1:2; 4:10).

Mahol [Ma'hol], *dance*—Father of three men noted for wisdom—Heman, Chalcol, and Darda (1 Kings 4:31). Solomon is described as being wiser than any of these three.

Mahseiah [Mah·sei'ah]—See Maaseiah No. 20.

Makaz [Ma'kaz], *an end*—A town under the supervision of the son of Dekar, one of Solomon's twelve food-purveyors (1 Kings 4:9).

Makheloth [Mak·he′loth], *assemblies*—An encampment of the Israelites in the wilderness (Num. 33:25–26).

Makkedah [Mak·ke′dah], *place of herdsmen*—A town in the lowland taken by Joshua (Josh. 15:41).

Maktesh [Mak′tesh], *mortar*—A valley in Jerusalem having a peculiar shape. The Targum calls it the Kidron Valley (Zeph. 1:11). Also called the "Mortar" (NASB, NRSV) and the "market district" (NIV).

Malachi [Mal′a·chi], *my messenger*—Old Testament prophet and author of the prophetic book that bears his name. Nothing is known about Malachi's life except the few facts that may be inferred from his prophecies. A Jewish tradition says that he was a member of the Great Synagogue. He apparently prophesied after the captivity, during the time when Nehemiah was leading the people to rebuild Jerusalem's wall and recommit themselves to following God's law. The people's negligence in paying tithes to God was condemned by both Nehemiah and Malachi (Neh. 13:10–14; Mal. 3:8–10).

Malcam [Mal′cam], *rule*—
    1. Son of Shaharaim, a Benjamite (1 Chron. 8:9).
    2. A god of the Ammonites (Zeph. 1:5). See Molech.

Malcham [Mal′cham]—See Malcam, also a form of Milcom (Zech. 1:5, KJV).

Malchiah [Mal·chi′ah]—See Malchijah.

Malchiel [Mal′chi·el], *God is king*—Son of Beriah and grandson of Asher (Gen. 46:17; Num. 26:45).

Malchijah, Malchiah [Mal·chi′jah, Mal·chi′ah], *Jehovah is king*—Ten Old Testament kings:
    1. A Levite of Gershom (1 Chron. 6:40).
    2. A descendant of Aaron. His house became the fifth course of priests in the time of David (1 Chron. 24:1, 6, 9).
    3. Son of Parosh who put away his foreign wife (Ezra 10:25).
    4. Son of Harim. He put away his foreign wife and labored on the wall of Nehemiah (Ezra 10:31; Neh. 3:11).
    5. A son of Rechab. He labored on the wall under Nehemiah (Neh. 3:14).

6. A goldsmith who labored on Nehemiah's wall (Neh. 3:31).

7. One who stood by Ezra when he explained the law (Neh. 8:4).

8. A priest who signed the covenant (Neh. 10:3).

9. A priest who participated in the dedication of the wall (Neh. 12:42).

10. Father of Pashur (Jer. 21:1; 38:1), who threw Jeremiah into the cistern. Pashur's father, Malchiah, was evidently a prince, and the cistern was in his courtyard (Jer. 38:6).

Malchiram [Mal·chi′ram], *God exalted*—A son of Jehoiachin, born in captivity (1 Chron. 3:18).

Malchishua [Mal′chi·shu′a], *my king is wealth*—A son of King Saul (1 Sam. 14:49; 31:2; 1 Chron. 8:33; 9:39).

Malchus [Mal′chus], *king*—Servant of the high priest. His ear was cut off by Peter at the time of Christ's arrest (John 18:10). According to Luke, Christ healed the severed ear (Luke 22:51).

Maleleel [Mal′e·leel]—See Mahalaleel.

Malkijah [Mal·ki′jah]—See Malchijah.

Mallothi [Mal·lo′thi], *I have uttered*—Son of Heman, one of the musicians in the tabernacle service at the time of King David (1 Chron. 25:4, 26).

Malluch [Mal′luch], *reigning* or *counselor*—Six Old Testament men:

1. A Levite of the house of Mushi, of the family of Merari, ancestor of Ethan (1 Chron. 6:44).

2. A son of Bani. He put away his foreign wife (Ezra 10:29).

3. A son of Harim who divorced his Gentile wife (Ezra 10:32).

4. A priest who signed the covenant (Neh. 10:4).

5. A chief of the people who signed the covenant (Neh. 10:27).

6. A chief of the priests who returned from Babylon with Zerubbabel (Neh. 12:2, 7); also called Malluchi (Neh. 12:14, NASB, NRSV), Melichu (NKJV), or Melicu (KJV).

Malluchi [Mal·lu′chi]—See Malluch No. 6.

Malta [Mal'ta], possibly *honey*—An island in the Mediterranean, located between Sicily and Africa. When Paul was being transported to Rome, his ship was caught in a storm and they were shipwrecked on this island (Acts 28:1, 11). He stayed there for about three months, using the time to preach the gospel and start another church. Malta is also called Melita (KJV).

Mammaias [Mam·mai'as]—See Shemaiah (Ezra 8:16).

Mamre [Mam're], *strength* or *fatness*—The name of a man and a place in the Old Testament:

1. An Amorite chief who formed an alliance with Abraham against Chedorlaomer (Gen. 14:13, 24). He along with his brothers helped to rescue Lot.

2. A place in the district of Hebron, west of Machpelah, where Abraham lived. It was noted for its "terebinth trees" (Gen. 13:18; 18:1), or "oaks" (NRSV). Near Mamre was the cave of Machpelah, in which Abraham, Isaac, and Jacob—and their wives, Sarah, Rebekah, and Leah—were buried (Gen. 49:13). The site of ancient Mamre has been identified as Ramet el-Khalil, about 3 kilometers (2 miles) north of Hebron.

Manaen [Man'a·en], Greek form of *Menahem*—A teacher in the church at Antioch (Acts 13:1), probably of a noble family because he was "brought up with Herod the Tetrarch."

Manahath [Man'a·hath], *rest*—

1. Son of Shobal, the Horite (Gen. 36:23).

2. A place where Benjamites of Geba were held captive (1 Chron. 8:6).

Manahathites [Man·a·ha'thites]—Variant of Manahethites.

Manahethites [Man·a·he'thites]—The descendants of Manahath, or else the inhabitants of Manahath (1 Chron. 2:52, 54).

Manasseh [Ma·nas'seh], *causing to forget*—The name of five men and a tribe in the Old Testament:

1. Joseph's firstborn son who was born in Egypt to Asenath the daughter of Potipherah, priest of On (Gen. 41:50–51). Like his younger brother, Ephraim, Manasseh was half Hebrew and half Egyptian. Manasseh's birth caused Joseph to forget the bitterness of his past

experiences. Manasseh and Ephraim were both adopted by Jacob and given status as sons just like Jacob's own sons Reuben and Simeon (Gen. 48:5).

2. The grandfather of the Jonathan who was one of the priests of the graven image erected by the tribe of Dan (Judg. 18:30).

3. The fourteenth king of Judah, the son of Hezekiah born to Hephzibah (2 Kings 21:1–18). Manasseh reigned longer (fifty-five years) than any other Israelite king and had the dubious distinction of being Judah's most wicked king. He came to the throne at the age of twelve, although he probably co-reigned with Hezekiah for ten years. His father's godly influence appears to have affected Manasseh only negatively, and he reverted to the ways of his evil grandfather, Ahaz.

Committed to idolatry, Manasseh restored everything Hezekiah had abolished. Manasseh erected altars to Baal; he erected an image of Asherah in the temple; he worshipped the sun, moon, and stars; he recognized the Ammonite god Molech and sacrificed his son to him (2 Kings 21:6); he approved divination; and he killed all who protested his evil actions. It is possible that he killed the prophet Isaiah; rabbinical tradition states that Manasseh gave the command that Isaiah be sawn in two (see also Heb. 11:37). Scripture summarizes Manasseh's reign by saying he "seduced them [Judah] to do more evil than the nations whom the Lord had destroyed before the children of Israel" (2 Kings 21:9).

Manasseh was temporarily deported to Babylon where he humbled himself before God in repentance (2 Chron. 33:11–13). Upon Manasseh's return to Jerusalem, he tried to reverse the trends he had set; but his reforms were quickly reversed after his death by his wicked son Amon.

4. A descendant, or resident, of Pahath-moab (Ezra 10:30). After the captivity he divorced his pagan wife.

5. An Israelite of the family of Hashum. Manasseh divorced his pagan wife after the captivity (Ezra 10:33).

6. Tribe of Manasseh. It comprised seven tribal families, one springing from Manasseh's son, Machir, and the others from his grandson, Gilead (Num. 26:28–34; Josh. 17:1–2). A half of the tribe was settled east of the Jordan and the other half west of the Jordan in the central section, north of Ephraim (Num. 32:33, 42; Deut. 3:13–15; Josh. 13:29–33).

Manasses [Man′as·ses]—Alternate spelling of Manasseh.
1. Manasseh, king of Judah (Matt. 7:10).
2. Manasseh, son of Joseph (Rev. 7:6).

Manassites, The [Man′as·sites]—The tribe of Manasseh; the descendants of Joseph's oldest son, Manasseh (Deut. 4:43; Judg. 12:4; 2 Kings 10:33).

Manoah [Ma·no′ah], *rest*—The father of Samson, a Danite of the town of Zorah (Judg. 13:1–25). When told of the announcement of the angel to his wife promising the birth of Samson, he prayed for the angel's return to give him instruction concerning the rearing of the child. The petition was granted.

Manuhoth [Man·u·hoth], unknown—Descendants of Caleb (1 Chron. 2:52).

Maoch [Ma′och], *oppressed*—Father of Achish, king of Gath (1 Sam. 27:2). See Achish.

Maon [Ma′on], *dwelling*—
1. Son of Shammai of Judah, founder of Beth-zur (1 Chron. 2:45).
2. A town of Judah, south of Hebron (Josh. 15:55; 1 Sam. 25:2).

Maonites [Ma′on·ites], *habitation*—A people mentioned in Judges 10:12 as oppressors of Israel.

Mara [Mar′a], *bitter*—The name by which Naomi asked to be called after her bitter experiences in Moab (Ruth 1:20).

Marah [Mar′ah], *bitterness*—One of the encampments of the Israelites before coming to Sinai (Ex. 15:23–24; Num. 33:8–9).

Maralah [Mar′a·lah], *trembling*—A place on the border of Zebulun (Josh. 19:11).

Mareal [Mar′eal]—See Maralah.

Mareshah [Ma·re′shah], *summit*—
1. The father of Hebron, among the descendants of Caleb (1 Chron. 2:42).
2. A town of Judah in the lowland (Josh. 15:44; 2 Chron. 14:9–10).

Marheshvan [Mar'hesh·van], unknown—Heshvan, the eighth month of the sacred year and the second month of the civil year, corresponding roughly to October/November.

Mark, John [Mark, John], *Jehovah is a gracious giver* and *a defense*—An occasional associate of Peter and Paul, and the probable author of the second gospel, also named Mark. Mark's lasting impact on the Christian church comes from his writing rather than his life. He was the first to develop the literary form known as the "gospel" and is rightly regarded as a creative literary artist.

John Mark appears in the New Testament only in association with more prominent personalities and events. His mother, Mary, was an influential woman of Jerusalem who possessed a large house with servants. The early church gathered in this house during Peter's imprisonment under Herod Agrippa I (Acts 12:12). Peter apparently went to this house often because the servant girl recognized his voice at the gate (Acts 12:13–16). Barnabas and Saul (Paul) took John Mark with them when they returned from Jerusalem to Antioch after their famine-relief visit (Acts 12:25). Shortly thereafter, Mark accompanied Paul and Barnabas on their first missionary journey as far as Perga. He served in the capacity of "assistant" (Acts 13:5), which probably involved making arrangements for travel, food, and lodging; he may have done some teaching too.

At Perga John Mark gave up the journey for an undisclosed reason (Acts 13:13); this departure later caused a rift between Paul and Barnabas when they chose their companions for the second missionary journey (Acts 15:37–41). Paul was unwilling to take Mark again and chose Silas; they returned to Asia Minor and Greece. Barnabas persisted in his choice of Mark, who was his cousin (Col. 4:10), and returned with him to his homeland of Cyprus (Acts 15:39; also Acts 4:36).

This break occurred about A.D. 49–50, and John Mark is not heard from again until a decade later. He is first mentioned again, interestingly enough, by Paul—and in favorable terms. Paul asks the Colossians to receive Mark with a welcome (Col. 4:10), no longer as an assistant but as one of his "fellow laborers" (Philem. 24). And during his imprisonment in Rome, Paul tells Timothy to bring Mark with him to Rome, "for he is useful to me for ministry" (2 Tim. 4:11). One final reference to Mark comes also from Peter in Rome; Peter affectionately refers to him as "my son" (1 Peter 5:13). Thus, in the later references to Mark in the New Testament, he appears to be reconciled to Paul and laboring with the two great apostles in Rome.

It has been suggested that Mark was referring to himself in his account of "a certain young man" in Gethsemane (14:51–52). Since all the disciples had abandoned Jesus (14:50), this little incident may have been a firsthand account.

Information about Mark's later life is dependent on early church tradition. Writing at an early date, Papias (A.D. 60–130), whose report is followed by Clement of Alexandria (A.D. 150–215), tells us that Mark served as Peter's interpreter in Rome and wrote his gospel from Peter's remembrances. Of his physical appearance we are only told, rather oddly, that Mark was "stumpy fingered." Writing at a later date (about A.D. 325), the church historian Eusebius says that Mark was the first evangelist to Egypt, the founder of the churches of Alexandria, and the first bishop of that city. So great were his converts, both in number and sincerity of commitment, says Eusebius, that the great Jewish philosopher Philo was amazed.

Market of Appius [App·i'us]—A marketplace outside of Rome, where believers came to meet Paul as he journeyed toward the city for prison and trial (Acts 28:15).

Maroth [Mar'oth], *bitterness*—A town of Judah not far from Jerusalem (Mic. 1:12).

Marsena [Mar·se'na]—One of the Persian princes in the court of Ahasuerus (Est. 1:14).

Mars' Hill—See Areopagus.

Martha [Mar'tha], *lady* or *mistress*—The sister of Mary and Lazarus of Bethany (Luke 10:38–41; John 11:1–44; 12:1–3). All three were sincere followers of Jesus, but Mary and Martha expressed their love for Him in different ways. The account of the two women given by Luke reveals a clash of temperaments between Mary and Martha. Martha "was distracted with much serving" (Luke 10:40); she was an activist busy with household chores. Her sister Mary "sat at Jesus' feet and heard His word" (Luke 10:39); her instinct was to sit still, meditate, and receive spiritual instruction.

While Martha busied herself making Jesus comfortable and cooking for Him in her home, Mary listened intently to His teaching. When Martha complained that Mary was not helping her, Jesus rebuked Martha. "You are worried and troubled about many things," He declared. "But one thing is needed, and Mary has chosen that good part, which will not be taken away from her" (Luke 10:41–42). He told her, in effect, that Mary was feeding her spiritual needs. This was more important than Martha's attempt to feed His body.

Jesus recognized that Martha was working for Him, but He reminded her that she was permitting her outward activities to hinder her spiritually. Because of her emphasis on work and her daily chores, her inner communion with her Lord was being hindered.

Mary [Ma'ry], *their rebellion*—The name of six women in the New Testament:

1. Mary, the mother of Jesus (Luke 1–2). We know nothing of Mary's background other than that she was a peasant and a resident of Nazareth, a city of Galilee. She must have been of the tribe of Judah and is assumed to be the daughter of Heli (Eli) and thus in the lineage of David (Luke 1:32), but of the line of Nathan, the royal rights of the Solomonic line being transferred through the daughter of Jeconiah and in this manner transferred from Mary to Jesus. The genealogies in Matthew 1 and Luke 3 do not say so, because they trace Joseph's genealogy rather than Mary's. We do know that Mary's cousin Elizabeth was the mother of John the Baptist.

When Mary was pledged to be married to Joseph the carpenter, the angel Gabriel appeared to her. Calling her "highly favored one" and "blessed . . . among women" (Luke 1:28), the angel announced the birth of the Messiah. After Gabriel explained how such a thing could be possible, Mary said, "Let it be to me according to your word" (Luke 1:38). That Mary "found favor with God" and was allowed to give birth to His child indicates she must have been of high character and faith.

At the home of Elizabeth, her kinswoman, she spoke her hymn of praise, "The Magnificat" (Luke 1:46–55). The angel's explanation to Joseph was in fulfillment of Isaiah's prophecy (Matt. 1:18–25). The "brethren of the Lord" were doubtless the children of Mary and Joseph. There were also sisters (Mark 6:3), so Mary was the mother of a large family.

When Jesus was born in Bethlehem of Judea, Mary "wrapped him in swaddling cloths, and laid Him in a manger" (Luke 2:7). She witnessed the visits of the shepherds and the wise men and "pondered them in her heart" (Luke 2:19) and heard Simeon's prophecy of a sword that would pierce through her own soul (Luke 2:35). Joseph and Mary fled to Egypt to escape Herod's murder of all males under two years old (Matt. 2:13–18). Neither Mary nor Joseph appear again until Jesus is twelve years old, at which time He stayed behind in the temple with the teachers (Luke 2:41–52). Both Mary and Joseph accepted Jesus' explanation, realizing He was Israel's Promised One.

Mary was present at Jesus' first miracle—the turning of water into wine at the wedding feast in Cana of Galilee (John 2:1–12). Mary seemed to be asking her Son to use His power to meet the crisis. Jesus warned her that His time had not yet come; nevertheless, He turned the water into wine. At another time Mary and Jesus' brothers wished to see Jesus while He was teaching the multitudes—perhaps to warn Him of impending danger. But again Jesus mildly rebuked her, declaring that the bond between Him and His disciples was stronger than any family ties (Luke 8:19–21).

The Scriptures do not mention Mary again until she stands at the foot of the cross (John 19:25–27). No mention is made of Joseph; he had likely been dead for some time. Jesus' brothers were not among His followers. Of His family, only His mother held fast to her belief in His messiahship—even though it appeared to be ending in tragedy. From the cross Jesus gave Mary over to the care of the beloved disciple, John. The last mention of Mary is in the Upper Room in Jerusalem, awaiting the coming of the Holy Spirit (Acts 1:14). We do not know how or when Mary died. The Tomb of the Virgin is in the Kidron Valley in Jerusalem, southeast of the temple area; but there is no historical basis for this site.

According to Scripture, Jesus had four brothers—James, Joses, Judas, and Simon—and unnamed sisters (Matt. 13:55–56; Mark 6:3). The Roman Catholic Church, however, claims that Mary remained a virgin and that these "brothers" and "sisters" were either Joseph's children by an earlier marriage or were cousins of Jesus. Legends concerning Mary began circulating in written form as early as the fifth century, but there is no valid historical evidence for them.

In reaction to the Roman Catholic teachings about Mary, many Protestants almost totally neglect her and her contribution. What can be said of her that is consistent with Holy Scripture?

God was in her womb. In conceiving and bearing the Lord Jesus Christ, she gave earthly birth not to mere man but to the Son of God Himself. She conceived as a virgin through the mysterious power of the Holy Spirit. We are to bless and honor her, for as she herself said under the inspiration of the Holy Spirit, "Henceforth all generations will call me blessed" (Luke 1:48).

As the first member of the human race to accept Christ, she stands as the first of the redeemed and as the flagship of humanity itself. She is our enduring example for faith, service to God, and a life of righteousness.

2. Mary Magdalene, the woman from whom Jesus cast out seven demons. The name Magdalene indicates that she came from Magdala, a city on the southwest coast of the Sea of Galilee. After Jesus cast seven demons from her, she became one of His followers. The Scriptures do not describe her illness. Mary Magdalene has been associated with the "woman in the city who was a sinner" (Luke 7:37) who washed Jesus' feet, but there is no scriptural basis for this. According to the Talmud (the collection of rabbinic writings that make up the basis of religious authority for traditional Judaism), the city of Magdala had a reputation for prostitution. This information, coupled with the fact that Luke first mentions Mary Magdalene immediately following his account of the sinful woman (Luke 7:36–50), has led some to equate the two women.

Mary Magdalene is also often associated with the woman whom Jesus saved from stoning after she had been taken in adultery (John 8:1–11)—again an association with no evidence. We do know that Mary Magdalene was one of those women who, having "been healed of evil spirits and infirmities," provided for Jesus and His disciples "from their substance" (Luke 8:2–3).

Mary Magdalene witnessed most of the events surrounding the crucifixion. She was present at the mock trial of Jesus; she heard Pontius Pilate pronounce the death sentence; and she saw Jesus beaten and humiliated by the crowd. She was one of the women who stood near Jesus during the crucifixion to try to comfort Him. The earliest witness to the resurrection of Jesus, she was sent by Jesus to tell the others (John 20:11–18). Although this is the last mention of her in the Bible, she was probably among the women who gathered with the apostles to await the promised coming of the Holy Spirit (Acts 1:14).

3. Mary of Bethany, sister of Martha and Lazarus (Luke 10:38–42). As with Martha, we know nothing of Mary's family background. Martha was probably older than Mary since the house is referred to as Martha's, but she could have inherited it from an unmentioned husband. All we really know is that Mary, Martha, and Lazarus loved one another deeply. When Jesus visited their house in Bethany, Mary sat at Jesus' feet and listened to His teachings while Martha worked in the kitchen. When Martha complained that Mary was no help, Jesus gently rebuked Martha.

When Lazarus died, Mary's grief was deep. John tells us that when Jesus came following Lazarus's death Mary stayed in the house. After she was summoned by Martha, she went to Jesus, fell at His feet weeping, and, like Martha, said, "Lord, if You had been here, my brother would not have died" (John 11:21, 32).

Following Lazarus's resurrection, Mary showed her gratitude by anointing Jesus' feet with "a pound of very costly oil of spikenard" (John 12:3) and wiping His feet with her hair. Judas called this anointing extravagant, but Jesus answered, "Let her alone; she has kept this for the day of My burial" (John 12:7). Jesus called Mary's unselfish act "a memorial to her" (Mark 14:9).

4. Mary, the mother of the disciple James and Joses (Matt. 27:55–61) and the wife of Clopas or Cleophas. In light of her presence at Jesus' death and resurrection, it is likely that Mary was one of the women who followed Jesus and His disciples and provided food for them (Luke 8:2–3). Since Mark 15:40 tells us that this Mary, along with Mary Magdalene, observed Jesus' burial, the "other Mary" (Matt. 27:61) must refer to this mother of James and Joses. Mary was one of the women who went to the tomb on the third day to anoint Jesus' body with spices and discovered that Jesus was no longer among the dead (Mark 16:1–8). It is the view of some that this Mary was the sister of the Virgin, but it seems very improbable that there would be two daughters in one family who were both named Mary.

5. Mary, the mother of John Mark (Acts 12:12). The mother of the author of the gospel of Mark opened her home to the disciples to pray for the release of Peter, who had been imprisoned by Herod Antipas. When Peter was miraculously released, the angel immediately delivered him to Mary's house. Tradition has it that Mary's house was a primary meeting place for the early Christians of Jerusalem. We know that Barnabas and Mark were related (Col. 4:10), but whether through Mark's mother or through his father (who is never mentioned), we do not know.

6. Mary of Rome (Rom. 16:6). All we know about this Christian woman of Rome is found in Paul's salutation: "Greet Mary, who labored much for us."

Mash [Mash], *drawn out*—A son of Aram, the son of Shem (Gen. 10:23). In 1 Chronicles 1:17 he is called Meshech.

Mashal [Ma'shal], *entreaty*—See Mishal (1 Chron. 6:74).

Maskil [Mas'kil]—Variant spelling of Maschil.

Masrekah [Mas·re'kah], *vineyard*—A city of Edom (Gen. 36:36; 1 Chron. 1:47).

Massa [Mas'sa], *burden*—A tribe of Arabia descended from Ishmael (Gen. 25:14; 1 Chron. 1:30).

Massah [Mas'sah], *testing*—A place in the Wilderness of Sin, near Mount Horeb. The Israelites murmured against Moses at Massah because of no water, indicating their lack of faith. At the command of God, Moses struck the rock with his rod to produce water. The place is also called Meribah, which means "rebellion, strife, contention" (Ex. 17:7).

Mathusala [Ma·thu'sa·la]—See Methuselah (Luke 3:37).

Matred [Ma'tred], *driving forward*—Mother-in-law of Hadar, king of Edom (Gen. 36:39; 1 Chron. 1:50).

Matri [Ma'tri], *rainy*—A family of Benjamin to which Kish and Saul belonged (1 Sam. 10:21).

Mattan [Mat'tan], *a gift*—Two Old Testament men:
   1. Father of Shephatiah (Jer. 38:1).
   2. A priest of Baal (2 Kings 11:18; 2 Chron. 23:17).

Mattanah [Mat·ta'nah], *a gift*—A station of the Israelites near Moab (Num. 21:18–19).

Mattaniah [Mat·ta·ni'ah], *gift of Jehovah*—Ten Old Testament men:

1. Son of King Josiah. He was the third of Josiah's sons to be on the throne of Judah. Nebuchadnezzar changed his name to Zedekiah (2 Kings 24:17). See Zedekiah.

2. Son of Heman in David's time; a singer (1 Chron. 25:4, 16).

3. A descendant of Asaph, a Levite, head of a branch of the family (2 Chron. 20:14).

4. A descendant of Asaph, a Levite. He assisted Hezekiah in his religious reforms (2 Chron. 29:13).

5. A son of Elam who put away his Gentile wife (Ezra 10:26).

6. A son of Zattu (Ezra 10:27) who divorced his pagan wife.

7. A son of Pahath-moab (Ezra 10:30) who divored his pagan wife.

8. A son of Bani (Ezra 10:37) who divorced his pagan wife.

9. A Levite, ancestor of Hanan who was treasurer of the storehouse in the days of Nehemiah (Neh. 13:13).

10. A singer among the Levites, descended from Asaph (1 Chron. 9:15; Neh. 11:17; 12:25, 35); he lived in Jerusalem after the captivity.

Mattathah [Mat'ta·thah], *gift*—Son of Nathan (Luke 3:31; Mattatha, KJV), listed in the genealogy of Christ. See Mattattah.

Mattathiah [Mat·ta·thi'ah], *gift of Jehovah*—Three Israelite men:

1. A priest and the founder of the Maccabee family (168 B.C.).

2. The name of two ancestors of Jesus (Luke 3:25–26; Mattathias, KJV, NASB, NIV, NRSV).

Mattathias [Mat·ta·thi'as]—See Mattathiah.

Mattattah [Mat'tat·tah], *gift*—Son of Hashum (Ezra 10:33), one who divorced his pagan wife (Mattathah, KJV).

Mattenai [Mat·te'nai], *gift of Jehovah*—

1. A son of Hashum (Ezra 10:33) who divorced his foreign wife.

2. A son of Bani (Ezra 10:37) who divorced his foreign wife.

3. A priest of the family of Joiarib in the time of Joiakim (Neh. 12:19).

Matthan [Mat'than], *gift*—An ancestor of Joseph, husband of Mary (Matt. 1:15).

Matthat [Mat'that], *gift of God*—Two ancestors of the family of Jesus (Luke 3:24, 29).

Matthew [Mat'thew], *gift of the Lord*—A tax collector who became one of the twelve apostles of Jesus (Matt. 9:9). Matthew's name appears seventh in two lists of apostles (Mark 3:18; Luke 6:15), and eighth in two others (Matt. 10:3; Acts 1:13).

In Hebrew, Matthew's name means "gift of the Lord," but we know from his trade that he delighted in the gifts of others as well. He was a tax collector (Matt. 9:9–11) who worked in or around Capernaum under the authority of Herod Antipas. In Jesus' day, land and poll taxes were collected directly by Roman officials, but taxes on transported goods were contracted out to local collectors. Matthew was such a person, or else he was in the service of one. These middlemen paid an agreed-upon sum in advance to the Roman officials for the right to collect taxes in an area. Their profit came from the excess they could squeeze from the people.

The Jewish people hated these tax collectors not only for their corruption but also because they worked for and with the despised Romans. Tax collectors were ranked with murderers and robbers, and a Jew was permitted to lie to them if necessary. The attitude found in the Gospels is similar. Tax collectors are lumped together with harlots (Matt. 21:31), Gentiles (Matt. 18:17), and, most often, sinners (Matt. 9:10). They were as offensive to Jews for their economic and social practices as lepers were for their uncleanness; both were excluded from the people of God.

It is probable that the Matthew mentioned in Matthew 9:9–13 is identical with the Levi of Mark 2:13–17 and Luke 5:27–32; the stories obviously refer to the same person and event. The only problem in the identification is that Mark mentions Matthew rather than Levi in his list of apostles (Mark 3:18), thus leading one to assume two different persons. It is possible, however, that the same person was known by two names (compare "Simon" and "Peter"), or, less likely, that Levi and James the son of Alphaeus are the same person, since Mark calls Alphaeus the father of both (Mark 2:14; 3:18). Following his call by Jesus, Matthew is not mentioned again in the New Testament.

Matthias [Matth·i'as], *gift of the Lord*—A disciple chosen to succeed Judas Iscariot as an apostle by drawing lots (Acts 1:23, 26).

Matthias had been a follower of Jesus from the beginning of His ministry until the day of His ascension and had been a witness of His resurrection. In this way he fulfilled the requirements of apostleship (Acts 1:21–22). Probably he was one of the "seventy" (Luke 10:1, 17). The New Testament makes no further mention of him after his election. One tradition says that Matthias preached in Judea and was stoned to death by the Jews. Another tradition holds that he worked in Ethiopia and was martyred by crucifixion.

Mattithiah [Mat·ti·thi′ah], *gift of Jehovah*—Four Old Testament men:

1. A son of Shallum of the branch of Korah, a Levite. He had charge of baked offerings (1 Chron. 9:31).
2. Son of Jeduthun, a Levite and harpist (1 Chron. 15:18, 21; 25:3, 21).
3. A son of Nebo who put away his foreign wife (Ezra 10:43).
4. One who stood by Ezra when he read the law (Neh. 8:4).

Mazzaroth [Mazz′a·roth], unknown—A word in Job 38:32, believed to denote the twelve signs of the zodiac. Also translated "constellations" (NIV).

Meah [Me′ah], *a hundred*—A tower of Jerusalem near the sheep gate (Neh. 3:1; 12:39), also called the Tower of the Hundred.

Mearah [Me·ar′ah], *a cave*—A place near Sidon (Josh. 13:4).

Mebunnai [Me·bun′nai], *built*—A warrior of David; a Hushathite (2 Sam. 23:27). In 1 Chronicles 11:29; 27:11 he is called Sibbecai.

Mecherathite [Me·che′ra·thite], *he of the dug-out*—A native or inhabitant of Mecherah (1 Chron. 11:36).

Meconah [Me·co′nah], *foundation*—A town of Judah (Neh. 11:28; Mekonah, KJV).

Medad [Me′dad], *love*—An elder who received the gift of prophecy (Num. 11:26–29).

Medan [Me′dan], *contention*—A son of Abraham and Keturah (Gen. 25:2; 1 Chron. 1:32).

Mede, Median [Me′de, Me′di·an], *middle land*—A native or inhabitant of Media (2 Kings 17:6; Est. 1:19; Dan. 5:28, 31). Darius, son of Ahasuerus (Dan. 5:31) is referred to as "the Median," and also "the Mede" (11:1).

Medeba [Me′de·ba], *water of quiet*—A town of Moab (Num. 21:30), assigned to Reuben (Josh. 13:9, 16). This town apparently went back and forth between Moabite and Israelite domination (2 Kings 14:25; 1 Chron. 19:7). By the time of Isaiah, the town was in Moabite control (Isa. 15:2).

Media [Me′di·a], *middle lane*—A country of Asia bounded on the north by the Caspian Sea, on the east by Parthia, and on the south by Elam; it was about six hundred miles in length and about two hundred and fifty miles broad. The area which was once Media is now parts of Iran, Iraq, and Turkey. A Median kingdom was established by the ninth and eighth centuries B.C., and Assyria battled with it, demanding tribute. Media was conquered by Tiglath-pileser of Assyria between 745 and 727 B.C.

The first mention of Media is in 2 Kings 17:6; 18:11, when Shalmanesar of Assyria deported the conquered Israelites there. Media was dominated by Assyria until 614–612 B.C., when the Babylonians and Medians formed an alliance and overthrew the Assyrian Empire. Intermarriage between the ruling families increased the strength of this bond. Some years later, the Babylonian Empire under Belshazzar was overthrown by the Medes and the Persians (Dan. 5:28). The laws of the Medes and Persians were considered unbreakable, even by the king (Est. 1:19). The religion of Media and Persia was Zoroastrianism.

Mediterranean Sea [Med′i·ter·ra′ne·an]—A large body of water in the Middle East bordered by many important nations, including Israel, Greece, Lebanon, and Italy. Its southern coastline stretches 2,200 miles from the coast of Palestine to the Straits of Gibraltar off the coast of Spain. The sea is 80 miles wide at its narrowest point between Sicily and North Africa. Many ancient civilizations grew up around this sea, using it for transportation and commerce. While the Israelites were wandering in the wilderness, they received instructions from God about the future boundaries of the land that God had promised to Abraham and his descendants.

The Mediterranean Sea was established as the western boundary of their territory (Num. 34:6). In the Bible, the Mediterranean is also referred to as "the Great Sea" (Josh. 1:4), "the Western Sea" (Deut. 11:24), and simply "the sea" (Josh. 16:8). The Romans called it *Mare Nostrum*, or "Our Sea," because of its importance to their empire in trade and commerce. In the time of Jesus and Paul, the Mediterranean was controlled by the Romans, who also used it to transport soldiers to the east to keep order in the provinces.

Perhaps the first people to exploit the trading advantages offered by the Mediterranean Sea were the Phoenicians. Through their fine port cities of Tyre and Sidon, they imported and exported goods from many nations of the ancient world. But the Israelites were never a seafaring people. Even Solomon, with all his wealth, formed an alliance with the Phoenicians under which they conducted import and export services for the Israelites (1 Kings 9:27). The Philistines also loved the sea. Some scholars believe they migrated to Palestine from their original home on the island of Crete, or Caphtor, in the Mediterranean. The Mediterranean is called "the Sea of the Philistines" in Exodus 23:31.

The Mediterranean also played a key role in the early expansion of Christianity. Paul crossed the Mediterranean during his missionary journeys and set sail from many of its ports, including Caesarea (Acts 9:30), Seleucia (Acts 13:4), and Cenchrea (Acts 18:18). He was shipwrecked in the Mediterranean while sailing to Rome in late autumn (Acts 27).

Megiddo [Me·gid′do], *place of troops*—A walled city east of the Carmel Mountain range where many important battles were fought in Old Testament times. Megiddo was situated on the main road that linked Egypt and Syria. Overlooking the valley of Jezreel (plain of Esdraelon), Megiddo was one of the most strategic cities in Palestine. All major traffic through northern Palestine traveled past Megiddo, making it a strategic military stronghold.

Megiddo is first mentioned in the Old Testament in the account of the thirty-one kings conquered by Joshua (Josh. 12:21). In the division of the land of Canaan among the tribes of the Hebrew people, Megiddo was awarded to Manasseh. But the tribe was unable to drive out the native inhabitants of the city (Josh. 17:11; Judg. 1:27; 1 Chron. 7:29).

During the period of the judges, the forces of Deborah and Barak wiped out the army of Sisera "by the waters of Megiddo" (Judg. 5:19). During the period of the united kingdom under Solomon, the Israelites established their supremacy at Megiddo. The city was included in the fifth administrative district of Solomon (1 Kings 4:12). Along with Hazor, Gezer, Lower Beth Horon, Baalath, and Tadmor, Megiddo was fortified and established as a chariot city for the armies of King Solomon (1 Kings 9:15–19). The original walls of the city were about thirteen feet thick, and they were apparently enlarged and reinforced at selected points to twice this thickness.

The prophet Zechariah mentioned the great mourning that would one day take place "in the plain of Megiddo" (Zech. 12:11; Megiddon, KJV). The fulfillment of Zechariah's prophecy is the battle at the end of time known as the battle of Armageddon. Armageddon is a compound word in Hebrew that means "mountain of Megiddo."

In the end times, God will destroy the armies of the Beast and the False Prophet in "the battle of that great day of God Almighty" (Rev. 16:14) when He shall gather them "together to the place called in Hebrew, Armageddon" (Rev. 16:16). Jesus Christ will ride out of heaven on a white horse (Rev. 19:11) as the "King of kings and Lord of lords" (Rev. 19:16).

Megiddon [Me·gid′don]—See Megiddo.

Mehetabeel [Me·het′a·beel], *favored of God*—Father of Delaiah (Neh. 6:10). Also see Mehetabel.

Mehetabel [Me·het′a·bel], *God blesses*—Wife of Hadar, king of Edom (Gen. 36:39; 1 Chron. 1:50). Also see Mehetabeel.

Mehida [Me·hi′da], *union*—Founder of a family of Nethinim (Ezra 2:43, 52).

Mehir [Me′hir], *price*—Son of Chelub of Judah, and the brother of Shuah (1 Chron. 4:11).

Meholathite [Me·ho′la·thite], *of dancing*—A native perhaps of Abel-meholah (1 Sam. 18:19; 2 Sam. 21:8).

Mehujael [Me·hu′ja·el], *smitten of God*—Son of Irad, the fourth in descent from Cain (Gen. 4:18).

Mehuman [Me·hu′man], *faithful*—A chamberlain in the service of Ahasuerus, one of the seven eunuchs who served as his personal servants (Est. 1:10).

Mehunim [Me·hu'nim]—See Meunim.

Me-jarkon [Me-jar'kon], *yellow waters*—A place in Dan near Joppa (Josh. 19:46).

Mekonah [Me·ko'nah]—See Meconah.

Melatiah [Mel·a·ti'ah], *Jehovah delivers*—A Gibeonite (Neh. 3:7).

Melchi [Mel'chi], *my king*—Two ancestors of Christ, one of whom was the father of Levi (Luke 3:24); the other the son of Addi (Luke 3:28).

Melchiah [Mel·chi'ah]—See Malchijah.

Melchisedec [Mel·chis'e·dec]—See Melchizedek.

Melchishua [Mel·chis'hua], possibly *my king is salvation*—A son of Saul (1 Sam. 14:49; 31:2). See Malchishua.

Melchizedek [Mel·chiz'e·dek], *king of righteousness*—A king of Salem (Jerusalem) and priest of the Most High God (Gen. 14:18–20; Ps. 110:4; Heb. 5:6–11; 6:20–7:28). Melchizedek's appearance and disappearance in the book of Genesis are somewhat mysterious. Melchizedek and Abraham first met after Abraham's defeat of Chedorlaomer and his three allies. Melchizedek presented bread and wine to Abraham and his weary men, demonstrating friendship and religious kinship. He bestowed a blessing on Abraham in the name of El Elyon ("God Most High"), and praised God for giving Abraham a victory in battle (Gen. 14:18–20).

Abraham presented Melchizedek with a tithe (a tenth) of all the booty he had gathered. By this act Abraham indicated that he recognized Melchizedek as a fellow-worshiper of the one true God as well as a priest who ranked higher spiritually than himself. Melchizedek's existence shows that there were people other than Abraham and his family who served the true God. In Psalm 110, a messianic psalm written by David (Matt. 22:43), Melchizedek is seen as a type of Christ. This theme is repeated in the book of Hebrews, where both Melchizedek and Christ are considered kings of righteousness and peace. By citing Melchizedek and his unique priesthood as a type, the writer shows that Christ's new priesthood is superior to the old Levitical order and the priesthood of Aaron (Heb. 7:1–10; Melchisedec, KJV).

Attempts have been made to identify Melchizedek as an imaginary character named Shem, an angel, the Holy Spirit, Christ, and others. All are products of speculation, not historical fact; and it is impossible to reconcile them with the theological argument of Hebrews. Melchizedek was a real, historical king-priest who served as a type for the greater King-Priest who was to come, Jesus Christ.

Melea [Mel'e·a], *my dear friend* or *object of care*—An ancestor of Christ. He lived shortly after the time of David (Luke 3:31).

Melech [Me'lech], *king*—Son of Micah, son of Mephibosheth (1 Chron. 8:35; 9:41).

Melichu, Melicu [Mel'i·chu, Mel'i·cu]—Forms of Malluch.

Melita [Mel'i·ta], *honey*—An island now called Malta on which Paul was shipwrecked (Acts 28:1). See Malta.

Melzar [Mel'zar], *steward*—The chief of the eunuchs who was given charge of Daniel and his companions (Dan. 1:11, 16).

Memphis [Mem'phis], *haven of the good*—The capital of Egypt. According to Herodotus it was built by Menes, the first king of Egyptian history. It was an important city. The Hebrews knew Memphis as Noph (Isa. 19:13). Some of the remnant, after the fall of Judah, settled in Memphis (Jer. 44:1). The prophets pronounced judgments against the city (Jer. 46:19; Ezek. 30:13, 16; Hos. 9:6).

Memucan [Me·mu'can], *dignified*—A prince of Persia who advised Ahasuerus concerning Vashti (Est. 1:14–15, 21).

Menahem [Men'a·hem], *comforter*—A son of Gadi and seventeenth king of Israel (2 Kings 15:14–23). Some scholars believe Menahem probably was the military commander of King Zechariah. When Shallum took the throne from Zechariah by killing him in front of the people, Menahem determined that Shallum himself must be killed. After Shallum had reigned as king of Israel for a month in Samaria, Menahem "went up from Tirzah, came to Samaria, and struck Shallum . . . and killed him; and he reigned in his place" (2 Kings 15:14).

When the city of Tiphsah refused to recognize Menahem as the lawful ruler of Israel, Menahem attacked it and inflicted terrible cruelties upon its people (2 Kings 15:16). This act apparently secured his position, because Menahem remained king for ten years (752–742 B.C.). His reign was evil, marked by cruelty, oppression, and idolatrous worship.

During his reign Menahem faced a threat from the advancing army of Pul (Tiglath-pileser III), king of Assyria. To strengthen his own position as king and to forestall a war with Assyria, he paid tribute to the Assyrian king by exacting "from each man fifty shekels of silver" (2 Kings 15:20). After Menahem's death, his son Pekahiah became king of Israel (2 Kings 15:22).

Menan [Men'an]—See Menna.

Meni [Meni], *fate* or *fortune*—A pagan god (Isa. 65:11).

Menna [Men'na], possibly *soothsayer* or *enchanted*—An ancestor of Christ after the time of David (Luke 3:31).

Menuhoth [Men·u'hoth]—See Manuhoth.

Meonenim [Me·o'ne·nim], *enchanters*—The name of the diviners' terebinth tree (Judg. 9:37). Micah 5:12 renders this word "soothsayers."

Meonothai [Me·o'no·thai], *my dwellings*—Father of Ophrah of Judah (1 Chron. 4:14), and one of the sons of Caleb's younger brother Othniel (Judg. 1:13).

Mephaath [Meph'a·ath], *splendor* or *height*—A town of Reuben assigned to the Merarite Levites (Josh. 13:18; 21:37; 1 Chron. 6:79).

Mephibosheth [Me·phib'o·sheth]. *from the mouth of* (the) *shame*(ful god Baal)—The name of two men in the Old Testament:

1. A son of Jonathan and grandson of Saul. Mephibosheth was also called Merib-baal (1 Chron. 8:34; 9:40), probably his original name, meaning "a striver against Baal." His name was changed because the word *Baal* was associated with idol worship.

Mephibosheth was only five years old when his father, Jonathan, and his grandfather, Saul, died on Mount Gilboa in the Battle of Jezreel (2 Sam. 4:4). When the child's nurse heard the outcome of the battle, she feared for Mephibosheth's life. As she fled for his protection, "he fell and became lame" (2 Sam. 4:4). For the rest of his life he was crippled.

After David consolidated his kingdom, he remembered his covenant with Jonathan to treat his family with kindness (1 Sam. 20). Through Ziba, a servant of the house of Saul, David found out about Mephibosheth. The lame prince had been staying "in the house of Machir the son of Ammiel, in Lo Debar" (2 Sam. 9:4). David then summoned Mephibosheth to his palace, restored to him the estates of Saul, appointed servants for him, and gave him a place at the royal table (2 Sam. 9:7–13).

When David's son Absalom rebelled, the servant Ziba falsely accused Mephibosheth of disloyalty to David (2 Sam. 16:1–4). David believed Ziba's story and took Saul's property from Mephibosheth. Upon David's return to Jerusalem, Mephibosheth cleared himself. David in turn offered Mephibosheth half of Saul's estates (2 Sam. 19:24–30), but he refused. David's return to Jerusalem as king was the only reward Mephibosheth desired.

2. A son of King Saul and Rizpah (2 Sam. 21:8). He was slain by the Gibeonites during the harvest (2 Sam. 21:8–9).

Merab [Me′rab], *increase*—Eldest daughter of Saul (1 Sam. 14:49). She was promised to David as the reward for slaying the giant, but Saul gave her to Adriel instead (1 Sam. 18:17–19). Later, he gave his younger daughter Michal to David.

Meraiah [Me·rai′ah], *rebellion*—A priest in the days of Joiakim (Neh. 12:12).

Meraioth [Me·rai′oth], *rebellious*—Three priests of the Old Testament:

1. A priest, son of Ahitub and father of Zadok (1 Chron. 9:11; Neh. 11:11).

2. A priest, son of Zerahiah (1 Chron. 6:6–7, 52). He lived during the time of Eli.

3. A priestly family in the time of Joiakim (Neh. 12:15).

Merari [Me·rar′i], *bitter*—The third and youngest son of Levi and the founder of the Merarites, one of the three Levitical families. Merari was the father of Mahli and Mushi (Ex. 6:16–19), who, in turn, were the founders of the Mahlites and the Mushites (Num. 3:33; 26:58).

Merarites [Me·rar′ites]—One of the three families of the tribe of Levi, descended from Merari. They had charge of portions of the tabernacle (Num. 3:36; 4:29–33; 7:8). The two divisions of the family were the Mahlites and Mushites (Num. 3:20, 33).

Merathaim [Mer·a·tha′im], *double rebellion*—A symbolic name given to Babylon (Jer. 50:21).

Mercurius [Mer·cu′ri·us]—See Mercury.

Mercury [Mer′cu·ry], *herald of the gods*—A Roman and Grecian deity (Acts 14:12). The Latin Mercury corresponds with the Greek Hermes.

Mered [Me′red], *rebellion*—Son of Ezrah. His wife was a daughter of Pharaoh (1 Chron. 4:17–18).

Meremoth [Mer′e·moth], *heights*—Three Old Testament men:
   1. Son of Uriah (Ezra 8:33; Neh. 3:4, 21).
   2. Son of Bani. He divorced his foreign wife (Ezra 10:36).
   3. A chief priest who returned from Babylon with the first expedition (Neh. 12:3, 7).

Meres [Me′res], *lofty*—One of the princes of Persia in the reign of Ahasuerus (Est. 1:14).

Meribah [Mer′i·bah], *contention*—The name of two different places where Moses struck a rock with his rod, and water gushed forth to satisfy the thirsty Israelites:
   1. A place "in Rephidim" at the foot of Mount Horeb. The Israelites camped here near the beginning of their forty years in the wilderness (Ex. 17:1–7).
   2. A second place where Moses struck a rock. This camp was in Kadesh, in the wilderness of Zin. The Israelites camped here near the end of their period of wilderness wandering (Num. 20:2–13). In Deuteronomy 32:51, this place is referred to as Meribath-kadesh (Meribah Kadesh, NIV).

Meribah-kadesh [Mer′i·bah-ka′desh], *contention* or *strife*—A place near Kadesh where the Israelites became angry at Moses because of the lack of water. Moses then struck a rock and water gushed forth (Num. 20:1–13; 27:14; Deut. 32:51).

Merib-baal [Mer'ib-ba'al], *contender against Baal*—(2 Sam. 9:6; 1 Chron. 8:34; 9:40) See Mephibosheth.

Merodach [Mer'o·dach], *death*—The god, Marduk, the patron deity of Babylon (Jer. 50:2); also known as Bel.

Merodach-baladan [Mer'o·dach-bal'a·dan], *Marduk has given a son*—Son of Baladan and king of Babylon. He seized the throne of Babylon in 722 B.C. when Israel, the Northern Kingdom, was overthrown by Assyria. He reigned eleven years (2 Kings 20:12–19; 2 Chron. 32:31; Isa. 39:1–8). He was driven from the throne by the son of Sargon. Also called Berodach-baladan.

Merom, Waters of [Me'rom], *a height*—A lake on the Jordan, about ten miles north of the Sea of Galilee. It was here that Joshua defeated the northern chiefs united under Jabin (Josh. 11:1–7).

Meronothite [Me·ro'no-thite]—The native of a place called Meronoth which has not been identified. The Bible names two Meronothites; Jehdeiah (1 Chron. 27:30); and Jadon (Neh. 3:7).

Meroz [Me'roz], *refuge*—In the conflict with Sisera this town failed to render assistance (Judg. 5:23).

Mesech [Me'sech]—See Meshech.

Mesha [Me'sha], *freedom*—Four Old Testament men:

1. The region inhabited by the descendants of Joktan (Gen. 10:30) in Arabia.

2. Son of Shaharaim of Benjamin. His mother was Hodesh (1 Chron. 8:8–9).

3. Son of Caleb of the family of Hezron and founder of Ziph (1 Chron. 2:42).

4. A king of Moab. He paid tribute to Ahab, king of Israel (2 Kings 3:4). When Israel was defeated in the attempt to recover Ramoth Gilead and Ahab was slain, Mesha refused to pay that year's tribute (2 Kings 1:1). The Moabites, Ammonites, and Edomites invaded Judah and were defeated by Jehoshaphat (2 Chron. 20:1).

Meshach [Me'shach], *guest of a king*—The Chaldean name given to Mishael, one of Daniel's companions (Dan. 1:7). Along with

Shadrach and Abed-nego, Meshach would not bow down and worship the pagan image of gold set up by Nebuchadnezzar. They were cast into "the burning fiery furnace," but were preserved from harm by the power of God.

Meshech [Me'shech], *drawing out*—A people of the line of Japheth (Gen. 10:2; 1 Chron. 1:5; Ezek. 38:2–3; 39:1; 27:13; Ps. 120:5).

Meshelemiah [Me·shel·e·mi'ah], *Jehovah awards*—A Levite of the branch of Kohath (1 Chron. 9:21; 26:1). He is called Shelemiah in 1 Chronicles 26:14. A porter or gatekeeper of the house of the Lord during the reign of David.

Meshezabeel [Me·shez'a·beel], *God delivers*—Three Old Testament men:
1. A man of Judah (Neh. 11:24).
2. One who sealed the covenant (Neh. 10:21).
3. Father of Berechiah (Neh. 3:4).

Meshezabel [Me·shez'a·bel]—See Meshezabeel.

Meshillemith [Me·shil'le·mith]—See Meshillemoth.

Meshillemoth [Me·shil'le·moth], *recompense*—Two Old Testament men:
1. Father of Berechiah, an Ephraimite who opposed the slavery of those brought from Judah by Pekah, king of Israel (2 Chron. 28:12).
2. A priest, the son of Immer (Neh. 11:13). In 1 Chronicles 9:12 he is called Meshillemith.

Meshobab [Me·sho'bab], *restored*—A prince of Simeon (1 Chron. 4:34–41).

Meshullam [Me·shul'lam], *ally* or *friend*—
1. Grandfather of Shaphan. He was appointed by Josiah to take charge of the funds to be used for temple repairs (2 Kings 22:3).
2. Son of Zerubbabel (1 Chron. 3:19).
3. A chief of Gad in Bashan (1 Chron. 5:13).
4. A descendant of Elpaal, a Benjamite (1 Chron. 8:17).
5. Son of Hodaviah (1 Chron. 9:7) or Joed (Neh. 11:7) father of Sallu.
6. Son of Shephatiah, a Benjamite (1 Chron. 9:8).

7. A priest whose descendants lived in Jerusalem. He was son of Zadok and father of high priest Hilkiah in the reign of Josiah (1 Chron. 9:11; Neh. 11:11).

8. Son of Meshillemith, a priest of the house of Immer (1 Chron. 9:12).

9. A Kohathite, an overseer of the temple repairs in the reign of Josiah (2 Chron. 34:12).

10. A chief sent by Ezra to Iddo to secure Levites to return to Jerusalem (Ezra 8:16).

11. One who opposed Ezra (Ezra 10:15).

12. A son of Bani who put away his foreign wife (Ezra 10:29).

13. Son of Berechiah; he labored on the wall of Nehemiah (Neh. 3:4, 30). His daughter married the son of Tobiah, the Ammonite (Neh. 6:18).

14. Son of Besodeiah. He repaired the old gate of the wall (Neh. 3:6).

15. One who stood by Ezra when he read the law (Neh. 8:4).

16. A priest who signed the covenant (Neh. 10:7).

17. One of the leaders of the people who sealed the covenant (Neh. 10:20).

18. A priest in the days of Joiakim, head of the house of Ezra (Neh. 12:13).

19. A priest, a son of Ginnethon (Neh. 12:16).

20. A gatekeeper in the days of Nehemiah (Neh. 12:25).

21. A leader of the people who took part in the dedication of the rebuilt wall (Neh. 12:33). Quite possibly the same person as No. 17.

Meshullemeth [Me·shul′le·meth], *friend*—Wife of Manasseh (2 Kings 21:19).

Mesobaite [Me·sob′a·ite]—See Mezobaite.

Mesopotamia [Mes·o·po·ta′mi·a], *a land between rivers*—The Greek name for the country located between the Euphrates and Tigris Rivers (Gen. 24:7–10).

Messiah [Mes·si′ah], *anointed one*—The Hebrew word *Messiah*, meaning "Anointed One," is translated, "the Christ" in the Greek language. In the Old Testament, the word is often associated with the anointing of a prophet, a priest, king, or other ruler. God's promise to Abraham that in him and his descendants all the world would be blessed (Gen. 12:1–3) created the expectancy of a kingdom of God on earth among the Hebrew people. The reign of David as king of Judah further shaped popular messianic expectations that the coming kingdom would be one like King David's (2 Sam. 7).

As the Hebrew kingdom divided after Solomon's time, the idea of a messianic deliverer became popular. The people of Israel looked for a political ruler to deliver them from their enemies. The "salvation" spoken of in the Psalms and some prophecies of Isaiah and Jeremiah was interpreted as referring to deliverance from Israel's enemies, especially threatening world powers (Ps. 69:35; Isa. 25:9; Jer. 42:11). The Hebrew people tended to overlook or ignore such prophecies as the Suffering Servant message of Isaiah 53, which foretold that the Messiah would suffer and die.

Major Old Testament passages indicated that the Messiah would be born of a virgin (Isa. 7:14), in Bethlehem (Mic. 5:2), and that He would be a descendant of the house of David (2 Sam. 7:12). He would be "a Man of sorrows" (Isa. 53:3) who would suffer rejection by His own people (Ps. 69:8), followed by betrayal by a friend (Ps. 41:9), and crucifixion between two thieves (Isa. 53:12).

As the Messiah died, His spirit would be commended to His Father (Ps. 31:5). He would be raised from the dead (Ps. 16:10) to take His place at God's right hand (Ps. 110:1). Jesus fulfilled these prophecies as Prophet, Priest, and King, but He came to deliver humankind from the reign of sin and bind us into God's family (Luke 4:18–19; Acts 2:36–42). "My kingdom is not of this world" (John 18:36), He told Pilate. He ruled by serving (Matt. 20:25–28). As a priest, He offered not the blood of animals, but Himself, as a full and final sacrifice for sins (John 10:11–18; Heb. 9:12).

Messias [Mes·si′as]—See Messiah.

Metheg-ammah [Meth′eg-am′mah], *bridle of the mother city*— A town of the Philistines (2 Sam. 8:1).

Methusael [Me·thu′sa·el]—See Methushael.

Methuselah [Me·thu′se·lah], *man of the dart*—The son of Enoch of the line of Seth and an ancestor of Jesus (Gen. 5:21–27). The oldest man in the Scriptures, he lived to be 969 years old.

Methushael [Me·thu′sha·el], *man of God*—Son of Mehujael, father of Lamech, fourth in descent from Cain (Gen. 4:18).

Meunim [Me·u′nim], *habitations*—One of the Nethinim, whose descendants served in the temple after the captivity (Ezra 2:50; Neh. 7:52).

Meunites [Me·u′nites], *habitations*—An Arabian tribe of tent dwellers. A group of them living in the valley of Gedor were attacked and wiped out by the Simeonites during the reign of Hezekiah (1 Chron. 4:24, 39–41). The Meunites were a Hamitic people. Previously, Uzziah had also battled with this group (2 Chron. 26:7).

Mezahab [Me′za·hab], *golden waters*—Grandfather of Mehetabel (Gen. 36:39; 1 Chron. 1:50).

Mezobaite [Me·zob′a·ite]—A term describing Jaasiel, who was one of David's mighty men (1 Chron. 11:47).

Miamin [Mi′a·min], *of the right hand*—See Mijamin.

Mibhar [Mib′har], *choice*—Son of Haggeri and one of David's warriors (1 Chron. 11:38).

Mibsam [Mib′sam], *sweet odor*—Two Old Testament men:
   1. A son of Ishmael, and a founder of a tribe (Gen. 25:13; 1 Chron. 1:29).
   2. Son of Shallum of Simeon (1 Chron. 4:25).

Mibzar [Mib′zar], *fortress*—A chieftain of Edom (Gen. 36:42; 1 Chron. 1:53).

Micah [Mi′cah], *who is like the Lord?*—The name of six men in the Old Testament:
   1. A man from the mountains of Ephraim during the period of the judges in Israel's history. He stole his mother's money but returned it. Part of it then was used to make an image. Micah appointed a Levite, Jonathan, to act as his personal priest. Micah's worship of false gods led the Danites into idolatry (Judg. 17–18).
   2. A descendant of Reuben who lived before the Exile (1 Chron. 5:5).

3. A son of Merib-baal listed in the family tree of King Saul of Benjamin (1 Chron. 8:34–35; 9:40–41). Micah was the father of Pithon, Melech, Tarea (or Tahrea), and Ahaz. His father Merib-baal (also called Mephibosheth, 2 Sam. 4:4) was a son of Jonathan and a grandson of Saul. He was also called Micha in 2 Samuel 9:12.

4. A son of Zichri and grandson of Asaph (1 Chron. 9:15). Micah is also called "Micha, the son of Zabdi" (Neh. 11:17; also Neh. 11:22) and "Michaiah, the son of Zaccur" (Neh. 12:35).

5. The father of Abdon (2 Chron. 34:20) or Achbor (2 Kings 22:12). Abdon was one of five men whom King Josiah of Judah sent to inquire of Huldah the prophetess when Hilkiah the priest found the Book of the Law. Micah is also called Michaiah (2 Kings 22:12).

6. An Old Testament prophet and author of the book of Micah. A younger contemporary of the great prophet Isaiah, Micah was from Moresheth-gath (Mic. 1:1, 14), a town in southern Judah. His prophecy reveals his country origins; he uses many images from country life (Mic. 7:1).

Micah spoke out strongly against those who claimed to be prophets of the Lord but who used this position to lead the people of Judah into false hopes and further errors: "The sun shall go down on the prophets, and the day shall be dark for them" (Mic. 3:6). Micah's love for God would not allow him to offer false hopes to those who were under His sentence of judgment.

Little else is known about this courageous spokesman for the Lord. He tells us in his book that he prophesied during the reigns of three kings in Judah: Jotham, Ahaz, and Hezekiah (Mic. 1:1). This would place the time of his ministry from about 750 to 687 B.C.

Micaiah [Mi·cai′ah], *who is like the Lord?*—The prophet who predicted the death of King Ahab of Israel in the battle against the Syrians at Ramoth Gilead (1 Kings 22:8–28; 2 Chron. 18:7–27). Ahab gathered about four hundred prophets, apparently all in his employment. They gave their unanimous approval to Ahab's proposed attack against the Syrian king, Ben-hadad.

King Jehoshaphat of Judah was unconvinced by this display. He asked, "Is there not still a prophet of the LORD here, that we may inquire of Him?" (1 Kings 22:7; 2 Chron. 18:6). Ahab replied, "There is still one man, Micaiah the son of Imlah, by whom we may inquire of the LORD but I hate him, because he does not prophesy good concerning me, but evil" (1 Kings 22:8; 2 Chron. 18:7). The prophet Micaiah was then summoned.

When Ahab asked this prophet's advice, Micaiah answered, "Go and prosper, for the LORD will deliver it into the hand of the king!" (1 Kings 22:15; 2 Chron. 18:14).

Micaiah's answer was heavy with sarcasm, irony, and contempt. Ahab realized he was being mocked; so he commanded him to speak nothing but the truth. Micaiah then said, "I saw all Israel scattered on the mountains as sheep that have no shepherd" (1 Kings 22:17; 2 Chron. 18:16). Ahab turned to Jehoshaphat and said, "Did I not tell you that he would not prophesy good concerning me, but evil?" (1 Kings 22:18; 2 Chron. 18:17).

Zedekiah then struck Micaiah on the cheek and accused him of being a liar. Ahab commanded that Micaiah be put in prison until the king's victorious return from Ramoth Gilead. Then Micaiah said, "If you ever return . . . the LORD has not spoken by me" (1 Kings 22:28; 2 Chron. 18:27).

Ahab did not return; he died at Ramoth Gilead, just as Micaiah had predicted.

Michael [Mi′cha·el], *who is like God?*—

1. Father of the Asherite spy sent to Canaan (Num. 13:13).

2. A descendant of Buz of Gad, head of a house in Gilead (1 Chron. 5:11–13).

3. Another Gadite (1 Chron. 5:14).

4. Son of Baaseiah and father of Shimea, a Levite of the family of Gershom (1 Chron. 6:40).

5. A chief of Issachar, of the family of Tola and house of Uzzi (1 Chron. 7:3).

6. A son of Beriah (1 Chron. 8:16).

7. A captain of Manasseh. He allied himself with David at Ziklag (1 Chron. 12:20).

8. Father of Omri, appointed by David as ruler of Issachar (1 Chron. 27:18).

9. A son of Jehoshaphat, king of Judah. He and his brothers were slain by Jehoram, their brother, when he became king (2 Chron. 21:2–4).

10. Father of Zebadiah. He returned to Jerusalem with Ezra (Ezra 8:8).

11. An archangel who was called the prince of Israel (Dan. 10:13, 21) and the great prince (Dan. 12:1). He is mentioned twice in the New Testament, once in Jude's puzzling reference to the dispute over Moses's body (Jude 9), and once in Revelation 12:7. "Michael and his angels" are described as struggling with Satan and his angels and throwing them out of heaven.

Michah [Mi'chah], *who is like God*—A Levite, a Kohathite of the house of Uzziel, who served during the time of David (1 Chron. 23:20; 24:24–25).

Michaiah [Mi·chai'ah]—

1. Father of Achbor (2 Kings 22:12; 2 Chron. 34:20).

2. Daughter of Uriel; wife of Rehoboam, king of Judah, and mother of Abijah (2 Chron. 13:2). She is also called Maacah.

3. A prince in the reign of Jehoshaphat (2 Chron. 17:7).

4. A descendant of Asaph (Neh. 12:35), also called Micah (1 Chron. 9:15), and Micha (Neh. 11:17, 22).

5. A priest and trumpeter (Neh. 12:41).

6. Son of Gemariah (Jer. 36:11–13).

Michal [Mi'chal], *brook*—Daughter of Saul, given to David on condition that he kill a hundred Philistines. Saul was hoping that David would be killed in the attempt, but instead David killed two hundred Philistines and came off unscathed. Saul saw that Michal was in love with David, and had to stand by his word and give her to him, but he became even more afraid of David's influence (1 Sam. 18:27–28). Michal helped David to escape from her father, but she did not accompany him on his flight. After a time David took two other wives; in the meantime Saul had given his daughter Michal to another man (1 Sam. 19:11–17; 25:44). After David became king, he demanded that Michal be returned to him. Her brother Ish-bosheth complied, taking her from Paltiel, her second husband, and sending her back to David. Paltiel apparently loved Michal very much; he followed after her weeping until he was finally turned back by Abner (2 Sam. 3:13–16). Michal's relationship with David had obviously soured; when David danced before the Lord as the ark was brought into Jerusalem, Michal ridiculed his enthusiasm. Because of her attitude, she was barren until she died (2 Sam. 6:20–23). Second Samuel 21:8 should probably read Merab, not

Michal (1 Sam. 18:19). Her five sons were slain to avenge Saul's wrongful killing of the Gibeonites.

Michmash [Mich′mash], *something hidden*—A town of Benjamin southeast of Beth-el (1 Sam. 13:2). Two hundred men from this town returned from the captivity (Ezra 2:27).

Michmethath [Mich′me·thath], *hiding place*—A town on the border of Ephraim and Manasseh (Josh. 16:6; 17:7).

Michri [Mich′ri], *worthy of price*—A Benjamite (1 Chron. 9:8).

Middin [Mid′din], *measures*—A village west of the Dead Sea in the wilderness of Judah (Josh. 15:61).

Middle Gate—A gate of Jerusalem. When Babylon conquered Judah and penetrated the city, the king of Babylon came and sat in this gate, along with the princes of Babylon (Jer. 39:3).

Midian [Mid′i·an], *strife*—The name of a man and a territory in the Old Testament:

1. A son of Abraham by his concubine Keturah (Gen. 25:1–6). Midian had four sons (1 Chron. 1:33).

2. The land inhabited by the descendants of Midian. Situated east of the Jordan River and the Dead Sea, the land stretched southward through the Arabian desert as far as the southern and eastern parts of the peninsula of Sinai.

Midianites [Mid′i·a·nites]—A nomadic people of northwestern Arabia. They are represented as descendants of Abraham and Keturah. Joseph was carried to Egypt by Midianite merchants (Gen. 37:28). Jethro, the father-in-law of Moses, was a Midianite (Ex. 3:1).

Migdal-el [Mig′dal-el], *tower of God*—A fortified city of Naphtali (Josh. 19:38).

Migdal-gad [Mig′dal-gad], *tower of fortune*—A town of Judah (Josh. 15:37).

Migdol [Mig′dol], *watchtower*—The name of two Egyptian sites in the Old Testament:

1. An encampment of the Israelites while they were leaving Egypt in the exodus led by Moses. "Speak to the children of Israel, that they

turn and camp before Pi Hahiroth, between Migdol and the sea, opposite Baal Zephon" (Ex. 14:2). Migdol lay west of the Red Sea in the eastern region of the Nile Delta.

2. A site in northeastern Egypt (Jer. 44:1; 46:14). After the destruction of Jerusalem by the Babylonians under Nebuchadnezzar, some Israelites fled to Egypt and lived in Migdol.

Migron [Mig'ron], *precipice*—A town of Benjamin north of Michmash (Isa. 10:28).

Mijamin [Mi'ja·min], *from the right hand*—Three Old Testament men:

1. A descendant of Aaron. In the time of David the family was the sixth course of the priests (1 Chron. 24:1, 6, 9).

2. A chief priest who returned from Babylon with the first expedition (Neh. 12:5, 7).

3. Son of Parosh (Ezra 10:25).

Mikloth [Mik'loth], *rods*—Two Old Testament men:
1. Son of Jeiel of Gideon, father of Shimeah (1 Chron. 8:32; 9:37–38).
2. A captain of the army (1 Chron. 27:4).

Mikneiah [Mik·nei'ah], *possession of Jehovah*—A Levite (1 Chron. 15:18, 21).

Milalai [Mil'a·lai], *eloquent*—A Levite (Neh. 12:36).

Milcah [Mil'cah], *queen*—The name of two women in the Old Testament:

1. A daughter of Haran and the wife of Nahor (Gen. 22:20–22).

2. One of the five daughters of Zelophehad, of the tribe of Manasseh. Zelophehad had no sons. When he died, his daughters asked Moses for permission to share their father's inheritance. Their request was granted, providing they married within their own tribe in order to keep the inheritance within Manasseh (Num. 36:11–12).

Milcom [Mil'com], *great king*—See Molech.

Miletus, Miletum [Mi·le'tus, Mi·le'tum], *pure white fine wool*—An ancient seaport in Asia Minor visited by the apostle Paul (Act 20:15, 17; 2 Tim. 4:20; Miletum, KJV). Situated on the shore of the Mediterranean Sea, Miletus was about 60 kilometers (37 miles) south of Ephesus and on the south side of the Bay of Latmus. Because of silting, the site is now more than 8 kilometers (5 miles) from the coast.

Colonized by Cretans and others, Miletus became a leading harbor during the Persian and Greek periods. It prospered economically and boasted a celebrated temple of Apollo. Although Miletus was still an important trade center in Roman times, the river was already silting in the harbor. The apostle Paul visited Miletus on his journey from Greece to Jerusalem. In Miletus Paul delivered a farewell message to the elders of the church of Ephesus (Acts 10:18–35).

Millo [Mil′lo], *a rampart* or *mound*—

1. A house or citadel at Shechem (Judg. 9:6, 20).

2. The place where Joash was killed; possibly the same as the preceding (2 Kings 12:20). A Jebusite city captured by David (2 Sam. 5:9; 1 Kings 9:15; 11:27; 2 Chron. 32:5).

Miniamin [Min·i′a·min], *from the right hand*—Three Old Testament Levites:

1. A Levite who had charge of the freewill offerings in the reign of Hezekiah (2 Chron. 31:15).

2. A priest in the days of the high priest Joiakim (Neh. 12:17).

3. A priest who blew the trumpet when the wall was dedicated (Neh. 12:41).

Minjamin [Min′ja·min]—See Miniamin.

Minni [Min′ni], *division*—A kingdom of Armenia referred to by Jeremiah (Jer. 51:27).

Minnith [Min′nith], *distribution*—A town of the Ammonites (Judg. 11:33).

Miphkadgate [Miph′kad·gate], *appointed place*—The name of a gate at Jerusalem (Neh. 3:31).

Miriam [Mir′i·am], *rebellion*—A Hebrew name whose Greek form is "Mary." Two Old Testament women:

1. Sister of Aaron and Moses (Ex. 15:20; Num. 26:59). When the Israelites passed through the Red Sea, she took a timbrel and sang a song of triumph (Ex. 15:20–21). In a spirit of jealousy, she and Aaron took a seditious attitude relative to the leadership of Moses, making the occasion of their murmuring Moses's marriage with a Cushite woman. Miriam was smitten with leprosy. Moses interceded for her and she was healed (Num. 12:1–16; Deut. 24:9). She was buried in Kadesh (Num. 20:1).

2. A man or woman named in the genealogy of Judah (1 Chron. 4:17).

Mirma [Mir'ma]—See Mirmah.

Mirmah [Mir'mah], *deceit*—Son of Shaharaim and Hodesh, a Benjamite (1 Chron. 8:10; Mirma, KJV).

Misgab [Mis'gab], *high fort*—A city of Moab (Jer. 48:1).

Mishael [Mi'sha·el], *who is what God is?*—The name of three men in the Old Testament:

1. A son of Uzziel and grandson of Kohath, of the tribe of Levi (Lev. 10:4).

2. An Israelite who helped Ezra read the Book of the Law to the people (Neh. 8:4).

3. One of the three friends of Daniel who were cast into the fiery furnace. "Now from among those of the sons of Judah were Daniel, Hananiah, Mishael, and Azariah." The Babylonians changed his name to Meshach (Dan. 1:6–7).

Mishal [Mi'shal], *entreaty*—A village of Asher, given to the Gershonite Levites (Josh. 19:26; 21:30; Misheal, KJV).

Misham [Mi'sham], *purification*—Son of Elpaal, a Benjamite (1 Chron. 8:12).

Misheal [Mi'she·al]—See Mishal.

Mishma [Mish'ma], *hearing*—Two Old Testament men:

1. A son of Ishmael and head of a tribe (Gen. 25:14; 1 Chron. 1:30).

2. Son of Mibsam, a Simeonite (1 Chron. 4:25).

Mishmannah [Mish·man'nah], *fatness*—A Gadite warrior who allied himself with David (1 Chron. 12:10).

Mishraites [Mish'ra·ites], *touching evil*—One of the four families of Kirjath-jearim (1 Chron. 2:53).

Mispar [Mis'par], *number*—One who returned to Jerusalem in the first expedition (Ezra 2:2). The feminine form, Mispereth, is used in Nehemiah 7:7.

Misperreth [Mis'per·reth]—See Mispar.

Misrephoth-maim [Mis're·photh-ma'im], *burning of waters*—When Joshua defeated the kings at Merom he pursued them to this place on the border of Zidon (Josh. 11:8; 13:6).

Mithcah [Mith'cah]—See Mithkah.

Mithkah [Mith'kah], *sweetness*—An encampment of the Israelites (Num. 33:28–29).

Mithnite [Mith'nite], *athlete*—The designation of Joshaphat, one of David's men (1 Chron. 11:43).

Mithredath [Mith're·dath], *given by Mithra*—

1. A Persian treasurer who, by the order of Cyrus, restored the sacred vessels to the Jews (Ezra 1:8).

2. One who wrote Artaxerxes, king of Persia, from Samaria in opposition to the Jews (Ezra 4:7).

Mitylene [Mit·y·le'ne], *mutilated*—The capital of Lesbos, an island situated in the Aegean Sea (Acts 20:13–15).

Mizar [Mi'zar], *small*—A proper name for a hill east of the Jordan (Ps. 42:6).

Mizpah [Miz'pah], *watchtower*—The name of six sites in the Old Testament:

1. One of three names given to a mound of stones erected as a memorial. Jacob set up this memorial in Gilead as a witness of the covenant between him and his father-in-law, Laban (Gen. 31:49). Both Jacob and Laban called this monument "heap of witness." The mound was also called Mizpah, meaning "watch[tower]." The stones were erected as a boundary marker between the two. God was the One who was to watch between them.

2. A district at the foot of Mount Hermon in the territory of Manasseh called "the land of Mizpah" and "the Valley of Mizpah" (Josh. 11:3, 8). The territory was inhabited by Hivites, a nation affiliated

with the northern confederacy which was defeated by Joshua at the waters of Merom.

3. A city of Judah (Josh. 15:38) in the Shephelah, or lowland plain.

4. A city of Benjamin in the region of Geba and Ramah (1 Kings 15:22). At Mizpah Samuel assembled the Israelites for prayer after the ark of the covenant was returned to Kirjath-jearim (1 Sam. 7:5–6). Saul was first presented to Israel as king at this city (1 Sam. 10:17). Mizpah was also one of the places that Samuel visited on his annual circuit to judge Israel (1 Sam. 7:16–17). Mizpah was one of the sites fortified against the kings of the northern tribes of Israel by King Asa (1 Kings 15:22). After the destruction of Jerusalem in 586 B.C., Gedaliah was appointed governor of the remaining people of Judah; his residence was at Mizpah (2 Kings 25:23, 25). After the fall of Jerusalem Mizpah became the capital of the Babylonian province of Judah. Mizpah also was reinhabited by Israelites after the Babylonian captivity (Neh. 3:7, 15, 19). The site is modern Tell en-Nasbch.

5. A town or site in Gilead known as Mizpah of Gilead and the home of Jephthah the judge (Judg. 11:29, 34). This site was probably known as Ramath Mizpah (Josh. 13:26)—the Ramoth in Gilead listed as one of the six cities of refuge (Josh. 20:8).

6. A city in Moab to which David took his parents for safety when King Saul sought to kill him (1 Sam. 22:3). Some scholars believe Mizpah of Moab was another name for Kir of Moab (present-day Kerak), the capital of Moab.

Mizpar [Miz′par]—See Mispar.

Mizpeh [Miz′peh]—See Mizpah.

Mizraim [Miz′ra·im]—The Hebrew word for Egypt, particularly upper Egypt (Gen. 10:6).

Mizzah [Miz′zah], *fear*—A duke of Edom (Gen. 36:13, 17; 1 Chron. 1:37).

Mnason [Mna′son], *remembering*—A native of Cyprus, in whose house Paul lodged in Jerusalem (Acts 21:16).

Moab [Mo′ab], *of my father*—The name of a man and a nation in the Old Testament:

1. A son of Lot by an incestuous union with his older daughter (Gen. 19:37). Moab became an ancestor of the Moabites.

2. A neighboring nation whose history was closely linked to the fortunes of the Hebrew people. Moab was situated along the eastern border of the southern half of the Dead Sea, on the plateau between the Dead Sea and the Arabian desert. It was about 57 kilometers (35 miles) long and 40 kilometers (25 miles) wide. Throughout much of its history, the northern border of Moab was the Arnon River and the southern border was the Zered. Although it was primarily a high plateau, Moab also had mountainous areas and deep gorges. It was a fertile area for crops and herds. To the south and west of Moab was the nation of Edom; to the north was Ammon. After the Israelites invaded the land, the tribe of Reuben displaced the Moabites from the northern part of their territory and the tribe of Gad pushed the Ammonites eastward into the desert.

Moabites [Mo'ab·ites]—Descendants of Lot's son, Moab. They were closely related to the Ammonites who were the descendants of Lot's son, Ammon (Gen. 19:37–38). By the time of the exodus they had become numerous and were in possession of the district from the plain of Heshbon to the wady Kurahi, east of the Jordan. Moses was forbidden to attack them because the Lord gave the land to the children of Lot (Deut. 2:9). It was on the plain of Moab the Israelites had their last encampment (Num. 22:1). Eglon, king of Moab, invaded Israel and oppressed the people until they were delivered by Ehud (Judg. 3:12–30; 1 Sam. 12:9). Ruth, the Moabitess, married Boaz of Bethlehem and became an ancestress of Jesus.

Moadiah [Mo·a·di'ah]—See Maadiah.

Modin [Mo'din], unknown—The hometown of the Maccabean family, made famous in the intertestamental period.

Moladah [Mo·la'dah], *birth*—A town in the extreme south of Judah (Josh. 15:26).

Molech [Mo'lech], *king*—An Ammonite deity (1 Kings 11:7) who was also called Milcom (1 Kings 11:5, 33) and Malcam (Jer. 49:1–3; Zeph. 1:5). This god was worshipped with human sacrifices (2 Kings 23:10).

Molid [Mo'lid], *begetter*—A man of Judah of the family of Hezron (1 Chron. 2:29).

Moloch [Mo'loch]—See Molech.

Molten Sea [Mol'ten]—A great basin made of brass which stood in the court of Solomon's temple (1 Chron. 18:8). It was decorated with flower-like ornaments. It was placed on the backs of twelve bronze oxen, had an estimated capacity of 16,000 gallons, and served the priests as a place for washing (1 Kings 7:23–26, 39; 2 Chron. 4:2–6).

Morashtite [Mo·rash'tite]—See Morasthite.

Morasthite [Mo·ras'thite], *possession of Gath*—One who lived in Moresheth (Jer. 26:18; Mic. 1:1).

Mordecai [Mor·de·ca'i], *related to Marduk*—The name of two men in the Old Testament:

1. One of the Jewish captives who returned to Jerusalem with Zerubbabel from Babylon (Ezra 2:2; Neh. 7:7).

2. The son of Jair and a descendant of Kish. The hero of the book of Esther. Mordecai was probably born in Babylonia during the years of the captivity of the Jewish people by this pagan nation. He was a resident of Susa (Shushan), the Persian capital during the reign of Ahasuerus (Xerxes I), the king of Persia (ruled 486–465 B.C.).

When Mordecai's uncle, Abihail, died (Est. 2:5), Mordecai took his orphaned cousin, Hadassah (Esther), into his home as her adoptive father (Est. 2:7). When two of the king's eunuchs, Bigthan and Teresh, conspired to assassinate King Ahasuerus, Mordecai discovered the plot and exposed it, saving the king's life (Est. 2:21–22). Mordecai's good deed was recorded in the royal chronicles of Persia (Est. 2:23).

Mordecai showed his loyalty to God by refusing to bow to Haman, the official second to the king (Est. 3:2, 5). According to the Greek historian Herodotus, when the Persians bowed before their king, they paid homage as to a god. Mordecai, a Jew, would not condone such idolatry.

Haman's hatred for Mordecai sparked his plan to kill all the Jews in the Persian Empire (Est. 3:6). Mordecai reminded his cousin, who had become Queen Esther, of her God-given opportunity to expose Haman to the king and to save her people (Est. 3:1–4:17). The plot turned against Haman, who ironically was impaled on the same stake that he had prepared for Mordecai (Est. 7:10).

Haman was succeeded by Mordecai, who now was second in command to the most powerful man in the kingdom. He used his new position to encourage his people to defend themselves against the scheduled massacre planned by Haman. Persian officials also assisted in protecting the Jews, an event celebrated by the annual Feast of Purim (Est. 9:26–32).

Moreh [Mo′reh], *teacher*—

1. The place where the sacred terebinth grew, near Shechem, where Abraham built an altar and the Lord appeared to him (Gen. 12:6; Deut. 11:30).

2. The hill of Moreh was in the valley of Jezreel (Judg. 7:1).

Moresheth-gath [Mo′resh·eth-gath], *possession of Gath*—The birthplace, hometown, or residence of the prophet Micah (Mic. 1:14). Micah is also called the Morasthite (Jer. 26:18, KJV; Mic. 1:1, KJV)—that is, a native or resident of Moresheth. The site of Moresheth-gath is identified with present-day Tell ej-Judeideh, in the lowland plain of Judah.

Moriah [Mo·ri′ah], *chosen by Jehovah*—The name of two sites in the Old Testament:

1. A land to which God commanded Abraham to take his son Isaac and to offer him as a burnt offering on one of the mountains. The mountains of this land were a three-day journey from Beersheba and were visible from a great distance (Gen. 22:2, 4).

2. The hill at Jerusalem where Solomon built "the house of the Lord," the temple. Originally this was the threshing floor of Ornan the Jebusite (2 Chron. 3:1), also called Araunah the Jebusite (2 Sam. 24:16–24), where God appeared to David. David purchased the threshing floor from Ornan (1 Chron. 21:15–22:1) and built an altar on the site. It was left to David's son (Solomon) to build the temple.

Some Jews believe the altar of burnt offering in the temple at Jerusalem was situated on the exact site of the altar on which Abraham intended to sacrifice Isaac. To them the two Mount Moriahs mentioned in the Bible are identical. The Muslim structure, the Dome of the Rock in Jerusalem, reputedly is situated on this site.

Morning Star—See Lucifer.

Moserah [Mo'se·rah], *bond*—One of the places where the Israelites camped in the wilderness (Deut. 10:6). Moseroth, the plural form, is used in Numbers 33:30.

Moseroth [Mo'se·roth]—See Moserah.

Moses [Mo'ses], *drawn out*—The Hebrew prophet who delivered the Israelites from Egyptian slavery and who was their leader and law-giver during their years of wandering in the wilderness. He was from the family line of Amram and Jochebed (Ex. 6:18, 20; Num. 26:58–59), Kohath and Levi. He was also the brother of Aaron and Miriam.

Moses was a leader so inspired by God that he was able to build a united nation from a race of oppressed and weary slaves. In the cov-enant ceremony at Mount Sinai, where the Ten Commandments were given, he founded the religious community known as Israel. As the interpreter of these covenant laws, he was the organizer of the commu-nity's religious and civil traditions. His story is told in the Old Testa-ment—in the books of Exodus, Leviticus, Numbers, and Deuteronomy.

Moses' life is divided into three major periods:

The Forty Years in Egypt: The Hebrew people had been in slavery in Egypt for some four hundred years. This was in accord with God's words to Abraham that his seed, or descendants, would be in a foreign land in affliction for four hundred years (Gen. 15:13). At the end of this time, God began to set His people free from their bondage by bringing Moses to birth. He was a child of the captive Hebrews, but one whom the Lord would use to deliver Israel from her oppressors.

Moses was born at a time when the pharaoh, the ruler of Egypt, had given orders that no more male Hebrew children should be allowed to live. The Hebrew slaves had been reproducing so fast that the king felt threatened by a potential revolt against his authority. To save the infant Moses, his mother made a little vessel of papyrus waterproofed with asphalt and pitch. She placed Moses in the vessel, floating among the reeds on the bank of the Nile River. By God's providence, Moses—the child of a Hebrew slave—was found and adopted by an Egyptian princess, the daughter of the pharaoh himself. He was reared in the royal court as a prince of the Egyptians: "And Moses was learned in all the wisdom of the Egyptians, and was mighty in words and deeds" (Acts 7:22). At the same time, the Lord determined that Moses should be taught in his earliest years by his own mother. This meant that he was founded in the faith of his fathers, although he was reared as an Egyptian (Ex. 2:1–10).

One day Moses became angry at an Egyptian taskmaster who was beating a Hebrew slave; he killed the Egyptian and buried him in the sand (Ex. 2:12). When this became known, however, he feared for his own life and fled from Egypt to the land of Midian. Moses was forty years old when this occurred (Acts 7:23–29).

The Forty Years in the Land of Midian: Moses' exile of about forty years was spent in the land of Midian (mostly in northwest Arabia), in the desert between Egypt and Canaan. In Midian Moses became a shepherd and eventually the son-in-law of Jethro, a Midianite priest. Jethro gave his daughter Zipporah to Moses in marriage (Ex. 2:21); and she bore him two sons, Gershom and Eliezer (Ex. 18:3–4; Acts 7:29). During his years as a shepherd, Moses became familiar with the wilderness of the Sinai Peninsula, learning much about survival in the desert. He also learned patience and much about leading sheep. All of these skills prepared him to be the shepherd of the Israelites in later years when he led them out of Egypt and through the wilderness of Sinai.

Near the end of his forty-year sojourn in the land of Midian, Moses experienced a dramatic call to ministry. This call was given at the burning bush in the wilderness near Mount Sinai. The Lord revealed to Moses His intention to deliver Israel from Egyptian captivity into a "land flowing with milk and honey" that He had promised centuries before to Abraham, Isaac, and Jacob. The Lord assured Moses that He would be with him, and that by God's presence, he would be able to lead the people out.

God spoke to Moses from the midst of a burning bush, but Moses doubted that it was God who spoke. He asked for a sign. Instantly his rod, which he cast on the ground, became a serpent (Ex. 4:3).

In spite of the assurance of this miraculous sign, Moses was still hesitant to take on this task. He pleaded that he was "slow of speech and slow of tongue" (Ex. 4:10), perhaps implying that he was a stutterer or a stammerer. God countered Moses' hesitation by appointing his brother, Aaron, to be his spokesman. Moses would be God's direct representative, and Aaron would be his mouthpiece and interpreter to the people of Israel. Finally Moses accepted this commission from God and returned to Egypt for a confrontation with Pharaoh.

Soon after his return, Moses stirred the Hebrews to revolt and demanded of Pharaoh, "Let My people go, that they may hold a feast to Me in the wilderness" (Ex. 5:1). But Pharaoh rejected the demand of this unknown God of whom Moses and Aaron spoke: "Who is the LORD, that I should obey His voice to let Israel go? I do not know the LORD, nor will I let Israel go" (Ex. 5:2). He showed his contempt of this God of the Hebrews by increasing the oppression of the slaves (Ex. 5:5–14). As a result, the people grumbled against Moses (Ex. 5:20–21).

But Moses did not waver in his mission. He warned Pharaoh of the consequences that would fall on his kingdom if he should refuse to let the people of Israel go. Then followed a stubborn battle of wills with Pharaoh hardening his heart and stiffening his neck against God's commands. Ten terrible plagues were visited upon the land of Egypt (Ex. 7:14–12:30), the tenth plague being the climax of horrors.

The ultimate test of God's power to set the people free was the slaying of the firstborn of all Egypt, on the night of the Passover feast of Israel (Ex. 11:1–12:30). That night Moses began to lead the slaves to freedom, as God killed the firstborn of Egypt and spared the firstborn of Israel through the sprinkling of the blood of the Passover lamb. This pointed to the day when God's own Lamb would come into the world to deliver, by His own blood, all of those who put their trust in Him, setting them free from sin and death "but with the precious blood of Christ, as of a lamb without blemish and without spot" (1 Peter 1:19).

After the Hebrews left, Pharaoh's forces pursued them to the Red Sea (or Sea of Reeds), threatening to destroy them before they could cross. A pillar, however, stood between the Israelites and the Egyptians, protecting the Israelites until they could escape. When Moses stretched his hand over the sea, the waters were divided and the Israelites passed to the other side. When the Egyptians attempted to follow, Moses again stretched his hand over the sea, and the waters closed over the Egyptian army (Ex. 14:19–31).

The Forty Years in the Wilderness: Moses led the people toward Mount Sinai, in obedience to the word of God spoken to him at the burning bush (Ex. 3:1–12). During the long journey through the desert, the people began to murmur because of the trials of freedom, forgetting the terrible trials of Egyptian bondage. Through it all, Moses was patient, understanding both the harshness of the desert and the blessings of God's provision for them.

In the wilderness of Shur the people murmured against Moses because the waters of Marah were bitter. The Lord showed Moses a tree. When Moses cast the tree into the waters, the waters were made sweet (Ex. 15:22–25). In answer to Moses' prayers, God sent bread from heaven—manna—and quail to eat (Ex. 16). In the Wilderness of Sin, when they again had no water, Moses performed a miracle by striking a rock, at a place called Massah (Testing) and Meribah (Contention), and water came out of the rock (Ex. 17:1–7). When they reached the land of Midian, Moses' father-in-law, Jethro, came to meet them. He gave Moses sound advice on how to exercise his leadership and authority more efficiently by delegating responsibility to subordinate rulers who would judge the people in small cases (Ex. 18).

When the Israelites arrived at Mount Sinai, Moses went up onto the mountain for forty days (Ex. 24:18). The Lord appeared in a terrific storm—"thunderings and lightnings, and a thick cloud" (Ex. 19:16). Out of this momentous encounter came the covenant between the Lord and Israel, including the Ten Commandments (Ex. 20:1–17).

In giving the law to the Hebrew people, Moses taught the Israelites what the Lord expected of them—that they were to be a holy people separated from the pagan immorality and idolatry of their surroundings. Besides being the lawgiver, Moses was also the one through whom God presented the tabernacle and instructions for the holy office of the priesthood. Under God's instructions, Moses issued ordinances to cover specific situations, instituted a system of judges and hearings in civil cases, and regulated the religious and ceremonial services of worship.

When Moses delayed in coming down from Mount Sinai, the faithless people became restless. They persuaded Aaron to take their golden earrings and other articles of jewelry and to fashion a golden calf for worship. When he came down from the mountain, Moses was horrified at the idolatry and rebellion of his people. The sons of Levi were loyal to Moses, however; and he ordered them to punish the rebels (Ex. 32:28). Because of his anger at the golden calf, Moses cast down the two tablets of stone with the Ten Commandments and broke them at the foot of the mountain (Ex. 32:19). After the rebellion had been put down, Moses went up onto Mount Sinai again and there received the Ten Commandments a second time (Ex. 34:1, 29).

After leaving Mount Sinai, the Israelites continued their journey toward the land of Canaan. They arrived at Kadesh-barnea, on the border of the promised land. From this site, Moses sent twelve spies, one from each of the twelve tribes of Israel, into Canaan to explore the land. The spies returned with glowing reports of the fruitfulness of the land. They brought back samples of its figs and pomegranates and a cluster of grapes so large that it had to be carried between two men on a pole (Num. 13:1–25). The majority of the spies, however, voted against the invasion of the land. Ten of them spoke fearfully of the huge inhabitants of Canaan (Num. 13:31–33).

The minority report, delivered by Caleb and Joshua, urged a bold and courageous policy. By trusting the Lord, they said, the Israelites would be able to attack and overcome the land (Num. 13:30). But the people lost heart and rebelled, refusing to enter Canaan and clamoring for a new leader who would take them back to Egypt (Num. 14:1–4). To punish them for their lack of faith, God condemned all of that generation, except Caleb and Joshua, to perish in the wilderness (Num. 14:26–38).

During these years of wandering in the wilderness, Moses' patience was continually tested by the murmurings, grumblings, and complaints of the people. At one point, Moses' patience reached its breaking point and he sinned against the Lord, in anger against the people. When the people again grumbled against Moses, saying they had no water, the Lord told Moses to speak to the rock and water would flow forth. Instead, Moses lifted his hand and struck the rock twice with his rod. Apparently because he disobeyed the Lord in this act, Moses was not permitted to enter the promised land (Num. 20:1–13). That privilege would belong to his successor, Joshua.

When Moses had led the Israelites to the borders of Canaan, his work was done. In "the Song of Moses" (Deut. 32:1–43), Moses renewed the Sinai Covenant with the survivors of the wanderings, praised God, and blessed the people, tribe by tribe (Deut. 33:1–29). Then he climbed Mount Nebo to the top of Pisgah and viewed the promised land from afar and died. The Hebrews never saw him again, and the circumstances of his death and burial remain shrouded in mystery (Num. 34:1–8).

After his death, Moses continued to be viewed by Israel as the servant of the Lord (Josh. 1:1–2) and as the one through whom God spoke to Israel (Josh. 1:3; 9:24; 14:2). For that reason, although it was truly the law of God, the law given at Mount Sinai was consistently called the law of Moses (Josh. 1:7; 4:10). Above all, Joshua's generation remembered Moses as the man of God (Josh. 14:6).

This high regard for Moses continued throughout Israelite history. Moses was held in high esteem by Samuel (1 Sam. 12:6, 8), the writer of 1 Kings (1 Kings 2:3), and the Jewish people who survived in the times after the captivity (1 Chron. 6:49; 23:14).

The psalmist also remembered Moses as the man of God and as an example of a great man of prayer (Ps. 99:6). He recalled that God worked through Moses (Ps. 77:20; 103:7), realizing that the consequence of his faithfulness to God was to suffer much on behalf of God's people (Ps. 106:16, 32).

The prophets of the Old Testament also remembered Moses as the leader of God's people (Isa. 63:12), as the one by whom God brought Israel out of Egypt (Mic. 6:4), and as one of the greatest of the interceders for God's people (Jer. 15:1). Malachi called the people to remember Moses' law and to continue to be guided by it, until the Lord Himself should come to redeem them (Mal. 4:4).

Jesus showed clearly, by what He taught and by how He lived, that He viewed Moses' law as authoritative for the people of God (Matt. 5:17–18). To the two disciples on the road to Emmaus, Jesus expounded the things concerning Himself written in the law of Moses, the Prophets, and the other writings of the Old Testament (Luke 24:27). At the transfiguration, Moses and Elijah appeared to Jesus and talked with Him (Matt. 17:1–4; Mark 9:2–5; Luke 9:28–33).

In his message before the Jewish Council, Stephen included a lengthy reference to how God delivered Israel by Moses and how Israel rebelled against God and against Moses' leadership (Acts 7:20–44).

The writer of the book of Hebrews spoke in glowing terms of the faith of Moses (Heb. 11:24–29). These and other passages demonstrate how highly Moses was esteemed by various writers of the Old and New Testaments.

The New Testament, however, shows that Moses' teaching was intended only to prepare humanity for the greater teaching and work of Jesus Christ (Rom. 1:16–3:31). What Moses promised, Jesus fulfilled:

"For the law was given through Moses, but grace and truth came through Jesus Christ" (John 1:17).

Most High—A title of God, indicating His superiority to any other being (Ps. 92:1; Isa. 14:14; Dan. 4:17). See God, Names of.

Mountain of the Valley—A mountain in the territory of Reuben, east of the Jordan (Josh. 13:19).

Mountains of the Amalekites—A place in the territory of Ephraim (Judg. 12:15).

Mountains of the Amorites—Near Kadesh-barnea, one of the places the twelve spies explored in the first venture into the promised land (Deut. 1:7, 20).

Mount Baal Hermon [Mount Ba'al Her'mon], *mount of destruction*—A mountain from which the Israelites were unable to expel the Hivites (Judg. 3:3). East of the Jordan River, the site marked the northern limit of the half-tribe of Manasseh. Some scholars believe the Hebrew text may originally have read "Baal Gad near Mount Hermon" (Josh. 13:5; 1 Chron. 5:23).

Mount Ephraim—See Ephraim, Mountains of.

Mount Heres [Her'es], *mountain of the sun*—A mountain near Aijalon and Shaalbim on the border between Judah and Dan (Judg. 1:35; in Aijalon, and in Shaalbim, NRSV).

Mount of Beatitudes—The mountain where Jesus delivered the "Sermon on the Mount" (Matt. 5:1–7:29). It is believed to be northwest of the Sea of Galilee.

Mount of Congregation—A mythical mountain in the far north which the Babylonians believed to be the home of the gods (Isa. 14:13).

Mount of Corruption—A hill on the southern ridge of the Mount of Olives. On the Mount of Corruption King Solomon built high places for his wives' pagan gods. These hill-shrines were destroyed in the religious reformation instituted by King Josiah (2 Kings 23:13; Hill of Corruption, NIV; mount of destruction, NASB).

Mount of Olives—A north-to-south ridge of hills east of Jerusalem where Jesus was betrayed on the night before His crucifixion. This prominent feature of Jerusalem's landscape is a gently rounded hill, rising to a height of about 830 meters (2,676 feet) and overlooking the temple.

The closeness of the Mount of Olives to Jerusalem's walls made this series of hills a grave strategic danger. The Roman commander Titus had his headquarters on the northern extension of the ridge during the siege of Jerusalem in A.D. 70. He named the place Mount Scopus, or "Lookout Hill," because of the view it offered over the city walls. The whole hill must have provided a platform for the Roman catapults that hurled heavy objects over the Jewish fortifications of the city.

In ancient times the whole mount must have been heavily wooded. As its name implies, it was covered with dense olive groves. It was from this woodland that the people, under Nehemiah's command, gathered their branches of olive, oil trees, myrtle, and palm to make booths when the Feast of Tabernacles was restored after their years of captivity in Babylon (Neh. 8:15).

The trees also grew on this mountain or hill in New Testament times. When Jesus entered the city, the people who acclaimed him king must have gathered the branches with which they greeted His entry from this same wooded area. Another summit of the Mount of Olives is the one on which the "men of Galilee" stood (Acts 1:11–12) as they watched the resurrected Christ ascend into heaven. Then there is the point to the south above the village of Silwan (or Siloam) on the slope above the spring. Defined by a sharp cleft, it faces west along the converging Valley of Hinnom. It is called the Mount of Offense, or the "Mount of Corruption" (2 Kings 23:13), because here King Solomon built "high places" for pagan deities that were worshiped by the people during his time (1 Kings 11:5–7).

Although the Mount of Olives is close to Jerusalem, there are surprisingly few references to this range of hills in the Old Testament. As David fled from Jerusalem during the rebellion by his son Absalom, he apparently crossed the shoulder of the hill: "So David went up by the ascent of the Mount of Olives" (2 Sam. 15:30). Support may be found in this account for the claim that the road from the Jordan Valley did not go around the ridge in Bible times but crossed over the ridge, allowing the city of Jerusalem to break spectacularly on the traveler's sight as he topped the hill.

The Mount of Olives is also mentioned in a reference by the prophet Zechariah to the future Day of the Lord: "In that day His feet will stand on the Mount of Olives, which faces Jerusalem on the east. And the Mount of Olives shall be split in two from east to west, making a very large valley; half of the mountain shall move toward the north and half of it toward the south" (Zech. 14:4). Christian tradition holds that when Christ returns to earth, His feet will touch first upon the Mount of Olives, the exact point from which He ascended into heaven (Acts 1:11–12).

In the New Testament the Mount of Olives played a prominent part in the last week of our Lord's ministry. Jesus approached Jerusalem from the east, by way of Bethphage and Bethany, at the Mount of Olives (Matt. 21:1; Mark 11:1). As He drew near the descent of the Mount of Olives (Luke 19:37), the crowd spread their garments on the road, and others cut branches from the trees and spread them before Him. They began to praise God and shout, "Hosanna to the Son of David!" (Matt. 21:9). When Jesus drew near Jerusalem, perhaps as He arrived at the top of the Mount of Olives, He saw the city and wept over it (Luke 19:41).

Jesus then went into Jerusalem and cleansed the temple of the moneychangers; He delivered parables to the crowd and silenced the scribes and Pharisees with His wisdom. Later, as He sat on the Mount of Olives, the disciples came to Him privately, and He delivered what is known as "the Olivet Discourse," a long sermon that speaks of the signs of the times and the end of the age, the Great Tribulation, and the coming of the Son of Man (Matt. 24:3–25:46; Mark 13:3–37).

After Jesus had instituted the Lord's Supper on the night of His betrayal, He and His disciples sang a hymn and went out to the Mount of Olives (Matt. 26:30; Mark 14:26), to the Garden of Gethsemane (Matt. 26:36; Mark 14:32). In this garden Jesus was betrayed by Judas and delivered into the hands of His enemies.

Moza [Mo'za], *going forth—*
  1. Son of Caleb of the family of Hezron (1 Chron. 2:46).
  2. Son of Zimri, a descendant of Jonathan (1 Chron. 8:36–37).

Mozah [Mo'zah], *fountain*—A town of Benjamin (Josh. 18:26).

Muppim [Mup'pim], *serpent*—A Benjamite (Gen. 46:21), a descendant of Rachel. He is also called Shupham and Shuppim (Num. 26:39; 1 Chron. 7:12, 15). See Shephuphan.

Mushi [Mu'shi], *yielding*—Son of Merari, a Levite (Ex. 6:19; Num. 3:20; 26:58; 1 Chron. 24:26, 30).

Mushites [Mu'shites]—Descendants of Mushi the Levite (Num. 3:20, 33).

Muster Gate, Mustering Gate—A gate of Jerusalem (Neh. 3:31), also called Miphkad Gate.

Myra [My'ra], *myrrh* or *myrtle juice*—A city of Lycia; Paul transferred ships here on his way to Rome (Acts 27:5–6).

Mysia [My'si·a], *land of beach trees*—A northwestern province of Asia Minor. One of its cities was Troas, and in coming to this point Paul and Silas passed through the province (Acts 16:7–8). Another city was Assos (Acts 20:13), and another was Pergamos, one of the seven churches of Revelation (Rev. 1:11; 2:12–17).

N

Naam [Na'am], *pleasantness*—Son of Caleb (1 Chron. 4:15).

Naamah [Na'a·mah], *pleasant*—
1. Daughter of Lamech and sister of Tubalcain (Gen. 4:22).
2. Wife of Solomon (1 Kings 14:21, 31; 2 Chron. 12:13).
3. A town of Judah (Josh. 15:41).

Naaman [Na'a·man], *pleasant*—The name of three or four men in the Old Testament:
1. A son of Benjamin (Gen. 46:21).
2. A son of Bela and the founder of a family, the Naamites (Num. 26:40). He may be the same person as No. 1.
3. A commander of the Syrian army who was cured of leprosy by the Lord through the prophet Elisha. Naaman was a "great and honorable man in the eyes of his master [Ben-hadad, king of Syria] . . . but he was a leper" (2 Kings 5:1–27). Although leprosy was a despised disease in Syria, as in Israel, those who suffered from the disease were not outcasts.

On one of Syria's frequent raids of Israel, a young Israelite girl was captured and became a servant to Naaman's wife. The girl told her mistress about the prophet Elisha, who could heal Naaman of his leprosy. Ben-hadad sent a letter about Naaman to the king of Israel. Fearing a Syrian trick to start a war, the king of Israel had to be assured by Elisha that Naaman should indeed be sent to the prophet. To demonstrate to Naaman that it was God, not human beings, who healed, Elisha refused to appear to Naaman. Instead, he sent the commander a message, telling him to dip himself in the Jordan River seven times. Naaman considered such treatment an affront and angrily asked if the Syrian rivers, the Abana and the Pharpar, would not do just as well. His servants, however, persuaded him to follow Elisha's instructions. Naaman did so and was healed. In gratitude, Naaman became a worshiper of God and carried two mule-loads of Israelite earth back to

Syria in order to worship the Lord "on Israelite soil," even though he lived in a heathen land. Before he departed for Damascus, however, Naaman asked Elisha's understanding and pardon for bowing down in the temple of Rimmon when he went there with Ben-hadad (2 Kings 5:18). Elisha said to him, "Go in peace" (v. 19), thus allowing Naaman to serve his master, the king.

4. A son of Ehud, of the tribe of Benjamin (1 Chron. 8:7).

Naamathite [Na·am′a·thite]—An inhabitant of Naamah (Job 2:11; 11:1; 20:1; 42:9).

Naamite [Na′a·mite]—The descendents of Benjamin's son Naaman (Num. 26:40).

Naarah [Na′a·rah], *maiden*—

1. A town east of Beth-el on the border of Ephraim (Josh. 16:7; Naarath, KJV), probably the same as Naaran (1 Chron. 7:28).

2. Wife of Ashur of Judah (1 Chron. 4:5–6).

Naarai [Na′a·rai], *handmaid*—One of David's mighty men, son of Ezbai (1 Chron. 11:37), also called Paarai (2 Sam. 23:35).

Naaran [Na′a·ran]—See Naarah.

Naarath [Na′a·rath]—See Naarah.

Naashon [Na·ash′on]—See Nahshon.

Naasson [Na·as′son]—(Matt. 1:4; Luke 3:32) See Nahshon.

Nabajoth [Na·ba·joth], unknown—Ishmael's firstborn son (1 Chron. 1:29), also called Nebajoth.

Nabal [Na′bal], *foolish*—A resident of Maon. He had large flocks of sheep and goats. David had protected his property and that of others from thieves. When persecuted by Saul, he sent ten of his band to Nabal asking for help. Nabal refused rudely, and only escaped being annihilated by David because of the clever intervention of his intelligent wife Abigail (1 Sam. 25:1–42). Nabal died of a stroke shortly thereafter, and Abigail became the wife of David.

Nabatea [Na·ba·te′a], unknown—A land between the Dead Sea and the Gulf of Aqaba. It is thought that Ishmael's eldest son Nabajoth was probably the ancestor of the Nabateans. The unique city of Petra was the capital of the Nabateans. When Paul was in Damascus, the "governor, under Aretas the king" was trying to apprehend Paul, and Paul's friends let him out of a window in the wall in a basket. This Aretas was Aretas IV (9 B.C.–A.D. 40), a Nabatean king. Rome did not annex Nabatea until A.D. 106, under the emperor Trajan.

Nabopolassar [Na·bo·po·lass'ar], *protect the son*—(2 Kings 25:1–7) Father of Nebuchadnezzar; reigned 626–605 B.C.

Naboth [Na'both], *fruits*—An Israelite of Jezreel who owned a vineyard next to the summer palace of Ahab, king of Samaria (1 Kings 21:1). Ahab coveted this property. He wanted to turn it into a vegetable garden to furnish delicacies for his table. He offered Naboth its worth in money or a better vineyard. But Naboth refused to part with his property, explaining that it was a family inheritance to be passed on to his descendants.

Jezebel obtained the property for Ahab by bribing two men to bear false witness against Naboth and testify that he blasphemed God and the king. Because of their lies, Naboth was found guilty; and both he and his sons (2 Kings 9:26) were stoned to death. Elijah the prophet pronounced doom upon Ahab and his house for this disgusting act of false witness (1 Kings 21:1–29; 2 Kings 9:21–26).

Nabuchodonosor [Na·bu·cho·don'os·or]—See Nebuchadnezzar.

Nachon [Na'chon], *prepared*—Nachon's Threshing Floor: the place where Uzzah was struck dead when he placed his hand on the ark in an attempt to steady it as it was being brought to Jerusalem (2 Sam. 6:6). Also called Nacon. The place was later called Perez-uzzah. See Perez-uzzah.

Nachor [Na'chor]—See Nahor.

Nacon [Na'con]—See Nachon.

Nadab [Na'dab], *liberal*—

1. Eldest son of Aaron (Ex. 6:23; Num. 3:2; 26:60; 1 Chron. 24:1). He and his brother, Abihu, were priests (Ex. 28:1). They offered strange fire to God and were instantly destroyed (Lev. 10:1–7; Num. 26:61).

2. Son and successor of Jeroboam, king of Israel (1 Kings 14:10–11, 20; 15:25–30).

3. Son of Shammai (1 Chron. 2:28, 30).

4. A son of Jehiel and Maachah of Benjamin (1 Chron. 8:29–30; 9:35–36).

Naggai [Nag′gai], *illuminating*—Son of Maath and an ancestor of Jesus (Luke 3:25; Nagge, KJV).

Nagge [Nag′ge]—See Naggai.

Nahalal [Na′ha·lal], *pasture*—A village of Zebulun (Josh. 21:35), also called Nahallal or Nahalol.

Nahaliel [Na·hal′i·el], *valley of God*—An encampment of the Israelites near Pisgah (Num. 21:19).

Nahallal [Na·hal′lal]—See Nahalal.

Nahalol [Na′ha·lol]—See Nahalal.

Naham [Na′ham], *solace*—A Calebite (1 Chron. 4:19).

Nahamani [Na·ha·ma′ni], *compassionate*—One who returned to Jerusalem (Neh. 7:7).

Naharai [Na′ha·rai], *snoring*—Joab's armorbearer, a Berothite (2 Sam. 23:37; 1 Chron. 11:39).

Nahari [Na′ha·ri]—See Naharai.

Nahash [Na′hash], *serpent*—

1. A king of the Ammonites. When he besieged Jabesh-gilead, he demanded as the price of peace that every man lose his right eye as a reproach to Israel (1 Sam. 11:1–11).

2. The probable father of David's sisters, Abigail and Zeruiah (2 Sam. 17:25). Scholars have guessed that Jesse was the second husband of David's mother.

3. A man of Rabbah, an Ammonite (2 Sam. 17:27).

Nahath [Na′hath], *rest*—

1. Son of Reuel, grandson of Esau and a chieftain of Moab (Gen. 36:3–4, 13, 17; 1 Chron. 1:37).

2. A Levite of the family of Kohath (1 Chron. 6:26), probably the same as Tohu (1 Sam. 1:1), and Toah (1 Chron. 6:34).

3. A Levite in charge of the offerings in the reign of Hezekiah (2 Chron. 31:13).

Nahbi [Nah'bi], *hidden*—The scout who represented Naphtali when the twelve went into Canaan to spy out the land preliminary to entering it (Num. 13:14).

Nahor [Na'hor], *snoring*—The name of two men and a city in the Old Testament:

1. Son of Serug, father of Terah, grandfather of Abraham (Gen. 11:22–25), and an ancestor of Jesus Christ (Luke 3:34; Nachor, KJV).

2. A son of Terah and a brother of Abraham and Haran (Gen. 11:26–29). Nahor had twelve children, eight by his wife Milcah (Lot's sister) and four by his concubine Reumah. One of his children was Bethuel, who became the father of Rebekah and Laban (Gen. 28:5).

3. A city mentioned in Genesis 24:10. Some confusion exists about the phrase "city of Nahor." This may refer either to the city called Nahor or to the city where Nahor lived. When Abraham and Lot migrated to Canaan, Nahor remained in Haran. Abraham sent his servant here to find a bride for Isaac from among Abraham's extended family (Gen. 24:10).

Nahshon [Nah'shon], *enchanter*—A prince of Judah (Num. 1:7; 2:3; 7:12, 17; 10:14). His sister was the wife of Aaron. He was the ancestor of Boaz, husband of Ruth (Ruth 4:20–22; 1 Chron. 2:10–12) and ancestor of Jesus (Matt. 1:4; Luke 3:32–33; Naason, KJV).

Nahum [Na'hum], *compassionate*—The name of two men in the Bible:

1. An Old Testament prophet and author of the book of Nahum whose prophecy pronounced God's judgment against the mighty nation of Assyria. Very little is known about Nahum. His hometown, Elkosh in the nation of Israel (Nah. 1:1), has not been located. But he must have lived some time shortly before 612 B.C., the year when Assyria's capital city, Nineveh, was destroyed by the Babylonians. Nahum announced that the judgment of God would soon be visited upon this pagan city.

The book of Nahum is similar to the book of Obadiah, since both these prophecies were addressed against neighboring nations. Obadiah spoke the word of the Lord against Edom, while Nahum prophesied against Assyria. Both messages contained a word of hope for God's covenant people, since they announced that Israel's enemies would soon be overthrown. While little is known about Nahum the man, his prophetic writing is one of the most colorful in the Old Testament. The book of Nahum is marked by strong imagery, a sense of suspense, and vivid language, with biting puns and deadly satire. Nahum was a man who understood God's goodness, but he could also describe the terror of the Lord against His enemies.

2. An ancestor of Jesus (Luke 3:25).

Nain [Na'in], *beauty*—A city of Galilee (Luke 7:11–17). Jesus raised a widow's son to life here.

Naioth [Nai'oth], *dwellings*—A community of prophets in Ramah who labored under the guidance of Samuel (1 Sam. 19:18–20:1).

Naomi [Na'o·mi], *my joy*—The mother-in-law of Ruth. After her husband, Elimelech, and two sons, Mahlon and Chilion, died, Naomi returned to her home in Bethlehem, accompanied by Ruth. Naomi advised Ruth to work for a near kinsman, Boaz (Ruth 2:1), and to seek his favor. When Boaz and Ruth eventually married, they had a son, whom they named Obed. This child became the father of Jesse, the grandfather of David, and an ancestor of Jesus Christ (Ruth 4:21–22; Matt. 1:5).

Naphathdor [Na'phath·dor]—See Dor.

Naphish [Na'phish], *inspiration*—Son of Ishmael (Gen. 25:15; 1 Chron. 1:31; Nephish, KJV).

Naphtali [Naph'ta·li], *my wrestling*—

1. The sixth son of Jacob (Gen. 35:25). Because Jacob's wife Rachel was barren and her sister Leah had borne four sons to Jacob, Rachel was distraught. She gave her maidservant Bilhah to Jacob. Any offspring of this union were regarded as Rachel's. When Bilhah gave birth to Dan and Naphtali, Rachel was joyous. "With great wrestlings I have wrestled with my sister," she said, "and indeed I have prevailed" (Gen. 30:8). So she called his name Naphtali, which means "my wrestling."

2. The tribe descended from the four sons of Naphtali (Gen. 46:24; Num. 26:48–49).

Naphtuhim [Naph·tu'him], *border people*—Descendants of Ham through Mizraim (Gen. 10:13; 1 Chron. 1:11); an Egyptian tribe.

Narcissus [Nar·cis'sus], *stupidity*—A Christian Roman family mentioned in Paul's greetings (Rom. 16:11).

Nathan [Na'than], *he gave*—The name of several men in the Old Testament:

1. A son of David and Bathsheba and an older brother of Solomon. Nathan was David's third son born in Jerusalem (2 Sam. 5:14). Six sons had been born to David earlier, while he was at Hebron. Through Nathan the line of descent passed from David to Jesus Christ (Luke 3:31). He was the father of Azariah and Zabud (1 Kings 4:5).

2. A prophet during the reign of David and Solomon. Nathan told David that he would not be the one to build the temple (1 Chron. 17:1–15). Using the parable of the "one little ewe lamb," Nathan confronted David ("You are the man!") with his double sin, the murder of Uriah the Hittite and his adultery with Bathsheba, Uriah's wife (2 Sam. 12:1–15). He also was divinely used to tell David that he would not build the temple, but that his son would (2 Sam. 7:1–7; 1 Chron. 17 1–15). Nathan, as the Lord's official prophet, named Solomon Jedidiah, which means "Beloved of the Lord" (2 Sam. 12:25). Nathan was also involved in David's arrangement of the musical services of the sanctuary (2 Chron. 29:25).

When David was near death, Nathan advised Bathsheba to tell David of the plans of David's son Adonijah to take the throne. Bathsheba related the news to David, who ordered that Solomon be proclaimed king (1 Kings 1:8–45). Nathan apparently wrote a history of David's reign (1 Chron. 29:29) and a history of Solomon's reign (2 Chron. 9:29).

3. A man from Zobah, an Aramean, or Syrian, kingdom between Damascus and the Euphrates River (2 Sam. 23:36). Father of Igal and warrior of David.

4. Father of two of Solomon's officials (1 Kings 4:5), perhaps the same person as No. 1 or No. 2.

5. Son of Attai of the Hazron family. A descendant of Jerahmeel, of the tribe of Judah (1 Chron. 2:36).

6. A brother of Joel and one of David's mighty men (1 Chron. 11:38) and probably the same man as No. 3.

7. A leader sent by Ezra at the river Ahava to find Levites for the temple in Jerusalem (Ezra 8:15–16).

8. A son of Bani (Ezra 10:34) who divorced his pagan wife after returning from the captivity in Babylon (Ezra 10:39), probably the same person as No. 7.

Nathanael [Na·than′a·el], *given of God*—One of the twelve apostles (John 21:2). When Jesus called Philip, the first thing Philip did was to go and find Nathanael. Nathanael was skeptical at first, ridiculing the idea that anything good could come out of Nazareth, but when he met Jesus, he changed his mind (John 1:45–51). He is probably the same person as Bartholomew (Matt. 10:3).

Nathan-melech [Na′than-me′lech], *given of the king*—An officer of the court. Josiah removed the horses dedicated to the sun from the entrance of the temple, near the chamber of Nathanmelech (2 Kings 23:11).

Naum [Na′um], *consolation*—Father of Amos in the maternal ancestry of Jesus (Luke 3:25). See Nahum.

Nazarene [Naz′a·rene]—A native or inhabitant of Nazareth (Matt. 2:23; 26:71; Mark 16:6). Jesus was born in Bethlehem, but He was brought up in Nazareth and was called a "Nazarene." The town and its people were held in low esteem (John 1:46).

Nazareth [Naz′a·reth], *watchtower*—A town of lower Galilee where Jesus spent His boyhood years (Matt. 2:23). For centuries Nazareth has been a beautifully secluded town nestled in the southernmost hills of the Lebanon Mountain range about 30 miles from the Mediterranean Sea. Situated in the territory belonging to Zebulun, the city must have been of late origin or of minor importance. It is never mentioned in the Old Testament, although artifacts discovered on the site indicate that Nazareth was a settled community at least 1,500 years before the New Testament era.

Nazareth lay close to the important trade routes of Palestine. It overlooked the plain of Esdraelon through which caravans passed as they traveled from Gilead to the south and west. North of the city was the main road from Ptolemais to the Decapolis, a road over which the Roman legions frequently traveled. This fact may account for the possible source of the name Nazareth in the Aramaic word meaning "watchtower."However, Nazareth itself was situated in something of a basin, a high valley about 366 meters (1,200 feet) above sea level over-looking the Esdraelon Valley. To the north and east were steep hills, while on the west the hills rose to an impressive 488 meters (1,600 feet). Nazareth, therefore, was somewhat secluded and isolated from nearby traffic. This apparent isolation of Nazareth as a frontier town on the southern border of Zebulun contributed to the reputation that Naz-areth was not an important part of the national and religious life of Israel. This, coupled with a rather bad reputation in morals and religion and a certain crudeness in the Galilean dialect, prompted Nathanael, when he first learned of Jesus of Nazareth, to ask, "Can anything good come out of Nazareth?" (John 1:46).

Although it was not an important town before the New Testament era, Nazareth became immortal as the hometown of Jesus the Messiah. It was here that the angel appeared to Mary and informed her of the forthcoming birth of Christ (Luke 1:26–38). Jesus was born in Bethle-hem (Luke 2). But after their sojourn in Egypt (Matt. 2:19–22) to escape the ruthless murders of Herod the Great (Matt. 2:13–18), Joseph and Mary brought the baby Jesus to Nazareth where they had lived (Matt. 2:23). Here Jesus was brought up as a boy (Luke 4:16) and spent the greater part of His life (Mark 1:9; Luke 3:23). Apparently Jesus was well received as a young man in Nazareth (Luke 2:42; 4:16). But this changed after He began His ministry. His own townspeople twice rejected Him (Mark 6:1–6; Luke 4:28–30).

Because of His close association with this city, Christ became known as "Jesus of Nazareth" (Luke 18:37; 24:19; John 1:45). There is prophetic significance as well to His being known as a "Nazarene." Matthew records that Joseph and Mary returned to their city during the reign of Herod Archelaus (ethnarch of Judea, Idumea, and Samaria, 4 B.C.–A.D. 6) "that it might be fulfilled which was spoken by the prophets, 'He shall be called a Nazarene' " (Matt. 2:23).

Modern Nazareth, known as En-Nasira, is a city of about 30,000 people. Its location on the site of old Nazareth makes it impossible to conduct extensive archeological excavations. The Church of the Annunciation, the major tourist attraction, has a special significance for all Bible students. This church consists of a cave where, according to legend, the angel Gabriel appeared to Mary (Luke 1:26–31). Rebuilding and excavation work on this site has turned up evidence that a Christian church existed at this location as early as the fourth century A.D.

Nazarite [Naz′a·rite]—See Nazirite.

Nazirite [Naz′i·rite], *separated*—The Nazirite vow was an oath to abstain from certain worldly influences and to consecrate oneself to God. Among the Jews, the vow was an option for all persons, and it could be taken for a short period or for life. When the specified period was completed, the Nazirite could appear before the priest for the ceremony of release. Nazirites who broke their vows could be restored only by observing specific restoration rites (Num. 6:9–20).

Nazirites expressed their dedication to God by (1) abstaining from all intoxicating drinks and grape products, (2) refusing to cut their hair, (3) avoiding contact with the dead, and (4) refusing to eat food regarded as unclean (Num. 6:3–7). Persons associated with this Nazirite vow in the Bible include Samson, Samuel, and John the Baptist. Samson's parents were told by the angel of the Lord that their son would be a Nazirite until his death (Judg. 13:7). Hannah dedicated Samuel to the Nazirite way of life even before his birth (1 Sam. 1:11, 28), although it is not clear from the Bible accounts whether Samuel ever actually became a Nazirite. The self-denying lifestyle of John the Baptist indicates that he may have been a Nazirite (Luke 1:15). John was so outspoken in his condemnation of sin in high places that he was executed by Herod, Roman governor of Palestine (Mark 6:17–28), at Herod's fortress palace in Machaerus.

Neah [Ne′ah], *shaking*—A place on the southern border of Zebulun (Josh. 19:13).

Neapolis [Ne·a′po·lis], *new city*—The seaport of the city of Philippi (Acts 16:11).

Neariah [Ne·a·ri′ah], *servant of Jehovah*—
1. A son of Shemaiah of the royal line of Judah (1 Chron. 3:22–23).
2. A son of Ishi and a Simeonite captain (1 Chron. 4:42).

Nebai [Ne·ba′i], *fruitful*—One of the leaders of the people who signed the covenant (Neh. 10:19).

Nebaioth [Ne·bai′oth], *heights*—The Arabian tribe descended from Ishmael's son Nebajoth (Isa. 60:7).

Nebajoth [Ne·ba'joth], *heights*—A son of Ishmael and the founder of a tribe (Gen. 25:13; 28:9; 36:3; 1 Chron. 1:29), also called Nebaioth.

Neballat [Ne·bal'lat], *hidden folly*—A town of Benjamin occupied after the return from Babylon (Neh. 11:34).

Nebat [Ne'bat], *aspect*—Father of Jeroboam (1 Kings 11:26; 12:2).

Nebo [Ne'bo], *prophet*—The name of two towns, a mountain, a man, and a god in the Old Testament:

1. A town in Moab east of the Jordan River, on or near Mount Nebo, that was captured and rebuilt by the tribe of Reuben (Num. 32:3, 38). Nebo is also mentioned on the Moabite Stone as having been taken back by Mesha, king of Moab.

2. A mountain of the Abarim range in Moab opposite Jericho (Num. 33:47). From Nebo, the highest point of Pisgah, Moses was permitted to view the promised land. He was buried in a nearby valley (Deut. 32:49, 50; 34:6).

3. A town mentioned immediately after Beth-el and Ai in the lists of Israelites who returned from the captivity (Ezra 2:29). Nehemiah calls it "the other Nebo," apparently to distinguish it from No. 1.

4. The ancestor of seven Israelites who divorced their pagan wives after the captivity (Ezra 10:43).

5. A god of the Babylonians (Isa. 46:1).

Nebuchadnezzar [Neb·u·chad·nez'zar], *may Nebo protect the crown*—Son of Nabopolassar and most famous of the Babylonian kings. In 625 B.C., his father founded the New Babylonian Empire which became one of the first of the world empires. In the battle of Carchemish the forces of Nabopolassar were under the command of his son and the Egyptians were defeated. This was in 605 B.C. (2 Kings 24:7; Jer. 46:2). In that year, upon the death of his father, Nebuchadnezzar ascended the throne. In biblical history he is linked with three great prophets: Jeremiah, Ezekiel, and Daniel. In 606 B.C., in the reign of Jehoiakim, he invaded Palestine, placed it under tribute (2 Kings 24:1), and carried away some of the people, one of whom was Daniel.

In 597 B.C., he returned and carried to Babylon the king, Jehoiachin, and many of the people, one of them Ezekiel. He placed Zedekiah on the throne (2 Chron. 36:6–10). Nebuchadnezzar received several prophetic dreams from God, which Daniel interpreted (Dan. 2; 4). His second dream foretold that unless he humbled himself before God, he would be humiliated before man. For a time, Nebuchadnezzar heeded this warning, but when he began to take glory for himself that belongs to God, he was stricken with insanity, and spent seven years living like an animal. At the end of this time, his reason was restored. He repented, gave glory to God, and was restored to his kingdom (Dan. 4:34–37).

Nebuchad-rezzar [Neb·u·chad-rez'zar]—See Nebuchadnezzar.

Nebushasban [Neb·u·shas'ban], *Nebo saves me*—An officer of Nebuchadnezzar (Jer. 39:11–14).

Nebushazban [Neb·u·shaz'ban]—See Nebushasban.

Nebuzaradan [Neb·u'zar·a'dan], *chief whom Nebo favors*—The chief commander of the troops of Nebuchadnezzar (2 Kings 25:8–11; 18–21; Jer. 39:9–10; 52:12–30).

Necho [Ne'cho]—(2 Chron. 35:20, 22; 36:4) See Pharaoh.

Nechoh, Neco, Necoh [Ne'choh, Ne'co, Ne'coh]—Variants of Necho.

Nedabiah [Ned·a·bi'ah], *abundance of Jehovah*—Son of Jeconiah (1 Chron. 3:18).

Negev, The [Neg'ev], *dry* or *parched*—A term used by some English translations of the Bible for the southern desert or wilderness area of Judah, south of Hebron, including about 4,500 square miles. Abraham journeyed in the Negev (Gen. 12:9; 13:1, 3; the South, NKJV). When the twelve spies explored the land of Canaan, they went up by way of the Negev (Num. 13:17, 22) and saw the Amalekites who lived there (Num. 13:29). The Canaanite king of Arad also lived in the Negev (Num. 21:1).

The prophet Isaiah described the Negev as a land of trouble and anguish, hardship and distress—a badland populated by lions and poisonous snakes (Isa. 30:6). Through its arid wastes donkey and camel caravans made their way to and from the land of Egypt. Negev is also spelled Negeb.

The Negev contained important copper deposits, and it connected Israel to trade centers in Arabia and Egypt. King Solomon built fortresses in the Negev to guard the trade routes. He also established at Ezion Geber, on the Gulf of Aqaba, a port from which he shipped goods to foreign lands. King Uzziah made great efforts to develop the region, building fortresses and expanding agriculture (2 Chron. 26:10).

In modern times, the desert is being made to "blossom as the rose" (Isa. 35:1); the Israelis have built an impressive irrigation system that channels life-giving water from northern Galilee to the dry, parched region of the Negev.

Nehelamite [Ne·hel′a·mite], *he of the dream*—A designation of uncertain meaning for Shemaiah (Jer. 29:24, 31–32).

Nehemiah [Ne·hem·i′ah]], *the Lord is consolation*—The name of three men:

1. A clan leader who returned with Zerubbabel from the captivity (Ezra 2:2; Neh. 7:7).

2. Son of Hachaliah (Neh. 1:1), the governor of Jerusalem who helped rebuild the wall of the city (Neh. 1:1; 8:9; 10:1; 12:26, 47). Nehemiah was a descendant of the Jewish population that had been taken captive to Babylon in 586 B.C. In 539 B.C. Cyrus the Persian gained control over all of Mesopotamia. He permitted the Jewish exiles to return to the city of Jerusalem. Nearly a century later, in Nehemiah's time, the Persian ruler was Artaxerxes I Longimanus (ruled 465–424 B.C.). Nehemiah was his personal cupbearer (Neh. 1:11).

In 445 B.C. Nehemiah learned of the deplorable condition of the returned exiles in Jerusalem (Neh. 1:2–3). The wall of the city was broken down, the gates were burned, and the people were in distress. Upon hearing this, Nehemiah mourned for many days, fasting and praying to God. His prayer is one of the most moving in the Old Testament (Neh. 1:5–11).

Nehemiah then received permission from Artaxerxes to go to Judah to restore the fortunes of his people. He was appointed governor of the province with authority to rebuild the city walls. Once in Jerusalem, Nehemiah surveyed the walls at night (Neh. 2:12–15). He gave his assessment of the city's condition to the leaders and officials and then organized a labor force to begin the work.

Nehemiah and his work crew were harassed by three enemies: Sanballat the Horonite (a Samaritan), Tobiah the Ammonite official, and Geshem the Arab (Neh. 2:10, 19; 6:1–14). But neither their ridicule

(Neh. 4:3) nor their conspiracy to harm Nehemiah (Neh. 6:2) could stop the project. The builders worked with construction tools in one hand and weapons in the other (Neh. 4:17). To the taunts of his enemies, Nehemiah replied: "I am doing a great work, so that I cannot come down" (Neh. 6:3). Jerusalem's wall was finished in fifty-two days (Neh. 6:14)—a marvelous accomplishment for such a great task. Nehemiah's success stems from the fact that he kept praying, "O God, strengthen my hands" (Neh. 6:9).

Nehemiah's activities did not stop with the completion of the wall. He also led many social and political reforms among the people, including a return to pure worship and a renewed emphasis on true religion. He had the Book of the Law read publicly, the Feast of the Tabernacles observed, the new walls dedicated, and a covenant to observe all obligations signed (Neh. 8–10).

3. A son of Azbuk and leader of half the district of Beth-zur (Neh. 3:16). After his return from the captivity, Nehemiah helped with the repair work on the wall of Jerusalem.

Nehum [Ne'hum], *consoled (by God)*—A leader of the Jews who returned from the captivity with Zerubbabel (Neh. 7:7), also called Rehum (Ezra 2:2).

Nehushta [Ne·hush'ta], *bronze*—Daughter of Elnathan. She was the wife of Jehoiakim (2 Kings 24:8).

Neiel [Nei'el], *moved by God*—A village of Asher (Josh. 19:27).

Nekeb [Ne'keb], *a cavern*—A border town of Naphtali (Josh. 19:33).

Nekoda [Ne·ko'da], *distinguished*—

1. One of the Nethinim, descendants of whom returned from Babylon (Ezra 2:48; Neh. 7:50).

2. Sons of Nekoda (Ezra 2:60; Neh. 7:62); this family could not prove its ancestry after the captivity.

Nemuel [Nem'u·el], *day of God*—Two Old Testament men:

1. Son of Eliab, and brother of Dathan and Abiram, of the tribe of Reuben (Num. 26:9).

2. Son of Simeon (Num. 26:12). Also called Jemuel (Gen. 46:10).

Nemuelites [Nem′u·el·ites]—The descendants of Nemuel, son of Simeon (Num. 26:12).

Nepheg [Neph′eg], *sprout*—Two Old Testament men:
1. Son of Izhar, family of Kohath (Ex. 6:21).
2. A son of David born in Jerusalem (2 Sam. 5:15; 1 Chron. 3:7; 14:6).

Nephilim [Neph′i·lim], possibly *aborted ones*—Giants. The Nephilim are something of a mystery. They are described in Genesis as the offspring of "the sons of God" and "the daughters of men." They were the "mighty men who were of old" and "men of renown" (Gen. 6:4). Exactly who the "sons of God" were remains unknown, but apparently the Nephilim did not die out with the Flood because the Israelites encountered them in the promised land. They were clearly giants, so tall that they made the Hebrews feel like grasshoppers (Num. 13:33).

Nephish [Ne′phish]—See Naphish.

Nephishesim [Ne·phish′e·sim], *refreshed of spices*—A family of Nethinim (Ezra 2:50; Neh. 7:52).

Nephisim, Nephusim, Nephushesim [Ne·phi′sim, Ne·phu′·sim, Ne·phush′e·sim]—Variants of Nephishesim.

Nephthalim [Neph′thal·im]—A form of Naphtali (Matt. 4:13, 15; Rev. 7:6).

Neph-toah [Neph-to′ah], *an opening*—A town or small stream on the border between Judah and Benjamin (Josh. 15:9; 18:15).

Ner [Ner], *light*—A Benjamite who was probably either the uncle or grandfather of Saul (1 Sam. 14:50; 1 Chron. 8:33).

Nereus [Ne′reus], *lamp*—A Christian at Rome (Rom. 16:15).

Nergal [Ner′gal], *hero*—A god of the Babylonians (2 Kings 17:30), a god of war and pestilence.

Nergal-sharezer [Ner′gal-sha·re′zer], *prince of fire*—A prince of Nebuchadnezzar (Jer. 39:3, 13).

Neri [Ne′ri], *Jehovah is my lamp*—Son-in-law of Jeconiah and father of Salathiel (Luke 3:27).

Neriah [Ne·ri'ah], *lamp of Jehovah*—Son of Maaseiah (Jer. 32:12; 36:4; 51:59).

Nero [Ne'ro], *brave*—The fifth Roman emperor (A.D. 54–68). Nero became emperor while still in his teens, succeeding his step-father, Claudius I. His mother was a ruthless woman, commonly supposed to have murdered her husband and engineered the crowning of her son. Although in his youth, Nero seems to have had some human impulses, and a desire to encourage the arts and improve society, he became a corrupt ruler, extravagant and with little management capability. His two deputies, Burrus and Seneca, did much of the actual administration of the government, while Nero gratified his pleasures with ever wilder and more riotous living. He crossed the line of proper decorum in the eyes of Rome, fulfilling his interest in the arts by acting on stage, and giving musical performances. He was as ruthless as his mother, and arranged to have her murdered when she became too interfering. He later had his wife killed as well, in order to marry the woman he had been having an affair with. He was a persecutor of the church, and is particularly remembered for the atrocious cruelties to Christians which he perpetrated after the fires in Rome in A.D. 64. Nero blamed the Christians for the fire, but it was widely believed that he started the fires himself in order to be able to direct the rebuilding of Rome on more artistic lines. He became more and more suspicious and distrustful of those around him, and continued to have inconvenient and threatening people murdered. In A.D. 68, his misrule finally sparked a revolt, and Nero cut his throat. He was thirty years old.

Netaim [Ne·ta'im], *among plants*—A place where potters dwelled, in the territory of Judah (1 Chron. 4:23).

Nethaneal [Neth'a·ne·al]—See Nethaneel.

Nethaneel [Neth'a·neel], *God hath given*—Also Nethanael and Nethanel.

1. A prince of Issachar (Num. 1:8; 2:5; 7:18, 23; 10:15).
2. David's brother, son of Jesse (1 Chron. 2:14).
3. A priest, one of the musicians at the time the ark was brought to Jerusalem (1 Chron. 15:24).
4. Father of Shemaiah, a Levite (1 Chron. 24:6).

5. Son of Obed-edom in the time of David (1 Chron. 26:4).

6. A prince commissioned by Jehoshaphat to teach the people of Judah (2 Chron. 17:7).

7. A Levite in the time of Josiah (2 Chron. 35:9).

8. A son of Pashur. He renounced his foreign wife (Ezra 10:22).

9. A priest in the time of Joiakim, the high priest (Neh. 12:21).

10. A Levite musician (Neh. 12:36).

Nethanel [Neth'a·nel]—See Nethaneel.

Nethaniah [Neth·a·ni'ah], *given of Jehovah*—Four Old Testament men:

1. Father of Ishmael who slew Gedaliah, Babylonian governor of Judah (2 Kings 25:23, 25).

2. An Asaphite Levite who was head of the fifth course of singers (1 Chron. 25:2, 12).

3. A Levite (2 Chron. 17:8).

4. Father of Jehudi (Jer. 36:14).

Nethinim [Neth'i·nim], *those set apart*—The name given those doing the more menial work of the sanctuary. They were temple servants or slaves. At an earlier time their ancestors, the Gibeonites, were hewers of wood and drawers of water for the tabernacle (Josh. 9:23). The office was founded by David but the word *Nethinim* occurs only in Ezra and Nehemiah. One other reference is in 1 Chronicles 9:2. A few hundred of these slaves returned from Babylon with Zerubbabel (Ezra 2:58; Neh. 7:60), and 220 more with Ezra 78 years later (Ezra 8:17–20).

Netophah [Ne·to'phah], *distillation*—A town of Judah near Bethlehem (1 Chron. 27:13, 15). One hundred eighty-eight people from Netophah and Bethlehem returned from Babylon with Zerubbabel (Ezra 2:22; Neh. 7:26).

Netophathite [Ne·toph'a·thite]—One who lived in Netophah (2 Sam. 23:28).

New Gate—A gate of the temple. Baruch read the words of Jeremiah's prophecy aloud to the people near this gate (Jer. 36:10).

New Jerusalem—See Jerusalem, New.

Neziah [Ne·zi′ah], *illustrious*—One of the Nethinim, descendants of whom returned from Babylon with Zerubbabel (Ezra 2:54; Neh. 7:56).

Nezib [Nez′ib], *idol* or *statue*—A town of the lowland district of Judah (Josh. 15:43).

Nibhaz [Nib′haz], *the barker*—An idol worshipped by the Avvites (2 Kings 17:31).

Nibshan [Nib′shan]—A town of Judah (Josh. 15:62).

Nicanor [Ni·ca′nor], *victor*—One of the seven deacons of the church of Jerusalem (Acts 6:5).

Nicodemus [Nic·o·de′mus], *conqueror of the people*—A Pharisee and a member of the Sanhedrin who probably became a disciple of Jesus (John 3:1, 4, 9; 7:50). Nothing is known of his family. He was described by Jesus as "the teacher of Israel," implying he was well trained in Old Testament law and tradition.

Nicodemus was a wealthy, educated, and powerful man—well respected by his people and a descendant of the patriarch Abraham. Yet Jesus said to him, "You must be born again" (John 3:7). The Greek adverb translated "again" can also mean "from the beginning" (suggesting a new creation) and "from above" (that is, from God). In other words, Jesus told Nicodemus that physical generation was not enough, nor could his descent from the line of Abraham enable him to be saved. Only as a person has a spiritual generation—a birth from above—will he be able to see the kingdom of God.

The next time Nicodemus appears in the gospel of John, he shows a cautious, guarded sympathy with Jesus. When the Sanhedrin began to denounce Jesus as a false prophet, Nicodemus counseled the court by saying, "Does our law judge a man before it hears him and knows what he is doing?" (John 7:51).

Nicodemus appears a third and final time in the gospel of John. Obviously a wealthy man, he purchased about a hundred pounds of spices to be placed between the folds of the cloth in which Jesus was buried (John 19:39). Nothing else is known of Nicodemus from the Bible. But there is reason to believe that he became a follower of Jesus.

Christian tradition has it that Nicodemus was baptized by Peter and John, suffered persecution from hostile Jews, lost his membership in the Sanhedrin, and was forced to leave Jerusalem because of his Christian faith. Further mention is made of him in the gospel of Nicodemus, an apocryphal narrative of the crucifixion and resurrection of Christ.

Nicolaitans [Nic·o·la′i·tans], *destruction of people*—It is probable that this sect or party followed the teachings of one called Nicolaus. In John's vision, Jesus commended the church in Ephesus for hating the teaching of the Nicolaitans (Rev. 2:6). The church at Pergamos was rebuked for allowing this doctrine to creep in. It appears that this teaching was associated with a kind of libertarianism, behaving exactly like Balaam and leading God's people into sexual immorality and idol worship (Rev. 2:14–15). This was contrary to and in defiance of the action of the Council at Jerusalem in A.D. 50 (Acts 15:29).

Nicolas [Nic′o·las], *victor of the people*—One of the seven deacons of the church of Jerusalem (Acts 6:5). Some have suggested that he started the Nicolaitan sect, but there is nothing to support this idea except the possible similarity of names.

Nicolaus [Nic′o·la·us]—See Nicolas.

Nicopolis [Ni·cop′o·lis], *city of victory*—There were several cities having this name, but the one where Paul expected to spend the winter and where he wrote the epistle to Titus was most likely the Nicopolis of Epirus, about four miles from Actium (Titus 3:12).

Niger [Ni′ger], *black*—The Latin surname of Simeon who taught in the church at Antioch (Acts 13:1). There is no evidence to support the theory, but some scholars have thought that this may be the same person as Simon of Cyrene, who carried Jesus's cross (Matt. 27:32).

Nile [Nile], *unknown*—The one great river of Egypt (Isa. 23:3). It has its source in two rivers, the White Nile flowing out of Lake Victoria, and the Blue Nile flowing out of Ethiopia. It flows northward, and empties into the Mediterranean Sea. This river had an enormous impact on the Egyptian civilization and culture. Its yearly flood deposited a layer of rich silt on the arable farmland along its banks; thus the river provided moisture and fertility for the crops of the coming year. Because of the Nile's importance to farming, and thus to the well-being of the people, it was worshipped as a god by the Egyptians. Several of the plagues of the exodus affected the Nile, clearly showing the superiority of the God of the Hebrews over the Egyptian god of the Nile (Ex. 7:20). The land promised to Abraham for his posterity was measured from the river of Egypt (the Nile) to the river Euphrates (Gen. 15:18).

Nimrah [Nim'rah], *limpid*—An abbreviation of Beth-nimrah (Num. 32:3, 36). See Beth-nimrah.

Nimrim [Nim'rim], *limpid*—A fertile district in Moab noted for its waters, southeast of the Dead Sea (Isa. 15:6; Jer. 48:34).

Nimrod [Nim'rod], *rebellion* or *the valiant*—A son of Cush and grandson of Ham, the youngest son of Noah (Gen. 10:8–12; 1 Chron. 1:10). Nimrod was a "mighty one on the earth"—a skilled hunter-warrior who became a powerful king. He is the first mighty hero mentioned in the Bible.

The principal cities of Nimrod's Mesopotamian kingdom were "Babel, Erech, Accad, and Calneh, in the land of Shinar" (Gen. 10:10). From the land of Babylon he went to Assyria, where he built Nineveh and other cities (Gen. 10:11). In Micah 5:6 Assyria is called "the land of Nimrod."

The origin and meaning of the name Nimrod is uncertain, but it is doubtful that it is Hebrew. It may be Mesopotamian, originating from the Akkadian (northern Babylonian) god of war and hunting, Ninurta, who was called "the Arrow, the mighty hero." Some scholars believe Nimrod was Sargon the Great, a powerful ruler over Accad who lived about 2400 B.C. Others think he was the Assyrian king Tukulti-Ninurta I (about 1246–1206 B.C.), who conquered Babylonia. However, if Nimrod was indeed a Cushite, he may have been the Egyptian monarch Amenophis III (1411–1375 B.C.).

Nimrod was more likely Assyrian. His fierce aggressiveness, seen in the combination of warlike prowess and the passion for the chase, makes him a perfect example of the warrior-kings of Assyria.

Nimshi [Nim'shi], *active*—Grandfather of Jehu (1 Kings 19:16; 2 Kings 9:21), also called his father (2 Kings 9:20).

Nineveh [Nin'e·veh], *abode of Ninus*—Founded by Nimrod, great-grandson of Noah (Gen. 10:6–12), Nineveh was for many years the capital city of the mighty Assyrian Empire. At the height of its prosperity,

Nineveh was a "great city" (Jonah 1:2; 3:2) with a population of 120,000 (Jonah 4:11). It would have taken a traveler three days to go around greater Nineveh, with its numerous outlying suburbs, and a day's journey to reach the center of the city (Jonah 3:4). The most famous biblical personality connected with ancient Nineveh was the prophet Jonah. Assyrian kings were cruel and ruthless.

This pagan nation had invaded and pillaged the homeland of the Israelites on numerous occasions by the time Jonah visited Nineveh about 760 B.C. The prophet wanted the city destroyed—not saved— because of its wickedness. But the people repented and were spared by a compassionate God (Jonah 3:10). God's love for a pagan people was deeper than His messenger could understand or accept.

Nineveh was eventually destroyed about 150 years after Jonah's visit—in 612 B.C. It fell after a long siege by an alliance of Medes, Babylonians, and Scythians. The attackers entered the city through walls made weak by a flooding of the Khosr and Tigris Rivers. The sun-dried bricks of its buildings were also dissolved. This was a remarkable fulfillment of the prophecy of Nahum: "The gates of the rivers are opened, and the palace is dissolved" (Nah. 2:6).

Significant archeological discoveries at Nineveh include the temples of Nabu and Ishtar, Assyrian gods, and the palaces of three Assyrian kings—Ashurbanipal, Ashurnasirpal, and Sennacherib. One of the most important discoveries was the royal library of Ashurbanipal, which contained over sixteen thousand cuneiform tablets. These include Mesopotamian stories of creation and the Flood, as well as many other religious and historical texts. It was to Nineveh that Sennacherib brought the tribute he exacted from King Hezekiah of Judah (2 Kings 18:13–15). Nineveh was one of the oldest cities of the ancient Near East. Excavations down to the virgin soil indicate the site was first occupied about 4500 B.C.

Ninevites [Nin'e·vites]—Those who dwelled in Nineveh (Luke 11:30).

Nisan [Ni'san], *their fight*—The first month of the Hebrew sacred year (Neh. 2:1; Est. 3:7).

Nisroch [Nis'roch], *the great eagle*—The god worshipped by Sennacherib (2 Kings 19:37; Isa. 37:38).

No [No]—See No-amon.

Noadiah [No·a·di′ah], *Jehovah convenes*—A man and a woman of the Old Testament:

1. A Levite, son of Binnui; he had charge of the vessels of the temple brought back from Babylon (Ezra 8:33).

2. A prophetess (Neh. 6:14).

Noah [No′ah], *rest* or *relief*—The name of a man and a woman in the Bible:

1. A son of Lamech in the line of Seth and the father of Shem, Ham, and Japheth. He was an ancestor of Jesus (Gen. 5:28–29). He was a hero of faith who obeyed God by building an ark (a giant boat), thus becoming God's instrument in saving mankind from total destruction by the Flood (Gen. 5:28–9:29). The line of descent from Adam to Noah was as follows: Adam, Seth, Enosh, Cainan, Mahalaleel, Jared, Enoch, Methuselah, Lamech, and Noah (Gen. 5:1–32). If this genealogy does not allow for any gaps, Noah was only nine generations removed from Adam; and his father, Lamech, was fifty-six years old at the time of Adam's death.

Noah lived at a time when the whole earth was filled with violence and corruption. Yet Noah did not allow the evil standards of his day to rob him of fellowship with God. He stood out as the only one who "walked with God" (Gen. 6:9), as was true of his great-grandfather Enoch (Gen. 5:22). Noah was a just or righteous man (Gen. 6:9). The Lord singled out Noah from among all his contemporaries and chose him as the man to accomplish a great work.

When God saw the wickedness that prevailed in the world (Gen. 6:5), He disclosed to Noah His intention to destroy the world by a flood. He instructed Noah to build an ark in which he and his family would survive the catastrophe. Noah believed God and obeyed Him and "according to all that God commanded him, so he did" (Gen. 6:22). He is therefore listed among the heroes of faith (Heb. 11:7).

With unswerving confidence in the word of God, Noah started building the ark. For 120 years the construction continued. During this time of grace, Noah continued to preach God's judgment and mercy, warning the ungodly of their approaching doom (2 Peter 2:5). He preached for 120 years, however, without any converts (1 Peter 3:20).

People continued in their evil ways and turned deaf ears to his pleadings and warnings until they were overtaken by the Flood.

When the ark was ready, Noah entered in with all kinds of animals "and the Lord shut him in" (Gen. 7:16), cut off completely from the rest of mankind.

Noah was grateful to the Lord who had delivered him from the Flood. After the Flood he built an altar to God (Gen. 8:20) and made a sacrifice, which was accepted graciously (Gen. 8:21). The Lord promised Noah and his descendants that He would never destroy the world again with a flood (Gen. 9:15). The Lord made an everlasting covenant with Noah and his descendants, establishing the rainbow as the sign of His promise (Gen. 9:12–17). The Lord also blessed Noah and restored the creation command, "Be fruitful and multiply, and fill the earth" (Gen. 9:1). These were the same words He had spoken earlier to Adam (Gen. 1:28).

Noah became the first tiller of the soil and keeper of vineyards after the Flood. His drunkenness is a prelude to the curse that was soon to be invoked on Canaan and his descendants, the Canaanites (Gen. 9:18–27). The Bible is silent about the rest of Noah's life after the Flood, except to say that he died at the age of 950 years (Gen. 9:28–29).

In the Gospels of the New Testament, the account of Noah and the Flood is used as a symbol of the end times. Warning His hearers about the suddenness of His return, Jesus referred to the sudden catastrophe that fell upon unbelievers at the time of the Flood: "As the days of Noah were, so also will the coming of the Son of Man be" (Matt. 24:37).

2. May mean *motion*. A daughter of Zelophehad of the tribe of Manasseh (Josh. 17:3).

No-amon [No-a·mon], *temple of Amon*—The name of the ancient Thebes, an Egyptian city. Its tutelary god was Amon, the worship of whom was denounced by Jeremiah (Jer. 46:25). It was on both sides of the Nile and was the capital of upper Egypt (Ezek. 30:14–16).

Nob [Nob], *high place*—A Levitical city in Benjamin (1 Sam. 22:19; Neh. 11:32) near Jerusalem (Isa. 10:32). The tabernacle was here for a time; in the days when Ahimelech was the priest, David came to the tabernacle as he was fleeing from Saul. Without knowing that he was running from Saul, Ahimelech gave him the showbread to eat and the sword of Goliath. David was betrayed by a loiterer named Doeg, and when Saul heard of how they had helped David, he had the priests and inhabitants slain. One priest, Abiathar, escaped and came to David (1 Sam. 21–22).

Nobah [No'bah], *barking*—A man and a town:
1. A man of Manasseh (Num. 32:42).
2. A town of Gad (Judg. 8:11).

Nobai [No·ba'i], possibly *fruitful*—A chief of the people who sealed the covenant (Neh. 10:19), also called Nebai.

Nod [Nod], *wandering*—An unidentified land east of the garden of Eden where Cain fled after he murdered his brother (Gen. 4:16).

Nodab [No'dab], *nobility*—An Arab tribe (1 Chron. 5:19).

Noe [No'e]—See Noah.

Nogah [No'gah], *shining*—A son of David born in Jerusalem (1 Chron. 3:7; 14:6).

Nohah [No'hah], *rest*—The fourth son of Benjamin, probably born in Egypt (1 Chron. 8:2).

Non [Non]—See Nun.

Noph [Noph], *presentability*—The Hebrew name for Memphis, an ancient Egyptian city on the western bank of the Nile and south of modern Cairo (Isa. 19:13).

Nophah [No'phah], *windy*—A town of Moab (Num. 21:30).

Nun [Nun], *fish*—Father of Joshua of the tribe of Ephraim (Ex. 33:11; Josh. 1:1).

Nymphas [Nym'phas], *sacred to the muses*—A Christian in Laodicea (Col. 4:15; also called Nympha).

O

Obadiah [O·ba·di'ah], *servant of the Lord*—The name of thirteen men in the Old Testament:

1. The governor of Ahab's palace (1 Kings 18:3–7, 16). He hid a hundred prophets in a cave when Jezebel was persecuting the prophets of God (1 Kings 18:3–4). During the drought he met Elijah, who had him inform Ahab of Elijah's presence. This led to the contest at Carmel (1 Kings 18:5–16).

2. A descendant of David and the head of a family (1 Chron. 3:21).

3. A son of Izrahiah, of the tribe of Issachar (1 Chron. 7:3).

4. A descendant of King Saul, son of Azel (1 Chron. 8:38).

5. A Levite, a son of Shemaiah (1 Chron. 9:16).

6. A Gadite captain who joined David at Ziklag (1 Chron. 12:9).

7. Father of Ishmaiah, a chief leader of the tribe of Zebulun during the reign of David (1 Chron. 27:19).

8. A prince and leader of Jehoshaphat commissioned to teach the Book of the Law to the cities of Judah (2 Chron. 17:7).

9. A Levite of the family of Merari who supervised workmen repairing the temple in the reign of Josiah (2 Chron. 34:12).

10. A son of Jehiel, a descendant of Joab (Ezra 8:9). He came with Ezra from Babylon.

11. A priest who sealed the covenant after the captivity with Nehemiah (Neh. 10:5).

12. A gatekeeper in Judah after the return from captivity (Neh. 12:25).

13. A prophet of Judah (Obad. 1). The fourth of the "minor" prophets, Obadiah's message was directed against Edom. Some scholars believe Obadiah was a contemporary of Jehoram, during whose reign (about 844 B.C.) Jerusalem was invaded by Philistines and Arabians (2 Chron. 21:16–17). Other scholars suggest a date following 586 B.C., the time of the destruction of Jerusalem by the Babylonians. Still others suggest an earlier Babylonian assault on Jerusalem, in 605 B.C.

Whatever date is assigned to Obadiah, he lived during a time of trouble for Jerusalem. His prophecy against Edom condemned the Edomites for taking sides against Jerusalem in its distress (Obad. 15). The strongest mountain fortresses would be no defense for the Edomites against the day—the time when God would bring His final judgment upon the world.

Obal [O′bal], *stripped bare*—Son of Joktan (Gen. 10:28).

Obed [O′bed], *serving*—

1. Son of Boaz and Ruth and grandfather of David (Ruth 4:17, 21–22).
2. Son of Ephlal of Judah (1 Chron. 2:37).
3. One of David's mighty men (1 Chron. 11:47).
4. Son of Shemaiah, a Levite of the house of Obed-edom and gatekeeper in David's time (1 Chron. 26:7).
5. Father of Azariah (2 Chron. 23:1).

Obed-edom [O′bed-e′dom], *serving Edom*—

1. A Gittite or Gathite, a native of the Levitical city of Gath-rimmon in Dan. The ark, when sent back by the Philistines, was placed in his house, which was situated between Kirjath-jearim and Jerusalem. It remained here three months (2 Sam. 6:10–12; 1 Chron. 13:13–14; 15:25), and he and his family were blessed during the time the ark stayed with them.
2. A Levite gatekeeper who was part of the procession bringing the ark into Jerusalem (1 Chron. 15:18–24; 26:4, 8)
3. A Levite musician who ministered before the Lord in the tabernacle in Jerusalem (1 Chron. 16:5).
4. Son of Jeduthun, a doorkeeper of the temple (1 Chron. 16:38).

Obil [O′bil], *camel driver*—An Ishmaelite who was appointed as royal camel keeper in David's stables (1 Chron. 27:30).

Oboth [O′both], *waterskins*—An encampment of the Israelites near Moab (Num. 21:10–11; 33:43–44).

Ochran [Och′ran]—See Ocran.

Ocran [Oc′ran], *troubled*—Father of Pagiel of Asher (Num. 1:13).

Oded [O′ded], *restoration*—

1. A prophet of Israel in the reign of Pekah (2 Chron. 28:9–15).
2. Father of the prophet Azariah (2 Chron. 15:1).

Odollam [O'dol·lam]—See Adullam.

Og [Og], *long-necked*—A king of the Amorites of the land of Bashan, a territory east of the Jordan River and north of the river Jabbok (Num. 21:33; 32:33). Og was king over sixty fortified cities, including Ashtaroth and Edrei. He was defeated by Moses and the Israelites (Deut. 3:6). Then his kingdom was given to the tribes of Reuben, Gad, and the half-tribe of Manasseh.

Og was the last survivor of the race of giants (Deut. 3:11). His huge iron bedstead was kept on display in Rabbah long after his death (Deut. 3:11).

Ohad [O'had], *united*—Son of Simeon (Gen. 46:10; Ex. 6:15).

Ohel [O'hel], *tent*—Son of Zerubbabel (1 Chron. 3:20).

Oholah [O·ho'lah], *her own tent*—A symbolic name for Samaria, capital of the Northern Kingdom, and the ten tribes that made up this nation (Ezek. 23:4–5, 36, 44). The prophet Ezekiel used the allegorical figure of two harlot sisters, Oholah (Aholah, KJV) and Oholibah (Aholibah, KJV), to represent Jerusalem and the kingdom of Judah. Oholah and Oholibah are pictured as lusting after the Assyrians, Babylonians, and Egyptians.

Oholiab [O·ho'li·ab], *father's tent*—A Danite who aided Bezaleel in making the furniture for the tabernacle (Ex. 31:6; 35:34–35).

Oholibah [O·hol'i·bah], *my tent is in her*—A symbolic name given by the prophet Ezekiel to Jerusalem, the capital of Judah (Ezek. 23:4–44), to signify its unfaithfulness to God.

Oholibamah [O·hol·i·ba'mah], *my tent in a high place*—Daughter of Anah, the Hivite, and wife of Esau (Gen. 36:2), also called Judith (Gen. 26:34).

Old Gate—A gate of Jerusalem (Neh. 3:6; 12:36).

Olivet [Ol'i·vet], *place of olives*—See Mount of Olives.

Olympas [O·lym'pas], *heavenly*—A Christian in Rome to whom Paul sent greetings (Rom. 16:15).

Omar [O'mar], *eloquent* or *talkative*—Son of Eliphaz (Gen. 36:11, 15).

Omri [Om'ri], *pupil of Jehovah*—The name of four men in the Old Testament:

1. The sixth king of the northern kingdom of Israel (885–874 B.C.) and the founder of the fourth dynasty. Omri is first mentioned as the commander of the army of Israel under King Elah. While Omri besieged the Philistine city of Gibbethon, another military figure, Zimri, conspired against Elah, killed him, and established himself as king. Zimri, however, had little support in Israel, and the army promptly made Omri its king. Omri returned to the capital with his army, besieged the city, and Zimri committed suicide. Tibni, the son of Ginath, continued to challenge Omri's reign, but after four years Tibni died and Omri became the sole ruler of Israel (1 Kings 16:21–28).

Omri was a king of vision and wisdom. From Shemer he purchased a hill on which he built a new city, Samaria, making it the new capital of Israel. Samaria was more defensible than Tirzah had been. Because it was strategically located, Omri was able to control the north–south trade routes in the region. Archaeological excavations at Samaria revealed buildings of excellent workmanship—an indication of the prosperity the city enjoyed during his reign. The Moabite Stone tells of Omri's success against King Mesha of Moab (2 Kings 3:4). But Omri's conflict with Syria proved to be less successful, and he was forced to grant a number of cities to the Syrians (1 Kings 20:34).

2. A member of the tribe of Benjamin and a son of Becher (1 Chron. 7:8).

3. A member of the tribe of Judah of the family of Perez, a son of Imri (1 Chron. 9:4).

4. The son of Michael and a prince of the tribe of Issachar during the time of David (1 Chron. 27:18).

On [On], *strength* or *vigor*—A city and a man of the Old Testament:

1. A city of lower Egypt on the east side of the Nile, about twenty miles north of Memphis. Being the seat of the worship of the sun, the Greeks called it Heliopolis. In Jeremiah it is called Beth-shemesh (Jer. 43:13).

2. Son of Peleth of Reuben (Num. 16:1).

Onam [O'nam], *strong*—Two Old Testament men:

1. A descendant of Seir, a Horite (Gen. 36:23; 1 Chron. 1:40).

2. Son of Jerahmeel of Judah (1 Chron. 2:26, 28).

Onan [O'nan], *strong*—The second son of Judah by the daughter of Shua the Canaanite (Gen. 38:2, 4). He refused to become the husband of the widow of his brother, Er, and was killed by the Lord.

Onesimus [O·nes'i·mus], *useful*—A slave of Philemon and an inhabitant of Colossae (Col. 4:9; Philem. 10). When Onesimus fled from his master to Rome, he met the apostle Paul. Paul witnessed to him, and Onesimus became a Christian. In his letter to Philemon, Paul spoke of Onesimus as "my own heart" (Philem. 12), indicating that Onesimus had become like a son to him.

Paul convinced Onesimus to return to his master, Philemon. He also sent a letter with Onesimus, encouraging Philemon to treat Onesimus as a brother rather than a slave. Paul implied that freeing Onesimus was Philemon's Christian duty, but he stopped short of commanding him to do so. Onesimus accompanied Tychicus, who delivered the epistle to the Colossians as well as the epistle to Philemon. Some scholars believe this Onesimus is Onesimus the bishop, praised in a letter to the second-century church at Ephesus from Ignatius of Antioch.

Onesiphorus [O·nes·iph'o·rus], *profit bearing*—A Christian who showed Paul great kindness when he was a prisoner at Rome (2 Tim. 1:16, 18; 4:19).

Onias [Oni'as], unknown—During the period between the Old and New Testaments, five high priests bore this name.

Ono [O'no], *strong*—A town of Benjamin (Neh. 11:35). It was rebuilt by Shamed (1 Chron. 8:12), and some of its inhabitants returned from Babylon with Zerubbabel (Ezra 2:33; Neh. 7:37).

Ophel [O'phel], *hill*—The site of the original city of the Jebusites. This triangular hill is located south of the temple area, and since it is surrounded by deep valleys on three sides, it was considered impregnable. David, however, was able to capture it, and Jerusalem became the religious and political center of Israel (2 Sam. 5:6–9). Jotham, one of the righteous kings of Judah, did extensive building on the wall of Ophel, the fortification on its eastern ridge, overlooking the Kidron Valley (2 Chron. 27:3). Later, Manasseh extended the city walls to completely enclose Ophel and the city of David (2 Chron. 33:14). After the captivity the Nethinim lived in this quarter (Neh. 3:26; 11:21).

Ophir [O'phir], *reducing to ashes*—A man and a region of the Old Testament:

    1. A son of Joktan and great-grandson of Shem (Gen. 10:29; 1 Chron. 1:23).

    2. A celebrated gold region (Job 22:24; 28:16; Isa. 13:12). Its exact location is a mystery; some have guessed that it may have been somewhere in India or Africa. Solomon and David both obtained gold from Ophir for use in the building of the temple and to augment Solomon's treasury (1 Kings 9:28; 1 Chron. 29:4; 2 Chron. 8:17–18; 2 Chron. 9:10). Many years later, Jehoshaphat, king of Judah attempted to send a fleet of ships to Ophir for gold as his ancestors had done, but the ships were wrecked and the venture came to nothing (1 Kings 22:48). The gold of Ophir is frequently used as a metaphor for beauty and value (Job 28:16; Ps. 45:9).

Ophni [Oph'ni], *moldy*—A town of Benjamin, the identity of which is uncertain (Josh. 18:24).

Ophrah [Oph'rah], *fawn*—Two cities and a man of the Old Testament:

    1. A town of Benjamin, the location of which is uncertain, perhaps north of Michmash (Josh. 18:23; 1 Sam. 13:17).

    2. A town of Manasseh east of the Jordan (Judg. 6:11, 13), the home of Gideon (Judg. 6–8).

    3. A son of Menothai of Judah (1 Chron. 4:14).

Oreb [Or'eb], *raven*—A prince of the Midianites put to death by Gideon (Judg. 7:25; 8:3; Ps. 83:11). The rock Oreb is where the Oreb and the Midianite army were defeated by Ephraim. It probably derived its name from the event (Isa. 10:26).

Oren [O'ren], *ash tree*—Son of Jerahmeel of Judah (1 Chron. 2:25).

Orion [O·ri'on], *the giant*—A constellation east of Taurus on the celestial equator, made up of eighty significant stars—seventeen of which are large and bright. The name comes from Greek mythology concerning Orion, the hunter; the constellation was also called "The Giant," named after Nimrod, the mighty hunter of the early post-flood world (Job 9:9; 38:31; Amos 5:8). Betelgeuse, Rigel, and Bellatrix are its brightest stars. The row of three stars making the Hunter's belt is the most recognizable feature of this constellation.

Ornan [Or'nan]—See Araunah.

Orontes [Or·on'tes], unknown—This river is not mentioned in the Bible, but the cities of Riblah (2 Kings 23:33–35), Hamath (1 Kings 8:65), and Kadesh were located on it.

Orpah [Or'pah], *gazelle*—A Moabite woman who married Chilion, one of the two sons of Elimelech and Naomi (Ruth 1:4). When Elimelech and his sons died in Moab, Orpah accompanied Naomi, her mother-in-law, part of the way to Bethlehem and then returned "to her people and to her gods" (Ruth 1:14) in Moab.

Osee [O'see]—Variant form of Hosea (Rom. 9:25).

Oshea [O'she·a]—See Hoshea, Joshua.

Osnapper [Os·nap'per]—See Asnapper.

Ostia [Os'tia], unknown—An ancient city located about fifteen miles from Rome, at the mouth of the Tiber River. It was a principal seaport for the city of Rome.

Othni [Oth'ni], *lion of Jehovah*—The son of Shemaiah, a Levite. In the days of David, Othni was a gatekeeper for the tabernacle (1 Chron. 26:7).

Othniel [Oth'ni·el], *powerful one of God*—The name of two men in the Old Testament:

1. The first judge of Israel (Judg. 1:13; 3:9, 11). Othniel was a son of Kenaz and probably was a nephew of Caleb. When the Israelites forgot the Lord and served the pagan gods of Canaan, the king of Mesopotamia oppressed them for eight years. When the Israelites repented of their evil and cried out to the Lord for deliverance, Othniel was raised up by the Lord to deliver His people. He won his wife Achsah, the daughter of Caleb, by capturing the town of Debir. Othniel was one of four judges (the other three were Gideon, Jephthah, and Samson) of whom the Scripture says, "The Spirit of the LORD came upon him" (Judg. 3:10).

2. An ancestor of Heldai (1 Chron. 27:15).

Ovens, Tower of the—Also called tower of the furnaces, a part of the wall of Jerusalem, restored in the days of Nehemiah by Malchijah and Hashub (Neh. 3:11; 12:38). It may have been a place where bread was baked commercially, or even more likely, it may have been a place where potters' or brickmakers' kilns were fired, or possibly metalwork was done.

Ozem [O'zem], *I shall hasten them*—Two Old Testament men:
   1. David's older brother, the sixth son of Jesse (1 Chron. 2:15).
   2. Son of Jerahmeel (1 Chron. 2:25).

Ozias [O·zi'as]—See Uzziah.

Ozni [Oz'ni], *attentive*—Son of Gad and founder of the tribal family of Oznites (Num. 26:16), also called Ezbon (Gen. 46:16).

Oznites [Oz·nites]—Descendants of Ozni (Num. 26:16).

P

Paarai [Pa′a·rai], *gaping*—One of David's mighty men (2 Sam. 23:35). A variant reading in 1 Chronicles 11:37 is Naarai.

Padan, Paddan [Pa′dan, Pad′dan]—Variants of Padan-aram.

Padan-aram [Pa′dan-a′·ram], *the plain of Aram*—The area of Upper Mesopotamia around Haran and the home of Abraham after he moved from Ur of the Chaldeans (Gen. 25:20; Paddan Aram, NIV; Paddan-aram, NRSV). Abraham later sent his servant to Padan-aram to find a bride for his son Isaac (Gen. 25:20). Isaac did the same by his son, sending Jacob to his mother's family in Padan-aram to look for a wife (Gen. 28:2, 5). Much later, Isaac's son Jacob fled to Padan-aram to avoid the wrath of his brother Esau and dwelled there with Laban (Gen. 28:2, 5–7). The region was also referred to as Padan (Gen. 48:7; Paddan, NIV, NRSV).

Padon [Pa′don], *freedom*—Head of a family of Nethinim who returned to Jerusalem with Zerubbabel (Ezra 2:44; Neh. 7:47).

Pagiel [Pa′gi·el], *meeting with God*—Son of Ocran of Asher (Num. 1:13; 2:27; 7:72, 77; 10:26), a leader who helped take the first census.

Pahath-moab [Pa′hath-mo′ab], *pit of Moab*—
1. Head of a family, members of which returned to Jerusalem with Zerubbabel (Ezra 2:6; 8:4; Neh. 7:11).
2. One who signed the covenant in the days of Nehemiah (Neh. 10:14).

Pai [Pa′i], *bleating*—An Edomite city, dwelling place of Hadad, king of Edom (1 Chron. 1:50). Also called Pau (Gen. 36:39).

Palal [Pa′lal], *judge*—Son of Uzai. He labored on the wall of Jerusalem (Neh. 3:25).

Palestina [Pal·es·ti′na]—See Palestine.

Palestine [Pal′es·tine]—The land of the Israelites, only once called Palestine (Joel 3:4, KJV; Philistia, NKJV). In the Old Testament the name signifies the "land of the Philistines." It was called Canaan by the Hebrews in distinction from Gilead, east of the Jordan. When taken by Joshua, it became known as the land of Israel (1 Sam. 13:19; Matt. 2:20). It is called the land of promise (Heb. 11:9) and the Holy Land (Zech. 2:12). During the Middle Ages, the name "Holy Land" was the most popular.

In those days, Palestine was considered to be the center of the earth, and in a sense this is perfectly true. It is strategically located on a tiny strip of land on the eastern coast of the Mediterranean Sea which unites three continents (Africa, Asia, and Europe). It was situated between the most dominant ancient kingdoms of the world (Egypt, Babylon, Assyria, and Persia). As occupied by the Israelites, the land extended from Mount Hermon on the north to Kadesh-barnea on the south and from the sea on the west to the Jordan and the region east of the river occupied by Reuben, Gad, and half-tribe of Manasseh. The Israelites never expanded their kingdom to include all the area promised to them in Numbers 34.

Pallu [Pal′lu], *distinguished*—A son of Reuben and head of a tribal family (Ex. 6:14; Num. 26:5), also called Phallu (Gen. 46:9, KJV).

Palluites [Pal′lu·ites]—The descendants of Reuben's son Pallu (Num. 26:5).

Palti [Pal′ti], *deliverance*—
1. The spy who represented Benjamin (Num. 13:9).
2. Same as Paltiel (2 Sam. 3:15).

Paltiel [Pal′ti·el], *seliverance of God*—
1. Prince of Issachar (Num. 34:26).
2. The man to whom Saul gave his daughter Michal, the wife of David (1 Sam. 25:44; 2 Sam. 3:3, 15), after David went into hiding. He is also called Phaltiel (KJV).

Paltite [Pal′tite], *escape*—A native of Beth-pelet (Josh. 15:27). One of David's mighty men was a Paltite (2 Sam. 23:26; also called a Pelonite, 1 Chron. 27:10).

Pamphylia [Pam·phyl'i·a], *a region of every tribe*—A Roman province on the southern coast of central Asia Minor. The province consisted mainly of a plain about 130 kilometers (80 miles) long and up to about 32 kilometers (20 miles) wide. The capital city of Pamphylia, its largest city, was Perga (Acts 13:13–14).

Pamphylia is first mentioned in the New Testament in Acts 2:10. People from Pamphylia were among those present in Jerusalem on the Day of Pentecost. In Pamphylia Paul and Barnabas first entered Asia Minor (Acts 13:13) during the first missionary journey. It was at Perga that John Mark left Paul and Barnabas (Acts 15:38). On his voyage to Rome, Paul sailed off the coast of Pamphylia (Acts 27:5).

Paphos [Pa'phos], *boiling* or *hot*—Capital of Cyprus and residence of the Roman proconsul. When Paul was talking to the Roman proconsul in Paphos, the magician Elymas (Bar-Jesus) did his best to turn Sergius Paulus against the gospel message. Paul told him that because of this sin, the Lord would blind him, and immediately Paul's words came true. Sergius Paulus was astonished at what he saw, and believed Paul's teaching (Acts 13:6–13).

Parah [Pa'rah], *heifer*—A village of Benjamin (Josh. 18:23).

Paran [Par'an], *place of caverns*—A wilderness region in the central part of the Sinai Peninsula. Although the boundaries of this desert region are somewhat obscure, it probably bordered the Arabah and the Gulf of Aqaba on the east. The modern Wadi Feiran in central Sinai preserves the ancient name.

Paran is frequently mentioned in the Old Testament. Chedorlaomer, one of the four kings who attacked Sodom, conquered as far as "El Paran, which is by the wilderness" (Gen. 14:6). After Hagar was driven from Abraham's household (Gen. 21:21), she fled to this wilderness with her son, Ishmael. The Israelites crossed Paran during their exodus from Egypt (Num. 10:12; 12:16), and Moses dispatched spies from Paran to explore the land of Canaan (Num. 13:3). After their mission, these spies returned "unto the wilderness of Paran, to Kadesh" (Num. 13:26).

Much later, after the death of Samuel, David fled to Paran (1 Sam. 25:1). After revolting from King Solomon, Hadad went through Paran on his flight to Egypt (1 Kings 11:18).

Parbar [Par'bar], *open apartment*—A section on the western side of the court of the temple (2 Kings 23:11; 1 Chron. 26:18).

Parmashta [Par·mash'ta], *superior*—A son of Haman (Est. 9:9).

Parmenas [Par'me·nas], *abiding*—One of the seven deacons selected to care for the temporal interests of the widows and financial matters of the early church (Acts 6:5).

Parnach [Par'nach], *delicate*—A man of Zebulun, father of Elizaphan (Num. 34:25).

Parosh [Par'osh], *a flea*—

1. The ancestor of 2,172 captives who returned with Zerubbabel (Ezra 2:3; Neh. 7:8, also called Pharosh). Another group of people descended from this man also returned with Ezra (Ezra 8:3).

2. A man who signed the covenant with Nehemiah (Neh. 10:14, also called Pharosh).

Parshandatha [Par·shan·da'tha], *given by prayer*—The eldest of Haman's ten sons (Est. 9:7).

Parthians [Par'thi·ans]—Inhabitants of Parthia (which means *a pledge*), a region which, in the fifth century B.C., corresponded closely to the modern Persian province of Khorasan. People from this area were present in Jerusalem at Pentecost (Acts 2:9). Parthia was one of the provinces of Persia which Darius set up (Dan. 6:1).

Paruah [Pa'ru·ah], *increase*—The father of a purveyor of Solomon in Issachar (1 Kings 4:17).

Parvaim [Par·va'im], *oriental regions*—The name of a place where gold was found, probably a locality in Ophir (2 Chron. 3:6).

Parzites [Par·zites]—The descendants of Perez, son of Judah (Num. 26:20; Perezite, NASB, NIV, NRSV; Pharzites, KJV).

Pasach [Pa'sach], *to divide*—A son of Japhlet of Asher (1 Chron. 7:33).

Pasdammim [Pas·dam'mim]—A place where David's mighty men defeated the Philistines (1 Chron. 11:13–14).

Paseah [Pa·se′ah], *lame—*

1. A son of Eshton of Judah (1 Chron. 4:12).

2. The head of a family of Nethinim (Ezra 2:49; Neh. 3:6; Phaseah, KJV).

Pashhur [Pash′hur], *freedom*—Several Old Testament men:

1. Head of a priestly family (Ezra 2:38; Neh. 7:41). Some of this family had married foreign women, whom they later divorced (Ezra 10:22). Probably the same as Pashur (1 Chron. 9:12).

2. A priest who sealed the covenant with Nehemiah (Neh. 10:3).

3. Son of Immer, a priest. He persecuted Jeremiah because of his predictions (Jer. 20:1–6).

4. Son of Melchiah and a bitter foe of Jeremiah (Jer. 21:1; 38:1, 4).

5. Father of Gedaliah and an opponent of Jeremiah (Jer. 38:1). He may be the same person as number 3 or 4.

Pashur [Pash′ur], *freedom*—Head of a priestly family who returned to Israel from Babylon (1 Chron. 9:12), probably the same as Pashhur No. 1.

Passover [Pass′o·ver], *passing over*—The first of the three annual Hebrew festivals at which all the men must appear at the sanctuary (Ex. 12:43; 13:3–10; Deut. 16:1). The Passover commemorated the sparing of the Hebrew firstborn in the tenth plague of Egypt, and the exodus. Moses warned the people that if they would save their firstborn sons from the angel of death, they must kill a lamb and spread its blood upon their doorposts. When the angel saw the blood, it would pass over them. They were to prepare the lambs at twilight, and eat the roasted meat with bitter herbs and unleavened bread. They must be dressed for travel, and eat in haste. Every year following, they were to repeat the Passover meal: roasted lamb, bitter herbs, and unleavened bread (Ex. 12:1–13:10).

The Passover meal is a clear type of Christ. Christ Himself is our "Passover Lamb," whose blood rescues us from death (1 Cor. 5:7). He is without blemish, pure and sinless (Ex. 12:5; 1 Peter 1:18–19); that a bone should not be broken (Ex. 12:46; John 19:36). The present-day Jewish Seder meal has many traditions added to the exodus account, and these also point to the Messiah.

Patara [Pat′a·ra], *scattering* or *cursing*—A city southwest of Lycia (Acts 21:1).

Pathros [Path′ros], *region of the south*—The name of upper (southern) Egypt (Isa. 11:11). Some Jews moved to Pathros after the fall of Judah (Jer. 44:1-2, 15-16). Ezekiel prophesied the judgment of the Egyptians, but also promised that God would one day return them to Pathros, their own land (Ezek. 29:14; 30:13-18).

Pathrusim [Path·ru′sim], *region of the south*—A people descended from Mizraim (Gen. 10:14; 1 Chron. 1:12).

Patmos [Pat′mos], *my killing*—A small rocky island in the Grecian Archipelago, one of the Sporades, to which the apostle John was banished and where he wrote the book of Revelation (Rev. 1:9). The island, about 16 kilometers (10 miles) long and 10 kilometers (6 miles) wide, lies off the southwest coast of Asia Minor (modern Turkey). Because of its desolate and barren nature, Patmos was used by the Romans as a place to banish criminals, who were forced to work at hard labor in the mines and quarries of the island. Because Christians were regarded as criminals by the Roman emperor Domitian (ruled A.D. 81-96), the apostle John probably suffered from harsh treatment during his exile on Patmos. An early Christian tradition said John was in exile for 18 months.

Patrobas [Pat′ro·bas], *paternal*—A Christian of the Roman church to whom Paul sent greetings (Rom. 16:14).

Pau [Pa′u], *bleating*—A town of Edom (Gen. 36:39); in 1 Chronicles 1:50 it is called Pai.

Paul, The Apostle, *small* or *little*—The earliest and most influential interpreter of Christ's message and teaching; an early Christian missionary; correspondent with several early Christian churches.

The Life of Paul: Paul was born at Tarsus, the chief city of Cilicia (southeast Asia Minor). He was a citizen of Tarsus, "no mean city," as he called it (Acts 21:39). He was also born a Roman citizen (Acts 22:28), a privilege that worked to his advantage on several occasions during his apostolic ministry. Since Paul was born a Roman citizen, his father must have been a Roman citizen before him. "Paul" was part of his

Roman name. In addition to his Roman name, he was given a Jewish name, "Saul," perhaps in memory of Israel's first king, a member of the tribe of Benjamin, to which Paul's family belonged.

His Jewish heritage meant much more to Paul than Roman citizenship. Unlike many Jews who had been scattered throughout the world, he and his family did not become assimilated to the Gentile way of life that surrounded them. This is suggested when Paul describes himself as "a Hebrew of the Hebrews" (Phil. 3:5), and confirmed by Paul's statement in Acts 22:3 that, while he was born in Tarsus, he was brought up in Jerusalem "at the feet of Gamaliel," the most illustrious rabbi of his day (Acts 5:34). Paul's parents wanted their son to be well grounded in the best traditions of Jewish orthodoxy.

Paul proved an apt pupil. He outstripped many of his fellow students in his enthusiasm for ancestral traditions and in his zeal for the Jewish law. This zeal found a ready outlet in his assault on the infant church of Jerusalem. The church presented a threat to all that Paul held most dear. Its worst offense was its proclamation of one who had suffered a death cursed by the Jewish law as Lord and Messiah (Deut. 21:22–23). The survival of Israel demanded that the followers of Jesus be wiped out.

The first martyr of the Christian church was Stephen, one of the most outspoken leaders of the new movement. Luke told how Paul publicly associated himself with Stephen's executioners and then embarked on a campaign designed to suppress the church. Paul himself related how he "persecuted the church of God beyond measure and tried to destroy it" (Gal. 1:13).

Conversion and Apostolic Commission: At the height of Paul's campaign of repression, he was confronted on the road to Damascus by the risen Christ. In an instant his life was reoriented. The Jewish law was replaced as the central theme of Paul's life by Jesus Christ. He became the leading champion of the cause he had tried to overthrow.

The realization that Jesus, whom he had been persecuting, was alive and exalted as the Son of God exposed the weakness of the Jewish law. Paul's zeal for the law had made him an ardent persecutor. He now saw that his persecuting activity had been sinful; yet the law, instead of showing him the sinfulness of such a course, had really led him into sin. The law had lost its validity. Paul learned that it was no longer by keeping the law that a person was justified in God's sight, but by faith in Christ. And if faith in Christ provided acceptance with God, then Gentiles might enjoy that acceptance as readily as Jews. This was one of the implications of the revelation of Jesus Christ that gripped Paul's mind. He was assured that he himself had received that revelation in order that he might proclaim Christ and His salvation to the Gentile world. Paul began to carry out this commission not only in Damascus but also in the kingdom of the Nabatean Arabs, to the east and south. No details are given of his activity in "Arabia" (Gal. 1:17), but he did enough to attract the hostile attention of the authorities there, as the representative of the Nabatean king in Damascus tried to arrest him (2 Cor. 11:32–33).

After leaving Damascus, Paul paid a short visit to Jerusalem to make the acquaintance of Peter. During his two weeks' stay there, he also met James, the Lord's brother (Gal. 1:18–19). Paul could not stay in Jerusalem because the animosity of his former associates was too strong. He had to be taken down to Caesarea on the Mediterranean coast and put on a ship for Tarsus.

Paul spent the next ten years in and around Tarsus, actively engaged in the evangelizing of Gentiles. Very few details of those years have been preserved. At the end of that time Barnabas came to Tarsus from Antioch and invited Paul to join him in caring for a young church there. A spontaneous campaign of Gentile evangelization had recently occurred at Antioch, resulting in the formation of a vigorous church. Barnabas himself had been commissioned by the apostles in Jerusalem to lead the Gentile evangelization in the city of Antioch.

About a year after Paul joined Barnabas in Antioch, the two men visited Jerusalem and conferred with the three "pillars" of the church there—the apostles Peter and John, and James the Lord's brother (Gal. 2:1–10). The result of this conference was an agreement that the Jerusalem leaders would concentrate on the evangelization of their fellow Jews, while Barnabas and Paul would continue to take the gospel to Gentiles.

The Jerusalem leaders reminded Barnabas and Paul, in conducting their Gentile mission, not to forget the material needs of the impoverished believers in Jerusalem. Barnabas and Paul (especially Paul) readily agreed to bear those needs in mind. This may have been the occasion when they carried a gift of money from the Christians in

Antioch to Jerusalem for the relief of their fellow believers who were suffering hardship in a time of famine (Acts 11:30).

Apostle to the Gentiles: The way was now open for a wider Gentile mission. Barnabas and Paul were released by the church of Antioch to pursue a missionary campaign that took them to Barnabas's native island of Cyprus and then into the highlands of central Asia Minor (modern Turkey), to the province of Galatia. There they preached the gospel and planted churches in the cities of Pisidian Antioch, Iconium, Lystra, and Derbe. The missionaries then returned to Antioch in Syria.

The great increase of Gentile converts caused alarm among many of the Jewish Christians in Judea. They feared that too many Gentiles would hurt the character of the church. Militant Jewish nationalists were already attacking them. A movement began that required Gentile converts to become circumcised and follow the Jewish law. The leaders of the Jerusalem church, with Paul and Barnabas in attendance, met in A.D. 48 to discuss the problem. It was finally decided that circumcision was not necessary, but that Gentile converts should conform to the Jewish code of laws in order to make fellowship between Jewish and Gentile Christians less strained (Acts 15:1–29).

After this meeting, Barnabas and Paul parted company. Paul chose Silas, a leading member of the Jerusalem church and a Roman citizen like himself, to be his new colleague. Together they visited the young churches of Galatia. At Lystra they were joined by Timothy, a young convert from Barnabas and Paul's visit some two years before. Paul in particular recognized qualities in Timothy that would make him a valuable helper in his missionary service. From that time to the end of Paul's life, Timothy was his most faithful attendant.

Paul and Silas probably planned to proceed west to Ephesus, but they felt the negative guidance of the Holy Spirit. They instead turned north and northwest, reaching the seaport of Troas. Here Paul was told in a vision to cross the north Aegean Sea and preach the gospel in Macedonia. This Paul and his companions did. By now their number had increased to four by the addition of Luke. The narrative reveals his presence at this point by using "we" instead of "they" (Acts 16:10).

Their first stop in Macedonia was the Roman colony of Philippi. Here, in spite of running into trouble with the magistrates and being imprisoned, Paul and his companions planted a strong church. They moved on to Thessalonica, the chief city of the province, and formed a church there, as well. But serious trouble broke out in Thessalonica. The missionaries were accused of rebelling against the Roman emperor by proclaiming Jesus as his rival. They were forced to leave the city quickly.

Paul moved south to Berea, where he was favorably received by the local synagogue, but his opponents from Thessalonica followed him, making it necessary for him to move on once more. Although churches of Macedonia would later give Paul much joy and satisfaction, he felt dejected at this time from being forced to flee city after city.

Paul, alone now, moved south into the province of Achaia. After a short stay in Athens, he came "in weakness, in fear, and in much trembling" (1 Cor. 2:3) to Corinth, the seat of provincial administration. Corinth had a reputation as a wicked city in the Greco-Roman world and it did not seem likely that the gospel would make much headway there. Surprisingly, however, Paul stayed there for 18 months and made many converts. While he was there, a new Roman proconsul, Gallio, arrived to take up residence in Corinth. The beginning of his administration can be accurately dated as July 1, A.D. 51. Paul was prosecuted before Gallio on the charge of preaching an illegal religion, but Gallio dismissed the charge. This provided other Roman magistrates with a precedent that helped the progress of the gospel over the next ten years.

The church of Corinth was large, lively, and talented but deficient in spiritual and moral stability. This deficiency caused Paul much anxiety over the next few years, as his letters to the Corinthians reveal. After his stay in Corinth, Paul paid a brief visit to Jerusalem and Antioch and then traveled to Ephesus, where he settled for the next three years. Paul's Ephesian ministry was perhaps the most active part of his apostolic career. A number of colleagues shared his activity and evangelized the city of Ephesus as well as the whole province of Asia (western Asia Minor). Ten years earlier there had been no churches in the great provinces of Galatia, Asia, Macedonia, or Achaia. Now Christianity had become so strong in them that Paul realized his work in that part of the world was finished. He began to think of a new area where he might repeat the same kind of missionary program. He wanted to evangelize territories where the gospel had never been heard before, having no desire to "build on another man's foundation" (Rom. 15:20). He decided to journey to Spain, and to set out as soon as he could. This journey would also give him a long-awaited opportunity to visit Rome on the way.

Before he could set out, however, an important task had to be completed. Paul had previously organized a relief fund among the Gentile churches to help poorer members of the Jerusalem church. Not only had he promised the leaders in Jerusalem to do such a thing, but he hoped it would strengthen the bond of fellowship among all the churches involved. Before leaving, Paul arranged for a member of each of the contributing churches to carry that church's donation. Paul himself would go to Jerusalem with them, giving the Jerusalem Christians an opportunity to see some of their Gentile brethren face-to-face in addition to receiving their gifts. Some of Paul's hopes and misgivings about the trip are expressed in Romans 15:25–32. His misgivings were well founded.

A few days after his arrival in Jerusalem, Paul was attacked by a mob in the area of the temple. He was rescued by a detachment of Roman soldiers and kept in custody at the Roman governor's headquarters in Caesarea for the next two years. At the end of that period he exercised his privilege as a Roman citizen and appealed to Caesar in order to have his case transferred from the provincial governor's court in Judea to the emperor's tribunal in Rome. He was sent to Rome in the fall of A.D. 59. The great apostle spent a further two years in Rome under house arrest, waiting for his case to come up for hearing before the supreme tribunal.

Paul, the Prisoner of Jesus Christ: The restrictions under which Paul lived in Rome should have held back his efforts to proclaim the gospel, but just the opposite actually happened. These restrictions, by his own testimony, "actually turned out for the furtherance of the gospel" (Phil. 1:12). Although he was confined to his lodgings, shackled to one of the soldiers who guarded him in four-hour shifts, he was free to receive visitors and talk to them about the gospel. The soldiers who guarded him and the officials in charge of presenting his case before the emperor were left in no doubt about the reason for his being in Rome. The gospel actually became a topic of discussion. This encouraged the Christians in Rome to bear more open witness to their faith, allowing the saving message to be proclaimed more fearlessly in Rome than ever before "and in this," said Paul, "I rejoice" (Phil. 1:18).

From Rome, Paul was able to correspond with friends in other parts of the Roman Empire. Visitors from those parts came to see him, bringing news of their churches. These visitors included Epaphroditus from Philippi and Epaphras from Colossae. From Colossae, too, Paul received an unexpected visitor, Onesimus, the slave of his friend Philemon. He sent Onesimus back to his master with a letter commending him "no longer as a slave but . . . as a beloved brother" (Philem. 16).

The letters of Philippi and Colossae were sent in response to the news brought by Epaphroditus and Epaphras, respectively. At the same time as the letter to Colossae, Paul sent a letter to Laodicea and a more general letter that we now know as Ephesians. The Roman captivity became a very fruitful period for Paul and his ministry. We have very little information about the rest of Paul's career. We do not know the outcome of his trial before Caesar. He was probably discharged and enjoyed a further period of liberty. It is not known whether he ever preached the gospel in Spain. It is traditionally believed that Paul's condemnation and execution occurred during the persecution of Christians under the Roman emperor Nero. The probable site of his execution may still be seen at Tre Fontane on the Ostian Road. There is no reason to doubt the place of his burial marked near the Basilica of St. Paul in Rome. There, beneath the high altar, is a stone inscription going back to at least the fourth century: "To Paul, Apostle and Martyr."

The Teaching of Paul: Paul is the most influential teacher of Christianity. More than any other disciple or apostle, Paul was given the opportunity to set forth and explain the revelations of Jesus Christ. Because Paul was called to teach Gentiles rather than Jews, he was in the unique position of confronting and answering problems that could only be presented by those completely unfamiliar with Jewish traditions. Several themes come through in his writings.

Christ, the Son of God: Paul knew that the one who appeared to him on the Damascus Road was the risen Christ. "Last of all He was seen by me also," he says (1 Cor. 15:8), counting this as the last of Christ's appearances.

Paul seems to have entertained no doubt of the validity of the appearance or of the words "I am Jesus" (Acts 9:5). Both the appearance and the words validated themselves in his later life. His whole Christian outlook on the world, like the gospel he preached, stemmed from that "revelation of Jesus Christ" (Gal. 1:12).

Christ was, in a unique sense, the Son of God. Other human beings became sons and daughters of God through their faith-union with Christ and their reception of the Spirit of Christ. From this point of view the Spirit was "the Spirit of adoption," enabling them to address God spontaneously as "Abba, Father" (Rom. 8:15).

Another token of the indwelling Spirit was giving Jesus the designation "Lord": "No one can say that Jesus is Lord except by the Holy Spirit" (1 Cor. 12:3). This designation is given by Paul to Jesus in the highest sense possible. It was bestowed on Jesus by God Himself when He rose to supremacy over the universe after His humiliation and death on the cross.

One striking designation that Paul gives to Christ—"the image of God" (2 Cor. 4:4) or "the image of the invisible God" (Col. 1:15)— appears to be closely associated with his conversion experience. Paul emphasizes the heavenly light that was such a memorable feature of that experience. Paul speaks of the minds of unbelievers being darkened to keep them from seeing "the light of the gospel of the glory of Christ, who is the image of God" (2 Cor. 4:4). This suggests that when "the glory of that light" (Acts 22:11) dispelled the darkness from Paul's own mind, he recognized the one who appeared to him as being the very image of God.

Christ is presented by Paul as the one "through whom are all things, and through whom we live" (1 Cor. 8:6), and in whom, through whom, and for whom "all things were created" (Col. 1:16).

This landmark known as the tomb of Caecilia Metella (wife of a Roman official) stood on the Appian Way when Paul went to Rome to appear before Nero (Acts 28:15, 16).

Displacement of the Law: After his conversion Paul said, "To me, to live is Christ" (Phil. 1:21). Before his conversion he might well have said, "To me, to live is law." In his mind he had judged Christ according to the Jewish law, finding Him condemned by it. Since the law pronounced a curse on one who was impaled on a stake (Deut. 21:23; Gal. 3:13), Paul took the side of the law and agreed that both Christ and His people were accursed.

After his conversion, Paul recognized the continuing validity of the Scripture that declared the impaled man to be accursed by God, but now he understood it differently. If Christ, the Son of God, subjected Himself to the curse pronounced by the law, another look at the law was called for. The law could not provide anyone with righteous standing before God, however carefully he kept it. Paul knew that his life under the law stood condemned in the light of his Damascus Road experience. It was not the law in itself that was defective, because it was God's law. It was instead the people with whom the law had to work who were defective. The righteous standing that the law could not provide was conferred on believers through their faith in Christ. That righteous standing was followed by a righteous life. In one tightly packed sentence Paul declared that God has done what the law, weakened by the flesh, could not do, "sending His own Son in the likeness of sinful flesh, on account of sin: He condemned sin in the flesh, that the righteous requirement of the law might be fulfilled in us who do not walk according to the flesh but according to the Spirit" (Rom. 8:3–4).

The law could lead neither to a righteous standing before God nor to a righteous life. Paul, while faithfully keeping the law, was condemned before God rather than justified. His life was not righteous but was sinful because he "persecuted the church of God" (1 Cor. 15:9). This situation radically changed when Paul believed in Christ and knew himself to "be found in Him, not having my own righteousness, which is from the law, but that which is through faith in Christ, the righteousness which is from God by faith" (Phil. 3:9).

Christ, then, "is the end of the law for righteousness to everyone who believes" (Rom. 10:4). The word *end* is ambiguous: it may mean "goal" or "completion." As the law revealed the character and will of God, it pointed to Christ as the goal. He was the fulfillment of all the divine revelation that had preceded Him: "All the promises of God in Him are Yes" (2 Cor. 1:20). But when the law came to be regarded as the way of salvation or the rule of life, Christ put an end to it. The law pronounced a curse on those who failed to keep it; Christ redeemed His people from that curse by undergoing it Himself. He exhausted the curse in His own person through His death.

According to Paul, the law was a temporary provision introduced by God to bring latent sin into the open. When they broke its individual commands, men and women would realize their utter dependence on divine grace. Centuries before the law was given, God promised Abraham that through him and his offspring all nations would be blessed. This promise was granted in response to Abraham's faith in God. The later giving of the law did not affect the validity of the promise. Instead, the promise was fulfilled in Christ, who replaced the law. The law had been given to the nation of Israel only, providing a privilege that set it apart from other nations. God's original promise embraced all nations and justified Paul's presentation of the gospel to Gentiles as well as Jews. The promise had wide implications: "Christ has redeemed us from the curse of the law . . . that the blessing of Abraham might come upon the Gentiles in Christ Jesus, that we might receive the promise of the Spirit through faith" (Gal. 3:13–14).

The Age of the Spirit: Those who believe God as Abraham did are not only justified by faith but also receive the Holy Spirit. The blessing promised to Abraham, secured through the redemptive work of Christ, is identified with the gift of the Spirit. The age of the Spirit has replaced the age of law.

It is common teaching in the New Testament that the age of the Spirit followed the completion of Christ's work on earth. Paul presents this teaching with his own emphasis. His negative evaluation of the place of law in Christian life naturally caused others to ask how ethical and moral standards were to be maintained. Paul answered that the Spirit supplied a more effective power for holy living than the law could ever supply. The law imposed bondage, but "where the Spirit of the Lord is, there is liberty" (2 Cor. 3:17). The law told people what to do, but could provide neither the will nor the power to do it; the Spirit, operating within the believer's life, can provide both the will and the power.

The Spirit is called not only the Spirit of God but also the Spirit of Christ. He is the Spirit who dwelled within Christ during His earthly ministry, empowering Him to accomplish merciful works and to teach wisdom and grace. The qualities that characterized Christ are reproduced by His Spirit in His people: "love, joy, peace, longsuffering, kindness, goodness, faithfulness, gentleness, self-control" (Gal. 5:22–23).

John the Baptist predicted that Christ would baptize men and women with the Holy Spirit (Matt. 3:11; Mark 1:8; Luke 3:16). The New Testament teaches that this prediction was fulfilled with the coming of the Holy Spirit at Pentecost (Acts 2:2–12). Paul accepted this teaching about baptism with the Spirit, but linked it with his teaching about the church as the body of Christ. "For by one Spirit," he wrote to his converts in Corinth, "we were all baptized into one body—whether Jews or Greeks, whether slaves or free" (1 Cor. 12:13).

In various ways Paul views the present indwelling of the Spirit as an anticipation of the coming glory. The Spirit's work in the lives of Christ's people differs in degree, but not in kind, from their full sharing of Christ's glory at His advent. It is through the work of the Spirit that they, "beholding . . . the glory of the Lord, are being transformed into the same image from glory to glory" (2 Cor. 3:18).

The Spirit is referred to by Paul as the one who identifies the people of God to secure them "for the day of redemption" (Eph. 4:30), as the "firstfruits" of the coming glory (Rom. 8:23), as the "deposit," "guarantee," or initial downpayment of the resurrection life that is their assured heritage (2 Cor. 1:22; 5:5).

The Body of Christ: Paul is the only New Testament writer who speaks of the church as a body. The members of the church, he suggests, are as interdependent as the various parts of the human body, each making its contribution in harmony with the others for the good of the whole. Just as a body functions best when all the parts follow the direction of the head, the church best fulfills its purpose on earth when all the members are subject to the direction of Christ. He is, by divine appointment, "head over all things to the church, which is His body" (Eph. 1:22–23). The Spirit of Christ not only dwells within each member but also dwells within the church as a whole, continually giving His life to the entire body together. The body cannot be thought of without the Spirit. "There is one body and one Spirit," and when the members show one another the love of God they "keep the unity of the Spirit in the bond of peace" (Eph. 4:3–4).

The source of Paul's concept of the church as the body of Christ has been long debated. One source may have been the Old Testament principle of "corporate personality"—the principle of regarding a community, nation, or tribe as a person to the point where it is named and described as if it were an individual. God said to Pharaoh through Moses, "Israel is My Son, My firstborn . . . Let My son go that he may serve Me" (Ex. 4:22–23).

Perhaps the most satisfactory source of Paul's concept can be found in the words of the risen Christ who appeared to him on the Damascus Road: "Why are you persecuting Me?" (Acts 9:4). Paul did not think he was persecuting Jesus, who was beyond his direct reach. But that is exactly what he was doing when he persecuted Jesus' followers. When any part of the body is hurt, it is the head that complains. Jesus' words may have sown the seed of that doctrine in Paul's mind. The Lord told Ananias of Damascus that He would show Paul "how many things he must suffer for My name's sake" (Acts 9:16). Paul later echoed this in his statement, "If one member suffers, all the members suffer with it" (1 Cor. 12:26).

The first time Paul wrote of this subject (1 Cor. 12:12–27), his purpose was to impress on his readers the fact that, as Christians, they have mutual duties and common interests that must not be neglected. When he next expounded on it (Rom. 12:4–8), he wrote of the variety of service rendered by the various members of the church. In accordance with their respective gifts, all members build up the one body to which they belong. The health of the whole body depends on the harmonious cooperation of the parts.

In his later letters, Paul dealt with the relation that the church, as the body of Christ, bears to Christ as head of the body. The well-being of the body depends on its being completely under the control of the head. It is from Christ, as head of the church, that "all the body, nourished and knit together by joints and ligaments, grows with the increase which is from God" (Col. 2:19).

Paul's doctrine of the church as the body of Christ is closely bound up with his description of believers as being "in Christ" at the same time as Christ is in them. They are in Him as members of His body, having been "baptized into Christ" (Gal. 3:27). He is in them because it is His risen life that animates them. Jesus once used another organic analogy when He depicted Himself as "the true vine" and His disciples as the branches (John 15:1–6). The relationship is similar to that between the head and the body. The branches are in the vine and the vine at the same time is in the branches.

Eschatology: Eschatology is the teaching about things to come, especially things to come at the end times.

Paul originally held the views of eschatology taught in the Pharisaic schools. When Paul became a Christian, he found no need to abandon the eschatological teaching he had received at the feet of Gamaliel. But his experience of Christ did bring about some important modifications of his views. The distinction between the present age and the age to come was basic to this teaching. The present age was subject to evil influences that affected the lives and actions of men and women. The God of righteousness and truth, however, was in control of the situation. One day He would bring in a new age from which evil would be banished. The Pharisees taught that the end of the present age and beginning of the new age would be marked by the resurrection of the dead. Whether all the dead would be raised or only the righteous among them was a matter of debate. In Acts 24:15 Paul stated before the governor, Felix, that he shared the hope "that there will be a resurrection of the dead, both of the just and the unjust." In his letters he spoke only of the resurrection of believers in Christ, perhaps because it was to such people that his letters were written.

An important question was the relation of this framework to the messianic hope. When would the Messiah, the expected ruler of David's line, establish His kingdom? His kingdom might mark the closing phase of the present age; it might be set up with the inauguration of the age to come; or it might occupy a phase between the two ages. There was no general agreement on this question. Another question on which there was no general agreement concerned the extent to which the Messiah would revoke or replace the law of Moses. When Paul was confronted with the risen Christ on the Damascus Road, he realized that the Messiah had come and that in Him the resurrection had begun to take place. Having been raised from the dead, Christ had now entered upon His reign. The age of the Spirit for His people on earth coincided with the reign of Christ in His place of exaltation in the presence of God. There "He must reign till He has put all enemies under His feet" (1 Cor. 15:25). The present age had not yet come to an end, because men and women, and especially the people of Christ, still lived on earth in mortal bodies. But the resurrection age had already begun, because Christ had been raised.

The people of Christ, while living temporarily in the present age, belong spiritually to the new age that has been inaugurated. The benefits of this new age are already made good to them by the Spirit. The last of the enemies that will be subdued by Christ is death. The destruction of death will coincide with the resurrection of the people of Christ. Paul wrote, "Each one in his own order: Christ the firstfruits, afterward those who are Christ's at His coming" (1 Cor. 15:23). The eternal kingdom of God will be consummated at that time.

The resurrection of the people of Christ, then, takes place at His coming again. In one of his earliest letters Paul said that, when Christ comes, "the dead in Christ will rise first. Then we who are alive and remain shall be caught up together with them in the clouds to meet the Lord in the air. And thus we shall always be with the Lord" (1 Thess. 4:16–17).

Further details are provided in 1 Corinthians 15:42–57. When the last trumpet announces the second coming of Christ, the dead will be raised in a "spiritual body," replacing the mortal body they wore on earth. Those believers who are still alive at the time will undergo a similar change to fit them for the new conditions. These new conditions, the eternal kingdom of God, are something that "flesh and blood cannot inherit"; they make up an imperishable realm that cannot accommodate the perishable bodies of this present life (1 Cor. 15:50).

The assurance that the faithful departed would be present at the second coming of Christ was a great comfort to Christians whose friends and relatives had died. But the question of their mode of existence between death and the Second Coming remained to be answered. Paul's clearest answer to this question was given shortly after a crisis in which he thought he faced certain death (2 Cor. 1:8–11).

Paul answered that to be "absent from the body" is to be "present with the Lord" (2 Cor. 5:8). Whatever provision is required for believers to enjoy the same communion with Christ after death as they enjoyed before death will certainly be supplied (2 Cor. 5:1–10). Or, as he put it when the outcome of his trial before Caesar was uncertain, "To live is Christ, and to die is gain," for to die would mean to "be with Christ, which is far better" (Phil. 1:21, 23).

The church as a whole and its members as individuals could look forward to a consummation of glory at the second coming of Christ. But the glory is not for them alone. In a vivid passage, Paul describes how "the creation eagerly waits for the revealing of the sons of God" (Rom. 8:19). This will liberate it from the change and decay to which it is subject at present and allow it to obtain "the glorious liberty of the children of God" (Rom. 8:21). In Genesis 3:17–19 man's first disobedience brought a curse on the earth. Paul looked forward to the removal of that curse and its replacement by the glory provided by the obedience of Christ, the "second Man" (1 Cor. 15:47).

This prospect is integrated into Paul's message, which is above all a message of reconciliation. It tells how God "reconciled us to Himself through Jesus Christ" (2 Cor. 5:18) and calls on people to "be reconciled to God" (2 Cor. 5:20). It proclaims God's purpose through Christ "to reconcile all things to Himself, . . . whether things on earth or things in heaven, having made peace through the blood of His cross" (Col. 1:20).

Paul and the Message of Jesus: Some critics charge that Paul corrupted the original "simple" message of Jesus by transforming it into a theological structure. But the truth is completely otherwise. No one in the apostolic age had a surer insight into Jesus' message than Paul.

A shift in perspective between the ministry of Jesus and the ministry of Paul must be recognized. During His own ministry Jesus was the preacher; in the ministry of Paul He was the one being preached. The Gospels record the works and words of the earthly Jesus; in Paul's preaching Jesus, once crucified, has been exalted as the heavenly Lord. Jesus' earthly ministry was confined almost entirely to the Jewish people; Paul was preeminently the Apostle to the Gentiles. Paul's Gentile hearers required that the message be presented in a different vocabulary from that which Jesus used in Galilee and Judea. The gospel of Jesus and the gospel preached by Paul are not two gospels but one—a gospel specifically addressed to sinners. Paul, like Jesus, brought good news to outsiders. This was the assurance that in God's sight they were not outsiders, but men and women whom He lovingly accepted. In the ministry of Jesus, the outsiders were the social outcasts of Israel. In the ministry of Paul the outsiders were Gentiles. The principle was the same, although its application was different. Paul's achievement was to communicate to the Greco-Roman world, in terms it could understand, the good news that Jesus announced in His teaching, action, and death. Paul did not have before him the Gospels as we know them, but he knew the main lines of Jesus' teaching, especially parts of the Sermon on the Mount. This teaching was passed orally among the followers of Jesus before it circulated in written form. If Jesus summed up the law of God in the two great commandments of love toward God and love toward one's neighbor, Paul echoed Him: "All the law is fulfilled in one word, even in this: 'You shall love your neighbor as yourself' " (Gal. 5:14; also Rom. 13:9).

Paul's Legacy: Paul was a controversial figure in his lifetime, even within the Christian movement. He had many opponents who disagreed with his interpretation of the message of Jesus. In the closing years of his life, when imprisonment prevented him from moving about freely, Paul's opponents were able to make headway with their rival interpretations. Even though Asia had been Paul's most fruitful mission field, at the end of his life he wrote, "All those in Asia have turned away from me" (2 Tim. 1:15).

In the following generation, however, there was a resurgence of feeling in Paul's favor. His opponents were largely discredited and disabled by the dispersal of the church of that city shortly before the destruction of Jerusalem in A.D. 70. Throughout most of the church Paul became a venerated figure. His letters, together with the Gospels, became the foundation of the Christian movement.

Paul's liberating message has proved its vitality throughout the centuries. Repeatedly, when the Christian faith has been in danger of being shackled by legalism or tradition, Paul's message has allowed the gospel to set people free. The relevance of Paul's teaching for human life today may be brought out in a summary of four of his leading themes:

1. True religion is not a matter of rules and regulations. God does not deal with men and women like an accountant, but He accepts them freely when they respond to His love. He implants the Spirit of Christ in their hearts so they may extend His love to others.

2. In Christ men and women have come of age. God does not keep His people on puppet strings but liberates them to live as His responsible sons and daughters.

3. People matter more than things, principles, and causes. The highest of principles and the best of causes exist only for the sake of people. Personal liberty itself is abused if it is exercised against the personal well-being of others.

4. Discrimination on the grounds of race, religion, class, or sex is an offense against God and humanity alike.

Paulos [Paul'os]—See Paul, the Apostle.

Paulus, Sergius [Paul'us, Ser'gi·us]—See Sergius Paulus.

Pedahel [Pe·dah'el], *God saves*—Son of Ammihud and prince of Naphtali (Num. 34:28).

Pedahzur [Pe·dah'zur], *a rock saves*—Father of Gamaliel, prince of Manasseh. He assisted Moses in numbering the people (Num. 1:10; 2:20; 7:54, 59; 10:23).

Pedaiah [Pe·dai'ah], *Jehovah hath saved*—

1. Maternal grandfather of Jehoiakim, king of Judah (2 Kings 23:36).

2. Brother of Shealtiel (Salathiel), possibly, but not probably, his son (1 Chron. 3:18–19); also held to be the father of Zerubbabel by the widow of Salathiel. A descendant of Jeconiah. See Zerubbabel.

3. Father of Joel, prince of Manasseh (1 Chron. 27:20).

4. A son of Parosh who labored on the wall of Jerusalem (Neh. 3:25).

5. One who stood by Ezra as he taught the people (Neh. 8:4).

6. A Benjamite of the family of Jeshaiah (Neh. 11:7).

7. A Levite, one of the treasurers in the time of Nehemiah (Neh. 13:13).

Pekah [Pe'kah], (God) *has opened the eyes*—The son of Remaliah and eighteenth king of Israel of the eighth dynasty (2 Kings 15:25–31; 2 Chron. 28:5–15). Pekah, a captain of the king, became king himself after he assassinated King Pekahiah. Pekah continued to lead Israel in the idolatrous ways of Jeroboam I (2 Kings 15:28).

Pekah took the throne at the time when Tiglath-pileser III, king of Assyria, was advancing toward Israel. To resist this threat, Pekah formed an alliance with Rezin, king of Syria. He also hoped to enlist the sister Israelite nation of Judah in the alliance. Under the counsel of the prophet Isaiah, however, Judah's kings, Jotham and later Ahaz, refused. Pekah and Rezin attempted to enlist Judah by force, marching first against Jerusalem. They were unsuccessful, and so they divided their armies. Rezin successfully captured Elath, and Pekah slew thousands in the districts near Jericho, taking many prisoners into Samaria. Later, these prisoners were returned to Jericho upon the advice of the prophet Oded. Pekah probably was unaware that he was God's instrument to punish Judah (2 Chron. 28:5–6).

As Tiglath-pileser III of Assyria advanced, King Ahaz of Judah met him to pay tribute and ask his help against Syria and Israel (2 Kings 16:10). Assyria planned to march against Syria, and so Damascus was taken and Rezin was killed. The Assyrians also invaded northern Israel, with city after city taken and their inhabitants deported to Assyria. Through the Assyrian army God brought His judgment on Israel and Syria, even as the prophet Isaiah had warned (Isa. 7:8–9).

Pekah was left with a stricken nation, over half of which had been plundered and stripped of its inhabitants. Soon Hoshea, son of Elah, conspired against Pekah and assassinated him. However, in his own writings Tiglath-pileser III claimed that he was the power that placed Hoshea on the throne of Israel, possibly indicating he was a force behind the conspiracy. Pekah's dates as king of Israel are usually given as 740–732 B.C.

Pekahiah [Pek·a·hi′ah], *the Lord has opened the eyes*—A son of Menahem and the seventeenth king of Israel (2 Kings 15:22–26). Pekahiah, of the seventhy dynasty, assumed the throne after his father's death. He was an evil king who continued the idolatrous worship first introduced by King Jeroboam I. After reigning only two years (about 742–740 B.C.), Pekahiah was killed by his military captain, Pekah, and fifty Gileadites. Pekah then became king.

Pekod [Pe′kod], *visitation*—A name applied to Babylonia, under divine judgment (Jer. 50:21; Ezek. 23:23).

Pelaiah [Pe·lai′ah], *distinguished by Jehovah*—
1. Son of Elioenai of Judah (1 Chron. 3:24).
2. One who helped explain the law to the people as Ezra read it aloud (Neh. 8:7).
3. A Levite who sealed the covenant (Neh. 10:10).

Pelaliah [Pel·a·li′ah], *Jehovah has judged*—A priest, a descendant of Malchijah (Neh. 11:12).

Pelatiah [Pel·a·ti′ah], *Jehovah has freed*—
1. Son of Hananiah, descendant of Salathiel (1 Chron. 3:21).
2. A Simeonite captain who participated in the war with the Amalekites, son of Ishi (1 Chron. 4:42).
3. A chief of the people who signed the covenant (Neh. 10:22).
4. Son of Benaiah. In a vision Ezekiel saw Pelatiah die as the prophet prophesied (Ezek. 11:1–13).

Peleg [Pe′leg], *division*—A descendant of Noah through Shem and a son of Eber (Gen. 10:25). Peleg was an ancestor of Jesus (Luke 3:35; Phalec, KJV). He was named Peleg (meaning "division"), because "in his days the earth was divided" (Gen. 10:25; 1 Chron. 1:19), probably referring to the scattering of Noah's descendants as God's judgment following the attempt to build the tower of Babel (Gen. 11:8, 16–19). Others surmise that it is a reference to a physical/geographical change on the earth's surface which possibly caused natural land bridges between continents to be flooded, thus dividing the earth. No one knows for sure exactly why Peleg received his name.

Pelet [Pe'let], *liberation*—
1. Son of Jahdai (1 Chron. 2:47).
2. Son of Azmaveth (1 Chron. 12:3).

Peleth [Pe'leth], *swiftness*—
1. A Reubenite, father of On (Num. 16:1).
2. Son of Jonathan (1 Chron. 2:33).

Pelethites [Pel'e·thites], *couriers*—Faithful soldiers who belonged to David's bodyguard (2 Sam. 15:18–22; 20:7).

Pella [Pel'la], unknown—One of the ten cities of the Decapolis. This city is not mentioned by name in the Bible, but the Decapolis is mentioned (Matt. 4:25; Mark 5:20; 7:31).

Pelonite [Pe'lo·nite], *a certain one*—Designations for Helez and Ahijah, two of David's mighty men (1 Chron. 11:27, 36). Helez was said to be of the tribe of Ephraim (1 Chron. 27:10). He is also called the Paltite in 2 Samuel 23:26.

Peniel [Pen'i·el]—See Penuel.

Peninnah [Pe·nin'nah], *coral*—The second wife of Elkanah, Samuel's father (1 Sam. 1:2–6). Peninnah ridiculed Elkanah's other wife, Hannah, because she was barren.

Pentecost [Pen'te·cost], *the fiftieth day*—A Jewish feast also known as the Feast of Weeks, which marked the completion of the barley harvest. On this annual holiday about fifty days after the resurrection of Jesus, Jewish people from throughout the Roman Empire were gathered in the city of Jerusalem to observe this great religious festival. When the Holy Spirit was poured out on the apostles, they began to speak with "other tongues," and all the people from other nations understood them perfectly (Acts 2:5–13). The different regions of the Roman Empire represented in Jerusalem on the Day of Pentecost included Judea, Lybia, Cyrene, Crete, Asia, Phrygia, Pamphylaia, Pontus, Cappadocia, Parthia, Media, Elam, Mesopotamia, Arabia, Egypt, and Rome herself.

Penuel [Pen'u·el], *face of God*—The name of a place and two men in the Old Testament:

1. A place north of the river Jabbok where Jacob wrestled with "a Man" until daybreak. Hosea 12:4 calls the "man" an "Angel." Jacob called the place Penuel, "For I have seen God face to face" (Gen. 32:30). A city was built there later, not far to the east of Succoth. When Gideon and his band of 300 men pursued the Midianites, the people of Succoth and Penuel insulted Gideon, refusing to give supplies to his army. Gideon later killed the men of the city (Judg. 8:17). Penuel is about 65 kilometers (40 miles) northeast of Jerusalem. It is also called Peniel (Gen. 32:30).

2. A son of Hur and grandson of Judah (1 Chron. 4:4).

3. A son of Shashak, of the tribe of Benjamin (1 Chron. 8:25).

Peor [Pe'or], *a cleft*—A mountain near Mount Nebo, northeast of the Dead Sea, in the land of Moab. Balak took Balaam to the summit of Peor (Num. 23:28) to encourage Balaam to curse the Israelites. Also the name of a god of the Moabites worshiped in Mount Peor, frequently called Baal-peor.

Peraea [Pe·rae'a]—See Perea.

Perazim [Pe·ra'zim]—See Baal-perazim.

Perea [Pe·re'a], *unknown*—The name given by Josephus to the region east of the Jordan.

Peresh [Pe'resh], *dung*—Son of Machir (1 Chron. 7:16).

Perez [Per'ez], *a breach*—A twin son of Judah and Tamar (Gen. 38:24–30), also called Pharez (KJV).

Perezites [Per'ez·ites]—See Parzites.

Perez-uzza, Perez-uzzah [Pe'rez-uz'za, Pe'rez-uz'zah], *(breach of Uzza)*—The place where Uzza died when he placed his hand upon the ark (2 Sam. 6:8; 1 Chron. 13:11).

Perga [Per'ga], *citadel*—The capital city of Pamphylia, a province on the southern coast of Asia Minor, twice visited by the apostle Paul.

During Paul's first missionary journey, he sailed to Perga from Paphos, on the island of Cyprus (Acts 13:13–14). Some time later, Paul and Barnabas stopped a second time at Perga (Acts 14:25).

Ruins of the walls and city gate at Perga, a city visited by Paul and Barnabas on their first missionary journey (Acts 13:13, 14).

Pergamos [Per′ga·mos], *citadel*—The chief city of Mysia, near the Caicus River in northwest Asia Minor (modern Turkey) and the site of one of the seven churches of Asia (Rev. 1:11; 2:12–17; Pergamum, NRSV, NIV, REB, NASB). The city, situated opposite the island of Lesbos, was about 24 kilometers (15 miles) from the Aegean Sea.

In its early history Pergamos became a city-state, then a powerful nation after Attalus I (241–197 B.C.) defeated the Gauls (Galatians). It stood as a symbol of Greek superiority over the barbarians. Great buildings were erected and a library containing over 200,000 items was established. The Egyptians, concerned with this library, which rivaled their own at Alexandria, refused to ship papyrus to Pergamos. As a result, a new form of writing material, Pergamena charta, or parchment, was developed.

In the days of Roman dominance throughout Asia Minor, Pergamos became the capital of the Roman province of Asia. In a gesture of friendship, Mark Antony gave Pergamos's library to Cleopatra; its volumes were moved to Alexandria. Not only was Pergamos a government center with three imperial temples but it was also the site of the temple of Asklepios (the Greco-Roman god of medicine and healing), and the medical center where the physician Galen worked (about A.D. 160). Here also was a temple to Athena and a temple to Zeus with an altar showing Zeus defeating snake-like giants.

In the book of Revelation, John issued the church at Pergamos a stern warning against compromise with evil (Rev. 2:13). As capital of the Roman province of Asia, the city became the first site where the cult of emperor worship was practiced, beginning in 29 B.C. John spoke of Pergamos as the place "where Satan's throne is" (Rev. 2:13). This could be a reference to the cult of emperor worship, because Pergamos was a center where this form of loyalty was pledged to the emperor of the Roman Empire. Refusal to burn incense before the Roman emperor's statue brought charges of disloyalty and possibly death. Antipas, a Christian leader, was martyred, perhaps for his refusal to worship the emperor (Rev. 2:13). Pergamos was also a center of other types of idolatry and pagan worship. The city featured temples dedicated to worship of the chief pagan god Zeus and to Aesculapius, the Greco–Roman God of healing.

The Christian community in Pergamos was too tolerant of evil. Some church teachers apparently advised Christians to participate in immoral sexual practices, as well as pagan worship (Rev. 2:14–15). John commanded, on behalf of the Lord, "Repent, or else I will come to you quickly and will fight against them with the sword of My mouth" (Rev. 2:16). Choice spiritual blessings were promised to those Christians who were faithful witnesses (Rev. 2:17).

The Pergamos of New Testament times has disappeared, although the site is occupied today by the town of Bergama in modern Turkey. Excavation of the old city has uncovered the ruins of the temple where the Roman emperor was worshipped and a huge temple of Zeus.

Pergamum [Per′ga·mum]—A variant of Pergamos.

Perida [Pe·ri′da]—See Peruda.

Perizzites [Pe·riz′zites], *villagers*—Inhabitants of the "forest country" (Josh. 17:15) in the territory of the tribes of Ephraim, Manasseh, and Judah (Judg. 1:4–5). The Perizzites, who lived in Canaan as early as the time of Abraham and Lot (Gen. 13:7), were subdued by the Israelites. After the conquest of the land of Canaan under Joshua, the Perizzites were allowed to live. They entered into marriages with their conquerors and seduced the Israelites into idolatry (Judg. 3:5–6). In the time of the judges, Bezek was their stronghold and Adoni-bezek was their leader (Judg. 1:4–5). In the days of King Solomon the Perizzites were recruited for the king's forced-labor force (1 Kings 9:20).

Persia [Per′sia], *pure* or *splendid*—A territory bounded on the north by Media, on the south by the Persian Gulf, on the west by Elam, on the east by Carmania. Persia became the second world empire and was brought into direct relation with the Jews. The Persians apparently sprang from a people from the hills of Russia who began to settle in upper Mesopotamia and along the Black Sea as early as 2000 B.C. Ancient Media was located in what is now northwestern Iran, west of the Caspian Sea. Cyrus the Great, first ruler of the Persian Empire, united the Medes and Persians to conquer Babylonia and Assyria, thus becoming the dominant power of the ancient world.

After his conquest of Babylonia about 539 B.C., Cyrus authorized the rebuilding of the temple at Jerusalem and the resettlement of the Jewish community in their homeland (2 Chron. 36:22–23). Many of the Israelites had been carried to Babylonia as captives after the fall of Jerusalem about 586 B.C. (2 Chron. 36:17–21). Of all the ancient peoples who lived in the upper reaches of the Tigris and Euphrates Rivers, the Medes and Persians probably had the greatest influence on the Israelites. The prophet Isaiah wrote that Cyrus, although he did not know God, was anointed by God for the special mission of returning God's people to Jerusalem (Isa. 45:1, 4).

Daniel 6:8–9 refers to "the law of the Medes and Persians." Once a Persian law was handed down by the king, it could not be changed or revoked. While he was a captive in the royal court of the Babylonians, Daniel predicted that Babylonia would fall to the Medes and Persians (Dan. 5). The book of Esther records events that occurred during the reign of King Ahasuerus, or Xerxes, of Persia in the fifth century B.C. By faithfully recording the manners and customs of the Persian Empire, the book serves as a reliable historical record of the period.

Among the nations of the ancient world, Persia is noted for its beautiful cities. Persepolis, the nation's ceremonial capital, was a showplace of Persian culture. Ecbatana, capital of the Median Empire, became a resort city for the Persians. Susa, called Shushan in the book of Esther, was the capital of the Elamites before it became the administrative capital of the Persian Empire. The book of Esther records events during the reign of King Ahasuerus (Xerxes) in the fifth century B.C. at Shushan (Susa), administrative capital of the Persian Empire. After the death of Darius I (the Persian king who had allowed any Jews who desired to return to their homeland to do so), his son Ahasuerus became king. Ahasuerus was the king who became dissatisfied with his queen Vashti and banished her, marrying Esther.

Royal Persian feasts were noted for their splendor and opulence. Esther describes the Persian custom of eating while reclining on beds or couches. All eating utensils were made of gold, "each vessel being different from the other" (Est. 1:7). Special laws protected the Persian king. Esther 1:14 refers to the seven princes who "had access to the king's presence." These were the chief nobles who were his advisors. Only a person summoned by the king could visit him, a custom which signified his royalty, as well as protected him from would-be assassins. Esther feared going to Ahasuerus without being called, because the punishment for such a visit was death (Est. 4:11).

The Persian Empire boasted a well-organized postal system (Est. 3:13). The king's ring (Est. 8:8) was the signet ring with which official documents were signed. In ancient Persia, documents were sealed in two ways: with a signet ring if they were written on papyrus, or with a cylinder seal if written on clay tablets. Among the objects excavated at the royal city of Persepolis was a cylinder seal, which belonged to King Xerxes. The book of Esther refers to "the laws of the Persians and Medes" (1:19). This phrase, also used in Daniel 6, again refers to the ironclad nature of the laws that governed the Persian Empire. Once a law was issued, it could not be changed or revoked—not even by the king himself, not even at the request of his beloved queen, not even if it was shown to have been made out of spite and injustice. That was why King Darius had to allow Daniel, who he knew was a faithful servant, to be put into the lions' den, and later King Ahasuerus found himself with the same situation in the case of Haman requesting a "law" to set a day to kill all the Jews. The king could not change the law, but he could provide a way for the Jews to protect themselves with his sanction, which effectively countered the earlier decree.

Persis [Per'sis], *a Persian woman*—A Christian of the Roman church (Rom. 16:12).

Peruda [Pe·ru'da], *a kernel*—A servant of Solomon (Ezra 2:55; also called Perida, Neh. 7:57).

Peter, Simon [Pe'ter Si'mon], *rock*—Son of Jonas (John 1:42; 21:15–16). The most prominent of Jesus' twelve apostles. The New Testament gives a more complete picture of Peter than of any other disciple, with the exception of Paul. Peter is often considered to be a big, blundering fisherman. But this is a shallow portrayal. The picture of his personality portrayed in the New Testament is rich and many-sided. A more fitting appraisal of Peter is that he was a pioneer among the twelve apostles and the early church, breaking ground that the church would later follow.

The First Apostle to Be Called: Peter's given name was Simeon or Simon. His father's name was Jonah (Matt. 16:17; John 1:42). Simon's brother, Andrew, also joined Jesus as a disciple (Mark 1:16). The family probably lived at Capernaum on the north shore of the Sea of Galilee (Mark 1:21, 29), although it is possible they lived in Bethsaida (John 1:44).

Peter was married, because the Gospels mention that Jesus healed his mother-in-law (Matt. 8:14–15). The apostle Paul later mentioned that Peter took his wife on his missionary travels (1 Cor. 9:5). Peter and Andrew were fishermen on the Sea of Galilee, and perhaps in partnership with James and John, the sons of Zebedee (Luke 5:10). In the midst of his labor as a fisherman, Peter received a call from Jesus that changed his life (Luke 5:8).

The gospel of John reports that Andrew and Peter were disciples of John the Baptist before they joined Jesus. John also reports that Peter was introduced to Jesus by his brother Andrew, who had already recognized Jesus to be the Messiah (John 1:35–42). Whether Andrew and Peter knew Jesus because they were disciples of John is uncertain. But it is clear that they followed Jesus because of His distinctive authority.

The First Among the Apostles: Jesus apparently gathered His followers in two stages: first as disciples (learners or apprentices), and later as apostles (commissioned representatives). Peter was the first disciple to be called (Mark 1:16–18) and the first to be named an apostle (Mark 3:14–16). His name heads every list of the Twelve in the New Testament. He was apparently the strongest individual in the band. He frequently served as a spokesman for the disciples, and he was their recognized leader (Mark 1:36; Luke 22:32). Typical of Peter's dominant personality was his readiness to walk to Jesus on the water (Matt. 14:28), and to ask Jesus the awkward question of how often he should forgive a sinning fellow believer (Matt. 18:21).

An inner circle of three apostles existed among the Twelve. Peter was also the leader of this small group. The trio—Peter, James, and John—was present with Jesus on a number of occasions. They witnessed the raising of a young girl from the dead (Mark 5:37; Luke 8:51); they were present at Jesus' transfiguration (Matt. 17:1–2); and they were present during Jesus' agony in Gethsemane (Matt. 26:37; Mark 14:33). During Jesus' final week in Jerusalem, two of the three, Peter and John, were sent to make preparations for their last meal together (Luke 22:8).

The First Apostle to Recognize Jesus as Messiah: The purpose of Jesus' existence in the flesh was that people would come to a true picture of who God is and what He has done for our salvation. The first apostle to recognize that was Peter. He confessed Jesus as Lord in the region of Caesarea Philippi (Matt. 16:13–17).

Jesus began the process that would lead to Peter's awareness by asking a nonthreatening question, "Who do men say that I, the Son of Man, am?" (Matt. 16:13). After the disciples voiced various rumors, Jesus put a more personal question to them, "But who do you say that I am?" (Matt. 16:15). Peter confessed Jesus to be the Messiah, the Son of God. According to Matthew, it was because of this confession that Jesus renamed Simon Cephas (in Aramaic) or Peter (in Greek), both meaning "rock."

Why Jesus called Simon a "rock" is not altogether clear. Peter's character was not always rock-like, as his denial of Jesus indicates. His new name probably referred to something that, by God's grace, he would become—Peter, a rock.

The First Apostle to Witness the Resurrection: How ironic that the one who denied Jesus most vehemently in His hour of suffering should be the first person to witness His resurrection from the dead. Yet according to Luke (Luke 24:34) and Paul (1 Cor. 15:5), Peter was the first apostle to see the risen Lord. We can only marvel at the grace of God in granting such a blessing to one who did not seem to deserve it. Peter's witnessing of the resurrection was a sign of his personal restoration to fellowship with Christ. It also confirmed His appointment by God to serve as a leader in the emerging church.

The First Apostle to Proclaim Salvation to the Gentiles: The earliest information about the early church comes from the book of Acts. This shows clearly that Peter continued to exercise a key leadership role in the church for a number of years. Indeed, the first eleven chapters of Acts are built around the activity of the apostle Peter.

When the Holy Spirit visited the church in Samaria, the apostles sent Peter and John to verify its authenticity (Acts 8:14–25). But this event was only a prelude to the one event that concluded Peter's story in the New Testament: the preaching of the gospel to the Gentiles (Acts 10–11). The chain of events that happened before the bestowal of the Holy Spirit on Gentile believers—beginning with Peter's staying in the house of a man of "unclean" profession (Acts 9:43), continuing with his vision of "unclean" foods (Acts 10:9–16), and climaxing in his realization that no human being, Gentile included, ought to be considered "unclean" (Acts 10:34–48)—is a masterpiece of storytelling. It demonstrates the triumph of God's grace to bring about change in stubborn hearts and the hardened social customs of Jewish believers.

Following the death of James, the brother of John, and Peter's miraculous release from prison (Acts 12), Peter drops out of the narrative of Acts. Luke reports that he "went to another place" (Acts 12:17). We know, however, that Peter did not drop out of active service in the early church.

Peter probably broadened his ministry, once the mantle of leadership of the Jerusalem church fell from his shoulders to those of James. Peter played a key role at the Council of Jerusalem (Acts 15; Gal. 2), which decided in favor of granting church membership to Gentiles without first requiring them to become Jews. Paul mentioned a visit of Peter to Antioch of Syria (Gal. 2:11), and he may refer to a mission of Peter to Corinth (1 Cor. 1:12). Peter dropped into the background in the book of Acts not because his ministry ended. Luke simply began to trace the course of the gospel's spread to Gentile Rome through the ministry of Paul.

Peter in Rome—The First to Inspire the Writing of a Gospel: According to early Christian tradition, Peter went to Rome, where he died. Only once in the New Testament do we hear of Peter's being in Rome. Even in this case, Rome is referred to as "Babylon" (1 Peter 5:13). Little is known of Peter's activities in Rome, although Papias, writing about A.D. 125, stated that Peter's preaching inspired the writing of the first gospel, drafted by Mark, who was Peter's interpreter in Rome. Peter was also the author of the two New Testament epistles that bear his name.

This early and generally reliable tradition supports the pioneer role played by Peter throughout his life and ministry. A number of other works—the Preaching of Peter, the Gospel of Peter, the Apocalypse of Peter, the Acts of Peter, and the Epistle of Peter to James—are apocryphal in nature. They cannot be accepted as trustworthy sources of information for the life and thought of the apostle.

Pethahiah [Peth·a·hi'ah], *freed by Jehovah*—

1. A priest whose family in the time of David became the nineteenth course of priests (1 Chron. 24:16).

2. A man of the family of Zerah of Judah, in the service of Artaxerxes. His work was relative to Jewish interests (Neh. 11:24).

3. A Levite (Ezra 10:23), probably the same as in Nehemiah 9:5.

Pethor [Pe'thor], *soothsayer*—A town in Mesopotamia (Num. 22:5; 23:7; Deut. 23:4).

Pethuel [Pe·thu'el], *enlarged of God*—Father of the prophet Joel (Joel 1:1).

Petra [Pet·ra], possibly *rock*—The unique red rock city south of the Dead Sea. Many of the buildings of this ruined city are carved directly into the face of the huge rock cliffs. It was the capital of Nabatea, and is believed by some scholars to be the Sela mentioned in Judges 1:36 and 2 Kings 14:7. Most of the monuments, temples, and buildings date from approximately 50 B.C. to A.D. 150. The beautiful pagan temple to the goddess Isis was commissioned by the emporer Hadrian in A.D. 131. The city is located in a basin only about one mile long and 3,000 feet wide, surrounded by high red rock cliffs. The only entrance to this secluded basin is a narrow gorge almost a mile long; this geographical arrangement made the city easy to defend against invasion.

Peullethai [Pe·ul'le·thai]—See Peulthai.

Peulthai [Pe·ul'thai], *work*—Son of Obed-edom, a Levite and porter of the tabernacle (1 Chron. 26:5).

Phalec [Pha'lec]—(Luke 3:35) See Peleg.

Phallu [Phal'lu]—See Pallu.

Phalti [Phal'ti]—See Palti.

Phaltiel [Phal'ti·el]—See Paltiel.

Phanuel [Pha·nu'el], *face of God*—Father of Anna, the prophetess (Luke 2:36).

Pharaoh [Pha'raoh], *great house*—The title of the kings of Egypt until 323 B.C. In the Egyptian language the word *pharaoh* means "great house." This word was originally used to describe the palace of the king. Around 1500 B.C. this term was applied to the Egyptian kings. It meant something like "his honor, his majesty." In addition to this title, the kings also had a personal name (Amunhotep, Rameses) and other descriptive titles (King of Upper and Lower Egypt).

The Egyptians believed their ruler was a god and the key to the nation's relationship to the cosmic gods of the universe. His word was law, and he owned everything in the land. When Pharaoh died, he became the ruler of the underworld and those who live after death. The Egyptians took great pains to prepare their dead for the afterlife. They perfected the intricate process of mummification. In lavish interiors of the great pyramids of Egypt the mummified bodies of royalty were buried, along with many of their earthly treasures. All in all there were thirty dynasties of pharaohs during Egypt's long history.

In several instances the Israelites came into contact with a pharaoh. Abram (Abraham) went to Egypt around 2000 B.C. because of a famine in the land of Canaan. Because Abram lied about Sarai (Sarah) being his sister, Pharaoh wanted to take her into his harem, but God stopped him by sending a plague (Gen. 12:10–20). About 200 years later Joseph was thrown into prison in Egypt because the wife of Potiphar, the captain of Pharaoh's guard, lied about Joseph's behavior (Gen. 39).

While in prison Joseph met two of Pharaoh's servants, the butler and the baker, who had been put in prison because they displeased the powerful pharaoh (Gen. 40). Joseph correctly interpreted the dreams of the butler and baker and later was brought from prison to interpret the dream of the pharaoh (Gen. 41). The Egyptian priestly magicians could not interpret Pharaoh's dream. But because God told Joseph the meaning of the dream, Joseph was appointed as second in command to collect one-fifth of the nation's crops during the seven years of plenty.

Because of the severity of the seven years of famine, the Egyptians had to sell their cattle, their property, and themselves to the pharaoh for grain; thus the pharaoh owned everything (Gen. 47:13–20). The pharaoh sent carts to bring Joseph's brothers to Egypt (Gen. 45:16–20) and settled them in the fertile land of Goshen (Gen. 47:1–6).

After about 300 more years in Egypt, a new dynasty came to power. Its kings did not acknowledge Joseph and his deeds to save Egypt (Ex. 1:8). Therefore all the Israelites but Moses were enslaved. He was raised in the pharaoh's own court (Ex. 1:11–2:10; Acts 7:21–22). At 80 years of age Moses returned to Pharaoh to ask permission to lead the Israelites out of Egypt. Pharaoh did not know or accept the God of the

Israelites and refused to obey Him (Ex. 5:1–2). On a second visit Moses functioned as God to Pharaoh by delivering a divine message (Ex. 7:1), but the miracles and initial plagues only hardened Pharaoh's heart (Ex. 7:8–13, 22; 8:15, 32). Each plague was carried out so the Israelites, the Egyptians, and the pharaoh would know that Israel's God was the only true God and that the Egyptian gods and their "divine pharaoh" were powerless before Him (Ex. 7:5, 17; 8:10, 22; 9:14, 29–30; 10:2).

Eventually Pharaoh admitted his sin, but before long he again hardened his heart (Ex. 9:27, 34; 10:16, 20). When Pharaoh's own "divine" firstborn son was killed in the last plague, he finally submitted to God's power and let the people go (Ex. 12:29–33). Pharaoh later chased the Israelites to bring them back, but he and his army were drowned in the Red Sea (Ex. 14:5–31).

Solomon formed an alliance with an Egyptian pharaoh through marriage with his daughter (1 Kings 3:1; 7:8; 9:24), thus demonstrating that Israel was a more powerful nation than Egypt. This pharaoh later gave the city of Gezer to his daughter (1 Kings 9:16). The next pharaoh had less friendly relationships with Solomon and gave refuge to Solomon's enemy, Hadad the Edomite (1 Kings 11:14–22). This may have been the pharaoh Shishak who protected Jeroboam (1 Kings 11:40) and captured Jerusalem in the fifth year of Rehoboam (1 Kings 14:25–28). Hoshea, the king of Israel, had a treaty with So, the king of Egypt (2 Kings 17:4). The pharaoh Tirhakah may have had a similar relationship with Hezekiah (2 Kings 19:9).

In 609 B.C. the pharaoh Necho marched north through Palestine to save the Assyrians. King Josiah opposed this move, so Necho killed him (2 Kings 23:29). Nebuchadnezzar later defeated Necho and took control of Judah (Jer. 46:2). It was possibly Pharaoh Hophra who challenged the Babylonians during the siege of Jerusalem in 587 B.C. (Jer. 37:5–10; 44:30; Ezek. 17:17).

The prophets Isaiah, Jeremiah, and Hosea condemned Pharaoh and the Israelites who trusted in him and his army (Isa. 30:1–5; 31:1; Jer. 42:18; Hos. 7:11). But the prophecies of Ezekiel are by far the most extensive (Ezek. 29–32). Pharaoh is quoted as saying, "My River is my own; I have made it for myself" (Ezek. 29:3). Because Pharaoh claimed the power and authority of God, Ezekiel declared, God will destroy Pharaoh and Egypt (Ezek. 29:19; 30:21; 31:2; 32:2, 12).

Pharaoh's Daughter [Pha'raoh]—Three Egyptian princesses are named in Scripture:

1. The daughter of Pharaoh who rescued the infant Moses and raised him as her own son (Ex. 2:5–10).

2. The bride of Solomon, king of all Israel. He built her a splendid house in Jerusalem (1 Kings 3:1; 7:8; 9:24).

3. The wife of Mered, a descendant of Judah (1 Chron. 4:18).

Pharaoh, Wife of [Pha'raoh]—(1 Kings 11:18–20) See Tahpenes.

Phares [Phar'es]—See Perez.

Pharisees [Phar'i·sees], *separated*—The Pharisees were one of the two major sects or special-interest groups among the Jews in New Testament times. These groups (the Pharisees and Sadducees) stood for different principles, but Jesus clashed with both parties at different times during His ministry. The word *Pharisee* means "separated." Their burning desire was to separate themselves from those people who did not observe the laws of tithing and ritual purity—matters they considered very important. The sect arose prior to the period of the Maccabees when there was a tendency on the part of the Jews to adopt Grecian customs.

In opposition to this, the Pharisees conformed in the strictest manner to the Mosaic institutions. The name "Pharisee" was first used in the time of John Hyrcanus. The Pharisees exerted strong influence in Jesus's time. The essential characteristic of their religion was conformity to the law. In addition to the Mosaic law they adhered strongly to traditions of the elders. They supported the scribes and rabbis in their interpretation of the Jewish law as handed down from the time of Moses. In Jesus's day, this interpretation of the law had become more authoritative and binding than the law itself. Jesus often challenged these traditional interpretations and the minute rules that had been issued to guide the people in every area of their behavior.

Jesus was also sensitive to the needs and hurts of individuals—an attitude that brought Him into conflict with the Pharisees. Matthew's gospel (23:1–36) contains Jesus's harsh words against the Pharisees. He accused them of placing too much emphasis on minor details, while ignoring "the weightier matters of the law," such as "justice and mercy and faith" (Matt. 23:23). The Pharisees often tried to trick Jesus into making statements that would be considered heretical or disloyal to Rome. On one occasion, Jesus used a denarius, a common coin of the day, to show that citizens of His country had responsibilities to ruling authorities, as well as to God.

Not all Pharisees were legalistic and hypocritical, however. Three Pharisees favorably recognized in the New Testament are Joseph of Arimathea (Luke 23:50–53), Nicodemas (John 3:1–21), and Gamaliel (Acts 5:34–39). The apostle Paul emphasized his own heritage as a Pharisee (Acts 22:3), but he also recognized the importance of abandoning this emphasis for the way of Christ (Phil. 3:1–14). The Pharisees were distinguished from the Sadducees in their doctrinal beliefs concerning belief in the resurrection and the immortality of the soul, and in angelic beings (Acts 23:8). See also Sadducees.

Pharosh [Phar'osh]—See Parosh.

Pharpar [Phar'par], *swift*—A river of Damascus mentioned by Naaman (2 Kings 5:12).

Pharzites [Phar·zites], *breach*—Those descended from Perez, the son of Judah and Tamar (Num. 26:20).

Phaseah [Pha·se'ah]—See Paseah.

Phebe [Phe'be]—See Phoebe.

Phenice [Phe·ni'ce]—See Phoenicia and Phoenix.

Phenicia [Phe·ni'ci·a]—See Phoenicia.

Phichol [Phi'chol], *mouth of all*—A captain of Abimelech (Gen. 21:22; 26:26).

Phicol [Phi'col]—See Phichol.

Philadelphia [Phil·a·del'phi·a], *brotherly love*—A city of the province of Lydia in western Asia Minor (modern Turkey) and the site of one of the seven churches of Asia to which John wrote in the book of Revelation (Rev. 1:11).

Philadelphia was situated on the Cogamus River, a tributary of the Hermus (modern Gediz) and was about 45 kilometers (28 miles) southeast of Sardis. It was founded by Attalus II (Philadelphus), who reigned as king of Pergamos from 159 B.C. until 138 B.C. Philadelphia was a center of the wine industry. Its chief deity was Dionysus, in Greek mythology the god of wine (the Roman Bacchus).

In the book of Revelation, John describes the church in Philadelphia as the faithful church and the church that stood at the gateway of a great opportunity (Rev. 3:7–13). Christ said to this church, "See, I have set before you an open door and no one can shut it" (v. 8). The "open door" means primarily access to God, but it also refers to opportunity for spreading the gospel of Jesus Christ. Still a city of considerable size, Philadelphia is known today as Alashehir.

Philemon [Phi·le′mon], *affectionate*—A wealthy Christian of Colossae who hosted a house church. Philemon was converted under the apostle Paul (Philem. 19), perhaps when Paul ministered in Ephesus (Acts 19:10). He is remembered because of his runaway slave, Onesimus, who, after damaging or stealing his master's property (Philem. 11, 18), made his way to Rome, where he was converted under Paul's ministry (Philem. 10).

Accompanied by Tychicus (Col. 4:7), Onesimus later returned to his master, Philemon. He carried with him the epistle to the Colossians, plus the shorter epistle to Philemon. In the latter, Paul asked Philemon to receive Onesimus, not as a slave but as a "beloved brother" (Philem. 16).

Philetus [Phi·le′tus], *beloved*—A teacher condemned by Paul for false teaching concerning the resurrection (2 Tim. 2:17–18).

Philip [Phil′ip], *lover of horses*—The name of four men in the New Testament:

1. One of the twelve apostles of Christ (Matt. 10:3; Mark 3:18; Luke 6:14) and a native of Bethsaida in Galilee (John 1:44; 12:21). According to the gospel of John, Philip met Jesus beyond the Jordan River during John the Baptist's ministry. Jesus called Philip to become His disciple. Philip responded and brought to Jesus another disciple, named Nathanael (John 1:43–51) or Bartholomew (Mark 3:18). Philip is usually mentioned with Nathanael.

Before Jesus fed the five thousand, He tested Philip by asking him how so many people could possibly be fed. Instead of responding in faith, Philip began to calculate the amount of food it would take to feed them and the cost (John 6:5–7).

When certain Greeks, who had come to Jerusalem to worship at the Feast of Passover, said to Philip, "Sir, we wish to see Jesus" (John 12:21), Philip seemed unsure of what he should do. He first told Andrew, and then they told Jesus of the request. Philip was one of the apostles who was present in the Upper Room following the resurrection of Jesus (Acts 1:13).

2. Philip the evangelist, one of the seven men chosen to serve the early church because they were reported to be "full of faith and the Holy Spirit" (Acts 6:5). Their task was to look after the Greek-speaking widows and probably all of the poor in the Jerusalem church. Following the stoning of Stephen, the first Christian martyr, many Christians scattered from Jerusalem (Acts 8:1). Philip became an evangelist and, in Samaria, preached the gospel, worked miracles, and brought many to faith in Christ (Acts 8:5–8).

Probably the most noted conversion as a result of Philip's ministry was the Ethiopian eunuch, an official under Candace, the queen of the Ethiopians. Philip met the eunuch on the road from Jerusalem to Gaza. The eunuch was reading from Isaiah 53, the passage about the Suffering Servant. Philip used this great opportunity to preach Jesus to him. The eunuch said, "I believe that Jesus Christ is the Son of God" (Acts 8:37). Then Philip baptized him.

After this event, Philip preached in Azotus (the Old Testament Ashdod) and Caesarea (Acts 8:40). He was still in Caesarea many years later when the apostle Paul passed through the city on his last journey to Jerusalem (Acts 21:8). Luke adds that Philip had "four virgin daughters who prophesied" (Acts 21:9).

3. Son of Herod the Great and half brother of Herod Antipas (Matt. 14:3; Luke 3:1).

4. Philip, the tetrarch. See Herod.

Philippi [Phi'lip·pi], *city of Philip*—A city in eastern Macedonia (modern Greece) visited by the apostle Paul. Situated on a plain surrounded by mountains, Philippi lay about 16 kilometers (10 miles) inland from the Aegean Sea. The Egnatian Way, the main overland route between Asia and the West, ran through the city. Philippi was named for Philip II of Macedonia, the father of Alexander the Great. In 356 B.C. Philip enlarged and renamed the city, which was formerly known as Krenides, meaning *wells* or *springs*. Philip resettled people from the countryside in Philippi and built a wall around the city and an acropolis atop the surrounding mountain. Although they date from later periods, other points of interest in Philippi include a forum the size of a football field, an open-air theater, two large temples, public buildings, a library, and Roman baths.

In 42 B.C. Mark Antony and Octavian (later Augustus Caesar) combined forces to defeat the armies of Brutus and Cassius, assassins of Julius Caesar, at Philippi. In celebration of the victory, Philippi was made into a Roman colony; this entitled its inhabitants to the rights and privileges usually granted those who lived in cities in Italy. Eleven years later, Octavian defeated the forces of Antony and Cleopatra in a naval battle at Actium, on the west coast of Greece. Octavian punished the supporters of Antony by evicting them from Italy and resettling them in Philippi. The vacated sites in Italy were then granted to Octavian's own soldiers as a reward for their victory over Antony.

The ruins of the city bear the marks of a rich Roman history, including an agora, or marketplace, where trade took place, and the western arch, or "gate," of the city, described in Acts 16:13. The agora was an important archeological discovery, with its seat of judgment, library, and adjacent jail site, possibly the very place where Paul and Silas were imprisoned (Acts 16:23–40).

The apostle Paul visited Philippi on his second missionary journey in A.D. 49 (Acts 16:12; 20:6). Evidently the city did not have the necessary number of Jewish males (ten) to form a synagogue, because Paul met with a group of women for prayer outside the city gate (Acts 16:13).

French excavations at Philippi between 1914 and 1938 unearthed a Roman arch that lay about one mile west of the city. This arch may have served as a zoning marker to restrict undesirable religious sects from meeting in the city. One of the women of Philippi who befriended Paul, named Lydia, was a dealer in purple cloth (Acts 16:14). A Latin inscription uncovered in excavations mentions this trade, thus indicating its economic importance for Philippi. Philippi also is mentioned or implied in Acts 20:16; Philippians 1:1; and 1 Thessalonians 2:2.

Philippians [Phi·lip′pi·ans]—Natives or inhabitants of Philippi (Phil. 4:15), a city of Macedonia situated about 113 kilometers (70 miles) northeast of Thessalonica (Acts 16:12; Phil. 1:1).

Philistia [Phi·lis'tia], *land of sojourners*—The land of the Philistines (Pss. 60:8; 87:4; Isa. 14:29). It was the maritime district of Canaan that extends from Joppa to Gaza.

Philistines [Phi·lis'tines]—An aggressive nation that occupied part of southwest Palestine from about 1200 to 600 B.C. The name Philistine was used first among the Egyptians to describe the sea people defeated by Rameses III in a naval battle about 1188 B.C. Among the Assyrians the group was known as Pilisti or Palastu. The Hebrew word *pelishti* is the basis of the name Palestine, a later name for Canaan, the country occupied by God's covenant people.

Little is known about the origins of the Philistines except what is contained in the Bible—that they came from Caphtor (Gen. 10:14), generally identified with the island of Crete in the Mediterranean Sea. Crete also was supposed to be the home of the Cherethites, who were sometimes associated with the Philistines (Ezek. 25:16). Philistine territory was considered Cherethite in 1 Samuel 30:14, suggesting that both peoples were part of the invading group defeated earlier by Rameses III of Egypt.

Liberal scholars have assumed that references to the Philistines during Abraham's time are incorrect historically and that the Philistine occupation actually occurred in the twelfth century B.C. More careful examination indicates there were two Philistine settlements in Canaan, one early and another later. Both these settlements were marked by significant cultural differences.

The Philistines of Gerar, with whom Abraham dealt (Gen. 20–21), evidently were a colony of the early settlement located southeast of Gaza in southern Canaan. This colony was situated outside the area occupied by the five Philistine cities after 1188 B.C. Gerar was also a separate city-state governed by a king who bore the name or title of Abimelech.

That Abimelech's colony was the chief one in the area seems probable from his title, "king of the Philistines" (Gen. 26:1, 8). This is different from a later period when the Philistines were governed by five lords. Unlike the later Philistines who were Israel's chief foes in the settlement and monarchy periods, the Gerar Philistines were peaceful. They encouraged the friendship of Abraham and Isaac. Finally, Gerar was not included among the chief cities of Philistia (Josh. 13:3). It was not mentioned as one of the places conquered by the Israelites. It is best, therefore, to regard the Genesis traditions as genuine historical records.

The early Philistine settlements in Canaan took on a new appearance when five cities—Ashkelon, Ashdod, Ekron, Gath, and Gaza—and the areas around them were occupied by the Philistines in the twelfth century B.C. Probably all of these except Ekron were already in existence when the sea peoples conquered them. These five Philistine cities formed a united political unit. Archaeological discoveries in the area have illustrated how they expanded to the south and east. Broken bits of Philistine pottery were found at archaeological sites in those areas.

The Philistines possessed superior weapons of iron when they began to attack the Israelites in the eleventh century B.C. The tribe of Dan moved northward to escape these Philistine attacks, and Judah also came under increasing pressure (Judg. 14–18). In Samuel's time the Philistines captured the ark of the covenant in battle. Although the ark was recovered later, the Philistines continued to occupy Israelite settlements (1 Sam. 10:5).

The threat of the Philistines prompted Israel's demands for a king. But even under Saul the united nation was still menaced by the Philistines—a threat that ultimately resulted in Saul's death (1 Sam. 31). David's slaying of Goliath, a giant from Gath, was a key factor in his rise to fame. By this time the Philistines had moved deep into Israelite territory. Archaeological evidence shows they had occupied Tell Beit Mirsim, Beth-zur, Gibeah, Megiddo, and Beth-shean. Yet by the end of David's reign their power had begun to decline significantly. By the time Jehoshaphat was made king of Judah (873–848 B.C.), the Philistines were paying tribute (2 Chron. 17:11), although they tried to become independent under Jehoshaphat's son, Jehoram (2 Chron. 21:16–17).

When the Assyrians began to raid Palestine in later years, the Philistines faced additional opposition. The Assyrian Adad-Nirari III (about 810–783 B.C.) placed the Philistine cities under heavy tribute early in his reign, while Uzziah of Judah (791–740 B.C.) demolished the defenses of several Philistine strongholds, including Gath. When he became king, Ahaz of Judah (732–715 B.C.) was attacked by Philistine forces, and cities in the Negev and the Judean lowlands were occupied. The Assyrian king Tiglath-pileser III responded by conquering the chief Philistine cities.

In 713 B.C. Sargon II, king of Assyria, invaded Philistia and con-quered Ashdod. The following year he launched another campaign against other Philistine cities. Hezekiah of Judah (716–686 B.C.) attacked Gaza (2 Kings 18:8), supported by the people of Ekron and Ashkelon, but in 701 B.C. Sennacherib brought Philistine territory under his control to prevent any Egyptian interference. When Nebu-chadnezzar came to power in Babylon, the Philistines formed an alli-ance with Egypt, but when the Jews were exiled to Babylonia between 597 and 586 B.C., the Philistines, too, were deported.

No Philistine literature has survived, making it difficult to recon-struct their religious beliefs or rituals. Old Testament records indicate they worshipped three gods, Ashtoreth, Dagon, and Baal-zebub—each of which had shrines in various cities (Judg. 16:23; 1 Sam. 5:1–7; 2 Kings 1:2). Philistine soldiers apparently carried images of their gods into bat-tle, perhaps as standards (2 Sam. 5:21). Like other Near Eastern peoples, the Philistines were superstitious. They respected the power of Israel's ark of the covenant (1 Sam. 5:1–12).

As depicted on Egyptian reliefs, Philistine soldiers wore short tunics, were clean-shaven, had crested or decorated helmets, carried round shields, and fought with spears and swords. In the days before David's reign, the Philistine cities were governed by a representative from each city. These authorities exercised complete power in both peace and war. This centralized control made the Philistines strong, in contrast to the loosely organized Israelites. The Philistines were impor-tant culturally because they adopted the manufacture and distribution of iron implements and weapons from the Hittites. Goliath's equip-ment was obviously of Philistine manufacture. The golden objects that were offered to Israel's God (1 Sam. 6:4–5) show that the Philistines were skilled goldsmiths as well.

The remains of Philistine furnaces have been uncovered at Tell Jemmeh and Ashdod. The area around Ashdod has produced some examples of typical Philistine pottery. This pottery reflected Greek as well as Egyptian and Canaanite styles. The Philistines loved beer. Large beer mugs decorated with red and black geometric designs were some of their important pottery products, along with large cups, bea-kers, and bowls. Some Philistine burial places discovered at Tell Far'ah reveal bodies encased in clay coffins shaped to match the human body.

The coffin lid was decorated with crude figures of the head and clasped arms of the deceased.

Philologus [Phi·lol'o·gus], *lover of words*—A Christian of the Roman church (Rom. 16:15).

Phinehas [Phin'e·has], *the Nubian*—the name of three men in the Old Testament:

1. A son of Eleazar and grandson of Aaron (Ex. 6:25). During the wilderness wandering, Phinehas killed Zimri, a man of Israel, and Cozri, a Midianite woman whom Zimri had brought into the camp (Num. 25). This action ended a plague by which God had judged Israel for allowing Midianite women to corrupt Israel with idolatry and harlotry. For such zeal Phinehas and his descendants were promised a permanent priesthood (Num. 25:11–13). Phinehas became the third high priest of Israel, serving for nineteen years. His descendants held the high priesthood until the Romans destroyed the temple in A.D. 70, except for a short period when the house of Eli served as high priests.

2. The younger of the two sons of Eli the high priest (1 Sam. 1:3). Phinehas and his brother, Hophni, were priests also, but they disgraced their priestly office by greed, irreverence, and immorality (1 Sam. 2:12–17, 22–25). The Lord told Eli his two sons would die (1 Sam. 2:34). They were killed in a battle with the Philistines. On the same day, the ark was captured, and his father fell, broke his neck, and died when he heard what had happened. When Phinehas's wife heard the news, she went into premature labor and died in childbirth. The child was named Ichabod, which means "The glory has departed from Israel!" (1 Sam. 4:22). Because of the evil actions of Phinehas and Hophni, the high priesthood later passed from Eli's family.

3. The father of a certain Eleazar, probably a priest (Ezra 8:33).

Phlegon [Phleg'on], *burning*—A Christian of the Roman church (Rom. 16:14).

Phoebe [Phoe'be], *radiant*—A deaconess of the church at Cenchreae, the eastern part of Corinth. She took up her residence at Rome and Paul recommended her to the Christians of Rome (Rom. 16:1–2).

Phoenicia [Phoe·ni'ci·a], *unknown*—A narrow strip of land on the eastern shore of the Mediterranean, north of Israel in the area which is modern-day Lebanon and coastal Syria. The lush vegetation of this area is mentioned by the prophets (Hos. 14:5–7), and the cedars of Lebanon were highly prized for building material. The Phoenician cities of Tyre and Sidon are mentioned often in the New Testament. Jesus healed a demon-possessed girl in this area (Matt. 15:21–28). Early Christian believers witnessed in Phoenicia after leaving Jerusalem (Acts 11:19). Paul often traveled through the area (Acts 15:3).

Phoenicians [Phoe·ni′ci·ans]—These people lived on a narrow strip of land northwest of Palestine on the eastern shore of the Mediterranean Sea in the area now known as Lebanon and coastal Syria. A group which once occupied the land of Canaan, the Phoenicians were driven out by Israel around 1380 B.C. and crowded onto this narrow strip of coastline. Hemmed in by the ocean and the mountains of Lebanon, the Phoenicians took to the sea to expand their empire. This led them to become distinguished seafaring merchants who founded many colonies along the Mediterranean. The nation was at the pinnacle of its power and prosperity from 1050 to 850 B.C.

With excellent ports such as Tyre and Sidon and a good supply of timber (cypress, pine, and cedar), the Phoenicians became noted shipbuilders and sea merchants (Ezek. 27:8–9). Since the Israelites were generally not seafarers, the Phoenicians generally enjoyed good working relations with Israel. Hiram of Tyre, a friend of David and Solomon, helped Israel equip its merchant fleet (1 Kings 9:26–28).

Phoenician religion was largely a carryover from the Canaanite worship system, which included child sacrifice. The gods were mainly male and female nature deities with Baal as the primary god. The marriage of King Ahab to Jezebel, a Phoenician woman, was a corrupting influence on Israel. Ahab allowed Jezebel to place the prophets of Baal in influential positions (1 Kings 18:19). Years before, King Solomon had lapsed into idolatry by worshipping Ashtoreth, the supreme goddess of the Sidonians (1 Kings 11:5).

Phoenix [Phoe′nix], *date palm*—The name of a harbor in Crete (Acts 27:12, 14; Phenice, KJV).

Phrygia [Phryg′i·a], *dry* or *barren*—A large province of the mountainous region of Asia Minor, visited by the apostle Paul (Acts 2:10; 16:6; 18:23). Because of its size, Phrygia was made a part of other provinces.

In Roman times the region was split between two provinces. The cities of Colossae, Laodicea, and Hierapolis belonged to Asia, while Iconium and Antioch belonged to Galatia.

The apostle Paul visited Phrygia on two journeys (Acts 13:14–14:5, 21; 16:6). He apparently also passed through Phrygia on his third journey (Acts 18:22–24), although his letter to the Colossians suggests he did not found a church there (Col. 2:1). Jews who were at Jerusalem on the Day of Pentecost may have been the first Phrygian converts (Acts 2:10). Jews settled in Phrygia during the Seleucid period. Some of them apparently adopted non-Jewish practices. Consequently, strict Jews became hostile to new ideas (Acts 13:44–14:6).

Phurah [Phu'rah]—See Purah.

Phurim [Phu'rim]—See Purim.

Phut [Phut]—See Put.

Phuvah [Phu'vah]—See Puah.

Phygellus, Phygelus [Phy·gel'lus, Phy·gel'us], *a little fugitive*— A Christian of Asia who deserted Paul when he was imprisoned (2 Tim. 1:15).

Pi-beseth [Pi-be·seth], *mouth of loathing*—A city of lower Egypt about 45 miles northeast of Cairo (Ezek. 30:17).

Pi-hahiroth [Pi-ha·hi'roth], *place where sedge grows*—The site of the final Israelite encampment in Egypt before they crossed the Red Sea. Pi-hahiroth is described as being "between Migdol and the sea" and "opposite" Baal-zephon (Ex. 14:2). Numbers 33:8 has Hahiroth, a shortened form of Pi-hahiroth.

Pilate, Pontius [Pi'late, Pon'tius], *of the sea and armed with a spear*—The fifth Roman prefect of Judea (ruled A.D. 26–36), who issued the official order sentencing Jesus to death by crucifixion (Matt. 27; Mark 15; Luke 23; John 18–19).

Pilate's Personal Life: The Jewish historian Josephus provides what little information is known about Pilate's life before A.D. 26, when Emperor Tiberius appointed him procurator of Judea. The sketchy data suggests that Pilate was probably an Italian-born Roman citizen whose family was wealthy enough for him to qualify for the middle class. Probably he held certain military posts before his appointment in Judea. He was married (Matt. 27:19), bringing his wife, Claudia Procula, to live with him at Caesarea, the headquarters of the province. Pilate governed the areas of Judea, Samaria, and the area south as far as the Dead Sea to Gaza. As prefect he had absolute authority over the non-Roman citizens of the province. He was responsible to the Roman governor who lived in Syria to the north (Luke 2:2).

Pilate never became popular with the Jews. He seemed to be insensitive to their religious convictions and stubborn in the pursuit of his policies. But when the Jews responded to his rule with enraged opposition, he often backed down, demonstrating his weakness. He greatly angered the Jews when he took funds from the temple treasury to build an aqueduct to supply water to Jerusalem. Many Jews reacted violently to this act, and Pilate's soldiers killed many of them in this rebellion. It may be this or another incident to which Luke refers in Luke 13:1–2. In spite of this, Pilate continued in office for ten years, showing that Tiberius considered Pilate an effective administrator.

Pilate's later history is also shrouded in mystery. Josephus tells of a bloody encounter with the Samaritans, who filed a complaint with Pilate's superior, Vitellius, the governor of Syria. Vitellius deposed Pilate and ordered him to stand before the emperor in Rome and answer for his conduct. Legends are confused as to how Pilate died. Eusebius reports that he was exiled to the city of Vienne on the Rhone in Gaul (France) where he eventually committed suicide.

Pilate's Encounter with Jesus: Since the Jews could not execute a person without approval from the Roman authorities (John 18:31), the Jewish leaders brought Jesus to Pilate to pronounce the death sentence (Mark 14:64). Pilate seemed convinced that Jesus was not guilty of anything deserving death, and he sought to release Jesus (Matt. 27:24; Mark 15:9–11; Luke 23:14; John 18:38–40; 19:12). Neither did he want to antagonize the Jews and run the risk of damaging his own reputation and career. Thus, when they insisted on Jesus' crucifixion, Pilate turned Jesus over to be executed (Matt. 27:26; Mark 15:12–15; Luke 23:20–25; John 19:15–16).

Pilate's Character: Pilate is a good example of the unprincipled achiever who will sacrifice what is right to accomplish his own selfish goals. Although he recognized Jesus' innocence and had the authority to uphold justice and acquit Jesus, he gave in to the demands of the crowd rather than risk a personal setback in his career. This is a real temptation to all people who hold positions of power and authority.

Pildash [Pil′dash], *flame of fire*—The son of Nahor (Gen. 22:22).

Pileha [Pi′le·ha]—See Pilha.

Pilha [Pil′ha], *millstone*—One who sealed the covenant with Nehemiah (Neh. 10:24).

Pillar of Fire and Cloud—The visible symbol of God's presence with the Israelites during the exodus. While they were escaping from the Egyptians, and wandering in the wilderness, they were led by a pillar of cloud by day, and a pillar of fire by night (Ex. 14:24; Num. 12:5; Deut. 31:15).

Piltai [Pil·ta′i], *my deliverance*—A priest of the house of Moadiah (Neh. 12:17).

Pinon [Pi′non], *darkness*—An Edomite chief (Gen. 36:41; 1 Chron. 1:52).

Piram [Pi′ram], *wild* or *swift*—A Canaanite king of Jarmuth who was defeated by Joshua (Josh. 10:3).

Pirathon [Pi·ra′thon], *princely*—A town of Ephraim where Abdon the judge lived (Judg. 12:13–15).

Pirathonite [Pi·ra′thon·ite]—An inhabitant or native of Pirathon (Judg. 12:13–15; 1 Chron. 27:14).

Pisgah [Pis′gah], *division*—A part of the Abarim range of mountains overlooking the northeastern end of the Dead Sea (Deut. 3:17, 27; 32:49; 34:1).

Pishon [Pi′shon]—See Pison.

Pisidia [Pi·sid′i·a], *pitchy*—A district of Asia Minor. Paul and Barnabas passed through this area on their first missionary journey, and again on their return (Acts 13:14; 14:24).

Pison [Pi′son], *increase*—One of the rivers of Eden (Gen. 2:11).

Pispah [Pis'pah], *disappearance*—Son of Jether of Asher (1 Chron. 7:38).

Pithom [Pi'thom], *the city of justice*—One of the supply cities, or store cities, in Lower Egypt built by the Israelites while they were slaves in Egypt (Ex. 1:11). Pithom was in the general area of Raamses. Some archaeologists, by the excavations of Naville, suggest that the temple, fortress, and storage chambers discovered at Tell el-Maskhutah, in the valley connecting the Nile River and Lake Timsah, are the remains of biblical Pithom. Others believe that Pithom should be identified with Tell er-Ratabah, about 16 kilometers (10 miles) to the west and closer to the land of Goshen. The site of Pithom remains a subject of doubt and debate.

It is possible that Pithom and Raamses (Ex. 1:11) were built during the reign of Pharaoh Rameses II (who ruled from about 1292–1225 B.C.). Rameses II, however, often made claims to "build" a city, when actually he "rebuilt" it, or strengthened its fortifications. Pithom is supposed by some scholars to be identical with Succoth (Ex. 12:37)—Pithom being the sacred or religious name and Succoth being the secular or civil name.

Pithon [Pi'thon], *harmless*—A descendant of Jonathan, the son of Saul (1 Chron. 8:35; 9:41).

Pleiades [Plei'a·des], *cluster*—A brilliant constellation of seven visible stars (Job 9:9; 38:31; Amos 5:8). It is located on the shoulder of Taurus.

Pochereth-hazzebaim [Po'che·reth-haz·ze·ba'im], *binder (or hunter) of gazelles*—A member of Solomon's body of servants, whose descendants returned from captivity with Zerubbabel (Ezra 2:57; Neh. 7:59). Possibly a reference to the town of Zeboim (Neh. 11:34).

Pollux [Pol'lux]—See Castor and Pollux.

Pontius Pilate [Pon·ti'us]—See Pilate, Pontius.

Pontus [Pon'tus], *the sea*—A large district of Asia Minor extending along the coast of the Black Sea. Six of its kings had the name Mithridates, the last of whom was in bitter conflict with the Romans until 63 B.C. There were many Jews in this district (Acts 2:9–10; 18:2; 1 Peter 1:1).

Pool of Gibeon [Gib·e·on]—See Gibeon, Pool of.

Poratha [Por·a'tha], *fruitfulness*—One of Haman's ten sons, slain in the conflict with the Jews (Est. 9:8).

Porcius Festus [Por'ci·us Fes'tus]—See Festus, Porcius.

Potiphar [Pot'i·phar], *dedicated to Ra*—The Egyptian to whom the Ishmaelites (Gen. 39:1) sold Joseph when he was brought to Egypt as a slave. Potiphar was a high officer of Pharaoh and a wealthy man (Gen. 37:36). In time, he put Joseph in charge of his household. But Potiphar's wife became attracted to Joseph and attempted to seduce him. When he rejected her advances, she falsely accused him and had him imprisoned (Gen. 39:6–19).

Potiphera [Po'ti·phe·ra]—Variant of Potipherah.

Potipherah [Po'ti·phe·rah], *unknown*—A priest of On, the father of Joseph's wife Asenath, and grandfather of Ephraim and Manasseh (Gen. 41:45–50; 46:20).

Potsherd Gate [Pot·sherd]—The gate of Jerusalem looking out over the Valley of the Son of Hinnom (Jer. 19:2).

Potter's Field [Pot'ter]—See Akeldama.

Preparation Day [Prep·a·ra'tion]—The day preceding the Sabbath, the Passover, and other sacred festivals (Mark 15:42; John 19:14, 31). Since no work was done on the Sabbath, extra work must be done the day before to prepare for it.

Prisca [Pris'ca]—A variant of Priscilla.

Priscilla [Pris·cil'la], *ancient*—The wife of Aquila and a zealous advocate of the Christian cause (Rom. 16:3; 1 Cor. 16:19). Her name is also given as Prisca (2 Tim. 4:19). Aquila and Priscilla left their home in Rome for Corinth when the emperor Claudius commanded all Jews to depart from the city (Acts 18:2). Thus, they were fellow passengers of the apostle Paul from Corinth to Ephesus (Acts 18:18), where they met Apollos and instructed him further in the Christian faith (Acts 18:26).

Prison, Gate of the—A gate in the reconstructed wall of Jerusalem (Neh. 12:39).

Prochorus [Proch'o·rus], *leader of the chorus*—One of the seven deacons of the early church (Acts 6:5).

Promised Land—The land of Canaan, which God gave to the Hebrews as their own. See Palestine.

Prophet, False—See False Prophet, The.

Ptolemais [Ptol·e·ma'is]—See Acco.

Ptolemy [Ptol'e·my], *warlike*—The name of the dynasty of Macedonian kings who ruled over Egypt from 305 to 31 B.C.

Pua [Pu'a]—See Puah.

Puah [Pu'ah], *scattered*—The name of two men and one woman in the Old Testament:

1. The second son of Issachar (1 Chron. 7:1), also called Puvah (Gen. 46:13, NRSV), Phuvah (KJV), and Pua (Num. 26:23, KJV). Founder of the family of Punites.

2. One of two midwives whom Pharaoh ordered to kill Hebrew males at their birth (Ex. 1:15). The midwives courageously disobeyed Pharaoh's command.

3. The father of Tola, of the tribe of Issachar (Judg. 10:1).

Publius [Pub'li·us], *popular*—A man of importance who lived on the island of Melita (Acts 28:7–8).

Pudens [Pu'dens], *modest*—A Christian at Rome who sent greetings to Timothy (2 Tim. 4:21).

Puhites [Pu'hites]—See Puthites.

Pul [Pul], *distinguishing*—

1. An African country that, according to the best evidence, should be identified with Phut or Put (Isa. 66:19).

2. A king of Assyria. See Tiglath-pileser.

Punites [Pun·ites]—The descendants of Puah, the son of Issachar (Num. 26:23).

Punon [Pu'non[], *darkness*—A place where the Israelites camped shortly before they entered Moab (Num. 33:42–43).

Purah [Pu'rah], *bough*—A servant of Gideon (Judg. 7:10–11).

Purim [Pu'rim], *lots*—An annual Jewish festival celebrating the deliverance of the Jews in Persia from the destruction planned by Haman. The event is narrated in the book of Esther.

Put [Put], *foreign bowman*—The name of a man and a land or people mentioned in the Old Testament:

1. One of the sons of Ham (Gen. 10:6; Phut, KJV; 1 Chron. 1:8). Put was a grandson of Noah.

2. The land where Put's descendants lived. This nation is mentioned in the Bible in connection with Egypt and Ethiopia (Cush). Some scholars identify this land with Punt, an area on the eastern shore of Africa (possibly Somaliland), famous for its incense. Since Put and Punt are not identical in spelling and because Put was known for its warriors rather than its incense, other scholars believe Put refers to certain Libyan tribes west of Egypt.

Men from Put and Lubim (Libya) were used as mercenary soldiers by the king of Tyre (Ezek. 27:10) and Magog (Ezek. 38:5). But most references in the Bible picture them as allies with Egypt (Jer. 46:9; Ezek. 30:5; Nah. 3:9). Although the warriors of Put were hired to help these different nations secure their borders and win their wars, the prophets point to the futility of such forces in the face of God's mighty power and judgment.

Puteoli [Pu·te'o·li], *wells*—The seaport in Italy where Paul was kindly treated by Christians (Acts 28:13).

Puthites [Pu'thites], *openness*—A family of Kirjath-jearim, descended from Shobal (1 Chron. 2:53; also called Puhites, KJV).

Putiel [Pu'ti·el], *afflicted of God*—Father-in-law of Eleazar, Aaron's son and successor (Ex. 6:25).

Puvah [Pu'vah]—See Puah.

Pyrrhus [Pyr'rhus], *fiery-red*—Father of Sopater of Berea (Acts 20:4). Because not all ancient Greek manuscripts contain Pyrrhus, some translations do not include his name.

Q

Quartus [Quar'tus], *fourth*—A Christian, probably of the Corinthian church (Rom. 16:23). Early church tradition taught that Quartus was one of the seventy sent out by Jesus in Luke 10:1–24, and later became a bishop.

Queen of Heaven—One of the false gods the Israelites worshipped in their days of rebellion. This fertility goddess particularly commanded the worship of wome (Jer. 7:18; 44:17–19, 25). "Queen of heaven" may have been a name for the goddess Ashteroth, also mentioned many times in the books of Kings and Chronicles.

Queen of Sheba [She'ba]—See Sheba.

Quicksands—(Acts 27:17) See Syrtis Sands.

Quirinius, Cyrenius [Qui·ri'ni·us, Cy·re'ni·us], *warrior*—A Roman who was governor of Syria (A.D. 6). He was in charge of the enrollment and the taxing that caused Joseph and Mary to go to Bethlehem just prior to the birth of Christ (Luke 2:1–5).

Qumran, Khirbet [Qum'ran, Khir'bet], *unknown*—The ruins of a community of Essene Jews from about 130 B.C.-135 A.D. This community collected and saved the famous Dead Sea Scrolls discovered in 1947 in caves near the ruins of Khirbet Qumran. See Essenes.

R

Raamah, Raama [Ra′a·mah, Ra′a·ma], *trembling*—
   1. A son of Cush (Gen. 10:7; 1 Chron. 1:9).
   2. A region of southwestern Arabia whose merchants traded with Tyre (Ezek. 27:22).

Raamiah [Ra·a·mi′ah]—See Reelaiah.

Raamses [Ra·am′ses]—See Rameses.

Rabbah [Rab′bah], *great*—Two ancient cites:
   1. A strong city east of the Jordan, chief city of the Ammonites. In David's conflict with them, Aramaeans were used by the Ammonites to attack the Israelites in the rear. Joab divided his army and defeated both forces (2 Sam. 10:8–9, 13–14; 1 Chron. 19:9). Joab later besieged Rabbah and the city was captured (2 Sam. 11:1; 12:26–31; 1 Chron. 20:1–3). The city was denounced by the prophets (Jer. 49:2–6; Ezek. 21:20).
   2. A city of Judah (Josh. 15:60).

Rabbi, Rabboni [Rab′bi, Rab′bo·ni], *my master*—A title of respect given by the Jews to their teachers (Matt. 23:7; John 1:38). It was also applied to doctors and other learned persons. This name was often used for Jesus (John 1:38, 49; 3:2; 6:25; 20:16) and once for John the Baptist (John 3:26).

Rabbith [Rab′bith], *multitude*—A village of Issachar (Josh. 19:20).

Rabboni [Rab′bo·ni]—A form of Rabbi.

Rabdai [Rad′da·i], *subjugating*—David's brother, son of Jesse (1 Chron. 2:14).

Rabmag [Rab′mag], unknown—The title of one of Nebuchadnezzar's chief princes, an official position rather than a proper name (Jer. 39:3, 13).

Rabsaris [Rab'sa·ris], *he who stands by the king*—A title signifying a chief official, not a proper name:

1. One of the officers sent by Sennacharib to lead the attack against King Hezekiah of Judah (2 Kings 18:17).

2. One of Nebuchadnezzar's chief princes (Jer. 39:3, 13); one of those who arranged for Jeremiah's release.

Rabshakeh [Rab'sha·keh]—The title of one of the Assyrian officials sent by Sennacherib to demand the surrender of Jerusalem (2 Kings 18:17; Isa. 36–37).

Racal [Ra'cal]—See Rachal.

Rachab [Ra'chab]—See Rahab.

Rachal [Ra'chal], *traffic*—A town of Judah (1 Sam. 30:29).

Rachel [Ra'chel], *lamb*—The younger daughter of Laban; the second wife of Jacob; and the mother of Joseph and Benjamin.

Jacob met Rachel, the beautiful younger daughter of his uncle Laban, at a well near Haran in Mesopotamia as he fled from his brother, Esau (Gen. 29:6, 11). Jacob soon asked Laban for Rachel as his wife (Gen. 29:15–18). However, it was customary in those days for the groom or his family to pay the bride's family a price for their daughter. Having no property of his own, Jacob served Laban seven years for Rachel, only to be tricked on the wedding day into marrying Rachel's older sister, Leah (Gen. 29:21–25). Jacob then had to serve another seven years for Rachel (Gen. 29:26–30).

Although Rachel was Jacob's favorite wife, she envied Leah, who had given birth to four sons—Reuben, Simeon, Levi, and Judah—while she herself had remained childless (Gen. 29:31–35). Her response was to give her handmaid Bilhah to Jacob. According to this ancient custom, the child of Bilhah and Jacob would have been regarded as Rachel's. Bilhah bore Dan and Naphtali (Gen. 30:1–8), but Rachel named them, indicating they were her children. Rachel's desperate desire to become fruitful is illustrated by her asking for Reuben's mandrakes, which she believed would bring fertility (Gen. 30:14–16). Mandrakes were considered love potions or magic charms by people of the ancient world.

Only after Zilpah, Leah's handmaid, produced two sons—Gad and Asher (Gen. 30:9–13)—and after Leah had borne two more sons and a daughter—Issachar, Zebulun, and Dinah (Gen. 30:17–21)—did Rachel finally conceive. She bore to Jacob a son named Joseph (Gen. 30:22–24), who became his father's favorite and who was sold into Egypt by his jealous brothers. Rachel died following the birth of her second son, whom she named Ben-oni (son of my sorrow). But Jacob later renamed him Benjamin (son of the right hand). Jacob buried Rachel near Ephrath (or Bethlehem) and set a pillar on her grave (Gen. 35:16–20). Jews still regard Rachel's tomb with great respect. The traditional site is about one mile north of Bethlehem and about four miles south of Jerusalem.

Although Rachel was Jacob's favorite wife, the line of David and ultimately the messianic line passed through Leah and her son Judah, not Rachel. "Rachel weeping for her children" (Jer. 31:15; Rahel, KJV; Matt. 2:18) became symbolic of the sorrow and tragedy suffered by the Israelites. Matthew points out that the murder of all the male children in Bethlehem, from two years old and under, by Herod the Great, was the fulfillment of Jeremiah's prophecy (Matt. 2:16–18).

Ragau [Ra'gau]—See Reu.

Raguel [Ra·gu'el]—See Reuel.

Rahab [Ra'hab], *breadth*—A harlot of Jericho who hid two Hebrew spies, helping them to escape, and who became an ancestor of David and Jesus (Josh. 2:1–21; 6:17–25; Matt. 1:5). Rahab's house was on the city wall of Jericho. Rahab, who manufactured and dyed linen, secretly housed the two spies whom Joshua sent to explore Jericho and helped them escape by hiding them in stalks of flax on her roof (Josh. 2:6).

Rahab sent the king's messengers on a false trail, and then let the two spies down the outside wall by a rope through the window of her house (Josh. 2:15). When the Israelites captured Jericho, they spared the house with the scarlet cord in the window—a sign that a friend of God's people lived within. Rahab, therefore, along with her father, her mother, her brothers, and all her father's household, was spared. Apparently she and her family were later brought into the nation of Israel.

Matthew refers to Rahab as the wife of Salmon (Ruth 4:20–21; Matt. 1:4–5; Luke 3:32; Salma, 1 Chron. 2:11). Their son Boaz married Ruth and became the father of Obed, the grandfather of Jesse, and the great-grandfather of David. Thus, a Canaanite harlot became part of the lineage of King David out of which the Messiah came (Matt. 1:5;

Rachab, KJV)—perhaps an early sign that God's grace and forgiveness is extended to all, that it is not limited by nationality or the nature of a person's sins.

The Scriptures do not tell us how Rahab, who came out of a culture where harlotry and idolatry were acceptable, recognized the Lord as the one true God. But her insights recorded in Joshua 2:9–11 leave no doubt that she did so. This Canaanite woman's declaration of faith led the writer of the epistle to the Hebrews to cite Rahab as one of the heroes of faith (Heb. 11:31), while James commended her as an example of one who has been justified by works (James 2:25).

According to rabbinic tradition, Rahab was one of the four most beautiful women in the world and was the ancestor of eight prophets, including Jeremiah and the prophetess Huldah.

Rahab-hem-shebeth [Ra'hab-hem-she'beth], *Rahab sits idle*— A symbolic name given to Egypt (Ps. 87:4; Isa. 30:7). See Rahab the Dragon.

Rahab the Dragon [Ra'hab]—A symbolic creature representing the forces of evil (Job 9:13; 26:12; Pss. 87:4; 89:10; Isa. 30:7; 51:9). The image of Rahab the dragon came to be used as a symbolic name—particularly for Egypt, the land which had held the Hebrews captive for so many years. The book of Revelation carries out the theme of the dragon representing evil (Rev. 20:2).

Raham [Ra'ham], *pity*—A man of the family of Hebron, a descendant of Caleb (1 Chron. 2:44).

Rahel [Ra'hel]—Variant of Rachel.

Rakem [Ra'kem], *varigated* or *multicolored*—A descendant of Manasseh and grandson of Machir and his wife Maacah (1 Chron. 7:16).

Rakkath [Rak'kath], *shore*—A city of Naphtali (Josh. 19:35).

Rakkon [Rak'kon], *the temple*—A town of Dan (Josh. 19:46).

Ram [Ram], *high*—
  1. Son of Hezron and brother of Jerahmeel, descendant of Pharez, of the tribe of Judah (Ruth 4:19; 1 Chron. 2:9; Matt. 1:3; Luke 3:33; Aram, KJV). He was an ancestor of Jesus.

2. Son of Jerahmeel and nephew of the preceding (1 Chron. 2:25–27).

3. Member of the family to which Elihu belonged (Job 32:2).

Rama [Ra′ma]—See Ramah.

Ramah [Ra′mah], *height*—The name of six cities in the Old Testament:

1. Ramah of Benjamin, one of the cities allotted to the tribe of Benjamin (Josh. 18:25) in the vicinity of Beth-el (Judg. 4:5) and Gibeah (Judg. 19:13). According to Judges 4:5, Deborah lived between Ramah and Beth-el.

Shortly after the division of the nation of Israel into two kingdoms, King Baasha of Israel fortified Ramah against King Asa of Judah (1 Kings 15:16–17). Ramah lay on the border between the two kingdoms. The fortification was done to guard the road to Jerusalem so no one from the Northern Kingdom would attempt to go to Jerusalem to worship. Baasha was also afraid these people would want to live in the Southern Kingdom.

When Asa learned that Baasha was fortifying the city, he bribed the Syrians to invade the north (1 Kings 15:18–21) so Baasha's attention would be turned away from Ramah. Meanwhile, Asa dismantled Ramah and used the stones to build two forts of his own nearby at Geba and Mizpah (1 Kings 15:22; 2 Chron. 16:6).

When Nebuchadnezzar invaded Judah, he detained the Jewish captives, including Jeremiah, at Ramah (Jer. 40:1). The captives who were too old or weak to make the trip to Babylonia were slaughtered here. This was the primary fulfillment of the prophecy, "A voice was heard in Ramah, lamentation and bitter weeping, Rachel weeping for her children" (Jer. 31:15), although Matthew also applies it to Herod's slaughter of children after the birth of Christ (Matt. 2:18). This city also figures in the prophecies of Isaiah (10:29) and Hosea (5:8).

2. Ramah of Ephraim, the birthplace, home, and burial place of the prophet Samuel (1 Sam. 7:17; 19:18–23; 28:3). It is elsewhere referred to as Ramathaim Zophim (1 Sam. 1:1). The exact location of this Ramah is unknown.

It was at Ramah that the elders of Israel demanded a king (1 Sam. 8:4) and Saul first met Samuel (1 Sam. 9:6, 10). David sought refuge from Saul in Ramah as well (1 Sam. 19:18; 20:1). In New Testament times the name of this town was Arimathea.

3. Ramah of Naphtali, one of the fortified cities of Naphtali (Josh. 19:36). Ramah appears to have been in the mountainous country northwest of the Sea of Galilee. It is identified with Khirbet Zeitun er-Rama, about 3 kilometers (2 miles) southwest of the modern village of er-Rama and about 17 miles east of Acre.

4. Ramah of Asher, a town on the border of Asher (Josh. 19:29). Ramah is mentioned only once in the Bible and was apparently near the seacoast. It has been identified both with er-Ramia, about 21 kilometers (13 miles) south of Tyre, and with an unknown site north of Tyre but south of Sidon.

5. Ramah of the South, a town of Simeon in the Negev (South country) of Judah (Josh. 19:8; Ramah in the Negev, NIV; Ramah of the Negeb, NRSV; Ramah of the Negev, NASB; Ramath-negeb, NEB; Ramath of the south, KJV). Joshua 19:8 identifies this town as Baalath Beer.

6. Ramah of Gilead (2 Kings 8:29; 2 Chron. 22:6), elsewhere known as Ramoth Gilead. This was an important town on the Syrian border, about 40 kilometers (25 miles) east of the Jordan River. King Ahab was killed in a battle for this site after failing to heed the prophet Micaiah's warning (1 Kings 22:1–40). Ahab's son Joram was wounded in a battle at Ramah (2 Kings 8:28). Here, too, Jehu was anointed to succeed Joram as king of Israel (2 Kings 9:1–13).

Ramath [Ra'math]—See Ramah.

Ramathaim-zophim [Ra·ma·tha'im-zo'phim], *twin heights*— The town of Ephraim where Samuel's father Elkanah lived with his two wives (1 Sam. 1:1). See Ramah No. 4.

Ramathite [Ra'math·ite]—A native of Ramah. Shimei, the overseer of David's vineyards was a Ramathite (1 Chron. 27:27).

Ramath-lehi [Ra'math-le'hi], *hill of the jawbone*—The place where Samson fought the Philistines, and killed a thousand of them with the jawbone of a donkey (Judg. 15:17).

Ramath-mizpah [Ra'math-miz'pah], *hill of the watchtower*—A town on the border of the territory of Dan (Josh. 13:26).

Ramath-mizpeh [Ra'math-miz'peh]—Variant of Ramath Mizpah.

Ramath-negeb [Ra'math-neg·eb]—See Ramah.

Ramath of the South—See Ramah No. 6.

Rameses [Ram'e·ses]—(Ramses)

1. A town in the land of Goshen in Egypt, a section of great fertility, where Joseph settled his people (Gen. 47:11). It was located on the Nile Delta. Since Joseph was well before the time of Rameses II, it has been suggested that the author of Genesis was using the "present day" name for the area, rather than the name used in Joseph's time. One of the supply cities the enslaved Israelites were forced to build was called Raamses (Ex. 1:11). Since the date for the exodus has been set for 1446 B.C., before the time of Rameses II, some think that this is another instance of a "modern" name being applied to the story. At the time of the exodus, the Israelites left from Rameses and marched to Succoth (Ex. 12:37).

2. Rameses, an Egyptian king. See Pharaoh.

Ramiah [Ra·mi'ah], *Jehovah exalted*—Son of Parosh. He renounced his foreign wife (Ezra 10:25).

Ramoth [Ra'moth], *heights*—

1. Son of Bani. He divorced his foreign wife (Ezra 10:29).

2. A Levitical city of Issachar, assigned to the Gershonites (1 Chron. 6:73). See Jarmuth.

3. A town of Gilead.

4. A town of Simeon (1 Sam. 30:27).

Ramoth Gilead [Ra'moth Gil'e·ad], *heights of Gilead*—An important fortified city in the territory of Gad near the border of Israel and Syria. It was approximately 40 kilometers (25 miles) east of the Jordan River. Ramoth Gilead was designated by Moses as one of the cities of refuge (Deut. 4:43; Josh. 20:8). In the time of Solomon, one of the king's 12 district officers was stationed at Ramoth Gilead to secure food for the king's household, since it was a commercial center.

Because of its strategic location near the border of Israel and Syria, Ramoth Gilead was frequently the scene of battles between the two nations. The Jewish historian Josephus says that the city was captured by King Omri from Ben-hadad I. It then changed hands several times. King Ahab enlisted the aid of King Jehoshaphat to retake the city, but he was mortally wounded in the attempt (2 Chron. 28–34). Ahab's son Joram was likewise wounded while attacking Ramoth Gilead (2 Kings 8:28). While Jehu was maintaining possession of Ramoth Gilead, Elisha sent his servant to anoint Jehu king of Israel (2 Kings 9:1–13).

Ramoth-mizpah [Ra′moth-miz′pah]—See Ramath-mizpah.

Ramoth-negeb [Ra′moth-ne′geb]—See Ramah.

Ramses [Ram′ses]—See Pharaoh and Rameses.

Rapha [Ra′pha], *tall*—Two men mentioned in the Old Testament:
1. Also called "the giant," the father of four Philistines from Gath who were killed by David's warriors (2 Sam. 21:15–22).
2. Fifth son of Benjamin (1 Chron. 8:2).

Raphael [Raph·a·el], *God heals*—Traditionally, one of the four angels around God's throne, along with Gabriel, Michael, and Uriel.

Raphah [Ra′phah], *heal*—A man of the tribe of Benjamin (1 Chron. 8:37; also called Rephaiah, 9:43).

Raphu [Ra′phu], *healed*—Father of Palti (Num. 13:9).

Reaia [Re·a′ia]—See Reaiah.

Reaiah [Re·a′iah], *Jehovah has seen*—
1. Son of Shobal (1 Chron. 4:2). He is called Haroeh in 1 Chronicles 2:52.
2. A Reubenite, son of Micah (1 Chron. 5:5); also called Reaia (KJV).
3. Founder of a family of Nethinim, some of whom returned from Babylon (Ezra 2:47; Neh. 7:50).

Reba [Re′ba], *fourth part*—A Midianite king who was slain by the Israelites (Num. 31:8; Josh. 13:21).

Rebecca [Re·bec′ca]—Greek variant of Rebekah (Rom. 9:10).

Rebekah [Re·bek′ah], *a noose* or figuratively speaking, *a maiden who ensnares men by her beauty*—Daughter of Laban and Bethuel. The wife of Isaac and the mother of Esau and Jacob. The story of

Rebekah (Gen. 24) begins when Abraham, advanced in age, instructs his chief servant to go to Mesopotamia and seek a bride for Isaac. Abraham insisted that Isaac marry a young woman from his own country and kindred, not a Canaanite.

When Abraham's servant arrived at Padan-aram, he brought his caravan to a well outside the city. At the well he asked the Lord for a sign that would let him know which young woman was to be Isaac's bride. When Rebekah came to the well carrying her water pitcher, she not only gave the servant a drink of water from her pitcher but she also offered to draw water for his camels. These actions were the signs for which the servant had prayed, and he knew that Rebekah was the young woman whom the Lord God had chosen for Isaac. When the servant asked Rebekah her name and the name of her family, he learned that she was the granddaughter of Nahor (Abraham's brother) and, therefore, was the grand-niece of Abraham. The servant then told Rebekah and her father the nature of his mission, and she chose to go to Canaan and become Isaac's wife. When a famine struck the land of Canaan, Isaac took Rebekah to Gerar, a city of the Philistines (Gen. 26:1–11). Fearful that Rebekah's beauty would lead the Philistines to kill him and seize his wife, he told them she was his sister. Abimelech, king of the Philistines, criticized Isaac for this deception. A similar story is told of Abraham and Sarah, who were scolded for their deception by Abimelech, king of Gerar (Gen. 20:1–18).

Nor was Rebekah above deception. When the time came for Isaac to give his birthright to Esau, she conspired with Jacob and tricked Isaac into giving it to Jacob instead. Jacob was forced to flee to Padan-aram to escape Esau's wrath. As a result of her scheming, Rebekah never again saw her son. Apparently she died while Jacob was in Mesopotamia. She was buried in the cave of Machpelah (Gen. 49:30–31), where Abraham, Isaac, Jacob, Sarah, and Leah were also buried.

Rebekah's name is spelled Rebecca in the New Testament (Rom. 9:10).

Recab [Re'cab]—See Rechab.

Recah [Re'cah]—See Rechah.

Rechab [Re'chab], *a horseman*—

1. A son of Rimmon, a Beerothite. He was one of the assassins of Ish-bosheth (2 Sam. 4:2, 6).

2. Father of Jehonadab who witnessed Jehu's zeal in destroying the worshippers of Baal (2 Kings 10:15, 23), and ancestor of the Rechabites.

3. Father of Malchijah, who helped rebuild the wall (Neh. 3:14).

Rechabites [Re′chab·ites]—Descendants of Jehonadab, son of Rechab (Jer. 35:1–19).

Rechah [Re′chah], *uttermost part*—An unidentified place of Judah (1 Chron. 4:12).

Red Sea—A long, narrow body of water which separates Arabia and Yemen from Egypt, the Sudan, and Ethiopia. It is approximately 1,300 miles long, and considered one of the hottest and saltiest bodies of water on earth. It has very little circulation of waters, and it is also situated over a volcanic area. It is called the Red Sea because of a form of algae which sometimes lends a reddish cast to the waters. Its northern end branches into two channels, the Gulf of Suez and the Gulf of Aqaba. Today, the Red Sea is used heavily for shipping since the Suez Canal has opened access to the Mediterranean.

The Red Sea appears in the Bible in the account of the Hebrew exodus from Egypt (Ex. 14:16; Num. 33:8; Deut. 11:4; Acts 7:36). The word translated "Red Sea" in most translations is the Hebrew *yam suph*, which actually means "sea of reeds." Many scholars agree that the translation "Red Sea" is not accurate. Papyrus reeds and other vegetation do not grow on the Red Sea, and thus it seems that the crossing could not have been here but rather some unidentified body of water bordered with marshy flats and reeds.

It is true, however, that later in Scripture the term *yam suph* is certainly applied to the Red Sea, reeds or no. Solomon had a seaport called Ezion Geber on the shore of the *yam suph* in the territory of Edom, clearly the Gulf of Aqaba, the eastern arm of the northern Red Sea (1 Kings 9:26). Jeremiah also mentions the *yam suph* in connection with Edom. This is not to say that the *yam suph* which the Israelites crossed was the Gulf of Aqaba—this would be highly unlikely, to say the least. It does tell us, however, that at least part of the Red Sea was called the *yam suph*. If the eastern arm was called by this name, it is reasonable to suppose that the western arm (the Gulf of Suez) could have been called *yam suph* also.

The exact place of the famous crossing is not known, speculation has included an unknown marshy lake, possibly in the area which was drained when the Suez canal was built. This area is directly opposite the wilderness of Shur where the Israelites made their first camp (Ex. 15:22).

Reelaiah [Re·el·ai'ah], *made to tremble*—One who came from Babylon with Zerubbabel (Ezra 2:2). In Nehemiah 7:7 he is called Raamiah.

Regem [Re'gem], *friend*—A son of Jahdai (1 Chron. 2:47).

Regem-melech [Re'gem-mel'ech], *friend of the king*—One sent from Beth-el to inquire of the priests concerning the continuation of weeping and fasting (Zech. 7:1–3).

Rehabiah [Re·ha·bi'ah], *Jehovah enlarges*—Son of Eliezer (1 Chron. 23:17; 24:21; 26:25).

Rehob [Re'hob], *open space*—The name of three cities and two men in the Old Testament:
   1. A city in northern Canaan in the upper Jordan River Valley (Num. 13:21). Rehob is the same place as Beth-rehob (Judg. 18:28; 2 Sam. 10:6). When the first spies explored the promised land, they penetrated as far north as this city.
   2. A city in the territory of Asher, near Sidon (Josh. 19:28).
   3. Another city in the territory of Asher (Josh. 19:30). The Israelites did not drive the Canaanites out of one of these Rehobs; the other Rehob was occupied by the Gershonite Levites.
   4. The father of Hadadezer (2 Sam. 8:3–12), king of Zobah. The latter was defeated by David (2 Sam. 8:3, 12).
   5. A Levite who sealed Nehemiah's covenant (Neh. 10:11).

Rehoboam [Re·ho·bo'am], *the people is enlarged*—The son and successor of Solomon and the last king of the united monarchy and first king of the Southern Kingdom, Judah (reigned about 931–913 B.C.). His mother was Naamah, a woman of Ammon (1 Kings 14:31). The Ammonites were the descendants of Lot, and therefore of the line of Arphaxad, of Shem, the line that through Abraham brought forth the Messiah (1 Kings 14:31).

Rehoboam became king at age forty-one (1 Kings 14:21) at a time when the northern tribes were discontented with the monarchy. They were weary of Solomon's heavy taxation and labor conscription. To promote unity, Rehoboam went to Shechem—center of much of the discontent among the northern tribes—to be made king officially and to meet with their leaders. They in turn demanded relief from the taxes and conscription.

Rehoboam first sought advice from older men who were of mature judgment and who had lived through Solomon's harsh years. They assured him that if he would be the people's servant, he would enjoy popular support. When he also sought the counsel of younger men, his arrogant contemporaries, he received foolish advice that he should rule by sternness rather than kindness. Misjudging the situation, he followed the foolish advice. The ten northern tribes immediately seceded from the kingdom and made Jeroboam king.

When Rehoboam attempted to continue his control over the northern tribes by sending Adoram to collect a tax from the people (1 Kin. 12:18), Adoram was stoned to death. Rehoboam fled in his chariot to Jerusalem. The prophet Shemaiah prevented Rehoboam from retaliating and engaging in civil war (1 Kings 12:22–24).

To strengthen Judah, Rehoboam fortified fifteen cities (2 Chron. 11:5–12) to the west and south of Jerusalem, undoubtedly as a defensive measure against Egypt. The spiritual life of Judah was strengthened, too, by the immigration of northern priests and Levites to Judah and Jerusalem because of the idolatrous worship instituted at Beth-el and Dan by Jeroboam (2 Chron. 11:13–17).

Rehoboam's military encounters were primarily with Jeroboam and Egypt. No specific battles with Jeroboam are described in the Bible, but "there was war between Rehoboam and Jeroboam all their days" (1 Kings 14:30). This warring probably involved border disputes over the territory of Benjamin, the buffer zone between the two kingdoms.

In Rehoboam's fifth year Judah was invaded by Shishak (Sheshonk I), king of Egypt, who came against Jerusalem and carried away treasures from the temple and from Solomon's house. When Shemaiah told him that this invasion was God's judgment for Judah's sin, Rehoboam humbled himself before God and was granted deliverance from further troubles (2 Chron. 12:1–12).

Rehoboam did not follow the pattern of David. Instead, he was an evil king (2 Chron. 12:14). During his 17-year reign, the people of Judah built "high places, sacred pillars, and wooden images" (1 Kings 1:23) and permitted "perverted persons" to prosper in the land (1 Kings 14:24). When he died, he was buried in the City of David (1 Kings 14:31).

Rehoboth [Re'ho·both], *broad places*—

1. A city built by Nimrod; apparently a suburb of Nineveh (Gen. 10:11). It was also called Rehoboth-ir.

2. One of three wells dug by Isaac in the valley of Gerar (Gen. 26:22). The first two were claimed by Philistine herdsmen. Since no claims were made on the third one, Isaac named it Rehoboth denoting room, or freedom. Rehoboth is probably present-day Wadi Ruheibeh, about 31 kilometers (19 miles) southwest of Beersheba.

3. A town which was the residence of Saul, king of Edom (Gen. 36:37; 1 Chron. 1:48). Also called Rehoboth by the River.

Rehoboth by the River [Re'ho·both]—See Rehoboth No. 3.

Rehoboth-ir [Re'ho·both-ir]—See Rehoboth No. 1.

Rehum [Re'hum], *beloved*—

1. One who returned with Zerubbabel from Babylon (Ezra 2:2); called Nehum in Nehemiah 7:7.

2. A Persian officer who was perhaps an official in Samaria. He wrote Artaxerxes, king of Persia, denouncing the building of the temple by the Jews (Ezra 4:8–9).

3. Son of Bani, a Levite. He labored on the wall (Neh. 3:17).

4. A chief of the people who signed the covenant with Nehemiah (Neh. 10:25).

5. A priest who returned with Zerubbabel from Babylon (Neh. 12:3, 7).

Rei [Re'i], *friendly*—One who refused to support Adonijah (1 Kings 1:8).

Rekem [Re'kem], *variegation*—Three men and a town of the Old Testament:

1. One of the five kings of Midian. He and Balaam were slain in the conflict with Moses (Num. 31:8; Josh. 13:21).

2. A town of Benjamin (Josh. 18:27).

3. A son of Hebron of Judah (1 Chron. 2:43).

4. A descendant of Machir, son of Manasseh (1 Chron. 7:16). He was also called Rakem.

Release, Year of—See Jubilee.

Remaliah [Rem·a·li'ah], *Jehovah adorns*—Father of Pekah, king of Israel (2 Kings 15:25; 16:1, 5).

Remeth [Rem'eth], *high place*—A town of Issachar (Josh. 19:21).

Remmon, Remmon-methoar [Rem'mon, Rem'mon-me·tho'ar]— See Rimmon.

Remnant [Rem'nant]—A small nucleus of God's people preserved by His unmerited grace, which form a foundation for a new community devoted to His redemptive work. Long before the prophets, a type of remnant theology may be seen in God's preservation of Noah and his family from the great flood (Gen. 7:1). In the same way, God used Joseph in Egypt to sustain a remnant during the worldwide famine (Gen. 45:7).

Remnant theology is also evident in the book of Deuteronomy where Moses warned Israel that they would be scattered, but the obedient remnant would eventually be restored to their homeland (Deut. 4:27–31). This concept was picked up by the prophets and applied to the Hebrew people when they were carried into captivity by the Assyrians and Babylonians. In the eighth century B.C., the prophet Amos proclaimed Israel's doom (Amos 5:15). In Isaiah's vision of Judah's judgment, the prophet warned, "Unless the LORD of Hosts had left to us a very small remnant, we would have become like Sodom" (Isa. 1:9). Isaiah even named one of his sons Shear-jashub, meaning "a remnant shall return" (Isa. 7:3). He predicted that the nation of Judah would be overthrown by a foreign power but that a remnant would survive to serve as a witness to God's continuing work of world redemption (Isa. 10:20–23). The prophet Micah, a contemporary of Isaiah, tied the restoration remnant to God's future reign in Zion (Mic. 2:12–13).

In the New Testament, the apostle Paul applied remnant theology to the church, indicating that God's new people would include both believing Jews and Gentiles (Rom. 9:22–27). Alluding to the seven thousand who had not worshipped Baal in Elijah's time (1 Kings 19:18),

Paul declared, "Even so then, at this present time there is a remnant according to the election of grace" (Rom. 11:5). Throughout history God has always preserved a remnant from among His people to serve as a lighthouse in the midst of a dark and sinful world.

Remphan [Rem'phan]—See Rephan.

Rephael [Reph'a·el], *God heals*—Son of Shemaiah, a Levite (1 Chron. 26:7).

Rephah [Re'phah], *riches*—Son of Beriah (1 Chron. 7:25).

Rephaiah [Re·phai'ah], *healed by Jehovah*—
1. The founder of a family registered with descendants of David (1 Chron. 3:21).
2. A captain of Simeon. He helped destroy a colony of Amalekites and then seized their land (1 Chron. 4:42–43).
3. Son of Tola of Issachar, head of a family (1 Chron. 7:2).
4. Son of Binea, a descendant of Jonathan, Saul's son (1 Chron. 9:43). In 1 Chronicles 8:37 he is called Rapha.
5. Son of Hur (Neh. 3:9).

Rephaim [Reph'a·im], *strong*—The name of a race of giants and a valley in the Old Testament:
1. A race of giants who lived in Palestine before the time of Abraham (Gen. 14:5; 15:20). When the Israelites entered Canaan, a remnant of this giant race seems to have been living among the Philistines (2 Sam. 21:16, 18, 20). The last survivor of the Rephaim was Og, king of Bashan (Deut. 3:11). The kingdom of Og—Gilead, Bashan, and Argob—was called "the land of the giants [Rephaim]" (Deut. 3:13).
2. The valley of Rephaim, called valley of the giants in Joshua 15:8; 18:16. Its fertility was famous (Isa. 17:5). It was here that David defeated the Philistines twice (2 Sam. 5:17–22; 23:13; 1 Chron. 11:15; 14:9). Rephaim lies between Jerusalem and Bethlehem (2 Sam. 23:13).

Rephan, Remphan [Re'phan, Rem'phan], *the shrunken*—A god worshipped by the Israelites in the wilderness (Acts 7:43).

Rephidim [Reph'i·dim], *rests* or *stays*—An Israelite encampment in the wilderness (Ex. 17:1–7). The Amalekites attacked the Israelites at Rephidim (Ex. 17:8–16). During the battle Moses stood on a hill and held the rod of God aloft. Aaron and Hur supported his arms until sundown, and the Israelites won the battle. Rephidim is probably the modern Wadi Feiran in south-central Sinai.

Resen [Re'sen], *bridle*—A suburb of Nineveh, built by Nimrod (Gen. 10:12).

Resheph [Re'sheph], *a flame*—
1. An Ephraimite, son of Beriah (1 Chron. 7:25).
2. A pagan god of the Canaanites, supposed to be lord of the underworld.

Reu [Re'u], *friend*—The son of Peleg in the line of Arphaxad (Gen. 11:18–26).

Reuben [Reu'ben], *behold a son*—
1. The firstborn son of Jacob, born to Leah, Jacob's first wife, in Padan-aram (Gen. 29:31–32; 35:23). Leah named her first son Reuben because the Lord had looked upon her sorrow at being unloved by her husband. By presenting a son to Jacob, she hoped he would respond to her in love.

The only reference to Reuben's early childhood is his gathering of mandrakes for his mother (Gen. 30:14). Years later, as the hatred of Jacob's sons for Joseph grew, it was Reuben who advised his brothers not to kill their younger brother. He suggested that they merely bind him, which would have allowed him to return later to release Joseph to his father (Gen. 37:20–22). It also was Reuben who reminded his brothers that all their troubles and fears in Egypt were their just reward for mistreating Joseph (Gen. 42:22).

When Jacob's sons returned from Egypt, Reuben offered his own two sons as a guarantee that he would personally tend to the safety of Benjamin on the next trip to Egypt (Gen. 42:37). In view of these admirable qualities, it is tragic that he became involved in incest with Bilhah, his father's concubine (Gen. 35:22).

As the firstborn, Reuben should have been a leader to his brothers and should have received the birthright—the double portion of the inheritance (Deut. 21:17). His act of incest, however, cost him dearly. He never lost his legal standing as firstborn, but he forfeited his right to the birthright. When Reuben made his descent into Egypt with Israel, he was father of four sons who had been born to him in Canaan (Gen. 46:9).

2. The tribe of Reuben had an inconspicuous place in Israelite history. The request of the Reubenites and Gadites that they be assigned the district east of the Jordan was granted on condition that they would do their part in the taking of the land. This they did (Num. 32:1–42; Josh. 4:12; 18:7).

Reubenites [Reu′ben·ites]—Descendants of Reuben, son of Israel (Num. 26:7; 1 Chron. 5:6, 26). See Reuben No. 2.

Reuel [Reu′el], *friend of God*—The name of four men in the Old Testament:

1. A son of Esau and Basemath, the daughter of Ishmael (Gen. 36:4, 10; 1 Chron. 1:35).

2. A priest of Midian who became Moses' father-in-law (Num. 10:29; Raguel, KJV). Reuel is also called Jethro (Ex. 3:1). See Jethro.

3. The father of Eliasaph of Gad (Num. 2:14), also called Deuel (Num. 10:20).

4. A son of Ibnijah (1 Chron. 9:8).

Rezeph [Re′zeph], *a hot stone*—A city near Haran mentioned by Sennacherib (2 Kings 19:12; Isa. 37:12).

Rezia [Re′zi·a]—See Rizia.

Rezin [Re′zin], *firm*—Two men mentioned in the Old Testament:

1. A king of Damascus in the time of Jotham and Ahaz of Judah and Pekah of Israel. He was allied with Pekah, their purpose being to dethrone Ahaz and place their own king upon the throne of Judah. Isaiah encouraged Ahaz not to fear these pagan kings (Isa. 7:1–9:12). Ahaz, however, did not listen to Isaiah, and secured the cooperation of Tiglath-pileser of Assyria who beseiged Damascus and killed Rezin (2 Kings 15:37; 16:6–9).

2. Head of a family of Nethinim (Ezra 2:48; Neh. 7:50).

Rezon [Re′zon], *prince*—Son of Eliadah of Zobah (1 Kings 11:23–25).

Rhegium [Rhe′gi·um], *breach*—A city opposite Messina in Sicily on the coast of Italy (Acts 28:13).

Rhesa [Rhe′sa], *head*—A descendant of Zerubbabel and ancestor of Christ (Luke 3:27).

Rhoda [Rho′da], *rose*—A servant of the mother of Mark (Acts 12:13–16).

Rhodes [Rhodes], *a rose*—A large island in the Aegean Sea off the southwest coast of Asia Minor visited by the apostle Paul (Acts 21:1). The island is about 68 kilometers (42 miles) long and about 24 kilometers (15 miles) wide; it lies about 19 kilometers (12 miles) off the coast of the province of Caria.

On the northeast corner of the island was the city of Rhodes, an important commercial, cultural, and tourist center for the Greeks as well as the Romans. At the entrance to the harbor of Rhodes stood the famous Colossus of Rhodes, a huge bronze statue of the sun-god Apollo built by the Greek sculptor Chares between 292 and 280 B.C. This towering statue was one of the seven wonders of the ancient world.

Because the island of Rhodes was on the natural shipping route from Greece to Syria and Palestine, the ship on which Paul traveled during his third missionary journey stopped at Rhodes (Acts 21:1). There is no evidence that Paul conducted any missionary activity on the island during his brief visit; he was in a hurry to get to Jerusalem for the Day of Pentecost. "For Paul had decided to sail past Ephesus" (Acts 20:16).

Ribai [Ri·ba′i], *contentious*—Father of Ittai, a Benjamite (2 Sam. 23:29; 1 Chron. 11:31).

Riblah [Rib′lah], *fertility*—A town of Hamath to which Jehoahaz, son of Josiah and king of Judah, was brought when taken from the throne by Pharaoh Necho (2 Kings 23:33).

Rimmon [Rim′mon], *pomegranate*—Two towns, a rock, a man, and a pagan god:

1. A town in the south of Judah (Josh. 15:32; 1 Chron. 4:32; Zech. 14:10). It was afterward assigned to Simeon (Josh. 19:7).

2. A town of Zebulun assigned to the Levites (Josh. 19:13; 1 Chron. 6:77), also called Rimmonmethoar (KJV).

3. The rock of Rimmon. A rock near Gibeah where the defeated Benjamites remained for four months (Judg. 20:45–47; 21:13). Ravines and caves afforded them safe shelter.

4. A Benjamite whose sons assassinated Ish-bosheth, king of Israel (2 Sam. 4:2).

5. A god of the Syrians (2 Kings 5:18).

Rimmon-methoar [Rim'mon-me·tho'ar]—See Rimmon No. 2.

Rimmon-parez [Rim'mon-par'ez]—See Rimmon-perez.

Rimmon-perez [Rim'mon-per'ez], *pomegranate of the cleft*—A place where the Israelites camped in the wilderness (Num. 33:19–20).

Rimmon, Rock of [Rim'mon]—See Rimmon No. 3.

Rinnah [Rin'nah], *a shout*—A son of Shimon of Judah (1 Chron. 4:20).

Riphath [Ri'phath], *spoken*—Son of Gomer and grandson of Japheth (Gen. 10:3). Also called Diphath in some translations (1 Chron. 1:6).

Rissah [Ris'sah], *a ruin*—A campsite of the Israelites in their wanderings (Num. 33:21–22).

Rithmah [Rith'mah], *health*—A campsite of the Israelites in the wilderness (Num. 33:18–19).

River of Egypt [E'gypt]—

1. The Nile (Gen. 15:18). This and the Euphrates are designated as the bounds of the land of promise, the inheritance of the chosen people.

2. The desert stream, called the river of Egypt (Num. 34:5; 1 Kings 8:65; 2 Kings 24:7). See Egypt, Brook of.

Rizia [Ri'zi·a], *delight*—Son of Ulla of Asher (1 Chron. 7:39).

Rizpah [Riz'pah], *a hot coal*—A concubine of Saul and daughter of Aiah, a Hivite. Her sons were hanged by the Gibeonites during the reign of David (2 Sam. 21:8–11).

Roboam [Ro·bo'am]—See Rehoboam.

Rodanim [Ro'da·nim]—See Dodanim.

Rogelim [Ro'ge·lim], *fullers*—A town in Gilead which was the residence of Barzillai (2 Sam. 17:27; 19:31).

Rohgah [Roh'gah], *clamor*—Son of Shamer of Asher (1 Chron. 7:34).

Romamti-ezer [Ro·mam'ti-e'zer], *I have raised a help*—A son of Heman, a singer (1 Chron. 25:4, 31).

Roman [Ro'man], *strong* or *powerful*—One who lived in Rome (Acts 2:10) or a representative of the Roman government (Acts 25:16; 28:17); anyone who had the rights of citizenship in the empire, irrespective of nationality.

Roman Empire—Modern Israel still bears many signs of the Roman occupation of that country. Ruins of the aqueduct and theater at Caesarea, the Roman encampment at Masada, and the Roman road at Emmaus bring to mind many mental pictures of what life under the Romans must have been like during New Testament times.

Rome was founded about 750 B.C., but it did not reach the status of a world power until several centuries later through victories over the Carthaginians and the Greeks. By New Testament times, the Romans were thoroughly entrenched as the ruling power of the ancient world. Throughout the entire New Testament period various emperors ruled over the Roman Empire. During the reign of Augustus, Christ was born (Luke 2:1). His crucifixion occurred during the reign of the succeeding emperor, Tiberius (Luke 3:1). The martyrdom of James, the brother of John, took place in the reign of the emperor Claudius (Acts 11:28; 12:1–2). Paul appealed his case to the emperor Nero (Acts 25:11). The destruction of Jerusalem prophesied by Jesus (Luke 19:41–44) was accomplished in A.D. 70 by the Roman general Titus, who later became emperor.

Thus, all of the New Testament story unfolded under the reign of Roman emperors. The entire territory around the Mediterranean Sea ruled by the Romans enjoyed a time of peace and prosperity during New Testament times. The great Roman roads were built mainly as military routes from the capital city of Rome into the provinces and territories Rome controlled. A stable money system and improved methods of banking and credit encouraged economic expansion. Rome sent its merchant ships throughout the ancient world, trading in wine, olive oil, and grain.

The general stability of these times contributed to the spread of Christianity throughout the Roman world. Paul could travel easily from one Roman province to another over the great Roman roads and sea routes to spread the gospel. While the Romans themselves worshipped pagan gods, they were generally tolerant of all religions among the peoples and nations whom they controlled.

The book of Acts shows how Christianity spread throughout the Roman Empire. Under Paul, the great missionary to the Gentiles, the gospel was preached as far west as the city of Rome and perhaps even into Spain (Rom. 15:28). By the time Paul wrote his epistle to the Romans, a large Christian community existed in the capital city of Rome (Rom. 1:7). In its early stages, Christianity was ignored by the Romans because they thought it was a harmless sect of Judaism. But this apparently changed when Nero became emperor of Rome.

Many Christians were arrested, tortured, crucified, and burned during his administration, seemingly in an attempt to blame them for the widespread rebellion and unrest that marked his years of rule. This persecution continued under the emperor Domitian.

The Romans worshipped many pagan gods: Jupiter, who was believed to control the universe; Mars, god of war; Juno, patron goddess of women; and Minerva, goddess of war, wisdom, and skill. The capital city of Rome was filled with shrines and temples devoted to worship of these pagan gods. Eventually, of course, the clash between dead idolatry and the living Christ broke down the original "Roman tolerance." But as Paul said, even that served to further the gospel (Phil. 1:12–18).

Rome, City of—Seat of the mighty Roman Empire. Rome was the largest and most magnificent city of its day, with a population of more than one million people in New Testament times. Situated near where the Tiber River meets the Mediterranean Sea, it was called *Urbis Septicollis* ("City of the Seven Hills") because of the seven hills upon which it is built.

When the apostle Paul entered Rome as a prisoner about A.D. 58, the city boasted of a history extending back more than eight hundred years. According to the legends of the Romans, the city was founded in 753 B.C. by Romulus, the son of the Roman god Mars. The city grew across the years as the Roman Empire expanded its power and influence throughout the ancient world.

Rome reached the height of its splendor under the emperor Augustus. Especially notable was the Forum, the center of the city with roads leading off in all directions, and the great outdoor theater known as the Colosseum, where Roman games and public events were held. The city featured more than four hundred temples dedicated to worship of pagan gods. It was also noted for its public buildings, baths, aqueducts, arches, temples, and roads.

To keep from being killed by hostile Jews at Jerusalem, and because he was a Roman citizen (Acts 22:27), Paul appealed to Caesar, an act that ultimately brought him to Rome as a prisoner to await trial. Paul must have seen many of Rome's pagan temples and spectacular public buildings when he entered the city on the famous road known as the Via Appia (Appian Way). He was kept at first under house arrest, and later, according to tradition, as a condemned prisoner in a dungeon near the Forum.

The Great Missionary to the Gentiles proclaimed the gospel to all classes of people while in Rome, especially to Greek-speaking easterners (called "Greeks" in Romans 1:16) and Jews. According to tradition, he was executed outside the city at a spot on the Via Ostia about A.D. 68.

Paul's first known connection with Rome had occurred several years before he actually visited the city. During his ministry at Corinth, he worked with Priscilla and Aquila, who had left Rome when the emperor Claudius expelled all Jews from the city (Acts 18:2). An active Christian church also existed at Rome several years before Paul arrived in the city; these were the Christians to whom Paul addressed his letter known as the epistle to the Romans.

In Paul's time the houses of the wealthy people of Rome were elaborately constructed and situated on the various hills of the city. But the common people lived in tenements, much like the crowded inner city of a modern metropolis. Thousands of people were crowded into these tenements, which were surrounded by narrow, noisy streets with a constant flow of traffic.

The citizens of Rome received food and entertainment from the government. Wine was cheap and plentiful. Admission to the Roman games was free. Thousands of people attended these games, which included contests among the gladiators, chariot races, and theatrical performances. Like Babylon, the city of Rome became a symbol of idolatry and paganism in the New Testament.

The Christians, with their steadfast loyalty to the one true God known through Jesus Christ, and who seemed such a threat to the emperors Nero and Domitian, left an indelible mark on Rome through their martyrdom. Many scholars believe that the eventual fall of Rome was linked to the kind of character that was willing to see "sport" in the death of the enemies of the state.

Rosh [Rosh], *the head*—

1. Son of Benjamin mentioned only in Genesis 46:21. He probably died childless, as a tribal family did not arise from him.

2. A word in Ezekiel 38:2–3; 39:1, translated *chief prince* in the KJV; possibly a northern tribal people.

Rufus [Ru′fus], *red*—Son of Simon of Cyrene who was compelled to carry the cross of Jesus (Mark 15:21; Luke 23:26). It is supposed that he is the same Rufus to whom Paul sent greetings (Rom. 16:13).

Ruhamah [Ru·ha′mah], *mercy is shown*—A name given to the daughter of Hosea. It was a symbolic reference to Israel by the prophet Hosea to indicate the return of God's mercy (Hos. 2:1, KJV, NASB; mercy is shown, NKJV).

Rumah [Ru′mah], *high place*—The residence of the grandfather of Jehoiakim, king of Judah, probably the same as Arumah (2 Kings 23:36).

Ruth [Ruth], *friendship*—The mother of Obed and great-grandmother of David. A woman of the country of Moab, Ruth married Mahlon, one of the two sons of Elimelech and Naomi. With his wife and sons, Elimelech had migrated to Moab to escape a famine in the land of Israel. When Elimelech and both of his sons died, they left three widows: Naomi, Ruth, and Orpah (Ruth's sister-in-law). When Naomi decided to return home to Bethlehem, Ruth chose to accompany her, saying, "Wherever you go, I will go" (Ruth 1:16).

In Bethlehem, Ruth was permitted to glean in the field of Boaz, a wealthy kinsman of Elimelech (Ruth 2:1). At Naomi's urging, Ruth asked protection of Boaz as next of kin—a reflection of the Hebrew law of Levirate marriage (Deut. 25:5–10). After a nearer kinsman waived his right to buy the family property and provide Elimelech an heir,

Boaz married Ruth. Their son, Obed, was considered one of Naomi's family, according to the custom of the day.

Ruth's firm decision—"Your people shall be my people, and your God, my God" (Ruth 1:16)—brought a rich reward. She became an ancestor of David and Jesus (Matt. 1:5).

S

Sabaoth [Sa·ba'oth], *hosts*—A word used as part of a name of God, literally "hosts" (Rom. 9:29; James 5:4). This is the word translated "hosts" in Psalm 44:9. "Lord Sabaoth" means "Lord of Hosts," signifying His control over all the powers of the universe.

Sabbath [Sab'bath], *rest*—The day on which labor ceases and attention is given to worshipping God. It occurs on the seventh day of the week because according to Genesis that was the day on which the Lord rested after creating the world (Gen. 2:1–3). Other sacred days and periods were also called "sabbaths," such as the Day of Atonement, the sabbatical year and the year of Jubilee. From the Flood to the exodus the Sabbath is not definitely mentioned, but before reaching Sinai and before the giving of the Decalogue containing legislation regarding the Sabbath, it appears in the record in connection with the manna in the Wilderness of Sin (Ex. 16:23–26). It was at Sinai that the law was first announced relative to maintaining the sanctity of the Sabbath. It was the fourth commandment (Ex. 20:8–11; 31:16–18; Deut. 5:15).

The Sabbath was to be a day for a holy convocation for divine worship (Lev. 23:3), a sign indicating they were sanctified by Jehovah (Ex. 31:13). When the Jews were restored to their land after the Exile and their Mosaic institutions were reestablished by Ezra and Nehemiah, they covenanted to keep the Sabbath. When traders brought their wares from Tyre to be sold in Jerusalem on the Sabbath, Nehemiah put a stop to it (Neh. 10:31; 13:15–22). In the time of Christ the Pharisees applied the law regarding Sabbath observance in the most scrupulous manner with the result that they missed the whole spirit and purpose of the Sabbath. In opposition to them, in the performance of works of necessity and mercy, our Lord stated that the Sabbath was made for man, that the Son of man is not the slave but the lord of the Sabbath.

Sabeans [Sa·be′ans], *drunkards*—Inhabitants of the kingdom of Sheba in southwestern Arabia (Job 1:15; Joel 3:8).

Sabtah, Sabta [Sab′tah, Sab′ta], *striking*—The third son of Cush, grandson of Ham (Gen. 10:7; 1 Chron. 1:9).

Sabteca [Sab·te′ca]—See Sabtecha.

Sabtecha [Sab·te′cha], *striking*—Son of Cush and grandson of Ham (Gen. 10:7; 1 Chron. 1:9), also called Sabteca or Sabetchah.

Sacar [Sa′car], *wages*—Two Old Testament men:
   1. Father of Ahiam and one of David's men, a Hararite (1 Chron. 11:35). He was called Sharar in 2 Samuel 23:33.
   2. Son of Obed-edom (1 Chron. 26:4).

Sachar [Sa′char]—See Sacar.

Sachia [Sa·chi′a]—See Sachiah.

Sachiah [Sa·chi′ah], *unknown*—A Benjamite, son of Hodesh (1 Chron. 8:10), also called Sachia, Sakia, Shachia.

Sadducees [Sad′du·cees], *followers of Zadok*—The Sadducees were one of the two major sects or special-interest groups among the Jews in New Testament times. These groups (the Pharisees and Sadducees) stood for different principles, but Jesus clashed with both parties at different times during His ministry.

The Sadducees took their name from Zadok, a high priest in the reign of David. They were the party of the priesthood for about two hundred years, ending with the fall of Jerusalem in A.D. 70. Most of the high priests of this time were Sadducees. They were the elite of Jewish society in the time of Jesus. As priests, merchants, and aristocrats, they supported the Roman authorities because they enjoyed a privileged status under Roman rule. In contrast to the Pharisees, they advocated loyalty to the original law of Moses, insisting that interpretation of the law could not be trusted. Also, unlike the Pharisees, they did not believe in the resurrection of the dead, the future state of the soul, or the theory of rewards or punishment after death—beliefs which Jesus challenged (Mark 12:18–27).

Sadoc [Sa′doc], *righteous*—An ancestor of Jesus who lived after the time of the Exile (Matt. 1:14). See Zadok.

Sakia [Sa·ki'a]—See Sachiah.

Sala [Sa'la]—See Shelah.

Salah [Sa'lah], *sprout*—The son of Arphaxad, grandson of Shem, and father of Eber (Gen. 10:24). Also called Shelah (1 Chron. 1:18, 24; Luke 3:35) and Sala (Luke 3:35, KJV). He is in the genealogy of Christ.

Salamis [Sal'a·mis], possibly *salt*—A city at the eastern end of the island of Cyprus (Acts 13:4–5). Tradition teaches that this was the hometown of Barnabas, and that he was eventually stoned to death here by a mob.

Salathiel [Sa·la'thi·el]—See Shealtiel.

Salcah [Sal'cah], *migration*—A town of Bashan (Deut. 3:10; Josh. 12:5; 13:11; 1 Chron. 5:11).

Salchah, Salecah [Sal'chah, Sal'e·cah]—See Salcah.

Salem [Sa'lem], *peaceful*—

    1. The city or area over which Melchizedek was king (Gen. 14:18; Heb. 7:1–2). Its location is uncertain, but many believe that the Salem of Melchizedek was the original Jebusite city of Jerusalem.

    2. An abbreviation of Jerusalem (Ps. 76:2). See Jerusalem and Melchizedek.

Salim [Sa'lim], *peace*—A place near Aenon where John the Baptist baptized (John 3:23).

Sallai [Sal·la'i], *weighed*—Two Old Testament men:

    1. Head of a priestly house after the Exile (Neh. 12:20). He is called Sallu in Nehemiah 12:7.

    2. A chief of the Benjamites (Neh. 11:8).

Sallu [Sal'lu], *weighed*—Two Old Testament men:

    1. Son of Meshullam, a Benjamite. He lived in Jerusalem after the Exile (1 Chron. 9:7; Neh. 11:7).

    2. Head of a priestly house after the Exile (Neh. 12:7). He is called Sallai in Nehemiah 12:20.

Salma [Sal'ma]—See Salmon.

Salmai [Sal'mai], *my thanks*—Head of a family of Nethinim (Ezra 2:46; Neh. 7:48), also called Shalmai, and Shamlai (Ezra 2:46).

Salmon [Sal'mon], raiment—A man and a hill of the Old Testament:

1. Father of Boaz, the husband of Ruth. Descended from Perez and Hezron, he was an ancestor of the family of Jesus (Ruth 4:18–21; Matt. 1:4; Luke 3:32), also called Salmah and Salma.

2. A wooded hill near Shechem where Abimelech cut timber to burn down the tower of Shechem (Ps. 68:14). It is called Zalmon in Judges 9:48.

Salmone [Sal·mo'ne], *clothed*—A point at the eastern extremity of Crete (Acts 27:7). Today it is called Cape Sidero.

Salome [Sa·lo'me], *peace*—The name of two women in the New Testament:

1. The daughter of Herodias by her first husband, Herod Philip, a son of Herod the Great. Her mother left Philip for his half brother, Herod Antipas, the man who imprisoned John the Baptist. The New Testament identifies her only as Herodias's daughter (Matt. 14:6–11; Mark 6:22–28). At the birthday celebration of Herod Antipas, who was now living with Herodias, Salome danced before the king and pleased him greatly. He offered to give her anything she wanted. At her mother's urging, Salome asked for John the Baptist's head on a platter. Salome later married her uncle Philip, tetrarch of Trachonitis (Luke 3:1), and then her cousin Aristobulus.

2. Wife of Zebedee and one of the women who witnessed the crucifixion of Jesus and who later brought spices to the tomb to anoint His body (Mark 15:40; 16:1). Salome apparently was the mother of James and John, two of the disciples of Jesus. She is pictured in the gospel of Matthew as asking special favors for her sons (Matt. 20:20–24). Jesus replied that Salome did not understand what kind of sacrifice would be required of her sons. Probably Mary's sister (John 19:25).

Salt, City of—A city near the Dead Sea allotted to the tribe of Judah (Josh. 15:62; Irmelach, REB). Many scholars identify this city with Khirbet Qumran, about 13 kilometers (8 miles) south of modern Jericho—a site made famous by the discovery of the Dead Sea Scrolls.

Salt Sea—An Old Testament name for the body of water at the southern end of the Jordan Valley (Gen. 14:3). It contains no marine life because of its heavy mineral content. The Salt Sea is also called the Sea of the Arabah (Deut. 3:17). Its modern name is the Dead Sea.

Salt, Valley of—A barren valley, probably south of the Dead Sea, where the nation of Israel won two important victories over the Edomites. The army of King David killed 18,000 Edomites (2 Sam. 8:13; Syrians, KJV, NKJV; Arameans, NASB) in the Valley of Salt. Two centuries later the army of King Amaziah of Judah killed another 10,000 Edomites in this valley (2 Kings 14:7).

Salu [Sa'lu], *exalted*—Father of Zimri. The son was slain for bringing a woman of the Midianites into the camp of Israel (Num. 25:14). See Phinehas.

Samaria, City of [Sa·mar'i·a], *lookout*—The capital city of the northern kingdom of Israel. This ancient city is second only to Jerusalem and Babylon in the number of times it is mentioned in the Bible. Samaria was one of the few major Jewish cities actually founded and built from the ground up by the Israelites. They took most of their cities from other nations and then either rebuilt or renovated them into distinctively Jewish population centers.

Built about 880 B.C. by Omri, the sixth king of Israel (1 Kings 16:24), Samaria occupied a 91-meter (300-foot) high hill about 68 kilometers (42 miles) north of Jerusalem and 40 kilometers (25 miles) east of the Mediterranean Sea. This hill was situated on the major north–south road through Palestine. It also commanded the east–west route to the plain of Sharon and the Mediterranean Sea. Because of its hilltop location, Samaria could be defended easily. Its only weakness was that the nearest spring was a mile distant, but this difficulty was overcome by the use of cisterns.

Samaria withstood an attack by Ben-hadad, king of Syria (2 Kings 6:24–25), but it finally fell to the Assyrians, in 722 B.C., and its inhabitants were carried into captivity. The city was repopulated by "people from Babylon, Cuthah, Ava, Hamath, and from Sepharvaim" (2 Kings 17:24), all bringing their pagan idolatries with them. Intermarriage of native Jews with these foreigners led to the mixed race of Samaritans so despised by full-blooded Jews during the time of Jesus (John 4:1–10).

In excavations of Samaria, archaeologists have uncovered several different levels of occupation by the Israelites. The first two levels, from the reigns of Omri and Ahab, show careful construction, apparently by Phoenician craftsmen. At this time, the city may have been 20 acres in extent, enclosed by an outer wall 6 to 8 meters (20 to 30 feet) thick, with a more narrow inner stone wall about 2 meters (5 feet) thick. A two-story palace was constructed at the higher western end of the hill around some courtyards. In one of these courtyards a pool about 5 by 9 meters (17 by 33 feet) was discovered. This may have been the pool where the blood of Ahab was washed from his chariot after he was killed in a battle against the Syrians (1 Kings 22:38).

The palace was described as an "ivory house" (1 Kings 22:39; Amos 3:15). Excavations near the pool uncovered a storeroom housing five hundred plaques or fragments of ivory used for inlay work in walls and furniture.

The third level of the city, from the period of Jehu (about 841–813 B.C.), gave evidence of additions and reconstruction. Levels four to six covered the period of Jereboam II and showed that repairs had been made to Samaria before the Assyrians captured it in 722 B.C. From this period came several pieces of pottery inscribed with administrative records describing shipments of wine and oil to Samaria. One potsherd recorded the name of the treasury official who received the shipment, the place of origin, and the names of the peasants who had paid their taxes. Structures from the Greek period can still be seen in ruined form. A round tower is a magnificent monument of the Hellenistic age in Palestine. Roman remains include a colonnaded street leading from the west gate, an aqueduct, a stadium, and an impressive theater.

The small village of Sebastiyeh—an Arabic corruption of the Greco-Roman name Sebaste—now occupies part of the ancient site of this historic city. Even after the Israelite residents of Samaria were deported, the city continued to be inhabited by several different groups under the successive authority of Assyria, Babylonia, Persia, Greece, and Rome. Herod the Great, ruler in Palestine (ruled 37 B.C.–A.D. 4) when Jesus was born, made many improvements to Samaria and renamed it Sebaste—the Greek term for Augustus—in honor of the emperor of Rome. This Herodian city is probably the "city of Samaria" mentioned in the book of Acts (8:5).

Samaria, Region of [Sam′ar·i·a], *guardianship*—By the time of Jesus, the land of Israel east of the Jordan was divided into three provinces: Galilee, Samaria, and Judea. Samaria was sandwiched between Galilee to the north and Judea to the south, but the animosity between Jews and Samaritans was so strong that Jews traveling from Galilee to Judea would cross the Jordan and travel through Decapolis and Perea rather than set foot in Samaritan territory.

Samaritan [Sam′ar·i·tan]—The inhabitants of the district of Samaria, between the districts of Judea and Galilee on the east side of the Jordan River. In the days of the divided kingdom, this was the territory of Ephraim and the half-tribe of Manasseh. When the Northern Kingdom fell into the hands of the Assyrians in 722 B.C., most of the inhabitants were deported and scattered through Assyria and Mesopotamia. The Assyrian king repopulated the land with foreigners (2 Kings 17:24) who intermarried with the remaining Israelites. These settlers were troubled by lions, and assumed that they were offending the god of the land, so they asked to have a priest of Israel come and teach them how to worship God (2 Kings 17:25–29). What developed was a strange mixture of Judaism and paganism. The Samaritans were neither pure religiously nor ethnically, and relationships with the rest of the Jews were strained. When the remnant returned under Zerubbabel, the Samaritans offered to help with the temple project.

Zerubbabel and the others refused this offer because the Samaritans were not Hebrews, and those who were had disobeyed God by marrying foreigners and participating in pagan worship. The Samaritans were offended and set about to hinder the work (Ezra 4:1–10). Later, when Nehemiah came back to work on the wall, the Samaritans continued to cause trouble. No doubt the divorcing of the pagan wives did not make the relationship any easier. Later, the Samaritans built a temple of their own on Mount Gerizim, rejecting the temple in Jerusalem and the religion of the returned captives. At some point, the pagan elements of 2 Kings 17:29 were weeded out of the Samaritan practice of religion. Today, Samaritans accept only the five books of Moses as authoritative, and reject the rest of the Old Testament and the Talmud. Very few Samaritans survived the upheaval and religious persecution of the Holy Roman Empire, but they still retain many of their ancient beliefs and continue to sacrifice a Passover lamb on Mount Gerizim every year.

Samgar-nebo [Sam'gar-ne'bo], *sword of Nebo*—An officer of Nebuchadnezzar who participated in the siege on Jerusalem (Jer. 39:3).

Samlah [Sam'lah], *a garment*—An Edomite king of the city of Masrekah (Gen. 36:36–37).

Samos [Sa'mos], *a sandy bluff*—An island in the Aegean Sea, near the coast of Lydia in Asia Minor (Acts 20:15).

Samothrace [Sam·o·thra'ce], *height of Thrace*—An island off the coast of Thrace in the Aegean Sea (Acts 16:11).

Samson [Sam'son], *sunny*—A hero of Israel known for his great physical strength as well as his moral weakness. The last of the "judges," or military leaders, mentioned in the book of Judges, Samson led his country in this capacity for about twenty years.

Samson lived in a dark period of Israelite history. After the generation of Joshua died out, the people of Israel fell into a lawless and faithless life. The author of the book of Judges summarized these times by declaring, "There was no king in Israel; everyone did what was right in his own eyes" (Judg. 17:6; 21:25). The standard of God's Word, His Law as handed down by Moses, was ignored.

Samson was a product of that age, but his parents gave evidence of faith in the Lord. During a time when the Philistines were oppressing the Israelites (Judg. 13:1), the Lord announced to Manoah and his wife that they would bear a son who would be raised as a Nazirite (Judg. 13:5, 7). This meant that Samson should serve as an example to Israel of commitment to God. Through most of his life, however, Samson fell far short of this mark.

Samson's mighty physical feats are well known. With his bare hands he killed a young lion that attacked him (Judg. 14:5–6). He gathered three hundred foxes (jackals; Judg. 15:4, REB) and tied them together, then sent them through the grain fields with torches in their tails to destroy the crops of the Philistines.

On one occasion, he broke the ropes with which the enemy had bound him (Judg. 15:14). He killed a thousand Philistine soldiers with the jawbone of a donkey (Judg. 15:15). And, finally, he carried away the massive gate of Gaza, a city of the Philistines, when they thought they had him trapped behind the city walls (Judg. 16:3).

But in spite of his great physical strength Samson was a foolish man. He took vengeance on those who used devious means to discover the answer to one of his riddles (Judg. 14). When deceived by his enemies, his only thought was for revenge, as when his father-in-law gave away his wife to another man (Judg. 15:6–7). He had not learned the word of the Lord, "Vengeance is mine" (Deut. 32:35).

Samson's life was marred by his weakness for pagan women. As soon as he became of age, he fell in love with one of the daughters of the Philistines. He insisted on marrying her, in spite of his parents' objection (Judg. 14:1–4).

This was against God's law, which forbade intermarriage of the Israelites among the women of Canaan. On another occasion he was almost captured by the Philistines while he was visiting a prostitute in the city of Gaza. Samson eventually became involved with Delilah, a woman from the valley of Sorek (Judg. 16:4), who proved to be his undoing (Judg. 16). The Philistines bribed her to find out the key to his strength. She teased him until he finally revealed that the secret was his uncut hair, allowed to grow long in accord with the Nazirite law. While Samson slept, she called the Philistines to cut his hair and turned him over to his enemies. Samson became weak, not only because his hair had been cut but also because the Lord had departed from him (Judg. 16:20).

After his enslavement by the Philistines, Samson was blinded and forced to work at grinding grain. Eventually he came to his senses and realized that God had given him his great strength to serve the Lord and his people. After a prayer to God for strength, he killed thousands of the enemy by pulling down the pillars of the temple of Dagon (Judg. 16:28–31). That one great act of faith cost Samson his life, but it won for him a place among the heroes of faith (Heb. 11:32). Out of weakness he was made strong by the power of the Lord (Heb. 11:34).

Samson was a person with great potential who fell short because of his sin and disobedience. Mighty in physical strength, he was weak in resisting temptation. His life is a clear warning against the dangers of self-indulgence and lack of discipline.

Samuel [Sam´u·el], *name of God*—The earliest of the great Hebrew prophets (after Moses) and the last judge of Israel. Samuel led his people against their Philistine oppressors. When he was an old man,

Samuel anointed Saul as the first king of Israel and later anointed David as Saul's successor. Samuel is recognized as one of the greatest leaders of Israel (Jer. 15:1; Heb. 11:32).

Samuel's birth reveals the great faith of his mother, Hannah (1 Sam. 1:2–22; 2:1). Samuel's mother, Hannah, was the second wife of her husband, and she had a great sorrow for she was barren. The other wife had both sons and daughters, and mocked Hannah because she was childless. In spite of the fact that she knew that her husband loved her very much, Hannah longed for children. Each year, Elkanah took his family to Shiloh to make sacrifices to the Lord, and one year Hannah went into the tabernacle and wept and prayed before the Lord. She vowed that if the Lord would give her a son, she would give that son back to the Lord. God granted her prayer, and a year later, Samuel was born.

Hannah stayed at home until Samuel was old enough to be weaned, and then she brought him to Shiloh, and left him in the care of the high priest. True to her vow, she was giving him back to the Lord. Every year, she returned with a new little robe for Samuel, and the Lord blessed her with five more children.

At a very early age, Samuel went to live with Eli the priest, who taught the boy the various duties of the priesthood. Here Samuel heard the voice of God, calling him to special service as a priest and prophet in Israel (1 Sam. 3:1–20). The first prophetic message he received was when he was still a child, concerning the wickedness of Eli's sons. After Eli's death, Samuel became the judge of Israel in a ceremony at Mizpah (1 Sam. 7). This event was almost turned to disaster by an attack from the Philistines, but the Lord intervened with a storm that routed the enemies and established Samuel as God's man. The godly Samuel erected a memorial stone, which he called "Ebenezer," meaning "Stone of Help." "Thus far the LORD has helped us," he declared (1 Sam. 7:12).

In the early part of his ministry, Samuel served as a traveling judge. With his home in Ramah, he made a yearly circuit to Beth-el, Gilgal, and Mizpah. In the person of Samuel, judges became more than military leaders called upon for dramatic leadership in times of national crises. Samuel became a judge with a permanent leadership office, an office approaching that of a king. When the people clamored for a king like those of the surrounding nations (1 Sam. 8:5), Samuel was reluctant to grant their request. He took this as a rejection of his long years of godly service on behalf of the people. He also was aware of the evils that went along with the establishment of a royal house. But the Lord helped Samuel to see the real issue: "Heed the voice of the people in all that they say to you; for they have not rejected you, but they have rejected Me, that I should not reign over them" (1 Sam. 8:7).

The person whom Samuel anointed as first king of Israel turned out to be a poor choice. Saul was handsome, likable, and tall. But he had a tragic flaw that led ultimately to his own ruin. He disobeyed God by taking spoils in a battle rather than wiping out all living things, as God had commanded (1 Sam. 15:18–26). Saul's false pride and extreme jealousy toward David also led him into some serious errors of judgment.

When God rejected Saul as king, He used Samuel to announce the prophetic words (1 Sam. 15:10–35). Samuel was faithful in presenting the stern words of rejection. Although he had no further dealings with Saul, Samuel mourned for him and for the death of the dream (1 Sam. 15:35). Samuel was then sent by the Lord to Bethlehem, to the house of Jesse, where he anointed the young man David as the rightful king over His people (1 Sam. 16:1–13).

In addition to his work as judge, prophet, and priest, Samuel is also known as the traditional author of the books of First and Second Samuel. He may have written much of the material contained in 1 Samuel during the early years of Saul's reign. After Samuel's death (1 Sam. 25:1), these books were completed by an unknown writer, perhaps Abiathar, the priest who served during David's administration.

When Samuel died, he was buried in his hometown of Ramah and was mourned by the nation (1 Sam. 25:1; 28:3). But he had one more message to give. After Samuel's death, Saul visited a fortune teller at Endor (1 Sam. 28). This fortune teller gave Saul a message that came from the spirit of Samuel: "The LORD has departed from you and has become your enemy" (1 Sam. 28:16). Even from the grave Samuel still spoke the word of God!

In many ways Samuel points forward to the person of the Savior, the Lord Jesus Christ. In the story of Samuel's birth, the direct hand of the Lord can be seen. In his ministry as judge, prophet, and priest, Samuel anticipates the ministry of the Lord as well as the work of his forerunner, John the Baptist. As Samuel marked out David as God's man, so John the Baptist pointed out Jesus as the Savior.

Sanballat [San·bal'lat], *strength*—A Horonite, probably a man of Beth-horon or of Horonaim in Moab. He had considerable influence in Samaria and served Artaxerxes (Neh. 2:10, 19; 4:2).

Sanctuary—A holy place, a place set apart. God commanded the Israelites to build Him a sanctuary, a place that would be set apart as holy and where His spirit would rest (Ex. 25:8; 36:1). After the Hebrews entered the land of Canaan, they set up the sanctuary at Shiloh (Josh. 18:1). Many years later, David prepared the materials for a permanent sanctuary, the temple which his son Solomon would build (1 Chron. 22:19). The psalmist also describes heaven as God's sanctuary (Ps. 102:119), and in the New Jerusalem there will be no temple or sanctuary because the "the Lord God Almighty and the Lamb are its temple" (Rev. 21:22).

Sanhedrin [San'he·drin], possibly *sitting together*—The Jewish Sanhedrin, also referred to as the Council, was the highest ruling body among the Jews in New Testament times. This group probably evolved from the council of advisors to the high priest during the years when the Jewish people lived under the domination of the Persians and the Greeks from about 500 to 150 B.C.

The Council originally was composed of leading priests and distinguished aristocrats among the Jewish people, but later scribes and Pharisees and Sadducees were added to the group. With an assembly of seventy-one members, the Council was headed by the high priest. The body was granted limited authority over certain religious, civil, and criminal matters by the Romans during their years of dominance in Palestine.

Most of the day-to-day business was left to the Sanhedrin, which was permitted to have its own police force. However, the Council was denied the right to exercise the death penalty (John 18:31). In spite of these restrictions, the Sanhedrin exercised considerable influence in religious matters.

The Council played a prominent role in the arrest and trial of Jesus, although it is not clear whether He was formally tried by the Council or given preliminary hearings. Christ was arrested by the temple police in the Garden of Gethsemane (Mark 14:43) and subjected to false accusations before the high priest (Matt. 26:59). Several of the apostles, including Peter, John, and Paul, were charged before the Sanhedrin (Acts 4:1–23; 5:17–41; 22–24) in later years.

Prominent members of the Sanhedrin mentioned in a favorable light in the New Testament were Joseph of Arimathea (Mark 15:43); Gamaliel (Acts 5:34); and Nicodemus (John 3:1; 7:50). During most of its history, the Council met at Jerusalem. But after A.D. 150, it convened at Tiberias, a Roman city on the shores of the Sea of Galilee.

Sansannah [San·san′nah], *palm leaf*—A town in the south of Judah (Josh. 15:31). It was probably the same as Hazar-susah in Joshua 19:5.

Saph [Saph], *a basin or threshold*—A giant of the Philistines. In a conflict at Gob he was slain by Sibbechai the Hushathite (2 Sam. 21:18). In 1 Chronicles 20:4 he is called Sippai.

Saphir [Saph′ir]—See Shaphir.

Sapphira [Sapph·i′ra], *beautiful*—The wife of Ananias. Together this couple sold a piece of real estate and donated part of the money to the apostles. Trying to give an appearance of sacrificial generosity, they pretended that the money they donated was the whole sum. Peter rebuked them for their dishonesty, and God struck both of them dead. This remarkable example of God's omniscience, and His intolerance of sin was a frightening lesson to the early church (Acts 5:1–10).

Sarah, Sarai [Sar′ah, Sar′a·i], *noble lady*—The name of two women in the Bible:

1. The wife of Abraham, and the mother of Isaac. Sarah's name was originally Sarai, but it was changed to Sarah by God, much as her husband's name was changed from Abram to Abraham. Ten years younger than Abraham, Sarah was his half sister; they had the same father but different mothers (Gen. 20:12).

Sarah was about 65 years old when she and Abraham left Haran (Gen. 12:5; 17:7). Passing through Egypt, Abraham introduced Sarah as his sister, apparently to keep himself from being killed by those who would be attracted by Sarah's beauty (Gen. 12:10–20; also see 20:1–18).

In spite of God's promise to Abraham that he would become the father of a chosen nation, Sarah remained barren. When she was 75, she decided that the only way to realize God's promise was to present to

Abraham her Egyptian maidservant, Hagar, by whom he could father a child. Hagar bore a son named Ishmael (Gen. 16:1–16).

When Sarah was 90 years old, far beyond her childbearing years, she gave birth to a son, Isaac—the child of promise (Gen. 21:1–7). After Isaac was born, Sarah caught Ishmael mocking the young child and, with God's approval, sent both Ishmael and Hagar into the wilderness.

At the age of 127, Sarah died at Kirjath-arba (Hebron) and was buried by Abraham in the cave of Machpelah (Gen. 23:1–20). Sarah is the only woman in the Bible whose age was recorded at death—a sign of her great importance to the early Hebrews. The prophet Isaiah declared Abraham and Sarah as the father and mother of the Hebrew people: "Look to Abraham your father, and to Sarah who bore you" (Isa. 51:2).

In the New Testament the apostle Paul pointed out that "the deadness of Sarah's womb" (Rom. 4:19) did not cause Abraham to waver in his faith; he believed the promise of God (Rom. 9:9). The apostle Peter cited Sarah as an example of the holy women who trusted in God, possessed inward spiritual beauty, and were submissive to their husbands (1 Peter 3:5–6). The writer of the epistle to the Hebrews also includes Sarah as one of the spiritual heroines in his roll call of the faithful (Heb. 11:11).

2. A daughter of Asher (Num. 26:46, KJV; Serah, NKJV, NIV).

Saraph [Sar'aph], *burning*—A descendant of Shelah, the son of Judah (1 Chron. 4:22).

Sardis [Sar'dis], *red ones*—A city of Asia Minor at the foot of Mount Tmolus, on the east bank of the Pactolus River (Rev. 1:11; 3:1, 4). It was the capital of Lydia, in western Asia (modern Turkey). The church in this city is one of the seven addressed in the beginning of Revelation.

Sardites [Sar'dites]—Those descended from Zebulon's son Sered (Num. 26:26).

Sarepta [Sa·rep'ta]—See Zarephath.

Sargon [Sar'gon], *prince of the sun*—Three kings of ancient Mesopotamia had this name, but only one is mentioned in the Bible. Sargon II was one of the greatest of Assyrian kings. His immediate predecessor was Shalmaneser IV, who had besieged Samaria for three years (2 Kings 17:3–6; 18:9–12). Sargon had apparently succeeded him by the time the city actually fell in 722 B.C., and according to an inscription found in his palace, he claimed the glory of victory for himself. The people of Samaria were carried away into captivity, and foreigners imported to take their place in the land (2 Kings 17:6, 24).

Sargon is only mentioned by name once in the Bible, in the book of Isaiah. The city of Ashdod had rebelled against Assyria, and Sargon retook the city. When this happened, God instructed Isaiah to walk around naked and barefoot as a sign of what would happen to Egypt and Ethiopia as they fought against Assyria. This may have been a warning to Judah to avoid entering the conflict.

Sarid [Sar'id], *survivor*—A village or landmark in the southern district of Zebulun (Josh. 19:10, 12).

Saron [Sa'ron]—(Acts 9:35) See Sharon.

Sarsechim [Sar'se·chim]—A prince of Nebuchadnezzar (Jer. 39:3).

Saruch [Sa'ruch]—See Serug.

Satan [Sa'tan], *adversary*—Satan, or Adversary, is the most frequently used name for the devil in the New Testament, appearing over fifty times. Devil, or Slanderer is used over thirty times. Satan, the personification of evil in this world, is the great superhuman enemy of God, His people, and all that is good. His character is vile and evil, and he is portrayed as the great deceiver. So sly is Satan in his deception that he sometimes transforms himself into an angel of light (2 Cor. 11:14).

Satan is mentioned first by name in Job 1:6–12; 2:1. His first appearance in the history of mankind was in Eden as the seducer of Adam and Eve (Gen. 3:1–6; 2 Cor. 11:3; Rev. 12:9). Regarded by many scholars as a fallen angel, Satan has a continuing ambition to replace God and have others worship him (Matt. 4:8–9). He constantly tempts people to try to entice them into sin (1 Thess. 3:5). In falling from God's favor, Satan persuaded other angels to join him in his rebellion (Rev. 12:9). When Christ returns, Satan will be defeated and ultimately cast into the lake of fire (Rev. 20:1–10).

The following names or titles for Satan in the New Testament throw further light on the devil's character: Beelzebub, ruler (or prince) of demons (Matt. 12:24); the wicked one (Matt. 13:19); the enemy (Matt. 13:39); murderer (John 8:44); a liar (John 8:44); ruler of this world (John

12:31; 14:30); god of this age (2 Cor. 4:4); Belial (which means wickedness, or ungodliness; found in the Old Testament: Deut. 15:9; Ps. 41:8; Prov. 19:28; as well as 2 Cor. 6:15); prince of the power of the air (Eph. 2:2); ruler of darkness (Eph. 6:12); the tempter (1 Thess. 3:5); the king of death (Heb. 2:14); a roaring lion and adversary (1 Peter 5:8); angel of the bottomless pit, Abaddon (Destruction), and Apollyon (Destroyer), (Rev. 9:11); the dragon (Rev. 12:7); accuser of our brethren (Rev. 12:10); serpent of old (Rev. 20:2); and the deceiver (Rev. 20:10).

Satan's character is one of cunning (Gen. 3:1 and 2 Cor. 11:3); he is slanderous (Job 1:9); fierce (Luke 8:29); deceitful (2 Cor. 11:14); powerful (Eph. 2:2); proud (1 Tim. 3:6); cowardly (James 4:7) and wicked (1 John 2:13). He has power over the wicked. They are his children (Acts 13:10; 1 John 3:10); they do his will (John 8:44), they are punished with him (Matt. 25:41). He possesses (Luke 22:3); blinds (2 Cor. 4:4); deceives (Rev. 20:7–8); and ensnares (1 Tim. 3:7).

Satan also has power over God's people to tempt (1 Chron. 21:1); afflict (Job 2:7); oppose (Zech. 3:1); sift (Luke 22:31); deceive (2 Cor. 11:3); and to disguise himself (2 Cor. 11:14–15). But the believers are not powerless; they can watch against Satan (2 Cor. 2:10–11); fight against him (Eph. 6:11–16); resist him (James 4:7; 1 Peter 5:9) and overcome him (1 John 2:13; Rev. 12:10–11). Best of all, Christ has triumphed over Satan. This was predicted (Gen. 3:15); portrayed (Matt. 4:1–11); proclaimed (Luke 10:18) and perfected (Mark 3:22–28). What this means to believers in Christ is thoroughly explained in the eighth chapter of Paul's epistle to the Romans. "There is now no condemnation to those who are in Christ Jesus [no falling into Satan's ways] who do not walk according to the flesh, but according to the Spirit" (Rom. 8:1). The last part of the chapter particularly talks about the believer's ability to live the Christian life, of Christ's intercession on the believer's behalf, and the fact that nothing can separate the believer from the love of God. This is a life lived with the knowledge of Satan and his enmity to the people of God, but it is not a life of fear.

Saul [Saul], *asked* (of God)—The name of three men in the Bible:

1. The sixth of the ancient kings of Edom (Gen. 36:36–38). He was called Shaul in 1 Chronicles 1:48.

2. The son of Kish and the first king of Israel (1 Sam. 9:2–31:12; 1 Chron. 5:10–26:28). Saul lived in turbulent times. For many years,

Israel had consisted of a loose organization of tribes without a single leader. In times of crisis, leaders had arisen; but there was no formal government. Samuel was Saul's predecessor as Israel's leader; but he was a religious leader, not a king. Threatened by the warlike Philistines, the people of Israel pressured Samuel to appoint a king to lead them in their battles against the enemy. Samuel gave in to their demands and anointed Saul as the first king of the nation of Israel.

Saul's Qualifications: Saul had several admirable qualities that made him fit to be king of Israel during this period in its history. He was a large man of attractive appearance, which led to his quick acceptance by the people. In addition, he was from the tribe of Benjamin, situated on the border between Ephraim and Judah. Thus, he appealed to both the northern and southern sections of Israel. Furthermore, he was a capable military leader, as shown by his victories early in his career.

One of the most important episodes of Saul's career was his first encounter with the Philistines. Saul took charge of 2,000 men at Michmash, leaving his son Jonathan with 1,000 men at Gibeah. After Jonathan made a successful, but unplanned, attack on a company of Philistines at Geba, the reaction of the Philistine forces drove the Israelites back to Gilgal. The Philistines gained control of central Canaan, and Saul's defeat seemed imminent. But Jonathan burst in unexpectedly upon the Philistines at Michmash, succeeding in starting a panic in their camp. Saul took advantage of this and routed the Philistines. This victory strengthened Saul's position as king.

Saul's Mistakes: Saul's first sin was his failure to wait for Samuel at Gilgal (1 Sam. 13:8–9). There he assumed the role of a priest by making a sacrifice to ask for God's blessing. His second sin followed soon afterward. After defeating Moab, Ammon, and Edom, Saul was told by Samuel to go to war against the Amalekites and to "kill both man and woman, infant and nursing child, ox and sheep, camel and donkey" (1 Sam. 15:3). Saul carried out his instructions well except that he spared the life of Agag, the king, and saved the best of the animals. When he returned, he lied and told Samuel that he had followed the instructions exactly.

Saul's disobedience in this case showed that he could not be trusted as an instrument of God's will. He desired to assert his own will instead. Although he was allowed to remain king for the rest of his life, the Spirit of the Lord departed from Saul. He was troubled by an evil spirit that brought bouts of madness. Meanwhile, Samuel went to Bethlehem to anoint David as the new king.

Saul and David: Saul's last years were tragic, clouded by periods of depression and gloom. David was brought into Saul's court to play soothing music to restore him to sanity. Saul was friendly toward David at first, but this changed as David's leadership abilities emerged. Enraged by jealousy, Saul tried to kill David several times. But David succeeded in eluding these attempts on his life for many years, often with the aid of Saul's son Jonathan and his daughter Michal.

Saul's Death: The closing years of Saul's life brought a decline in his service to his people and in his personal fortunes. Rather than consolidating his gains after his early victories, Saul wasted his time trying to kill David. Meanwhile, the Philistines sensed Israel's plight and came with a large army to attack the Hebrew nation. Saul's army was crushed, and three of his sons, including Jonathan, were killed. Wounded in the battle, Saul committed suicide by falling on his own sword.

An Appraisal of Saul: Saul is one of the most tragic figures in the Old Testament. He began his reign with great promise but ended it in shame. As Israel's first king, he had the opportunity to set the pattern for all future leaders. His weakness was his rebellious nature and his inability to adapt to the necessity of sharing power and popularity.

Saul also used his power to pursue unworthy purposes and wasted much time and energy in fruitless attempts on David's life. Commercial enterprises were not encouraged during his reign. As a result, the economic condition of the nation was not good. Saul also failed to unite the various tribes into one nation. Saul allowed the religious life of his people to deteriorate as well. However, he did provide distinct services to his people through his military actions. His victories paved the way for the brilliant career of his successor, David.

3. The original name of Paul, a persecutor of the church, who became an apostle of Christ and a missionary of the early church (Acts 7:58–9:26; 11:25–13:9).

Sceva [Sce′va], *mind reader*—A Jewish chief priest in Ephesus at the time of Paul (Acts 19:14–16). His seven sons attempted to cast out demons in the name of "Jesus whom Paul preaches." The demons recognized their lack of authority, and the demon-possessed man attacked them, wounding them and forcing them to flee naked and bleeding.

Scythian [Scyth′i·an], *rude* or *rough*—A native of Scythia, the region north of the Black Sea (Col. 3:11).

Sea, Brazen—See Brazen Sea.

Sea, Chinnereth [Chin·ner·eth]—See Galilee, Sea of.

Sea, Dead—See Dead Sea.

Sea, Molten—See Brazen Sea.

Sea of Galilee [Gal·i·lee]—See Galilee, Sea of.

Sea of Glass—The sea before the throne of God in the throne room of heaven (Rev. 4:6; 15:2). When Moses and the elders of Israel went up on the mountain at Sinai, they saw God standing on a "paved work of sapphire stone, and it was like the very heavens in its clarity" (Ex. 24:10). Ezekiel's vision of God describes the firmament of heaven as a clear crystal (Ezek. 1:22–28).

Sea of Jazer [Ja′zer]—A sea mentioned in Jeremiah's prophecy against Moab (Jer. 48:32). See Jazer.

Sea, Salt—See Dead Sea.

Sea, The Great—Another name for the Mediterranean Sea, a major body of water along the western coast of the land of Palestine (Josh. 15:47).

Sea, Tiberius [Ti′ber·i·us]—See Tiberias.

Seba [Se′ba], *drink thou*—The oldest son of Cush and ancestor of a Cushite tribe (Isa. 43:3; 45:14).

Sebam [Se′bam]—See Shebam.

Sebat [Se′bat]—See Shebat.

Secacah [Se·ca′cah], *inclosure*—A town in the wilderness of Judah (Josh. 15:61).

Sechu [Se′chu], *watchtower*—A place near Ramah (1 Sam. 19:22).

Second Death—Another name for the lake of fire, or hell (Rev. 20:14).

Second Quarter, The—A district of Jerusalem in which Huldah the prophetess lived (2 Kings 22:14; Second District, NIV). This district lay in the angle formed by the west wall of the temple and the ancient wall of the city. It was later included within the wall restored by Nehemiah.

Secu [Se′cu]—See Sechu.

Secundus [Se·cun′dus], *second*—A Christian of Thessalonica; one of Paul's party when Paul went from Macedonia into Asia Minor (Acts 20:4).

Segub [Se′gub], *exalted*—Two Old Testament men:
   1. Son of Hezron and father of Jair. His mother was the daughter of Machir (1 Chron. 2:21–22).
   2. Son of Hiel. Joshua declared that anyone attempting to rebuild Jericho would be cursed. When Hiel set up the gates of the city, Segub, his son, died (Josh. 6:26; 1 Kings 16:34).

Seir [Se′ir], *hairy or rough*—The name of two places and one person in the Old Testament:
   1. The mountainous country stretching from the Dead Sea to the Red Sea, east of the gorge called the Arabah (Gen. 14:6). The elevations of Seir range from 183 meters (600 feet) to 1,830 meters (6,000 feet).

Two of Seir's outstanding features are Mount Hor, where Aaron died (Num. 20:27–28), and the ancient city of rock, Petra or Sela (Isa. 16:1). The region was named after a Horite (Hurrian) patriarch whose descendants settled in this area.

God gave this land to Esau and his descendants, who drove out the Horites, or Hurrians (Deut. 2:12). Esau and his descendants, the Edomites, lived in Seir (Deut. 2:29). This explains why God directed the people of Israel not to invade this territory when they moved from Egypt toward the promised land (Deut. 2:4–5).

Although Seir was originally the name of the mountain range in Edom, the name came to signify the entire territory of Edom south of the Dead Sea (2 Chron. 20:10). King David made these people his servants (2 Sam. 8:14).

Later, in the days of King Jehoshaphat of Judah, the people of Mount Seir (the Edomites) joined the Ammonites and the Moabites in an invasion against Judah (2 Chron. 20:10, 22–23). Later, the prophet

Ezekiel predicted God's destruction of "Mount Seir" because of their strong hatred of Israel and their desire to possess the lands of Israel and Judah (Ezek. 35:1–15).

2. The grandfather of Hori, ancestor of the Horites (1 Chron. 1:39).

3. A mountain on the northern border of the territory of Judah (Josh. 15:10). Some have identified Seir with the rocky point near Chesalon on which the present-day village of Saris stands, about 19 kilometers (12 miles) west of Jerusalem.

Seirah [Se·i′rah], *shaggy*—A place in Ephraim to which Ehud fled after slaying Eglon at Jericho (Judg. 3:26–27).

Seirath [Se·i′rath]—See Seirah.

Sela [Se′la], *rock or cliff*—The name of three places in the Old Testament:

1. A fortress city, the capital of Edom, situated on the Wadi Musa ("the Valley of Moses") between the Dead Sea and the Gulf of Aqaba (2 Kings 14:7; Selah, KJV). A rock formation about 1,160 meters (3,800 feet) above sea level, now known as Umm el-Bayyarah, the great acropolis of the Nabatean city of Petra, dominates the site.

Sela was near Mount Hor, close to the wilderness of Zin. Its name was changed to Joktheel by Amaziah, king of Judah, after he captured it (2 Kings 14:7). Amaziah's men took 10,000 of the people of Seir (Edomites), "brought them to the top of the rock, and cast them down . . . so that they all were dashed in pieces" (2 Chron. 25:12).

2. A place apparently in the territory of Judah near the boundary of the Amorites (Judg. 1:36; the rock, KJV). Some scholars believe the site was in Amorite territory.

3. An unidentified site in Moab mentioned by Isaiah in a prophecy of doom (Isa. 16:1).

Sela-hammahlekoth [Se·la-ham·mah′le·koth], *rock of division*—A cliff in the wilderness of Maon where David escaped from Saul (1 Sam. 23:28).

Seled [Se′led], *exultation*—A descendant of Jerahmeel (1 Chron. 2:30).

Seleucia [Se·leu′ci·a], *white light*—A seaport near Antioch of Syria from which Paul and Barnabas began their first missionary journey.

Apparently they also landed at Seleucia when they returned to Antioch (Acts 14:26). Seleucia was an important Roman city because of its strategic location on the trade routes of the Mediterranean Sea. It was originally built by Seleucus Nicator, founder of Syria. Nicator built other cities and called them by the same name.

Sem [Sem]—See Shem.

Semachiah [Sem·a·chi′ah], *sustained by Jehovah*—Son of Shemaiah, son of Obed-edom, a Levite and porter (1 Chron. 26:7).

Semei [Sem′e·i], possibly *hearing* or *obeying*—Father of Mattathias, ancestor of Christ (Luke 3:26).

Semein [Sem′e·in]—See Semei.

Senaah [Sen′a·ah], *thorny*—The head of a family—3,680 of whom returned to Israel with Zerubbabel (Ezra 2:35).

Seneh [Sen′eh], *bramble*—One of the two rocks in the mountain pass of Michmash. It was climbed by Jonathan and his armorbearer when they surprised the garrison of the Philistines (1 Sam. 14:4–5).

Senir [Se′nir], *snow mountain*—Possibly the Ammonite name for Mount Hermon (Deut. 3:9) or a peak near Mount Hermon (1 Chron. 5:23; Song 4:8). The fir trees from this area were used for shipbuilding (Ezek. 27:5).

Sennacherib [Sen·nach′er·ib], *Sin multiplied brothers*—Son of Sargon. He ascended the throne of Assyria when his father was assassinated (705 B.C.). He put down the revolt of Merodach-baladan of Babylon and placed Belibni on the throne. About twenty years after the capture of Samaria by his father, he invaded Judah and, according to his account, he captured 46 towns and carried away over 200,000 captives. He attacked the city of Jerusalem, boasting against the Lord and saying that the God of Israel was not powerful enough to save Jerusalem from his hand. The prophet Isaiah told the righteous king Hezekiah that in fact God would deliver them, and a short time later the angel of the Lord went through the Assyrian camp and killed 185,000 soldiers. Sennecherib abandoned the siege and returned to Nineveh (2 Kings 18:17–19:37). Later he again captured Babylon, massacred the people, and ruined the city. He built a great palace in Nineveh, 1,500 feet long and 700 broad and brought water into the city by a system of canals. In 680 B.C. he was assassinated by two of his sons which brought another son, Esar-haddon, to the throne (2 Kings 19:37; 2 Chron. 32:21).

Senuah [Sen'u·ah]—See Hassenuah.

Seorim [Se·or'im], *barley*—A descendant of Aaron. In the time of David his family constituted the fourth course of the priests (1 Chron. 24:1, 6, 8).

Sephar [Se'phar], *numbering*—A place, probably in southern Arabia, located on the boundary of the territory of the descendants of Joktan (Gen. 10:30).

Sepharad [Se·phar'ad], *separated*—A place, believed by some to be Sardis in Asia Minor. The captives of Judah were taken here (Obad. 20).

Sepharvaim [Se·phar·va'im], *enumeration*—A city under the rule of Assyria. Inhabitants of this city were brought to settle Samaria after the Israelites were taken away (2 Kings 17:24, 31). It has been identified with the city of Sippar, ruins of which were found at Abu Habbah, southwest of Baghdad, near the Euphrates.

Sepharvites [Se·phar'vites]—Inhabitants of Sepharvaim. They sacrificed their children by fire to their gods Adrammalech and Anammalech (2 Kings 17:31).

Serah [Se'rah], *abundance*—A daughter of Asher, son of Jacob and Leah's handmaid, Zilpah (Gen. 46:17; 1 Chron. 7:30).

Seraiah [Se·rai'ah]—
1. A scribe who lived in the reign of David (2 Sam. 8:17). See Shavsha.
2. The chief priest, son of Azariah. When Jerusalem was taken by Nebuchadnezzar, Seraiah was sent to him at Riblah and was put to death (2 Kings 25:18–21; 1 Chron. 6:14; Jer. 52:24–27).
3. The son of Tanhumeth, a Netophathite. He was one of those Gedaliah advised to yield to the Chaldeans (2 Kings 25:23; Jer. 40:8).
4. Son of Kenaz (1 Chron. 4:13).
5. Son of Asiel and father of Josibiah of the tribe of Simeon; ancestor of Jehu (1 Chron. 4:35).
6. One who returned with Zerubbabel (Ezra 2:2).

7. An ancestor of Ezra (Ezra 7:1).

8. A son of Hilkiah, a priest (Neh. 11:11).

9. A priest who returned from Babylon with Zerubbabel (Neh. 12:1, 7).

10. Son of Azriel. He was ordered by Jehoiakim to arrest Baruch and Jeremiah (Jer. 36:26).

11. Son of Neriah. He was taken to Babylon with Zedekiah, Judah's last king. He is described as "a quiet prince." Jeremiah the prophet gave him a book which contained the prophecy of doom for Babylon (Jer. 51:59–64).

Seraphim [Ser'a·phim], *burning*—Seraphim are mentioned in Isaiah 6 when Isaiah received his commission from God. The word *seraphim* comes from the verb *seraph* ("to burn") and appears in the context of holiness. Isaiah sensed his own lack of holiness in the light of the seraphim's ascription of praise to God: "Holy, holy, holy!" Seraphim are seen as burning with holiness. Some scholars believe cherubim and seraphim are not really that different. In fact, the living creatures in Revelation seem to have some characteristics of both. It should be underscored that the study of angels is not theoretical; it should be practical and encouraging. Hebrews 1:14 gives believers a wonderful assurance: "Are they not all ministering spirits sent forth to minister for those who will inherit salvation?"

Sered [Se'red], *fear*—A son of Zebulun and head of a tribal family (Gen. 46:14; Num. 26:26).

Seredites [Se'red·ites]—See Sardites.

Sergius Paulus [Ser'gi·us Pau'lus], *earth-born* or *born to wander*—The Roman proconsul, or governor, of Cyprus who was converted to Christianity when the apostle Paul visited that island on his first missionary journey, about A.D. 46 (Acts 13:7). Luke describes Sergius Paulus as an intelligent man. This Sergius Paulus may have been the same man as L. Sergius Paulus, a Roman official in charge of the Tiber during the reign of the emperor Claudius (ruled A.D. 41–54).

Serpent Well [Ser'pent]—A well outside of Jerusalem between the Valley Gate and the Refuse Gate (Neh. 2:13), also called "dragon well" and "Dragon's Spring."

Serug [Se'rug], *branch* or *shoot*—The son of Reu and great-grand-father of Abraham, in the line of Arphaxad, son of Shem, and ancestor of Jesus (Gen. 11:20, 23; 1 Chron. 1:26; Luke 3:35; Saruch, KJV).

Seth [Seth], *appoint or compensate*—The third son of Adam and Eve, born after Cain murdered Abel (Gen. 4:25–26; 5:3–8; Sheth, KJV). The father of Enosh (or Enos) and an ancestor of Jesus Christ (Luke 3:38), Seth died at the age of 912.

Sethur [Se'thur], *hidden*—Son of Michael. He was a spy, the representative of Asher, sent to Canaan by Moses from Kadesh-barnea (Num. 13:13).

Seven Churches of Revelation—The book of Revelation contains special messages directed to churches in seven specific cities throughout the Roman province of Asia. These cities were important trade and communication centers, which were connected by major roads in New Testament times. Interestingly, John addressed the churches in exactly the order they would be if he had traveled the road, from Ephesus north to Pergamos, then south all the way to Laodicea. Some scholars believe that Revelation was a circular letter that would have been read first by the Ephesian church, then passed on the next church on the route. John received his vision and wrote the Revelation while he was in exile on Patmos, an island in the Aegean Sea. The message themes that he delivered to each church are as follows, each in their order:

1. Message to Ephesus: "You have left your first love" (2:4).

2. Message to Smyrna: "Be faithful until death, and I will give you the crown of life" (2:10).

3. Message to Pergamos: "I have a few things against you" (2:14).

4. Message to Thyatira: "Hold fast what you have until I come" (2:25).

5. Message to Sardis: "You have a name that you are alive, but you are dead" (3:1).

6. Message to Philadelphia: "I have set before you an open door" (3:8).

7. Message to Laodicea: "You are neither cold nor hot" (3:15).

Seveneh [Se·ve'neh]—See Syene.

Shaalabbin [Sha·al'ab·bin], *foxes*—A city of the Amorites in the territory of Dan (Judg. 1:35; 1 Kings 4:9).

Shaalbim [Sha·al′bim]—See Shaalabbin.

Shaalbonite [Sha·al·bo′nite]—A native of a place called Shaalbon or Shaalbim. Eliahba, one of David's mighty men, was a Shaalbonite (2 Sam. 23:32; 1 Chron. 11:33).

Shaalim, Shalim [Sha′a·lim, Sha′lim], *foxes*—A district in Ephraim or Benjamin in which Saul searched for his father's asses (1 Sam. 9:4).

Shaaph [Sha′aph], *division*—Two Old Testament men:
  1. A son of Jahdai of Judah, in the registry of Caleb (1 Chron. 2:47).
  2. Son of Caleb (1 Chron. 2:49).

Shaaraim [Sha·a·ra′im], *two gates*—Two Old Testament towns:
  1. A town of Simeon (1 Chron. 4:31).
  2. A town of Judah in the lowland west of Socoh (1 Sam. 17:52), also called Sharaim (Josh. 15:36).

Shaashgaz [Sha·ash′gaz], *servant of the beautiful*—A eunuch or chamberlain in the court of Ahasuerus, king of Persia (Est. 2:14).

Shabbethai [Shab′be·thai], *sabbatical*—A chief Levite of Jerusalem after the Exile. He was an overseer of the temple and helped interpret the law. However, he opposed Ezra in the matter of the Israelites divorcing the foreign women (Ezra 10:15; Neh. 8:7; 11:16).

Shachia [Sha·chi′a], *announcement*—Son of Shaharaim of Benjamin (1 Chron. 8:10).

Shad′dai [Shad′dai], commonly *almighty*—A name of God, denoting Almighty (Gen. 48:3; 49:25; Ex. 6:3).

Shadrach [Sha′drach], *command of* (the god) *Aku*—The name that Ashpenaz, the chief of Nebuchadnezzar's eunuchs, gave to Hananiah, one of the Jewish princes who was carried away to Babylon in 605 B.C. (Dan. 1:7; 3:12–30).

Shadrach was one of the three faithful Jews who refused to worship the golden image that King Nebuchadnezzar of Babylon set up (Dan. 3:1). Along with his two companions, Meshach and Abednego, Shadrach was "cast into the midst of a burning fiery furnace" (Dan. 3:11, 21). But they were protected by a fourth "man" in the fire

(Dan. 3:25), and they emerged without even the smell of fire upon them (Dan. 3:27).

Shagee, Shage [Sha'gee, Sha'ge]—See Shageh.

Shageh [Sha'geh], possibly *erring*—A Hararite, the father of Jonathan who was one of David's mighty men (1 Chron. 11:34; also see Shammah, 2 Sam. 23:11).

Shaharaim [Sha·ha·ra'im], *double dawn*—A man of Benjamin, father of nine tribal leaders (1 Chron. 8:8–11).

Shahazimah [Sha·ha·zi'mah], *heights*—A town of Issachar (Josh. 19:22–23).

Shahazumah [Sha·ha·zu'mah]—See Shahazimah.

Shalem [Sha'lem], *peace* or *safety*—A town near Shechem (Gen. 33:18, KJV). Modern translations render this word as "peace" or "safely" rather than as the name of a town.

Shalim [Sha'lim]—See Shaalim.

Shalisha [Shal'i·sha], *the third*—A district mentioned in connection with Saul's search for his father's donkeys, probably in Ephraim (1 Sam. 9:4).

Shalishah [Shal'i·shah]—See Shalisha.

Shallecheth [Shal'le·cheth], *casting out*—A western gate of Solomon's temple (1 Chron. 26:16).

Shallum [Shal'lum], *retribution*—Thirteen or fourteen Old Testament men:

1. King of Israel, son of Jabesh. He slew Zechariah, son of Jeroboam II and the last king of the fifth dynasty (2 Kings 15:10).

2. A son of Tikvah. He was the husband of the prophetess Huldah in the reign of Josiah and an official of the temple (2 Kings 22:14; 2 Chron. 34:22).

3. Son of Josiah, king of Judah. His other name was Jehoahaz. He followed Josiah on the throne (2 Kings 23:30–34; 1 Chron. 3:15). See Jehoahaz.

4. Son of Sisamai and descendant of Judah (1 Chron. 2:40–41).

5. Son of Shaul, grandson of Simeon (1 Chron. 4:25).

6. Son of Zadok, high priest and father of Hilkiah and ancestor of Ezra (1 Chron. 6:12–13; Ezra 7:2). In 1 Chronicles 9:11 he is called Meshullam.

7. Son of Naphtali (1 Chron. 7:13). In Genesis 46:24 he is called Shillem.

8. A descendant of Kore and a porter of the sanctuary in the time of David (1 Chron. 9:17–18). He may be the same as Meshelemiah or Shelemiah (1 Chron. 26:1, 14).

9. Father of Jehizkiah (2 Chron. 28:12).

10. A Levite, gatekeeper of the temple, who divorced his foreign wife in the time of Ezra (Ezra 10:24).

11. A son of Bani. He renounced his Gentile wife (Ezra 10:42).

12. A son of Hallohesh, ruler of the half of Jerusalem. He labored with his daughters on the wall of Jerusalem (Neh. 3:12).

13. Uncle of Jeremiah, father of Hanameel (Jer. 32:7–8), possibly the same as No. 2.

14. Father of Maaseiah (Jer. 35:4).

Shallun [Shal′lun], *retribution*—Son of Colhozeh (Neh. 3:15).

Shalmai [Shal′mai]—See Salmai.

Shalman [Shal′man], *fire-worshipper*—An abbreviation of Shalmaneser, king of Assyria (Hos. 10:14).

Shalmaneser [Shal·man·e′ser], *fire-worshipper*—There were four kings by this name in Assyrian history, only one of whom is mentioned by name in the Old Testament—Shalmaneser V. He succeeded Tiglath-pileser III in 727 B.C. He demanded tribute from Hoshea, king of Israel, and when Hoshea attempted to rebel, he laid a siege on Samaria which lasted for three years. Samaria fell in 722 B.C., but apparently Shalmaneser died shortly before the victory, and his successor, Sargon, arranged the deportation of the inhabitants and claimed the victory as his own. See Sargon.

Shama [Sha′ma], *obedient*—A son of Hotham, one of David's mighty men (1 Chron. 11:44).

Shamariah [Sham·a·ri′ah]—See Shemariah.

Shamed [Sha'med]—See Shemed.

Shamer [Sha'mer]—See Shemer.

Shamgar [Sham'gar], *sword*—the third judge of Israel (Judg. 3:31) who delivered the nation from oppression by the Philistines. Using an ox goad (or sharp stick) as a weapon, Shamgar killed six hundred Philistines who were terrorizing the main travel routes. Shamgar was a "son of Anath"—which may mean he was a resident of Beth-anath (Judg. 1:33), a fortified city in the territory of Naphtali.

Shamhuth [Sham'huth], *desolation*—A captain of David's army (1 Chron. 27:8).

Shamir [Sha'mir], *a thorn*—Two towns and a man of the Old Testament:

1. A town of Ephraim, the residence and burial place of Tola, a judge of Israel (Judg. 10:1–2).

2. A town in the mountain region of Judah (Josh. 15:48), possibly thirteen miles southwest of Hebron.

3. Son of Micah, a Levite (1 Chron. 24:24).

Shamlai [Sham'lai]—See Salmai.

Shamma [Sham'ma], *desolation*—Son of Zophah (1 Chron. 7:37).

Shammah [Sham'mah], *desolation*—Four Old Testament men:

1. A son of Reuel, son of Esau. He became a duke of Edom (Gen. 36:3–4, 13, 17).

2. A son of Jesse, brother of David (1 Sam. 16:9; 17:13). He is called Shimea in 1 Chronicles 20:7.

3. A son of Agee, a Hararite (2 Sam. 23:11), a captain of David. Perhaps he is the same as Shage (1 Chron. 11:34).

4. A warrior of David, a Harodite (2 Sam. 23:25). He is also called Shammoth (1 Chron. 11:27), and Shamhuth (1 Chron. 27:8).

Shammai [Sham'ma·i], *waste*—Three Old Testament men:

1. Son of Onam of Judah (1 Chron. 2:28).

2. Son of Rekem of Judah (1 Chron. 2:44).

3. Son of Ezra of Judah (1 Chron. 4:17).

Shammoth [Sham'moth]—See Shammah.

Shammua, Shammuah [Sham′mu·a, Sham′mu·ah], *fame—*

1. Son of Zaccur, the representative of Reuben sent to spy the land of Canaan (Num. 13:4).

2. David's son by Bath-sheba (2 Sam. 5:14; 1 Chron. 3:5). In the latter passage he is called Shimea.

3. The father of Abda (Neh. 11:17), also called Shemaiah (1 Chron. 9:16).

4. A priest of the family of Bilgah in the time of the high priest, Joiakim (Neh. 12:18).

Shamsherai [Sham′she·rai], *sunlike—*A son of Jeroham, a Benjamite (1 Chron. 8:26).

Shapham [Sha′pham], *bold—*A chief of the Gadites in the days of Jotham (1 Chron. 5:12).

Shaphan [Sha′phan], *coney—*

1. The scribe and secretary of King Josiah of Judah (2 Kings 22:8–14; Jer. 26:24; 39:14).

2. The father of Ahikam, who stood by Jeremiah to prevent him from being killed (Jer. 26:24). Akikam went with Shaphan the scribe (No. 1) to inquire of Huldah the prophetess concerning the books of the Law which had been found. It is quite likely that Shaphan No. 2 is the same as Shaphan No. 1. Ithikam's son Gedaliah, the grandson of Shaphan, took Jeremiah from prison and took him home (Jer. 39:14).

3. The father of Elasah who carried Jeremiah's letter to the captives (Jer. 29:3). Probably the same as Shaphan No. 1.

4. A scribe and the father of Gemariah, in whose chamber Baruch stood to read the words of Jeremiah's scroll to the people (Jer. 36:10–12). Probably the same as Shaphan No. 1.

5. The father of Jaazaniah, an elder who took part in "wicked abominations" in the Lord's house (Ezek. 8:9, 11).

Shaphat [Sha′phat], *hath judged—*Five Old Testament men:

1. Son of Hori. He represented Simeon in the group of spies sent to scout in the land of Canaan (Num. 13:5).

2. Father of Elisha, the prophet (1 Kings 19:16; 2 Kings 3:11).

3. A son of Shemaiah of Judah (1 Chron. 3:22).

4. A chief of the Gadites in Bashan (1 Chron. 5:12).

5. Son of Adlai, the herdsman in charge of David's herds in the valleys (1 Chron. 27:29).

Shapher [Sha'pher]—See Shepher.

Shaphir, Saphir [Sha'phir, Sa'phir], *beautiful*—An unidentified town of Judah (Mic. 1:11).

Sharai [Shar·a'i], *releaser*—A son of Bani who divorced his foreign wife (Ezra 10:40).

Sharaim [Sha·ra'im]—See Shaaraim.

Sharar [Shar'ar], *enemy*—A Hararite and father of Ahiam (2 Sam. 23:33). He is called Sacar in 1 Chronicles 11:35.

Sharezer [Sha·re'zer], *prince of fire*—

1. Son of Sennacherib. He and another son murdered their father and then fled, leaving their brother to ascend to the throne (2 Kings 19:37; Isa. 37:38).

2. A man of Beth-el (Zech. 7:2).

Sharon [Shar'on], *a plain*—The name of a plain and a district in the Old Testament:

1. The chief coastal plain of Palestine, running approximately 80 kilometers (50 miles) from south of the Carmel Mountain range to the vicinity of Joppa (1 Chron. 27:29). This lowland region was extremely fertile and was known for its agriculture (Isa. 33:9).

In ancient times, an important caravan route ran along the plain of Sharon, connecting Egypt, Mesopotamia, and Asia Minor. The flowers of Sharon (Isa. 35:2), particularly the rose of Sharon (Song 2:1), were beautiful. Sharon is also called Lasharon (Josh. 12:18).

2. A district in Transjordan, the area east of the Jordan River, occupied by the tribe of Gad (1 Chron. 5:16).

Sharonite [Shar'on·ite]—One who dwells in Sharon. The herdsman in charge of David's herds which fed in Sharon was called a Sharonite (1 Chron. 27:29).

Sharuhen [Sha·ru'hen], *refuge of grace*—A village of Simeon (Josh. 19:6). Also called Shilhim (Josh. 15:32) and Shaaraim (1 Chron. 4:31).

Shashai [Sha'shai], *pale*—A son of Bani who divorced his foreign wife (Ezra 10:40).

Shashak [Sha'shak], *longing*—Son of Beriah, in the family tree of King Saul (1 Chron. 8:14).

Shaul [Sha'ul], *asked*—

1. Son of Simeon. His mother was a Canaanite woman (Gen. 46:10; Ex. 6:15; 1 Chron. 4:24). He was the head of a tribal family (Num. 26:13).

2. A king of Edom from Rehoboth (Gen. 36:37). He is also called Saul.

3. A Levite descended from Korah (1 Chron. 6:24).

Shaulites [Shaul'ites]—The descendants of Simeon's son Shaul (Num. 26:13).

Shaveh [Sha'veh], *a plain*—A valley, called also the "king's dale," near Jerusalem (Gen. 14:17–18; 2 Sam. 18:18).

Shaveh Kiriathaim [Sha'veh Kir·i·a·tha'im], *plain of Kiriathaim*—A plain of Moab near the city of Kiriathaim (Gen. 14:5; Josh. 13:19).

Shavsha [Shav'sha], *nobility*—A scribe of David and Solomon (1 Chron. 18:16; 1 Kings 4:3). He was probably the same as Seraiah (2 Sam. 8:17) and Sheva (2 Sam. 20:25).

Sheal [She'al], *asking*—A son of Bani who divorced his pagan wife (Ezra 10:29).

Shealtiel [She·al'ti·el], *I have asked of God*—Son of Jeconiah and father of Zerubbabel (1 Chron. 3:17; Ezra 3:2, 8; 5:2; Neh. 12:1). He was an ancestor of the family of Christ (Matt. 1:12; Luke 3:27; Salathiel, KJV).

Sheariah [She·a·ri'ah], *valued by Jehovah*—A son of Azel, a descendant of Saul (1 Chron. 8:38).

Shear-jashub [She'ar-jash'ub], *a remnant shall return*—A symbolic name given to a son of the prophet Isaiah in the days of King Ahaz of Judah (Isa. 7:3). The name emphasized Isaiah's prophecy that a remnant of the nation would return to the land after their years of captivity in a foreign country (Isa. 10:21–22).

Sheba [She'ba], *fullness* or *completeness*—

1. A son of Raamah, son of Cush (Gen. 10:7; 1 Chron. 1:9).

2. A son of Joktan and grandson of Eber, of the family of Shem (Gen. 10:28; 1 Chron. 1:22). His descendants settled in southern Arabia, and founded the kingdom of Sheba.

3. A son of Jokshan and grandson of Keturah and Abraham (Gen. 25:3; 1 Chron. 1:32).

4. A town assigned to Simeon (Josh. 19:2), possibly the same as Beersheba.

5. A son of Bichri, a Benjamite. He supported Absalom in his rebellion. After it was crushed, he blew a horn to assemble the ten tribes to induce them to renounce their allegiance to David. He entered the fortress of Abel of Beth-maacah but was besieged and beheaded by the inhabitants. His head was tossed over the wall (2 Sam. 20:1–22).

6. A kingdom in southwestern Arabia whose queen heard of the fame of Solomon and came to Jerusalem to see and hear for herself. Sheba exported perfumes and incense, and sent out trading caravans to the nations of the Middle East. See Sheba, Queen of.

7. A Gadite chief who lived in Gilead in Bashan during the time of Jeroboam II of Israel (1 Chron. 5:13, 16).

Sheba, Queen of [She'ba], *fullness* or *completeness*—A queen who came to visit King Solomon. She tested him with "hard questions" and found that Solomon's wisdom and prosperity exceeded his fame (1 Kings 10:1–13). Some scholars believe she represented the region of Ethiopia, south of Egypt. But others insist she ruled among the tribes of southwestern Arabia. In the New Testament, Jesus referred to her as "the queen of the South," who "came from the ends of the earth to hear the wisdom of Solomon" (Matt. 12:42).

Shebah [She'bah], *seven* or *oath*—The well dug by Isaac's servants at Beersheba, after he had sworn an oath of friendship with Abimelech (Gen. 26:33).

Shebam [She'bam], *fragrance*—A city assigned to Reuben and Gad, east of the Jordan near Heshbon (Num. 32:3). Probably the same place as Shibmah (Num. 32:38) and Sibmah (Josh. 13:19).

Shebaniah [Sheb·a·ni'ah], *reared by Jehovah*—Four Levites of the Old Testament:

1. A Levite who blew the trumpet when the ark was brought by David to Jerusalem (1 Chron. 15:24).

2. A Levite who sealed the covenant and offered the prayer at the Feast of Tabernacles (Neh. 9:4–5; 10:10).

3. A priest who sealed the covenant (Neh. 10:4; 12:14).

4. Another Levite who sealed the covenant (Neh. 10:12).

Shebarim [Sheb'a·rim], *ruins*—Possibly stone quarries near Ai (Josh. 7:5).

Shebat [She'bat], possibly *a rod*—Eleventh month of the sacred year and the fifth month of the civil year, corresponding roughly to January/February (Zech. 1:7). Also called Sebat (KJV).

Sheber [She'ber], *fracture*—Son of Caleb; his mother was Maacah, Caleb's concubine (1 Chron. 2:48).

Shebna [Sheb'na], *vigor*—An official in the court of Hezekiah of Judah in whom was vested considerable authority as minister of the household (Isa. 22:15). Later he was given a secretarial position, while his former position was taken by Eliakim (2 Kings 18:18, 26, 37; 19:2; Isa. 36:3; 37:2).

Shebuel [She·bu'el], *captive of God*—Two Old Testament men:

1. Son of Gershom and grandson of Moses (1 Chron. 23:16; 26:24). In 1 Chronicles 24:20 he is called Shubael.

2. A son of Heman, a musician in the time of David (1 Chron. 25:4). In 1 Chronicles 25:20 he is called Shubael.

Shecaniah, Shechaniah [Shec·a·ni'ah, Shech·a·ni'ah], *Jehovah has dwelt*—Eight Old Testament men:

1. A descendant of David (1 Chron. 3:21–22).

2. A descendant of Aaron. In the time of David his family was the tenth course of priests (1 Chron. 24:1, 6, 11).

3. A priest and a distributor of tithes in the reign of Hezekiah (2 Chron. 31:15).

4. The head of a family who returned with Ezra (Ezra 8:3).

4. A son of Jahaziel who returned with Ezra from Babylon (Ezra 8:5).

5. A son of Jehiel, of the sons of Elam. He proposed to Ezra that foreign wives be renounced (Ezra 10:2–3).

6. The father of Shemaiah (Neh. 3:29).

7. The father-in-law of Tobiah, the Ammonite, and son of Arah (Neh. 6:17–18).

8. A priest who returned to Jerusalem with Zerubbabel (Neh. 12:3).

Shechem [She′chem], *shoulder*—The name of a city and three men in the Bible:

1. An ancient fortified city in central Canaan and the first capital of the northern kingdom of Israel. Its name means "shoulder," probably because the city was built mainly on the slope, or shoulder, of Mount Ebal. Situated where main highways and ancient trade routes converged, Shechem was an important city long before the Israelites occupied Canaan. The city has been destroyed and rebuilt several times through the centuries.

Shechem is first mentioned in connection with Abraham's journey into the land of Canaan. When Abraham eventually came to Shechem, the Lord appeared to him and announced that this was the land He would give to Abraham's descendants (Gen. 12:6; Sichem, KJV). This fulfilled God's promise to Abraham at the time of his call (Gen. 12:1–3). In response, Abraham built his first altar to the Lord in Canaan at Shechem (Gen. 12:7). Because of this incident, Shechem is an important place in the religious history of the Hebrew people.

Upon his return from Padan-aram, Jacob, a grandson of Abraham, also built an altar to the Lord at Shechem (Gen. 33:18–20). This marked Jacob's safe return to the promised land from the land of self-imposed exile. According to Jewish tradition, Jacob dug a deep well here (John 4:12). Jacob's Well is one of the few sites visited by Jesus that is identifiable today.

After the Israelites conquered Canaan under the leadership of Joshua, an altar was built at Shechem. Its building was accompanied by a covenant ceremony in which offerings were given and the blessings and curses of the law were recited (Josh. 8:30–35). This was done in obedience to the command of Moses, given earlier in Deuteronomy 27:12–13. Because Shechem was situated between Mount Ebal and

Mount Gerizim, this covenant ceremony took on a symbolic meaning. To this day Mount Gerizim is forested while Mount Ebal is barren. Thus the blessings of faithfully keeping the covenant were proclaimed from Mount Gerizim, while the curses of breaking the covenant were proclaimed from Mount Ebal.

At the close of his life, Joshua gathered the tribes of Israel at Shechem. Here he reviewed God's gracious dealings with Israel and performed a covenant-renewing ceremony on behalf of the nation. He closed his speech with his famous statement, "Choose for yourselves this day whom you will serve . . . but as for me and my house, we will serve the LORD" (Josh. 24:15).

The significance of Shechem in Israel's history continued into the period of the divided kingdom. Rehoboam, successor to King Solomon, went to Shechem to be crowned king over all Israel (1 Kings 12:1). Later, when the nation divided into two kingdoms, Shechem became the first capital of the northern kingdom of Israel (1 Kings 12:25). Samaria eventually became the permanent political capital of the Northern Kingdom, but Shechem retained its religious importance. It apparently was a sanctuary for worship of God in Hosea's time in the eighth century B.C. (Hos. 6:9).

At Shechem (sometimes identified with Sychar) Jesus visited with the Samaritan woman at Jacob's Well (John 4). The Samaritans had built their temple on Mount Gerizim, where they practiced their form of religion. To this outcast woman of a despised sect Jesus offered salvation. This is a vivid example of the truth that the gospel of Christ is meant for all people.

2. A son of Hamor, a Hivite prince (Gen. 33:19; 34:1–31). Shechem raped Dinah, the daughter of Jacob. When Shechem later wanted to marry her, Dinah's half brothers, Simeon and Levi, agreed to give Shechem permission only if "every male of you is circumcised" (Gen. 34:15). When Hamor, Shechem, and their followers agreed to the procedure, Simeon and Levi killed them before the circumcision operations had healed.

3. A son of Gilead, grandson of Manasseh, and head of a tribal family (Num. 26:31; Josh. 17:2).

4. A son of Shemida, of the tribe of Manasseh (1 Chron. 7:19).

Shechemites [Shech'em·ites]—Family and descendents of Shechem, son of Gilead (Num. 26:31).

Shedeur [Shed'e·ur], *sending of light*—Father of Elizur (Num. 1:5; 2:10).

Sheep Gate—A gate of Jerusalem, at which point Nehemiah began the building of the wall (Neh. 3:1).

Sheerah, Sherah [She'e·rah, She'rah], *kinswoman*—A daughter of Ephraim (1 Chron. 7:24).

Shehariah [She·ha·ri'ah], *drawing of Jehovah*—A son of Jeroham of Benjamin (1 Chron. 8:26).

Shelah [She'lah], *prayer*—

1. Son or grandson of Arphaxad (Gen. 10:24; 11:12–15; 1 Chron. 1:18). He was an ancestor of Abraham and the family of Christ (Luke 3:35–36, also called Sala, KJV).

2. The third son of Judah by the daughter of Shush. He was head of a tribal family (Gen. 38:2, 5, 11, 14, 26; Num. 26:20).

3. A pool by the King's Garden (Neh. 3:15), also translated Siloah (KJV) and Siloam (NIV). See Siloam.

Shelanites [She'la·nites]—Descendents of Shelah, the youngest son of Judah (Num. 26:20).

Shelemiah [Shel·e·mi'ah], *Jehovah rewards*—Nine Old Testament men:

1. A porter of the tabernacle in David's time (1 Chron. 26:14). In 1 Chronicles 9:21 he is called Meshelemiah.

2. A descendant of Bani. He divorced his foreign wife (Ezra 10:39).

3. Another descendant of Bani. He divorced his foreign wife (Ezra 10:41).

4. Father of the Hananiah who labored on the wall of Jerusalem (Neh. 3:30).

5. A priest appointed by Nehemiah to take charge of and distribute the tithes (Neh. 13:13).

6. Grandfather of Jehudi. He was sent by the princes to ask Baruch to read to them the roll of Jeremiah (Jer. 36:14).

7. Son of Abdeel. He was ordered by Jehoiakim to arrest Baruch and Jeremiah (Jer. 36:26).

8. Father of Jucal, or Jehucal (Jer. 37:3; 38:1).

9. Son of Hananiah and father of Irijah (Jer. 37:13).

Sheleph [She'leph], *a drawing forth*—A son of Joktan (Gen. 10:26; 1 Chron. 1:20).

Shelesh [She'lesh], *triplet*—Son of Helem and a descendant of Asher (1 Chron. 7:35).

Shelomi [She·lo'mi], *peaceful*—Father of Ahihud, a prince of Asher (Num. 34:27).

Shelomith, Shelomoth [She·lo'mith, She·lo'moth], *peaceful*—Seven Old Testament men and women:

1. The daughter of Dibri, or Dan. She was mother of the man put to death for blasphemy at the time of the exodus (Lev. 24:11).

2. Daughter of Zerubbabel (1 Chron. 3:19).

3. A son of Shimei, a Levite of the family of Gershon (1 Chron. 23:9).

4. A descendant of Eliezer, son of Moses. In the reign of David he was a temple treasurer (1 Chron. 26:25–26).

5. A Levite of the family of Kohath, of the house of Izhar in the time of David (1 Chron. 23:18). In 1 Chronicles 24:22 he is called Shelomoth.

6. The son or daughter of Rehoboam (2 Chron. 11:20).

7. Son of Josiphiah (Ezra 8:10).

Shelumiel [She·lu'mi·el], *peace of God*—A prince of Simeon in the wilderness. He was the son of Zurishaddai (Num. 1:6; 2:12; 7:36, 41; 10:19).

Shem [Shem], *renown*—The son of Noah and brother of Ham and Japheth. He was probably the firstborn. Shem was born after Noah became 500 years old (Gen. 5:32). He was one of eight people who entered Noah's ark and survived the Flood (Gen. 7:7, 13). Shem was married at the time of the Flood. He was 100 years old, but had no children. After the Flood he became the father of Elam, Asshur, Arphaxad, Lud, and Aram (usually identified by scholars as Persia, Assyria, Chaldea, Lydia, and Syria, respectively). Thus Shem was the ancestor of the people of the ancient Near East generally, and the Hebrews specifically. Some time after the Flood Shem and Japheth respectfully covered their father's nakedness during a time when Noah was very drunk. Because of this they received his blessing (Gen. 9:23–37).

Shem died at the age of 600 (Gen. 11:10–11). He is listed by Luke as an ancestor of Jesus Christ (Luke 3:36; Sem, KJV).

Shema [She′ma], *rumor*—Four men and a town of the Old Testament:

1. A town in the south of Judah (Josh. 15:26), also called Sheba (Josh. 19:3).

2. Son of Hebron of Judah (1 Chron. 2:43–44). See Mareshah.

3. A son of Joel of Reuben (1 Chron. 5:8).

4. A son of Elpaal, a Benjamite and head of the house in Aijalon (1 Chron. 8:13).

5. One who assisted Ezra when he read the law (Neh. 8:4).

Shemaah [Shem′a·ah], *rumor*—A man of Gibeah who allied himself with David at Ziklag (1 Chron. 12:3).

Shemaiah [Shem·ai′ah], *Jehovah heard*—The name of a number of Old Testament men:

1. A prophet in the reign of Rehoboam who told the king he should not attack the kingdom of Israel (1 Kings 12:22–24; 2 Chron. 11:2–4). He also explained the invasion of Shishak of Egypt as divine punishment for the sins of Judah (2 Chron. 12:5–8). He wrote a history of this reign (2 Chron. 12:15).

2. The son of Shechaniah, of the tribe of Judah (1 Chron. 3:22).

3. Father of Shimri, a Simeonite (1 Chron. 4:37).

4. The son of Joel and father of Gog (1 Chron. 5:4), possibly the same as Shema No. 3.

5. Son of Hasshub. He was a Levite of the Merari family (1 Chron. 9:14) and overseer of the business of the house of God in the time of Nehemiah (Neh. 11:15).

6. Father of Obadiah, a Levite (1 Chron. 9:16), also called Shammua (Neh. 11:17).

7. Son of Elizaphan, a Levite. He participated in the removal of the ark to Jerusalem (1 Chron. 15:8–11).

8. A Levite, son of Nethaneel and a scribe in the time of David (1 Chron. 24:6).

9. Son of Obed-edom (1 Chron. 26:4-8) and a doorkeeper of the sanctuary in the time of David.

10. A Levite commissioned by Jehoshaphat to teach the people (2 Chron. 17:8).

11. A descendant of Jeduthun. In the reign of Hezekiah he assisted in purifying the temple (2 Chron. 29:14-15). Possibly the same person as No. 6.

12. A Levite. In the reign of Hezekiah he had charge of the freewill offerings (2 Chron. 31:15).

13. A Levite in the reign of Josiah. He and others contributed generously to the offerings of the Passover (2 Chron. 35:9).

14. A son of Adonikam. He and his two brothers came with Ezra to Jerusalem from Babylon (Ezra 8:13).

15. One sent by Ezra to Iddo to secure Levites to accompany the Israelites to Jerusalem (Ezra 8:16).

16. A priest descended from Harim. He renounced his foreign wife (Ezra 10:21).

17. Son of another Harim, a layman, who divorced his foreign wife (Ezra 10:31).

18. A son of Shechaniah, a Levite who assisted Nehemiah in building the wall of Jerusalem (Neh. 3:29).

19. A false prophet. He was the son of Delaiah and grandson of Mehetabeel. Tobiah and Sanballat of Samaria bribed him to get Nehemiah to seek safety in the temple to escape assassination (Neh. 6:10-13).

20. One of the priests who sealed the covenant with Nehemiah (Neh. 10:8).

21. A chief priest who returned from Babylon with Zerubbabel (Neh. 12:6-7, 18).

22. A prince of Judah who had a part in the dedication of the wall of Jerusalem (Neh. 12:34).

23. A Levite of the line of Asaph (Neh. 12:35).

24. A Levite musician who assisted in the dedication of the wall of Jerusalem (Neh. 12:36).

25. A priest who blew the trumpet when the wall of Jerusalem was dedicated (Neh. 12:42).

26. Father of Urijah, the prophet of Kirjath-jearim whom Jehoiakim put to death because of his true prophecies (Jer. 26:20-23).

27. A Nehelamite, a false prophet among the captives in Babylon, who declared they would return in a short time to Jerusalem. Jeremiah predicted Shemaiah would not live to the end of the Exile (Jer. 29:24–32).

28. Father of Delaiah, a prince in the reign of Jehoiakim who heard Baruch read the roll of Jeremiah (Jer. 36:12).

Shemariah [Shem·a·ri′ah], *Jehovah hath kept*—Four Old Testament men:

1. A man of Benjamin who joined David at Ziklag (1 Chron. 12:5).

2. A son of Rehoboam. His mother was Abihail (2 Chron. 11:19; also called Shamariah).

3. A son of Harim in the time of Ezra. He renounced his Gentile wife (Ezra 10:32).

4. A son of Bani (Ezra 10:41).

Shemeber [Shem·e′ber], *lofty flight*—The king of Zeboiim in the days of Abraham. He was defeated by Chedorlaomer (Gen. 14:2, 8, 10).

Shemed [She′med], *destruction*—A descendant of Shaharaim through Elpaal, a Benjamite (1 Chron. 8:12; Shamed, KJV).

Shemer [She′mer], *preserved*—Three Old Testament men:

1. A Levite of the family of Merari and son of Mahli, also called Shamer (1 Chron. 6:46).

2. A man of Asher, also called Shomer or Shamer (1 Chron. 7:32, 34).

3. The man who sold Omri the hill of Samaria (1 Kings 16:24).

Shemida [She·mi′da], *fame of wisdom*—A descendant of Manasseh (Num. 26:32; Josh. 17:2; 1 Chron. 7:19).

Shemidah [She·mi′dah]—See Shemida.

Shemidaites [She·mi′da·ites]—Descendants of Shemida of the tribe of Manasseh (Num. 26:32).

Shemiramoth [She·mi′ra·moth], *an exalted name*—Two Levites of the Old Testament:

1. A Levite singer who lived in the time of David (1 Chron. 15:18, 20).

2. A Levite appointed by Jehoshaphat of Judah to teach the people (2 Chron. 17:8)

Shemuel [She·mu'el], *name of God*—

1. Son of Ammihud. He represented the tribe of Simeon at the time of the division of the land of Canaan (Num. 34:20).

2. A form of the name Samuel, used once for Samuel the prophet (1 Chron. 6:33, KJV).

3. A descendant of Tola of Issachar (1 Chron. 7:2).

Shen [Shen], *a tooth*—A place near the spot where Samuel set up the memorial stone called Ebenezer (1 Sam. 7:12).

Shenazar [Shen·a'zar]—See Shenazzar.

Shenazzar [Shen·az'zar], possibly *splendid leader*—A son of Jeconiah (Jehoiachin) and brother of Salathiel (1 Chron. 3:18; Shanazzar, KJV).

Shenir [She'nir]—See Senir.

Sheol [She'ol]—Everyone who reads the Old Testament is agreed that *Sheol* has to do with a place or state to which one (or one's body) goes after death. Because of differing theological views, however, there is agreement on little else regarding this word.

The Hebrew word is apparently related to *shaal* "to ask," but exactly how is unknown. It occurs sixty-four times in the Old Testament. The KJV translates about half of them by "grave," nearly half by "hell," and three by "pit." Most modern versions, such as NKJV, also sometimes transliterate the Hebrew word, and frequently do so in footnotes.

Sheol as the Grave: Jacob uses the term four times in Genesis in reference to his being brought down in sorrow "to the grave" (Gen. 42:38). This meaning is undoubted. It frequently occurs in a parallel construction with *qeber,* "grave." Job's description of *Sheol* as a place of darkness, dust, worms, and decay certainly describe the physical grave (Job 17:13–16; 21:13; 24:19–20).

Peter quoted Psalm 16:10 in Acts 2:27 to prove that Christ arose from the grave, and Paul quoted Hosea 13:14 in 1 Corinthians 15:55 to teach the resurrection of Christians from the grave.

Sheol as Hell: When the context suggests a negative, fearful future, the translation "hell" is called for. For example, using "grave," or "Sheol," rather than "hell" in Psalm 9:17 would weaken that text considerably: "The wicked shall be turned into hell *and* all the nations that forget God." Righteous people also go to the grave and the unseen world, so punishment for disobedience must inspire a more fearful response. Proverbs 7:27 describes the harlot's temptations as "the way to hell." "Grave" could be used here, but would not provide as forceful a warning to a young man.

Sheol is paired with *abaddon* ("destruction") in both Proverbs 15:11 and 27:20. This is capitalized as "Hell and Destruction" in the NKJV to indicate personification. Since even the wise go to the grave, it is likely that avoiding eternal punishment in hell is meant here: "The way of life *winds* upward for the wise, that he may turn away from hell below" (Prov. 15:24).

Several of the occurrences of *Sheol* translated "hell" in the KJV probably refer to the grave. Unfortunately, when these are changed, some people insist that the translators do not believe in the doctrine of hell. This is certainly not true for the translators of the NASB, NIV, and NKJV, all of whose translators held orthodox views on eternal punishment (however unpopular that doctrine may be to modern man).

Sheol as Pit: In Numbers 16:30, 33, Korah and his fellow rebels went "down alive into the pit." KJV and NKJV translators believed this should be taken in quite a physical sense, as the ground opened up to swallow the rebels. The KJV's third occurrence of *Sheol* as "pit" (Job 17:16) in the NKJV is translated to allow other interpretations, since the second line of the parallelism uses "dust," which would suggest "grave" to many Bible readers. See Gehenna.

Shepham [She'pham], *bald*—An unidentified place on the eastern boundary of Canaan (Num. 34:10–11).

Shephatiah [Sheph·a·ti'ah], *Jehovah judges*—Nine Old Testament men:

1. A son of David born at Hebron. His mother was Abital (2 Sam. 3:4; 1 Chron. 3:3).

2. Son of Reuel, a Benjamite. After the Exile he lived at Jerusalem (1 Chron. 9:8; Shephathiah, KJV).

3. A Benjamite, a Haruphite, who joined David at Ziklag (1 Chron. 12:5).

4. Son of Maacah. In the time of David he was the head of the tribe of Simeon (1 Chron. 27:16).

5. A son of Jehoshaphat of Judah (2 Chron. 21:2).

6. Head of a family, a large number of whose members returned to Jerusalem with Zerubbabel and in the second expedition with Ezra (Ezra 2:4; 8:8; Neh. 7:9).

7. A servant of Solomon. His descendants returned with Zerubbabel from Babylon (Ezra 2:57; Neh. 7:59).

8. A descendant of Judah (Neh. 11:4).

9. Son of Mattan. He was a prince of Judah who advised Zedekiah, the king, to imprison Jeremiah because of his prophecies (Jer. 38:1).

Shepher [She'pher], *beauty*—A station of the Israelites in the wilderness (Num. 33:23–24; Shapher, KJV, REB).

Shephi, Shepho [She'phi, She'pho], *bold*—A son of Shobal and grandson of Seir (Gen. 36:23; 1 Chron. 1:40).

Shephupham [She·phu'pham]—See Shephuphan.

Shephuphan [She·phu'phan], *serpent*—Head of a Benjamite family (Num. 26:39; 1 Chron. 8:5). The name also appears as Muppim and Shuppim (Gen. 46:21; 1 Chron. 7:12, 15; 26:16).

Sherah [She'rah]—See Sheerah.

Sherebiah [Sher·e·bi'ah], *Jehovah has scorched*—Three Old Testament Levites:

1. Head of a Levitical family who returned with Ezra (Ezra 8:18).

2. A Levite who aided Ezra when he read the law to the people (Neh. 8:7; 9:4).

3. A Levite who returned from Babylon with Zerubbabel. He was the head of a family of musicians (Neh. 10:12; 12:8, 24).

Sheresh [She'resh], *root*—Son of Machir of Manasseh (1 Chron. 7:16).

Sherezer [She·re'zer]—See Sharezer.

Sheshach [She'shach], *thy fine linen*—A code word for Babel, or Babylonia. The code operates according to the ancient Hebrew system known as atbash (the first letter of the Hebrew alphabet stands for the last, the second stands for the next to last, etc.). This code word was used by the prophet Jeremiah when he predicted the downfall of the Babylonian Empire (Jer. 25:26; 51:41).

Sheshai [She'shai], *whitish*—A son of Anak who lived in Hebron (Num. 13:22).

Sheshan [She'shan], *noble*—A son of Ishi of the family of Hezron of Judah (1 Chron. 2:31).

Sheshbazzar [Shesh·baz'zar], *worshipper of fire*—The "prince of Judah," who brought the golden vessels from Babylon and who helped to lay the foundation of the second temple (Ezra 1:8, 11; 5:14–16). The name may be the Babylonian equivalent of Zerubbabel. Some regard him as the latter's uncle.

Sheth [Sheth], *unknown*—
    1. One of the sons of Adam and head of the messianic line (1 Chron. 1:1). See Seth.
    2. A chief of the Moabites (Num. 24:17).

Shethar [She'thar], *a star*—One of the princes of Persia attached to the court of Ahasuerus (Est. 1:14).

Shethar-bozenai [She'thar-boz'e·nai]—See Shethar-boznai.

Shethar-boznai [She'thar-boz'·nai], *star of splendor*—A Persian officer of high rank who, in the reign of Darius, joined others to prevent the Jews from rebuilding the temple (Ezra 5:3, 6; 6:6).

Sheva [She'va], *Jehovah contends*—Two Old Testament men:
    1. David's secretary (2 Sam. 20:25), also called Seraiah (2 Sam. 8:17) and Shavsha (1 Chron. 18:16).
    2. A man of Judah of the house of Caleb, son of Maacah (1 Chron. 2:49).

Shibmah [Shib'mah]—See Shebam.

Shicron [Shic'ron], *drunkenness*—A town on the northern border of Judah (Josh. 15:11), also written Shikkeron.

Shihor [Shi'hor], *black* or *turbid*—The eastern boundary of the promised land, described as being "east of Egypt" (Josh. 13:3) and also "in Egypt" (1 Chron. 13:5). It is uncertain whether this is referring to a branch of the Nile or to the Wadi el-'arish, the Brook of Egypt (Isa. 23:3; Jer. 2:18).

Shihor-libnath [Shi'hor-lib'nath], *turbid*—A small river near Carmel (Josh. 19:26).

Shikkeron [Shik'ke·ron]—See Shicron.

Shilhi [Shil'hi], *missive*—The father of Azubah, the mother of Jehoshaphat of Judah (1 Kings 22:42).

Shilhim [Shil'him], *fountains*—A town in the south of Judah (Josh. 15:32), possibly the place to which David pursued the Philistines (1 Sam. 17:52; 1 Chron. 4:31).

Shillem [Shil'lem], *retribution*—Son of Naphtali (Gen. 46:24; Num. 26:49). In 1 Chronicles 7:13 he is called Shallum.

Shillemites [Shil'le·mites]—The descendants of Naphtali's youngest son, Shillem (Num. 26:49).

Shiloah [Shi·lo'ah]—See Siloam.

Shiloh [Shi'loh], *rest*—A city in the territory of Ephraim that served an Israelite religious center during the days before the establishment of the united kingdom. Shiloh was "north of Bethel, on the east side of the highway that goes up from Bethel to Shechem, and south of Lebonah" (Judg. 21:19). This pinpoints Khirbet Seilun, about 16 kilometers (10 miles) northeast of Beth-el.

At Shiloh the tabernacle received its first permanent home, soon after the initial conquest of Canaan by the children of Israel (Josh. 18:1). This established Shiloh as the main sanctuary of worship for the Israelites during the period of the judges (Judg. 18:31). Here the last seven tribes received their allotments of land (Josh. 18:8–10).

Hannah prayed for a son at Shiloh (1 Sam. 1:3, 11). God granted her request by giving her Samuel. During his boyhood, Samuel worked with the high priest Eli at Shiloh. One of the most beautiful stories of the Old Testament is the account of Samuel's response to the voice of the Lord. Thinking his master Eli was calling him, he awakened the high priest to find out what the high priest wanted. Finally Eli realized that it was God calling Samuel, and Samuel's response to God's next call was as Eli had directed: "Speak, LORD, for your servant hears" (1 Sam. 3:1–10).

Samuel eventually succeeded Eli as the judge over Israel. The tabernacle, with the ark of the covenant, was still located in Shiloh during Samuel's early years as priest and prophet (1 Sam. 1:9; 4:3–4). However the ark was captured by the Philistines because God had forsaken Shiloh as the center of worship (Ps. 78:60).

When the ark was returned to the Israelites by the Philistines, it was not returned to Shiloh (2 Sam. 6:2–17). Archaeologists have determined that Khirbet Seilun (Shiloh) was destroyed about 1050 B.C. After the ark was moved to another city, Shiloh gradually lost its importance. This loss was made complete when Jerusalem was established as capital of the kingdom. After the division of the kingdom, Jeroboam established worship centers at Dan and Beth-el; but Ahijah, the prophet of the Lord, still remained at Shiloh (1 Kings 14:2, 4). From here, Ahijah pronounced the doom of Jeroboam's rule (1 Kings 14:7–16).

In the days of the prophet Jeremiah, Shiloh was in ruins (Jer. 7:12, 14), although some people continued to live on the site of this former city (Jer. 41:5). Shiloh became an inhabited town again in the days of the Greeks and Romans several centuries later.

Shiloni [Shi·lo′ni], *peace bringer*—The father of Zechariah, a man of the tribe of Judah who lived in Jerusalem after the captivity (Neh. 11:5), also translated "the Shilonite."

Shilonite [Shi′lo·nite]—

1. A native or resident of Shiloh, such as Ahijah the prophet (1 Kings 11:29).

2. A member of the house of Shelah (Gen. 38:5; Num. 26:20; 1 Chron. 9:5; Neh. 11:5).

Shilshah [Shil′shah], *triad*—Son of Zophah of Asher (1 Chron. 7:37).

Shimea, Shimeah [Shim′e·a, Shim′e·ah], *fame*—

1. David's brother, the third son of Jesse (2 Sam. 13:3), father of Jonadab and Jonathan (2 Sam. 13:3, 32; 21:21). Also called Shammah (1 Sam. 16:9) and Shimma (1 Chron. 2:13).

2. Son of David by Bath-sheba (1 Chron. 3:5), also called Shammua (2 Sam. 5:14; 1 Chron. 14:4).

3. Son of Uzza, a Levite of the family of Merari (1 Chron. 6:30).

4. A Levite of the family of Gershom (1 Chron. 6:39, 43).

5. A descendant of Jeiel, a Benjamite (1 Chron. 9:38), also called Shimeah (1 Chron. 8:32).

Shimeam [Shim′e·am], *their fame*—Son of Mikloth of Benjamin (1 Chron. 9:38). In 1 Chronicles 8:32 he is called Shimeah.

Shimeath [Shim′e·ath], *report*—A woman of Ammon; mother of one of those who killed Joash (2 Kings 12:21).

Shimeathites [Shim′e·a·thites], *report*—A family of scribes who lived at Jabez in Judah (1 Chron. 2:55).

Shimei [Shim′e·i], *famous*—A number of Old Testament men:

1. Son of Gershon and grandson of Levi (Ex. 6:17; Num. 3:18, 21).

2. Son of Gera of Benjamin, of the house of Saul. He lived on the eastern side of the Mount of Olives. When David was passing down the mount leaving Jerusalem in the time of Absalom's rebellion, Shimei hurled insults at him. David forgave him but he was put to death later by Solomon for disobeying a royal order (2 Sam. 16:5–13; 1 Kings 2:8–9, 36–46).

3. The son of Elah. He remained loyal to Solomon when Adonijah attempted to seize the throne (1 Kings 1:8).

4. Solomon's purveyor in the territory of Benjamin (1 Kings 4:18).

5. A brother of Zerubbabel, of the royal line of Judah (1 Chron. 3:19).

6. Son of Zacchur of Simeon. He had twenty-two children (1 Chron. 4:24–27).

7. Son of Gog and father of Micah of Reuben (1 Chron. 5:4).

8. A Levite family of Merari (1 Chron. 6:29).

9. Son of Jahath, a Levite of the family of Gershon (1 Chron. 6:42).

10. A Benjamite (1 Chron. 8:21; Shimha, KJV; or Shema, 1 Chron. 8:13).

11. A family of Gershom (1 Chron. 23:6–9).

12. Son of Jeduthun. He was head of the tenth division of singers in the reign of David (1 Chron. 25:3–17).

13. A Ramathite. He had charge of David's vineyards (1 Chron. 27:27).

14. A son of Heman, a Levite. In the reign of Hezekiah he assisted in the cleansing of the temple (2 Chron. 29:14–16).

15. The brother of Conaniah, a Levite. He had charge of the offerings in the reign of Hezekiah (2 Chron. 31:12–13). He may be the same as the preceding.

16. A Levite in the time of Ezra who divorced his foreign wife (Ezra 10:23).

17. A son of Hashum who divorced his foreign wife (Ezra 10:33).

18. A son of Bani who divorced his foreign wife (Ezra 10:38).

19. Son of Kish of Benjamin, an ancestor of Mordecai (Est. 2:5).

Shimeites [Shim'e·ites]—See Shimites.

Shimeon [Shim'e·on], *a hearing*—A son of Harim who divorced his foreign wife (Ezra 10:31).

Shimhi [Shim'hi]—See Shimei.

Shimi [Shim'i]—See Shimei.

Shimites [Shim·ites]—Descendants of Shimei, grandson of Levi (Num. 3:21).

Shimma [Shim'ma]—See Shimea.

Shimon [Shi'mon], *desert*—A man of Judah. His genealogy is obscure (1 Chron. 4:20).

Shimrath [Shim'rath], *guarding*—Son of Shimei of Aijalon (1 Chron. 8:21), a Benjamite.

Shimri [Shim'ri], *watchful*—Four Old Testament men:

1. Son of Shemaiah of Simeon (1 Chron. 4:37).

2. Father of Jediael, one of David's warriors (1 Chron. 11:45).

3. Son of Hosah, a Levite of Merari; gatekeeper in the time of David (1 Chron. 26:10; Simri, KJV).

4. Son of Elizaphan, a Levite who assisted in Hezekiah's reforms (2 Chron. 29:13).

Shimrith [Shim'rith], *vigilant*—Mother of one of the murderers of Joash; a Moabitess (2 Chron. 24:26). Also called Shomer (2 Kings 12:21).

Shimrom [Shim'rom]—See Shimron No. 1.

Shimron [Shim'ron], *a guard*—

1. Son of Issachar and head of a tribal family (Gen. 46:13; Num. 26:24).

2. A town on the border of Zebulun (Josh. 11:1; 19:15).

Shimronites [Shim'ron·ites]—Descendants of Issachar's son Shimron (Num. 26:24).

Shimron-meron [Shim'ron-me'ron], *watch-height of Meron*— A town of the Canaanites conquered by Joshua (Josh. 12:20), possibly the same as Shimron No. 2.

Shimshai [Shim'shai], *sunny*—A scribe who, with others, made a complaint to Artaxerxes protesting against the rebuilding of the wall (Ezra 4:8).

Shinab [Shi'nab], *splendor of the father*—The king of Admah (Gen. 14:2, 8, 10).

Shinar [Shi'nar], *country of two rivers*—The plain of Babylon (Gen. 10:10; 11:2; Dan. 1:2).

Shion [Shi'on], *ruin*—A town of Isaachar (Josh. 19:19; Shihon, KJV).

Shiphi [Shi'phi], *abundant*—Son of Allon and father of Ziza of Simeon. He lived in the time of Hezekiah (1 Chron. 4:37).

Shiphmite [Shiph'mite], *fruitful*—Probably a native of Shepham or Siphmoth (1 Chron. 27:27).

Shiphrah [Shiph'rah], *splendor*—A Hebrew midwife who refused to obey the order of Pharaoh to kill the male infants (Ex. 1:15).

Shiphtan [Shiph'tan], *judicial*—Father of Kemuel of Ephraim (Num. 34:24).

Shisha [Shi'sha]—See Shavsha.

Shishak [Shi'shak]—See Pharaoh.

Shitrai [Shit·ra'i], *my officers*—The Sharonite who had charge of David's herds (1 Chron. 27:29).

Shittim [Shit'tim], *acacia*—

1. The last encampment of the Israelites in the plains of Moab, east of the Jordan (Num. 25:1). It was while the Israelites were here that the Moabite king Balak tried to hire Balaam to curse them (Num. 22–24) and here the people sinned and were punished (Num. 25). The second census was taken at this point and laws were given regarding the inheritance of daughters. From this point Joshua sent the spies to Jericho (Josh. 2:1).

2. A barren valley near Jerusalem and the Dead Sea, probably the lower Kidron Valley (Joel 3:18).

See Abel Acacia Grove.

Shiza [Shi'za], *splendor*—A Reubenite and father of Adina who was one of David's warriors (1 Chron. 11:42).

Shoa [Sho'a], *rich*—A country and its people mentioned by Ezekiel as future enemies of Judah (Ezek. 23:23).

Shobab [Sho'bab], *rebellious*—Two Old Testament men:

1. The son of Caleb and grandson of Hezron of Judah. His mother was Azubah (1 Chron. 2:18).

2. A son of David (2 Sam. 5:14).

Shobach [Sho'bach], *pouring out*—The general of Hadarezer, king of Zobah (2 Sam. 10:16). Also called Shophach (1 Chron. 19:16, 18).

Shobai [Sho·ba'i], *taking captive*—A Levite (Ezra 2:42; Neh. 7:45).

Shobal [Sho'bal], *flowing*—Two Old Testament men:

1. The second son of Seir and one of the Horite princes (Gen. 36:20, 29).

2. A son of Caleb of Judah (1 Chron. 2:50; 4:1).

Shobek [Sho'bek], *forsaking*—One of the peoples' leaders who sealed the covenant with Nehemiah (Neh. 10:24).

Shobi [Sho'bi], *glorious*—An Ammonite, son of Nahash of Rabbah (2 Sam. 17:27).

Shocho, Shochoh, Socoh [Sho'cho, Sho'choh, So'coh]—See Sochoh.

Shoham [Sho'ham], *onyx*—Son of Jaaziah (1 Chron. 24:27).

Shomer [Sho'mer], *keeper*—
1. Son of Heber of Asher (1 Chron. 7:32). See Shemer.
2. The mother of one of the murderers of King Joash, a Moabitess (2 Kings 12:21). See Shimrith.

Shophach [Sho'phach]—See Shobach.

Shophan [Sho'phan]—See Atroth-shophan.

Shua [Shu'a], *wealth*—A man and a woman of the Old Testament:
1. A Canaanite. His daughter was the wife of Judah and the mother of Er, Onan, and Shelah (Gen. 38:2, 12).
2. A daughter of Heber of Asher (1 Chron. 7:32).

Shuah [Shu'ah], *pit*—A son of Abraham and Keturah (Gen. 25:2; 1 Chron. 1:32). Also see Shuhah.

Shual [Shu'al], *fox*—
1. A district near Beth-el invaded by the Philistines (1 Sam. 13:17).
2. Son of Zophah of Asher (1 Chron. 7:36).

Shubael [Shu'ba·el]—See Shebuel.

Shuhah [Shu'hah], *pit*—A man of Judah (1 Chron. 4:11; also called Shuah).

Shuham [Shu'ham], *depression*—Son of Dan and head of a tribal family (Num. 26:42). In Genesis 46:23 he is called Hushim.

Shuhamites [Shu'ham·ites]—Descendants of Dan's son Shuham (Num. 26:42).

Shuhite [Shu'hite], *wealth*—The surname of Bildad, one of Job's friends (Job 2:11; 8:1; 18:1; 25:1; 42:9).

Shulamite [Shu'la·mite], *the perfect*—A young woman mentioned in Song of Solomon 6:13 (Shulammite, NRSV, NIV, REB, NASB). Many scholars interpret Shulamite as Shunammite—a woman from the city of Shunem (1 Sam. 28:4).

Others believe this woman was Abishag, the lovely young Shunammite brought to David in his old age (1 Kings 1:1–4, 15) and who later apparently was a part of Solomon's harem (1 Kings 2:17–22).

Shulammite [Shu'lam·mite]—See Shulamite.

Shumathites [Shu'ma·thites]—One of the families of Kirjath-jearim (1 Chron. 2:53).

Shunammite [Shu·nam'mite], *double resting place*—A native of Shunem. Two Shunammite women are mentioned in the Bible. The first is Abishag, the beautiful young woman brought in to care for David in his last days (1 Kings 1:3; 2:17, 21). The second is the woman whose child Elisha restored to life (2 Kings 4:8, 12; 8:1).

Shunem [Shu'nem], *double resting place*—A border town of Issachar, some sixteen miles southwest of the Sea of Galilee (Josh. 19:18). It was the place where the Philistines camped before their victory over Saul (1 Sam. 28:4).

Shuni [Shu'ni], *quiet*—A son of Gad and head of a tribal family (Gen. 46:16; Num. 26:15).

Shunites [Shu'nites]—The family descended from Gad's son Shuni (Num. 26:15).

Shupham [Shu'pham]—See Shephupham.

Shuphamite [Shu'pham·ite]—The family descended from Shuphim or Shephupham (Num. 26:39).

Shuppim [Shup'pim], *serpents*—
  1. A man of Benjamin (1 Chron. 7:12, 15). See Shephupham.
  2. A Levite doorkeeper of the temple (1 Chron. 26:16).

Shur [Shur], *wall*—A place or district on the border of Egypt mentioned in connection with Abraham, Hagar, and the sons of Ishmael (Gen. 16:7; 20:1; 25:18).

Shushan [Shu'shan], *lily*—The Persian capital (Neh. 1:1; Est. 1:2; Dan. 8:2). It was also called Susa.

Shushanchites [Shu·shan'chites]—Inhabitants of Susa (Ezra 4:9).

Shuthalhites [Shu·thal'hites]—See Shuthelah.

Shuthelah [Shu·the'lah], *noise of breaking*—

1. Son of Ephraim and head of a tribal family (Num. 26:35–36; 1 Chron. 7:20).

2. A descendant of Ephraim (1 Chron. 7:21).

Sia, Siaha [Si'a, Si'a·ha], *assembly*—A Nethinim family (Siaha, Ezra 2:44; Sia, Neh. 7:47).

Sibbecai [Sib'be·cai]—See Sibbechai.

Sibbechai [Sib'be·chai], *weaver*—A Hushathite and one of David's mighty men (1 Chron. 11:29).

Sibmah [Sib'mah], *coolness*—A town of Reuben east of the Jordan (Josh. 13:19). See Shebam.

Sibraim [Sib'ra·im], *twofold hope*—An unidentified place on the northern boundary of Palestine (Ezek. 47:16).

Sichem [Si'chem]—See Shechem.

Siddim [Sid'dim], *field* or *plain*—A valley in the region of the Dead Sea (Gen. 14:3, 8).

Sidon [Si'don], *hunting*—A city of Phoenicia, north of Tyre. It is called Sidon in the New Testament and Zidon in the Old Testament. It was the northern limit of Zebulun and Asher (Gen. 49:13; Josh. 19:28; Judg. 1:31).

In the course of time the city was subject to Tyre, to Sennacherib in 701 B.C., to Alexander the Great in 333 B.C., and to Rome in 64 B.C. The city supplied cedar for the building of the second temple (Ezra 3:7). It was repeatedly denounced by the prophets (Isa. 23:12; Ezek. 28:21–22). Persons from Sidon heard Jesus preach in Galilee and once Jesus visited this vicinity (Matt. 15:21; Mark 3:8). Paul landed at Sidon on his voyage to Rome as a prisoner (Acts 27:3). See Tyre and Sidon.

Sidonians [Si'don·i·ans]—Inhabitants of Sidon (Deut. 3:9). The Israelites were supposed to drive the Sidonians out of the land, but they failed to do so (Josh. 13:4, 6; Judg. 3:3). The Sidonians were skillful lumbermen (1 Kings 5:6).

Sihon [Si'hon], *warrior*—A king of the Amorites defeated by the Israelites during their journey toward the land of Canaan. Moses asked Sihon to let the Israelites pass peacefully through his kingdom, located east of the Jordan River. Sihon refused and later attacked the Israelites at Jahaz. In the battle that followed Sihon and his army were killed (Num. 21:21–32), and his territory was given to the tribes of Gad and Reuben (Num. 32:33). Sihon's defeat is mentioned often in the Old Testament (Deut. 1:4; Josh. 2:10; Ps. 135:11; Jer. 48:45).

Sihor [Si'hor]—See Shihor.

Silas [Si'las], *woody*—The contracted form of Silvanus. Silas was a member of the church at Jerusalem (Acts 15:22), probably a Hellenistic Jew. He was commissioned by the Council at Jerusalem to report its decision about circumcision to the church of Antioch (Acts 15:22, 27, 32). When Paul and Barnabas disagreed regarding Mark, Silas became Paul's companion on the second journey (Acts 15:40). At Philippi they were imprisoned (Acts 16:19, 25). He remained with Timothy at Berea and both joined Paul at Corinth (Acts 18:5). In the Epistles he is called Silvanus.

Silla [Sil'la], *twig* or *basket*—A place near the house of Millo (2 Kings 12:20).

Siloam [Si·lo'am], *sent* or *conducted*—A famous pool of Jerusalem, also called the upper pool to distinguish it from the nearby old or lower pool (Isa. 7:3; 22:9), and probably identical with the king's pool (Neh. 2:14). It was south of the temple area and just west of the Kidron Valley (John 9:6–7). See also Hezekiah's Water Tunnel.

Siloam, Tower of [Si·lo'am]—A tower mentioned by Jesus. It had recently collapsed, and eighteen people were killed (Luke 13:4). It was probably near the Pool of Siloam, but its exact location is unsure. It may have been on the site of the modern village of Siloam, across the valley from the Gihon spring.

Silvanus [Sil·va'nus]—See Silas.

Simeon [Sim'e·on], *(God) hears*—The name of five men and a tribe in the Bible:

1. The second son of Jacob and Leah (Gen. 29:33). Simeon's descendants became one of the twelve tribes of Israel. He and his brother Levi

tricked the Hivites of Shechem and massacred all the males because one of them had raped Dinah, their sister (Gen. 34:2, 25, 30). Later Jacob deplored this deed (Gen. 49:5–7). Simeon was the brother whom Joseph kept as security when he allowed his brothers to leave Egypt and return to their father, Jacob, in the land of Canaan (Gen. 42:24).

2. A devout Jew who blessed the infant Jesus in the temple (Luke 2:25, 34). The Holy Spirit had promised Simeon that he would not die until he had seen the long-awaited Messiah. Simeon recognized the child as the Messiah when Mary and Joseph brought Him to the temple to present Him to the Lord.

3. The son of Judah and an ancestor of Joseph listed in the genealogy of Jesus Christ (Luke 3:30).

4. A Christian prophet or teacher in the church at Antioch of Syria (Acts 13:1). Some scholars believe Simeon was the same person as Simon of Cyrene, who bore Jesus' cross (Luke 23:26).

5. A variant of Simon Peter (Acts 15:14). See Peter, Simon.

6. The tribe descended from the sons of Simeon. The six sons were Jemuel, Janim, Jachin, Zohar, Shaul, and Ohad, and all but the latter founded a tribal family (Gen. 46:10; Num. 26:12–14; 1 Chron. 4:24). The tribe was located in the extreme south of Judah and eventually was absorbed by the tribe of Judah (Josh. 19:1, 2, 9).

Simon [Si'mon], *(God) hears*—The name of nine men in the New Testament:

1. Simon Peter, the Galilean fisherman who became an apostle of Christ (Matt. 4:18; 10:2). Simon was the son of Jonah (Matt. 16:17; John 21:15) and a brother of the apostle Andrew (John 1:40). See Peter, Simon.

2. Another of the Twelve, called the Canaanite to distinguish him from Simon Peter. The name may also indicate he was a member of a fanatical Jewish sect, the Zealots (Matt. 10:4; Mark 3:18; Luke 6:15; Acts 1:13). Members of this group were fanatical opponents of Roman rule in Palestine. As a Zealot, Simon would have hated any foreign domination or interference.

3. One of Jesus' brothers (Matt. 13:55).

4. A former leper in whose house Mary, the sister of Lazarus, anointed Jesus' feet with a precious ointment, spikenard (Matt. 26:6–13; Mark 14:3–9; John 12:1–8). It is probable that Jesus cured his leprosy. Mary, Martha, and Lazarus were present when this happened, and

Martha took an active part in serving the dinner. This has led to speculation that Simon was a member of the family or at least was a very close friend.

5. A man of Cyrene who was forced to carry Jesus' cross (Matt. 27:32; Mark 15:21; Luke 23:26). Simon was the father of Alexander and Rufus, men who were known to the early Christians in Rome (Rom. 16:13).

6. A Pharisee in whose house Jesus ate (Luke 7:36–50). On that occasion a woman who was a sinner anointed Jesus' feet. Simon felt that Jesus should not have allowed her to come near Him. But Jesus explained that sinners like her were the very ones who needed forgiveness.

7. The father of Judas Iscariot (John 13:2). Both father and son are called Iscariot. The NRSV has "Judas the son of Simon Iscariot" (John 6:71; 13:26).

8. A sorcerer known as Simon Magus, or Simon the magician, who tried to buy spiritual powers from the apostle Peter who chastised him for trying (Acts 8:9–24). Simon's feats were so impressive that the people of Samaria declared, "This man is the great power of God" (Acts 8:10), and followed him. But when Philip the evangelist preached, the Samaritans believed and were baptized. Simon also believed and was baptized.

Later the apostles Peter and John visited Samaria to make sure these believers received the power of the Holy Spirit. When Simon saw that the Holy Spirit was bestowed by the laying on of hands, he attempted to buy this power. Peter rebuked him, "Your money perish with you, because you thought that the gift of God could be purchased with money! You have neither part nor portion in this matter, for your heart is not right in the sight of God" (Acts 8:20–21).

9. A tanner of Joppa. Peter was staying at his house when he had the vision of the clean and unclean animals and received the summons from Cornelius (Acts 9:43; 10:6, 17, 32).

Simon Peter [Si'mon Pe'ter]—See Peter, Simon.

Simri [Sim'ri]—See Shimri.

Sin [Sin], possibly *thorn* or *clay*—A fortified city on the border of Egypt (Ezek. 30:15–16).

Sin, Wilderness of—A wilderness through which the Israelites passed on their way to Mount Sinai (Ex. 16:1; 17:1; Num. 33:12). God first sent the manna while they were in this area, and also the quail.

Sina [Si′na]—Sinai in the Greek form (Acts 7:30, 38).

Sinai [Si′nai], *thorny*—The name of a peninsula, a wilderness, and a mountain in the Bible. All three of these played a prominent role in the life of God's covenant people as they searched for the Land of Promise following their miraculous deliverance from enslavement in Egypt.

The Peninsula: Shaped like a triangle, the peninsula of Sinai is an area of great contrasts. It appears to hang from the southeast corner of the Mediterranean Sea with its base serving as the land bridge between Egypt and Israel. The peninsula is bounded on the west by the Gulf of Suez and on the east by the Gulf of Aqaba.

The Sinai peninsula is about 240 kilometers (150 miles) wide at the northern end and about 400 kilometers (250 miles) long. Its land area is desert and a tableland rising to about 762 meters (2,500 feet). On the north the Sinai plateau slopes away to the Mediterranean Sea. Near the south end of the peninsula a series of granite mountains rise 1,209 to 2,743 meters (4,000 to 9,000 feet) high, in striking contrast to the surrounding wastelands.

The Wilderness: Exodus 19:1 indicates that "in the third month after the children of Israel had gone out of the land of Egypt, on the same day, they came to the Wilderness of Sinai." This phrase may refer only to the particular desert that lies at the foot of Mount Sinai and in which the Israelites pitched their camp. But the phrase may also refer in a broader sense to the entire desert area of the Sinai Peninsula. If this is the case, it would include the Wilderness of Sin, through which the Israelites passed between Elim and Mount Sinai (Ex. 16:1); the wilderness of Paran, in the central Sinaitic Peninsula (Num. 10:12); the wilderness of Shur, east of Egypt in the northern Sinai (Gen. 16:7); and the wilderness of Zin, close to the border of Canaan (Num. 13:21).

The Mountain: Perhaps the most frequent use of the word *Sinai* is in connection with the mountain. This was the mountain where God met Moses and gave him the law (Ex. 19:3, 20). This mountain is to be identified with Mount Horeb (Ex. 3:1), or perhaps Horeb refers to a mountain range or ridge and Sinai to an individual summit on that ridge. The name Sinai is used at the time when the Israelites were actually at the foot of the mountain (Ex. 19:11), whereas Horeb is used upon reflection about the events that happened here.

Although several mountains have been identified as possibilities, there are only two serious contenders for the title—Jebel Serbal (2,070 meters; 6,791 feet) in central Sinai and Jebel Musa (2,286 meters; about 7,500 feet) in southern Sinai. One of a cluster of three peaks, Jebel Musa, Arabic for "Mount Moses," has a broad plain at its base, where the Israelites may have camped.

Biblical References: After the Israelites left Egypt, they camped first in the Wilderness of Sin, then at Rephidim, and finally at Sinai. Moses climbed the mountain and received the tablets of the law from God. A stirring atmospheric disturbance accompanied God's meeting with the people (Ex. 19:18–19; 20:18).

During their years of wandering in the Sinai wilderness, the census was taken (Num. 1:1–46), the firstborn were redeemed (Num. 3:40–51), the office and duties of the Levites were established (Num. 4:1–49), and the first tabernacle was built (Num. 9:15).

Sinim [Si′nim], *thorns*—A distant land from which exiles shall return (Isa. 49:12).

Sinite [Si′nite], *thorn* or *clay*—A Canaanite tribe (Gen. 10:17).

Sion [Si′on]—

    1. An ancient name for Mount Hermon (Deut. 4:48).

    2. The Greek form of Zion. This term is used to specifically apply to the temple mount, and more generally to the city of Jerusalem (Rom. 9:33).

Siphmoth [Siph′moth], *fruitful*—A place where David took refuge when persecuted by Saul (1 Sam. 30:28).

Sippai [Sip′pa·i]—See Saph.

Sirah [Si′rah], *retreat*—A well near Hebron where Joab and his brother murdered Abner (2 Sam. 3:26).

Sirion [Si′ri·on], *coat of mail*—The name by which Hermon was known to the Sidonians (Deut. 3:9; Ps. 29:6).

Sisamai [Sis′a·mai]—See Sismai.

Sisera [Sis'e·ra]—The name of two men in the Old Testament:

1. The commander of the army of Jabin, king of Canaan. Deborah and Barak defeated Jabin's army under Sisera's command at the river Kishon. He fled and hid in the home of Heber the Kenite. Sisera was soon after killed by Jael, Heber's wife, who drove a tent peg into his temple (Judg. 4:1–22).

2. One of the Nethinim who returned from the captivity with Zerubbabel (Neh. 7:55).

Sismai [Sis'mai], unknown—Son of Eleasah of the line of Jerahmeel of Judah (1 Chron. 2:40; Sisamai, KJV).

Sithri [Sith'ri], *a hiding place*—A Levite of the family of Kohath (Ex. 6:22).

Sitnah [Sit'nah], *enmity*—A well in the Philistine country near Gerar (Gen. 26:21).

Sivan [Si'van], *their covering*—The third month of the sacred year and ninth of the civil year, corresponding roughly to May/June (Est. 8:9).

Siyon [Si'yon]—See Zion.

Skull, Place of the—See Calvary.

Slaughter, Valley of—See Tophet.

Smyrna [Smyr'na], *myrrh*—A city of Ionia. Smyrna was a center for emperor worship. They had built a temple dedicated to Tiberius Caesar in 23 B.C., and under such emperors as Nero and Domitian, persecution of Christians was severe. (Rev. 1:11; 2:8–11).

So [So], possibly *a measure for grain*—A king of Egypt to whom Hoshea of Israel sent letters (2 Kings 17:4).

Sochoh, Socoh, Soco [So'choh, So'coh, So'co], *hedge*—

1. A town in the lowland of Judah (Josh. 15:35), also spelled Shochoh or Shoco.

2. A town in the hill country of Judah (Josh. 15:48).

3. A city under the jurisdiction of Ben-hesed, one of Solomon's twelve food purveyors (1 Kings 4:10).

4. A man of Judah, son of Heber (1 Chron. 4:18; Shocho, KJV), or possibly the same as No. 1, and not a person.

Sodi [So'di], *intimate*—Father of the spy who represented Zebulun (Num. 13:10).

Sodom [Sod'om]—A city at the southern end of the Dead Sea destroyed because of its wickedness (Gen. 10:19; Rom. 9:29). Together with her sister cities—Gomorrah, Admah, Zeboiim, and Zoar—Sodom formed the famous pentapolis of the plain or circle of the Jordan (Gen. 10:19; 13:10; 14:2) in the valley that surrounded the Dead Sea (Gen. 14:3). It was famous for its wickedness, particularly its extremely promiscuous homosexuality.

Although Sodom was a notoriously wicked city, when Lot separated himself and his herdsmen from Abraham, he chose to pitch his tent toward Sodom (Gen. 13:5–13). This was because the fertile plain that surrounded the city "was well watered everywhere" (Gen. 13:10).

When Sodom was plundered by Chedorlaomer, the goods and captives he carried away had to be rescued by Abraham (Gen. 14:11, 21–24). However, the wickedness of the people of the city continued, and God finally had to destroy Sodom.

Fire and brimstone fell from heaven and consumed Sodom and Gomorrah and the other cities of the plain. Lot's wife disobeyed the word of the two angels who had been sent to rescue them by looking back at Sodom, and she was instantly changed into a pillar of salt (Gen. 19:26).

Early tradition held that the northern end of the Dead Sea was the valley of Sodom. But the geological conditions of the southern end of the Dead Sea matched those of the area around Sodom. Salt formations, asphalt, and sulfur are found in large quantities here. Many scholars believe the cities of the plain may be located beneath the shallow end of the Dead Sea. The basin surrounding the shallow southern end of the Dead Sea is fed by five streams, including the Wadi Zered (Num. 21:12), which would have provided for a fertile, well-watered plain. In addition, Zoar, one of the cities of the plain (Gen. 13:10), is reported by the Jewish historian Josephus to have been visible during his time at the southern end of the sea. Other scholars have recently claimed that the most likely site for the cities of the plain is on the eastern shore of the Dead Sea opposite Masada.

The sin, vice, and infamy of Sodom and the judgment of God on this city are referred to often throughout the Bible (Isa. 1:9–10; Ezek. 16:46–49; Amos 4:11; Rom. 9:29).

Sodomite [Sod′om·ite]—An inhabitant of the city of Sodom (Gen. 19:5). The word has come to mean anyone who engages in homosexual acts.

Solomon [Sol′o·mon], *peaceful*—The builder of the temple in Jerusalem and the first king of Israel to trade commercial goods profitably to other nations; author of much of the book of Proverbs and perhaps also the author of the Song of Solomon and Ecclesiastes.

Solomon succeeded David, his father, as the third king of a unified Israel. Solomon's rise met with widespread approval from the people, but David's officials were slow to accept the new king. They did warm up considerably, however, when they realized David was determined to anoint Solomon as his heir. Solomon became Israel's king because God had told David that Saul's heirs would not follow him to the throne. Thus, Solomon became king although there was no clear precedent for his succession. According to the chronology in 1 Kings 11:42, Solomon was about twenty years old when he was crowned. He assumed leadership of Israel at a time of great material and spiritual prosperity. During his forty-year reign (970–931 B.C.), he expanded his kingdom until it covered about 50,000 square miles—from Egypt in the south to Syria in the north to the borders of Mesopotamia in the east.

Great Beginnings: One of the first things Solomon did as king was to go to Gibeon to offer sacrifices to the Lord. God appeared to the new king at night and asked him, "What shall I give thee?" Solomon asked for an understanding heart to judge the people of Israel and the ability to tell good from evil. God not only granted Solomon's request but He also promised him riches and honor if he would walk in the steps of his father (1 Kings 3:4–15).

Solomon organized Israel much as David had done, but he enlarged and expanded its government. He divided the country into twelve districts, each of which was responsible for providing the court with regular supplies one month out of the year, with a supply officer in charge of each district. As the years passed, Solomon's court reached a standard of luxury that had never existed in Israel's history.

Wisdom: Solomon is usually remembered as a wise man. His Proverbs and his Song of Songs demonstrate his deep knowledge of the natural world (plants, animals, etc.). He also had a profound knowledge of human nature, as demonstrated by the two women who claimed the same child. His suggestion that the child be physically divided between the two was a masterful strategy for finding out who was the real mother (1 Kings 3:16–28). Solomon's concern with the ethics of everyday life is evident in his Proverbs. They show that Solomon loved wisdom and was always trying to teach it to others. They also indicate he was a keen observer who could learn from the mistakes of others.

Solomon's sayings in these Proverbs are so true that they sound almost trite today. Their clarity sometimes hides their depth. During his lifetime, Solomon's fame as a man of wisdom spread to surrounding lands, and leaders came from afar to hear him speak. When the queen of Sheba came to test his wisdom, he answered all her questions with ease. After she saw the extent of his empire and the vastness of his knowledge, she confessed that she had underestimated him (2 Chron. 9:1–12).

Solomon's Temple: One of Solomon's first major feats was the construction of the temple his father, David, started in Jerusalem as a place for worship of the God of Israel. The task was enormous, involving much planning and many workers. A work force of 30,000 was employed in cutting timber from the cedars of Lebanon. Also working on this massive project were 80,000 cutters of stone in the quarries of Jerusalem, 70,000 ordinary workers, and many superintendents. Gold, silver, and other precious metals were imported from other lands. Hiram, king of Tyre, sent architects and other craftsmen to assist with the project. The building was completed after seven years. The temple was famous not for its size—since it was relatively small—but for the quality of its elaborate workmanship (1 Kings 6–7).

After the temple was completed, Solomon planned an elaborate program of dedication. He invited the leaders of all twelve tribes to attend as he presided over the ceremony. The ark of the covenant was brought into the most sacred place in the temple as a cloud filled the room to hide God's presence. King Solomon then blessed the crowd, recounted the history of the building of the temple, and offered long prayers of dedication while standing at the altar. This reveals the admirable spirit of devotion in Solomon's heart. The dedication ceremony lasting seven days was followed by observance of the Feast of Tabernacles (1 Kings 8–9).

Immediately after the dedication, the Lord appeared to Solomon once again. He assured the king that his prayers had been heard and that the temple had been blessed. He also warned Solomon that the divine favor and protection that had been bestowed upon Israel would continue only if their faith remained uncorrupted by other beliefs. If idolatry should be introduced, Israel would be punished and the temple would be destroyed (1 Kings 9:1–9).

Other Buildings: After completing the temple, Solomon built the palace complex, a series of five structures that took thirteen years to complete. He also built many cities to assist the development of his trade empire. Among these were Tadmor (also called Palmyra) and Baalath (also called Baalbek) in Syria. To protect his kingdom, he built fortresses and lodgings for his army. These fortifications, especially the ones at Jerusalem, Gezer, Megiddo, and Hazor, had strong double walls and massive gateways.

Commercial Enterprises: Trade with other nations was another of Solomon's contributions to the nation of Israel. The international situation was favorable for a strong leader to emerge in Israel; traditional centers of strength in Egypt and Syria were at an all-time low. Solomon entered into trade agreements with a number of nations, increasing Israel's wealth and prestige.

Although Solomon had a strong army and strong navy, he relied upon a system of treaties with his neighbors to keep the peace. Egypt was allied with Israel through the marriage of Solomon to the daughter of the pharaoh. The seafaring cities of Tyre and Sidon were also united to Israel by trade agreements. Some of Israel's trade was conducted overland by way of camel caravans. But the most significant trade was by sea across the Mediterranean Sea through an alliance with Tyre. Solomon's ships apparently went as far west as Spain to bring back silver. Soon Solomon became the ruler of a huge commercial empire. Archaeologists believe that Solomon's trading may have brought him into conflict with the queen of Sheba. One purpose of her famous visit to Solomon may have been to establish trade agreements between Solomon's kingdom and her own nation (1 Kings 10:1–13).

Solomon's Sins: Solomon's reign brought changes not only to Israel but also to his own life. Near the end of his life, the king lost the ideals of his youth, becoming restless and unsatisfied. The book of Ecclesiastes, proclaiming that "all is vanity" ("meaningless," NIV), supports the view that the world's wisest man had become a jaded figure in his old age.

Solomon's greatest sin was his loss of devotion to the God of the Hebrew people. In this, he fell victim to his own trade agreements. By custom, beautiful women were awarded to the most powerful member of a treaty to seal the covenant. The constant influx of wives and concubines in Solomon's court led eventually to his downfall. Thus, Solomon broke the Mosaic law and violated the warning not to stray from the path of his father, David. The large number of foreign women in Solomon's court made many demands upon the king. He allowed these "outsiders" to practice their pagan religions. The result was that Jerusalem, and even its holy temple, was the scene of pagan practices and idol worship (1 Kings 11:1–13).

Solomon's own faith was weakened. Eventually he approved of, and even participated in, these idolatrous acts. The example he set for the rest of the nation must have been demoralizing. This unfortunate error was a severe blow to the security of Solomon's throne and to the nation he had built.

The End of Solomon's Throne: Years before Solomon's death, his heavy taxation of the people brought unrest and rebellion. Surrounding nations began to marshal their forces to free themselves of Israel's tyranny, but the most serious uprising came from within the nation itself. When Solomon's son Rehoboam ascended the throne after his father, Jeroboam, a young leader who had been exiled to Egypt, returned to lead a successful civil war against him. The result was a division of Solomon's united kingdom into two separate nations—the southern kingdom of Judah and the northern kingdom of Israel.

Solomon's Character: In many ways, Solomon's forty-year reign as king of the Hebrew people is a puzzle. In his early years he was both noble and humble—undoubtedly one of the best rulers of his day. Although he was surrounded by wealth and luxury as a young man, he seemed to be a person of honor and integrity. He was the first king in Israel who was the son of a king. The glory of his empire was a reflection of his own royal tastes, which he satisfied through a shrewd and successful foreign policy.

Unfortunately, Solomon was not strong enough to withstand the temptations that go along with a long life of luxury. His contribution to the nation of Israel is figured largely in material terms. He made Jerusalem one of the most beautiful cities of the ancient world, and he will always be remembered as a great builder. The tragedy is that after the building of the temple, Solomon did very little to promote the religious life of his people.

Solomon's Porch [Sol'o·mon]—The outer corridor on the east side of Herod's temple (John 10:23; Acts 3:11). It was so named because of a supposed connection with Solomon's temple.

Son of God—One of the titles of the Messiah. In the New Testament it occurs nearly fifty times and is expressive of the relation that exists between the Father and the eternal Son (Matt. 16:16; 27:43; Mark 1:1; John 3:18). He has all the perfections of God and is equal with God (John 1:1–14; 5:17–25; Phil. 2:6). In receiving the commission of the Father, in His mode of operation He is subordinate, but not inferior (John 3:1, 17; 8:42; Gal. 4:4; Heb. 1:2). It was because He claimed He was the Son of God that He was charged with blasphemy by the Sanhedrin (Matt. 26:63–66; Mark 14:61). At His baptism and transfiguration He was divinely acknowledged as the Son of God (Matt. 3:16–17; 17:5).

Son of Man—This title was applied by Christ to Himself. This title does not mean that He was merely human and not divine. He identified Himself with man in His human nature and in His sufferings for mankind (Matt. 20:28; John 1:14).

Sons of God—A designation for certain godlike beings or angels (Gen. 6:2–4; Job 1:6; 2:1).

Sopater [So'pa·ter], *savior of his father*—A Christian of Berea. On Paul's return from his third missionary journey he accompanied the apostle from Philippi to Asia. His father's name was Pyrrhus (Acts 20:4).

Sophereth [So'phe·reth], *scribe*—A family among the descendants of Solomon's servants, members of which came with Zerubbabel from Babylon (Ezra 2:55; Neh. 7:57, also called Hassophereth).

Sorek [So'rek], *vine*—A valley about twelve miles west of Jerusalem which follows a northerly twisting course to the Mediterranean. It was through this valley the ark was taken to Beth-shemesh (1 Sam. 6:7–13; Judg. 16:4).

Sosipater [So·sip′a·ter], *a savior of a father*—A Christian who sent greetings to the church at Rome (Rom. 16:21).

Sosthenes [Sos′the·nes], *of full strength*—The ruler of the synagogue at Corinth during the apostle Paul's first visit to this city (Acts 18:17). When the Roman ruler of the area refused to deal with the angry mob's charges against Paul, they beat Sosthenes. This may be the same Sosthenes as the one greeted by Paul in one of his Corinthian letters (1 Cor. 1:1). If so, he must have become a Christian sometime after the mob scene in his city.

Sotai [So·ta′i], *one of deviates*—A servant of Solomon. His descendants returned from exile with Zerubbabel (Ezra 2:55; Neh. 7:57).

South, The—See Negev.

South Gate—A gate of the temple, assigned to Obed-edom, one of the gatekeepers in the time of David (1 Chron. 26:15).

South Ramoth [Ra′moth]—See Ramah No. 6.

Spain [Spain], *scarceness*—The territory now called Spain and Portugal. In his epistle to the Romans Paul expressed his desire to visit Spain (Rom. 15:24, 28).

Spirit—When the Bible says we were created in God's image, it does not mean God looks like us—a most carnal theory—for God in essence is Spirit (John 4:24). We are like God in creative personality, having intellect, sensibility, and will. In addition God has given us marvelously working bodies to work and live in the world he created for mankind. Body, soul, and spirit are meant to work in harmony for the glory of God. We can only imagine what Adam and Eve were like before the fall. On this side of the garden of Eden, we struggle with our will, our emotions, and our bodies, and especially with our relationship to God as we deal with sin.

In 1 Thessalonians 5:23, the apostle Paul differentiates among three components: ". . . . may your whole spirit, soul, and body be preserved blameless as the coming of our Lord Jesus Christ." As we think of these three parts "being preserved" it helps to think of the things one might do to keep them "blameless" before Christ. It is very hard for a believer to separate "soul" and "spirit" but if one thinks of the soul as the thinking, feeling part of a living being, and the spirit as the part that relates to God, it helps some. One can have wrong thinking, wrong actions (things done in the body) and a wrong or neglected relationship with God. In all of these areas we need the help of the Holy Spirit to live blamelessly.

Spirit (*pneuma*) has the same double meaning in both Testaments: Hebrew *ruah* and Greek *pneuma* both mean "wind" or "spirit." This explains Jesus's play on words in John 3 in His discussion on being born from above by the Spirit, and the wind blowing where it wills.

The spirit is that part of humans that differentiates us from animals; it is the part that seeks a relationship with God. Animals obviously have bodies, and they also have "souls" in the sense of sentient life, but what animal has ever built a church or even prayed to God? The spiritual aspect of human beings is the most important. Our spiritual growth and knowledge will last for all eternity.

Soul (*psyche*) is the Greek word that has spawned many an English derivative beginning with *psycho*. The main usages of *psyche* are "soul" (in its many meanings, including "person" and "life." There are passages where it is hard to know which of these is the better translation. For example, when Jesus asked "What shall a man give in exchange for his [*psyche*]?" He could have referred to man's soul or to his life here on earth and the rewards that come from living for God.

We are so used to using "soul" for the personality that will last forever that we miss another meaning. We say, "Make the most of your life [*psyche*] for the Lord." The best and "most" we can make of our life is to believe in the Lord Jesus Christ so that we can live eternally with Him. If we are not believers we cannot serve God acceptably. However, since *psyche* also refers to our personality and our "aliveness" on earth, we must also make the most of our lives so that we can give glory to God, teach others about Him, and have a reward for our labors in the Day of Christ.

Body (*soma*): There is far too much stress on the body in today's culture. We work out, we diet, we struggle for the perfect shape and color, we use cosmetics and surgery in our search for perfection. This is all supported by gigantic industries. But in reacting to this, we must not fail to take good care of our bodies. They are tools that God has designed for His good purposes on earth, for us to use and use well. Anyone who has struggled with health problems has a deep appreciation for a body that works well without pain. The human body is a masterpiece of divine engineering and should be properly maintained for health to serve God and our fellow man. Not only that, we are very familiar with the faces, the hands, the characteristics of the walk or smile of our friends and families. It is the body which identifies us in this physical world.

And when someone dies and the body is left, we look at the shell and know how much it was the soul and spirit that made that person lovable to us. The body is not really the person, and yet, it was through the body that we related to one another. It is in this body, and this body only that we have the chance to secure eternal life and live the life of faith in Jesus Christ, and it was His body that bore our sins on the cross. In the resurrection, believers will receive perfect bodies with none of the weaknesses of mortality. We know that these immortal bodies will not be just like our earthly bodies, yet they will clearly be "ours," just as the body we wear now is "ours." In the end, we can do no better than repeat Paul's prayer: "Now may the God of peace Himself sanctify you completely; and may your whole spirit, soul, and body be preserved blameless at the coming of our Lord Jesus Christ (1 Thess. 5:23).

Spirit, Holy—See Holy Spirit.

Stachys [Stach′ys], *ear of grain*—A Christian at Rome (Rom. 16:9).

Star of Bethlehem [Beth′le·hem]—The special star which led the wise men from the east to Bethlehem to find the King of the Jews (Matt. 2:2, 7, 9–10). This may be the star of Balaam's prophecy in Numbers 24:17.

Stephanas [Steph′a·nas], *crowned*—A man of Corinth who was converted. He and his household were baptized by Paul, thus becoming the first of Paul's converts in Achaia. He was with Paul when he wrote the First Epistle to the Corinthians in Ephesus (1 Cor. 1:16; 16:15, 17).

Stephen [Ste′phen], *a crown*—One of the first seven deacons of the early church and the first Christian martyr. The story of Stephen is found in Acts 6:7–7:60. His Greek name would indicate that he was a Hellenist but his birthplace is unknown.

In the period following Pentecost, the number of Christians in the New Testament church grew steadily. Followers were eventually recruited not only from among the Jews in Palestine but also from among the Jews in Greek settlements. The church had to appoint several men to handle the work of providing aid to these needy Christians.

Stephen was one of the first seven "good and worthy men" chosen to provide relief to these needy Christians from Greek backgrounds. Since Stephen is mentioned first in the list of the seven administrators, he was probably the most important leader in this group. Although they are not specifically named as deacons, these seven men are considered to be the forerunners of the office of deacon that developed later in the early church. Stephen assumed a place of prominence among these seven leaders as the church grew (Acts 6:7).

Stephen was probably critical of the system of Old Testament laws, claiming they had already lost their effectiveness because they had reached fulfillment in Christ. This viewpoint, which Stephen argued very skillfully, brought him into conflict with powerful leaders among the Jewish people. Stephen became well known as a preacher and a miracle-worker (Acts 6:8). His work was so effective that renewed persecution of the Christians broke out.

Members of certain Jewish synagogues felt that Stephen had blasphemed Moses and God. They accused him of being disloyal to the temple and rejecting Moses. He was also accused of hostility toward Judaism—a charge that had never been made before against other disciples. In debates the Jews were no match for Stephen; even Saul was outwitted by him. Thus, they resorted to force. Stephen was arrested and brought before the Sanhedrin, the Jewish council, where charges were placed against him. False witnesses testified against him. The high priest then asked Stephen if these things were true. Stephen was not dismayed. When he stood before them his face was "as the face of an angel" (Acts 6:15).

The lengthy speech Stephen made in his own defense is reported in detail in Acts 7:2–53. Stephen summarized Old Testament teachings, showing how God had guided Israel toward a specific goal. He reviewed Israel's history in such a way that he replied to all the charges made against him without actually denying anything. This amounted to a criticism of the Sanhedrin itself. Stephen denounced the council as "stiff-necked and uncircumcised in heart and ears" and accused them of resisting the Holy Spirit. Then he charged that they had killed Christ, just as their ancestors had killed the prophets. He accused them of failing to keep their own law (Acts 7:51–53).

Stephen's speech enraged the Sanhedrin so that they were "cut to the heart, and they gnashed at him with their teeth" (Acts 7:54). At this moment Stephen had a vision of God in heaven, with Jesus on His right hand. Stephen's fate was sealed when he reported this vision to his enemies. The crowd rushed upon him, dragged him out of the city, and stoned him to death (Acts 7:55–58).

Among the people consenting to Stephen's death that day was Saul, who later became the apostle Paul—great Christian missionary to the Gentiles. As he was being stoned, Stephen asked God not to charge his executioners with the sin of his death (Acts 7:59–60).

Stephen's martyrdom was followed by a general persecution that forced the disciples to flee from Jerusalem into the outlying areas. This scattering led to the preaching of the gospel first to the Samaritans and then to the Gentiles in the nations surrounding Palestine.

Straight Street—The street of Damascus where Paul stayed after his blinding vision on the road leading to the city (Acts 9:11). Ananias visited him there, and laid hands on him, healing his blindness.

Suah [Su'ah], *sweepings*—A son of Zophah and head of the tribe of Asher (1 Chron. 7:36).

Sucathite [Su'ca·thite]—See Suchathite.

Succoth [Suc'coth], *booths*—Two geographical locations:
1. The place of the first encampment of the Israelites after leaving Rameses in Egypt (Ex. 12:37; 13:20; Num. 33:5–6). It is believed that this is the Hebrew name of the Egyptian Thuku, the chief city of the district.
2. A place east of the Jordan where Jacob, returning from Padan-aram, built a house with booths for his cattle (Gen. 32:22; 33:17).

Succoth-benoth [Suc'coth-be'noth], *the daughter's booth*—An idol set up in Samaria and worshipped by settlers from Babylon (2 Kings 17:30–31).

Suchathite [Su'cha·thite], *unknown*—A family of scribes at Jabez (1 Chron. 2:55).

Sukkiim [Suk'ki·im], *possibly booth dwellers*—An African tribe which fought with the army of the pharaoh Shishak when he attacked Jerusalem during the reign of Rehoboam, king of Judah (2 Chron. 12:3).

Sukkites [Suk'kites]—See Sukkiim.

Sundial of Ahaz—See Dial of Ahaz.

Suph [Suph], *reeds*—A place in the wilderness where Moses delivered his farewell address (Deut. 1:1).

Suphah [Su'phah], *honeycomb*—A place somewhere east of the Jordan, near Moab (Num. 21:14).

Supper, Lord's—See Lord's Supper.

Sur [Sur], *turning aside*—A gate of Solomon's temple, called "the gate of the foundation" (2 Kings 11:6; 2 Chron. 23:5).

Susa [Su'sa]—See Shushan.

Susanchites [Su·san'chites]—See Shushanchites.

Susanna [Su·san'na], *lily*—A woman who followed and ministered to Jesus (Luke 8:3).

Susi [Su'si], *a horseman*—Father of Gaddi, who represented the tribe of Manasseh when Moses appointed the twelve spies (Num. 13:11).

Sychar [Sy'char], *drunken*—A town in Samaria near Jacob's well (John 4:5).

Sychem [Sy'chem]—See Shechem.

Syene [Sy·e'ne], *her veiling*—A town of Egypt, far in the south, near the border of Ethiopia (Ezek. 29:10; 30:6).

Symeon [Sy'me·on]—See Simon.

Syntyche [Syn'ty·che], *with fate*—A Christian woman of Philippi who seemed to be at variance with another woman named Euodia. Paul exhorted them to come to a state of harmony (Phil. 4:2).

Syracuse [Syr'a·cuse], *a Syrian hearing*—A city of importance on the east coast of Sicily. On his voyage to Rome Paul touched at this port (Acts 28:12).

Syria [Syr'i·a], *exalted*—A somewhat indefinite region bounded in general by the Taurus Mountains, the Euphrates River, the Syrian and

Arabian deserts, northern Palestine, and the Mediterranean (2 Sam. 8:6; 15:8; Luke 2:2; Acts 15:23, 41). Its political history is interwoven with the Assyrian, Babylonian, Persian, Greek, Roman, and Mohammedan empires.

Syrian [Syr'i·an]—An inhabitant of Syria (Gen. 28:5).

Syrophoenician [Sy'ro·phoe·nic'i·an]—A Gentile woman whose daughter was healed by Jesus (Mark 7:26). She was from Phoenicia, a nation northeast of Palestine that had been incorporated into the Roman province of Syria—thus the term Syro-Phoenician. Although she was not a citizen of the Jewish nation, she believed Jesus could heal her daughter. Jesus commended her because of her great faith. She was called a woman of Canaan in Matthew 15:22.

Syrtis Sands, The [Syr'tis], commonly *quicksands*—Syrtis Major, a dangerously shallow area off the African coast. A smaller area of shallows is further west. The ship which carried Paul to Rome was caught in a terrible storm, and the sailors feared they would run aground on these treacherous sandbars (Acts 27:17).

T

Taanach [Ta'a·nach], *sandy*—An ancient royal city of the Canaanites whose king was conquered and slain by Joshua, but whose inhabitants were not driven out of the land (Josh. 12:21; Judg. 1:27). Tanaach was occupied by the tribe of Manasseh and was assigned to the Levites of the family of Kohath (Josh. 17:11–13; 21:25; Tanach, KJV). According to the Song of Deborah, the kings of Canaan fought against Deborah and Barak at Taanach, but they were defeated (Judg. 5:19).

The ruins of Taanach, Tell Taannek, are on the southwestern edge of the valley of Jezreel about 8 kilometers (5 miles) southeast of Megiddo.

Taanath-shiloh [Ta'a·nath-shi'loh], *approach to Shiloh*—A border town on the northern boundary of Ephraim (Josh. 16:6).

Tabbaoth [Tab·ba'oth], *rings*—A Nethinim. His descendants returned from Babylon with Zerubbabel (Ezra 2:43; Neh. 7:46).

Tabbath [Tab'bath], *celebrated*—A place mentioned in connection with the defeat of the Midianites by Gideon (Judg. 7:22).

Tabeel [Tab'e·el], *God is good*—

1. Father of the man whom Pekah, king of Israel, and Rezin, king of Syria, intended to place on the throne of Judah in the place of Ahaz (Isa. 7:6). It was in this connection that Isaiah spoke the prophecy of the one to be born of a virgin.

2. A Persian official in Samaria (Ezra 4:7).

Taberah [Tab'e·rah], *burning*—A place in the wilderness of Paran (Num. 11:1–3; Deut. 9:22).

Tabernacle of Meeting—The tent which Moses set up outside the camp to serve as a sanctuary until the tabernacle could be completed to God's specifications (Ex. 33:7). The finished tabernacle was also called by this name; it indicated the fact that this tent was the place where God met with His people (Ex. 27:21; 38:8).

Tabernacle of the Congregation—See Tabernacle of Meeting.

Tabernacles, Feast of—One of the three great annual festivals at which the men of Israel were required to appear (Deut. 16:16; 2 Chron. 8:12–13; Zech. 14:16). During this time, the celebrants lived in tents (tabernacles) in commemoration of the period of wandering in the wilderness (Lev. 23:40–42).

Tabitha [Tab′i·tha]—See Dorcas.

Tabor [Ta′bor], *mound*—

1. A mountain in the plain of Esdraelon and on the boundary of Issachar, conical in shape, about thirteen hundred feet high. It is about twelve miles north of Mount Gilboa and six miles southeast of Nazareth. While a notable mountain (Ps. 89:12), it is greatly inferior in size to Hermon. Here the forces of Barak gathered for the conflict with Sisera (Judg. 4:6, 12, 14), and here the Midianite kings killed Gideon's brothers (Judg. 8:18–19). Mount Tabor is on the adjoining borders of Issachar, Zebulun, and Naphtali. Hosea the prophet speaks of judgment to fall upon Israel and Judah because they had been "a net spread on Tabor" (Hos. 5:1). From this it may be construed that a sanctuary for pagan worship may have been situated on this mountain.

2. The terebinth or plain of Tabor (1 Sam. 10:3), a place located in the territory of Benjamin, and mentioned in connection with Saul's journey homeward after Samuel met him and anointed him as the first king of Israel.

3. A town of Zebulun assigned to the Levites of the Merari family (1 Chron. 6:77).

Tabrimmon [Tab·rim′mon], possibly *good is Rimmon*—Father of Ben-hadad, king of Syria (1 Kings 15:18; Tabrimon, KJV).

Tachmonite [Tach′mo·nite], *thou will make me wise*—Josheb-basshebeth, one of David's mighty men, is called "the Tachmonite (2 Sam. 23:8; also Tachemonite or Tahkemonite). Some believe that this should read "Hachmonite," because the corresponding list of David's mighty men in 1 Chronicles lists a man with a very similar name: "Jashobeam the son of a Hachmonite." See Hachmoni.

Tadmor [Tad'mor], *palm*—A city built by Solomon in the wilderness (1 Kings 9:18; 2 Chron. 8:4). It was a part of the northeastern border of his empire, about 120 miles northeast of Damascus and strategically situated on both the north-south and east-west trade routes of Canaan and Mesopotamia. After Solomon's death, and the shrinking of the kingdom, Tadmor passed into the hands of other rulers. The Greeks and Romans called the city Palmyra; it was eventually destroyed by Rome in the third century A.D. and remains an impressive ruin.

Tahan [Ta'han], *camp*—The head of a tribal family of Ephraim (Num. 26:35), and ancestor of Joshua son of Nun (1 Chron. 7:25-27).

Tahanites [Ta'han·ites]—The descendants of Ephraim's son Tahan (Num. 26:35).

Tahapanes [Ta·hap·an'es]—See Tahpanhes.

Tahash [Ta'hash]—See Thahash.

Tahath [Ta'hath], *station*—Three men and a geographical location of the Old Testament:

1. A place where the Israelites encamped in the wilderness (Num. 33:26-27).

2. A Levite of the family of Kohath. He was the son of Assir and the father of Uriel (1 Chron. 6:22, 24).

3. Son of Bered of Ephraim (1 Chron. 7:20).

4. Son of Eladah and probably grandson of the preceding (1 Chron. 7:20).

Tahchemonite [Tah'che·mon·ites]—See Tachmonite.

Tahkemonite [Tah'ke·mon·ite]—See Tachmonite.

Tahpanhes [Tah'pan·hes], *thou will fill hands with pity*—A city of Egypt on the Nile. After the assassination of Gedaliah, many of the Jewish remnant fled from the Chaldeans. In spite of Jeremiah's advice, they went to Tahpanhes in Egypt, and they forced Jeremiah to come with them (Jer. 2:16; 43:7-9; 44:1; 46:14; Ezek. 30:18). Some seem to have settled there permanently.

Tahpenes [Tah'pe·nes], *wife of the king*—A queen of Egypt whose sister became the wife of Hadad, a descendant of the king of Edom and the adversary of Solomon (1 Kings 11:18-25).

Tahrea [Tah're·a]—See Tarea.

Tahtim-hodshi [Tah'tim-hod'shi], *lowest-moon*—A region between Gilead and Dan-jaan (2 Sam. 24:6), mentioned in the description of King David's census of the fighting men of Israel.

Talmai [Tal'mai], *furrowed*—Two men of the Old Testament:
1. Descendant of Anak (Num. 13:22; Josh. 15:14; Judg. 1:10).
2. A king of Geshur, whose daughter Maacah was a wife of David and the mother of Absalom (2 Sam. 3:3; 13:37). His kingdom was in Bashan.

Talmon [Tal'mon], *oppressed*—The head of a family of porters (1 Chron. 9:17).

Tamah [Ta'mah]—See Temah.

Tamar [Ta'mar], *palm*—The name of three women and a city in the Bible:
1. The widow of Er and Onan, sons of Judah (Gen. 38:6–30; Matt. 1:3; Thamar, KJV). According to the law of Levirate marriage, Judah's third son, Shelah, should have married Tamar; their first child would have been regarded as his brother's and would have carried on his name. However, Judah withheld his third son from marrying Tamar. Undaunted, Tamar disguised herself as a harlot and offered herself to Judah. Twin sons, Perez and Zerah, were born of their union. Judah and Tamar became ancestors of Jesus through Perez (Matt. 1:3).
2. The lovely daughter of David by Maacah and sister of Absalom (2 Sam. 13:1–22, 32; 1 Chron. 3:9). Tamar was raped by her half brother Amnon. She fled to Absalom, who plotted revenge. Two years later Absalom got his revenge for Tamar by arranging Amnon's murder.
3. Absalom's only surviving daughter, possibly named after his sister Tamar (2 Sam. 14:27).
4. A place on the southern border of the land promised Ezekiel by the Lord, southwest of the Dead Sea (Ezek. 47:19; 48:28).

Tammuz [Tam'muz], *sprout of life*—
1. A deity worshipped by Babylonians, Assyrians, and Phoenicians. Ezekiel speaks of the women "weeping for Tammuz" (Ezek. 8:14). In his vision they were at the gate of the temple in Jerusalem. The wife of this

deity was the goddess Ishtar. Tammuz was the god of flocks and of shepherds.

2. The fourth month of the Jewish sacred year, tenth month of the civil year. It corresponded roughly with June/July.

Tanach [Ta'nach]—See Taanach.

Tanhumeth [Tan·hu'meth], *consolation*—The father of Seraiah, a Netophathite (2 Kings 25:23; Jer. 40:8).

Taphath [Ta'phath], *ornament*—A daughter of Solomon. Her husband was Benabinadab (1 Kings 4:11).

Tappuah [Tap'pu·ah], *an apple*—A man and two towns of the Old Testament:

    1. A son of Hebron of the line of Caleb (1 Chron. 2:43).

    2. A town on the border of Manasseh and Ephraim (Josh. 16:8; 17:7–8).

    3. A town in the Shephelah (lowland) of Judah (Josh. 15:34.)

Tarah [Ta'rah]—See Terah.

Taralah [Tar'a·lah], *reeling*—A town of Benjamin (Josh. 18:27).

Tarea [Tar'e·a], *chamber of a neighbor*—A descendant of Saul through Jonathan (1 Chron. 8:35; also called Tahrea, 1 Chron. 9:41).

Tarpelites [Tar'pe·lites], *they of the fallen (or wonderous) mountain*—A people which Shalmaneser of Assyria settled in Samaria after the Israelites were taken captive (Ezra 4:9), also called "men from Tripolis" (NIV).

Tarshish [Tar'shish], *jasper*—The name of a type of ship, a city or territory, three men, and a precious stone in the Old Testament:

    1. The Hebrew name for a type of cargo ship fitted for long sea voyages (1 Kings 10:22; Tharshish, KJV).

    2. A city or territory in the western portion of the Mediterranean Sea with which the Phoenicians traded (2 Chron. 9:21; Ps. 72:10). Tarshish is believed by some to be Tartessus, in southern Spain, near Gibraltar. When Jonah fled from God's instruction to go to Nineveh, he boarded a ship bound for Tarshish, in the opposite direction from Nineveh (Jonah 1:3; 4:2). Tarshish was famous for its ships (Ps. 48:7; Isa.

2:16), which carried gold, silver, iron, tin, lead, ivory, apes, and monkeys (1 Kings 10:22; Jer. 10:9).

Because the ships of Tarshish carried such great riches, they became symbols of wealth, power, and pride. When God judged the nations for their sinful ways, He destroyed their "ships of Tarshish" to humble them and to demonstrate His great power (2 Chron. 20:35–37; Isa. 2:16–17).

3. Son of Javan, grandson of Japheth, and great-grandson of Noah (Gen. 10:4; 1 Chron. 1:7; also called Tarshishah).

4. Son of Bilhan of Benjamin (1 Chron. 7:10).

5. A high official at Shushan (Susa). He was one of seven princes of Persia and Media "who had access to the king's presence" (Est. 1:14). Tarshish was one of those present at the royal banquet of King Ahasuerus that Vashti, the queen, refused to attend.

6. The Hebrew name of a precious stone (Ex. 28:20; Ezek. 28:13). Its brilliant color is associated with the glorious appearance of God Himself (Ezek. 1:16; Dan. 10:6).

Tarshisha [Tar′shis·ha]—See Tarshish No. 1.

Tarsus [Tar′sus], *a flat basket*—The birthplace of the apostle Paul (Acts 21:39; 22:3), formerly known as Saul of Tarsus (Acts 9:11). Tarsus was the chief city of Cilicia, a province of southeast Asia Minor. This important city was situated on the banks of the Cydnus River about 16 kilometers (10 miles) north of the shore of the Mediterranean Sea.

Because of its strategic location, protected on the north by the Taurus Mountains and open to navigation from the Mediterranean, the city of Tarsus was a prize location for the Hittites, Mycenean Greeks, Assyrians, Persians, Seleucids, and Romans. In the post-Roman period it dwindled to a small city in the wake of battles between various Christian and Muslim powers.

St. Paul's Gate at Tarsus: The chief city of Cilicia in eastern Asia Minor, Tarsus was the birthplace of the apostle Paul (Acts 21:39).

During the Seleucid period, however, Tarsus became a free city (about 170 B.C.), and was open to Greek culture and education. By the time of the Romans, Tarsus competed with Athens and Alexandria as the learning center of the world. "I am a Jew from Tarsus, in Cilicia," wrote the apostle Paul, "a citizen of no mean city" (Acts 21:39).

North of Tarsus were the famous Cilician Gates, a narrow gorge in the Taurus Mountains through which ran the only good trade route between Asia Minor and Syria. The location of Tarsus in a fertile valley brought great wealth to the city. The apostle Paul spent his early years at Tarsus (Acts 9:11; 21:39; 22:3) and revisited it after his conversion to Christianity (Acts 9:30; 11:25).

Tartak [Tar'tak], *prince of darkness*—An idol worshipped by the Avvites in Samaria (2 Kings 17:31).

Tartan [Tar'tan]—A title of the commander-in-chief of the Assyrian army (2 Kings 18:17; Isa. 20:1).

Tattenai [Tat'te·nai], *possibly gift*—A Persian governor who opposed the plan of Zerubbabel and others to build the second temple (Ezra 5:3, 6; 6:6, 13).

Taverns, Three—See Three Inns.

Tebah [Te'bah], *slaughter*—The son of Nahor and his concubine Reumah (Gen. 22:24).

Tebaliah [Teb·a·li'ah], *Jehovah has purified*—The son of Hosah (1 Chron. 26:11).

Tebeth [Te'beth], *goodness*—The tenth month of the Hebrew sacred year (Est. 2:16), and fourth month of the civil year. It corresponds roughly with December/January.

Tehaphnehes [Te·haph'ne·hes]—See Tahpanhes.

Tehinnah [Te·hin'nah], *grace*—A descendant of Chelub and founder of the city of Ir-nahash (1 Chron. 4:12).

Tekoa [Te·ko'a], *trumpet blast*—The birthplace of the prophet Amos. Situated in Judah (1 Chron. 2:24; 4:5), Tekoa is identified today with Khirbet Taqu'a, about 10 kilometers (6 miles) southeast of Bethlehem and about 16 kilometers (10 miles) south of Jerusalem. It was built on a hill in the wilderness of Tekoa toward En Gedi (2 Chron. 11:6; 20:20).

Tekoa is first mentioned in the Bible in connection with Joab employing a "wise woman" (2 Sam. 14:2) to bring reconciliation between David and Absalom (2 Sam. 14:2, 4, 9; Tekoah, KJV). Later Rehoboam, king of Judah (ruled 931–913 B.C.), fortified the site in order to prevent an invasion of Jerusalem from the south (2 Chron. 11:6).

Because of its elevation—about 850 meters (2,790 feet) above sea level—Tekoa became a station for warning Jerusalem of the approach of its enemies (Jer. 6:1). From Tekoa a person can see the Mount of Olives in Jerusalem and Mount Nebo beyond the Dead Sea. About 2 miles from Tekoa, Herod the Great (ruled 37–4 B.C.) built a fortress, the Herodium, in the Judean wilderness.

Tekoah [Te·ko′ah]—See Tekoa.

Tekoite [Te′ko·ite]—A native of Tekoa (2 Sam. 23:26; 1 Chron. 11:28; 27:9).

Tel-abib [Tel-a′bib], *hill of grain*—A place in Babylon on the river Chebar. Ezekiel and some of the captives were settled there (Ezek. 3:15).

Telah [Te′lah], *breach*—A descendant of Ephraim (1 Chron. 7:25).

Telaim [Te·la′im], *young lambs*—A place where Saul mustered his troops before his fight with the Amalekites (1 Sam. 15:4).

Telassar [Tel′as·sar], *hill of Asshur*—A city in the northwestern part of Mesopotamia (2 Kings 19:12; Thelasar, KJV).

Telem [Te′lem], *oppression*—

1. A town on the southern border of Judah (Josh. 15:24), possibly the same as Telaim.

2. A porter of the temple who renounced his foreign wife (Ezra 10:24).

Tel-haresha [Tel-har′esh·a]—See Tel-harsha.

Tel-harsa [Tel-har′sa]—See Tel-harsha.

Tel-harsha [Tel-har′sha], *mound of the forest* or *mound of magic*—A town of Babylonia from which some Jews returned to Palestine (Ezra 2:59; Neh. 7:61; Tel Harsa, KJV).

Tel-melah [Tel-me′lah], *hill of salt*—A place in Babylonia (Ezra 2:59; Neh. 7:61).

Tema [Te′ma], *desert*—

1. A son of Ishmael (Gen. 25:15; 1 Chron. 1:30).

2. A town or district about 200 miles north of Medina (Job 6:19; Isa. 21:14; Jer. 25:23).

Temah [Te'mah], possibly *laughter*—Head of a family of Nethinim (Ezra 2:53; Neh. 7:55; Thamah, KJV).

Teman [Te'man], *the south*—

1. Son of Eliphaz, grandson of Esau (Gen. 36:11), and a chief of Edom (Gen. 36:15; 1 Chron. 1:36).

2. A tribe and their district in northeast Edom (Gen. 36:34). The members of the tribe were noted for their wisdom (Jer. 49:7, 20) and were mentioned by several prophets (Ezek. 25:13; Amos 1:12; Obad. 9; Hab. 3:3).

3. Another chief of Edom (Gen. 36:42; 1 Chron. 1:53).

Temani [Te'man·i]—See Temanite.

Temanite [Te'man·ite], *southward*—A member of the tribe of Teman or inhabitant of the land (Gen. 36:34; Temani, KJV). Eliphaz, one of the friends with whom Job debated, was a Temanite (Job 2:11).

Temeni [Te'me·ni], *southern*—A son of Ashur and Naarah and founder of the town of Tekoa (1 Chron. 4:5–6).

Tent of Meeting—See Tabernacle of Meeting.

Terah [Te'rah], *station*—The name of a man and a place in the Bible:

1. The father of Abraham and an ancestor of Christ (Gen. 11:26–27; Luke 3:34; Thara, KJV). Descended from Shem, Terah also was the father of Nahor and Haran. He lived at Ur of the Chaldeans most of his life; at Ur he probably worshipped the moon-god (Josh. 24:2). From Ur, Terah migrated with his son Abraham, his grandson Lot (Haran's son), and his daughter-in-law Sarah (Abraham's wife) to Haran, a city about 800 kilometers (500 miles) north of Ur and about 445 kilometers (275 miles) northeast of Damascus. Terah died in Haran, another city where the moon-god was worshipped, at the age of 205 (Gen. 11:24–32).

2. An encampment of the Israelites in the wilderness (Num. 33:27–28; Tarah, KJV).

Teresh [Te'resh], *severe*—One of the eunuchs who planned to assassinate Ahasuerus (Est. 2:21–23; 6:2). Mordecai learned of the plot and warned the king in time to avert the danger.

Tertius [Ter'tius], *third*—The secretary or scribe who took Paul's dictation of the book of Romans (Rom. 16:22).

Tertullus [Ter·tul′lus], *diminutive form of Tertius*—A lawyer employed by the Jews to make the accusation against Paul (Acts 24:1–8).

Tetrarch [Te′trarch]—Originally the ruler of the fourth part of a country. The term also applied to subordinate princes or petty kings. The title was applied to Herod Antipas, ruler of Galilee and Perea (Matt. 14:1; Luke 3:1, 19; 9:7; Acts 13:1).

Thaddaeus [Thad·dae′us], *large hearted* or *courageous*—One of the twelve apostles of Jesus (Matt. 10:3; Mark 3:18; Thaddeus, KJV), also called Lebbaeus (Matt. 10:3) and Judas the son of James (Luke 6:16; Acts 1:13). He is carefully distinguished from Judas Iscariot (John 14:22). Nothing else is known about this most obscure of the apostles, but some scholars attribute the epistle of Jude to him.

Thahash [Tha′hash], *dugong*—Son of Nahor. His mother was Reumah (Gen. 22:24).

Thamah [Tha′mah]—See Temah.

Thamar [Tha′mar]—See Tamar.

Thara [Thar′a]—See Terah.

Tharshish [Thar′shish]—See Tarshish.

Thebes [Thebes]—See No-amon.

Thebez [The′bez], *splendor*—A fortified city of Ephraim near Shechem (Judg. 9:50–55; 2 Sam. 11:21).

Thelasar [Thel·a′sar]—See Telassar.

Theophilus [The·oph′i·lus], *lover of God*—A Christian to whom Luke dedicated the gospel of Luke and the book of Acts (Luke 1:3; Acts 1:1). The fact that Luke spoke of Theophilus as "most excellent" indicates that he was a prominent man of high rank and possibly a Roman. He may have chosen the name when he was converted to Christianity. According to tradition, both Luke and Theophilus were natives of Antioch in Syria. Much speculation surrounds Theophilus, but little is known for certain about him.

Thessalonica [Thess·a·lo′ni·ca], *victory of falsity*—A city in Macedonia visited by the apostle Paul (Acts 17:1, 11, 13; 27:2; Phil. 4:16).

Situated on the Thermaic Gulf, Thessalonica was the chief seaport of Macedonia. The city was founded in about 315 B.C. by Cassander, who resettled the site with inhabitants from twenty-six villages that he had destroyed. He named the city after his wife, the sister of Alexander the Great and daughter of Philip II of Macedonia. The Egnatian Way, the main overland route from Rome to the east, ran directly through the city and can still be traced today.

Under Roman rule, Thessalonica achieved prominence. In 167 B.C. the Romans divided Macedonia into four districts, Thessalonica becoming capital of the second district. Some twenty years later Macedonia became a Roman province with Thessalonica as its capital. After the battle of Philippi in 42 B.C., when Octavian and Mark Antony defeated Brutus and Cassius, the assassins of Julius Caesar, Thessalonica became a free city. It was the most populous city of Macedonia.

In the third century A.D. Thessalonica was selected to oversee a Roman temple, and under Decius (ruled A.D. 249–251), infamous for his persecution of Christians, the city achieved the status of a Roman colony, which entitled it to the rights and privileges of the Roman Empire. The city was surrounded by a wall, stretches of which still stand. Archaeologists have uncovered a paved Roman forum some 63 by 99 meters (70 by 110 yards) in size, dating from the first or second centuries A.D. Roman arches stood at Thessalonica's two entrances to the Egnatian Way. The one built in A.D. 297 to honor the Roman emperor Galerius remains intact. The modern wall was built after Paul's time, but it was constructed on the foundations of the old city wall from the New Testament era.

The apostle Paul visited Thessalonica in A.D. 49 or 50 during his second missionary journey (Acts 17:1–9). Paul's evangelistic efforts met with success. Within a short time a vigorous Christian congregation had blossomed, consisting of some members of the Jewish synagogue as well as former pagans.

The book of Acts leads some to assume that Paul stayed in Thessalonica only a few weeks before being forced to leave because of Jewish opposition. But in reality he probably stayed at least two or three months. A shorter stay would scarcely account for Paul's receiving two gifts of aid from the Philippians (Phil. 4:16), or for the depth of affection that developed between Paul and the Thessalonians, as is evidenced by the language in the first letter to them (1 Thess. 2:1–12). Thessalonica was also the home of two of Paul's coworkers, Aristarchus and Secundus (Acts 20:4; 27:2). The church that he worked with here consisted of former members of the Jewish synagogue, as well as non-Jews from pagan backgrounds.

Theudas [Theu′das], *God-given*—The leader of about four hundred men in an unsuccessful Jewish revolt against Rome (Acts 5:36).

Thimnathah [Thim′na·thah]—See Timnah.

Thomas [Thom′as], *twin*—One of the twelve apostles of Jesus; also called *Didymus,* the Greek word for "twin" (Matt. 10:3; Mark 3:18; Luke 6:15). Thomas is probably best known for his inability to believe that Jesus had indeed risen from the dead. For that inability to believe, he forever earned the name "doubting Thomas."

Thomas was not present when Jesus first appeared to His disciples after His resurrection. Upon hearing of the appearance, Thomas said, "Unless I see in His hands the print of the nails, and put my finger into the print of the nails, and put my hand into His side, I will not believe" (John 20:25). Eight days later, Jesus appeared again to the disciples, including Thomas. When Jesus invited him to touch the nail prints and put his hand into His side, Thomas's response was, "My Lord and my God!" (John 20:28). Of that incident the great church father Augustine remarked, "He doubted so that we might believe."

Thomas appears three other times in the gospel of John. (Except for the listing of the disciples, Thomas does not appear in the other three gospels.) It was he who expressed concern for the safety of Jesus when the latter went to Bethany at the time of the death of Lazarus. When Jesus made known His intention to go into Judea, Thomas urged his fellow disciples, "Let us also go, that we may die with Him" (John 11:16). Knowing that His earthly life would soon end, Jesus said He was going to prepare a place for His followers and that they knew the way. Thomas asked, "Lord, we do not know where You are going, and how can we know the way?" (John 14:5). To that Jesus gave His well-known answer: "I am the way, the truth, and the life" (John 14:6).

After the resurrection, Thomas was on the Sea of Galilee with six other disciples when Jesus signaled to them from the shore and told them where to cast their net (John 21:2). Thomas was also with the other disciples in the Jerusalem Upper Room after the ascension of Jesus.

According to tradition, Thomas spread the gospel in Parthia and Persia, where he died. Later tradition places Thomas in India, where he was martyred. The Mar Thoma Church in India traces its origins to Thomas.

Three Inns—A station on the Appian Way (Acts 28:15).

Three Taverns—See Three Inns.

Thunder, Sons of—The nickname Jesus gave to the sons of Zebedee, James and John (Mark 3:17).

Thyatira [Thy·a·ti′ra], *odor of affliction*—A city of Asia Minor, located on the banks of the Lycus River, between Pergamum and Sardis. Lydia, the first convert in Philippi, was from Thyatira (Acts 16:14). The book of Revelation also mentions this city; one of the letters to the seven churches was addressed to Thyatira (Rev. 1:11; 2:18–24).

Tiberias [Ti·be′ri·as], *from the Tiber (as river-god)*—A city on the Sea of Galilee built by Herod Antipas, and named after Tiberius who was then emperor. It was the capital of Galilee until the reign of Herod Agrippa II. The Sea of Galilee is also called the Sea of Tiberias (John 6:1; 21:1).

Tiberias, Sea of [Ti·be′ri·as]—See Tiberias and Galilee, Sea of.

Tiberius Caesar [Ti·be′ri·us Cae′sar]—See Caesar.

Tibhath [Tib′hath], *slaughter*—A city of Aramzobah (1 Chron. 18:8). In 2 Samuel 8:8 it is called Betah.

Tibni [Tib′ni], *intelligent*—The son of Ginath (1 Kings 16:21–22).

Tidal [Ti′dal], *great son*—One of the kings who joined with Chedorlaomer, the ancient king of Elam, in a raid into Palestine (Gen. 14:1–10).

Tiglath-pileser [Tib′lath-pi·le′ser], *thou will uncover the wonderful bond*—An Assyrian king who reigned from 745 to 727 B.C. Under the name of Pul, he also reigned as king of Babylonia from 729–727 B.C. (2 Kings 15:19). He is also called Tilgath-pilneser (1 Chron. 5:6, 26; 2 Chron. 28:20).

Tiglath-pileser led Assyria in a period of expansion and military greatness. In the last period of the northern kingdom of Israel, Assyria came against the nation and its king, Menahem. In order to deal with the threat of Assyrian invasion, Menahem paid an exorbitant tribute of 1,000 talents of silver in tribute to Tiglath-pileser. He exacted this money from all the wealthy of the land (2 Kings 15:17–20).

During the reign of Pekah, the assassin who murdered Menahem's son and took over the throne, Tiglath-pileser came against Israel again and captured many of its towns. The entire tribe of Naphtali was carried off into captivity at this time (2 Kings 15:29). Pekah later made an alliance with Syria and came against Judah. Ahaz, king of Judah, appealed to Tiglath-pileser for help, offering him the silver and gold from the house of the Lord. This relationship with Assyria proved to be a means of introducing more pagan worship to Judah. On a visit of state to Damascus, Ahaz was impressed by a heathen altar he saw there, had a copy made, and proceeded to offer sacrifices on it. He also rearranged many of the articles of the temple in order to make it more like the things he had seen in Assyria (2 Kings 16:7–20).

Tigris [Ti′gris], unknown—A major river of southwest Asia. Flowing about 1,850 kilometers (1,150 miles) from the Taurus Mountains of eastern Turkey, the Tigris joins the Euphrates River north of Basra. The Tigris and Euphrates flow roughly parallel to each other for hundreds of miles in the "Land of the Two Rivers," or Mesopotamia. The Tigris is identical with Hiddekel (Gen. 2:14, KJV, NKJV), one of the four branches of the river that flowed from the garden of Eden.

Tikvah [Tik′vah], hope—
1. Son of Harhas and father of Shallum whose wife was Huldah, the prophetess (2 Kings 22:14). He is called Tikvath in 2 Chronicles 34:22.
2. The father of Jahaziah (Ezra 10:15).

Tikvath [Tik′vath]—See Tikvah.

Tilgath-pilneser [Til′gath-pil·ne′ser]—See Tiglath-pileser.

Tilon [Ti′lon], gift—A son of Shimon of Judah (1 Chron. 4:20).

Timaeus [Ti·mae′us], highly prized—Father of Bartimaeus, the blind man Jesus healed (Mark 10:46).

Timeus [Ti·me'us]—See Timaeus.

Timna [Tim'na], *restrained*—

1. A chief of Edom (Gen. 36:40; 1 Chron. 1:51).

2. The daughter of Seir and concubine of Eliphaz (Gen. 36:12, 22; 1 Chron. 1:39). Also called Timnah (1 Chron. 1:51; Gen. 36:40).

Timnah [Tim'nah], *portion*—

1. See Timna No.2.

2. A town in the hill district of Judah (Josh. 15:57). It was near this place that Tamar met Judah (Gen. 38:12–14). The town was captured by the Philistines (2 Chron. 28:18).

3. A town of Dan, later held by the Philistines (Josh. 15:10). Samson's wife lived in this town (Judg. 14:1, 2, 5; 15:6). Also called Thimnathah (Josh. 19:43).

Timnath-heres [Tim'nath-he'res]—See Timnath-serah.

Timnath-serah [Tim'nath-se'rah], *portion of the sun*—A city of Ephraim in the mountains; the inheritance of Joshua son of Nun, and his burial place (Josh. 19:50; 24:30). In Judges 2:9 it is called Timnath-heres. It is thought to be the modern town of Khirbet Tibneh.

Timnite [Tim'nite]—A native of Timnah (Judg. 15:6).

Timon [Ti'mon], *worthy*—One of the seven deacons appointed to serve in the church in Jerusalem (Acts 6:5).

Timotheus [Ti·moth'e·us]—A variant of Timothy.

Timothy [Tim'o·thy], *honored by God*—Paul's friend and chief associate, who is mentioned as joint sender in six of Paul's epistles (2 Cor. 1:1; Phil. 1:1; Col. 1:1; 1 Thess. 1:1; 2 Thess. 1:1; Philem. 1).

Timothy first appears in the second missionary journey when Paul revisited Lystra (Acts 16:1–3). Timothy was the son of a Gentile father and a Jewish-Christian mother named Eunice, and the grandson of Lois (Acts 16:1; 2 Tim. 1:5). Timothy may have been converted under Paul's ministry, because the apostle refers to him as his "beloved and faithful son in the Lord" (1 Cor. 4:17) and as his "true son in the faith" (1 Tim. 1:2). Timothy was held in high regard in Lystra and Iconium, and Paul desired to take him along as a traveling companion. To forestall criticism of Timothy on the part of the Jews, Paul caused him to be circumcised (Acts 16:3).

Timothy played a prominent role in the remainder of the second missionary journey. When Paul was forced to leave Berea because of an uproar started by Jews from Thessalonica, Silas and Timothy were left behind to strengthen the work in Macedonia (Acts 17:14). After they rejoined Paul in Athens (Acts 18:5), Paul sent Timothy back to the believers in Thessalonica to establish them and to encourage them to maintain the faith (1 Thess. 3:1–9). Timothy's report of the faith and love of the Thessalonians greatly encouraged Paul.

During Paul's third missionary journey, Timothy was active in the evangelizing of Corinth, although he had little success. When news of disturbances at Corinth reached Paul at Ephesus, he sent Timothy, perhaps along with Erastus (Acts 19:22), to resolve the difficulties. The mission failed, perhaps because of fear on Timothy's part (1 Cor. 16:10–11). Paul then sent the more forceful Titus, who was able to calm the situation at Corinth (2 Cor. 7). Later in the third journey, Timothy is listed as one of the group that accompanied Paul along the coast of Asia Minor on his way to Jerusalem (Acts 20:4–5).

Timothy also appears as a companion of Paul during his imprisonment in Rome (Phil. 1:1; Col. 1:1; Philem. 1). From Rome, Paul sent Timothy to Philippi to bring back word of the congregation that had supported the apostle so faithfully over the years.

Timothy's strongest traits were his sensitivity, affection, and loyalty. Paul commends him to the Philippians, for example, as one of proven character, faithful to Paul like a son to a father, and without rival in his concern for the Philippians (Phil. 2:19–23; also 2 Tim. 1:4; 3:10). Paul's warnings, however, to "be strong" (2 Tim. 2:1) suggest that Timothy suffered from fearfulness (1 Cor. 16:10–11; 2 Tim. 1:7) and perhaps youthful lusts (2 Tim. 2:22). But in spite of his weaknesses, Paul was closer to Timothy than to any other associate.

Writing about A.D. 325, Eusebius reported that Timothy was the first bishop of Ephesus. In 356 Constantius transferred what was thought to be Timothy's remains from Ephesus to Constantinople (modern Istanbul) and buried them in the Church of the Apostles, which had been built by his father, Constantine.

He was the recipient of two of Paul's epistles, and his name appears with Paul's in the greetings of six of Paul's other epistles

(2 Corinthians; Philippians; Colossians; 1 and 2 Thessalonians; and Philemon).

Tiphsah [Tiph'sah], *fording place*—

1. A town at the extreme eastern limit of Solomon's dominions (1 Kings 4:24). It has been identified with the city of Thapsacus on the Euphrates. The ford was used by Cyrus and Alexander.

2. A place probably not far from Tirzah (2 Kings 15:16).

Tiras [Ti'ras], *desire*—A son of Japheth (Gen. 10:2; 1 Chron. 1:5).

Tirathites [Ti'ra·thites], *men of the gate*—The designation of a family of scribes who lived at Jabez (1 Chron. 2:55).

Tirhakah [Tir'ha·kah]—See Pharaoh.

Tirhanah [Tir·ha'nah], *favor*—Son of Caleb by his concubine Maachah (1 Chron. 2:48).

Tiria [Ti'ri·a], *fear*—A son of Jehaleleel, of the tribe of Judah (1 Chron. 4:16).

Tirshatha [Tir'sha·tha], commonly *your excellence*—A Persian title given to Zerubbabel and Nehemiah at the time they governed Judah (Ezra 2:63; Neh. 7:65, 70; 8:9; 10:1).

Tirzah [Tir'zah], *delight*—The name of a woman and a city in the Old Testament:

1. The youngest of the five daughters of Zelophehad (Num. 26:33; Josh. 17:3).

2. One of thirty-one ancient Canaanite cities west of the Jordan River conquered by Joshua (Josh. 12:24). Tirzah was the capital of the northern kingdom of Israel from the time of Jeroboam I until the time of Omri (reigned 885–874 B.C.), who moved the capital to Samaria after reigning in Tirzah six years (1 Kings 16:23).

Tishbite [Tish'bite], *captivity*—The designation of Elijah, the prophet (1 Kings 17:1; 21:17, 28; 2 Kings 1:3, 8; 9:36).

Tishri [Tish'ri], possibly *beginning*—First month of the Jewish civil year, seventh month of the sacred year, roughly corresponding to September/October. Also called Ethanim (1 Kings 8:2).

Titius Justus [Tit'i·us Jus'tus], *just* (Justus)—A man of Corinth who lived next door to the synagogue and with whom Paul stayed (Acts 18:7; NRSV, NIV, REB, NASB). He is also called Justus (KJV, NKJV).

Titus [Ti'tus], *nurse*—A "partner and fellow worker" (2 Cor. 8:23) of the apostle Paul. Although Titus is not mentioned in the book of Acts, Paul's letters reveal that he was the man of the hour at a number of key points in Paul's life.

Paul first mentions Titus in Galatians 2:1–3. As an uncircumcised Gentile, Titus accompanied Paul and Barnabas to Jerusalem as a living example of a great theological truth: Gentiles need not be circumcised in order to be saved.

Titus next appears in connection with Paul's mission to Corinth. While Paul was in Ephesus during his third missionary journey, he received disturbing news from the church at Corinth. After writing two letters and paying one visit to Corinth, Paul sent Titus to Corinth with a third letter (2 Cor. 7:6–9). When Titus failed to return with news of the situation, Paul left Ephesus and, with a troubled spirit (2 Cor. 7:5), traveled north to Troas (2 Cor. 2:12–13).

Finally, in Macedonia, Titus met the anxious apostle with the good news that the church at Corinth had repented. In relief and joy, Paul wrote yet another letter to Corinth (2 Corinthians), perhaps from Philippi, sending it again through Titus (2 Cor. 7:5–16). In addition, Titus was given responsibility for completing the collection for the poor of Jerusalem (2 Cor. 8:6, 16–24; 12:18).

Titus appears in another important role on the island of Crete (Titus 1:4). Beset by a rise in false teaching and declining morality, Titus was told by Paul to strengthen the churches by teaching sound doctrine and good works, and by appointing elders in every city (Titus 1:5). Paul then urged Titus to join him in Nicopolis (on the west coast of Greece) for winter (Titus 3:12). Not surprisingly, Titus was remembered in church tradition as the first bishop of Crete.

A final reference to Titus comes from 2 Timothy 4:10, where Paul remarks in passing that Titus has departed for mission work in Dalmatia (modern Croatia).

Titus was a man for the tough tasks. According to Paul, he was dependable (2 Cor. 8:17), reliable (2 Cor. 7:6), and diligent (2 Cor. 8:17); and he had a great capacity for human affection (2 Cor. 7:13–15).

Possessing both strength and tact, Titus calmed a desperate situation on more than one occasion. He is a good model for Christians who are called to live out their witness in trying circumstances.

Titus Justus [Ti'tus Jus'tus]—See Titius Justus.

Tizite [Ti'zite], *thou shall go forth*—The designation of Joha, son of Shimri, and one of David's mighty men (1 Chron. 11:45).

Toah [To'ah], *low* or *lowly*—Son of Zuph and ancestor of Samuel and Heman. He was a Levite of the family of Kohath (1 Chron. 6:34). He is also called Tohu (1 Sam. 1:1) and Nahath (1 Chron. 6:26).

Tob [Tob], *good*—A land east of the Jordan River between Gilead and the Syrian desert. Jephthah fled to Tob from his half brothers, who did not want him to share in their inheritance. And it was from Tob that Jephthah was called to lead the eastern tribes of Israel against the Ammonites (Judg. 11:3, 5).

Tob-adonijah [Tob-ad·o·ni'jah], *pleading to Jehovah*—A Levite (2 Chron. 17:8).

Tobiah [To·bi'ah], *Jehovah is good*—Two men mentioned in the Old Testament:
1. Head of a family, some of whom returned from Babylon with Zerubbabel. They were unable to establish their descent as true Israelites (Ezra 2:60; Neh. 7:62).
2. An Ammonite who opposed Nehemiah in building the wall of Jerusalem (Neh. 2:10; 4:3, 7).

Tobijah [To·bi'jah], *Jehovah is good*—Two Old Testament men:
1. A Levite appointed by Jehoshaphat to teach the people of Judah (2 Chron. 17:8).
2. A Jew from whom the prophet Zechariah secured the silver and gold for the crowns to place on the head of Joshua the high priest (Zech. 6:10, 14).

Tochen [To'chen], *a measure*—A city of Simeon (1 Chron. 4:32).

Togarmah [To·gar'mah], *thou wilt break her*—A son of Gomer, the son of Japheth who survived the Flood (Gen. 10:3). His descendants are mentioned by Ezekiel as traders in horses and mules (Ezek. 27:14).

Tohu [To'hu], *lowly*—A son of Zuph and an ancestor of Samuel (1 Sam. 1:1). See Tohu.

Toi [To'i], *terror*—King of Hamath (2 Sam. 8:9–12; also called Tou, 1 Chron. 18:9–11).

Tokhath [To'khath]—See Tikvah.

Tola [To'la], *worm*—Two Old Testament men:

1. Son of Issachar. He was the head of a tribal family (Gen. 46:13; Num. 26:23; 1 Chron. 7:1–2). In the time of David, the Tolaites numbered 22,600 fighting men.

2. A judge of Israel (Judg. 10:1–2).

Tolad [To'lad]—See Eltolad.

Tolaites [To'la·ites]—The descendants of Issachar's son, Tola (Num. 26:23).

Tophel [To'phel], *mortar*—A station of the Israelites in the wilderness. It is associated with the last words of Moses to the nation (Deut. 1:1).

Tophet [To'phet], *spitting out*—A place southeast of Jerusalem, in the Valley of Hinnom, where child sacrifices were offered and the dead bodies were buried or consumed (Isa. 30:33; Jer. 7:31–32; 19:6, 11–14; Topheth, 2 Kings 23:10). Chemosh, a Moabite god (1 Kings 11:7, 33; 2 Kings 23:13), and Molech, an Ammonite god (1 Kings 11:7; 2 Kings 23:10), were worshipped at Tophet through a practice despised by God—infant sacrifice (2 Kings 16:3; Jer. 7:31; 19:5; 32:35).

Two kings of Judah—Ahaz, or Jehoahaz (2 Kings 16:3), and Manasseh (2 Kings 21:6)—made their own sons "pass through the fire." Godly King Josiah stopped this horrible practice (2 Kings 23:10), possibly by dumping the garbage of Jerusalem at Tophet.

The prophet Isaiah used Tophet as a symbol of the death and destruction God would use as judgment against the king of Assyria (Isa. 30:33). Jeremiah proclaimed that God's judgment would fall upon the people of Judah for sacrificing their infants to Baal (Jer. 19:5–6). The burial of slaughtered Judahites at this place would be so great, said Jeremiah, that the name Tophet would be changed to "Valley of Slaughter" (Jer. 7:31–32; 19:6). Jeremiah also announced that God would make

Jerusalem itself a defiled place like Tophet because of the idolatry of the city (Jer. 19:6, 11–14).

Topheth [To'pheth]—See Tophet.

Tou [To'u]—See Toi.

Tower of Babel [Bab'el]—See Babel, Tower of.

Tower of the Furnaces—See Ovens, Tower of the.

Trachonitis [Trach·o·ni'tis], *rough*—A lava region south of Damascus; Herod's brother Philip was tetrarch over this area (Luke 3:1).

Transjordan—The area on the east side of the Jordan River. The word *Transjordan* is not actually used in the Bible, the area is usually referred to as "beyond the Jordan" (Gen. 50:10–11). The tribes of Reuben, Gad, and the half-tribe of Manasseh settled in this area (Deut. 3:12–20; Josh. 1:12–16). In the New Testament era, this area was known as the Decapolis and Perea (Matt. 4:15; Mark 3:8). The King's Highway was a road which passed through the Transjordan from north to south (Num. 20:17; 21:22).

Tree of Knowledge—A tree in the center of the garden of Eden, the one tree from which God had forbidden Adam and Eve to eat, or they would die (Gen. 2:9, 17). Satan, in the form of a serpent, tempted Eve to eat the fruit, encouraging her first to doubt God, and then to disobey. He told her that by knowing good and evil, she would be like God, and this seemed desirable to Eve (Gen. 3:5–6). She took the fruit and ate it, Adam followed her example, and both God's warning and the serpent's promise came true—in a way. Adam and Eve now had experiential knowledge of the difference between good and evil, the great gulf between innocence and sin. They knew more, but the serpent lied when he said it would make them more like God. God's warning came true just as He had said: Adam and Eve experienced spiritual death on the day they ate the fruit. They also lost the right to eat from the Tree of Life, and were banished from the garden, to work hard until they finally died physically.

Tree of Life—The second tree in the center of the garden of Eden, along with the Tree of Knowledge (Gen. 2:9, 16). Adam and Eve were free to eat from this tree until they disobeyed God. Then they were cast from the garden and denied the fruit of the tree. Happily, this is not the end of the story. God loved the world, and made a way of redemption (John 3:16). At the end of time, when the new heavens and earth are made, and all that is old is passed away, the Tree of Life will once again be free for all to eat from. The curse will be ended (Rev. 22:2–3).

Tribulation, The Great—A terrible time of unprecedented trouble on earth when the wrath of God will be poured out on sinful humans (Mark 13:14–23). Some believers will live through this time (Rev. 7:14). Afterward, the sun and moon will be darkened, and Christ will return in power and great glory (Mark 13:24). According to the prophet Daniel, this time will last for one "seven," or a period of seven years. It is divided into two parts: a time of apparent peace, and then a time of abomination, wrath, and destruction (Dan. 9:27). The book of Revelation speaks of a similar period of seven years. See Antichrist.

Trinity—The theological term describing the unique three-in-one God of the universe, a unified being made up of three persons: Father, Son, and Holy Spirit. The three persons are eternal, coexistent, and equal. The three persons are the same substance but different in subsistence. All parts of the Godhead possess deity, but all have different functions. This is not a doctrine of three gods, but one God in three persons.

The word *trinity* never appears in the Bible, but the doctrine is nevertheless clearly set forth. The deity of God the Father is undoubted (John 6:27; 1 Peter 1:2). The deity of the Son is shown as He portrays the attributes of God (Matt. 9:4; 28:8, 20); as He is addressed as God (John 1:1; 8:58; 20:28); and as He is doing things only God can do (John 1:3; 12:9; Col. 1:17). The deity of the Holy Spirit is taught as He is called God (Acts 5), and seen with the attributes of God (1 Cor. 6:19).

Tripolis, Men of the [Trip'o·lis]—See Tarpelites.

Troas [Tro'as], *a Trojan*—A seaport of Mysia, some distance south of the Troy of Homer. Paul visited Troas several times (Acts 16:8–11; 20:6; 2 Tim. 4:13). Paul was in this city when he had the vision of the man from Macedonia, asking him to come and help them. Troas was also the location of the miraculous healing of Eutychus, who fell out of an upstairs window and was picked up dead (Acts 20:5–12).

Trogyllium [Tro·gyl′li·um], *a cache*—A city on the western coast of Asia Minor, south of Ephesus. Paul stayed in this city on his return from his third missionary journey (Acts 20:15).

Trophimus [Troph′i·mus], *nourishing*—A native of Ephesus who was a Gentile Christian and a companion of Paul on his third journey (Acts 20:4). He inadvertently caused a riot in Jerusalem, as the Jews assumed that Paul had brought him into the temple, defiling the holy place with a Gentile presence. They seized Paul and would have killed him if it had not been for the timely intervention of the Romans. Trophimus accompanied Paul again as he traveled to Rome as a prisoner, but fell sick and had to stay in Miletus (2 Tim. 4:20).

Trumpets, Feast of—On the first day of the seventh month, a Sabbath rest was taken, and the trumpets were blown as a memorial. Offerings of fire were made, and no work was done (Lev. 23:24–32). The offering was to consist of one young bull, one ram, seven yearling lambs, a grain offering, and a goat kid as a sin offering. In addition, the ordinary New Moon offerings were to be made (Num. 29:1–6).

Tryphaena [Try·phae′na]—See Tryphena.

Tryphena [Try·phe′na], *luxurious*—A Christian woman at Rome (Rom. 16:12). See Tryphosa.

Tryphosa [Try·pho′sa], *delicate*—A Christian woman at Rome to whom Paul sent greetings. She and Tryphena may have been sisters, or they may have labored together as deaconesses (Rom. 16:12).

Tubal [Tu′bal], *thou will be brought*—
    1. Son of Japheth (Gen. 10:2; 1 Chron. 1:5).
    2. A tribe probably descended from the preceding. It is believed to have spread into Russia and perhaps into Spain (Isa. 66:19; Ezek. 32:26).

Tubal-cain [Tu′bal-cain], *thou will be brought of Cain*—A son of Lamech and Zillah, a descendant of Cain. Tubal-cain was the "father" of all metalworkers and is described as "an instructor of every craftsman in bronze and iron" (Gen. 4:22).

Tychicus [Tych′i·cus], *fateful*—A fellow-laborer of the apostle Paul who went to Troas to await Paul's coming to that city at the close of the third journey (Acts 20:4). He carried Paul's epistles to the churches at Ephesus and Colosse (Eph. 6:21; Col. 4:7).

Tyrannus [Ty·ran'nus], *sovereign*—A man who had a school in Ephesus which he permitted Paul to use for his teaching during his two years in that city (Acts 19:9).

Tyre [Tyre], *rock*—An ancient seaport city of the Phoenicians situated north of Israel. Tyre was the principal seaport of the Phoenician coast, about 40 kilometers (25 miles) south of Sidon and 56 kilometers (35 miles) north of Carmel. It consisted of two cities: a rocky coastal city on the mainland and a small island city. The island city was just off the shore. The mainland city was on a coastal plain, a strip only 24 kilometers (15 miles) long and 3 kilometers (2 miles) wide.

Behind the plain of Tyre stood the rocky mountains of Lebanon. Tyre was easily defended because it had the sea on the west, the mountains on the east, and several other rocky cliffs (one the famous "Ladder of Tyre") around it, making it difficult to invade.

In the fifteenth century B.C. it was under the dominion of Egypt, and it was a strong city when the Israelites came into Canaan under Joshua (Josh. 19:29). At no time did it come into the hands of the Israelites.

In the time of David and Solomon very friendly relations existed between Israel and Tyre. Hiram, king of Tyre, furnished David with materials and craftsmen for his palace (2 Sam. 5:11). He also provided materials for Solomon's temple and other building enterprises (1 Kings 5:1; 9:10–14; 2 Chron. 2:3, 11). Sometime after the kingdom was divided in 921 B.C., Ahab, the second king of the fourth dynasty of Israel, married the daughter of Ethbaal, king of the Sidonians (1 Kings 16:31). The Tyrians were not a warlike people; like all Phoenicians they were dominantly interested in commerce, colonization, and manufacture. They traded with the remotest peoples, their productions consisting of glassware, dyes, and metalwork. In the ninth century B.C. Carthage was founded by Tyrians and became one of Rome's strongest rivals.

Throughout the history of Israel, the two Phoenician cities of Tyre and Sidon had a generally good relationship with God's people. Why, then, did the prophet Ezekial utter such bitter words against Tyre (Ezra 26)? It was probably because of the taunting attitude Tyre demonstrated when the nation of Judah was overrun by the Babylonians in 586 B.C.

(Ezra 26:2). Judah's collapse meant that Phoenicia was a region with little competition in central Palestine. Their trade monopoly complete, Tyre and Sidon rejoiced. Their insatiable greed and prideful attitude led Ezekiel to issue his bitter condemnation.

When Ezekiel spoke these words, the cities of Tyre and Sidon had no peers on the Mediterranean shores. As early as 1000 B.C. the two cities had emerged as important population centers. As the leader of a group of small city-states, Sidon first grew to prominence in trade. After a time, it was eclipsed by Tyre, which established an empire based on maritime trade. The ships of Tyre sailed as far away as Great Britian and North Africa on trading ventures.

As predicted by Ezekiel, the cities of Tyre and Sidon were eventually judged by God. Tyre was thought to be invincible because part of the city was located offshore, completely surrounded by the sea. But the Greek conqueror Alexander the Great built a causeway to the city and destroyed it in 332 B.C. After the Romans became the dominant world power, they rebuilt Tyre. The ruins of this city are visible today. Both Tyre and Sidon are mentioned in the New Testament. Jesus visited both cities during His ministry (Matt. 15:21–28). Paul also visited a Christian community in Tyre, staying with believers there for a week during his third missionary journey (Acts 21:1–6).

Ucal [U'cal], *devoured*—One of the two unknown persons to whom Agur addressed a proverb (Prov. 30:1).

Uel [U'el], *will of God*—A son of Bani who put away his foreign wife (Ezra 10:34).

Ulai [U'lai], *my leaders (mighties)*—A river of Persia. Daniel was standing by this river in his second prophetic vision from God when he saw the ram and the male goat (Dan. 8:2, 16).

Ulam [U'lam], *their leader* or *vestibule*—Two Old Testament men:
1. Son of Sheresh of the tribe of Manasseh (1 Chron. 7:16–17).
2. Son of Eshek and a descendant of Saul (1 Chron. 8:39–40).

Ulla [Ul'la], *a yoke*—A man of the tribe of Asher (1 Chron. 7:39).

Ummah [Um'mah], *union*—A city which was part of the inheritance of Asher (Josh. 19:30).

Unni [Un'ni], *afflicted*—Two Old Testament Levites:
1. A Levite musician who lived in the time of David (1 Chron. 15:18, 20).
2. A Levite who returned to Jerusalem with Zerubbabel (Neh. 12:9). He is called Unno in the Revised Version.

Unno [Un'no]—See Unni.

Uphaz [U'phaz], *desire of fine gold*—A region from which gold was exported (Jer. 10:9; Dan. 10:5), thought by some to be the same as Ophir.

Upper Gate—A gate of the temple which was rebuilt by Jotham, king of Judah (2 Kings 15:38).

Ur [Ur], *flame*—A city and a man of the Old Testament:

1. A city in northern Mesopotamia slightly west of the Euphrates, halfway between the Persian Gulf and modern-day Baghdad. It was the place in which Abraham lived before moving to Canaan (Gen. 11:28, 31; 15:7; Neh. 9:7). After the Chaldeans came into Babylonia, Ur was called "Ur of the Chaldeans." This did not happen until after the days of Abraham, so it seems clear that this was a "modern term" used by Moses when writing the account of Abraham's life. Ur was a bustling metropolis in Abraham's day; archeological finds among its ruins show that its culture was highly developed.

2. The father of Eliphal (1 Chron. 11:35).

Urbane [Ur'bane]—See Urbanus.

Urbanus [Ur·ba'nus], *polite* or *of the city*—A Christian of the Roman church (Rom. 16:9).

Uri [U'ri], *fiery*—

1. The father of Bezalel of Judah. Bezalel was one of the men who worked on the tabernacle (Ex. 31:2).

2. The father of Geber, Solomon's tax gatherer in Gilead (1 Kings 4:19).

3. A temple porter who divorced his foreign wife (Ezra 10:24).

Uriah [U·ri'ah], *the Lord is my light*—The name of three men in the Old Testament:

1. A Hittite married to Bathsheba. Uriah was one of David's mighty men (2 Sam. 11:3–26; 12:9–10, 15; 1 Kings 15:5; Matt. 1:6; Urias, KJV).

Judging from the usual interpretation of his name and good conduct, Uriah was a worshiper of God. David's adultery with Uriah's wife, Bathsheba, occurred while Uriah was engaged in war at Rabbah, the Ammonite capital. She became pregnant and Uriah was immediately recalled to Jerusalem to hide what had happened, but his sense of duty and loyalty only frustrated the king. Failing to use Uriah as a shield to cover his sin with Bathsheba, David ordered this valiant soldier to the front line of battle, where he was killed. David then married Bathsheba (2 Sam. 11:1–27; Matt. 1:6), but the child died.

2. A priest, the son of Koz and father of Meremoth. Uriah helped rebuild the wall of Jerusalem under Nehemiah. He stood with Ezra the scribe as Ezra read the law and addressed the people (Ezra 8:33). The NKJV spells his name Urijah in Nehemiah 3:4, 21; 8:4.

3. A priest, one of two faithful witnesses to a scroll written by the prophet Isaiah concerning Maher-shalalhashbaz (Isa. 8:2).

Uriel [U′ri·el], *light of God*—Two Old Testament men:

1. A Levite of the Kohath family and house of Izhar (1 Chron. 6:24).

2. The father of Micaiah, the mother of Abijah and wife of Rehoboam (2 Chron. 13:2).

Urijah [U·ri′jah], *light of Jehovah*—

1. A priest in Jerusalem who built an altar for King Ahaz, a copy of an altar Ahaz saw in Damascus on a visit of state to Tiglath-pileser (2 Kings 16:10–16). Urijah apparently made no protest at the placing of this copy of a pagan altar in the temple courts, and making all sacrificial offerings on the new altar.

2. Son of Shemaiah and a prophet of Kirjath-jearim. Jehoiakim sought to kill him for the judgment he predicted would fall upon Judah. He fled to Egypt but was brought back and put to death (Jer. 26:20–23).

Uthai [U′thai], *helpful*—Two Old Testament men:

1. Son of Ammihud of the family of Pharez, son of Judah (1 Chron. 9:4).

2. A son of Bigvai. He returned to Jerusalem with Ezra (Ezra 8:14).

Uz [Uz], *wooded*—Three men and a geographical area:

1. A son of Aram (Gen. 10:23; 1 Chron. 1:17) and grandson of Shem.

2. A son of Nahor and Milcah (Gen. 22:21), also called Huz (KJV).

3. A son of Dishan and grandson of Seir (Gen. 36:28).

4. The land of Uz, the home of Job (Job 1:1). The exact location is not known, but it has been suggested that Uz was east of the Jordan River, either between Edom and northern Arabia, or the area south of Damascus.

Uzai [U′zai], *I shall have my sprinklings*—The father of Palal, one who worked on repairing the wall of Jerusalem (Neh. 3:25).

Uzal [U′zal], *I shall be flooded*—A son of Joktan (Gen. 10:27; 1 Chron. 1:21).

Uzza, Uzzah [Uz′za, Uz′zah], *strength*—The name of five men in the Old Testament:

1. A son of Abinadab of Kirjath-jearim. When the ark was on its way to Jerusalem in the reign of David, it was jolted by the stumbling of the oxen. Uzzah put forth his hand to steady it and was struck dead. The place was called Perez-uzzah, meaning the breaking out against Uzzah (2 Sam. 6:3–8; 1 Chron. 13:7–14).

2. A person in whose garden Manasseh, king of Judah, and Amon (Manasseh's son), also king of Judah, were buried (2 Kings 21:18, 26).

3. A Levite of the family of Merari (1 Chron. 6:29).

4. A descendant of Ehud mentioned in the family tree of King Saul (1 Chron. 8:7).

5. An ancestor of a family of Nethinim (temple servants) who returned with Zerubbabel from the captivity (Ezra 2:49; Neh. 7:51).

Uzza, Garden of [Uz′za]—A garden near the palace of Manasseh, king of Judah in which Manasseh and his son, Amon, were buried (2 Kings 21:18, 26).

Uzzen-sheerah [Uz′zen-she′e·rah], possibly *portion of Sherah*— A town built by Sheerah, the daughter of Ephraim (1 Chron. 7:24). Its exact location is not known.

Uzzi [Uz′zi], *strong*—

1. Son of Bukki and father of Zerahiah; a descendant of Aaron and an ancestor of Ezra (1 Chron. 6:5–6, 51; Ezra 7:4).

2. Son of Tola of Issachar (1 Chron. 7:2–3).

3. Son of Bela (1 Chron. 7:7).

4. Son of Michri, a Benjamite and father of Elah (1 Chron. 9:8).

5. Son of Bani, a Levite, and overseer of the Levites in the time of Nehemiah (Neh. 11:22).

6. A priest of the house of Jedaiah who lived in the time of Joiakim, the high priest (Neh. 12:19). He may have been the same as the following.

7. A priest who had a part in the dedication of the wall of Jerusalem (Neh. 12:42); possibly the same as No. 6.

Uzzia [Uz·zi′a], *strength of Jehovah*—One of David's mighty men, of the town of Ashtaroth (1 Chron. 11:44).

Uzziah [Uz·zi′ah], *the Lord is my strength*—The name of five men in the Old Testament:

1. The son of Amaziah and Jecholiah; ninth king of Judah and father of Jotham (2 Kings 15:1–7; 2 Chron. 26). Uzziah is also called Azariah (2 Kings 14:21; 15:1–7).

Uzziah ascended the throne at age sixteen and reigned longer than any previous king of Judah or Israel—fifty-two years. He probably co-reigned with his father and had his son Jotham as his co-regent during his final years as a leper. A wise, pious, and powerful king, he extended Judah's territory and brought the nation to a time of great prosperity. In the south he maintained control over Edom and rebuilt port facilities at Elath on the Gulf of Aqaba. To the west he warred against the Philistines, seizing several cities. He also apparently defeated and subdued the Ammonites. The foolishness of Uzziah's father, Amaziah, in fighting Joash, the king of Israel, had left the city of Jerusalem in a vulnerable position (2 Chron. 25:23). So Uzziah focused his attention on securing the defenses of both his capital and his country. He reinforced the towers of the city gates. On these towers and walls he placed huge catapults capable of shooting arrows and hurling stones at the enemy (2 Chron. 26:15). He also maintained a well-equipped army and fortified strategic places in the desert. His successes were directly related to his spiritual sensitivity, because he sought the Lord through a prophet who encouraged him to honor and obey God (2 Chron. 26:5).

However, Uzziah's heart was lifted up in pride. No longer satisfied to be a mortal king, he desired to be like some of his contemporaries— a divine king. He entered the temple to burn incense. When Azariah the high priest and eighty associates confronted him, he responded in anger instead of repentance. God judged him by striking him with leprosy. Uzziah was forced to live the rest of his life in a separate place, with his son Jotham probably acting as king. At Uzziah's death the prophet Isaiah had a transforming vision of the Lord, high and lifted up on a throne (Isa. 1:1; 6:1–13; 7:1).

2. A Levite of the family of Kohath, Uzziah was the son of Uriel and the father of Shaul (1 Chron. 6:24).

3. The father of Jehonathan (1 Chron. 27:25). Jehonathan was an officer of David over the storehouses.

4. Son of Harim, a priest commanded by Ezra to divorce his pagan wife (Ezra 10:21).

5. The father of Athaiah. He was a man of Judah who lived in Jerusalem after the captivity (Neh. 11:4).

Uzziel [Uz'zi·el], *might of God*—

1. A son of Kohath (Ex. 6:18, 22; Num. 3:19, 27, 30). He was a kinsman of Aaron (Lev. 10:4).

2. Son of Ishi. He was a captain of the tribe of Simeon. In the reign of Hezekiah he helped defeat the Amalekites (1 Chron. 4:41–43).

3. A Benjamite of the family of Bela (1 Chron. 7:7).

4. A musician in David's reign (1 Chron. 25:4). Also called Azarel.

5. A son of Jeduthun, a Levite. He labored with Hezekiah in his religious reforms (2 Chron. 29:14).

6. Son of Harhaiah. He was a goldsmith and labored on the wall of Jerusalem with Nehemiah (Neh. 3:8).

Uzzielites [Uz'zi·el·ites]—The descendants of the Uzziel, son of Aaron's son Kohath (Num. 3:27; 1 Chron. 26:23).

V

Vaheb [Va'heb], *now, come on* and *do thou give*—A place in the region of the Arnon, mentioned only in the Revised Version (Num. 21:14–15).

Vajezatha [Va·jez'a·tha], *strong as the wind*—One of the ten sons of Haman (Est. 9:9).

Valley Gate—A gate of Jerusalem. Uzziah, king of Judah, built a fortified tower at this gate (2 Chron. 26:9; Neh. 2:13).

Valley of Slaughter—See Tophet.

Vaniah [Va·ni'ah], *Jehovah is praise*—A son of Bani who put away his foreign wife (Ezra 10:36).

Vashni [Vash'ni], *strong*—The eldest son of Samuel (1 Chron. 6:28; probably the same as Joel in 1 Sam. 8:2; 1 Chron. 6:33).

Vashti [Vash'ti], *beautiful*—The beautiful queen of King Ahasuerus of Persia (Xerxes I, reigned 486–465 B.C.) who was banished from court for refusing the king's command to exhibit herself during a period of drunken feasting (Est. 1:11). Her departure allowed Esther to become Ahasuerus's new queen and to be used as God's instrument in saving the Jewish people from destruction.

Vedan [Ve'dan], *and Dan*—A place which traded with Tyre (Ezek. 27:19). It is rendered "Dan also" in the KJV.

Via Dolorosa [Via Dol·o·ro'sa], *way of sorrow*—The road traveled by Jesus as He carried the cross from Pilate's judgment hall to Golgotha. Many years of tradition have marked out the way, and also fourteen "stations of the cross," or events which happened during the short journey. However, the exact route the soldiers took is not recorded in the Gospels, nor are the fourteen "stations." Since Jerusalem was destroyed in 70 A.D., it is a little unlikely that the real "via dolorosa" could be found.

Vineyards, Plain of—See Abel-keramim.

Vophsi [Voph'si], *rich*—The father of Nahbi (Num. 13:14).

Weeks, Feast of—One of the three annual feasts at which time all the men of Israel were required to present themselves at the sanctuary (Ex. 34:22–23). It fell seven weeks after the waving of the sheaf and is also called Pentecost (Acts 2:1) or the feast of harvest because the firstfruits of the wheat harvest were presented (Ex. 23:16; 34:22; Num. 28:26). All labor was avoided and the day was observed as a Sabbath (Lev. 23:21). Sacrifices attended the offering of the loaves (Lev. 23:17–19).

Wilderness of the Wandering—The land in which the Israelites wandered for forty years before entering Canaan. It was in the peninsula of Sinai formed by the Gulf of Suez and the Gulf of Akabah, the two branches of the Red Sea. About Mount Sinai was the granite region, while along the shore of the Mediterranean was the sandy region. The northern and central districts consisted of limestone (Ex. 16:1–35; Num. 14:25, 33–45; 20:2–13).

Willows, Brook of the—A brook in Moab lined with willows (Isa. 15:7).

Wise Men—The men who came from the east to worship the newly born Jesus (Matt. 2:1) were of a priestly caste, a tribe of Media, who retained an important place after the Medes were conquered by the Persians. They worshipped fire, the earth, water, air. They wore white robes. They claimed to be mediators between God and man and to have the gift of prophecy. Also called Magi or Magus.

Xerxes [Xer′xes]—See Ahasuerus.

Y

Yah [Yah]—An abbreviation of Yahweh (Ps. 68:4; Jah, KJV).

Yahweh [Yah′weh]—See Lord, and God, Names of.

Year of Jubilee—See Jubilee.

Yhwh—The Hebrew name of God, probably pronounced "Yahweh." See Lord and God, Names of.

Z

Zaanaim [Za·a·na'im]—See Zaanannim.

Zaanan [Za'a·nan], *place of flocks*—A city of Judah (Mic. 1:11). See Zenan.

Zaanannim [Za·a·nan'nim], *removings*—A place in Naphtali near Kedesh (Josh. 19:33).

Zaavan [Za'a·van], *disquiet*—A son of Ezer and a Horite chief (Gen. 36:27). In 1 Chronicles 1:42 he is called Zavan.

Zabad [Za'bad], *has endowed*—Six Old Testament men:

1. A descendant of Sheshan of the family of Hezron. He was one of David's warriors (1 Chron. 2:31, 34–37; 11:41).

2. Son of Tahath of Ephraim (1 Chron. 7:21).

3. Son of Shimeath and one of the two assassins of Joash, king of Judah (2 Chron. 24:26). When Amaziah came to the throne, the two were executed. His mother was a woman of Ammon. The name is more correctly written Jozachar in 2 Kings 12:21.

4. A Hebrew who, in the time of Ezra, divorced his foreign wife (Ezra 10:27).

5. Another Hebrew who, in the time of Ezra, divorced his foreign wife (Ezra 10:33).

6. Yet another Hebrew who, in the time of Ezra, divorced his foreign wife (Ezra 10:43).

Zabbai [Zab·ba'i], *pure*—A son of Bebai and the father of Baruch (Neh. 3:20).

Zabbud [Zab'bud], *given*—A son of Bigvai. He returned with Ezra (Ezra 8:14).

Zabdi [Zab'di], *gift of Jehovah*—Four Old Testament men:

1. Son of Zerah, of Judah (Josh. 7:1, 17). He is called Zimri in 1 Chronicles 2:6.

2. A son of Shimhi of the tribe of Benjamin (1 Chron. 8:19).

3. An inhabitant of Shepham (a Shiphmite), who had charge of David's wine cellars (1 Chron. 27:27).

4. A son of Asaph, a Levite. He lived in the time of Nehemiah (Neh. 11:17).

Zabdiel [Zab'di·el], *gift of God*—Two Old Testament men:

1. The father of Jashobeam, the latter an officer of David's army (1 Chron. 27:2).

2. Son of Haggedolim. He was overseer of 128 warriors in the time of Nehemiah (Neh. 11:14).

Zabidah [Ze·bi'dah]—See Zebudah.

Zabud [Za'bud], *given*—Son of Nathan (1 Kings 4:5), a principal officer and the king's (Solomon) friend.

Zabulon [Za·bu'lon]—See Zebulun.

Zaccai [Zac·ca'i], *pure*—The head of a family, a large number of whom returned to Palestine with Zerubbabel (Ezra 2:9; Neh. 7:14).

Zacchaeus [Zac·chae'us], *pure*—A chief tax collector of Jericho who had grown rich by overtaxing the people. When Jesus visited Jericho, Zacchaeus climbed a tree in order to see Jesus (Luke 19:3). Jesus asked him to come down and then went to visit Zacchaeus as a guest. As a result of Jesus' visit, Zacchaeus became a follower of the Lord, repented of his sins, and made restitution for his wrongdoing. He gave half of his goods to the poor and restored fourfold those whom he had cheated. In associating with people like Zacchaeus, Jesus showed that He came to call sinners to repentance.

Zacchur [Zac'chur]—See Zaccur.

Zaccur [Zac'cur], *mindful*—Seven Old Testament men:

1. Father of Shammua, the spy of the tribe of Reuben (Num. 13:4).

2. Son of Hamuel of the tribe of Simeon (1 Chron. 4:26). He is also called Zacchur.

3. A son of Jaaziah of the family of Merari, a Levite (1 Chron. 24:27).

4. A son of Asaph, family of Gershom, a Levite and leader of the third course of musicians in the time of David (1 Chron. 25:2, 10; Neh. 12:35).

5. A son of Imri. He labored on the wall of Jerusalem under Nehemiah (Neh. 3:2).

6. A Levite who sealed the covenant (Neh. 10:12).

7. A Levite, son of Mattaniah (Neh. 13:13).

Zachariah [Zach·a·ri′ah]—See Zechariah.

Zacharias [Zach·a·ri′as], *remembered of Jehovah*—Two righteous men, one of the Old Testament, one of the New.

1. Greek spelling of Zechariah, son of Barachias, the prophet who wrote the book of Zechariah. He was referred to by Jesus as a righteous man who was put to death by the Jews at the temple (Matt. 23:35; Luke 11:51). Some scholars think this could also refer to Zechariah, a priest who was the son of Jehoida, at the time of Joash, king of Judah (2 Chron. 24:20–22).

2. Father of John the Baptist. He was a priest of the course of Abia (Luke 1:5). His wife, Elizabeth, was related to the mother of Jesus. They lived in the hill country of Judea, probably at Juttah (Luke 1:39–40). While he was engaged in burning incense at the hour of prayer, an angel assured him that his prayer for a son was answered. On account of the age of Elizabeth he was doubtful and asked for a sign. As a result he became dumb until John was born. When he spoke, he praised God (Luke 1:18–22, 62–64).

Zacher [Za′cher]—See Zechariah.

Zadok [Za′dok], *just or righteous*—The name of several men in the Bible:

1. A high priest in the time of David. Zadok was a son of Ahitub (2 Sam. 8:17) and a descendant of Aaron through Eleazar (1 Chron. 24:3). After the death of Saul, he and others of his father's house went to David at Hebron (1 Chron. 12:27–28). During David's reign he served jointly as high priest with Abiathar (2 Sam. 8:17).

Both Zadok and Abiathar fled from Jerusalem with David when the king's son Absalom attempted to take over the throne. They brought the ark of the covenant out with them. After Absalom had been killed, David asked Zadok and Abiathar to urge the people to recall David to the throne (2 Sam. 19:11).

When David was dying, another of his sons, Adonijah, tried to take the throne. This time only Zadok remained faithful to the king. When David heard of the plot, he ordered Zadok and the prophet Nathan to anoint Solomon king (1 Kings 1:7–8, 32–45).

Consequently, Abiathar was deposed and Zadok held the high priesthood alone (1 Kings 2:26–27). In this way the high priesthood was restored to the line of Eleazar, son of Aaron.

2. The grandfather of Jotham, king of Judah (2 Kings 15:33; 2 Chron. 27:1). Also the father of Jerusha and the wife of Uzziah.

3. A high priest in Solomon's temple and father of Shallum (1 Chron. 6:12; 9:11).

4. A valiant warrior who joined David's army at Hebron (1 Chron. 12:28).

5. A son of Baana who helped repair part of the Jerusalem wall after the captivity (Neh. 3:4). He may be the same person as No. 7.

6. A son of Immer, a priest who helped repair Jerusalem's wall (Neh. 3:29). He may be the same person as No. 9.

7. An Israelite who sealed the covenant with Nehemiah (Neh. 10:21). He may be the same person as No. 5.

8. A son of Meraioth (Neh. 11:11).

9. A scribe in the time of Nehemiah (Neh. 13:13). Zadok was appointed a treasurer over the storehouse.

10. An ancestor of Jesus (Matt. 1:14; Sadoc, KJV).

Zaham [Za'ham], *loathing*—A son of Rehoboam and Abihail (2 Chron. 11:19).

Zair [Za'ir]. *little*—A place in Edom, east of the Dead Sea (2 Kings 8:21).

Zalaph [Za'laph], *fracture*—The father of Hanun. The son labored on the wall (Neh. 3:30).

Zalmon [Zal'mon], *shady*—An Old Testament man and a forest.

1. One of David's warriors; an Ahohite (2 Sam. 23:28). In 1 Chronicles 11:29 he is called Ilai.

2. A forest near Shechem (Judg. 9:48). In Psalm 68:14 it is called Salmon.

Zalmon, Mount [Zal'mon], *shady*—The place where Abimelech and his warriors each cut a bough from a tree to use in their siege against the tower of Shechem (Judg. 9:48).

Zalmonah [Zal·mo'nah], *shady*—A place southeast of Edom, one of the stopping places on the wilderness journey (Num. 33:41–42).

Zalmunna [Zal·mun'na], *shade denied*—A king of Midian (Judg. 8:4–28; Ps. 83:11). See Zebah.

Zamzummim [Zam·zum'mim], possibly *plotters*—A tribe of Rephaim that occupied a region east of the Jordan, which afterward was held by the Ammonites (Deut. 2:20).

Zanoah [Za·no'ah], *bog*—Two towns of Judah.
    1. A town in the hill country of Judah about ten miles southwest of Hebron (Josh. 15:56).
    2. A town in the lowland of Judah (Josh. 15:34).

Zaphenath-paneah [Zaph'e·nath-pa·ne'ah]—Variant spelling of Zaphnath-paaneah.

Zaphnath-paaneah [Zaph'nath-pa·a·ne'ah], *treasury of the glorious rest*—The name given Joseph by Pharaoh (Gen. 41:45).

Zaphon [Za'phon], *north*—A town in the territory of Gad, east of the Jordan (Josh. 13:27).

Zara, Zarah [Zar'a, Zar'ah]—See Zerah.

Zareathite [Za·re'a·thite]—See Zorathite.

Zared [Zar'ed]—See Zered.

Zarephath [Zar'e·phath], *refinement*—A town of Phoenicia near Sidon where the widow who sheltered and sustained Elijah lived. Her jar of oil and bin of meal did not run out until the Lord sent rain, "according to the word of the Lord which he spoke by Elijah" (1 Kings 17:9–16). This town is also mentioned in Obadiah, verse 20, as one of the border towns that the "captives of the host of the children of Israel shall possess as far as"; Jesus refers to this widow and this incident when He talks of a prophet not receiving honor in his own country (Luke 4:26; Sarepta, KJV).

Zaretan [Zar'e·tan], *their distress*—A village near Adam and Beth-shean close to the place where the Israelites under Joshua crossed the Jordan (Josh. 3:16; 1 Kings 4:12). The metal ornaments for Solomon's temple were cast near here (1 Kings 7:46; 2 Chron. 4:17). The Midianites fled toward this town when Gideon and his three hundred warriors routed them (Judg. 7:22). Also called Zartanah and Zarethan (KJV).

Zarethan [Zar'e·than]—See Zaretan.

Zareth-shahar [Zar'eth-sha'har]—See Zereth-shahar.

Zarhite [Zar'hite], *unknown*—Two families of the Old Testament:
   1. One belonging to the family of Zerah, a son of Simeon (Num. 26:13, 20).
   2. One belonging to the family of Zerah, a son of Judah. Achan, the man who took plunder for himself at Jericho was of this family (Josh. 7:17).
   3. One of the twelve captains of Israel was a Zarhite, but it does not say which family he was from (1 Chron. 27:11, 13).

Zartanah [Zar·ta'nah]—See Zaretan.

Zarthan [Zar'than]—See Zaretan.

Zattu [Zat'tu], *brightness of him*—The head of a family, a large number of whom returned from Babylon with Zerubbabel (Ezra 2:8; 10:27; Neh. 7:13; 10:14).

Zavan [Za'van]—See Zaavan.

Zaza [Za'za], *brightness* or *fulness*—A son of Jonathan (1 Chron. 2:33).

Zealot [Zeal'ot], *zealous one*—Nickname of the other Simon of the Twelve (Luke 6:15; Acts 1:13), which may refer to his interest in a patriotic party originated by Judas the Galilean. Like the Pharisees, the

Zealots were devoted to the law, but they were also violently opposed to submission to Rome. In their fanatical dedication to overthrowing Rome, they took over Jerusalem in A.D. 66, which resulted in the last siege and fall of Jerusalem to Rome in A.D. 70. Masada, the last Zealot fortress, was taken over by Rome in A.D. 73.

Zebadiah [Zeb·a·di'ah], *the Lord has given*—The name of nine men in the Old Testament:

1. A Benjamite, one of the sons of Beriah (1 Chron. 8:15).

2. A Benjamite, one of the sons of Elpaal (1 Chron. 8:17).

3. A son of Jeroham of Gedor (1 Chron. 12:7). With his brother, Zebadiah joined David at Ziklag.

4. A son of Meshelemiah, a Korhite Levite, who was a gatekeeper of the sanctuary in David's time (1 Chron. 26:2).

5. A captain of the fourth division of David's army (1 Chron. 27:7). Zebadiah took command of this division after Asahel, his father, was killed by Abner.

6. A Levite leader sent by King Jehoshaphat to teach the law in the cities of Judah (2 Chron. 17:7–8).

7. A son of Ishmael in the time of King Jehoshaphat (2 Chron. 19:11) who held a high judicial position under Jehoshaphat.

8. A son of Michael, a descendant of Shephatiah, who returned with Ezra from the captivity (Ezra 8:8).

9. A priest of the house of Immer (Ezra 10:20) who divorced his foreign wife.

Zebah and Zalmunna [Ze'bah, Zal'mun·na], *sacrifice*—These were the kings of Midian who Gideon was fighting with his three hundred selected warriors. The warriors were weary, but they crossed the Jordan, took the two kings, and routed the whole army. The men of Succoth had refused to give Gideon's warriors bread, so when Gideon returned to Succoth with the captured kings, he punished the men of Succoth for ridiculing him and his men. He then questioned the kings of Midian and when he discovered that they had killed his own brothers, Gideon killed them (Judg. 8:4–28). This battle is also referred to in Psalm 83:11 and Isaiah 9:4; 10:6.

Zebaim [Ze'ba·im], *gazelles*—One of Solomon's servants. Descendants of Zebaim are named as those who came back from the Babylonian captivity with Zerubbabel (Ezra 2:57; Neh. 7:59).

Zebedee [Zeb′e·dee], *gift (of the Lord)*—The father of James and John (Matt. 4:21–22; Mark 1:19–20). Apparently Zebedee's wife was named Salome (Matt. 20:20; Mark 15:40). He was a fisherman on the Sea of Galilee, perhaps living in Capernaum or Bethsaida. Zebedee was probably wealthy since he had "hired servants" (Mark 1:20). In later references to Zebedee, he appears in the phrase "sons [or son] of Zebedee" (Matt. 10:2; Mark 10:35; Luke 5:10; John 21:2).

Zebina [Ze·bi′na], *acquired* or *bought*—A descendant of Nebo, one of those who put away the pagan wife he had taken during the Babylonian captivity (Ezra 10:43).

Zeboiim [Ze·boi′im], *gazelles*—One of the five cities of the plain in the Valley of Siddim destroyed along with Sodom and Gomorrah (Gen. 10:19; 14:2). Its king, Shemeber, was defeated by Chedorlaomer. The prophet Hosea used Admah and Zeboiim (Hos. 11:8; Zeboim, KJV) as examples of God's judgment on wicked cities. Many scholars believe Zeboiim was situated near the southern end of the Dead Sea in an area presently covered by water. Others believe it was located near the eastern shore of the Dead Sea.

Zebudah [Ze·bu′dah], *bestowed*—A daughter of Pedaiah of Rumah, mother of King Jehoiakim of Judah (2 Kings 23:36).

Zebul [Ze′bul], *exalted*—A lieutenant of Abimelech, who was a son of Gideon by his concubine (Judg. 9:28–41).

Zebulun [Ze·bu′lun], *habitation*—The name of a man and a territory in the Old Testament:

1. The tenth of Jacob's twelve sons; the sixth and last son of Leah (Gen. 30:19–20; 35:23; 1 Chron. 2:1). Zebulun had three sons: Sered, Elon, and Jahleel (Gen. 46:14; Num. 26:26–27). These are the only details about Zebulun that appear in the Bible.

2. The territory in which the tribe of Zebulun lived. The land allotted to Zebulun after the conquest of Canaan was bounded by Issachar and Manasseh on the south, by Asher on the west, and by Naphtali on the north and east (Josh. 19:10–16, 27, 34). Zebulun was fertile. It included part of the mountainous area of lower Galilee and the northwest corner of the fertile plain of Esdraelon (valley of Jezreel).

Zebulunite [Ze·bu'lun·ite]—A member of the tribe of Zebulun (Num. 26:27; Judg. 12:11–12).

Zechariah [Zech·a·ri'ah], *the Lord remembers*—The name of about thirty-one men in the Bible:

1. The fifteenth king of Israel (2 Kings 14:29; 15:8, 11; Zachariah, KJV), the last of the house of Jehu. The son of Jeroboam II, Zechariah became king when his father died. He reigned only six months (about 753/52 B.C.) before being assassinated by Shallum.

2. The father of Abi or Abijah, mother of Hezekiah (2 Kings 18:2; Zachariah, KJV; 2 Chron. 29:1).

3. A chief of the tribe of Reuben when Tiglath-pileser invaded Israel (1 Chron. 5:7).

4. A son of Meshelemiah (1 Chron. 9:21; 26:2, 14) and a Levite doorkeeper in the days of David. His wisdom as a counselor is mentioned in 1 Chronicles 26:14.

5. A son of Jeiel, of the tribe of Benjamin (1 Chron. 9:37), also called Zecher (1 Chron. 8:31). Also the brother of Kish and uncle of Saul.

6. A Levite musician in the days of David who played a psaltery when the ark was brought to Jerusalem by David and who, afterward, was in the service of the tabernacle (1 Chron. 15:18).

7. A priest and trumpeter in the days of David when the ark was brought from the house of Obed-edom (1 Chron. 15:24).

8. A son of Isshiah, a Levite of the family of Kohath; a descendant of Uzziel who lived in the time of David (1 Chron. 24:25).

9. A son of Hosah, a Levite of the family of Merari. He lived in the reign of David (1 Chron. 26:11).

10. A Manassite of Gilead and the father of Iddo (1 Chron. 27:21). He lived during the reign of David.

11. A prince sent by King Jehoshaphat to teach the people of Judah (2 Chron. 17:7).

12. Son of Benaiah and father of Jahaziel, a Levite of Gershom who encouraged Jehoshaphat against Moab (2 Chron. 20:14).

13. A son of King Jehoshaphat (2 Chron. 21:2).

14. Son of Jehoiada, the high priest. He lived in the time of the reign of Athaliah, wife of Jehoram, who headed the revolt that brought Joash to the throne. Zechariah, like his father, was a righteous man. When his

father died, the people forgot Jehovah and when Zechariah reproved them the king had him killed (2 Chron. 24:20–22).

15. A prophet who counseled Uzziah, king of Judah, who followed his advice for a time (2 Chron. 26:5).

16. A Levite who helped cleanse the temple during the reign of King Hezekiah of Judah (2 Chron. 29:13). He was descended from Asaph.

17. A Levite of the family of Kohath who supervised temple repairs during Josiah's reign (2 Chron. 34:12).

18. A prince of Judah and ruler of the temple in the days of Josiah (2 Chron. 35:8).

19. A prophet in the days of Ezra (Ezra 5:1; 6:14; Zech. 1:1, 7; 7:1, 8) and author of the book of Zechariah. A leader in the restoration of the nation of Israel following the captivity, Zechariah was a contemporary of the prophet Haggai, the governor Zerubbabel, and the high priest Joshua. Zechariah himself was an important person during the period of the restoration of the community of Israel in the land of Palestine after the captivity.

The book of Zechariah begins with a note concerning the prophet. He is named as a grandson of Iddo, one of the heads of the priestly families who returned with Zerubbabel from Babylon (Zech. 1:1, 7; also Ezra 5:1; 6:14). This means that Zechariah himself was probably a priest and that his prophetic activity was in close association with the religious center of the nation. His vision of Joshua the high priest (Zech. 3:1–5) takes on added importance, since he served as a priest in association with Joshua. Zechariah began his ministry while still a young man (Zech. 2:4) in 520 B.C., two months after Haggai completed the prophecies that are recorded in the book of Haggai.

20. A descendant of Parosh and a leader of the Jews who, with 150 males returned to Palestine with Ezra after the captivity (Ezra 8:3).

21. A son of Bebai, he was the chief of twenty-eight men who returned with Ezra from the captivity (Ezra 8:11).

22. A leader of Israel after the captivity. Ezra sent him to secure the Levites and Nethinim (Ezra 8:16). He may be the same person as No. 20 or No. 21.

23. Son of Elam, an Israelite who divorced his pagan wife after the return from the captivity (Ezra 10:26).

24. A man, probably a priest, who stood with Ezra at the public reading of the law (Neh. 8:4).

25. A descendant of Perez, of the tribe of Judah (Neh. 11:4).

26. Son of Shiloni, a person whose descendants lived in Jerusalem after the captivity (Neh. 11:5).

27. An ancestor of Adaiah and a priest descended from Pashhur (Neh. 11:12).

28. Son of Jonathan, a Levite who led a group of musicians at the dedication of the rebuilt wall of Jerusalem (Neh. 12:35–36).

29. A priest who took part in the dedication ceremony for the rebuilt wall of Jerusalem (Neh. 12:41).

30. A son of Jeberechiah (Isa. 8:2) and a witness who recorded a prophecy given to Isaiah.

31. A prophet whom the Jews stoned (Matt. 23:35; Luke 11:51). He may be the same as No. 14.

Zecher [Ze′cher]—See Zechariah.

Zedad [Ze′dad], *mountain side*—A place on the northern border of Palestine (Num. 34:8; Ezek. 47:15).

Zedekiah [Zed·e·ki′ah], *the Lord my righteousness*—The name of five men in the Old Testament:

1. A false prophet, son of Chenaanah, who advised King Ahab of Israel to attack the Syrian army at Ramoth Gilead (1 Kings 22:11). When Micaiah, the prophet of Jehovah, advised the king against this, saying that he would fail in his attempt, he was struck by the false prophet. Zedekiah's flattery and unfounded optimism proved to be lies; the king was mortally wounded in the battle.

2. The last king of Judah (597–586 B.C.). The third son of Josiah, Zedekiah was successor to Jehoiachin as king (2 Kings 24:17–20; 25:1–7; 2 Chron. 36:10–13). After Jehoiachin had reigned only three months, he was deposed and carried off to Babylonia. Nebuchadnezzar installed Zedekiah on the throne as a puppet king and made him swear an oath that he would remain loyal (2 Chron. 36:13; Ezek. 17:13). Zedekiah's original name was Mattaniah, but Nebuchadnezzar renamed him to demonstrate his authority over him and his ownership of him (2 Kings 24:17). Although Zedekiah reigned in Jerusalem for eleven years, he was never fully accepted as their king by the people of Judah.

Because Zedekiah was a weak and indecisive ruler, he faced constant political unrest. Almost from the first he appeared restless about his oath of loyalty to Babylon, although he reaffirmed that commitment in the fourth year of this reign (Jer. 51:59). However, he was under constant pressure from his advisors to revolt and look to Egypt for help. A new coalition composed of Edom, Moab, Ammon, and Phoenicia was forming against Babylonia and they urged Judah to join (Jer. 27:3). Adding to the general unrest was the message of false prophets who declared that the yoke of Babylon had been broken (Jer. 28).

In his ninth year Zedekiah revolted against Babylonia. King Nebuchadnezzar invaded Judah and besieged Jerusalem. While Jerusalem was under siege, other Judean cities were falling to the Babylonians (Jer. 34:7).

The final months of the siege were desperate times for Zedekiah and the inhabitants of Jerusalem. The king made frequent calls on the prophet Jeremiah, seeking an encouraging word from the Lord. Jeremiah's message consistently offered only one alternative: Surrender to Nebuchadnezzar in order to live in peace and save Jerusalem. To his credit, Zedekiah was not arrogant and heartless (Jer. 36:22–23). But he regarded God's prophetic word superstitiously and "did not humble himself before Jeremiah the prophet, who spoke from the mouth of the Lord" (2 Chron. 36:12).

In 586 B.C. the wall of Jerusalem was breached, and Zedekiah fled the city. The army of the Babylonians pursued the king, overtaking him in the plains of Jericho. He was brought before Nebuchadnezzar and forced to watch the slaying of his sons. Then his own eyes were put out and he was led away to Babylonia (2 Kings 25:6–7). Zedekiah died during the years of the captivity of the Jewish people in Babylon. His reign marked the end of the nation of Judah as an independent, self-governing country.

3. A son of Jeconiah and grandson of Jehoiakim, king of Judah (1 Chron. 3:16). It is the view of some that he was son in the sense of successor; others hold he was his actual son who died prior to the Exile.

4. A prominent Jewish official who sealed the covenant with Nehemiah after returning from the captivity (Neh. 10:1; Zidkijah, KJV).

5. Son of Maaseiah. An immoral false prophet denounced by the prophet Jeremiah (Jer. 29:21). Nebuchadnezzar destroyed him by fire.

6. A prince of Judah, son of Hananiah, in the days of the prophet Jeremiah and Jehoiakim, king of Judah (Jer. 36:12). He was one of several who learned through Michaiah the contents of the roll which had been read by Baruch.

Zeeb [Zeeb], *wolf*—A prince of Midian, one of those killed by the men of Ephraim during Gideon's campaign against the Midianites with his three hundred specially chosen warriors (Judg. 7:25).

Zelah [Ze'lah], *side*—A town of Benjamin where the bones of Saul and Jonathan in the tomb of Kish, Saul's father (2 Sam. 21:14).

Zelek [Ze'lek], *a cleft*—One of David's mighty warriors, an Ammonite (2 Sam. 23:37; 1 Chron. 11:39).

Zelophehad [Ze·loph'e·had], *first-born*—Son of Hepher of Manasseh. He had five daughters and no sons which, at his death, brought up the question of the inheritance of daughters when there was no son (Num. 26:33; 27:1–8).

Zelotes [Ze·lo'tes], *full of zeal*—(Luke 6:15; Acts 1:13, KJV) See Zealot.

Zelzah [Zel'zah], *shade*—A town of Benjamin and the location of Rachel's sepulchre (1 Sam. 10:2).

Zemaraim [Zem·a·ra'im], *double fleece*—A town and a mountain:

1. An ancient town of Benjamin, west of the Jordan and a few miles north of Jericho; to be identified probably with es-Sumrah (Josh. 18:22).

2. A mountain of Ephraim from which Abijah, king of Judah, addressed his troops before battling the forces of Israel (2 Chron. 13:4).

Zemarite [Zem'a·rite], *double woolens*—A tribe from the sons of Canaan, son of Ham, son of Noah (Gen. 10:18; 1 Chron. 1:16).

Zemirah [Ze·mi'rah], *music*—A son of Becher of Benjamin (1 Chron. 7:8; Zemira, KJV).

Zenan [Ze'nan], *pointed*—A town of Judah (Josh. 15:37).

Zenas [Ze'nas], *gift of Zeus*—A lawyer who traveled with Apollos in Crete. Paul asks for these two men to be sent to him (Titus 3:13).

Zephaniah [Zeph·a·ni'ah], *Jehovah has hidden*—Four Old Testament Men:

1. A Levite of the family of Kohath. He was an ancestor of Samuel (1 Chron. 6:36–38).

2. Son of Maaseiah and a priest in the reign of King Zedekiah (Jer. 21:1). He was one of Jeremiah's loyal friends and frequently served as a messenger between the prophet and King Zedekiah. After the capture of Jerusalem he was killed by the Babylonians at Riblah (Jer. 21:1; 29:25, 29; 37:3; 52:24–27).

3. A prophet living at the time of King Josiah (639–608 B.C.). He described himself as the son of Cushi and the great-great-grandson of Hezekiah (Hizkiah) who is believed to be the same as King Hezekiah. It is believed that he began prophesying at about the age of twenty-five (Zeph. 1:1).

4. The father of a Josiah who lived at the time of Zerubbabel and Zechariah, the prophet (Zech. 6:10, 14).

Zephath [Ze'phath], *watchtower*—A town of the Canaanites near the border of Edom. The men of Judah and Simeon attacked the Canaanites who inhabited Zephath and destroyed it; the city was then called Hormah, which means *destruction* (Judg. 1:17).

Zephathah [Zeph'a·thah], *watchtower*—A valley near Mareshah in which Asa, king of Judah, fought Zerah the Ethiopian (2 Chron. 14:10).

Zephi, Zepho [Ze'phi, Ze'pho], *watch*—A son of Eliphaz and grandson of Esau. He was a duke of Edom (Gen. 36:11, 15; 1 Chron. 1:36).

Zephon [Ze'phon], *watching*—The eldest son of Gad and the head of a tribal family (Num. 26:15).

Zer [Zer], *rock* or *flint*—A fortified town of Naphtali, not otherwise identified (Josh. 19:35).

Zerah [Ze'rah], *dawn*—Six men of the Old Testament:

1. Son of Reuel, grandson of Esau, and a duke of Edom (Gen. 36:3–4, 13, 17; 1 Chron. 1:37).

2. The twin brother of Pharez and son of Judah and Tamar (Gen. 38:30; 46:12; Num. 26:20; Josh. 7:1, 17). His descendants were called Zarhites. Also called Zarah and Zara (KJV).

3. Son of Simeon (Num. 26:13). In Genesis 46:10 and Exodus 6:15 he is called Zohar.

4. A Levite (1 Chron. 6:21).

5. Another Levite (1 Chron. 6:41).

6. The king of Ethiopia who in the time of King Asa invaded Judah with a great army. Asa's forces met him in the valley of Zephathah and defeated the Ethiopians with great loss (2 Chron. 14:8–15).

Zerahiah [Zer·a·hi′ah], *Jehovah has risen*—Two Old Testament men:

1. Son of Uzzi. He was a descendant of Aaron and ancestor of Ezra (1 Chron. 6:6, 51; Ezra 7:4).

2. Father of Elihoenai. His descendants returned from exile with Ezra (Ezra 8:4).

Zered [Zer′ed], *luxuriance*—A valley crossed by the Israelites at the close of their wandering (Num. 21:12; Deut. 2:13–14). Also called Zared (KJV).

Zereda [Zer′e·da], *fortress*—An Ephramite town. Jeroboam, who became king of the northern kingdom of Israel, was from this town (1 Kings 11:26).

Zeredah [Zer′e·dah], *God has regarded*—A town in the plain of Jordan. The bronze castings for the temple were made in clay molds in the plain between the towns of Zeredah and Succoth (1 Kings 7:46; 2 Chron. 4:17; Zeredathah, KJV).

Zeredathan [Zer′e·da·than]—See Zeredah.

Zererah [Zer′e·rah], unknown—The town toward which the Midanites fled when routed by Gideon and his three hundred picked warriors (Judg. 7:22; Zererath KJV).

Zererath [Zer′e·rath]—See Zererah.

Zeresh [Ze′resh], *gold*—The wife of Haman, who encouraged him in his wicked plans (Est. 5:10; 6:13).

Zereth [Ze′reth], *brightness*—Son of Ashur of Judah (1 Chron. 4:5–7).

Zereth-shahar [Zer′eth-sha′har], *splendor of dawn*—A town of Reuben situated on a mountain (Josh. 13:19).

Zeri [Ze'ri], *built*—A son of Jeduthun (1 Chron. 25:3), a Levite and harpist. In 1 Chronicles 25:11 he is called Izri.

Zeror [Ze'ror], *bundle* or *pouch* or *particle of stone*—An ancestor of King Saul (1 Sam. 9:1).

Zeruah [Ze·ru'ah], *leprous*—The mother of Jeroboam, first king of the northern kingdom of Israel (1 Kings 11:26).

Zerubbabel [Ze·rub'ba·bel], *offspring of Babylon*—Head of the tribe of Judah at the time of the return from the Babylonian captivity; prime builder of the second temple.

Zerubbabel is a shadowy figure who emerges as the political and spiritual head of the tribe of Judah at the time of the Babylonian captivity. Zerubbabel led the first group of captives back to Jerusalem and set about rebuilding the temple on the old site. For some twenty years he was closely associated with prophets, priests, and kings until the new temple was dedicated and the Jewish sacrificial system was reestablished. As a child of the captivity, Zerubbabel's name literally means "offspring of Babylon." He was the son of Shealtiel or Salathiel (Ezra 3:2, 8; Hag. 1:1; Matt. 1:12) and the grandson of Jehoiachin, the captive king of Judah (1 Chron. 3:17). Zerubbabel was probably Shealtiel's adopted or Levirate son (1 Chron. 3:19). Whatever his blood relationship to King Jehoiachin, Zerubbabel was Jehoiachin's legal successor and heir.

A descendant of David, Zerubbabel was in the direct line of the ancestry of Jesus (Matt. 1:12; Luke 3:27). Zerubbabel apparently attained considerable status with his captors while living in Babylon. During the early reign of Darius, he was recognized as a "prince of Judah" (Ezra 1:8). Zerubbabel was probably in the king's service since he had been appointed by the Persians as governor of Judah (Hag. 1:1).

With the blessings of Cyrus (Ezra 1:1–2), Zerubbabel and Jeshua the high priest led the first band of captives back to Jerusalem (Ezra 2:2). They also returned the gold and silver vessels that Nebuchadnezzar had removed from the ill-fated temple (Ezra 1:11). Almost immediately they set up an altar for burnt offerings, kept the Feast of Tabernacles, and took steps to rebuild the temple (Ezra 3:2–3, 8).

After rebuilding the temple foundation the first two years, construction came to a standstill for seventeen years. This delay came principally because of opposition from settlers in Samaria who wanted to help with the building (Ezra 4:1–2). When the offer was refused because of the Samaritans' association with heathen worship, the Samaritans disrupted the building project (Ezra 4:4). Counselors were hired who misrepresented the captives in court (Ezra 4:5), causing the Persian king to withdraw his support (Ezra 4:21). The delay in building also was due to the preoccupation of Zerubbabel and other captives with building houses for themselves (Hag. 1:2–4).

Urged by the prophets Haggai and Zechariah (Ezra 5:1–2), Zerubbabel diligently resumed work on the temple in the second year of the reign of Darius Hystaspes of Persia (Hag. 1:14). This renewed effort to build the temple was a model of cooperation involving the captives, the prophets, and Persian kings (Ezra 6:14). Zerubbabel received considerable grants of money and materials from Persia (Ezra 6:5) and continuing encouragement from the prophets Haggai and Zechariah (Ezra 5:2).

The temple was finished in four years (516/515 B.C.) and dedicated with great pomp and rejoicing (Ezra 6:16). The celebration was climaxed with the observance of the Passover (Ezra 6:19). If there was a discordant note, it likely came from older Jews who had earlier wept because the new temple lacked the splendor of Solomon's temple (Ezra 3:12).

For some mysterious reason, Zerubbabel is not mentioned in connection with the temple dedication. Neither is he mentioned after this time. Perhaps he died or retired from public life upon completion of the temple. His influence was so great, however, that historians designate the second temple as "Zerubbabel's Temple."

God was apparently pleased with Zerubbabel's role in bringing the captives home and reestablishing temple worship (Ezra 3:10). On God's instructions, Haggai promised Zerubbabel a special blessing: "I will take you, Zerubbabel My servant, the son of Shealtiel, says the Lord, and will make you as a signet ring; for I have chosen you" (Hag. 2:23).

Zeruiah [Zer·u·i'ah], *balsam*—David's sister or half sister and the mother of Joab, Abishai, and Asahel (1 Sam. 26:6; 2 Sam. 2:13, 18; 8:16; 1 Chron. 2:16).

Zetham [Ze'tham], *olive*—Son of Laadan; a Levite of the family of Gershom (1 Chron. 23:8).

Zethan [Ze'than], *olive*—A Benjamite of the family of Jediael (1 Chron. 7:10).

Zethar [Ze'thar], *star*—A chamberlain who was one of the seven eunuchs in the court of King Ahasuerus of Persia (Est. 1:10).

Zeus [Zeus], *a father of help*—A principal deity of the Greeks, the father of other gods. Zeus is typically portrayed as the sky god with a thunderbolt. A statue of Zeus in Olympia was one of the seven wonders of the ancient world. Zeus is equated with the Roman god Jupiter, and is so translated in Acts (KJV). The people of Lystra, impressed with the miracle done through Paul, called Barnabas Zeus and Paul Hermes. Paul and Barnabas were appalled, and quickly set the crowd straight, but even so they could barely keep them from offering sacrifices to them (Acts 14:12–13; 19:35).

Zia [Zi'a], *motion*—A Gadite of Bashan (1 Chron. 5:13).

Ziba [Zi'ba], *statue*—A servant of King Saul. He had a large family (2 Sam. 9:10). After the death of Jonathan, David's friend, David inquired of Ziba if there was any of the house of Saul to whom he could show kindness. Ziba brought Mephibosheth, Jonathan's crippled son, and Ziba was appointed steward of Saul's land for Mephibosheth (2 Sam. 9:9–12).

Zibeon [Zib'e·on], *dyed*—Father of Anah. He is called a Hivite and a Horite (Gen. 36:20, 24, 29). He was the grandfather of Aholibamah, the wife of Esau (Gen. 36:2).

Zibia [Zi'bi·a], *roe*—The son of Shaharaim, a Benjamite. His mother was Hodesh (1 Chron. 8:9).

Zibiah [Zi'bi·ah], *roe*—The wife of Ahaziah and mother of Jehoash, king of Judah. She was a native of Beersheba (2 Kings 12:1; 2 Chron. 24:1).

Zichri [Zich'ri], *famous*—Twelve men of the Old Testament:
1. Son of Izhar, a Levite of the family of Kohath (Ex. 6:21).
2. Son of Shimhi of Benjamin (1 Chron. 8:19).
3. Son of Shashak of Benjamin (1 Chron. 8:23).
4. Son of Jeroham of Benjamin (1 Chron. 8:27).

5. Son of Asaph (1 Chron. 9:15). In Nehemiah 11:17 he is called Zabdi, and in Nehemiah 12:35 he is called Zaccur.

6. A Levite and a descendant of Moses (1 Chron. 26:25).

7. A member of the tribe of Reuben in the time of David (1 Chron. 27:16).

8. The father of Amasiah of Judah. The son was a captain in the army of Jehoshaphat (2 Chron. 17:16).

9. The father of Elishaphat, who with the aid of Jehoiada, overthrew Queen Athaliah and placed Joash on the throne (2 Chron. 23:1). He was possibly the same as the preceding.

10. A man of Ephraim in the army of Pekah, king of Israel. He slew Maaseiah, the son of Ahaz, king of Judah, and two of the king's officers (2 Chron. 28:7).

11. The father of Joel, the latter a chief man of the Benjamites when they returned from Babylon (Neh. 11:9).

12. A priest of the family of Abijah when Joiakim was high priest (Neh. 12:17).

Ziddim [Zid'dim], *sides*—A city of Naphtali (Josh. 19:35), a few miles west of the Sea of Galilee.

Zidkijah [Zid·ki'jah]—See Zedekiah.

Zidon [Zi'don]—See Sidon.

Zidonians [Zi'don·i·ans]—Those who lived in Sidon. See Sidonians.

Zif [Zif]—See Ziv.

Ziha [Zi'ha], *draught*—Two Old Testament men:

1. One of the Nethinim, descendants of whom returned from Babylon after the Exile (Ezra 2:43; Neh. 7:46).

2. A chief of the Nethinim after the return to Palestine from Babylon (Neh. 11:21).

Ziklag [Zik'lag], possibly *winding*—A town in the southernmost part of Judah (Josh. 15:31), first assigned to Judah, then given to Simeon (Josh. 19:5; 1 Chron. 4:30). It belonged to the Philistines during Saul's reign, and to it David fled when he was a fugitive from Saul. Achish of Gath gave him the town as his residence. When the Amalekites plundered and burnt Ziklag, David pursued them, routed them, and recovered all the booty and prisoners. The booty he distributed among a number of Hebrew cities. Eventually the town was brought under the jurisdiction of the kings of Judah (1 Sam. 27:6; 30:1–31).

Zillah [Zil'lah], *a shadow*—A wife of Lamech of the line of Cain and mother of Tubal-cain (Gen. 4:19, 22–23).

Zillethal, Zilthai [Zil'le·thal, Zil'thai]—Two Old Testament men:
1. Son of Shimhi (Shimei) of Benjamin (1 Chron. 8:20).
2. A captain of a contingent of warriors who allied themselves with David at Ziklag (1 Chron. 12:20).

Zilpah [Zil'pah], *a drop*—The mother of Gad and Asher (Gen. 30:9–13; 35:26). Zilpah was one of the female slaves of Laban, the father of Leah and Rachel. When Leah married Jacob, Laban gave her Zilpah to serve as her maid (Gen. 29:24; 46:18). Later, Leah gave Zilpah to Jacob as a concubine (Gen. 30:9), and she gave birth to both Gad and Asher.

Zilthai [Zil'thai]—See Zillethal.

Zimmah [Zim'mah], *counsel*—Two Old Testament men:
1. Son of Shimei and grandson of Jahath of the family of Gerahom (1 Chron. 6:20, 42–43).
2. A Gershonite Levite (2 Chron. 29:12).

Zimran [Zim'ran], *musician*—A son of Abraham and Keturah (Gen. 25:2; 1 Chron. 1:32).

Zimri [Zim'ri], *(God is) my protection*—The name of four men and a tribe or district in the Old Testament:
1. A son of Salu, a Simeonite prince (Num. 25:14). In an outrageous move, Zimri brought a Midianite woman, Cozbi, into the camp while Israel was repenting for having worshipped Baal. When Phinehas, the son of Eleazar, saw Zimri take her to his tent, he was enraged, took a javelin in his hand, went into Zimri's tent, and thrust both of them through.
2. The fifth king of Israel (1 Kings 16:8–20). Before he became king, Zimri was a servant of King Elah and commander of half of his chariots. One day, Zimri killed the drunken Elah and proclaimed himself king. When Omri, the commander of Elah's army, heard about the assassination, he abandoned the siege of Gibbethon and besieged

Tirzah, the capital city. When Zimri saw that the city was taken, he "burned the king's house down upon himself" (1 Kings 16:18). Zimri's reign lasted only seven days (1 Kings 16:15).

3. The oldest of the five sons of Zerah, grandson of Judah (1 Chron. 2:6).

4. A Benjamite, son of Jehoaddah (1 Chron. 8:36) or Jarah (1 Chron. 9:42). Zimri was a descendant of King Saul and of King Saul's son Jonathan.

5. Unknown area, listed in Jeremiah as "all the kings of Zimri" along with the kings of Elam, the Medes, etc. as one of the nations who would drink of the cup of God's fury (Jer. 25:25).

Zin [Zin], *flat*—A wilderness through which the Israelites passed on their journey to Canaan (Num. 13:21; 20:1). The wilderness of Zin stretched along the extreme southern limits of the promised land (Num. 13:21). In it was Kadesh-barnea.

Zina [Zin'a], *well-fed*—One of the sons of Shimei, a Gershonite (1 Chron. 23:10).

Zion [Zi'on], *possibly citadel* or *sunny mount*—The city of David and the city of God. The designation of Zion underwent a distinct progression in its usage throughout the Bible.

The first mention of Zion in the Bible is in 2 Samuel 5:7: "David took the stronghold of Zion (that is, the City of David)." Zion, therefore, was the name of the ancient Jebusite fortress situated on the southeast hill of Jerusalem at the junction of the Kidron Valley and the Tyropoeon Valley. The name came to stand not only for the fortress but also for the hill on which the fortress stood. After David captured "the stronghold of Zion" by defeating the Jebusites, he called Zion "the City of David" (1 Kings 8:1; 1 Chron. 11:5; 2 Chron. 5:2). It was here that David brought the ark of the covenant (2 Sam. 6:12).

When Solomon built the temple on Mount Moriah (a hill distinct and separate from Mount Zion), and moved the ark there, the word *Zion* expanded in meaning to include also the temple and the temple area (Pss. 2:6; 48:2, 11–12; 132:13). It was only a short step until Zion was used as a name for the city of Jerusalem, the land of Judah, and the people of Israel as a whole (Isa. 40:9; Jer. 31:12). The prophet Zechariah spoke of the sons of Zion (Zech. 9:13). By this time the word *Zion* had come to mean the entire nation of Israel.

The most important use of the word *Zion* is in a religious or theological sense. Zion is used figuratively of Israel as the people of God (Isa. 60:14). The spiritual meaning of Zion is continued in the New Testament, where it is given the Christian meaning of God's spiritual kingdom, the church of God, the heavenly Jerusalem (Heb. 12:22; Rev. 14:1; Sion, KJV).

Zior [Zi'or], *smallness*—A town of Judah near Hebron (Josh. 15:54).

Ziph [Ziph], *battlement*—Two towns and an Old Testament man:
   1. A town at the most southerly point of Judah (Josh. 15:24).
   2. A town near a wilderness to which David fled from Saul (1 Sam. 23:14). It was later fortified by Rehoboam, king of Judah (2 Chron. 11:8).
   3. A son of Jehaleleel of Judah (1 Chron. 4:16).

Ziphah [Zi'phah], *battlement*—Son of Jehaleleel and brother of Ziph (1 Chron. 4:16).

Ziphims [Ziph'ims]—See Ziphites.

Ziphion [Ziph'i·on], *lookout*—A son of Gad, also called Zephon (Gen. 46:16).

Ziphites [Ziph'ites]—The inhabitants of Ziph (1 Sam. 23:19; 26:1). The inhabitants of Ziph went to Saul and told him that David was hiding in their area. This is referred to in the title of Psalm 54, which is David's cry to God in this circumstance.

Ziphron [Ziph'ron], *fragrance*—A place on the northern boundary of Palestine (Num. 34:9).

Zippor [Zip'por], *bird or sparrow*—The father of Balak (Num. 22:2; Josh. 24:9). Balak was the king of Moab who hired Balaam the soothsayer (Josh. 13:22) to curse Israel.

Zipporah [Zip'po·rah], *female bird*—A daughter of Jethro, priest of Midian, and wife of Moses (Ex. 2:21–22; 4:25; 18:2–4). Their sons were Gershom and Eliezer. When the Lord sought to kill Moses because Eliezer had not been circumcised, Zipporah grabbed a sharp stone and immediately circumcised the child. She and the two sons must have returned to Jethro rather than continuing on to Egypt with Moses, because she is not mentioned again until after the exodus. Along with Jethro, she and her two sons visited Moses in the wilderness after the Hebrew people left Egypt (Ex. 18:1–5).

Zithri [Zith'ri]—See Sithri.

Ziv [Ziv], *bloom*—The second month of the Jewish sacred year, and eighth month of the civil year. Also called Iyon.

Ziz, Ascent of [Ziz], *a flower*—A steep ascent in a pass that runs from the western shore of the Dead Sea, at a point slightly north of En Gedi, into the wilderness of Judah, toward Tekoa. Through the ascent of Ziz (2 Chron. 20:16) the allied forces of Ammon, Moab, and Mount Seir made their journey from En Gedi to attack the army of Jehoshaphat, king of Judah.

Ziza [Zi'za], *abundance*—Two Old Testament men:
1. Son of Shiphi, a Simeonite. He lived in the reign of Hezekiah (1 Chron. 4:37).
2. Son of Rehoboam. His mother was Maacah (2 Chron. 11:20).

Zizah [Zi'zah], *abundance*—Son of Shimei, a Levite of the family of Gershom (1 Chron. 23:11). In 1 Chronicles 23:10 he is called Zina.

Zoan [Zo'an], *place of departure*—An ancient city in Egypt that dates back to the time of Abraham. It was situated on the Tanitic branch of the Nile in the delta region. Built seven years after Hebron (Num. 13:22), Zoan has often been identified with one of the royal cities in northern Egypt, and was the capital of Egypt in the early days of the twelfth dynasty. It was also the capital of the Hyksos kings. Following the end of that dynasty, it lost its importance for several centuries but regained its distinction under the kings of the nineteenth dynasty. It was in Zoan that Moses met Pharaoh (Ps. 78:12, 43). It was a city of importance in the time of Isaiah and Ezekiel (Isa. 19:11, 13; 30:4; Ezek. 30:14).

The Greek translation of the Old Testament identified Zoan with Tanis, a city that is sometimes associated with an ancient capital of Egypt, Ramses (Ex. 1:11). Now many scholars identify Ramses with Qantir, while Zoan is probably the nearby San el-Hagar.

Zoar [Zo'ar], *little*—An ancient city apparently situated on the eastern shore of the Dead Sea (Gen. 13:10), and also known as Bela (Gen. 14:2, 8). It was one of five city-states in the area, each with its own king.

Zoar figures prominently in the story of Lot and the destruction of the wicked "cities of the plain" (Gen. 13:12; 19:29). Warned to flee to the mountains, Lot sought further mercy by asking to go instead to Zoar. His reasoning was that Zoar is only a "little" city (hence its name). His request was granted and Zoar was spared, while the four other cities (Sodom, Gomorrah, Admah, and Zeboiim) were destroyed (Gen. 19:22–23, 30).

Many scholars believe the site of Zoar to be es-Safi, at the foot of the mountains of Moab, about 7 kilometers (4.5 miles) up the river Zered from where it empties into the Dead Sea.

Zoba, Zobah [Zo'ba, Zo'bah], *station*—A region of Syria between Hamath and Damascus. The inhabitants of this area fought bitterly against the Jewish nation (1 Sam. 14:47; 2 Sam. 8:3, 5, 12; 10:6, 8; 1 Kings 11:23; 1 Chron. 18:3, 5, 9). It is called Hamath-zobah in 2 Chronicles 8:3 and Aram-zobah in the title of Psalm 60.

Zobebah [Zo·be'bah], *slow movement*—The second child of Hakkos (Coz) of Judah (1 Chron. 4:8).

Zohar [Zo'har], *whiteness*—Two Old Testament men:

1. Father of Ephron, a Hittite (Gen. 23:8). It was from Ephron that Abraham purchased the cave of Machpelah.

2. Son of Simeon (Gen. 46:10). In Numbers 26:13 he is called Zerah.

Zoheleth [Zo'he·leth], *serpent*—A rock by En-rogel where Adonijah killed oxen and sheep (1 Kings 1:9).

Zoheth [Zo'heth], *releasing*—A son of Ishi (1 Chron. 4:20).

Zophah [Zo'phah], *a cruse*—Son of Helem of Asher (1 Chron. 7:35–36).

Zophai [Zo'phai], *honeycomb*—Son of Elkanah in the Levitical line (1 Chron. 6:26).

Zophar [Zo'phar], *sparrow*—The third of the "friends" of Job to speak. He is called a Naamathite (Job 2:11; 11:1; 20:1; 42:9), indicating he was from Naamah, in northern Arabia. Zophar's two discourses are found in Job 11:1–20 and 20:1–29. He accused Job of wickedness and hypocrisy, urged Job to turn from his rebellion, and charged that God was punishing Job far less than his sins deserved (Job 11:6). In the end the Lord rebuked Zophar and his two companions because, "you have not spoken of Me what is right, as My servant Job has" (Job 42:9).

Zophim [Zo'phim], *watchers*—A field on the top of the mountain peak Pisgah (Num. 23:14).

Zorah [Zor'ah], *hornet*—A town of Judah which was inhabited by people of Dan (Josh. 15:33; 19:41; Zoreah, KJV). Here Samson was born and buried (Judg. 13:2, 25; 16:31). It overlooked Sorek. Rehoboam, king of Judah, fortified it, and exiles who returned from Babylon lived there (Neh. 11:29).

Zorathite [Zor'a·thite]—A native of Zorah (1 Chron. 2:53; 4:2).

Zoreah [Zor'e·ah]—See Zorah.

Zorites [Zor·ites], *hornet*—A member of the clans of Caleb, a descendant of Salma (1 Chron. 2:54).

Zorobabel [Zo·ro'ba·bel]—See Zerubbabel.

Zuar [Zu'ar], *smallness*—The father of Nethaneel and chief of the tribe of Issachar when the Israelites were in the wilderness (Num. 1:8; 2:5; 7:18, 23; 10:15).

Zuph [Zuph], *honeycomb*—An Old Testament man and a region:
1. A Levite of the family of Kohath and ancestor of Samuel (1 Sam. 1:1; 1 Chron. 6:35).
2. A district probably south of the border of Benjamin where Saul searched for his father's asses (1 Sam. 9:4–6).

Zur [Zur], *a rock*—Two Old Testament men:
1. Son of Jehiel who founded Gibeon (1 Chron. 8:30; 9:36).
2. A king of Midian and father of Cozbi, the woman who was brought into the camp of Israel and slain by Phinehas (Num. 25:15). Zur was slain in the conflict with the Israelites (Num. 31:8; Josh. 13:21).

Zuriel [Zu'ri·el], *God is a rock*—Son of Abihail, a Levite. He was chief of the Levites of Merari when Israel was in the wilderness (Num. 3:35).

Zurishaddai [Zu·ri·shad′dai], *my rock is the Almighty*—Father of Shelumiel, the chief of the Simeonites in the wilderness (Num. 1:6; 2:12; 7:36, 41; 10:19).

Zuzim, The [Zu′zim], *roving creatures*—An ancient people who dwelt in Ham, east of the Jordan. They were conquered by Chedorlaomer (Gen. 14:5).

Bibliography

Katharine Harris. *World's Bible Dictionary*. (Nashville: World Publishing 2004).

Ronald F. Youngblood. *Unlock the Bible: Keys to Discovering the People and Places*. (Nashville: Thomas Nelson 2011).

Bible Study Tools.com. *Brown, Driver, Briggs, Gesenius Lexicon*. Hendrickson Pub; Complete and Unabridged, fully searchable, with Strong Numbers and interactive Index edition (June 1996). http://www.biblestudytools.com/lexicons/hebrew/.

Bible Study Tools.com. *Thayer's Lexicon* and *Smith's Bible Dictionary*. Hendrickson Pub; Rei Sub edition (June 1996), AND Hendrickson Publishers; Rev Sub edition (July 1, 1990) http://www.biblestudytools.com/lexicons/greek/.

Studylight.org. *Holman Bible Dictionary*, Broadman & Holman Publishers (January 1991). http://www.studylight.org/dic/hbd/.

Net Bible. *Online Study Dictionary*. Multiple Sources (Hitchcock, Nave's, EBD, Smith's, ISBE, Strong's Greek & Hebrew Lexicon). http://classic.net.bible.org/bible.php.